GAZETTEER OF THE STATE OF NEW JERSEY

Comprehending a General View of its Physical and Moral Conditions, Together with a Topographical and Statistical Account of its Counties, Towns, Villages, Canals, Rail Roads, Etc., Accompanied by a Map.

By
Thomas F. Gordon

CLEARFIELD

Originally published
Trenton, New Jersey, 1834

Reprinted for
Clearfield Company, Inc. by
Genealogical Publishing Co., Inc.
Baltimore, Maryland
2001

International Standard Book Number: 0-8063-5109-8
Made in the United States of America

CONTENTS

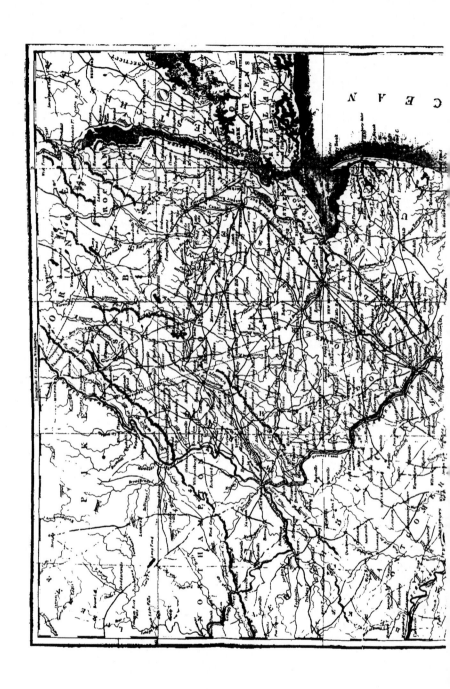

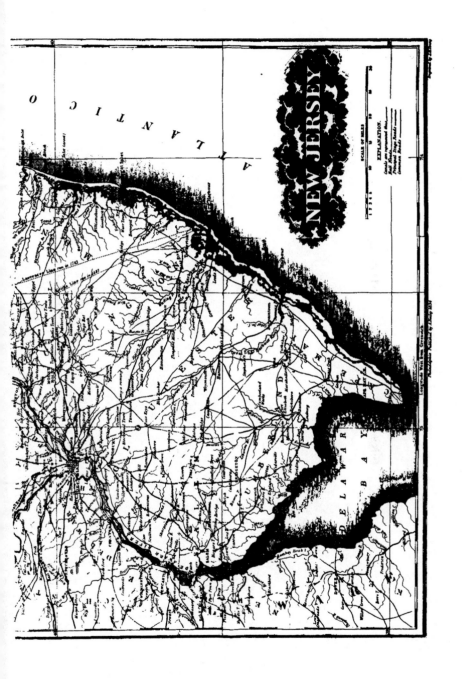

ADVERTISEMENT.

—••◦◉◦••—

THE author of the following work has sought to present to the public, a full and correct portraiture of the State in the year 1833. To this end, he has, personally, visited almost every portion of it; communed with many of its most distinguished and enlightened citizens, and collected, from numerous but scattered sources, a mass of useful and curious information, which must prove alike grateful to the present and succeeding generations. Errors will undoubtedly be discovered in the work; for such a work is peculiarly liable to them; being exposed, not only to the misconceptions of the author, but, to those of his thousand informants. Distance of places from each other, and the area of the townships and counties are, specially, subject to misstatement. The first has been given from the returns of the General Post-Office, measures upon the map, and verbal information of residents; the only and best sources, save actual admeasurement. The area of the townships has been obtained from calculation of their contents, as delineated on Mr. Gordon's map, by means of a reticulated scale of square miles. The result corresponds, so nearly, with the returns of the assessors of such townships, as contain no unimproved lands, as to give considerable confidence in its approximation to the truth. It must be observed, however, that this area comprises roads, lakes, ponds, marshes and, in a word, every thing within the lines.

The abstract which has been given of the laws relating to the administration of the government, generally, and of the counties and townships, specially, will appear, to many, trite and familiar; but to the great mass of the people, particularly, to the rising generation, it will not prove the least acceptable portion of the work. To those about to enter on the duties of the citizen, it will communicate much valuable knowledge; and will be useful to all, for occasional reference; comprising, in a small compass, matter of daily interest, which must, elsewhere, be sought, in many volumes. More of this species of information might have been usefully given; but, the volume collected, exceeds, by one-third, the quantity originally proposed; and to get it within the size of a convenient manual, resort has been had to a small type for the prefatory chapters.

To the many gentlemen to whom the author is indebted for communications, he tenders his unfeigned thanks; and solicits from them, and others, such corrections and additions as may render the next edition of his work, still more valuable.

Philadelphia, January 1, 1834.

GAZETTEER OF NEW JERSEY.

PREFATORY CHAPTER.

PART I.

Containing a Physical View of the State.

I. *General Boundary.*—II. *Principal Divisions.*—III. *Southern and Alluvial Division.*— *Bounds—Surface—Nevisink Hills—Sandy Hook—Sea Beach—Bays or Lagunes— Soil: Forest—Pine Lands—Oak—Cedar Swamp—Marl—Ferruginous Sand—Proportions of Marl used in Agriculture.—Cultivation of the Alluvial District.—Bog Ore—Streams.*—IV. *Middle and Secondary District: Bounds—Area—Formation— Trap Ridges—Bergen Ridge—First and Second Mountains—Bituminous Coal— Mountains from Springfield to Pluckemin.—Pompton Plain: Abundance of Minerals there—Ridges extending to the Delaware.—Character of the surrounding Country—Quarries of Freestone near Princeton—Sandy Hill—Primitive Rocks near Trenton.—Copper Mines: at Belleville, Brunswick, Somerville, Greenbrook.— V. Mountainous District: Extent—Blended Geological Formation—Limits—Primitive Ridges, Minerals of—Tongue of Transition Formation, Minerals of—Primitive resumed—Valley of the Wallkill, or of Sparta—Singular Geology and Mineralogy—Valley of Paulin's Kill—Alternation of Slate and Limestone—Blue or Kittatinney Mountains—Transition Limestone on Delaware River—Precious Marbles—Manganese—Rivers and Lakes of the Third Section—Timber of the Middle and Northern Sections.*—VI. *Turnpike Roads.*—VII. *Rail Roads: Camden and Amboy, West Jersey, Patterson and Hudson, Patterson Junction, Patterson and Fort Lee, Elizabethtown and Somerville, New Jersey, Hudson and Delaware, Delaware and Jobstown.*—VIII. *Canals: Morris, Delaware and Raritan, Manasquan, Salem.*—IX. *Population—Increase—Tables—Slavery.*—X. *Statistical Table.* XI. *Agriculture, Manufactures and Commerce.*—XII. *Climate.*

I. The State of New Jersey is bounded on the N. E. by Orange and Rockland counties, of the State of New York; on the E. by Hudson River and Bay, Staten Island Sound, Raritan Bay and the Atlantic Ocean; on S. E. and S. by the Atlantic; on S. W. by the Delaware Bay, dividing it from the State of Delaware; and on the W. and N. W. by the Delaware River, separating it from Pennsylvania. The N. E. line from Carpenter's Point, at the mouth of the Nevisink, or Mackackomack River, in north lat. 41° 21', to a point on the Hudson River, in 41° north latitude; is in length 45 miles; the E. 60; the S. E. from Sandy Hook to Cape May, 120; and the S. W., W. and N. W. from Cape May to Carpenter's Point, 220 miles—making the extent of its exterior limit 445 miles. The extreme length of the State, by a line almost due north from Cape May, to the northern angle on the Delaware, is 164 miles; its greatest breadth due E. and W. through Salem, Gloucester, Burlington and Monmouth counties, about 75 miles; and through Warren, Sussex, Morris and Bergen counties, to the extreme N. E. point, on the Hudson River, about 60 miles. It may be crossed, however, by a direct line from S. W. to N. E., from Bordentown to South Amboy, in about 30 miles. The nearest approximation we can make to its area, measuring the map by a reticulated scale of square miles, is about 7,276 square miles, or 4,656,330 acres, contained between 38° 58' and 41° 21' northern latitude.*

II. This area is distributed into three strongly marked divisions; the alluvial and southern; the secondary, hilly and middle; and the mountainous and northern, comprising primitive and transition formations.

III. The triangular peninsula, or southern division, bordered on the S. and E. by Delaware Bay and the Ocean, on the N. and W. by the Delaware River, about 110 miles in length, and 75 in breadth, is entirely alluvial. South of the Nevisink Hills, the surface seldom rises 60 feet above the sea. Those hills, adjacent to the Ocean, are 310 feet above its level; and stand where the waves formerly rolled, resting in some places on banks of oyster shells and other marine relics, blended with clay and

---

* Morse gives 8,320 square miles, or 5,324,800 acres; Smith's Hist. N. J. 4,800,000 acres; and Darby 6,851 square miles, or 4,384,000 acres.

A

sea mud. A sandy earth, highly coloured by oxide of iron, and imbedding reddish brown sand and puddingstone, cemented by iron, composes the higher strata; and large rocks and beds of ferruginous sandstone, apparently in place, of a more recent formation than the alluvial below, containing sufficient metal to be called an ore of iron, are of frequent occurrence. Particles of iron are blended with the sands of the beach ; and some of the streams which descend from the top of the clay strata, are red with iron oxide. Efflorescences of the sulphates of iron and alumine, are often observed ; and flame, proceeding from the spontaneous combustion of gases, generated, probably, in beds of sulphuret of iron, has been noticed here. The strata of the steep eastern declivity are exposed by frequent land slips.

A small portion, only, of these hills is cultivated. They are rough, broken, and covered with wood, in which deer still find covert. From their summit, a view is disclosed of the ocean, unrivalled in grandeur upon the seaboard of this State ; and the coast on the N. E. and S. may be seen as far as the eye can reach. The land prospect, though not so extensive, is scarce less interesting. In this hill, on the side of a branch of the Nevisink River, is a remarkable cave, 30 feet long by 15 broad, divided into three apartments. The entrance and roof are low, the latter arched, and of soft rock, through which the water percolates; the bottom is of loose sand.

Sandy Hook, east of, and divided from, the Nevisink Hills by a narrow bay, is six miles in length. It was formerly, and is now, isolated by a channel running from Shrewsbury River, which was first opened in 1778, closed in 1810, but reopened in 1830. The beach running northward several miles from Long Branch, invites to a promenade on the hard sand when the tide is low ; but the wrecks of vessels, visible at short intervals, oppress the spectators with recollections of the perils of the sea. From the Hook, this beach extends 125 miles to Cape May, varying in width from half a mile to two miles, but broken in several places by channels communicating with the sea. South of Manasquan it covers a number of bays or salt water lakes, of which Barnegat, Little Egg Harbour, and Great Egg Harbour, are the chief. West of these runs a belt of marsh, in some places from four to five miles wide, intersected by small rivers, with broad and shallow estuaries.

The soil of this alluvial district consists of sand and clay, sometimes one overlaying the other; but frequently intimately blended, forming a tolerably fertile loam, which prevails on its northern and western border with a variable breadth. Above Salem, this breadth is from five to twelve miles, but below that town it is sometimes contracted to a mile. East of this strip of loam, and west of the marsh which girds the sea shore, lies an immense sandy plain, scarce broken by any inequality, and originally covered by a pine and shrub-oak forest—a great portion of which has been once, and some of it twice, cut over. There are many square miles on which there is not a human inhabitant, and where the deer, foxes and rabbits are abundant, and the wolf and the bear find a lair to protect their race from extirpation. But in many places the echo is awakened by the woodman's axe, and the louder din of the forge hammer, and the forest glares with the light of the furnace or glass house. In this sandy desert there are found veins of generous soil, which yield a compensatory crop of corn and rye to the labours of the husbandman.

This immense forest covers probably four-fifths of the alluvial district; and forty years ago a large portion of it was not worth more than from six to ten cents the acre. There was little demand for the timber, oak being preferred for architectural and economical uses, nor was the land worth clearing for agricultural purposes. The establishment of furnaces and glass manufactories first gave additional value to the woodland near their locations ; but for a while they made little apparent reduction of the vast wilderness. Then came the steamboats, which for some years traversed our waters, propelled by timber from New Jersey, without sensibly diminishing the density of the forest. In a few years more, however, their number was doubled, trebled, quadrupled. Their huge maws, though fed with thousands of shallop loads of pine wood, were insatiable. The demand for fuel became immense; the almost worthless pine lands rose rapidly in value, and the hitherto almost idle population of the sea-board, found abundant and profitable employment in supplying the growing markets. The introduction of anthracite coal diminished the consumption of oak wood as fuel, but increased that of pine, vast quantities of charcoal being required to ignite the fossil. Yet the invention of the simple portable culinary furnace increased the demand still more, thousands of these convenient utensils being constantly, during the summer months, fed by charcoal. These circumstances have produced an entire revolution in the value of pine lands. They have risen from ten cents, to an average price of six dollars the acre; and, where very well timbered, and convenient to market, bring from fifteen to twenty-five dollars. Indeed, the soil, denuded of the timber, is worth from four to sixteen dollars the acre, the purchaser looking to the growth of wood for profit on his investment. Where the forest has been felled, an extraordinary change takes place in the subsequent product. The oak springs up where the pine has flourished, and pine where the oak has grown. The second growth becomes fit for the axe, in a space varying from 25 to 40 years.

Upon the clay and loam soils, oak grows abundantly; frequently of great size, and of quality much valued in the construction of ships. It is the common timber of the western border, and covers almost exclusively the central portion of the county of Cape May. In the sandy region, are extensive swamps which bear the beautiful and valuable white cedar, much sought for fencing, and which sells readily at from one to three hundred dollars the acre.

Throughout a great portion of the alluvial district, from four to twenty feet beneath the surface, is a species of greenish blue earth, mixed with shells, and generally known as marl. As this substance is of great importance to the agricultural interest of the section, some remarks on its physical properties and use will not be out of place here. The essential ingredient of marl, as a manure, is lime; and its value depends upon the proportion of calcareous matter which it contains. When this abounds in connexion with sand only, it produces indurated marl, classed with the limestones, and frequently forming marble of great variety and beauty. We have discovered none of this precious character; but shell limestone, similar to that of the alluvion of North Carolina, Georgia, and Mississippi Territory, has been discovered in several places, and is burned for lime on the banks of the Rancocus, between Eayrstown and Vincent-town. The Jersey marls, at present, are chiefly known as the shell, clay and stone marls. The first is composed of testaceous matter, in various quantities and degrees of combination; and sometimes imbeds bones of marine and land animals.* The quantity of clay in union with calcareous substances, gives name to the second sort. This absorbs and retains moisture better than other kinds, and varies greatly in colour—being brown, blue, red and yellowish. In the third species, sand is combined with calcareous and argillaceous matter, giving hardness proportionate to its quantity; when of thin and laminar structure, this is termed slate marl. From the clay they contain, all these species are softened by water, and, when exposed to the atmosphere, gradually fall into powder.

By reason of their calcareous principle, all marls effervesce with acids; but as water, alone, frequently produces the same effect when poured on dry clay, it may be necessary, in order to guard against mistake, in making trials upon substances supposed to be marl, to let them remain a short time in mixture with water, previous to the test of acids. The best marls containing the largest proportion of calcareous earth, it is important to know how to ascertain the quantity. Some are so poor as to have only a thirtieth part of their weight of lime. A simple method has been suggested, founded on the fact, that marl commonly contains about forty per cent. of its weight of fixed air or carbonic acid. It is merely by saturating the marl with muriatic or some other acid, and marking correctly the loss of weight which it sustains by the extrication of the fixed air. So, also, if the substance supposed to be marl falls readily to powder when exposed to the air; if the powder, when dry and thrown on hot coals, crackles like salt; and if, when dry, and mixed with water, it have a soapy feel and effervesces much, its quality may be pronounced good.

Some marls in England, and probably here, have eighty-four per cent. of carbonate of lime, which is more than limestone generally possesses; and the refuse being often of peaty substances, is more useful as manure than that of limestone, which is mostly sand or clay. Such marl may be converted into quicklime by burning; and its solution changes vegetable colours to green, possessing all the other properties of caustic lime. Marl is further distinguished by its feeling fat and unctuous, and appearing when dry, after exposure to the weather, as if covered with hoar frost, or sprinkled with fine salt; and even when mixed with the land, giving to the whole surface a whitish appearance.

The farmers in Staffordshire, England, consider the soft blue marl, commonly

---

* Among the latter, it is said, are bones of the rhinoceros and other animals of the eastern continent, some of them of extinct species; elephant's teeth, deer's horns, bones of the whale, shark's teeth, and entire skeletons of fish, together with graphytes, belemnites, cardites, and various shell-fish.

found under clay, or low black ground, at the depth of seven or eight feet, the best
for arable land, and the grey sort for pasture.   But that which is of a brownish
colour, with blue veins, and small lumps of chalk or limestone lying under stiff clays
and very hard to dig, is most esteemed in Cheshire.   The marl having a light sand
in its composition, usually found at the depth of two or three feet, on the sides of
hills, and in wet, boggy grounds, is fat and close, and reckoned the strongest and
most beneficial on sandy lands.   It is usually called peat or delving marl.   What is
sometimes called paper marl, frequently lies near coals, and flakes like leaves or
pieces of brown paper, being of somewhat lighter colour.   That which some call
clay marl is very fat, and is sometimes mixed with chalk stones.   There is another
sort of marl, which breaks of itself into square cubical bits.   The two last kinds generally lie under sand and clay ; sometimes about a yard deep under the former, but
often much deeper under the latter.   The stone, slate or flag marl, which is a kind
of soft stone, or rather slate, of a bluish colour, is generally allowed very good.   It
easily breaks down, and dissolves with frost or rain ; is found near rivers and on the
sides of hills, and is very lasting when used as manure.

In many places marl discovers itself to the most negligent eye, particularly on the
sides of broken hills or deep hollow roads.   Many rivers are bordered with a vast
treasure of this sort, which is plundered by every flood.   Boggy lands frequently
cover it, and in them it seldom lies above three feet deep.   It is somewhat lower
under stiff clays and marshy levels.   The lowest parts of most sandy lands abound
with it, at the depth of three, seven, nine or more feet.   The depth of the marl
itself can seldom be found ; for when the upper crust is removed, all that can be
seen or dug is marl, to so great a depth that there are few if any instances of a pit
having been exhausted.   Much of the preceding description of the English marls
is applicable to those of New Jersey.

The marl region of this State, is classed by some authors with the ferruginous sand
formation of the United States.   It may be located, so far as it has yet been explored,
between two lines ; one drawn from Amboy Bay to Trenton, the other from Deal, on
the Atlantic, to the mouth of Stow Creek, in Cumberland county, upon the Delaware River : but there is much reason to believe that this formation occupies a great
portion of the triangular peninsula south of the Raritan River.   Much of the ferruginous sand region, however, is overlaid by deposites of clay containing lignite.
Above these is an almost uniform covering of grey sand ; yet in many places the
marl, with its peculiar fossil, is found immediately beneath the soil.   This formation
has been traced southward in many places, and most probably extends nearly the
whole length of the Atlantic frontier of the United States.

In all its localities, it has been identified by similar genera and species of organic
remains, though all the genera do not exist in every locality.   Thus, at the Deep Cut
of the Delaware and Chesapeake Canal, the strata are characterized by great numbers of ammonites, baculites, and other multilocular univalves.   These remarks apply
to various parts of Burlington and Monmouth counties, in New Jersey.   Near New
Egypt, are ten or twelve beds, one above the other, with the genera terebratula and
gryphæa.   (*Ostrea*, Say.)   Near Horner's Town, the marl is extremely indurated ;
and contains terebratulæ exclusively.   Near Walnford, the fossils are chiefly exogyræ
and belemnites ; while at Mullica Hill, in Gloucester county, the beds contain bi-
valves, and quantities of belemnites ; and the calcareous beds of this county contain
gryphæa, teredo, alcyonium ? sparangus, and several species of Linnæan madrepores.

The mineralogical characters vary considerably.   Of the species of marl in minute
grains, loose and friable, and of an uniform dull bluish or greenish colour, often with
a shade of grey, and called gunpowder marl, Mr. Seybert has given the following
constituents : silex 49.83, alumine 6.00, magnesia 1.83, potash 10.12, water 9.80,
protoxide of iron 51.53, loss 89=100 grains.   A less cautious analysis by Mr. J. P.
Wetherill and Dr. S. G. Morton, of a specimen, apparently similar, from another locality, gave silex 49.00, protoxide of iron 50.00, alumine 5.50, lime 4.70 ; the remainder being chiefly water and carbonic acid.   Hence the predominant constituents
of these marls are silex and iron.   They often contain beds of a dark bluish tenacious
clay, sometimes mixed with the marl, forming marley clay ; at others, the marl and
clay alternate.

Again, marl is seen of a yellowish brown colour, friable or compact, and filled
with green specks of the silicate of iron.   Some of the greenish varieties are also
very compact, rendering it extremely difficult to separate the fossils from their

matrix. The friable blue marls often contain a large proportion of mica, in minute scales.

Other localities present beds of silicious gravel, the pebbles varying from the size of coarse sand, to one and two inches in diameter, cemented together by oxide and phosphate of iron, and containing fossils, similar to those above described. The most striking instance of this kind is at Mullica Hill. Some of the blue marls, which effervesce strongly with acids, contain but five per cent. of lime. But we find large beds of calcareous marl, containing at least thirty-seven per cent.; the remainder being silex, iron, &c. Also a hard, well characterized, subcrystalline limestone, filled with zeophytes. All these diversified appearances pass, by insensible degrees, into each other, exhibiting an almost endless variety of mineralogical character.

The mineral substances found in these beds, are iron pyrites in profusion; chert in the calcareous beds, amber, retinasphalt, lignite and small spherical masses of a dark green colour, and compact texture, apparently analogous to those found in the green sand of France. Their structure does not appear to be organic, although they have, often, a shark's tooth, or a small shell for a nucleus. Larger spherical bodies also occur, resembling the nodules of clay in ironstone, common in some parts of England.

As the quality of the marl varies greatly, so does the quantity used in manuring lands. In Monmouth county, south of the Shrewsbury River, there is marl so strong, that five cart-loads the acre are as much as the land will bear advantageously : in other places, from twenty to one hundred and forty loads to the acre are profitably used. It is asserted, that a good dressing will last from twelve to twenty years. It would be difficult to calculate the advantages which the state has gained, and will yet derive from the use of marl. It has already saved some districts from depopulation, and increased the inhabitants of others; and may, one day, contribute to convert the sandy and pine deserts into regions of agricultural wealth.

Pine lands, in the counties of Columbia, Albany, and Saratoga, and other parts of the state of New York, of a character similar to those of New Jersey, have been rendered very valuable by gypsum, and rotation of crops, often producing from twenty to twenty-five bushels of wheat to the acre. The sandy soil is in time changed to a rich vegetable mould—and gypsum, therefore, may probably be used with marl to render the pine lands of this State productive.

The occupation of a vast proportion of the inhabitants of this section is agricultural. Upon the loam soils large quantities of grass and grain, particularly rye, corn and oats, are produced; and the sandy lands, treated with marl, also give abundant crops of grain and grass. In convenient situations for supplying the markets of New York and Philadelphia, the farmers give much attention to the more profitable culture of garden vegetables, potatoes, melons, fruit, &c. The peach orchards of E. and W. Jersey, give abundance of that delicious fruit to both cities; so low, at times, as fifty cents the bushel. At a distance from the navigable waters, and from market, the grain is commonly fed to stock, and few portions of the United States, of equal area, produce more, or better, pork, than the counties of Monmouth, Burlington and Gloucester; scarce less famed for the quality of their horses. In the counties of Gloucester, Cumberland and Salem, upon the fresh waters of their streams whose shores are subject to overflow by the tides, many thousand acres have, by embankment, been converted into productive meadows, which maintain large herds of cattle, and furnish adequate means for enriching the upland. Adjacent to the Delaware Bay and sea coast, are wide tracts of salt meadow, some of which have also been reclaimed by embankment; and the rest afford abundance of coarse hay, free in many places to all who seek it, and valuable in the maintenance of stock and making manure. The climate is so mild, near the coast, that herds of cattle subsist, through the winter, upon these meadows, and in the neighbouring thickets, without expense to the proprietors. The sea coast is said also to be favourable to the production of good mutton and wool. The great inducements to enterprise and industry constantly operating in the markets upon the borders of this section, have already produced wonderful effects, and cannot fail to excite the inhabitants to still greater efforts to improve the advantages they possess.

Extensive beds of the variety of argillaceous oxide of iron, called bog ore, are common throughout this district, which when mixed with mountain ore, in the furnace, makes good iron for castings and the forge. From these furnaces, and those of the glass-houses, fed by the wood of the forest, a considerable portion of the annually growing wealth of the district is derived; and if we add to these, the cord wood, and lumber, and vessels built upon its southern waters, we shall have enumerated the chief sources of the prosperity of the peninsula. In this part of the state, 14 furnaces, including cupolas, and 14 forges, one extensive rolling and slitting mill and nail factory, and 11 glass manufactories, engaged in the manufacture of window-glass and hollow ware, provide a valuable and steady market for large portions of the agricultural product.

The whole of this district is tolerably well watered; but the streams are neither large nor rapid, and are remarkable for the depth of their beds, which cause, indeed, almost the only inequalities of its surface. Those of the northern part of the peninsula interlock their sources in various ways; some flow N. and N. E. as the Millstone and the South Rivers, with their many tributaries; some E. to the Atlantic, as the Swimming, Shark, Manasquan, Metetecunk and Tom's Rivers; whilst others seek the Delaware, as the Assunpink, the Crosswicks, the Rancocus, Cooper's, Big Timber, Mantua and Oldman's Creeks. Those on the south either flow S. E. to the ocean, as the Mullica, Great Egg Harbour and Tuckahoe rivers, or run S. W. into the bay, as Salem, Stow and Cohansey creeks and Maurice River. Most of the streams have a crooked course, and flowing through a flat country, are commonly navigable some miles from their mouth. Unlike the rivers of hilly countries, they are steady in their volumes, and uniform supplies of water can be more confidently relied upon.

IV. The second of our divisions of the State is included by a line drawn from Hoboken, running S. of New Brunswick to Trenton, and another from the Ramapo Mountains, on the boundary of New York, curving by the Pompton Mountain or Highlands, Morristown, Baskingridge and Flemington, to the Delaware, between Alexandria and Milford. This section, from N. E. to S. W. has about 70 miles in length, and an average breadth of about twenty miles. It possesses considerable variety of surface and soil, but is strikingly distinguished by its geological formation, which is chiefly secondary or old red sandstone, upon which rest hills of greater or less elevation, crowned with trap or greenstone rock. Its area includes four-fifths of Bergen county, the whole of Essex, a small portion of Morris, nearly all of Somerset, one-half of Middlesex, and one-half of Hunterdon counties. The sandstone base is found in various states of induration and aggregation. Generally, on the eastern portion of the section, from the Palisades, on the North River, westerly to Hunterdon county, it is compact, hard, and well adapted for building, frequently assuming the form of puddingstone and wacke, and occasionally affording considerable organic remains. Between the south branch of the Raritan and Delaware, still underlaying mountain and valley, the red rock assumes a slaty, shaly form, has more clay in its composition, and, taken from whatever depth, readily disintegrates into loam more fertile than that formed from the harder stone. But for the trap hills which have been thrown upon it, the whole of this section would be a vast plain, whose only inequalities would be formed by the excavations made by the streams in their tortuous and generally sluggish passage to the Ocean.

From this general formation, however, we must admit the following exceptions. The alluvial borders the first south-eastern trap ridge, known as the first Newark Mountain, from Boundbrook to Springfield, and westward it approaches the Raritan within two miles, forming the bed of that river a little below Brunswick. Wherever excavations have been made in this alluvial tract, strata of sand, gravel, and clay are disclosed, but no rocks in place. Ochres of good quality have been found in many parts of it, and at Uniontown, near Springfield, compact peat of superior quality, resting on marl, supposed to extend through a morass of five hundred acres. Bones of the mastodon were discovered a few years since in this swamp. Extensive beds of white pipe clay, composed principally of alumine, and infusible, have been observed between Woodbridge and Amboy, and marine shells in various parts of the district.

The alluvial section we have just described, is connected with another five miles in breadth by twenty in length, formed of the deposits of the Hackensack and Passaic Rivers, between the secondary valley and the Bergen ridge. In this tract, the depth of the deposit is from 12 to 20 feet, its basis sand and shells like the shore of the sea. The whole was formerly covered with wood, of which some groves of cedar still remain, and bodies of trees but little decayed are frequently found at various depths. Indeed, so abundant and sound are the logs on these marshes, that they are used for the foundation of the New Jersey Rail-road, now being constructed here. In this bog, N. of the turnpike road, between Newark and Jersey City, rises an island (*Secaucus*) about four miles long by one wide, composed, like the adjacent shores, of red and grey sandstone, and having a promontory at either end. That on the south known as Snake Hill, has a conical form, is of trap rock on sandstone rising into mural precipices, and having cubical masses of the trap piled at its southern base. From its wood clad, rocky and precipitous summit, the spectator may behold the Hackensack and Passaic Rivers almost at his feet, and for several miles dragging their slow length through a sea of verdure; on the west, populous villages and ranges of mountains; on the east the great city of New York, and on the south the wide expanded ocean. Through the grey sandstone of this island, micaceous iron ore is abundantly dispersed; and pectenites and other marine shells are found on its elevated parts.

The trap ridges which traverse this division excite much interest. Trapstone is known in many cases to have an igneous origin. Whether it may be ascribed to the same cause in all, is still a vexed question. That it has been found here subsequently to the sandstone on which it reposes, is most obvious; but when or how it has been poured over its base, throughout such great extent of country, in Connecticut, New York, and Pennsylvania, will probably never be discovered. We observe the first mountainous range of this district, on the eastern border adjacent to the Hudson River. It rises gradually from Bergen Point, bounds the State for about 28 miles, and runs a greater distance into the State of New York. In this State this ridge has an average width of two and a half miles, with a summit of table land. From its western brow there is a gradual descent into the valley of the Hackensack and Passaic. On its eastern side it is uniformly precipitous. At Weehawk, four miles N. of the City of Jersey, the mountain presents a perpendicular wall, elevated 200 feet above the Hudson, commanding a fine view of the surrounding country. From Weehawk to Fort Lee, a distance of about 7 miles, there is an alternation of precipitous ledges and steep declivities, mostly clothed with various verdure. The hills, retiring at intervals from the shore, give room for narrow but fertile and well cultivated strips of ground, adorned with neat dwellings, environed by fruit trees and diversified crops. From Fort Lee to the state line, the mountain has a uniform appearance. The eastern front rises perpendicularly from 200 to 550 feet; numerous vertical fissures cross each other at various angles, forming basaltic columns, from which the name of Palisades has been derived. The face of the ledge is bare, but vegetation is occasionally seen in the crevices. From the base of the precipice to the edge of the water, a distance of 3 or 400 feet, there is a steep declivity covered with angular blocks of stone fallen from the heights, and shaded with trees. The summit of the mountain is slightly undulating table land, gradually rising to the north, with an average width of about two miles, generally covered with wood in all the wildness of nature. The western side of the mountain has a very gradual descent, is cleared and well cultivated, and neat farm houses of freestone line its base, like a village street, for near 20 miles. The prospect is one of the most delightful; numerous farms, rich in luxuriant vegetation, and extensive alluvial meadows through which the Hackensack and its tributaries flow, are bounded by the mountain ranges of the west. The greenstone of this mountain, resting on sandstone, is not so dark as that of New Haven, and is an aggregate of hornblende, feldspar, and epidote, with which prehnite compact and radiated is sometimes associated. At the base of the mountain bordering the river, in many places, secondary argillaceous shist, conglomerate, red, white, yellow and purple sandstone, and indurated clay, alternate, exhibiting a stratification nearly horizontal, the underlaying inclination being from 8 to 10 degrees. These layers are sometimes visible on the mountain's side, at considerable elevations above the river. The sandstone is generally a coarse aggregate of quartz and feldspar, often friable, but sometimes very firmly combined; exhibiting winding vertical fissures. In this base may be observed, in some few places, a compact white sandstone, resembling the Portland stone of England.

A metallic vein was worked, at Fort Lee, at the commencement of the revolutionary war, under the impression that it contained gold; but Dr. Torrey has determined, that the ore is pyritous and green carbonate of copper; and the matrix quartz, dipping under the greenstone.

Two other prominent mountain ranges intersect the country now under view. They rise near the primitive highlands, two miles north of Pompton, and run about sixty miles in an almost semicircular course. The first ridge, at its commencement, is about twenty miles E. from the Palisades; but at, and south of Patterson, it is not

more than twelve, from the North River. The most elevated point of these mountains is six miles N. W. from Patterson, where a sugar-loaf peak rises near 1000
feet above the level of the ocean. Its trap rock is generally covered with a thin
mould and verdant surface; and a walnut grove, without underwood, occupies,
exclusively, about forty acres upon the summit, from which there is a very extensive view, towards the E. N. E. and N. over a tolerably level country. On the N.
W. the waving tops of the Preakness ridge are observed, extending for several
miles, indented by ponds of considerable magnitude and depth. North of this ridge
is another high and detached hill, sweeping in a semicircle, rising and terminating
near the Highlands. Many of the summits are under cultivation, and afford fine
views of the great secondary valley, bounded by the Highlands, the Hudson and
the Preakness ridge. On the east of the last chain is another section of the trap
ranges, called the Totoway mountain. It rises near the Preakness mountain, six
miles from Patterson, and unites with the Newark chain, at the Great Falls. It is
in many places free from rocks, but on the east side are precipices of considerable
height and extent, with waving or denticulated mural faces, presenting columns of
basaltic regularity. An insulated semicircular wall of greenstone, with projecting
columns, bearing some resemblance to a castle or fort in ruins, occupies a summit of
the Totoway ridge. Sandstone quarries are opened in several places at the base
of the greenstone; and one, three miles from Patterson, on the Preakness mountain, affords the best freestone of New Jersey. Fine red and grey sandstone sprinkled with mica, alternates with argillaceous strata, dipping under the greenstone,
with a western inclination of about 12°. Bituminous coal, in layers two inches
thick, has frequently been found in this and other parts of the Preakness ridge, in
connexion with sandstone and shale, and the neighbourhood is supposed to exhibit
indications of more valuable beds of this combustible. Gneiss, granite, pudding
and sandstone, in rolled masses, abundantly cover the surface, in many parts of
this region. The greenstone of the Preakness range rarely offers interesting imbedded minerals; but prehnite, agate, chalcedony, and a mineral resembling cach-
elong, have been discovered in it.

At the falls of the Passaic, in Patterson, perpendicular mural precipices of greenstone, with wide vertical fissures and amorphous masses at their base, may be observed. The lower strata of this rock contain much argillaceous matter, which partially takes the place of hornblende. The ledges rest on porous rocks, horizontally
posited, resembling the toadstone of Derbyshire. Carbonate of lime and other minerals, subject to decay, are imbedded in it; and by their decomposition give a cellular and volcanic appearance. A friable amygdaloid, with an argillaceous base, enclosing nodules of carbonate of lime of a spheroidal oval or almond shape, from the
size of a pea to that of a walnut, may also be noticed. The nodules, easily disen-
gaged from the base, exhibit a smooth dark green surface of chlorite. The layers
beneath the amygdaloid, are red and grey conglomerate, connected with red sandstone, too porous for use, absorbing much moisture and breaking by the expansive
power of frost. Good freestone in nearly a horizontal position, is the basis layer,
and forms the bed of the Passaic. In many places the greenstone occupying the
summit appears but a few feet in thickness; and it is not arranged in columns of ba-
saltiform regularity. Prehnite, calcareous spar and carbonate of copper, zeolite,
stilbite, analcime and datholite, have been found here.

Mural precipices of dark fine grained fissile greenstone, are observed at the Little
Falls of the Passaic, five miles above Patterson. Vertical seams cross each other
here, at various angles, in the ledges, giving to detached pieces a regular prisma-
tic form, with three or four sides, often truncated on one or more of the lateral
edges—the tabular form is common. Rock of similar character is observable in
other parts of the Preakness ridge. Marine organic remains, such as *orthocerites*,
madrepores, tubipores, pectenites, terebratulas, encrinites, bilabites, serpulites,
and other species, generally in an argillaceous base, in mountain and valley, have
been observed here, as in other parts of this region.

From Patterson to Springfield, the trap ridges are called first and second Newark mountains, and Caldwell mountain. Their direction is nearly south, with
great uniformity of altitude; their eastern declivity steep, their western descent
gradual, as is common with mountains of North America. Mural precipices are
rarely seen, except at Patterson and Springfield. Wherever ledges appear, the
mountain side is covered with small amorphous stones. The red sandstone appears
in place, both upon the sides and base. Much of the eastern side is under cultiva-

tion; the summit and western declivity are generally covered by coppice of small oak, chesnut, walnut, butternut and cedar. The second Newark mountain runs a parallel course with, and is distant from, the first, about a mile. It is less elevated and rocky, and has a more gradual ascent than the other. The view from the first embraces the thickly settled and highly cultivated valley, whose surface appears like a plain, painted with meadows, grain fields and orchards, and studded with the villages of Bloomfield, North and South Orange, and the large towns of Newark and Elizabeth;—beyond which we have in sight the salt meadows, the city and harbour of New York, parts of Long and Staten Islands and the distant ocean. In this valley, fine red and grey freestone alternates with shale. Bituminous coal, in thin layers, is associated with argillaceous shale, in freestone quarries, adjacent to the Passaic. At the termination of the Newark Mountain, at Springfield, and in many parts of the trap ranges, smoke, and in some instances, flame issuing from the crevices of the rock, have been observed by the inhabitants; proceeding probably from carbonated hydrogen gas indicating coal below. Animal and vegetable organic remains have been observed in this freestone. Near Belleville a tooth, almost two inches in length, was discovered, some years since, fifteen feet below the surface.

The Newark Mountains terminate at Springfield, where the continuity of the trap range is broken. From this place the greenstone ridges take a S. W. direction of seventeen miles to the vicinity of Boundbrook, and thence, N. W. about ten more to Pluckemin: the second mountain following the curvature of the first. Secondary greenstone is, exclusively, the rock, in place, of the summits and sides of both ridges, but it seldom appears in ledges of magnitude. Sandstone is as usual the base, and has been observed under the greenstone, in nearly a horizontal position, with a small dip, sometimes alternating with secondary compact limestone, in layers, from two inches to two feet in thickness. Prehnite is found in considerable quantities, near the foot of the mountain, in amygdaloid with a greenstone base, much of it partly decomposed. It is sometimes imbedded in the rock, in long parallel columns in various directions, its fibres radiating from the centre. Zeolite, stilbite, crystals of quartz, and carbonate of lime, are frequently seen in the valley between the mountains. North of Scotch Plains, sulphat of barytes appears associated with carbonate of lime. A small portion only of these ranges is cleared and cultivated.

The mountain, running a S. W. course from Springfield, has been termed, by some geologists, the Granite Ridge. It is described as passing through the State, bordering the oceanic alluvial, and having its highest point near Hoboken—alluding, doubtless, to the height near Weehawk. The *Greenstone Ridge* would be the more appropriate name. For excepting the serpentine, at Hoboken, there are no primitive rocks in place, between the Hudson and Highland chains; the summit rock of all the ranges being, uniformly, secondary greenstone. The Highland chain runs from S. E. to N. W., the general direction of the primitive strata; but none of the secondary ranges of New Jersey pursues a course parallel with the primitive. The latter, in many places, preserve for miles an even summit of table-land, whilst the Highland ridges display sugar loaf eminences, and a waving profile, characteristic of the primitive. The extensive secondary range commencing near Pompton, within half a mile of the Highlands, and extending in a semi-circular course until it again approaches them, corroborates, by its direction and the character of its summit, the correctness of these positions. The broad valley, encircled by the Greenstone ridge and the Highlands, contains much fresh water alluvial. Many of its small hills have no rock in place. The plain bordering the Passaic is generally extensive—in some places four miles wide. Peat is observed in several places between the source of the river and Little Falls; and a considerable quantity has been cut, adjacent to the Newark and Morristown turnpike, and the bed discovered to be more than six feet deep.

Pompton Plain, near twenty miles in circumference, and environed by mountains, presents a decided fresh water alluvion—strata of gravel, sand, and clay, without rocks in place, have uniformly been found wherever wells have been dug; and it was, probably, at a remote period, the bed of a lake. The waters of the Pequannock Long Pond and Ramapo Rivers pass through it. The southern and much of the western part of the plain is marshy, and embraces about 1500 acres of peat ground, apparently of good quality, judging by a ditch of four miles in length which has been dug through it. In the southern part of the plain, good granular argillaceous oxide

B

of iron, or pea ore, is found over a space of about 200 acres. The Highlands form the west and north-west boundary of the plain, which in other directions is skirted by the Pacganack Mountain, pursuing a serpentine course from North Pompton, to the vicinity of Morristown, separating the wide alluvial plains watered by the Pompton and Passaic Rivers. Upon this range, the summit rock, in place, is, uniformly, a fine grained dark secondary greenstone, often in a state of partial decomposition, exhibiting mural precipices of considerable height and extent, with sandstone at the sides and base. The first contains prehnite, zeolite, analcime, chalcedony, agate, amethyst, jasper, crystals of quartz, and narrow veins of satin spar, in jasper. The part of this range adjacent to Pompton Plains, may, perhaps, from the abundance of these minerals, be useful to the lapidary, as well as to the mineralogist. The agates are from the size of a pin's head to three pounds weight, mostly chalcedony—The eyed and fortification agate has been observed here in a few instances. A mineral specimen was found in this mountain by Judge Kinsey, of near 16 pounds weight, containing agate, amethyst, and white quartz.

Another greenstone range, of minor extent, called Long Hill, is situate in the great valley, under review, rising near Chatham, and running westerly about ten miles. The trap of this ridge is in such state of decay, that rocks seldom appear in place. The Passaic pursues a winding course along the base of the mountain, sometimes concealed in groves, at others glancing sheen in the verdant meadows. About the centre of Long Hill are mural precipices, composed of what the farmers call shell rock, resembling the stone on the banks of the Raritan.

This secondary formation accompanies the Highlands to the Delaware, and is pierced in several places by broken ridges of the same trap character we have described. Such is the Rocky or Nashanic Mountain, the heights near Rocktown, Lambertville, Belmont, Herberttown, and Woodville, and Rocky Hill, immediately north of Princeton. The sandstone, generally, in this portion of the section, differs materially from that of the Passaic. It extends northerly to the first primitive ridge, north of Flemington, and forms the soil of the broad red shale valley, spreading from that ridge to the Rocky Hills, underlays the last, and extends south of Penington. Its colour is of a darker red than the Newark stone—it appears to be without grain, yields a strong argillaceous odour when breathed upon, and is readily decomposed by exposure to air and moisture. It is, probably, composed of iron, alumine, and silex, with a small portion of sulphur, and may be termed ferruginous shist. The rock is stratified, splitting readily into thin brittle laminæ, and is said to rest in some places on good freestone. But on the S. E. near Princeton, are quarries of excellent red and white freestone, similar to that of the Preakness ridge.

Sandy Hill, an elevation of the secondary region, situate between Kingston and Brunswick, is alluvial, like the Nevisink Hills, composed of sand, white and coloured clay, containing beds of ferruginous sand and puddingstone.

Upon the south-western angle of this district, and particularly at and around Trenton, there is a small portion of primitive, rising through the secondary, into abrupt rocks of granitic character, varying from loose micaceous shale to massive granite, but composed chiefly of hard and compact gneiss. This rock forms the Falls of the Delaware at the head of tide, and stretches away in a S. W. direction through Pennsylvania. From a mass in the bed of the river, large and beautiful specimens of zircon have been taken.

The portion of New Jersey which we have now described, is the most populous, and perhaps the most wealthy of the State. Its soil is not so productive as the limestone of the primitive and transition regions; but there is less of it waste, than in those regions, and it is divided into smaller farms, and more assiduously laboured, under the excitement of proximity to the markets of New York and Philadelphia, and that created in the eastern portion by its own manufacturing towns; as Patterson, Little Falls, Godwinsville, New Prospect, Bloomfield, Belleville, North and South Orange, Springfield, Plainfield, Newark, Elizabethtown, Rahway, Woodbridge, New Brunswick, Princeton, Trenton, &c.

Besides the minerals already mentioned, large deposits of copper ore have been discovered in this section, at Belleville, at Griggstown, near Brunswick, Woodbridge, Greenbrook, Somerville, and Pluckemin; and it would seem probable that a vein of this metal extends S. W. across the secondary region from Fort Lee.

The following account of the mine near New Brunswick is extracted from Morse's Gazetteer:—

" About the years 1748, 1749, 1750, several lumps of virgin copper, from 5 to 30 lbs. weight, (in the whole upwards of 200 lbs.) were ploughed up in a field belonging to Philip French, Esq., within a quarter of a mile of the town. This circumstance induced Mr. Elias Boudinot to take a lease of the land of Mr. French, for 99 years, with a view to search for copper ore. A company was formed, and about the year 1751, a shaft was commenced in the low ground 300 yards from the river. The spot selected had been marked by a neighbour, who, passing it in the dark, had observed a flame rising from the ground, nearly as large as the body of a man. At about 15 feet, the miners struck a vein of blue stone, about two feet thick, between loose walls of red sand stone, covered with a sheet of pure copper, somewhat thicker than gold leaf. The stone was filled with grains of virgin copper, much like copper filings, and occasionally lumps of virgin copper of from 5 to 30 pounds were found in it. This vein was followed about thirty feet, when the accumulation of water exceeded the means of the company to remove it. A stamping mill was erected, where, by reducing the ore to powder, and washing it, many tons of pure copper were obtained and exported to England. Sheets of copper of the thickness of two pennies, and three feet square, have been taken from between the rocks, within four feet of the surface, in several parts of the hill. At about fifty or sixty feet deep, a body of fine solid ore was struck in the same vein, but between rocks of white flinty spar, which was soon worked out."

Some efforts were made to renew the mining operations here, at various periods, but never with encouraging success. The excavations have been extensive. A shaft of great depth is yet visible; an adit, it is said, was driven several hundred yards beneath the bed of the river, and hydraulic pumps were worked by Lyell's Brook to free the mine from water. The stones around the vicinage are every where coloured by the oxide of copper, and beautiful copper pyrites are obtained from the neighbouring quarries.

The Schuyler copper mine, near Belleville, on the left bank of the Passaic, seven miles from Jersey City and Hoboken, was discovered about the year 1719, by Arent Schuyler. The ore cropping out on the side of a hill was easily raised; and as the policy of Great Britain prohibited every species of manufacture in the colonies, it was exported in the crude state to England. From the books of the discoverer, it appears that before the year 1731, he had shipped 1,386 tons to the Bristol copper and brass works. His son, Col. John Schuyler, prosecuted the work with more numerous and skilful hands; but the quantity of ore raised by him is unknown, his books having been lost during the war.

In 1761, the mine was leased to a company, who erected a steam engine, of the imperfect construction then in use, and worked the mine profitably for four years. In 1765, however, a workman, who had been dismissed, having set fire to the engine-house, the works were discontinued. Several gentlemen in England, acquainted with the superior quality of the ore of this mine, obtained permission from the crown to erect works for smelting and refining copper in America, and offered to purchase the estate of Mr. Schuyler, containing the mine, at £100,000 sterling. This offer he refused, but agreed to join them in rebuilding the engine and working the mine. But the revolutionary war, and the deranged state of the country subsequent thereto, and other circumstances, caused the mine to be neglected until 1793, when a new company undertook the work with much vigour, but it would seem with little prudence. They collected miners from England and Germany, purchased a freehold estate, convenient for the erection of furnaces and manufactories, with an excellent stream of water, rebuilt the engine, and commenced and partly completed other works. Their labours were interrupted by the death of the principal shareholder in the company, the whole interest of which soon after was vested in Mr. Nicholas I. Roosevelt, whose many engagements debarred him from prosecuting this enterprise.

Another company, organized in 1825, procured some Cornish miners, and cleared out two adit levels, three old shafts, and sunk one new one about 60 feet deep; erected a new steam engine, and prepared most of the necessaries for working the mine in the deep levels. But, when they were ready to break out ore, some inefficient machinery designed to pump the water from the vein to the great shaft, gave way, and the funds or patience of the company were insufficient to prosecute the enterprise further. Their lease, conformable to its terms, was forfeited. We understand that during the present year (1833), a new association has been formed for working this mine.

There are many veins well worth working, particularly those near the surface, containing what is termed stamp ore. The principal vein, which has proved very profitable, is imbedded in a stratum of freestone, from 20 to 30 feet thick, and is called a pipe vein. It dips about 12 degrees from the horizon, rather by steps than a straight line, and increases in richness with its depth. It has been followed 212 feet below the surface, and about 112 feet beneath the adit cut for draining ; hence, the water must be pumped to that level. A large shaft has been sunk 140 feet below the adit, 30 feet of which have been filled with mud and rubbish. The engine at the mine has a cylinder 31½ inches in diameter, and eight feet stroke, and has ample power to free the mine from water. Excellent cast iron pumps are fixed from the level of the vein to the adit, and from the adit to the surface, for supplying the engine. The vein has been worked about 150 feet, horizontally, from the shaft, declining from the entrance a few feet : hence, though the leakage is inconsiderable, some method is required to carry it into the shaft, which may be readily done if the shaft be cleared to the bottom.

The ore of the principal vein, it is said, yields from 60 to 70 per cent. of copper ; and the vein will produce, it is supposed, from 100 to 120 tons of ore annually, which yields from four to seven ounces of silver to the hundred pounds; and, like most copper ores, a small portion of gold. When pure copper was sold in England at £75 sterling the ton, the ore of this mine was shipped from New York for that market at £70 the ton. The quality of the ore, and condition of the mine, are attested by several respectable persons, who have skill and proper means to judge of them.

If the statement respecting the proportion of silver in this ore be correct, it is more productive than many of the much-worked and highly valued mines of Mexico. The mines of Biscayna, of Royas, of Tehuilotepec, and of Gautla, do not yield more than three ounces of pure silver to one quintal of the ore; whilst the remarkable rich mines of the Count de la Valenciana, at Guanaxuato, gave only 5.1-10 ounces the quintal. The mean product of the whole Mexican mines, when in their best condition, did not exceed 2½ ounces the quintal; and that of the ores of Peru was still less; giving at most at Potosi, 53-100, and at Pasco, 1.3-50 ounces, the quintal. If the ores of the Schuyler mine give from four to seven ounces of silver the quintal, and are abundant, they must be better worth working for the silver alone than most of the silver mines of the world; and the copper product must add enormously to their value.

The copper mine in the trap ridge, two miles north of Somerville, commonly known as Cammam's, has been wrought at intervals for many years, but without profit; more, it is said, because of the want of capital, and public confidence in the operators, than from the poverty of the ores. The following, according to Dr. Torrey, are the principal minerals found here, viz : native copper in irregular masses, weighing from one ounce to eight pounds, and one block has been obtained of 23 pounds ; phosphate of copper, massive, and of a verdigris colour, generally accompanying native copper ; carbonate of copper, green, in connexion with the phosphate ; red oxide of copper ; the massive variety of which is the common ore of the mine, found crystallized in octahedra, whose surfaces are extremely brilliant and beautiful; native silver, in small masses, disseminated through the phosphate and crystallized oxide; green quartz, in tabular, partly noded masses, a beautiful mineral, resembling chrysoprase; prehnite, in cavities in the greenstone, very fine ; and mountain leather, in thin plates, very tenacious when moistened. Drifts have been made in various directions in this mine, and the ore is said to be abundant, yielding from 25 to 75 per cent. of pure metal.

North of the village of Greenbrook, in the same ridge, a vein of copper, many years since, was wrought to a considerable extent ; but it, too, has been long abandoned.

To these locations of copper, we are now to add another, lately discovered, near Flemington, in a vein remarkably, but not yet extensively, explored.

V. The third section, into which we have divided the State, and which we have called the mountainous, is in breadth from 10 to 40 miles, measured at right angles with the direction of the mountains. This district is the most interesting, as it is the most varied, in its geological formation, surface, soil, mineral and vegetable productions.

The geological formations here are much blended and confounded ; and the most we can attempt is to designate and describe the strongly marked divisions. The secondary section we have above noticed, is bounded on the N. W. throughout its range by a broad district of primitive ; containing, however, a large proportion of transition. The southern limits of this district are marked by the chain of highlands running S. W. from the Ramapo and Pompton Mountains, on the line of New York, by Morristown, Baskingridge and Flemington to, and across, the Delaware, near Saxtonville. The extension, northward, is limited to a line running west of the Wallkill Mountains, and thence crossing the Delaware in the neighbourhood of Belvidere. A belt of transition, having an average breadth of about six miles, including Long Pond, Raffenberg and Greenpond Mountains, continues, we believe, along the eastern foot of Musconetcong and Schooley's Mountains, across the State. The continuity of the eastern ridges of the primitive, with its belt of transition, is interrupted in many places by the streams; yet the hills form few valleys of considerable extent, and are generally less elevated in this State than in the vicinity of the Hudson River, where they rise to 1600 feet. They are usually crowned by sugarloaf eminences, forming a waving profile, characteristic of primitive regions. The summits are commonly covered with masses of rock, which render them unfit for culture.

The primitive ridges contain rocks of pretty uniform character; in general coarse, well crystallized aggregates of quartz and feldspar; often enclosing shorl, garnets, hornblende and epidote, with little mica; and in many places, for a considerable extent, none. These simple materials, variously combined, form granite, gneiss and sienite. Primitive greenstone is observable also in some cases.

In the transition section, grauwacke and grauwacke slate, are the most common rocks. The extensive ranges in Bergen and Morris counties, of Long Pond, Raffenberg, and Green Pond Mountains, for miles present stupendous mural precipices, facing the east, of a reddish brown grauwacke, composed of red and white quartz, red and grey jasper, and indurated clay. The rocks are stratified, inclining to the north-west at an angle of about 40°. They are scattered in abundance on the banks of the Pequannock, from Newfoundland to Pompton. Grauwacke, in place, is sometimes observed, resting on sienite adjacent to the Pequannock. Extensive beds of magnetic iron ore are found on these ranges at Ringwood and Mount Pleasant, and at Suckasunny, at the mines of General Dickenson, being on the strata which extends 300 miles from the White Hills of Newhampshire, to the end of the primitive ridge near Black River. These beds are from 8 to 12 feet thick; and the ore from the mine of General Dickenson produces the best iron manufactured from highland ore. Calcareous spar and asbestos are frequent, and sulphuret of iron abounds in various parts of the Highlands. Probably, the most extensive bed of the last is in Morris county, near the eastern base of Copperas Mountain, and opposite to Green Pond. Copperas was manufactured here extensively during the late war with Great Britain. Many rich beds of iron ore in this region, are rendered useless for the forge by sulphur. Graphite or black lead, in various stages of purity, is common.

At Monro Iron Works, (N. Y.) on the River Ramapo, large plates of black mica, crystallized in hexaedral form, are seen sometimes a foot in diameter. Compact feldspar and epidote, are in the elevated primitive ranges west of the transition district, and compact limestone at various parts of the transition range; and in the vicinity of New Germantown, and on a line running N. E. and S. W. from that point, pudding limestone, not inferior in beauty to that employed in the capitol of Washington, is abundant, and frequently converted into lime. In the primitive range of Morris county, west of Pompton Plains, called Stony Brook Mountains, chlorite slate is common, and granular limestone has recently been found in the same mountain. The latter is in colour clear white, admits of good polish, and is often associated with beautiful amianthus and talc, alternating in narrow veins. In the same vicinity there is a greyish white marble, rendered porphyritic by grains of noble serpentine disseminated through it. It is hard and receives a fine polish. In the talc, metallic crystals supposed to be chromate of iron, have been observed. From the last mentioned mineral an acid is extracted, which, united with lead, forms chromate of lead, a valuable pigment. Galena has been observed in the grauwacke ranges adjacent to Green Pond, and beautiful tremolite is connected with the white granular limestone of Stoneybrook.

North-west of the transition, the primitive resumes its empire, and includes the Wallkill and Hamburg Mountains, which are continued in Schooley's and the Musconetcong Mountains, from the line of New York to the line of Pennsylvania, undivided by any stream. In this ridge and the portion of the primitive sections west of it, the primitive, the transition, and the secondary formations seem combined. This region also includes Marble Mountain, Scott's Mountain, Jenny Jump, Furnace Mountain, Pimple Hill, Pochuck Mountain, and other innominate hills. This, also, is a remarkable mineral district. Schooley's Mountain and the Musconetcong, abound with highly magnetic iron ore, blended however with foreign substances,

which render liquefaction difficult. Along the valleys and hill sides of this mountain there is an abundance of excellent flints suitable for guns.

West of the Hamburg Mountain lies the valley of the Wallkill, or, as it is sometimes called, the Valley of Sparta; running east of north twenty miles to the State
of New York, much noted for the number and variety of its minerals. A white
crystalline limestone and marble occupies the bottom of the valley, and rises on the
west into a low subsidiary ridge following the course of the stream eight or nine miles.
The metalliferous deposits, however, claim the greatest interest. The first or eastern
bed, which at Franklin appears like a black mountain mass, contains an ore of iron
commonly little magnetic, and, as a new metalliferous combination, has received the
name of Franklinite, and is composed of 66 per cent. of iron, 16 of zinc, and 17 of
the red oxide of manganese. On its supposed richness the great furnace of Franklin was built, but it was soon discovered that this ore was not only irreducible to
metallic iron, but that it obstructed the fusion of other ores. If employed in quantity exceeding one-tenth of the magnetic oxide of iron with which it was economi-
cally mixed, there resulted what the smelters term a *salamander;* an alloy of iron
with manganese, which resisted fusion and crystallized even under the blast, so that
all the metal was lost, the hearth demolished, and 10 or 12 yoke of oxen required
to drag away the useless mass. At Franklin, it is but sparingly intermixed with
the red oxide of zinc. About two miles north, the bed ceases to be apparent at the
surface, but may be traced seven miles to the south-east. Three miles from the furnace, at Stirling, is another huge mass of this mineral, but so combined with the red
oxide of zinc, that the crystals of Franklinite are imbedded in the zinc, forming a
metalliferous porphyry. This ore, merely pounded and mixed with copper, was
profitably employed during the late war for forming brass. Often, within a few feet
west of the Franklinite, appear beds of well characterized magnetic oxide of iron,
but always accompanied by hornblende rock. A species of this last ore, found near
the furnace, is intimately blended with plumbago. Here, also, are curious beds of
yellow garnet, imperfect sienitic granite, in which are beautiful opaque blackish
brown masses of garnet of a high resinous lustre, and crystallized on the surface,
accompanied with laminated epidote; white and compact massive or minutely laminated augite, in some parts intimately blended with specks of violet, granular feldspar, resembling petrosilex; sphene, brown garnet, dark green granular augite, like
the cocolite of Lake Champlain; phosphate of lime; spinelle and black spinelle or
fowlerite, from Dr. Fowler, of Franklin, its discoverer; specular iron ore; brucite,
bronzite, pargazite and idocras, zircon, tremolite, imbedded in crystals of white augite; actynolite, short crystals of augite almost black, like those of volcanic rocks;
apatite, a beautiful apple green feldspar, in crystalline carbonate of lime, accompanied with perfect crystals of mica, and hexagonal plates of plumbago, soft and
almost as fusible as hornblende; a very brilliant pale green hornblende, passing into
actynolite, which has been denominated maclureite, in honour of him who has done
so much for American geology, and natural science in general;—blue and white
sapphire, enormous green crystals of augite, at least an inch and a half in diameter, presenting hexaedral or octahedral prisms, with almost equal faces, and termi-
nated by oblique tetrahedral pyramids, accompanied, near the junction of granite
and crystallized carbonate of lime, with large crystals of feldspar; scapolite, or wernerite; arsenical pyrites, mixed with others resembling the sulphuret of cobalt, or
nickel, with a substance like blende, accompanied by dendrodite, and argillaceous
fluate of lime.

The crystalline calcareous rock which here alternates with granitines of feldspar
and quartz, or with beds of sienitic granite, at other places, disappears, and a conflu-
ent grauwacke, almost porphyritic, and contemporaneous, apparently, with the other
formations, is observed, directly overlaid by a bed of leaden, minutely granular, secondary limestone, containing organic remains of the usual shells and corallines,
and layers of blackish hornstone or petrosilex. This rock, as well as the grauwacke *beneath* has disseminated crystals of blue fluate of lime. In the limestone
the cavities are sometimes very numerous, and lined both with pseudomorphous
masses and cubes, and white fluate and quartz crystals. Thus we have here before
us, as at Lake Champlain, the rare and interesting spectacle of an union of every
class of rocks, but passing decidedly into each other, as if almost contemporaneous.
This singular formation, to which slate should be added, extends into Orange county, State of New York. Immense masses, some miles in length, of the red oxide
of zinc, lie in the mountains, near Sparta; and as this ore may be easily converted

into metal, they will probably one day add greatly to the wealth of this portion of the State. The white crystalline limestone, which is so interesting a feature of this region, has been distinctly traced from Mounts Adam and Eve, in the state of New York, to Byram township of Sussex county, in an uninterrupted line of twenty-five miles, with a width varying from two and a half miles, to that of a few rods, its greatest breadth being at the state line. Its inclination, except at Mounts Adam and Eve, is low, often falling below the adjoining limestone of more recent date. It crops out, only here and there, in large masses; and its continuity is to be observed, solely, by boulders and loose stones, scattered over the surface. It most probably extends, with occasional breaks, to Easton on the Delaware. Silver and gold are asserted to have been found in several places of the primitive region, and attempts have been made at various times, by the ignorant, who have been self-deceived, and by the knavish who have deceived others, to work veins of pyrites, which have a resemblance to those metals.

Among these primitive ridges, we must notice, upon the S. W., Scott's Mountain, and Jenny Jump, in both of which, are extensive deposits of magnetic iron ore, and other interesting minerals. In the first, near Oxford furnace, the mining of iron was many years ago very extensively conducted, and shafts of great depth, and drifts of great length, are still visible. The works, however, had been long abandoned, when Messrs. Henry and Jordan, from Pennsylvania, with praiseworthy enterprise recommenced them in 1832. They are now prosecuting a vein of productive magnetic ore, blended with carbonate of lime, from 10 to 12 feet wide, enclosed by parietes of mica shale. Throughout these mountains, the elements of primitive rock may be found variously and curiously combined; but we are not aware, that they have been subjected to minute examination by the naturalist.

N. W. of the primitive hills we have described, there lies a valley, having an average breadth of about 10 miles, but broadest near the Delaware, extending over the northern parts of Sussex and Warren counties. It is drained for the greatest part by Paulin's Kill, flowing to the Delaware, and may, therefore, properly be termed Paulin's Kill Valley. It is bounded on the N. W. by the Blue Mountain. The valley is covered with knolls and low ridges, at first view apparently in much confusion, but which may be traced on the inclination of the mountains. Transition limestone alternates here with slate. A notable ridge of the latter bounds the Paulin's Kill on the S. E. side, from near its mouth to Newton, whilst the N. W. side is as strikingly distinguished by its range of limestone, which may be traced to Orange county, New York. North of the limestone, there is another ridge of slate, of a character well adapted for roofing and ciphering slate, quarries of which are extensively worked on the Delaware. Between this slate and the Blue Mountain lies a bed of grauwacke. The mountain contains the usual species of transition rocks, grauwacke, in every variety of aggregation, slate, mountain limestone, and greenstone, and rising from 1400 to 1600 feet high, is covered with wood, in which the deer, bear, wolf, and most wild animals, indigenous, still roam. N. W. of the mountain, bounded by the Delaware River, lies a fertile tract of transition limestone land, watered by the Flat Kill, and varying in width from one to seven miles.

The mountains of this third section are, generally, in a state of nature. There are, however, some cultivated spots, which reward the husbandman. But the valleys form the most fertile portions of the State. They are generally based on limestone; and since lime has been extensively adopted as manure, they have rapidly improved. This is especially the case among the Highlands, at Clinton, New Germantown, in the valleys of the north and south branches of the Raritan and of Lamington rivers, in the valleys of the Musconetcong, the Pohatcong, the Pequest and its tributaries, and valleys of Paulin's Kill and Flat Kill. All these produce wheat in abundance, and where wheat abounds and finds a ready way to market, no other good thing is absent. Wheat and iron are the staples of the country, which in the lower part of the section, seek the market by the Morris canal. There were, in 1832, by the report of the assessors, fifteen furnaces and eighty-seven forge fires in operation in the counties of Sussex, Warren, Morris and Bergen. By the completion of the Morris canal, the iron mines are growing into vast importance; great demand for the ores having been created in West Jersey, Pennsylvania and New York. From the valley of the Musconetcong immense quantities of wheat are exported, individual farmers raising from one thousand to three thousand bushels per annum.

Marble for ornamental architecture is abundant in this district. At Mendham.

Morris county, it occurs with dendritic impressions in which it resembles the beautiful marble of Florence. White marble and noble serpentine, we are told, are found in large masses on the Pompton Mountain, and also near Phillipsburg. Manganese, too, is said to be abundant in various parts of the section, and a water lime, similar to that of New York, has been discovered at Mendham and other places.

South-east of the Musconetcong Mountain, this district is drained by the Ramapo River, which divides the primitive formation from the secondary, in Bergen county; by Longpond or Ringwood River, which rises in Longpond or Greenwood Lake; by the Pequannock, which has its source in the Wallkill Mountains : these streams uniting in Pompton and Saddle River townships, Bergen county, form the Pompton River, which joins the Passaic, about four miles N. W. of the Little Falls. The Passaic receives also the Rockaway, Whippany and Dead Rivers. The remainder of this part of the section is tributary to the Raritan River, which receives from it, three of its main branches; the North, the Lamington and the South; each of which has a tortuous course, and waters a great extent of surface, but all having their source S. W. of the Musconetcong and Hamburg Mountains, which separate entirely the whole of the section.

There are several lakes, of from four to six miles in compass, and others larger. The principal is Greenwood Lake, upon the confines of New York, about 16 miles in circumference ; lying in a narrow valley of the Highlands, scarce a mile wide. Mackepin, in the southern part of Pompton township, covers less surface, and is supposed to be 600 feet above the waters of an adjacent mountain valley. Greenpond, on the south of the Hamburg turnpike and near the valley of Newfoundland, is a beautiful sheet of water, about eight miles in circumference, bounded E. by the woodclad Copperas Mountain, and W. by a high and savage hill, which bears its name. Two or three farm houses, pleasantly situated, on a sandy beach, on its northern bank, serve as an hostelrie, for the sportsmen of Morris and Bergen counties, when resorting to this their favourite spot. Some of the lakes in the transition region have their borders girded by lofty walls of grauwacke, and rival in their romantic scenery the celebrated sheets of Cumberland and Westmoreland. Budd's Pond upon Schooley's Mountain is also remarkable for its fish, as were Hurds and Hopatcong Lakes ; but the last is now celebrated as the perennial source of the supply of water for the Morris Canal, being on the summit level, and the principal feeder. In its natural state the Hopatcong poured forth its waters to the Delaware, only, by the Musconetcong Creek, which courses the north-western base of the Musconetcong Mountain.

The streams that drain the interval, between the Musconetcong and the Blue Mountain, westwardly, are, the Musconetcong, Pohatcong, Lapatcong, Pequest, and Paulinskill; and eastwardly, the Wallkill. In this valley there are also several small lakes; the most curious of which are the White Ponds, near Marksboro', and Pimple Hill, both noted for the quantity of the shells of the small white fresh water snail, which covers the bottom and banks. At the first, the mass of these shells is enormous, covering the sides and bottom of the pond many feet thick. North of the Blue Mountain the only stream worth special notice is the Flatkill.

Oak, walnut, beach, birch, ash, elm and sugar maple, are the predominant timber of the third section. Pine, hemlock, and cedar, are scattered through the forest, adjacent to the lakes and streams. On the high points of ground, walnut and oak are the most common trees. Shrub oak is the most frequent in the transition highland district which passes through Morris county. It occupies almost exclusively an extensive level interval on the north of Suckasunny Plain, attaining the height of six or eight feet, and forming an entangled thicket, beneath which the ground is covered with loose stones.

We have already mentioned the number of peach orchards in the alluvial of the State, and we may observe here, that the apple orchards of the secondary, primitive, and transition sections, are not less worthy of notice. The cider of New Jersey is justly preferred to any other of the United States, and the quantity of ardent spirit distilled from it, may be conjectured by a glance at the list of distilleries in the general statistical table.

For a more particular notice of the rivers of the State, and of the bridges which cross them, we refer the reader to the names of the streams, respectively, in the subsequent part of the work. But we will conclude this physical sketch by a view of the turnpike roads, rail roads, and canals, which traverse the State.

VI. Turnpikes. Since March, 1801, authority has been given for making 54 turnpike roads. The object of these improvements seems threefold. 1. The facilitating the communication between the great cities of New York and Philadelphia. 2. The more ready approach from the interior to the markets of New York and Easton, for the products of agriculture and the mines ; and 3. The drawing the produce of the Delaware river, to the waters of East Jersey and New York, all which has been much aided by the capital of that great city. The following list gives the titles of these acts, the dates of their enactment, with their respective supplements. Those marked with an asterisk, (*) have been wholly, or partially, carried into effect.

1801, March 9. *1. Morris Turnpike, from Elizabethtown, through Morristown and Newton, over the Minisink Mountain, at Culver's Gap, to the Delaware, opposite Milford. Supplement, Nov. 10, 1803.

1802, Nov. 30. *2. Hackensack and Hoboken. Supplement, Nov. 16, 1807.

1804, Feb. 23. *3. Union, from Morristown to Sparta.

1806, Nov. 11. *4. Union continued from Sparta, through Culver's Gap, to the Delaware. Supplement, Feb. 4, 1815.

1804, Nov. 14. *5. Trenton and New Brunswick. Supplement, Nov. 28, 1806. Feb. 1, 1814.

1804, Dec. 1. *6. City of Jersey and Hackensack. To which the state subscribed $12,500. Supplement, Nov. 4, 1808.

1806, Feb. 24. *7. Newark and Pompton. Supplement, Nov. 28, 1806. Jan. 28, 1830.

„ 27. *8. Newark and Mount Pleasant. Supplement, May 9, 1820.

„ *9. Jersey, from New Brunswick to Easton Bridge, on the Delaware. Supplement, Nov. 28, 1806. Feb. 22, 1811. Feb. 14, 1815. Feb. 15, 1816. Feb. 16, 1831.

„ March 3. *10. Essex and Middlesex, from New Brunswick to Newark. Supplement, Nov. 17, 1821.

„ „ *11. Washington, from Morristown to the Delaware, opposite to Easton. Supplement, Nov. 15, 1809.

„ „ *12. Patterson and Hamburg, from Acquackanonck landing to Deckertown. Supplement, Nov. 26, 1806. Nov. 23, 1822.

1806, March 3. 14. Springfield and Newark.

„ *15. Franklin, from New Prospect to the New York line.

„ March 12. 16. Hunterdon and Sussex.

1807, Dec. 3. *17. Princeton and Kingston—branch of Trenton and New Brunswick turnpike.

„ „ 18. Jefferson, through Berkshire valley to the Patterson and Hamburg road.

„ Nov. 16. 19. Belleville, from Belleville bridge to the Newark and Pompton road, between Bloomfield and Cranetown.

1808, Nov. 22. *20. Perth Amboy, to Boundbrook. Supplement, Feb. 18, 1820.

„ „ *21. Woodbridge, from New Brunswick, through Piscataway and Woodbridge, to Rahway.

„ Nov. 24. 22. Burlington, through Bordentown, to intersect the Trenton and New Brunswick turnpike. Supplement, November, 1809. Feb. 6, 1811.

„ Nov. 28. 23. Jersey and Acquackanonck, from Acquackanonck to Belleville turnpike.

„ 28. *25. Deckertown and Milford. Supplement, Feb. 10, 1813. Dec. 7, 1825. Dec. 16, 1826.

1809, Nov. 28. *13. Patterson and Hamburg, continued from Deckertown over the Blue Mountain, to the Delaware opposite to Milford. Supplement, Feb. 11, 1815. Feb. 15, 1816. January 23, 1818.

„ 29. *24. Parsippany and Rockaway, from Vanduyns, through Rockaway, to the Union turnpike.

1811, Feb. 8. 26. Water Gap, from the Morris and Sussex turnpike, near the 34 mile post, through Milton and Hope, to the Delaware, near the Water Gap. Supplement, Feb. 3, 1813.

„ 9. *27. Ringwood and Longpond, and division line between the 29th and 30th mile stones. Supplement, Feb. 10, 1813. Feb. 6, 1819.

C

1811, Feb. 9. 28. Farmers, from Springfield, through New Providence, Long
                    Hill, Pluckemin, to the Jersey turnpike near Potterstown.
      „   11. *29. Newark and Morris, from Newark, through S. Orange to Bot-
                    tle Hill or Morristown. Supplement, Feb. 12, 1817. Jan.
                    15, 1818. Feb. 7, 1820. Dec. 5, 1823.
      „   14. 30. Vernon, from the division line, near Decay's, to the Patterson
                    and Hamburg turnpike.
      „   31. New Milford, from the division line between the 29th and 30th
                    mile stones.
1813, Jan. 12. 32. Dover, to Suckasunny.
      „   *33. Spruce Run, from Clinton, in Hunterdon county, to the Wash-
                    ington turnpike road, near Sherard's mill, in Sussex county.
                    Supplement, Jan. 26, 1814. Jan. 27, 1818.
      „ Feb. 11. 34. Hope and Hackettstown.
      „   *35. New Germantown, from Bayle's Mill and White House to New
                    Germantown.
1814, Jan. 27. *36. Deckertown and Newton. Supplement, Feb. 4, 1817. Feb. 4,
                    1831.
      „   37. Vernon and Newton, from Decay's, in the division line, by
                    Hamburg, to Sussex Court House.
      „ Feb. 11. 38. New Brunswick and Middleburg.
1815, Jan. 18. *39. Hackensack and Hoboken. Supplement, Jan. 21, 1818.
      „ Feb. 6. *40. Patterson and Hackensack. Supplement, Feb. 27, 1824. Nov.
                    6, 1827.
      „ Feb. 11. 41. Mount Hope and Longwood. Feb. 7, 1820.
      „   42. New Providence, from Morristown to Scotch Plains.
1816, Feb. 15. 43. Georgetown and Franklin. Supplement, Jan. 20, 1819. Dec.
                    12, 1823. Feb. 25, 1828.
      „ Feb. 16. *44. Bordentown and South Amboy. Supplement, January 20,
                    1817. Nov. 6, 1819. Dec. 8, 1826.
      „   45. Belleville, to the Newark and Pompton road, at the Little Falls.
      „   46. Woodbridge, to the New Blazing Star.
      „   47. Patterson and Hamburg, to the Hudson, from Acquackanonck
                    Bridge, to the Hackensack and Hoboken roads near the
                    Three Pigeons. Supplement, Dec. 7, 1824.
1817, Feb. 12. *48. Pochuck, from Hamburg to Goshen, N. Y.
1819, Jan. 21. 49. Columbia and Walpack, to intersect the Sussex and Morris
                    turnpike.
      „ Feb. 6. 50. Newton, from near Andover furnace, through Newton, to the
                    third district of the Morris and Essex turnpike, near the Blue
                    Mountain.
1825, Nov. 23. 51. Patterson and New Prospect.
      „   52. Patterson and New Antrim, from Patterson through Saddle
                    River and Franklin townships.
1828, Jan. 23. 53. Hackensack and Fort Lee.
      „   54. Passaic, from Patterson to Little Falls.

Not more than half the projects for roads, which have received legislative sanction, have been executed; but in some instances the new laws were wholly, or
partly, substituted for others, of which the designated routes had been abandoned.
There have been made, however, about 550 miles of turnpike road, principally of
earth and gravel. We do not recollect to have seen, in any direction, five conti-
nuous miles of road paved with stone. The main highways of the State are preserved in pretty good condition, and generally during the summer and fall seasons
may be travelled with pleasure, in every direction. Some of them are preferable to
the turnpikes, particularly such as pass over the slate and sandstone regions, where
the hard rock approaches the surface.

VII. Up to the year 1833, nine companies have been chartered for making rail-
roads, with authority to employ the sum of $7,140,000 towards these objects. The
Camden and Amboy Rail-road Company was incorporated under the act of February
4th, 1830, authorizing a capital stock of $1,000,000, with privilege to increase it
$500,000, divided into shares of $100 each, to be employed in the construction of
rail-road or roads, with all necessary appendages, from the Delaware River, at some

point between Cooper's and Newton Creeks, in the county of Gloucester, to some point on the Raritan Bay; the road to be one hundred feet wide, with as many set of tracks as may be necessary, with a lateral road to Bordentown; reserving to the legislature the right to subscribe one-fourth, or less, of the capital stock, within a limited time—which right was not exercised—with condition, also, that the road should be commenced within two, and be completed within nine, years; and that the company should make quarterly returns of the number of passengers, and tons of merchandise, transported upon the road, to the state treasurer; and pay a transit duty of ten cents for each passenger, and fifteen cents for each ton of merchandise, in lieu of all other taxes. The company was empowered to decide upon the description of carriages to be used on the road, the weight to be transported on each, the times of starting and rates of travelling, and to regulate the tolls; and was required to provide suitable steam or other vessels, at either extremity of the road, for the transportation of passengers. The State, also, reserved to itself the right to purchase the road at and after the expiration of thirty years, at a valuation to be made according to law; stipulating, that if the legislature shall authorize the construction of any other rail-road for the transportation of passengers across the State from New York to Philadelphia, which road shall be constructed and used, and which shall commence and terminate within three miles of the commencement and termination of the road authorized by the act, then the transit duties shall cease; and that such other rail-road shall be liable to a tax not less than the amount payable to the State by this company.

By an act passed 4th February, 1831, it was further stipulated between the State and the company, that the latter should transfer to the former 1000 shares of the capital stock, the instalments thereon to be paid by the company; the State to appoint one director, on condition, that it should not be lawful to construct any rail-road for the transportation of passengers across the State, within three miles of the road of the company, until after the expiration of the term of nine years from the date of the act of incorporation, (Feb. 4th, 1830.) And that when any other rail-road for the transportation of passengers and property between New York and Philadelphia shall be constructed and used, by virtue of any law of this State or of the United States, authorizing or recognising such road, that the dividends on the stock should cease, and the stock be retransferred to the company.

By the act of 15th February, 1831, the Camden and Amboy Rail-road and the Delaware and Raritan Canal Companies were consolidated, for the purposes of completing the canal and road, subject to the provisions, reservations and conditions of their respective charters; the directors appointed under which are empowered to manage the affairs of the companies in joint meeting; and the companies are jointly liable on the contracts made by either; and are prohibited from charging more than three dollars for the transportation of passengers from and to the cities of New York and Philadelphia. This act further provides that the canal and rail-road shall be completed within the time specified in the respective charters; and that if one of the works at the expiration of such time be completed without the other, that the work completed shall be forfeited to the State.

By the act of 2d March, 1832, 1000 shares of the joint capital stock are transferred to the State; and the companies contract that, if within one year from the time that the rail-road shall be completed, the transit duty received by the acts incorporating such companies, and the dividends on the stock so transferred, shall not amount to $30,000, the companies shall pay the deficiency to the State; and so, annually, out of the joint funds, and before any dividend be made to the stockholders, so as to secure to the State the sum of $30,000 at least, annually, during the charter; and that the State may appoint one director to represent the stock, but shall not vote thereon at any election of the stockholders. The state directors are appointable by the governor. The companies further covenant to construct a lateral rail-road from the village of Spottswood to the city of New Brunswick, to be completed so soon as any rail-road shall be made from that city to the Hudson River; and that they will not charge more than $2.50 for every passenger carried to and from the cities of New Brunswick and Philadelphia. The condition of these grants, however, is, that it shall not be lawful at any time during the rail-road charter, to construct any other rail-road in the State, without the consent of the companies, which shall be intended or used for the transportation of passengers or merchandise between the cities of New York and Philadelphia, or to compete in business, with the Camden and Amboy Rail-road.

The united companies have completed one track of rail-road from a point below Bordentown, on the Delaware River, to South Amboy, passing through, or rather over, Hight's Town and by Spottswood, a distance of 35 miles, at an expense, it is said, of more than $18,000 the mile. Upon this road passengers and merchandise have been carried since February, 1833. It is constructed in a very substantial manner of cast iron rails, supported upon blocks of stone, or wooden sleepers, placed three feet distant from each other in the line. Until September, 1833, the carriages were commonly drawn by horses; at that time steam locomotives were applied to one of the three daily lines which traverse it.

The remainder of the road from Bordentown to Camden is in progress, and is being constructed of wood, faced with iron bars; it being supposed that it will not be employed more than two or three months in the year, and will therefore not require the strength of the portion between Bordentown and New York.

By the power which this company has to regulate the tolls on the road, they are enabled to exclude all other persons from its use, and to secure to themselves a monopoly thereof; and this they have effected.

The West Jersey Rail-road was designed to be connected with the Camden and Amboy Rail-roads, at Camden; and to run, thence, to any point upon the Delaware River, in the township of Penn's Neck, in the county of Salem. The company was authorized to have a capital of half a million, and to increase it to one million of dollars; and the road was to be commenced within two years from the passage of the act, (12th February, 1831,) and to be completed within five years. The road not having been commenced, the charter may be deemed void.

The Patterson and Hudson River Rail-road Company, was incorporated under the act of 21st January, 1831, with a capital of $250,000, and the privilege to extend it to half a million; and was authorized to make a rail-road or lateral roads from one or more suitable places in the town of Patterson, one at least of which to commence at or pass in its course within 50 feet of the corner of the present lower race-way in the town of Patterson, at the intersection of Congress and Mill streets, near the Catholic Chapel, to Weehawkin; and from thence to any other suitable place or places on the Hudson River opposite to the city of New York, within 50 feet of high-water mark, not exceeding 66 feet wide, with as many tracks as they may deem necessary, crossing the Hackensack River upon or near the bridge of the New Barbadoes Company. By act 18th November, 1831, the company was empowered to locate the road from the east side of Berry's Hill, in the county of Bergen, to the Hudson River, and on making a tunnel through Bergen Hill, to charge additional toll.

The company are empowered also to purchase and employ all means necessary in the transportation of merchandise, passengers, &c. upon the road, but the road is declared a public highway, free to all persons paying the prescribed toll, and may be purchased by the State after the expiration of fifty years from its completion. The treasurer of the company is required to make to the State treasurer annual returns of the number of passengers, and tons of merchandise, &c. transported on the road, and after the expiration of five years from the passing of the act, to pay to the State, annually, one-quarter of one per cent., and after the expiration of ten years, one-half per cent. on the capital stock paid in, in lieu of all taxation.

By an act of 3d February, 1831, the Patterson Junction Rail-road Company was incorporated with a capital of $20,000, which may be increased to $40,000, and a power to construct a rail-road or lateral roads from the Morris Canal, distant not more than one and a half miles from the corner of Congress and Mill streets, in the town of Patterson, to intersect the Patterson and Hudson River Rail-road, within the town of Patterson. This is also declared a public highway, and the company are required, when the road shall be completed, to file a statement of its cost in the office of the secretary of state, and annually thereafter to report to the legislature the proceeds of the road, until they shall amount to seven per cent. upon its cost, and afterwards annually to pay to the State a tax of one-half per cent. on such cost in lieu of all taxes. And the legislature have reserved the right to purchase such road upon terms similar to those annexed to the charter of the Patterson and Hudson River Rail-road Company; and the charter of this, as of that company, is declared void, if the road be not commenced in one year, and finished in five years from the 4th July, 1831.

The Patterson and Fort Lee Rail-road Company, incorporated by the act of 8th March, 1832, has authority to employ a capital of $200,000 in making a road from the town of Patterson to Fort Lee, on the Hudson River, not further than 50 feet from high-water mark; to be commenced within one year from the 4th July, 1832, and completed within six years from that time, under penalty of forfeiture of the charter; and subject to be purchased by the State at the expiration of thirty years from the completion of the road, and to a transit duty of the one-quarter of one per cent. yearly, after the expiration of six years from the passage of the act, and the half of one per cent. after the expiration of ten years, upon the capital stock, in lieu of all other taxes.

The Elizabethtown and Somerville Rail-road Company, by the act of 9th February, 1831, was empowered to construct a road from the village of Somerville to Elizabethtown, passing as near as practicable by Boundbrook, Plainfield, Scotch Plains and Westfield, subject to a tax of one-half of one per cent. upon the cost, annually, after the proceeds of the road shall yield seven per cent. thereon, and to the avoidance of the charter in case the road be not completed within seven years from the 4th July, 1831. This road is to be a public highway, and may be purchased by the State on the terms established in the case of the Patterson and Hudson road, and the State may subscribe $25,000 to the stock of the company, at any time before, or within, twelve months after the road shall be completed.

The capital stock originally permitted to the company, was $200,000, with the privilege of increase to $400,000; but, by the act of 8th February, 1833, authority was given to add $500,000 immediately to the stock, and, eventually, should it be found necessary, $500,000 more; and to extend the road from the village of Somerville, by the village of Clinton, in the county of Hunterdon, to the Delaware River, opposite to the village of Belvidere, in the county of Warren, with a branch, if the company deem it expedient, to the Delaware River, between the mouth of the Musconetcong Creek and the Easton Delaware Bridge; subject to all the restrictions and reservations made by the original act. The great object of this extension of the road, is to unite it with the North-western Rail-road, which it is proposed to commence at the Delaware, opposite Belvidere, and to run through the Blue Mountain at the Water Gap, and by Stroudsburg, through a densely wooded country to Pittston, on the Susquehanna; being located for about 18 miles upon an inexhaustible coal bed. From this coal region, the road may be connected with several *authorized* roads into western New York. If this road be executed, it will open a convenient way to the New York market, not only from one of the most fertile and interesting portions of the State of New Jersey, but will give a direction to the produce of a portion of New York territory, otherwise destined to reach the city of Philadelphia. A portion of the stock for this route has, we understand, been subscribed.

The New Jersey Rail-road and Transportation Company was incorporated by the act of 7th March, 1832, with a capital of $750,000, and the privilege to double it, divided into shares of $50 each; with power to make a rail-road not more than 66 feet wide, with as many tracks as they may deem proper, from such point in the city of New Brunswick, as shall be agreed upon by them and the corporation of that city, through or near the villages of Rahway and Woodbridge, within half a mile of the market house, in Elizabethtown, and through Newark, by the most practicable route, and thence contiguous to, or south of the bridges, over the Hackensack and Passaic River; crossing Bergen Ridge, south of the turnpike road to some convenient point not less than 50 feet from high-water mark, on the Hudson river, opposite to the city of New York: and to make a branch road to any ferry on the Hudson opposite to New York, which shall join the main road within 100 yards of the Hackensack River, if the main road cross that river within 100 yards of the present bridge: but if more than 100 yards from that bridge, then the branch to join it, at such point, west of the river, as shall best give to the ferries equal facilities of communication with Newark. And if the company do not construct such branch, as soon as the main road from Newark to the Hudson shall be made, then the law authorizes the owner of the ferry so to do, with the same power and liabilities as the company. The act, also, empowers the company to regulate the time and manner of transporting goods and passengers, the description and formation of carriages; and the rates and modes of collecting toll within the following limits; viz. for empty carriages, weighing less than a ton, two cents; more than one, and less than two tons, four cents; above three tons, eight cents per mile; and in addition thereto, six cents per ton for goods, and three cents for each passenger, per mile. Provided, that no farmer of the State shall pay toll for carrying the produce of his farm, in his own wagon, not weighing more than a ton, when such produce does not weigh more than 1000 lbs.: but shall pay, only, for carriages, as if empty. It also authorizes the company to construct branches to any landing, on or near the Passaic, not north of Belleville, and to any place in the township of Newark; and requires them to commence the road at Jersey City and New Brunswick, within one year, and to complete the whole route in five years, under penalty of forfeiture of their charter. The company are further empowered to purchase any turnpike road and bridges on the route; but the act reserves to the State and individual stockholders of the Newark Turnpike Company, the right, at any time, within two years from the opening of the books, to take stock of the company in exchange, or to sell to the company, at market value; but the Newark turnpike and the bridges over the Raritan, Passaic and Hackensack, are to be kept as public roads, without obstruction: to build or purchase carriages for the transportation of persons or property; but not to charge more than six cents a mile for transporting passengers and each ton of goods, nor more than $1.25 for carrying passengers from New York to New Brunswick: to hold real estate, at the commencement and termination of their roads, not exceeding three acres at each place; and to build thereon, warehouses, stables, machine shops, &c. and over the Hackensack and Passaic Rivers, such bridges, piers, &c. as may be necessary. The State has reserved the right to purchase the road after the expiration of the charter, (30 years) and of subscribing one-fourth of the stock, and has imposed an annual tax of 1-4 per cent. upon the capital paid in; and should the road be continued across the State, a transit duty of 8 cents for each passenger and 12 cents for every ton of goods transported over the whole road. By a supplement to the act relative to the Delaware and Raritan Canal, and Amboy Rail-road, the companies are required to construct a lateral rail-road from the village of Spottswood to the city of New Brunswick, as soon as a rail-road shall be made from New Brunswick to the Hudson River; consequently, when the Camden and Amboy Rail-road and the New Jersey Rail-road shall be completed, there must be a rail-road through the state, from Jersey City to Philadelphia.

The New Jersey Rail-road Company commenced operations in the summer of 1832, and have confident expectations of completing the road from Hackensack River, through Newark to Elizabethtown, by the fall of '1833; and from the Hudson to Elizabethtown in the summer of 1834; and the whole line, from the Hudson to New Brunswick, within two years. The estimated cost of the whole road for one track, with suitable passing places, including the purchase from the Bridge and Newark Turnpike Companies, the bridges over the Hackensack, Passaic and Raritan, and the moving power, cars, &c. as per report of N. Beach, the engineer, is   -   -   -   -   -   -   - $718,912

Cost of superstructure for a second track on the whole line, 30 miles, at $4,710 80 per mile,   -   -   -   -   -   141,324

Total,   -   -   - $860,236

Upon this capital, the company, after paying for annual repairs, cost of moving power, cars, &c. the sum of $35,640 per annum, anticipate to receive a profit of $134,775, equal to 15½ per cent.

By an arrangement with the Patterson Rail-road Company, the road for both companies, from the west side of Bergen Ridge, through the Deep Cut, and across the heavy embankments, on the east of the Ridge, and to the Hudson River, is to be constructed under the charter of this company, as joint property of the two companies; the Patterson company paying two-fifths, and this company three-fifths of the expense of construction, each company using the road without accounting to the other. This arrangement reduces the expense of the New Jersey Company $55,171.

The company, in order to avoid litigation, has purchased of the United Passaic and Hackensack Bridge Companies their stock, at $150,000, equal to $150 per share, upon which amount it had, for some years, paid seven per cent. and created a surplus fund of $30,000. With this stock, they obtained also all the right which the bridge company possessed, to pass the Passaic and Hackensack Rivers, by bridges, for sixty years to come. A very large majority of the stockholders of the bridge companies used the right of election stipulated for, to take rail-road stock, and have thus become identified in interest with the company.

The New Jersey, Hudson and Delaware Rail-road Company was incorporated by an act of 8th March, 1832, with a capital stock of $1,000,000, and authority to increase it to $2,000,000, to be employed in making a rail-road and public highway, commencing at any point on the Delaware River, between the New York state line and the mouth of Paulin's Kill, (and constructing a bridge over said river,) and to run thence to Snufftown, in the county of Sussex, and thence to the Hudson River, opposite the city of New York; or to join any rail-road chartered or to be chartered, leading to or terminating at the Hudson River, opposite the city of New York : but if extended to the Hudson, not to cross the Passaic south of the village of Belleville, nor to approach any point within three miles of the present bridge over the Passaic, at Newark, nor to run south of the turnpike road, a causeway leading from Newark to Jersey City ; such road to be commenced within two and finished within twenty years ; and when the dividends upon its stock shall amount to seven per cent. to be subject to a tax of one-half of one per cent. per annum on the cost of the road and appendages, in lieu of all taxes ; reserving to the State the right, at any time within three years after the expiration of ninety-nine years, of taking the road and appendages at cost.

The Delaware and Jobstown Rail or Macadamized Road Company, was incorporated under the act of 11th February, 1833, with a capital of $60,000, and liberty to increase it to $200,000, for the purpose of making a public road from the mouth of Craft's Creek, upon the Delaware River, by the villages of Columbus, Jobstown and Juliustown, to New Lisbon, a distance of 13 miles ; the road to be commenced within three and completed within ten years from the passage of the act, on penalty of forfeiture of the charter: and when the annual net proceeds shall amount to more than seven per cent. to pay half per cent. tax annually to the State ; reserving the right to the State to purchase the road upon appraisement after the expiration of fifty years. The stock of this road, we are told, is subscribed.

VIII. There are four canals in the State completed or about to be completed, viz. the Morris Canal, the Delaware and Raritan Canal, the Salem Creek Canal, and the Manasquan Canal.

The Morris Canal is among the most original and boldest efforts of the spirit of internal improvement. The idea of making it was first conceived by George P. M'Culloch, Esq. of Morristown, whilst on a fishing party at the Hopatcong Lake, near the summit of the Musconetcong Mountain, more than 900 feet above the level of the sea, and the enterprise was commenced through his zealous and active exertions. This lake, the source of the Musconetcong River, in its original state covered an area of about five square miles. To dam up its outlet, husband the spring freshets, to double its capacity, and by leading its accumulated waters to the eastern declivity and valley of the Rockaway, to pursue the western descent until a practical route could be obtained across the country to Easton, were the means he proposed to open the way to market for the rich mineral products and the iron manufactured at the many furnaces and forges of this mountainous district. At one period, 81 forges and 12 furnaces flourished in the district, but when the canal was proposed, 30 of the former and 9 of the latter had fallen into ruins; whilst the remainder were greatly limited in their operations by the growing scarcity of fuel and increasing cost of transportation. A ton of iron might have been brought to New York from Archangel on the White Sea, at nearly the same price it could have been transported from Berkshire valley ; and thus, this great branch of manufacture, alike interesting to the State and the Union, was in imminent danger of perishing.

But how might a canal penetrate from the Delaware to the Hudson, 100 miles, through the mountainous chain repeatedly crossing its path? How might the elevation, rapid and unavoidable, be surmounted, and how should the pecuniary sources be provided for an enterprise vast, novel, hazardous and expensive? The lake at the summit level would supply water to be sure ; but to raise boats 900 feet high, and again to lower them to their first level of lockage, would have required an amount of money for the construction, and of time in the passage, alike fatal to the enterprise. Mr. M'Culloch, therefore, adopted the expedient of inclined planes for the greater lifts, and locks for the less. Such planes had never before been applied to boats of much magnitude, nor to an operation so extensive.

Mr. M'Culloch endeavoured to induce the State to adopt the enterprise ; and at the instance of him and others, the legislature, by act 15th November, 1822, appointed G. M'Culloch, Charles Kinsey, of Essex, and Thomas Capner, Esqrs. commissioners, with authority to employ a scientific engineer and surveyor to explore, survey and level the most practicable route for this canal ; and to report an estimate of the expense thereof, with such information relative to the minerals along its lines as they could obtain, and to deposit specimens thereof in the state library. The commissioners reported, in 1823, and received the thanks of the legislature for the intelligence, industry and zeal displayed in the execution of their commission. But that cautious and prudential policy which has hitherto prevented the State from yielding her treasury and resources to the blandishment of projectors, charm they ever so wisely, deterred her from making the Morris Canal a state enterprise. A private company was therefore formed, and incorporated under the act of 31st December, 1824, with a capital of $1,000,000, and the right to increase it to $1,500,000, for canal purposes; and, likewise, to employ in banking operations, additionally, the sum of $200,000, for every $200,000 actually expended on the canal, so that the banking capital did not exceed a million of dollars.

The route of the canal was selected, and the estimate of cost made, by Major Ephraim Beach, under whose direction the work was executed. This route, and the estimate of cost, were approved by General Bernard and Major Totten, of the engineer corps of the United States, and by Judge Wright; and the plan of inclined planes, suggested by professor James Renwick, of Columbia College, New York, also received the sanction of the like authority; but much modification was afterwards found necessary in this particular.

In 1825, the excavations were prosecuted with alacrity, while the planes were deferred; an arrangement which experience proves should have been reversed, since the latter could be perfected only by many and tedious experiments. The erection of the planes, too, was entrusted to ordinary mechanics, who, deficient in scientific knowledge and manual skill, caused much disappointment, which was aggravated by great and useless expenditure; but, finally, proper engineers were employed, and the planes have become effectual to establish a regular intercourse along the line of the canal with the Delaware and Lehigh Rivers, and with the Hudson The machinery of the inclined plane, so far as we have examined it, consists of a double railway connecting the upper and lower portions of the canal, up which a carriage supporting a boat is drawn by means of iron chains, wound round a cylinder, set in motion by a water wheel turned by a stream from the upper level; whilst another chain regulates the descent of another boat to the lower level, if there be one to pass, or if none, of the empty cradle.

The cost of the canal, originally estimated at $817,000, has been about $2,000,000. The length completed is about 90 miles from the Passaic River, at Newark, to the Delaware, at Philipsburg, opposite to Easton; 11¾ miles between Jersey City and Newark remain to be executed, and are estimated to cost $100,000; but the cost will, as usual, probably exceed the estimate. This excess of cost over the estimate is not peculiar to the Morris Canal, but is common, perhaps unavoidable, in all the public works of the country. The engineer can judge only from an imperfect knowledge of the surface of the ground through which he is to make his way: an unexpected bed of stone, a limestone sink, a quicksand, a sudden freshet or frost, may mock his calculations. Adventurers, therefore, in canals and rail-roads, should be content when their agents display reasonable intelligence and full fidelity. The canal was completed to Newark in August, 1831. It is deeply in debt, and pays no dividend to the stockholders; but its use has been most beneficial upon the business of the country through which it passes, and its portage will increase with population and business; and should the anthracite coal be successfully applied to the extraction of iron from ore, the consumption of that article alone will add greatly to the tolls. The transportation of the Lehigh coal to the New York market, originally counted on by the projectors of this canal, will be effected by the Delaware and Raritan Canal. The Morris Canal was adapted to boats of 25 tons only, which in many cases have proved too heavy for the chains of the inclined planes. The passage from Easton to Newark has been performed in less than five days.

The width of the canal is 32 feet at top, and 20 feet at bottom, four feet deep. The locks are 75 feet long between the mitre sills, and nine feet wide. The line is naturally divided into two divisions, the Eastern and Western. The first has 12 planes, whose united elevations make 748 feet, and 18 locks rising, together, 166 feet, making the whole rise, 914 feet. The highest lift by planes is 80 feet. There are two of that height, one at Boonton Falls, and another at Drakeville; and the highest lift of the locks is 10 feet. This division now ends at the Passaic River, near Newark—the section designed to connect it with the Hudson, 11¾ miles, has not yet been commenced. The length of the division is 51 miles 32-100ths. The western division has 11 planes rising 691 feet, and 7 locks, whose aggregate lifts are 69 feet—total, 760 feet. Its length from the summit level to the Delaware, is

38 miles, 91-100ths, making the length of the whole line 90 miles 23-100ths. The
annexed table shows at one view the number of the planes and locks, their location,
elevation, grade of the planes, and lift of the locks; and is, perhaps, the best exposition that can be given of the work short of an engraved profile.

EASTERN DIVISION.

Plane.	Lock.	No. of the plane or lock.	LOCATION.	No. of the section.	Elevation of plane in feet.	Inclination of the plane.	Lift of the Lock in feet.
1		1	Summit.	2	50	1-12	
1		2	Drakeville.	4	80	1-10	
1		3	Near do.	5	38	1-12	
	2	1 and 2	do. do.	6			20
1		4	Baker's Mills.	12	52	1-8	
	1	3	Near do.	13			8
1		5	Above Dover.	15	66	1-9	
	1	4	do.	16			9
	1	5	do.	17			9
	2	6 and 7	At do.	19			18
1		6	Rockaway.	25	52	1-12	
	1	8	Near do.	29			7
	2	9 and 10	Powerville.	34			15
	1	11	Booneton.	36			10
		7	Booneton Falls.	37	80	1-10	
	1	12	Near do.	38			12
1		8	Montville.	40	76	1-11	
1		9	do.	41	74	1-11	
1		10	Near Pompton.	48	56	1-12	
	1	13	do.	42			8
		11	Bloomfield.	84	54	1-12	
	1	14	Near do.	86			10
	1	15	Above Newark.	95			10
1		12	Newark.	96	70	1-12	
	3	16, 17, 18	do.	97			30
					748		
12	17				166		166
			Planes and Locks.		914		

WESTERN DIVISION.

Plane.	Lock.	No. of the plane or lock.	LOCATION.	No. of the section.	Elevation of plane in feet.	Inclination of the plane.	Lift of the Lock in feet.
1		1	Great Meadow.	3	58	1-10	
1		2	Stanhope.	5	70	1-11	
	1	1	Near Sayers.	6			12
		3	do. do.	6	55	1-12	
		4	Old Andover.	10	80	1-8	
	1	2	Guinea Hollow.	16			10
1		5	Near Anderson.	38	64	1-12	
1		6	Monté Rose.	41	50	1-10	
	1	3	Near do.	43			10

D

Western Division, continued.

Plane.	Lock.	No. of the plane or lock.	LOCATION	No. of the section.	Elevation of plane in feet.	Inclination of the plane.	Lift of the Lock in feet.
1		7	Pohatcong.	47	75	1-10	
	1	4	Near N. Village.	61			10
1		8	Hulzesers.	63	62	1-11	
1		9	Near Bridleman's				
			Brook.	67	100	1-10	
1		10	Nr. Green's mills.	70	44	1-12	
	1	5	do. do.	71			9
1	1 and 2	6 and 7	do. do.	72			18
1		11	Delaware River.	74	33	1-12	
11					691		69
					69		
			Planes and Locks.		760		

RECAPITULATION.

PLANES. Eastern Division,   12   748
Western Division,   11   691

     —   ——   1439 feet.
     22

LOCKS. Eastern Division,   17   166
Western Division,   7   69

     —   ——   235
   24 locks.   ——
             1674 feet.

Of the interesting works on the line of the canal, our limits permit us only to notice, the aqueduct of stone of a single arch, 80 feet span, 50 feet above the river, over the Passaic at the Little Falls, built of beautiful dressed freestone, in the most substantial and durable manner—and the wooden aqueduct 236 feet long, supported by nine stone piers, over the Pompton River.

The State is indebted, as we have already observed, for the inception of this great work, to the genius and zeal of George M'Culloch, Esq., and she is not less indebted to the skill and perseverance of Cadwallader D. Colden, Esq., the actual president of the company, for its completion.

The Delaware and Raritan Canal, one of the great links of the chain of internal navigation, which is to give to the domestic trade of the country the greatest facility and security, has for years been a subject of deep interest to all who have reflected on the means of increasing our prosperity. The construction of this canal has been a favourite project,—with speculators desirous to deal in a marketable commodity; with capitalists seeking for safe and profitable investments; and with many statesmen of New Jersey, who believed they saw, in it, the means of creating a permanent and large revenue for the State, which would forever relieve her citizens from taxation, for the ordinary support of government.

So early as the year 1804, the project of a canal to connect the waters of the Delaware and Raritan Rivers, was earnestly considered. A route was then examined by a company of experienced and intelligent gentlemen, and a law passed authorizing its construction by a private company; but the state of our trade, and our inexperience in works of this character, prevented its execution. In 1816 and in 1823, commissioners, appointed by the legislature, explored the route, and by accurate examination demonstrated its practicability. At a subsequent period, a second joint-stock company was authorized to make this canal, and paid to the State treasury, for the privilege so to do, the sum of $100,000; but failing to obtain the sanction of the State of Pennsylvania to the use of the waters of the Delaware, they were compelled to abandon the enterprise, receiving back from New Jersey the premium they had paid. Many citizens of the State rejoiced in this failure, by which the power of making the canal reverted to her; anticipating that she would immediately use it. To this end, many petitions were presented to the legislature, at their session of 1828–9; and a committee appointed thereon, made an able and elaborate report, accompanied by a bill, authorizing the canal to be constructed by the State. But the settled policy of the State, safe at least, if not eminently prosperous or sagacious, which carefully eschews all prospective advantages to be purchased by loans, or by the taxation of her citizens, marred this measure. Finally, by the act of 4th February, 1830, the enterprise was again committed to a joint-stock company, with certain beneficial reservations to the State. The act provides, that a capital stock be created of $1,000,000, which may be enlarged to $1,500,000, divided into shares of $100 each, and that the company have all the powers necessary to perfect an expeditious and complete line of communication from Philadelphia to New York : That, if the capital were not subscribed within one year, or the canal and feeder not commenced within two, and completed within eight, years, the charter should become void : That, the company might make the canal between, and improve the rivers below, where the canal shall empty into them; the canal to be at least 50 feet wide at the water line, and at least five feet deep, and the feeder not less than 30 feet wide and four feet deep : That they may charge tolls for the transport of persons and merchandise, not exceeding five cents per mile for the first, nor four cents per ton per mile for the second, nor more than half those rates respectively on the feeder : That they may alter the route of the canal ; that it shall be a public highway; and that, no other canal shall be constructed within five miles of any point of the canal or feeder, without the assent of the company : That at the expiration of thirty years from the completion of the canal and feeder, a valuation of them shall be made by six appraisers, appointed by the company and State ; who, in case of difference, may choose an umpire ; that such appraisement shall not exceed the first cost, with the lands and appendages, and that the State shall have the privilege for ten years of taking the canal and feeder at the appraisement, upon payment of the amount thereof : That the treasurer of the company shall, on oath, make quarterly returns of the number of passengers and tons of merchandise transported on the canal across the State, and pay to the treasurer of the State, eight cents for each passenger, and eight cents for each ton of merchandise so transported thereon, except for coal, lumber, lime, wood, ashes, and similar low priced articles, for which two cents only per ton shall be paid; and that no other impost shall be levied upon the company.

By the act of 3d February, 1831, in consideration, that the company would make the canal 75 feet wide on the water line, seven feet deep throughout, and the locks at least 100 feet in length, by 24 feet in width in the clear, the State extended the time after which the appraisement should be made, to 50 instead of 30 years, and engaged that neither the company, nor any other person, should construct any railroad across the State, between the Delaware and Raritan Rivers, within five miles of any point of the canal, until after the expiration of the period allowed for the construction of the canal, reserving existing rights.

As we have already mentioned, when speaking of the Camden and Amboy Railroad, the Canal and Rail-road Company were consolidated pursuant to the act of 15th February, 1831. By act 2d March, 1832, the united company, in consideration, that no other rail-road should be constructed which might compete with that road, covenanted to convey to the State one thousand shares of the joint stock, and guaranteed to the State an annual income of $30,000 at least, should not the dividends on stock and the transit duties amount to that sum; and engaged that they would annually divide the whole of the net profits, except such surplus fund as might be necessary, not exceeding $100,000.

Under these provisions the canal was commenced, and has progressed nearly to its completion. (Oct. 1833.) It begins at the confluence of the Crosswicks Creek and the Delaware, at Bordentown, and runs thence, through the city of Trenton and the valley of the Assunpink, crossing the creek by a noble stone culvert, to Lawrence's Meadows, whence it passes into the valley of Stony Brook; thence down the right side thereof, one mile S. of Princeton, to the junction of Stony Brook with the Millstone River; thence across the river by an aqueduct of eight arches, and by the right bank of the river to the Raritan River; thence along the right bank of the Raritan to New Brunswick, where it unites with the tide. It passes through or near Bordentown, Lamberton, Trenton, Princeton, Kingston, Griggstown, Millstone, Somerville, and Boundbrook. Its whole length is 42 miles, within which there are 116 feet lockage, viz: 58 between Trenton and the Delaware River, overcome by seven locks; one at Trenton of seven feet; one at the State Penitentiary of seven feet; three at Lamberton of nine feet each; one below Lamberton of seven feet, and one at Bordentown of 10 feet, lift. The last, by reason of the badness of the foundation, has cost an extraordinary portion of time, labour and money, in its construction. The lockage between Trenton and New Brunswick is also 58 feet, and is overcome by seven locks; one at Kingston, one at Griggstown, and one at the mouth of the Millstone, each of eight feet; two opposite to Boundbrook, seven feet each; one two miles below Boundbrook, of eight feet, where a dam has been constructed across the river to use it as a feeder, and one at New Brunswick, of twelve feet, lift. At this city, there is also a tide lock sufficiently capacious to admit a steamboat, and a basin extending the whole front of the town, formed by an embankment in the river. By turning the river into the canal, a water power will have been gained at Brunswick, equal, it is supposed, to 400 horse power. Upon the line of the main canal, there are 17 culverts, some of them very large; one aqueduct, and 29 pivot bridges. The canal is 75 feet wide on the water line, and seven feet deep, and the depth may be increased to eight feet should it be found necessary. To avoid bridging, the company have purchased a large quantity of land, in many cases whole farms, at great expense.

The feeder commences at Bull's Island, in the Delaware River, and runs thence along the left bank of the river to Trenton, where it intersects the canal, a distance of 23 miles, with an inclination of two inches in the mile. The works, beside the excavation, consist of a lift lock of 10 feet at Lambertsville; two guard locks, one at Bull's Island, and the other at Prallsville; 15 culverts, and 37 pivot bridges. The width of the excavation is throughout 50 feet; at the water line, its depth six feet; but, where it could be effected without great expenditure, the width has been increased to 60 feet, and thus three-fourths of the distance will afford good sloop navigation. A large basin has been constructed by the company, upon the feeder near the centre of Trenton, for the accommodation of the city.

The canal is adapted to vessels exceeding 150 tons burden, and has been executed in the most substantial manner. Its cost is now estimated at two millions of dollars. The estimate, when the proposition was made to the State to undertake the enterprise, was stated at $1,142,741; but the present canal is every way larger than that originally proposed.

The Manasquan River and Barnegat Bay Canal Company, was authorized under the act of 21st February, 1833, with a capital of $5,000, to make a canal 40 feet wide and five feet deep, from the mouth of the Manasquan River to the head waters of Barnegat Bay, at Layton's pond or ditch, in the county of Monmouth; to erect tide gates, and to take toll for passing through the canal for every scow, eight cents per ton; sail boat or small craft 10 cents per ton; and for every fish boat or skiff, 25 cents per ton; provided that the canal be commenced within two, and finished within five years.

A short canal of about four miles in length, in Upper and Lower Penn's Neck Township, Salem County, connects the Salem Creek with the Delaware River, about four miles above Kinseyville, and saves to sloops that ply in the creek, from 15 to 20 miles of the distance to Philadelphia.

IX. The population of New Jersey, derived from European ancestry, is composed chiefly of the descendants of the Dutch, Swede, English, and New England settlers. For nearly half a century, the country was in the undisturbed possession of the Dutch, who, in that period, spread themselves extensively over East Jersey; not, however, without an intermixture of their New England neighbours, who very early displayed a disposition to abandon their sterile soil for more fertile lands and milder skies; and who had also found their way to the shores of the Delaware, and made one attempt, at least, to colonize them. After the year 1664, the English authority was established over the province, and the settlement of West Jersey was then zealously commenced by English emigrants, chiefly of the sect called Quakers. The liberality of the provincial government must necessarily have drawn population from other European sources; but such acquisitions were not great, inasmuch as her aspiring and successful neighbours, New York and Pennsylvania, possessed greater attractions.

These attractions, too, have operated to prevent that increase of population in the State, which must otherwise have taken place from natural causes. Abounding in all that is necessary to the comfortable enjoyment of life, and stimulated to industry by the growth of the neighbouring cities, whose wants she in no inconsiderable degree supplied, New Jersey, had not her sons and daughters gone forth to people other lands, would have been covered with inhabitants, who, by natural increase, doubling their numbers in about 23 years, would, at this period, have exceeded 700,000 souls. But the State has been an *officina gentium*, a hive of nations, constantly sending out swarms, whose labours have contributed largely to build up the two greatest marts of the Union, and to subdue and fertilize the western wilds. Instead, therefore, of being distinguished for the growth of numbers within her borders, she is remarkable for the paucity of their increase. By adverting to the periodical census, a copy of which we have annexed, it will be perceived that the ratio of increase from 1790, to 1820, has been about 18½ per cent. for each decennial term, and 15½ per cent. for that ending in 1830. The augmentation in the last period may be ascribed to the growth of manufactures, the improvement of agriculture in the northern, and the accession of labour in clearing the forest of the southern, portion of the State. In the first half of the eighteenth century, the ratio of her increase was about 30 per cent. in about eight years; at which she would have doubled her population in 26 8-12ths years. This is apparent from the census in the annexed tables of the years 1737, and 1745.

CENSUS OF 1737.

COUNTIES.	WHITES.					SLAVES AND OTHER NEGROES.					Total of both.
	Males above 16.	Females above 16.	Males under 16.	Females under 16.	Total whites.	Males above 16.	Females above 16.	Males under 16.	Females under 16.	Total slaves.	
West Jersey — Morris,	1,618	1,230	1,270	1,170	5,288	75	53	49	42	219	5,570
Hunterdon,	1,487	1,222	1,190	996	4,895	134	87	58	64	343	5,238
Burlington,	930	757	782	676	3,145	42	24	32	24	122	3,267
Gloucester,	1,069	1,331	1,313	1,327	5,700	57	56	40	31	184	5,884
Salem,	261	219	271	211	962	12	10	9	11	42	1,004
Cape May,											
East Jersey — Bergen,	939	822	820	708	3,289	256	203	187	160	806	4,095
Essex,	1,118	1,720	1,619	1,494	6,644	114	114	84	63	375	7,019
Middlesex,	1,134	1,085	1,086	956	4,261	181	124	91	107	503	4,764
Monmouth,	1,508	1,339	1,289	1,295	5,431	233	152	129	141	655	6,086
Somerset,	967	940	999	867	3,773	255	175	170	132	732	4,505
	11,631	10,725	10,639	9,700	43,388	1,359	998	849	775	3,981	47,402

CENSUS OF 1745.

COUNTIES.	WHITES.					SLAVES.			Increase since 1737.
	Males above 16.	Females above 16.	Males under 16.	Females under 16.	Quakers	Males.	Females.	Whole number.	
West Jersey — Morris,	1,109	1,190	957	1,087	22	57	36	4,436	} 8,080
Hunterdon,	2,302	2,182	2,117	2,090	240	244	216	9,151	
Burlington,	1,786	1,528	1,605	1,454	3,237	233	197	6,803	1,565
Gloucester,	913	786	797	808	1,436	121	81	3,506	239
Salem,	1,716	1,746	1,603	1,595	1,090	90	97	6,847	963
Cape May,	306	284	272	274	54	30	22	1,188	184
	8,132	7,716	7,331	7,308	6,079	775	649	31,911	11,031
East Jersey — Bergen,	721	494	590	585	0	379	237	3,006	
Essex,	1,694	1,652	1,649	1,548	35	244	201	6,988	
Middlesex,	1,728	1,651	1,659	1,695	400	483	396	7,612	2,848
Monmouth,	2,071	1,975	1,783	1,899	3,131	513	386	8,627	2,541
Somerset,	740	765	672	719	91	194	149	3,239	
	6,954	6,537	6,353	6,446	3,557	1,813	1,369	29,472	
	15,086	14,253	13,684	13,754	9,636	2,588	2,018	61,383	

CENSUS OF 1800.

COUNTIES	FREE WHITE MALES					FREE WHITE FEMALES					All other Free Persons, except Indians not taxed.	Slaves.	Total number.
	Under 10 years.	Of 10 and under 16.	Of 16 and under 26.	Of 26 and under 45.	Of 45 and upwards.	Under 10 years.	Of 10 and under 16.	Of 16 and under 26.	Of 26 and under 45.	Of 45 and upwards.			
Hunterdon,	3,363	1,558	1,698	1,872	1,366	3,031	1,509	1,929	1,965	1,230	520	1,220	21,261
Sussex,	4,080	1,981	1,926	2,061	1,381	3,779	1,717	2,013	1,853	1,127	102	514	22,534
Burlington,	3,569	1,637	1,742	2,229	1,289	3,459	1,418	1,933	2,166	1,121	770	188	21,524
Essex,	3,343	1,663	1,928	2,084	1,285	3,344	1,718	1,857	2,088	1,240	198	1,521	22,269
Monmouth,	3,144	1,353	1,375	1,864	1,190	3,106	1,309	1,412	1,736	1,282	468	1,633	19,872
Morris,	2,998	1,318	1,405	1,503	1,197	2,905	1,277	1,564	1,616	1,032	100	775	17,750
Middlesex,	2,819	1,307	1,419	1,564	1,083	2,619	1,278	1,397	1,577	995	263	1,564	17,890
Gloucester,	2,561	1,332	1,230	1,578	936	2,661	1,169	1,285	1,511	845	646	61	16,115
Bergen,	2,887	920	665	1,560	925	2,048	1,008	649	1,410	857	202	2,825	15,956
Somerset,	1,798	819	879	1,027	822	1,804	767	968	1,115	778	175	1,863	12,815
Salem,	1,759	946	856	1,329	500	1,876	745	895	1,276	497	607	85	11,371
Cumberland,	1,672	783	844	961	453	1,541	685	844	941	459	271	75	9,529
Cape May,	487	242	334	264	197	449	227	272	279	137	80	98	3,066
	34,780	15,859	16,301	19,956	12,629	32,632	14,827	17,018	19,533	11,000	4402	12,422	211,949

CENSUS OF 1790.

COUNTIES	Free White Males of 16 years and upwards.	Free White Males under 16 years.	Free White Females, including Heads of Families.	All other Free Persons.	Slaves.	Total Number.
Hunterdon,	4,966	4,379	9,316	191	1,301	20,153
Sussex,	4,963	4,939	9,094	65	439	19,500
Burlington,	4,625	4,164	8,481	598	227	18,095
Essex,	4,339	3,972	8,143	160	1,171	17,785
Monmouth,	3,843	3,678	7,448	353	1,596	16,918
Morris,	4,092	3,938	7,502	48	636	16,216
Middlesex,	3,995	3,375	7,128	140	1,318	15,956
Gloucester,	3,287	3,311	6,232	342	191	13,363
Bergen,	2,865	2,299	4,944	192	2,301	12,601
Somerset,	2,819	2,300	5,130	147	1,810	12,296
Salem,	2,679	2,396	4,816	374	172	10,437
Cumberland,	2,147	1,966	3,877	138	120	8,248
Cape May,	631	609	1,176	14	141	2,571
	45,251	41,416	83,287	2762	11,423	184,139

CENSUS OF 1810.

COUNTIES	FREE WHITE MALES					FREE WHITE FEMALES					All other free persons except Indians not taxed.	Slaves.	Total number.
	Under 10 years.	Of 10 and under 16.	Of 16 and under 26.	Of 26 and under 45.	Of 45 and upwards.	Under 10 years.	Of 10 and under 16.	Of 16 and under 26.	Of 26 and under 45.	Of 45 and upwards.			
Hunterdon,	3664	1827	2114	2074	1769	3572	1608	2240	2188	1694	687	1119	24,556
Sussex,	4472	1927	2510	2188	1627	4301	1851	2339	2120	1413	269	478	25,549
Burlington,	4108	1789	2060	2221	1716	3868	1853	2310	2428	1590	946	93	24,972
Essex,	3795	1867	2535	2375	1640	3519	1967	2448	2335	1616	758	1129	25,984
Monmouth,	3356	1698	1655	1876	1557	3286	1452	1808	1851	1475	632	1504	22,150
Morris,	3625	1983	1813	1969	1315	3374	1750	1820	1882	1237	204	856	21,828
Middlesex,	2878	1697	1675	1751	1402	2860	1642	1286	1778	1449	665	1298	20,381
Gloucester,	3249	1531	1821	1714	1290	3154	1411	1722	1738	1154	886	74	19,744
Bergen,	2122	1037	1180	1338	1202	2130	1040	1232	1276	1081	785	2180	16,603
Somerset,	2003	1022	1226	1128	951	1762	1016	1228	1224	881	316	1968	14,726
Salem,	2014	1050	1141	1146	674	1865	835	1175	1114	681	1037	29	12,761
Cumberland,	1911	1157	1183	1230	662	1811	1128	1244	1108	647	547	42	12,670
Cape May,	617	285	318	384	199	563	234	332	317	191	111	81	3632
	37,814	18,914	21,231	21,394	16,004	36,065	17,787	21,184	21,359	15,109	7843	10,851	245,555

CENSUS OF 1820.

COUNTIES	FREE WHITE MALES						FREE WHITE FEMALES					MALE SLAVES				FEMALE SLAVES				FREE COLOURED PERSONS—MALES				FREE COLOURED PERSONS—FEMALES				All other free persons except Indians not taxed.	Total number.
	Under 10 years.	Of 10 and under 16.	Between 16 and 18.	Of 16 and under 26.	Of 26 and under 45.	Of 45 and upwards.	Under 10 years.	Of 10 and under 16.	Of 16 and under 26.	Of 26 and under 45.	Of 45 and upwards.	Under 14 years.	Of 14 and under 26.	Of 26 and under 45.	Of 45 and upwards.	Under 14 years.	Of 14 and under 26.	Of 26 and under 45.	Of 45 and upwards.	Under 14 years.	Of 14 and under 26.	Of 26 and under 45.	Of 45 and upwards.	Under 14 years.	Of 14 and under 26.	Of 26 and under 45.	Of 45 and upwards.		
Hunterdon,	4194	1940	586	2539	2515	1967	4175	1907	2547	2646	2024	24	135	81	55	21	148	92	60	351	134	117	109	356	155	131	90	91	28604
Sussex,	5901	2435	723	3053	3034	1931	5458	2371	3174	2276	1768	37	75	40	20	42	77	60	27	139	55	35	30	119	39	30	26		32752
Burlington,	4334	2176	661	2542	2459	2022	4082	2201	2854	2759	2050	14	12	10	4	10	24	2	6	241	173	146	100	252	139	128	82		28882
Essex,	4337	2185	720	3100	2502	1999	4162	2244	2930	2934	2051		181	99	64		126	117	72	391	118	118	118	397	115	131	80		30793
Monmouth,	3777	1758	543	2189	2030	1770	3645	1747	2150	2076	1666	328	233	109	65	129	179	134	71	205	68	82	78	223	86	77	73		25038
Morris,	3218	1639	536	1855	1857	1522	3110	1556	2096	1917	1484	126	122	46	50	81	103	85	44	139	38	37	32	113	40	34	24		21368
Middlesex,	2999	1430	431	1791	1938	1517	2877	1491	1882	1941	1559	134	168	111	81	111	178	130	100	257	77	77	85	273	108	80	67		21470
Gloucester,	3779	1829	451	2161	2051	1531	3384	1704	2194	1979	1356	11	4			6	6	6	3	203	107	138	104	187	120	119	86	18	23089
Bergen,	2416	1154	302	1330	1489	1435	2306	1148	1406	1465	1247	152	376	218	167	157	241	217	155	389	59	44	56	346	73	50	42	40	18178
Somerset,	2140	1091	308	1342	1319	1096	2044	985	1403	1395	1083	23	269	200	112	27	192	190	109	511	99	99	57	502	99	74	66		16506
Salem,	2193	1047	350	1340	1289	738	2025	963	1368	1289	754	2	3	3	5	3	5	1	4	222	133	107	91	166	129	74	79		14022
Cumberland,	2065	960	266	1026	1201	747	1999	880	1231	1156	780	5	1			2	1	2		138	64	65	48	125	80	46	37		12668
Cape May,	702	326	79	371	434	262	654	308	402	360	213	4	4		5	3	5		5	52	17	25	24	34	15	24	14		4265
	42055	19970	5956	24639	24418	18537	39921	19504	25637	24093	18035	860	1583	917	628	592	1285	1036	656	3328	1116	1090	892	3093	1198	987	766	149	277575

CENSUS, 1830.

Showing the Aggregate Amount of each description of Persons within the District of New Jersey, by Counties.

FREE WHITES.

MALES.

Names of Counties.	Under 5 years.	Above 5 under 10.	Above 10 under 15.	Above 15 under 20.	Of 20 under 30.	Of 30 under 40.	Of 40 under 50.	Of 50 under 60.	Of 60 under 70.	Of 70 under 80.	Of 80 under 90.	Of 90 under 100.	Of 100 and upwards.
Bergen	1558	1401	1268	1082	1778	1270	779	509	415	173	61	5	1
Essex	3024	2572	2482	2571	4062	2522	1449	818	477	211	48	4	
Morris	1900	1603	1459	1200	2025	1387	906	565	347	170	53	4	
Sussex	1898	1590	1342	1140	1752	1045	665	445	225	103	28	2	
Warren	1614	1363	1205	1090	1773	1062	670	341	234	95	14	3	
Somerset	1140	1074	1000	921	1255	809	585	434	269	129	46	1	
Middlesex	1561	1411	1378	1227	1886	1190	813	487	371	183	35	8	
Hunterdon	2345	2079	1899	1592	2376	1550	1121	685	500	232	78	3	
Burlington	2389	2053	1926	1580	2638	1660	1041	733	441	196	50	2	
Monmouth	2491	1893	1776	1419	2290	1528	950	731	435	221	64	3	
Gloucester	2513	1928	1856	1551	2546	1452	907	629	354	151	26	3	
Cape May	411	359	341	227	418	284	178	93	63	22	4		
Salem	1067	874	892	785	1090	761	500	253	143	66	11	1	
Cumberland	1160	1004	921	738	1112	711	479	330	181	69	16	2	1
	25071	21204	19745	17123	27001	17231	11043	7053	4458	2021	534	44	2

FEMALES.

Names of Counties.	Under 5 years.	Of 5 under 10.	Of 10 under 15.	Of 15 under 20.	Of 20 under 30.	Of 30 under 40.	Of 40 under 50.	Of 50 under 60.	Of 60 under 70.	Of 70 under 80.	Of 80 under 90.	Of 90 under 100.	Of 100 and upwards.
Bergen	1519	1374	1154	983	1656	1102	750	494	402	140	49	11	1
Essex	2867	2506	2316	2367	3735	2331	1503	923	606	289	63	5	
Morris	1837	1525	1332	1187	1856	1304	827	609	370	170	58	5	
Sussex	1840	1502	1218	1146	1624	977	626	375	232	79	31	4	
Warren	1507	1268	1128	1042	1467	959	566	387	246	100	23	2	
Somerset	1152	1029	938	854	1259	887	619	438	319	164	56	2	
Middlesex	1507	1398	1285	1239	1831	1203	812	569	401	186	51	5	
Hunterdon	2191	1931	1797	1736	2509	1612	1216	821	473	274	81	11	
Burlington	2283	2037	1848	1665	2780	1683	1105	789	520	235	66	11	
Monmouth	2296	1904	1603	1363	2212	1454	951	640	437	205	58	8	
Gloucester	2331	1844	1618	1513	2324	1374	871	592	315	148	30	8	
Cape May	405	353	321	264	373	260	175	85	43	25	4	2	
Salem	1065	822	836	707	1100	765	498	277	156	67	7		
Cumberland	1137	986	873	718	1091	712	488	308	185	75	9		1
	23937	20479	18267	16784	25817	16623	11007	7307	4705	2160	586	63	2

E

CENSUS, 1830 (continued).

Legend — SM = Slaves, Males; SF = Slaves, Females; FM = Free Coloured Persons, Males; FF = Free Coloured Persons, Females. Age groups: U10 = Under 10 years; 10–24 = Of 10 under 24; 24–36 = Of 24 under 36; 36–55 = Of 36 under 55; 55–100 = Of 55 under 100; 100+ = Of 100 and upwards.

Names of Counties	SM U10	SM 10–24	SM 24–36	SM 36–55	SM 55–100	SM 100+	SF U10	SF 10–24	SF 24–36	SF 36–55	SF 55–100	SF 100+	FM U10	FM 10–24	FM 24–36	FM 36–55	FM 55–100	FM 100+	FF U10	FF 10–24	FF 24–36	FF 36–55	FF 55–100	FF 100+	Total
Bergen	1	3	102	120	79	1	3	2	79	110	86		413	409	136	64	38	1	341	302	97	58	36	1	22,412
Essex		2	36	40	29			4	36	41	34		291	297	162	134	36	2	272	360	174	159	53	1	41,911
Morris		2	30	28	15			1	44	26	14		132	182	55	50	17		117	134	48	44	21		23,666
Sussex	4		11	5	5			5	9	14	6		65	86	27	19	9		69	69	26	20	11		20,346
Warren		3	7	5	2	1	3	1	9	4	5		83	63	34	24	9		58	72	38	26	14		18,627
Somerset		1	71	81	60		3	1	78	98	57	3	312	408	107	73	45	2	325	366	115	70	37	2	17,689
Middlesex			53	45	32			1	70	67	38		297	319	119	112	55		258	333	136	113	72		23,157
Hunterdon			33	25	18			3	39	36	17		266	314	138	104	47		279	299	165	113	45		31,060
Burlington			4	2	1	1	1	2	7	5	1		190	203	139	108	54		199	195	105	103	58		31,107
Monmouth			45	32	20		1	1	53	45	29	1	385	382	119	129	79		336	306	137	130	69	1	29,233
Gloucester										3	1		228	172	174	179	81		203	175	161	118	56		28,431
Cape May													32	35	21	18	12		23	33	16	19	16		4,936
Salem		1	2							2			216	243	146	101	67	1	209	153	140	83	48	1	14,155
Cumberland			1										123	121	81	81	24		122	88	70	57	18		14,093
Total	5	12	395	383	261	3	8	20	424	451	288	4	3033	3234	1458	1196	573	7	2811	2890	1428	1113	554	6	320,823

CENSUS, 1830 (continued).

Names of Counties.	WHITE PERSONS INCLUDED IN THE FOREGOING.					SLAVES & COLOURED Included in the foregoing.			
	Deaf and Dumb under 14 years.	Deaf and Dumb above 14 and under 25 years.	Deaf and Dumb above 25 years.	Blind.	Aliens.	Deaf and Dumb under 14 years.	Deaf and Dumb above 14 and under 25 years.	Deaf and Dumb above 25 years.	Blind.
Bergen	6	2	2	12	213	3			5
Essex	7	11	9	22	1176				1
Morris	2	6	12	11	497	2	1	1	1
Sussex	1	2	3	14	89				
Warren	2	2	1	12	286			5	2
Somerset	4	4	6	17	118				3
Middlesex	5	4	3	7	174				3
Hunterdon	11	11	12	19	210				2
Burlington	5	7	8	41	129		1	1	2
Monmouth	8	5	6	14	81			1	1
Gloucester	11	13	5	22	357				2
Cape May		1							
Salem	2	2	2	7	8				
Cumberland		1	3	7	27				
	64	71	72	205	3365	5	2	8	22

The vice of slavery was early introduced into the State, and took deep root, particularly, in the eastern portion. In the county of Bergen, in 1790, the slaves amounted to near one-fifth of the population; and in Essex, Middlesex, and Monmouth, they were very numerous, the counties having most Dutch population being most infected. In the counties settled by "Friends," Burlington, Gloucester, Salem, Cumberland, and Cape May, there were, comparatively, few slaves: the first, at that period, had only 227: the second, 191: the third, 120; and the last, 141. The whole number in the State was then, 11,423. At the subsequent census, the number had increased to 12,422. The small increase of 999, in ten years, proves that the inhabitants, generally, had discovered the moral and physical evils of slavery, and had applied themselves to diminish them. This became more apparent by the act of 15 Feb. 1804, entitled "An Act for the gradual Abolition of Slavery," under which the number of slaves was reduced, in 1810, to 10,851; and in 1820, to 7,557. This act is supplied by the act of 24th February, 1820, which embraces and extends its principles, and provides, that every child, born of a slave, within the State, since the 4th of July, 1804, or which shall be thereafter born, shall be free; but shall remain the servant of the owner of the mother, as if it had been bound to service by the overseers of the poor; if a male, until the age of 25; if a female, to the age of 21 years: that the owner shall, within 9 months after the birth of such child, deliver to the clerk of the county, a certificate, subscribed by him, containing the name and addition of the owner; the name, age and sex of the child, and the name of the mother; which certificate, whether delivered before or after the nine months, must be recorded by the clerk. The owner neglecting to file such certificate, within the nine months, is liable to a fine of five dollars, and the sum of one dollar per month afterward; but not exceeding in the whole $100, to any one suing therefor, one half to the prosecutor, and the other half to the poor of the township; and for delivering a certificate containing a false relation of the time of the birth of such child, $100, recoverable in the same manner: one-half in favour of the child, and the other, of the township. The time of birth may be inquired into, notwithstanding the certificate.

The traffic in slaves, between this and other states, was prohibited by the act of 14th March, 1798, and by act of 1820, last recited, under the forfeiture of vessels, and severe penalties on persons concerned therein. But slaves may still be brought into the State, by persons removing thereto, with a view to settled, or temporary residence; during the stay of the master only, in the latter case. By these acts, also, the manumission of slaves was permitted under certain formalities therein prescribed. And such has been the beneficial operation of these provisions, that in 1830, the State contained 2,254 slaves only; the counties of Gloucester and Cumberland, none; the county of Cape May, 2; and Salem, 1. So that it is probable, that in another 20 years, this pest will be entirely eradicated from the State.

We may remark, as a curious fact, and one that may prove most encouraging to the southern states, in an attempt at the abolition of slavery, that the coloured population, under the system of manumission adopted by this State, has increased in 40 years only, about 44 per cent. including the free and the slaves; whilst the whites have increased in the ratio of nearly 75 per. cent. In considering this subject, it must be observed, on one hand, that the coloured population has uniformly been treated with humanity and indulgence; and upon the other, that the great cities have absorbed a portion of their increase. But yet, the white population of the State has been kept down in a much greater degree by emigration. Indeed, New Jersey has received a large and unwelcome increase of coloured population from the fugitive slaves of Delaware, Maryland, and the southern states.

To complete our view of the physical condition of the State, we annex a table, framed from abstracts returned by the assessors of the several counties, showing the species and the amount of taxable property, and the amount of tax raised for state, county and township purposes. The returns from several counties have not been as full as they should have been, for our purpose; particularly, in respect to township charges; and we have been compelled, in some cases, to estimate the amount of road and poor tax, in some townships, by the ratio of population compared with that of others.

STATISTICAL TABLE OF THE STATE.

Names of Counties	Total Number of Acres	Acres of unimproved Land	Lots of and under 10 acres	Householders	Single Men	Taxables	Merchants and Traders	Grist Mills—run of Stones	Saw Mills	Fulling Mills	Paper Mills	Oil, Hemp and Slitting Mills	Furnaces	Forge Fires	Cotton Factories	Woollen Factories	Carding Machines	Cider Distilleries	Tan Vats	Male Slaves	Neat Cattle over 3 years	Horses & Mules over 3 ys.	Stud Horses	Chairs, Sulkies, and Dearborns	Coaches, Phaetons, and Chaises	Covered Wagons	Two and Four Horse Stages	Ferries and Toll Bridges	Fisheries	Township Taxes — Poor Dolls.	Township Taxes — Road Dolls.	Township Taxes — School Dolls.	County Tax Dolls.	State Tax Dolls.	Population, 1830.	Represent. in Assembly†
Bergen	207,500	108,766	660	1,262	533	5,706	75	84	93				4	16	16	5	10	12	127	158	1,287	446	14	320	17	977	4	8	7	2,500	600	100	5,000	2,631.43	22,412	3
Burlington	533,002	123,524	1,867	3,236	1095	6,549	86	91	46				4	3	3		11	40	350	2	14,210	6,055	19	579	34	148	1	2	16	3,450	*		15,000	4,607.12	31,107	5
Cape May	161,300	59,528	188	669	182	1,000	28	8	16	1			1						6	1	2,053	673		72				2		1,125	1,650		2,000	646.01	4,936	1
Cumberland	335,460	209,380	475	774	333	2,742	51	44	91	1			5	1		1	2	4	223		5,713	2,053	9	75	4			8	2	3,150	4,000		4,115	1,586.18	14,093	3
Essex	154,660	205,913	3,316	3,370	1412	8,100	306	42	41	10	2		5	10	22	13	5	5	158	40	9,783	3,849	7	715	30	967	4	9	21	9,261	13,860		10,000	3,822.04	41,911	5
Gloucester	713,320		1,113	3,075	978	5,600	102	75	63	6			2			2	5	29	594		9,478	4,640	13	235				2	17	4,993	15,100		9,993	3,379.26	28,431	4
Hunterdon	324,572	6,272	1,167		673	6,000	85	80	71			13	3		1	2	17	58	243	51	12,492	7,538	50	894	59	56				6,850	8,300		10,000	4,535.84	31,060	5
Middlesex	217,000	127,505	1,143	841	477	6,000	99	67	20				3			2	17	39	238	32	7,075	3,684	13	522	81	380	1	1		5,850	3,000		4,000	3,253.96	23,157	4
Monmouth	665,000		786	1,385	663	6,000	103	67	52						1		17	46	309	31	12,068	4,942	19	192		5				6,650	9,646		11,769	3,723.68	29,233	4
Morris	292,900	58,989	254	1,053	528	4,836	83	33	71				5	43	5		11	53	119	78	11,820	4,056	23	309	6	663		1		5,650	10,900		7,100	3,171.93	23,666	4
Salem	204,936			437	490	3,092	47	61	11				2				11	15	211	5	7,300	3,103	18	278	32	32				5,076	4,620		7,000	2,156.60	14,155	3
Somerset	189,800	135,555	196	608	391	3,500	68	64	44								21	27	227	12	8,634	4,621	25	218	2	16	1	3		4,476	5,837		6,000	2,642.86	17,689	3
Sussex	352,300	135,555	196	1,075	449	3,611	87	84	55				3	28			18	35	235	6	13,070	3,875	17	218				1		3,400	8,600	766	5,475	2,025.70	20,346	3
Warren	224,360	89,356	132	1,062	411	3,489	56		41					7	2	2	16	25	235		7,772	4,324	28	61						5,700	6,146	500	6,714	2,185.50	18,627	3
	4,656,390	1,125,788	11,734	19,623	8541	66,315	1252	857	1655	72	13	13	28	108	106	45	135	588	2876	394	192,805	53,865	236	4400	275	3287	71	59	35	78,131	92,859	1366	104,166	40,366.71	320,823	50

* Township generally.   † Each county sends one member to Council.

There are in the State—17 Oil Mills—6 Calico Printing Works—4 Plaster Mills—13 Glass and 1 Delf Work—11 Grain Distilleries.

The number of acres in each county in the above table, is given from the measurement of the area of the county upon Gordon's map, with a reticulated scale of square miles. The result corresponds sufficiently well with the returns of the assessor from the counties in which there are no unimproved lands. But in the others, the returns of the assessors fall much short of the estimate in the table. We do not know, exactly, what is meant by "unimproved lands," in the returns of the assessors. We have copied from them.

XI. It will be seen by reference to the preceding table, that the State is, 'in the aggregate, agricultural; and such is the character of all the counties, except Essex, part of Bergen, and part of Morris. The glass and iron manufactures of the counties of Burlington, Gloucester, and Cumberland, are not sufficient to exempt them from this classification. Of the agricultural products of the several portions, we have already spoken, and will observe, only, generally, here, that the valleys of the two northern sections are well adapted to wheat, and that under the improved mode of culture they may become equally productive with any lands east of the mountains. The southern district, composed of the alluvial country, is productive, chiefly of corn, rye, fruits, grass, and vegetables; and sends to market large quantities of pork, cured in a manner that can scarcely be surpassed. New Jersey hams, bacon, and barrelled pork, bear the highest prices in all markets. Nor is the reputation of the farmers of this district, much less for their beef, and especially for their veal. Its gardens and orchards supply the Philadelphia markets with the best fruits. Indeed the whole state is remarkable for the abundance and quality of its peaches and apples, and the quantity of cider, and brandy made from the latter. Notwithstanding the influence of Temperance Societies upon distilling, and it has been confessedly great, there are yet in the State 388 cider distilleries. The counties of Burlington, Gloucester, Monmouth, Hunterdon, Warren, and Sussex, are renowned for the number and quality of the horses which they breed.

Yet, notwithstanding this agricultural character of the State, she claims no mean rank in manufactures. By the preceding table, 28 furnaces are given; but 12 of these, only, we believe, are blast furnaces, employed in making iron from the ore; the remainder are cupola furnaces, used in the reduction of pig and other metal to castings. The furnaces of New Jersey, by the report of the committee of the tariff convention, holden in New York, October, 1831, produced in 1830, 1,671 tons of pig iron, and 5,615 tons of castings; and her 108 forges, 3000 tons of bar iron.

The first valued at $30 the ton, yields - - - - -	$50,130
The second, at $60, - - - - - - - -	336,900
The third, at $90 the ton, - - . - - - -	270,000
Making - - -	$657,030

for her manufacture of iron in pigs, castings and bars. This iron, however, is further improved in value by the aid of 10 rolling and slitting mills, 16 cupola furnaces, and the extensive machine shops of Patterson. And we shall not, we presume, underrate the annual value of the iron manufacture of the State, when we state it at one million of dollars; all of which is obtained from her mines, her forests, and her labour, not one cent of foreign matter entering into the composition.

There are in the State,

1 flint glass manufactory, producing annually, - - - -	$80,000
12 glass houses, employed on hollow ware and window glass, estimated each to produce annually $30,000, - - - - -	360,000
	440,000
And 1 delf ware establishment, whose product may exceed $ -	50,000
	$490,000

Beside several extensive clay potteries.

We may set down, therefore, the annual product of glass and pottery ware at full half a million.

Of the 25 woollen manufactories most are small; and having no data for determining their respective products, we conjecturally average them at $10,000 per annum.

From the Abstracts of the Assessors, we obtain but 45 cotton manufactories in the State; but the Committee of the New York Convention, of 1831, return 51—of which they give the following interesting results:

Capital employed	$2,027,644	Pounds of cloth	1,877,418
Number of spindles	62,979	Males employed	2,151
Number of power-looms	815	Wages per week, each	$6 00
Pounds of yarn sold	3,212,184	Females employed	3,070
Yards of cloth	5,133,776	Wages per week, each	$1 90

Children under 12 years of age	217	Bushels of charcoal	820
Wages per week, each	$1 40	Gallons of oil	13,348
Pounds of cotton used	5,832,204	Value of other articles	18,208
Bbls. of flour, for sizing	975	Spindles building	11,000
Cords of wood	671	Hand weavers	1,060
Tons of coal	1,007	Total dependants	12,750

The price of the raw material, viz. 5,832,204 lbs. at 11 cts. was $641,542
Price of yarn sold, 3,212,184 lbs. at 30 cts. the lb. average, was $963,655
Price of cloth, 5,133,776 yards, at 15 cts.   770,066

Gross return of cotton manufacture $1,733,721

The six calico bleaching and printing establishments, belong to the cotton manufacture. Some of these, as at Patterson, Belleville, and Rahway, are very extensive, but we have not the means to give their results.

The four machine factories at Patterson alone, employ above 400 hands ; and the Phœnix Manufacturing Company, in addition to their cotton establishment, have 1,616 spindles employed in spinning flax, consuming 493,000 lbs., and employing 196 hands. The flax is manufactured into duck and bagging. In the cotton establishment of Mr. John Colt, there were manufactured in 1831-2, 460,000 yards of cotton duck.

The 29 paper mills produce large returns. Some of these mills, as at Patterson, Springfield, Mount Holly, &c. are built on the best models, and employ the most improved machinery.

The manufacture of leather from the hide into the various articles of its use, is very extensively conducted. There are 2,876 tan vats ; and the fabric of shoes, boots and harness, gives employment and wealth to many individuals in Newark, Bloomfield, Rahway, Burlington, &c. &c. ; and its product forms a large item in the exports of the commonwealth. Hats and clothing for the southern market, are also made in the first three towns last mentioned ; and, also, in large quantities in the thriving village of Plainfield.

Coaches, cabinetware and chairs, form also large articles of export both from East and West Jersey, from Camden, and from Newark and Rahway.

Unfortunately, we do not possess the means of giving in detail, or in gross, the results of many of these valuable branches of business ; for we want, in relation to this state, the usual data for determining the quantum of surplus production, which an account of her exports would afford. Her whole foreign trade, and the far greater proportion of her domestic business, centers in New York and Philadelphia, to swell the business tables of these two great marts. But we are assured that, from Rahway alone, the amount furnished to the general coasting trade is not less than a million of dollars annually ; whilst the products of the manufactures of Belleville and its vicinity, are valued at 2,000,000, and those of Patterson at more than double that amount. By the treasury report of 1832, the whole tonnage was 573 90.100, registered, and 32,499 24.100, enrolled and licensed. And the whole amount of exports, foreign and domestic, $11,430 ; but of the tonnage of the State, 5,000 are said to be enregistered in the New York districts.

We confess, that the view we have thus given of the condition of the State is very imperfect ; but it suffices to show, that, in agriculture, in manufactures, in the great improvements by canals and rail-roads, she nobly maintains a course of emulation with her great adjacent sister states. By the Morris and Raritan Canals, and by the rail-way of the Trenton Falls Company, new and great acquisitions of water power for machinery have been attained, with increased facilities of communication with the best markets ; and there remain unemployed upon the mountain streams, now cheaply accessible, a vast number of mill sites, among which we may mention those at Belvidere and Clinton as entitled to great attention. The Musconetcong river throughout its course may also be profitably employed, since ready communication may be had with the Morris Canal from all points. The upper falls of the Passaic, the waste waters of the Rockaway, the Pequannock and Ramapo Rivers, will all, probably, be brought into use by the improvements already made and projected. Her mines, her limestones, her marbles, her marls, nay her very sands and clay, will be shortly all better known and more highly valued, and will greatly increase her wealth ; her copper profusely scattered over a large area, accessible as any in the world; her inexhaustible and unsurpassed beds of iron; her stupendous veins of zinc will, at no distant day, give employment to additional thousands of intelligent and contented labourers, and instead of pouring forth her population to fertilize, enrich, and bless other lands, she will give to her sons full employment, and the means of wealth, within her own limits. Already has the reflux of population commenced. Newark, Patterson, Bloomfield, Trenton, Boonton and Rahway, will, in ten years, have doubled their population; and New Jersey will, we believe, at the census of 1840, have increased her inhabitants in a ratio equal to that of any of the original states; and among the stars which form the bright constellation of the Union, though small, she will not be the least brilliant.

CLIMATE.—It is supposed that the climate of our country has undergone, and is still undergoing, a material change; that thunder and lightning are less frequent; the cold of our winters, and heat of our summers, less, and more variable; the springs colder, and the autumns more temperate. It is possible, but we think doubtful, that the variability of the climate has increased; but the average severity of heat and cold has not been diminished. The following description of the weather, by a settler of East Jersey, in 1683, will be recognised as true at the present day. "As for the temperature of the air, it is wonderfully suited to the humours of mankind; the wind and weather rarely holding in one point, or one kind, for ten days together. It is a rare thing for a vessel to be windbound for a week together, the wind seldom holding in a point more than 48 hours; and in a short time we have wet and dry, warm and cold weather, which changes we often desire in England, and look for before they come."* Alternations of cold and mild winters, of hot and cool summers, of early and late commencements of frosts, of drought and superabundant rain, have been continued, from the earliest period to which our knowledge of the country extends. A review of the seasons from 1681, shows no less than 39 years in which the navigation was obstructed by ice, in the month of December. On the 10th of that month, 1678, the good ship *The Shield*, moored to a tree before the town of Burlington; and, on the following morning, her passengers walked to the shore upon the ice, so hard had the river suddenly frozen. In 1681, December 10th, the Bristol Factor arrived at Chester; and, on the next day, her passengers, also, went on shore on the ice. On the 19th December, 1740, the navigation was stopped, and the river remained closed until the 13th March. In 1790, it closed on the 8th, and in 1797, on the 1st of that month. In 1831, rigorous cold weather began in November; and the Delaware was frozen fast on the 7th December. In 1780, in the month of January, the mercury stood, for several hours, at 5° below 0, F.; and, during the month, except on one night, never rose in the city of Philadelphia to the freezing point. In 1817, February 7, the water froze in most of the hydrant plugs, and some of the street mains, in that city. The earliest notice we have seen of the weather, on the shores of the Delaware, is in the Journal of De Vries. He left the Texel on the 12th December, 1630, and arrived in the Delaware at the close of January, or commencement of February, the period of our coldest weather; when, unimpeded by the season, which he reports as so mild that his men could work in the open air, in their shirt sleeves, he erected, on Lewis's Creek, the fortress of *Oplandt*. The winter of 1788-9, was also uncommonly mild; but there was ice sufficient to obstruct the navigation. On the 22d March, the orchards were in full bloom, and the meadows as green as ordinarily in the month of June; but, on the 23d, snow fell two feet deep, destroying nearly all the fruits of the year. In 1827-8, the navigation of the Delaware was altogether unobstructed. The atmosphere was filled with dense fog, in the months of December, January and February; during which, including days when the sun was apparent for some hours, there were not more than 17 days of clear weather. By a table for January, during 20 years, from 1807 to 1827, the mean temperature of the month varied from 42° to 27°; and the mean of the whole period was 39° of Fahrenheit.

There are seldom more than from 20 to 30 days, in summer, in which the mercury rises above 80°, or, in winter, falls below 30°. The warmest part of the day is from 2 to 3 o'clock; from which time the heat gradually diminishes until the ensuing morning. The coldest part of the four-and-twenty hours is at the break of day. There are seldom more than three or four nights of the summer, in which the heat of the air is nearly the same, as in the preceding day. After the hottest days, the evenings are generally agreeable, and often delightful. The higher the mercury

---

* Smith's N. J. 169.

rises in the day, the lower it falls the succeeding night. From 80°, it commonly falls to 66°; but from 60° only to 50°. This disproportion between the temperature of the day and night, in summer, is always greatest in the month of August, when the dews are heavy in proportion to the coolness of the evening. They are sometimes so considerable as to wet the clothes; and marsh meadows and creeks, drained by the heat, have been supplied with their usual water from this source, in this month and the first weeks of September. The violent heats of summer seldom continue more than two or three days, without intermission. They are generally broken by showers of rain, sometimes accompanied by thunder and lightning, and succeeded by a north-west wind, which produces an agreeable and invigorating coolness in the air.

The warmest weather is generally in July; but intensely hot days are often felt in May, June, August and September, and the mean heat of August has been greater than that of July. The transitions from heat to cold are often sudden, and sometimes to very distant degrees. After a day in which the mercury has been at 86° and even at 90°, it has fallen in the course of a single night to 60°, and fires have been found necessary the ensuing morning, especially if the change in the temperature of the air has been accompanied by rain and a S. E. wind. In a summer month, the mercury has been known to fall 20° in an hour and a half. There are few summer months in which fires are not agreeable in some part of them. Mr. Rittenhouse informed Dr. Rush, that there was not a summer during his residence in the country, in which he did not discover frost in every month.

The weather is equally variable during the winter. The mercury has fallen from 37 to 4½° below 0 in 24 hours. In this season, nature seems frequently to play at cross-purposes. Heavy falls of snow are often succeeded by a thaw, which, in a short time, wholly dissolves them. The rivers are frozen sufficiently hard to bear horses and carriages, and thawed so as to be navigable, several times in the course of the winter. Ice is commonly formed gradually, and seldom until the rivers have been chilled with snow. Yet, sometimes its production is sudden, and the Delaware has frequently been frozen over in a night, so as to bear the weight of a man.

In the alluvial district of New Jersey, frost and ice appear in the latter end of October, or beginning of November. But intense cold is rarely felt, until about Christmas. Hence the vulgar saying, "as the day lengthens, the cold strengthens."

The coldest weather is from the middle of January, to the middle of February. As in summer there are often days in which fires are agreeable, so in winter they sometimes are incommodious. Vegetation has been observed in all the winter months. Garlic was tasted in butter in January, 1781; the leaves of the willow, the blossom of the peach, and the flowers of the dandelion, were all seen in February, 1779, and Dr. Rush says, that 60 years since, he saw an apple orchard in full bloom, and small apples on many of the trees in the month of December. In February, 1828, we gathered flowers from the unprotected garden, and saw cattle cropping good pasturage in the fields. A cold day is often the precursor of a moderate evening. The greatest degree of cold recorded in Philadelphia, is 5° below zero, and of heat 95° F. The standard temperature of Southern Jersey may be 52°, which is that of our deepest wells and the mean heat of common spring water.

The spring is generally unpleasant. In March, the weather is stormy, variable and cold; in April, and sometimes far in May, moist and raw. From the variableness of the spring, vegetation advances with unequal pace in different seasons. The colder the spring, the more favourable the prospect of fruit. The hopes of the farmer from his fruit-trees, are, in a warm spring, often blasted by frost in April or May, and sometimes even by snow, at a later period. The colder the winter, the greater is the delay of the return of spring. Sometimes the weather, during the spring months is cloudy and damp, attended occasionally with gentle rain resembling the spray from a cataract.

June is the only month of the year which resembles the spring in the southern countries of Europe. Then, generally, the weather is temperate, the sky serene, and the verdure of the country universal and delightful.

The autumn is the most agreeable season of the year. The cool evenings and mornings, which begin about the middle of September, are attended with a moderate temperature of the air during the day. This kind of weather continues, with an increase of cold scarcely perceptible, till the middle of October, when it is closed by rain, which sometimes falls in such quantities as to produce destructive freshets; at others, in gentle showers, which continue, with occasional interruption by a few fair

F

days, for two or three weeks. These rains are the harbingers of winter, and the Indians long since taught us, that, the cold of that season is proportionate to the quantity of rain which falls during the autumn. From this account, it is apparent, that there are seldom more than four months of the year in which the weather is agreeable without fire. In winter the winds generally come from the N. W. in fair, and from the N. E. in foul weather. The N. W. winds are dry and cold. The winds, in fair weather in the spring, and in warm weather in the summer, blow from the S. W. and W. N.W. The S. W. winds usually bring with them refreshing showers of rain in spring and summer, which moderate the heat when succeeded by a N. W. wind. Sometimes showers come from the W. and N. W.

The moisture of the air is said to be greater than formerly; occasioned, probably, by the exhalations which fell in the form of snow, now descending in rain. The depth of the snow is sometimes between two and three feet; in 1828-9, it was near four, but in general it is from six to nine inches. Hail frequently falls with snow in the winter. At intervals of years, heavy showers of hail fall in the spring and summer, running commonly in veins from 40 to 50 miles long, and from half a mile to two miles in breadth. On such occasions, destruction of grain, grass and windows, to great value, is not unfrequent. From sudden changes of the air, rain and snow often fall together, forming what is commonly called sleet. In the northern parts of the State, in protected spots, snow sometimes lies until the first of April. The backwardness of the spring has been ascribed to the passage of the air over the ice and snow which remain, after the winter months, on the plains and waters of the north-west country.

The dissolution of the ice and snow is sometimes so sudden, in the spring, as to swell the creeks and rivers to such a degree as to lay waste the hopes of the husbandman, and in some instances to sweep his barns, stables, and even his dwelling into their currents. Of this power of the flood, the years 1784 and 1832, afford memorable examples. The wind, during a general thaw, comes from the S. W. or S. E.

The air, when dry, has a peculiar elasticity, which renders the heat and cold less insupportable than the same degrees of both in moister countries. It is only when summer showers are not succeeded by N. W. winds, that the air becomes oppressive by combination with moisture. With the removal of the forest the waters have decreased considerably.

The average quantity of water which falls yearly, is from 24 to 26 inches, according to the statement of Dr. Rush: but this would seem much too small, since a table of 20 years, from 1810 to 1829, inclusive, 14 of which were kept by P. Legeaux, Esq. at Springmills, and 6 at the Pennsylvania Hospital, give 35.16 inches; and a table for 10 years, ending 1827, kept by Dr. Darlington, of West Chester, gives 49.92. In the first table, the highest was 43.135 inches, in 1814; and the lowest, 23.354, in 1819. In the last table the highest was 54.1 inches in 1824, and the lowest 39.3 inches in 1822.

From the foregoing remarks we may justly conclude that, in New Jersey no two successive years are alike; that even the successive seasons and months differ from each other every year. Perhaps there is but one steady trait in the character of our climate, and that is, that it is never steady, but uniformly variable. The foregoing remarks apply generally to the whole State, yet with some variation. Thus, in the low flat country in the alluvial district, the climate is warmer in winter and hotter in summer, than in the more northern and elevated lands of the other sections. The heat of the summer and the cold of the winter are, however, tempered by the waters which bound it on three sides. In summer, upon the ocean and bay, the sea breeze prevails, and with the prostration of the forest, it finds its way yearly further interior. As the country north of Trenton rises in aerial height, as well as in latitude, its temperature necessarily decreases from both causes. The change, however, is not very considerable until we reach the mountains, where the diminution of heat is apparent in the difference of the seasons. Vegetation in the spring is from one to two weeks later than in the lower country, and the approach of winter is so much earlier. It is to their altitude more than latitude, that the mountains owe their cool and invigorating breezes which render them attractive in the summer season.

PREFATORY CHAPTER.

PART II.

Containing a Moral View of the State.

Division of the Political Power into Three Great Branches.—I. *Legislative Council and Assembly—by whom Elected—Nominations—Form of Elections—Legislative Council —how Composed—Powers—Assembly—how Constituted—Powers.*—II. *Executive Branch—What—Governor—his Powers and Duties—Secretary of State—Powers and Duties—Treasurer—Powers and Duties—Revenue and Expenditures of the State— Burden on the Citizens—Attorney General—Sheriff—Coroner—Officers of State Prison —Political Division of Counties and Townships—of Township Officers—Services in Taxation—Relief of the Poor—Making and Repairing Roads—Executive Duties of County Clerk—Militia System.*—III. *Judiciary—Courts for Trials of Small Causes— Court of Quarter Sessions—Common Pleas—Orphans' Court—Supreme and Circuit Courts—Court of Chancery—Court of Appeals—Compensation of Officers.*—IV. *Provisions for Religious, Moral, and Intellectual Improvement—Religious Societies—Literary Institutions established by Individual Largess—Common Schools established by the State—Publication of the Laws—Newspapers in the State.*

In the organization of the Commonwealth, the political power here, as elsewhere in well constituted States, has been divided into three great branches; the Legislative, Executive, and Judicial. But, in the existing constitution, these divisions have not been well preserved, the first having received the greater proportion of the province of the second, and having the third wholly dependent upon it.

I. The legislative power is vested in a council and assembly, chosen by qualified electors, on the second Tuesday of October, and the day succeeding, annually. The election is then holden for State officers, and on the first Tuesday of November, when occasion requires, for members of congress and electors of president and vice president. Such electors must be free white citizens, of full age, who have resided within the county in which they claim to vote, for twelve months immediately preceding the election, and who have paid a tax or been enrolled on any duplicate list of the last State or county tax, and possess fifty pounds, clear estate. But, from the requisite of taxation or enrolment, as the case may be, are exempted persons who may have arrived at the age of twenty-one years since the date of the last duplicate; persons removing from the township where they have paid tax, to another in the same county; and persons who have been inadvertently overlooked by the assessor; the names of the last being immediately entered upon the tax list. The property qualification, though demanded by the constitution, has been virtually annulled by the act of 1st June, 1820, providing that every person paying a State or county tax, whose name shall be enrolled on such duplicate list, shall be taken to be worth fifty pounds clear estate; and thus by the omnipotence of the legislature, things essentially different are made the same.

The electors vote only in the township in which they reside. An attempt to vote a second time, is punishable by a fine of fifty dollars to the use of the poor, recoverable by the overseer of the township. The assessor or collector enrolling one under age, or non-resident in the township, with intent to admit him to vote, is subject to the penalty of $100 to the like use, and recoverable in like manner.

Such elections are conducted after the following mode. The clerks of the respective courts of Common Pleas, attend at the court house, on the first Mondays of September, annually, to receive from voters, lists of candidates for public suffrage, signed by the nominator, and transmitted by letter or delivered in person. From these, the clerk makes a general list of the nominees for the several offices, a copy whereof he sends, within a week from the nomination, to the clerks of the several precincts of the county; and, in case of nominations for congress or electors of president, a copy to the governor, who transmits a copy of all the nominations to the clerk of every county, who sends these also to the township clerks. At the election, no vote can be given unless for such nominee.

The precinct clerks, by public advertisement fourteen days before that of the election, make known the time and place of holding it, and the names of the candidates, when and where the election officers, viz. the judge, assessor, collector, and town clerk, attend. The clerk posts on the door of the house where the election is holden, the list of the nominees, and the other officers open the polls at 10 o'clock of the day. If any one of such officers be in nomination, he is disqualified from assisting at the election, unless before its commencement he publicly decline; and should he assist, and be elected, his election is void. The town clerk, with the approbation of his fellow officers, may appoint a substitute; or, if he be absent, dead, or otherwise disqualified, and no substitute have been appointed, such officers may nominate a clerk for the occasion. And if the judge, assessor, or collector be absent or disqualified, his place may be filled by the voters present, and the absentee is subject to punishment by fine, unless he satisfactorily excuse himself to the court of common pleas. Malfeasance by an officer of the election, is punishable by a fine of $100 for the use of the poor. Each officer swears or affirms to the faithful performance of his duty, and may administer like oath or affirmation to his fellows. For the preservation of order, the judge and inspectors may commit riotous or disorderly persons either to the charge of the constable, or to the common gaol for any time not exceeding twenty-four hours.

The poll is open for two days; but may be adjourned for short periods, as occasion may require, in case no voters appear. On the evening of the first day, it is closed at 9 o'clock; and opened on the morning of the 2d at 8; and is finally closed at 7 o'clock of the evening of the second day.

All elections, for representatives in Congress, electors of President and Vice-President of the United States, members of council and assembly, sheriffs and coroners, are by ballot, which may be written or printed, or partly both, and must be delivered by the voter to the judge or either of the inspectors; and the name of such voter, being pronounced, by the officer, in an audible voice, and being unobjected to, is entered upon the poll-list, and the ballot deposited in the ballot-box.

When the poll is closed, the poll-list is signed by the officers, the ballots read, registered, and filed. If there be a greater number of ballots than names on the list, no more ballots are enumerated than names: if two or more ballots be folded, or rolled together, or a ballot contain more names than it ought, or otherwise appear to be fraudulent, it is rejected, and as many numbers, deducted from the poll-list as there are ballots, cast away. The number of votes being ascertained, the election officers, or any two of them, certify the number for each candidate, after a prescribed form; a duplicate of which, duly attested, is filed in the office of the town clerk, with the poll-list; and the original is transmitted to the clerk of the pleas, on or before the Saturday, next after the day of election; who makes a list of the votes for each candidate, from the several certificates, and ascertains who are duly elected, by a plurality of votes; files the certificates and list in his office, and makes a certificate of the election of each officer, a copy of which, with a copy of the list filed, he transmits to the governor.

In case the election be for members of Congress, or electors of President, the governor, within five days of the receipt of the list, before a privy council, determines the persons elected, whom the governor commissions under the seal of the State.

In case two or more candidates, nominated for council, assembly, sheriff, or coroner, have an equal number of votes, there not being a sufficient number having a plurality, the county clerk proclaims, by advertisement, that he will attend at the county court-house, at a day certain, to receive nominations of persons to supply the vacancy; and the nomination and the election, holden thereon, are conducted in the manner already described; except that, the nominations are made ten days, only, previous to the election.

In case of vacancy in the council, or assembly, the vice-president of council, or speaker of the house, as the case may be; or in case there be no vice-president or speaker, the governor, causes the vacancy to be filled; unless it be probable that the services of the member will not be required during the remainder of the unexpired legislative year. But if the board of freeholders, of the county in which the vacancy happens, desire that the vacancy be filled, it is done without delay. Thus, if a member refuse to take his seat pursuant to his election, or to send a satisfactory excuse within twenty days after the meeting of the legislature, die, remove from the state, or be expelled, the vice-president, or speaker, as the case may be, issues his warrant, to the clerk of the county, who takes measures similar to those above described, for filling the vacancy.

The legislative council consists of the governor, who is its perpetual president, having a casting voice; of a vice-president elected by the members, who presides in the absence of the president; and a member from each county, elected annually. It has powers co-ordinate with the assembly, except in the preparation or alteration of money bills, which is reserved to the latter. It is convened, from time to time, by the governor, or vice-president, and must be convened at all times, when the assembly sits; its members must be, and have been, for one whole year, next before election, inhabitants and freeholders in the county for which they are respectively chosen, and worth at least one thousand pounds of real and personal estate, within such county. Seven members form a quorum for business. This property qualification, in practice, is scarce more respected than that of the voters.

The assembly is composed of such number of delegates, from each county, as the legislature may, from time to time, direct; making together, not less than thirty-nine. The delegate must be, and have been, for one whole year next before his election, an inhabitant of the county he represents, and worth five hundred pounds, in real and personal estate, therein. The assembly have power to choose a speaker, and other their officers; to judge of the qualifications and election of their own members; sit on their own adjournments; prepare bills to be passed into laws; and to empower their speaker to convene the members when necessary.

No judge of the Supreme, or other court, sheriff, or person holding any post of profit under the government, other than justices of the peace, may sit in the assembly. On the election of such person his office becomes vacant.

On the second Tuesday next after the day of election, the council and assembly meet, separately, and the consent of a majority of all the representatives in each body, is requisite to the enactment of a law. At their first meeting, after each annual election, the council and assembly, jointly, by a majority of votes, elect the governor; they appoint the field, and general officers of the militia; the judges of the Supreme Court for seven years, the judges of the inferior courts of Common Pleas, justices of the peace, clerks of the Supreme Court, and of the Common Pleas and Sessions, the attorney general and secretary of state, for five years; and the state treasurer, for one year; all of whom are commissioned by the governor; are capable of reappointment, and are liable to be dismissed, when convicted by the council on the impeachment of the assembly. Each member of council and assembly makes oath, that he will not assent to any law, vote, or proceeding which shall appear to him injurious to the public welfare, nor that shall annul or repeal that part of the third section of the constitution which makes the election of members of the legislature, annual; nor that part of the twenty-second section, which provides for trial by jury; nor the eighteenth and nineteenth sections which relate to religion. And such oath may be administered to the members by any member of the respective houses. The oath of the legislators being to preserve a part only of the constitution, sound construction warrants the induction, that they have a constitutional authority to change all other parts of that instrument; and thus, their power is unrestrained, as much as that of the British Parliament, which may, by a simple act of legislation, remodel the State, as has been lately done in Great Britain.

II. The executive power is vested in the governor, secretary of state, treasurer, the attorney general, and county prosecutors, and in the officers of the several townships, counties, and other precincts, viz: in the township clerks, assessors, collectors, commissioners of appeals, surveyors and overseers of the highways, pound keepers, overseers of the poor, judges of elections, township committees, and constables: and in the chosen freeholders of the county, the county clerk, collector, sheriff, coroners, and the militia.

By the 8th article of the constitution, the governor is said to have the supreme executive power; but his executive duties are circumscribed by very narrow limits, and in their performance he may be aided, perhaps controlled, by any three or more of the council, whom he is authorized to call as his privy council. Before entering on his office he swears faithfully and diligently to execute his office, and to promote the peace and prosperity, and to maintain the lawful rights of the State to the best of his ability. He is captain-general, and commander-in-chief of all the militia, and other military force of the State, and is by special act of assembly, trustee of the school fund. He is empowered, when the post of vice president of council, or speaker of assembly is vacant, to cause vacancies in the respective chambers to be filled. He may proclaim rewards of not more than $300 for one offender, for the apprehension of any person charged with murder, burglary, robbery, or other dangerous outrage upon the person or property of the citizen, for the apprehension of their accessories, and for the arrest of any unknown perpetrator of such offences;

may demand fugitives from justice from this State, and draw his warrant for the expenses of their reclamation; may remit costs of prosecution and debts due to the State, from any criminal, on the recommendation of the inspectors of the State prison; may suspend the execution of the sentence of death against any criminal until the rising of the next meeting, thereafter, of the governor and council; and in conjunction with the legislative council, may grant pardon for any offence after condemnation; he may authorize the owner of a slave condemned for certain offences, to send him from the State; distribute copies of the laws to the United States and other States; license pedlars; appoint notaries, who hold their offices during good behaviour; appoint inspectors of flour in certain cities, removable at his pleasure; order out the militia in case of invasion or other emergency, when and so long as he may deem necessary, not exceeding two months; and perform other duties specially imposed upon him by the legislature.

The secretary of state, as we have seen, is elected by the assembly in joint meeting, for five years. Before entering on the duties of his office, he makes oath that he will faithfully perform them, and gives bond conditioned to like effect. He must reside at Trenton. He must file in his office the laws of the State as they are enacted, so that those of each session be kept in separate bundles, and give copies of them when required, under his hand and seal of office; and, within four weeks from the end of every session, deliver a copy of the laws therein passed, to the printer thereof, assist him in comparing the proof sheets with the laws, and make marginal notes thereto. He must record all papers which come to his hands pertaining to his office; and tri-monthly report to the governor, an account of the business done in his office, relating to the record of wills, letters of administration and guardianship, and of the unfinished business therein; and must lay a general statement of the business in his office before the legislature at their first session, annually; must keep the books and papers of the late auditor's office, and settle the accounts, if any be unsettled, of any of the agents of forfeited estates; must record all deeds delivered to him for record, duly acknowledged and proved, and must index such deeds; must in all cases, where money is paid into the public treasury, and the receipt of the treasurer therefor is brought to him, enter the same in the public books in his office, in an account with the treasurer, and indorse such entry upon the receipt, without which it is not available against the State. He must prosecute clerks of courts, on the report of the treasurer, who fail to return the abstracts of fines, amercements and judgments on forfeited recognizances for use of the State. He is register of the prerogative office and court, and is required to record the names of testators of all wills, and of intestates, the inventories of whose estates he may receive, and to file such wills and inventories. He must record bonds given by the keeper of State prison; and the partition lines of townships and counties, as returned by the commissioners of survey. He is also clerk of the court of appeals, and trustee of the school fund; and he must keep suspended for public view a list of the fees payable in his several offices.

The treasurer, before entering on his office, is required to take and subscribe an oath of office, and give bond with sufficient sureties approved by the legislature, in the sum of fifty thousand dollars, conditioned for the faithful performance of his duties and for the fidelity of those employed by him; which oath and bond are to be made before the vice president or justice of the Supreme Court, and to be deposited in the office of the secretary of state. His duty is to receive and keep the monies of the State, and to disburse them agreeably to law; to take receipts for all payments; to keep accounts of receipts and expenditures, and of all debts due to, and from the State; to make reports and give information to either branch of the legislature in person or in writing, as he may be required, respecting matters referred to him by the council or assembly, or appertaining to his office; and generally to perform all services relative to the finances which he may be directed to perform; to state, in books, the account of monies which he shall receive for taxes, or other account in behalf of the State, or which he shall pay, in pursuance of the acts and resolutions of the legislature, so that, the net produce of the whole revenue, as well as of each branch thereof, and the amount of disbursements, may distinctly appear; and to lay such accounts, from time to time, before the legislature; to receive reports of clerks of courts, of fines, amercements and judgments on forfeited recognizances, and within two days after the first day of November, annually, to return the name of every delinquent clerk, to the secretary for prosecution; to cause to be set up in his office, that clause of the act of 19th Nov. 1799, which requires the treasurer's receipt for monies paid him, to be entered in the office of the secretary, and endorsed by him; to receive taxes collected for the State from the county collector, and to prosecute for the same when wrongfully withheld; to prosecute for the recovery of the tax upon bank stock, when not paid according to law; to sue for all sums of money which may become due to the State, and receivable in his office, and to make distribution, annually, of the laws of the State according to law; he is also a trustee of the school fund.

The following abstract from the report of the State Treasurer made to the Legislature, Oct. 1832, exhibits the condition of the Treasury, and the sources of its revenue, with the exception, that $30,000 at least is to be added to receipts of the current and future years, for the annual bonus of the Camden and Amboy Rail-road, and the Delaware and Raritan Canal. It will also be observed, that besides the $40,000 tax levied directly upon the State, there is a further sum of about $11,000 annually, but indirectly, levied upon the holders of Bank stock, and appropriated to the school fund. We append, also, the treasurer's report on the banks, exhibiting in detail the income derived from that source, and the actual condition of this branch of business in the State. We may also remark, here, that the only property possessed by the State, save a small tract of land at Patterson, and some lots and buildings at Trenton, and the oyster beds in her rivers and on her coasts, and the stocks mentioned in the treasurer's report, consists of 2000 shares of Camden and Amboy Rail-road stock and Delaware and Raritan Canal stock, valued at par at $200,000.

DR.

1832.   Dolls. Cts.

Surplus monies loaned		$20,000 00		
Commissioners for negotiating loan		50 00		
Deaf and Dumb, amount of account		2,089 04		
State Library, do.		117 48		
Jurisdiction, amount of account for defence of suit against New York in relation to boundary		1,401 36		
Legislature, amount of account		18,728 98		
Printing account, do.		2,253 00		
State Prison, do.		5,800 20		
Salaries, do.		6,636 00	57,076 06	
Incidentals, do.		1,716 91		
Transportation of Criminals, do.		1,758 43		
Pensions, do.		856 86		
Inquisitions, do.		1,637 36		
Militia, do.*		398 78		
State account, including salaries of Governor, Judges, &c.		4,019 00		
Constable's account		15 00		
Bills receivable—				
Due from T. G.	$1000			
Due from Presbyterian Church at Patterson	150			
		1,150 00	10,552 34	
Trenton Bank,				
Due from Bank		9,779 91		
Due from State Bank at Morris		195 47		
Due from State Bank at Newark		87 45		
Due from George Sherman		300 00	10,362 83	
			$77,991 23	

Trenton, October 23d, 1832.

* The annual charge for militia expenses is $620—viz: $30 to the brigade inspector of each county, and $200 to the quartermaster and inspector generals.

CONTRA.   CR.

1832.   Dolls.   Cts.

Bills receivable—			
Received for surplus money loaned		$20,000 00	
Received for commissions paid, being part of interest		50 00	
Balance on hand, October 25th, 1831		14,819 66	
Taxes—			
Received from the several counties		40,000 00	
Debts outstanding—			
Amount received on this account	$ 509 34½		
Amount due this account	1,150 80		
		1,659 34½	
Fines and forfeitures—			
Received on this account		760 00	
			77,289 00½
Premiums—			
Received on this account		306 22½	
Revised laws—			
Received for one copy sold		3 00	
Pedlar's license—			
Received for this account		585 00	
Interest account—			
Received balance of interest for use of surplus money loaned		808 00	
			1,702 22½
			78,991 23
Balance due as above per contra—			
Deposited in Trenton Bank			9,779 91
Do. State Bank at Morris			195 47
Do. State Bank at Newark			87 45
Due from George Sherman, for advance made for printing law reports now in progress			300 00
Balance on settlement			10,362 23

When chartered.	INSTITUTIONS.	Amount of capital.	Amt. stock paid in, now subject to tax.	Amt. of tax at one-half of one per cent.	Amount of Bonus.	Amt. of Bonus paid to State Treasurer.
1804,	Newark Banking and Insurance Company	$ 800,000	$ 350,000 00	$ 1,750 00	$ 1,482 00	$ 1,482 00
"	Trenton Banking Company	600,000	214,740 00	1,073 70	(A)	
1807,	New Brunswick Bank	200,000	90,000 00	450 00	6,000 00	6,000 00
1812,	State Bank at Camden	800,000	300,000 00	1,500 00	25,000 00	25,000 00
"	State Bank at New Brunswick	400,000	88,000 00	440 00	7,000 00	7,000 00
"	State Bank at Elizabeth	200,000	132,924 00	664 62	2,625 50	2,625 50
"	State Bank at Newark	400,000	280,000 00	1,400 00	4,025 00	4,025 00
"	State Bank at Morris	200,000	78,440 23	392 20	1,000 00	1,000 00
1815,	Patterson Bank	(B)			6,000 00	6,000 00
1816,	Cumberland Bank at Bridgeton	200,000	52,025 00	260 12	(C)	
"	Farmers Bank at Mount Holly	200,000	100,000 00	500 00	3,500 00	3,500 00
1818,	Sussex Bank	100,000	27,500 00	137 50	(D)	
1822,	Commercial Bank at Amboy	100,000	30,000 00	150 00	No Bonus.	
"	Salem Banking Company	75,000	30,000 00	150 00	do.	
1824,	People's Bank at Patterson	250,000	75,000 00	375 00	7,000 00	4,000 00
"	Morris Canal and Banking Company*	1,000,000	40,000 00		No Bonus.	
1825,	Washington Bank, Hackensack	200,000	93,460 00	467 30	8,000 00	(E) 5,000 00
1828,	Farmers and Mechanics Bank at Rahway	100,000	60,000 00	300 00	No Bonus.	
"	Orange Bank	100,000	80,000 00	400 00	do.	
1830,	Farmers and Mechanics Bank at Middletown Point	50,000	10,000 00	50 00	do.	
"	Belvidere Bank	50,000	25,000 00	125 00	do.	
1831,	Mechanics Bank at Newark	250,000	200,000 00	1000 00	do.	
1832,	Union Bank at Dover	100,000	50,000 00	(G)		
		$6,525,000	$2,317,089 23	$11,595 44	$71,632 50	$65,632 50

* Eleven years after the charter, to pay one-half of one per cent. per annum, on the stock paid in for banking purposes.

(A) Trenton Banking Company—no bonus given—the State reserving the right of subscribing for 1200 shares; which shares were subscribed, and, on the 2d of February, 1825, sold to the Trenton Banking Company.

(B) Patterson Bank. This bank was chartered in 1815, with a capital of $200,000. It has recently closed its concerns.

(C) Cumberland Bank—40 shares of $50 each, given as a bonus.

(D) Sussex Bank—20 shares, of $50 each, given as a bonus.

(E) Formerly the Weehawk Bank at Weehawk. A supplement was passed 30th of November, 1825, changing its name to Washington Bank, and locating it at Hackensack.

(G) Union Bank at Dover. This institution has lately commenced operations.

G

STATEMENT RELATIVE TO INSOLVENT BANKS.

When chartered.	INSTITUTIONS.	Amount of capital.	Amount of capital paid in.	Amount of Bonus.	Amt. of Bonus paid to Treasurer.
1812,	State Bank at Trenton	$ 300,000	$ 92,400	$ 1,601	$ 1,601
1818,	Jersey Bank at Jersey City	200,000			
1822,	Salem and Philadelphia Manufacturing and Banking Company	75,000	The amount of notes circulated not known.		
1823,	New Jersey Manufacturing and Banking Company at Hoboken	150,000	150,000	4,000	4,000
1824,	Franklin Bank of New Jersey at Jersey City	500,000	300,000	25,000	15,000
"	Monmouth Bank at Freehold	200,000	40,000	4,000	800
"	New Jersey Protection and Lombard Bank	400,000	50,150	25,000	
"	Hoboken Banking and Grazing Company	300,000			
		$2,125,000	$832,550	$59,601	$21,401

Perhaps no country of equal territorial extent and population, in the world, is governed at less cost than the State of New Jersey; and if the happiness of the people be the object and evidence of good government, we do not hesitate to say, that none is better governed. The sum actually levied on the people directly and indirectly, for the maintenance of the State government, exclusive of the township and county polity, will not exceed $ 55,000, and is more likely to be diminished than increased. The whole population, at the present period, 1833, is not less than 330,000, which gives to each individual 16 2-3 cents tax; or dividing the number of individuals by six, for the number of families, gives one dollar for every head of a family in the State. This, it will be observed, is only the tax levied by the State, as contradistinguished from township and county taxes. To ascertain the burden actually supported by the people, we must include not only the latter, but also the sums paid for the maintenance of the militia, and of religious instruction. An opportunity is thus afforded, we trust, of settling, satisfactorily, the question which has lately been agitated, relative to the proportions paid by the inhabitants of the North American republics, and the subjects of European kingdoms, for the maintenance of the social relations.

By the singular character of our political association, each citizen contributes to the maintenance of two governments. The sum paid to the general government, by the whole community of the United States, is the net amount of duties after the deduction of drawbacks.

Taking that amount at twenty-five millions,* and dividing it by fourteen millions, the probable population of the United States, in January, 1834, we have a charge of $ 1 78½ nearly. But a more favorable view may be taken of this subject. The extent of revenue, required for a liberal administration of the government, is estimated at fifteen millions of dollars, and it is highly probable, that the nation will not, for many years, consent to pay a larger sum than is requisite, and which, from accumulation, may become dangerous to her welfare. This sum would impose a tax, supposing it be collected from commerce alone, and the proceeds of lands to be divided among the states, of $ 1 06 and a fraction upon each individual.

From the general statistical table of the State, it appears, that for the year 1832, there were levied, for State purposes, exclusive of the tax on banks, $ 40,366 71

Tax on banks, per treasurer's report, - - - -			11,585 44
County tax, as per return of assessors, - - - - -			104,166 00
Township taxes, viz : Poor, - - -	78,131 00		
Road, - - - -	192,859 00		
School, - - -	1,366 00		
			271,386 00
			427,504 15

The militia expenses, actually paid by the treasury of the State, are included in the foregoing amount; but the time devoted, we had like to have said, wasted, in militia duties, together with the money uselessly expended, cannot be estimated at less than one dollar for every prescribed day of service, for each person enrolled, or placed on the exempt list. There are three training days in the year. The fine for non-attendance is two dollars per day, and the sum paid by the exempt is five dollars per annum, in form of tax. Every officer and private expends, on the day of service, more than would support him at home. The military force of the State, by the adjutant general's report for 1832, amounted to $ 35,360; that number multiplied by four dollars, which we take as the mesne expense of each officer, private, and exempt, gives a total annual amount of - - - - 141,440 00

The annual cost of religious instruction, according to the statement hereinafter given, - - - - - - -	120,000 00
General government for duties at 179 per head, - - - -	590,700 00
State charges, including township and county rates, at one dollar twenty-nine cents and five mills per head, nearly, - -	427,504 15
	$ 1,279,644 15

* The receipts of the treasury, for the three first quarters of 1832, were $ 21,730,717 19; and the treasurer's estimate, for 1833, was twenty-one millions; but it is generally supposed that the receipt will much exceed the estimate.

This sum divided by the number of inhabitants, (330,000,) gives a charge of $ 3 86,* nearly, upon each inhabitant,—for the payment of principal and interest of the public debt—the pension list—for the support of the General and State governments—for the maintenance of schools in part—for the support of the clergy, and the founding and preservation of churches—for the support of the poor—for making and repairing all other than turnpike roads, and the erection of bridges by the townships and counties—and in a word, for all kinds of public expenditure.

The attorney general is the representative of the State in all the courts of the commonwealth, and prosecutes in her name all offenders against her peace and dignity, and sues and defends all suits in which she has an interest. Deputy attornies are appointed by the legislature for the counties respectively, whose term of office is five years; they are vested in their respective districts with the same powers, entitled to the same fees, and subject to the same penalties as the attorney general. Yet, notwithstanding such appointment, he may act in such counties when present; and any court is empowered to appoint a special substitute, for the term, in case neither the attorney general nor the general deputy shall attend. For neglect of duty, in prosecuting forfeited recognisances, fines, debts, &c. due to the State, he may, on conviction before council, on impeachment by the assembly, be disabled to act as attorney or solicitor in any court of the State, for one year. The attorney general is one of the trustees of the school fund.

A sheriff is annually elected by each county, who is eligible three times consecutively, but who, after the third year, cannot be again re-elected, until after the lapse of three years. He must be, and have been, an inhabitant and freeholder of his county for at least three years next preceding his election; must give bond to the State with five sureties in the sum of $20,000, approved by the judges of the Common Pleas, conditioned for the faithful performance of his duty, and make oath or affirmation to like effect; both of which are filed in the office of the county clerk. If he fail to give such bond and take such oath, a new election may be had; but this done, he may act before receipt of commission from the governor. When occasion requires, suits may be instituted on his bond, by order of that officer. He is *par excellence* the executive officer of his county, is the chief conservator of its peace, and has authority to call forth and direct its physical force to maintain the laws. He has charge of the jails of the county, and is responsible for the conduct of their keepers. He summons all juries, and executes all process civil and criminal issuing from the courts, and carries their judgments into effect. He may appoint deputies, who give bond and make oath for faithful performance of their duties, and have their appointment filed with the county clerk. At the request of the United States, and by the statute of this State, he has charge of prisoners committed by authority of the general government. He may not, during the continuance of his office, act as justice of the peace or keep tavern; nor become bail in any suit. In case of his death, removal or disability, a new election is had upon certificate thereof by a justice of the peace, to the county clerk; and during the vacancy, the duties of his office may be performed by the coroner.

Three coroners are annually elected in each county, must be inhabitants and freeholders, and be commissioned by the governor; but may act before commission; and must take oath, faithfully to execute their duties. The coroner, as we have seen above, is the substitute for the sheriff where the office of the latter is vacant, or where under particular circumstances, as when the sheriff is interested or

* The *Revue Britanique*, No 12, for 1831, avers, that notwithstanding the asserted economy of the American republic, its expenses exceeded, proportionably to its population, those of the French monarchy. The charge upon each individual in France is admitted, by the reviewer, to be 31 francs, and that in the United States is asserted, to be 35 francs. The French estimate does not include ecclesiastical expenses, the sums paid for the extinction of the public debt, the maintenance of the poor, the charges for education and other expenses, whilst our estimate contains all these. Valuing the dollar at 5 francs 33 centimes, the charge on each individual in the State of New Jersey would be 20 francs 69 cts. But if we include, in the American impost, no other charges than those of the French estimate, the American citizen, by the rate paid in this State, does not pay for every species of taxation, more than one-third of the amount of the French subject, whose burden is less than that of the subject of any other of the principal monarchies in Europe. The burden on the people of New Jersey is, perhaps, something less than that upon the citizens of some of the other States, which may have contracted considerable debts; but it is larger than is imposed in most of the Western States, and, we think, may be taken as a fair average of charges throughout the Union.

has not given bond, he is disqualified. Where any writ from any court is directed to the coroner, the return made and signed by one of them is sufficient, but such return does not prejudice or affect the rest. The most ordinary duty of the coroner, however, is to take inquests relative to deaths in prison, and of all violent, sudden or casual deaths within his county; which he performs through a jury summoned on his writ, by the constable, and over which he presides.

The constable is the next in grade, but is not the least important of the executive officers. He is annually elected by the qualified voters of the township, of which he may be considered the sheriff. He makes oath or affirmation, and gives bond to the township, for the faithful performance of his duty. He executes all process from the justices' courts, and that issued by coroner on inquest of death; and he is charged with various executive duties, the performance of which moves from himself. Thus, he is a conservator of the peace, and may arrest and confine persons found in breach of it, or contravening the act for the suppression of vice and immorality; may call out the inhabitants to extinguish fires in forests, &c.; may make proclamation in case of riots, and seize rioters; may arrest and disperse slaves meeting together in an unlawful manner, and the like.

All officers of the State appointed by the legislature in joint meeting, must reside within the State, and execute in person such office; except, that, the surrogate general may appoint deputies; officers of counties must reside within their respective counties, and are prohibited from farming out their offices to others, under penalty of five hundred pounds. Such officers desirous of resigning, must make their resignation during the sitting of the legislature, and to the members thereof in joint meeting, attending in person for that purpose, or by letter. And every officer issuing or executing a warrant for removing a prisoner out of the State, an inhabitant thereof, as prohibited by the habeas corpus act, is disqualified to hold office, and is punishable by fine and imprisonment at hard labour. The civil office of any person held under the State, is vacated by election and acceptance by the incumbent of a seat in congress; the office of governor is also vacated, if incumbent accept of any office or appointment under the United States, except such as may be for defence of the State or adjoining posts; and the seat of a member of council or assembly is also vacated by such election and acceptance, and by the acceptance of any appointment under the government of the United States. All officers elected in joint meeting neglecting or refusing to qualify themselves for the space of two months after information of their election, make void their posts. No alien can hold, or elect to any office.

The officers of the state prison are essential arms of the executive power, since they aid in executing the judgments of the law. They consist of three inspectors, two of whom make a quorum, appointed annually, in joint meeting by the assembly; the keeper nominated and removable by the inspectors, and his deputies and assistants appointed by him and approved by the inspectors. The inspectors are empowered to examine the accounts of the keeper, and any witness in relation thereto, including the keeper, upon oath; to appoint annually or oftener, one of their number acting inspector; to meet as often as shall be necessary, and at least quarterly; and the acting inspector is required to attend the prison, at least once a week to inspect the management thereof, and the conduct of the keeper and his deputies; to make regulations to give effect to the law, for the punishment of crimes and the good government of the prison; to punish prisoners in case of refractory, disorderly behaviour, or disobedience to the rules of the prison, by confinement in the cells and dungeons on bread and water for any time not exceeding twenty days for one offence, and for prevention or escapes, to put prisoners in irons; to appoint an agent where they may deem proper, for the sale of articles manufactured in the prison. If any vacancy happen in the board during the recess of the legislature, it may be filled by the governor. The inspectors are allowed one dollar and fifty cents per day, for every day necessarily employed in the duties of their office.

The keeper, before entering on the duties of his office, is required to give bond to the State treasurer, with two sureties in the sum of $1,000, conditioned that he, his deputy and assistants, shall faithfully perform their trusts, to be filed in the office of the secretary of state. He receives a salary of $1,000, and his six assistants each $475, per annum. The keeper is required to receive all prisoners duly committed to his custody, to treat them as directed by law and the rules of the prison; to provide, with the approbation of the inspectors, stock, materials and tools for prisoners; to contract for their clothing and diet, and for the sale of the produce of their labour; to keep accounts of the maintenance of offenders, of the materials furnished, and manufactures produced, subject to the inspection of inspectors, and to furnish an abstract thereof to the legislature. He may punish offenders guilty of assaults, where no dangerous wound or bruise is given, of profane cursing or swearing, indecent behaviour, idleness, negligence or wilful mismanagement in work, or disobedience to regulations, by confining offenders in the cells or dungeons on bread and water, for a time not exceeding two days; and in case of offences which he is not authorized to punish, he is required to make report to the inspectors. The keeper, his deputy or assistant, who shall obstruct the inspectors in the exercise of their powers, is subject to a fine of $30, and removal from office.

It is not within the scope of this work to detail the system of criminal jurisprudence in the State. But we may, with propriety, observe, that so early as 1789, she adopted the humane principles which now characterize the criminal laws of the Union; abolishing the punishment of death in all cases, save treason and murder, and applying imprisonment and hard labour to the correction of other offences in proportion to their enormity, and seeking to reclaim the offender from the evil of his ways. With these views she has constructed and regulated her penitentiary, and advancing with the improvements of the age, has, in the year 1833, directed the building of a new State prison upon the latest and most approved models.

The first steps in the science of reforming criminals in this, as in other States, have been unsteady, uncertain, and tending to thwart, rather than to effect, the proposed object. The prisons have every where been too small, and have not been constructed upon plans which would admit of the indispensable separation of the prisoners; and have, from the free intercommunion of the criminals, been converted into schools of vice, instead of asylums for repentance, where the convict might securely and unimpeded by ridicule or seduction, pursue the work of his own regeneration. The effects of this system are but too truly stated by the late governor De Vroom, in his message to the legislature of 1832. "The situation of our prison," he says, "is such as to invite to the commission of crime within our State. Its condition is well known to that class of offenders who are familiar with punishments. It offers to them all the allurements of that kind of society which they have long been accustomed to, freed from the restraints to which they would be obliged to submit in other places of confinement, and at the same time holds out a prospect of speedy escape. To this may be attributed the great number of our convicts, and as long as it continues, we may expect our prisons to be filled. Within the last three years, the number has increased from eighty-seven to one hundred and thirty, being an increase of fifty per cent. The remedy for these evils, now obvious, was the adoption of a system of penitentiary discipline, combining solitary confinement at labour, with instruction in labour, in morals, and religion." This system has been partially adopted by the act of 13th February, 1833, authorizing the construction of a penitentiary on the plan of the Eastern Penitentiary of Pennsylvania, with such alterations and improvements as the commissioners may approve, adhering to the principle of separate confinement of the prisoners, with hard labour. The estimate of the cost of this building is $150,000, and it is to be of sufficient capacity for the confinement of one hundred and fifty persons. The system will be further perfected by modelling the criminal law to the new species of punishment, when the prison shall have been completed. That the reader may have some idea of the plan of the penitentiary now being erected on the lot belonging to the State, near the old state prison, we give the following description of its model.

"The Eastern State Penitentiary is situated on one of the most elevated, airy, and healthy sites in the city of Philadelphia. The ground occupied by it, contains about 10 acres. The material with which the edifices are built is gneiss, in large masses; every room is vaulted, and fire proof. The design and execution, impart a grave, severe and awful character to the external aspect. The effect on the imagination of the spectator is peculiarly impressive, solemn and instructive. The architecture is in keeping with the design. The broad masses, the small and well proportioned apertures, the continuity of lines, and the bold simplicity which characterize the façade, are happily and judiciously combined. This is the only edifice in this country, which conveys an idea of the external appearance of those magnificent and picturesque castles of the middle ages, which contribute so eminently to embellish the scenery of Europe. The front is composed of large blocks of hewn stone; the walls are 12 feet thick at the base, and diminish to the top, where they are 2 3-4 feet in thickness. A wall of forty feet in height, above the interior platform, incloses an area 640 feet square; at each angle of the wall is a tower, for the purpose of overlooking the establishment; three other towers are situated near the gate of entrance. The façade or principal front is 670 feet in length, and reposes on a terrace, which, from the inequalities of the ground, varies from three to nine feet in height; the basement or belting course, which is 10 feet high, is scarped, and extends uniformly the whole length. The central building is 200 feet in length, consists of two projecting massive square towers, 50 feet high, crowned by projecting embattled parapets, supported by pointed arches, resting on corbels or brackets. The pointed, munnioned windows in these towers, contribute in a high degree to their picturesque effect. The curtain between the towers is 41 feet high, and is finished with a parapet and embrasures. The pointed windows in it are very lofty and narrow. The great gateway in the centre is a very conspicuous feature; it is 27 feet high, and 15 wide, and is filled by a massive wrought iron portcullis, and double oaken gates, studded with projecting iron rivets, the whole weighing several tons; nevertheless, they can be opened with the greatest facility. On each side of this entrance, (which is the most imposing in the United States,) are enormous solid buttresses, diminishing in offsets, and terminating in pinnacles. A lofty octangular tower, 80 feet high, containing an alarm bell and clock, surmounts this entrance, and forms a picturesque proportional centre. On each side of this main building, (which contains the apartments of the warden, keepers, domestics, &c.) are screen wing walls, which appear to constitute portions of the main edifice; they are pierced with small blank pointed windows, and are surmounted by a parapet; at their extremities are high octangular towers, terminating in parapets, pierced by embrasures. In the centre of the great court is an observatory, whence long corridors, eight in number, radiate. On each side of these corridors, the cells are situated, each at right angles to them, and communicating with them only by small openings, for the purpose of supplying the prisoner with food, &c., and for the purpose of inspecting his movements without attracting his attention; other apertures, for the admission of cool or heated air, and for the purpose of ventilation, are provided. A novel and ingenious contrivance in each cell, prevents the possibility of conversation, preserves the purity of the atmosphere of the cells, and dispenses with the otherwise unavoidable necessity of leaving the apartment, except when the regulations permit—flues conduct heated air from large cockle stoves to the cells. Light is admitted by a large circular glass in the crown of the arch, which is raking, and the highest part 16 feet six inches above the floor, (which is of wood, overlaying a solid foundation of stone.) The walls are plaistered, and neatly whitewashed; the cells are 11 feet nine inches long, and seven feet six inches wide; at the extremity of the cell, opposite to the apertures for inspection, &c., previously mentioned, is the door-way, containing two doors; one of lattice work or grating, to admit the air and secure the prisoner; the other, composed of planks, to exclude the air, if required; this door leads to a yard (18 feet by eight, the walls of which are 11½ feet in height,) attached to each cell. The number of the latter, erected on the original plan, was only 266, but it may be increased to 818 without resorting to the addition of second stories."

For the better administration of the government, the State has been divided into counties, townships, cities and boroughs. The object of these divisions is to allocate and circumscribe the duties of the various administrative officers, in the enforcement of the laws, civil and criminal, the collection of the revenues required by the commonwealth and its subdivisions, and, more especially, the better to enable the citizens to promote their own happiness by the improvement of the roads, bridges, &c., the education of their offspring, and the maintenance of the indigent. The division into counties is the most general, and embraces the others, all of which were readily adopted by the first English settlers, upon their coming hither, from models to which they had been accustomed in Europe. Several of the counties were organized before the year 1709; but many inconveniences having arisen from the imperfect definition of their boundaries, the limits of Bergen, Essex, Somerset, Monmouth, Middlesex, Burlington, Gloucester, Salem, and Cape May, were accurately designated by an act of assembly, passed 21st January, of that year. These limits have been since modified, in the erection of Hunterdon, Morris, Salem, Sussex, Warren, and Cumberland counties (for which see the titles respectively of these counties). By an act of 9th March, 1798, provision has been made for ascertaining the bounds of each county and township, in case of any dispute in relation to them.

The State contains at present 14 counties and 125 townships. The use of these divisions will be better understood by examining first the constitution of the townships. These are made bodies corporate by the act of 21st February, 1798; and new ones are created, and so constituted, by special laws, as the public convenience requires. They are thus empowered to sue, and be sued, by process left with the county clerks. And the qualified inhabitants are authorized to hold town meetings in their respective townships, upon specified days, and, also, on special convocation, at such places as the electors may from time to time appoint. At such meetings, every white male citizen of the State, of the age of twenty-one years, having resided within the township six calendar months, and paid taxes therein; or being seized of a freehold, or having rented a tenement, of the yearly value of five dollars, for the term of one year therein, is entitled to vote. A presiding officer, appointed by a plurality of voices, directs the business of the meeting, and determines who have or have not the right to participate therein; and to preserve order he may expel, and fine not exceeding one dollar, the unruly, and even imprison an offender during the session of the meeting. The voters of the township may make regulations and by-laws, from time to time, as they may deem proper, for improving their common lands in tillage or otherwise, and for the making and maintaining pounds; and may enforce such regulations by fine, not exceeding twelve dollars, for each offence; the regulations to be recorded by the clerk of the township, in a book kept for the purpose. Such meeting may, also, provide and allow rewards for the destruction of noxious animals; may raise money for the support of the indigent, and education of poor children; the building and rearing of pounds, the making and repairing of roads, the ascertaining the lines of the township, defending its rights, and for other necessary charges and legal objects and purposes as the major part may deem proper; being such as are expressly vested in the inhabitants of the several townships, by some act of the legislature. The meeting may elect annually, and whenever there shall be a vacancy, one clerk, one or more assessors, one or more collectors, who must give bond, with surety, for the faithful performance of their duties; three or more freeholders, to determine appeals relative to assessments in taxation; three school committee men; two freeholders, commonly called chosen freeholders; two surveyors of the highways; one or more overseers of the poor; one or more constables; so many overseers of the highways, and poundkeepers, as they shall judge necessary; one reputable freeholder as judge of elections; and five freeholders, denominated the township committee—whose duty is to examine and report to the town meeting the accounts and vouchers of the township officers, to superintend the expenditure of monies of the township, and in case of neglect of the township meeting to supply vacancies, to fill such vacancies, among the township officers as may occur. Service in a township office for one year, or payment of a fine for refusal to serve, excuses the party from services in such office for five years thereafter.

The townships being thus empowered to select their officers, and to provide for their wants, are made responsible for the proper performance of duty by their agents; and may be fined for the bad condition of the roads, and compelled to make good any loss sustained in the collection of state and county taxes, by the unfaithfulness of the collectors.

The chosen freeholders of the several townships of each county, form the administrative council, or board of the county. They are, also, incorporated, by the act of 13th February, 1798, with power, to sue and liability to be sued; to hold lands and chattels, &c. in trust for their respective counties, and for such uses as may be designated by law, and to sell and dispose of the same; to make and enforce such regulations as may be necessary for the government of their respective corporations, not contrary to the laws of the State; to raise, at their annual or other meeting held for the purpose, monies for the building, purchase or repairs of poor-houses, gaols, court-houses and bridges; the surveying and ascertaining the lines, the prosecuting and defending the rights, defraying the public and other necessary charges, and executing the legal purposes and objects of the county, as the major part of them shall deem proper; which monies are expended under the direction of the corporation: to elect, annually, and pro tempore in case of absence or refusal to act, a director to preside at the meeting of the board; to meet, annually, upon the second Wednesday in May, at the county town; to elect a clerk annually, who shall record the proceedings of the board; and a county collector, a freeholder and resident of the county, who shall give bond, with sureties, for the faithful performance of his duty;

to raise monies voted by the board, by precepts to the assessors of the respective townships, commanding them to assess such amount on the inhabitants and their estates, agreeably to the law for the time being, for raising money by taxation for the use of the State.

When the lines of the county have not been surveyed and distinctly marked, the freeholders, by prescribed form, may apply to the Supreme Court for commissioners to survey them. They may, also, at their discretion, build or purchase a workhouse within their county, and provide for its government, and the employment of its inhabitants; and may establish a market, once or oftener in every year, within the county, for the sale of live stock, to continue not more than four days, and establish laws for its regulation.

From all assessments, an appeal lies to the commissioners of appeal, who hold stated and special meetings at the usual place of the respective town meetings, attended by the proper assessor, and have power to summon and qualify witnesses, and whose decision upon the case is final.

The township collector is charged, with the collection, within his precinct, of all taxes, whether levied by the township, county or state; to make return of defaulters in payment, on oath, to a justice of the peace, who is required to issue his warrant, to the constable of the township, for levying the tax by distress and sale of the goods, or imprisonment of the delinquent; and the constable must account with the township collector. And such collector and constable are respectively required to render to the people, in township meeting, an account of monies by them received, and to pay, according to their direction, any overplus which may be in their hands.

All monies levied for county use are to be paid by the respective township collectors, on or before the 22d day of December, annually, to the proper county collector, who, in case of default, may proceed summarily against them. Monies levied for State use, are to be paid to the state treasurer by the county collector on or before the 30th December, annually; and such tax money, as he may receive from sheriffs, within ten days after the same shall have been paid; and in case of the default of any county collector, the state treasurer may recover from him, for the use of the State, the penalty of fifty dollars, before a justice of the Supreme Court, who has exclusive cognizance thereof; and when such collectors shall not have paid over monies received by them, the same may be recovered by the state treasurer by proper action at law. The counties are responsible for all monies belonging to the State, received by the county treasurer, and not paid over by him to the state treasurer. And it is the duty of the latter to add the annual deficiency of each county, to the quota of the county for the subsequent year; and of the county collector to charge such deficiency, and also deficiency of county tax, to the delinquent township.

The county collector disburses the monies of the county upon the orders of the board of chosen freeholders, and for neglect or refusal so to do, or to perform any of the duties connected with the levy of taxes imposed by such board, he is subjected to a penalty of 300 dollars.

Thus, in these subdivisions of the State, we have examples of a pure democracy and simple representative government. The people in their township meetings, (and the word township comprehends precincts and wards,) discuss their common wants, propose the remedies, and appoint the agents to give them effect. In the larger districts, where legislation in their proper persons would prove inconvenient, as well by the distance of the people from each other, as from their number when collected, the citizens have devolved the necessary legislative power upon agents, endowed also with an adequate executive capacity. This system works well, and might, possibly, be beneficially extended, by enlarging the sphere of action of the chosen freeholders, particularly in giving effect to a general and uniform system of education.

Having thus incidentally noticed the taxation of the townships and counties, we may give here the provisions for raising revenues for the State, to which those in other cases are analogous. [See Note A.]

1. The legislature annually ascertains what sum of money will be requisite for State expenses during the succeeding year, and passes an act apportioning such sum among the several counties, in a ratio of their wealth and population, and fixes a day for the payment of the respective quotas.

2. On certain subjects of taxation, they direct specific sums to be levied, viz: on stud horses above three years old, any sum not exceeding 10 dollars; on other horses and mules of like age, any sum not exceeding six cents; and on neat cattle three years old and upwards, any sum not exceeding four cents.

H

3. The following subjects of taxation are valued and rated at the discretion of the assessor, viz : tracts of land at any sum not exceeding 100 dollars the hundred acres.

But houses and lots of ten acres and under, are rated with regard to their yearly rent and value.*

Householders, (under which description all married men are included, the estimated value of whose rateable estate does not exceed 30 dollars,) three dollars over and above their certainties and other rateable estate ; merchants, shopkeepers and traders, not exceeding ten dollars ; fisheries, ten dollars ; grist mills, six dollars the run of stones ; cotton manufactories thirty dollars ; sail duck manufactories, ten dollars ; woollen manufactories, ten dollars ; carding machines, unconnected with cotton or woollen manufactories, and propelled by water or steam, three dollars ; all furnaces, (other than blast) ten dollars; blast furnaces, thirty dollars; saw mills, for each saw, eight dollars; forges that work pig iron, and forges and bloomeries that work bar iron immediately from ore or cinders, for each fire, six dollars ; rolling and slitting mills, ten dollars ; paper mills, eight dollars; snuff and oil mills, nine dollars ; powder mills, fifteen dollars; fulling mills, unconnected with woollen manufactory, four dollars ; every ferry or toll bridge, twenty dollars; tan yards, each vat, thirty cents; every single man, two dollars; but if he possess rateable estate, the tax whereof amounts to that sum, then for such estate only ; no person taxed as a single man may be taxed as a householder ; every male slave, able to labour, under the age of sixty years, one dollar ; distillery for grain, molasses or other foreign material, thirty-five dollars; other distillery, nine dollars ; coach or chariot, five dollars; phæton, coachee or four-wheeled chaise, with steel or iron springs, four dollars; four horse stage wagon, five dollars; two horse stage wagon, two dollars and fifty cents; covered wagon, with frame or fixed top, one dollar ; two horse chair, curricle, and every two horse riding chair, with steel or iron springs, one dollar and fifty cents; riding chair, gig, sulkey or pleasure wagon, dearborn wagon, with steel, iron or wooden springs, seventy-five cents; printing, bleaching and dying company, five dollars ; glass factory, five dollars.

The assessor is required to enter in his tax book and duplicate, a valuation of the real estate, having regard to the yearly rent and value thereof, and the amount of tax assessed in each township, above that raised from the certainties, is to be levied by a per centage upon such valution.

He is required between the 20th of June and 20th August, annually, to make an exact list of the persons, lands, chattels and estates, including certainties, made rateable by law in that year, by which all assessments during the year is regulated ; and persons refusing to render an account, or rendering a false one, are liable to be doubly taxed.

The assessors of the several townships of the county meet at the seat of justice, on the first Monday of September, annually, to ascertain the amount of the certainties, and to estimate the estates, real and personal, taken by the assessors of each township, at such valuation as a majority present shall think just, according to law, and thereby to adjust and fix the quota of tax to be levied in each township ; and it is their duty at such meeting to make out two abstracts of the rateables in each township, signed by the assessors present, and to deliver the same to the county treasurer, who is required to lay one of such abstracts before the legislature during the first week of their stated annual session ; and within fifteen days after their meeting, a duplicate of such assessment shall be delivered by the assessors to the township and county collectors; the last of whom is required also to lay such duplicate, at the time abovementioned, before the legislature.

The amount of the certainties being deducted from the quota of each township,

---

* The rationale of this arbitrary limitation to the value of the lands, is not very apparent. It is not possible in any case, due regard to relative value being preserved, that the valuation can approximate to the true marketable value of lands, which is in many cases more than fifty times the maximum of the statutory limitation. The assessor must make his valuation by adopting a maximum or minimum, always arbitrary, from which to commence his gradation, and determine the value of the several classes of property by the best comparison in his power. If the rule for valuation be uniform in all the counties, the taxation will be equal? But how is this uniformity to be obtained—to what standard shall an appeal be made. It is certain that this mode of valuation affords no means of judging of the wealth of the several counties, nor of comparing the value of lands in this state with that of lands in other states. If the standard of valuation were the marketable value of lands, though a variable one, it would be one of easy attainment ; and inequality, designed or accidental, could be detected by a standard that was notorious.

the remainder, with the fees of assessment, collection and paying over to the treasurer, is assessed on the other taxable property within the township, at such rate per dollar as will produce the sum required. Any party aggrieved by such assessment, may seek redress from the commissioners of appeal, who, for that purpose, meet on the second Tuesday of November, annually.

The township collector is required, within thirty days after receipt of the duplicate, to demand payment of the tax from each individual of his township, in person or by notice left at his place of residence, and also to give notice of the time and place of the meeting of the commissioners of appeal; and to pay the taxes, fines and forfeitures by him received, by virtue of any law of the State, to the collector of the county, by the 22d December, annually; and such sums as may be recovered by prosecution, thereafter, as soon as received. If the taxes be not paid at the time appointed, the collector is to make return to a justice of the peace, on the 22d December, annually, of delinquents, with the sums due from them, declaring on oath that he had in relation to them, respectively performed his duty according to law; and to take a receipt for such list from the justice.

Within five days after receipt of such list, it is the duty of the justice to deliver warrants to the constables, requiring them to levy the tax in arrears, with costs, &c. by distress and sale of chattels of delinquent—or, in default of chattels, to imprison the body until payment be made; giving four days notice, at least, by advertisement, of the time and place of such sale. And it is the duty of the constable to pay such tax to the township collector, within forty-five days from the date of the warrant; to return the warrant to the justice, with an account of the manner of his executing the same; a copy of which warrant and return, the justice shall, if demanded, give to the collector, and return the original warrant, if not fully executed, to the constable.

The constable is liable for so much of the taxes, which by such warrant he was required to collect, as shall not be paid over to the collector, unless the deficiency happen without neglect, fraud or default, on his part, in suit, by township collector, before a judge of the Common Pleas; and like suit may be brought against township collector, by the county collector, for monies collected by him, or received from constable, and not paid over, according to law; and in case the constable be prosecuted, such warrant, on cause shown, may be taken from him, and transferred to another.

Tenants or persons having charge of lands, and tenements and their chattels, are liable for taxes imposed on such lands; and on payment, may deduct the amount from their rent, or recover it by suit, where no contract prevents; and when the tax is on unimproved or untenanted land, or the tenant is unable to pay, the tax may be levied by the constable on the warrant of a justice, at the instance of the collector, by sale of timber, wood, herbage, or other vendible property of the owner, on the premises.

The justices, constables and township collectors, render to the township committee, when required, an account of the monies they or any of them may have received on any assessment, and not paid to the county collector, and must pay to such committee, on demand, such monies; and in default, are liable to suit by the clerk of the township, in the name of the inhabitants thereof.

Due provision is made for the compensation of the respective township and county officers, for enforcing performance of their duties by proper sanctions, and for levying monies becoming due from them by virtue of their official stations.

Another prominent use made of the township and county division, is in the system for the maintenance of the poor.

The provisions for this purpose, like the political subdivisions themselves, have, in their principal features, been copied from Great Britain. The wisdom of this system is less than equivocal, but the genius of legislation has not yet been able to substitute a better. Each township, or precinct, is required to maintain the poor *settled* within it. A settlement is gained by the acquisition of a freehold estate of fifty pounds value, and residence of a year; apprenticeship, or servitude by indenture, for a year; residence of one year by a mariner, or a person arriving directly from Europe; and such residence and notice to the overseer, recorded by the town clerk, in case of other persons. From these provisions are excepted servants procured from gaols and hospitals in other states. Bastard children have the settlement of the mothers. Penalties are inflicted upon such inhabitants as receive into their houses, vagabonds, vagrants, sturdy beggars, and idle strolling and disorderly persons; and they are liable to maintain such wanderers, and to pay the expenses of their funerals in case of death. A person may remove from one precinct to another, bearing the certificate of the overseers of the poor of the precinct in which he has a settlement, attested and allowed by two justices of the peace, declaring such settlement, and delivering such certificate to the overseers of the district into which he shall remove. But such person, becoming chargeable, may be returned to his place of settlement; residence under the certificate not giving settlement; and expenses incurred by the township for maintenance, relief or burial of such resident, must be paid by the precinct in which he has a legal settlement.

Relief is granted to paupers, on the order of a justice, at the application of the overseers; the order fixing the amount, and serving as the voucher for expenditure. And, as a check upon the overseers, they are required to register the name and description of the pauper, and such order, in the township book, together with the account of monies received or disbursed for the use of the poor, and registry of transactions of their office, and to lay such book before the inhabitants in town meeting.

Before relief granted, the goods of the applicant are to be inventoried, and in case of death, sold; and the proceeds applied to reimburse the expenditure for the pauper.

Poor children, who have no parents, or whose parents are applicants for relief, and children of paupers brought up in sloth and ignorance, may, by the overseers, with the assistance and application of two justices, be bound apprentices for such number of years as they may think proper, males until 21, and females until 18 years; inserting in the indenture, a clause binding the master to cause such apprentice to be instructed to read and write. And the overseers and justices continue the guardians of the apprentice.

Where the father deserts his family, or a widow her children, leaving them a public charge, and leaving estate, real or personal, such estate may be taken by the overseers, upon the warrant of two justices, and the rents of the land, and the proceeds of the sale of the chattels, applied to the maintenance of the deserted family.

The overseers, with the assent of the town meeting, may purchase or rent a workhouse, in which to employ and maintain the poor of the precinct, applying the proceeds of their labour to the poor fund; and such house may be erected by two or more townships conjointly. Or the overseers of the township may contract with the overseers of any other place, for the maintenance and employment of the poor of such other place; or the chosen freeholders of the county may purchase or build a poorhouse for the whole county. Persons claiming relief and refusing to be lodged, kept to work, and maintained in such house, are rejected.

When the overseers have reason to believe, that any person not having a settlement in their precinct is, or is likely to become, chargeable, they may bring him, by warrant from two justices, directed to and served by the constable, before such magistrates, who shall examine such person on oath touching his last place of settlement, and direct him to remove thither by a stated time; and on his neglect or refusal to comply with such order, may issue their warrant to the constable, commanding him to convey such person to the constable of the next precinct; and so, from precinct to precinct, until he reach the place of his legal settlement. And in case such person return to the place from which he was removed, and does not depart therefrom, within 24 hours after notice given, such person, if male, is liable, on the order of a magistrate, to receive fifteen lashes; if female, in the discretion of the magistrate, to be sent away again, or committed to close confinement, and fed, at the expense of the township, on bread and water only; and both to be sent back to the place to which they may have been first ordered. But if any person complained of, as a pauper, give bond with two sufficient sureties, conditioned to indemnify the precinct against the charge of his maintenance, he shall not be removed.

The overseers of the township, to which such pauper shall be legally removed, are required to receive him, under penalty of five pounds, on conviction of refusal, before a justice, to the use of the place from which the removal was made. An appeal from the order of removal lies by the pauper, or other person aggrieved, to the sessions.

An idle vagrant, vagabond, or beggar, strolling and begging through the country, may be apprehended by the constable, or any inhabitant, and carried before a justice, who is required to examine him on oath; and if it appear that he have a settlement, to grant a warrant for removal as abovementioned, but if he have no settlement in the State, then to direct by such warrant that he be conveyed back by every precinct through which he had wandered, until he be transported out of the State: and such vagrant returning into the State, is liable to punishment by whipping. These provisions respecting the removal of indigent persons, though in force, are not often executed.

The fund for maintenance of the poor is augmented by fines imposed for breach of the laws, and by the personal estates of such persons as may die intestate, without any representative. The pauper may sue without costs, and have counsel appointed him by the court, who shall conduct his cause without fee or reward. Authority is given to the respective townships to raise, as for other township purposes, such sum of money as may be deemed proper for the education of pauper children and children of paupers.

The father and grandfather, mother and grandmother, child and grandchild, when competent, are liable to maintain the pauper.

A third essential benefit, promoted by the territorial subdivision of townships and counties, is the formation and preservation of roads. The common roads of the country are either public or private. When ten or more freeholders deem a new public road necessary, or one existing, unnecessary or proper to be altered, they may by petition, after giving ten days public notice in the townships through which the road is intended to pass, obtain from the court of Common Pleas the appointment of six surveyors of the highways, having regard to those of the township in which the road lies or is to be made. When the road is to be on the county line, the application must be made to, and the surveyors appointed by, the Supreme Court, three being taken from each county. The surveyors, after a prescribed notice has been given, meet and view the road or ground proposed for the road, and lay out, vacate or alter it, as the case may require; and return a map thereof, with the time when the same may be opened, to the clerk of the Common Pleas, or to the clerk of the Supreme Court, as the case may be, who records the return, and the road so laid out and opened becomes, or if vacated ceases to be, a public highway; unless a caveat be entered thereto within fifteen days, which operates as a supersedeas of proceedings until the succeeding court.

Upon the complaint of any one alleging himself aggrieved, the court will appoint six of the chosen freeholders of the county, who, after due notice as prescribed by law, also view the road proposed to be made, vacated or altered, and concurring in report with the surveyors, it is definitively confirmed, so that no further proceedings may be had thereon for one year. But, if their report differ from that of the surveyors, the latter becomes void, and the road or alteration may be again applied for under a year. If no caveat have been entered, or the person entering it do not prosecute it according to law, or the freeholders make no unfavourable report, or be equally divided in their opinions, the proceedings of the surveyers become valid. If the application for review be in Cape May county, and the proposed or actual road run through lands of any of the chosen freeholders, one or more justices of the peace may be appointed on the review. And where the application relative to the road is in the Supreme Court, three such freeholders from each county are appointed to review, and like proceedings are had in regard to their report, as in the former case. Any neglect of the officers in regard to these proceedings, is punishable by a fine of sixteen dollars, to the use of the prosecutor. Four of the surveyors or freeholders, where the road proposed to be made or altered is in one county, and two from each of the counties, where there are more than one, are necessary to, and sufficient for, the return.

The proceedings for making, vacating, or altering private roads, are similar in most respects, to those in the case of public ones. Such roads, however, are made and preserved at the expense of those interested in them, who may hang gates thereon, which are protected by a penalty against those injuring them. By-roads, if shut up, may be laid out by three of the chosen freeholders, and remain as private roads until vacated, or altered in the manner abovementioned.

For the purpose of making or repairing roads, the township committee assign, in writing to the overseers of the roads respectively, their several limits of the highways within the township. And it is the duty of such overseers to provide labourers, animals, implements and materials for the work, and to erect such bridges as can be built by common labourers; the monies for which are raised by order of the town meeting, as in other cases of township expense, and the overseer accounts with the town meeting.

If the township be fined upon the presentment of the grand jury, or information of attorney general, for the bad condition of the roads, the overseer within whose limits the cause arose, is responsible therefor with costs, or he may be proceeded against in the first instance. The road tax payable by any individual, may be paid in labour on the road by himself or substitute; and the roads over mill-dams are to be kept in good and safe condition by the owners of the mills respectively, so long as they shall be upheld.

The town meeting may determine whether the highways shall be maintained by hire or by labour. But if the resolution be to maintain the roads by labour, the township committee divide the highways, in their township, into convenient districts, and assign the inhabitants to them, in equitable proportions. And whatever mode be thus adopted, must be continued for three years. Inhabitants who neglect to perform their quota of work, are each finable one dollar per day, for absence themselves; one dollar and a half for a horse and cart, and two dollars for wagon or cart with two horses or oxen, which have been warned out and shall be absent. If the township vote to maintain the roads by hire, but do not supply the money therefor, the overseers must resort to the labour system. If the overseer neglect his duty, he is liable to an action, and the magistrate on complaint of three freeholders, may issue his precept against overseer, and on conviction, fine him any sum not over twenty, nor under five dollars. The board of freeholders is authorized, at the county's expense, to erect guide posts and mile stones, where they may deem expedient.

When bridges are required in a township, or between two townships, they are built at the county expense, and if between two counties, at their joint expense. Where the cost does not exceed thirty dollars, the overseer and chosen freeholders of the township, are competent to order its execution; where the cost does not exceed one hundred and fifty dollars, the approbation of the overseers of the township, and of the chosen freeholders of that, and of the two adjacent townships, are necessary; and where the expense will exceed one hundred and fifty dollars, the assent of the overseers of the highway, and of the board of chosen freeholders of the county, is required.

In addition to his services as register of the proceedings of the Circuit Courts, the Court of Sessions and Common Pleas, the county clerk performs many other executive duties. We have already noticed his ministry in general elections. He is the recorder of deeds, mortgages, and other conveyances of lands in his county, and register of marriages returned to him by justices of the peace and ministersof the gospel; the receiver of monies for tavern licenses, which he pays over to the county freeholders; and is the depository of the dockets of the justices of his county, after their deaths. He is forbidden to act as surrogate, or practice as an attorney, within his county.

The township clerk records the proceedings of the town meetings, registers estrays, and receives for the use of the township its share of money produced by the sale of unclaimed beasts impounded for damage feasance; and registers all births and deaths in his township duly communicated to him.

The present militia system of the State, is founded on the act of 18th February, 1815, and the supplements of 1818, 1819, and 1830; which require, that every free able bodied white male inhabitant, of the age of 18, and under 45, years, shall be enrolled by the commanding officer of the company within whose bounds he may reside. From this requisition are exempted, ministers of the gospel; the vice president of the United States; the officers, judicial and executive, of the government of the United States; the judges of the Supreme Court of this State; the members of both houses of congress, and their respective officers; all custom house officers, with their clerks; all post officers and stage drivers employed in the transit of the mail; ferrymen; inspectors of exports; pilots; mariners actually employed in the sea service of any merchant within the United States; all students of divinity and students of the two colleges in this State, except in cases of actual invasion; and persons who shall have served ten years in any uniform corps of the State; and, at the discretion of the brigade board, an officer who has held a commission for one year in the army of the United States, or under the authority of any one of the States, and any soldier who may have faithfully served 18 months in the late war.

A brigade is formed in each county, except Cape May; in that, there is an independent regiment, under the command of a lieutenant colonel, whose field officers form a regimental board, with the power of a brigade board, in many particulars. The brigades are formed into four divisions, of which those of Burlington, Gloucester, Salem and Cumberland, with the Cape May regiment, make the first; those of

Bergen, Essex, and Morris, the second; those of Somerset, Middlesex, and Monmouth, the third; and those of Hunterdon and Sussex, the fourth.

The governor is commander in chief. There is a general staff, of which he appoints his four aids-de-camp, with the rank of lieutenant colonel; one quartermaster and one adjutant general, with the rank of brigadier; and, when the service may require it, one deputy adjutant, and one deputy quartermaster general, to each brigade or division, with rank of lieutenant colonel. To each division there is one major general, and two aids-de-camp appointed by him, with the rank of major; to each brigade, one brigadier general, with a brigade inspector, acting also as brigade major, one aid-de-camp taken from the line, appointed by the general, judge advocate, paymaster and quartermaster; to each regiment, one colonel; to each battalion or squadron, one major; to each company of infantry, light infantry and grenadiers, one captain, one lieutenant, one ensign, four sergeants, four corporals, one drummer, and one fifer; to each troop of horse, one captain, two lieutenants, one cornet, four sergeants, four corporals, one saddler, one farrier, one trumpeter, and the foot and cavalry companies contain not more than 64, nor less than 40, privates. Companies of horse can be raised only by permission of the commander in chief. To each company of artillery there are a captain, two lieutenants, four sergeants, four corporals, one drummer, one fifer, not more than six, nor less than three, gunners and bombardiers, nor more than 62, nor less than 15, matrosses. The regimental staff consists of one adjutant and quartermaster, ranking as lieutenants, taken from the subalterns of the regiment, a paymaster to each battalion; a surgeon, surgeon's mate, chaplain, sergeant major, drum major, fife major, and quartermaster sergeant; all of whom, except the paymasters, are appointed by the field officers. To each company of riflemen there belong a captain, three lieutenants, four sergeants, four corporals, and drummer, fifer, or bugler. Such companies are attached to the battalion in whose bounds a majority of the members reside. To each troop of horse artillery, there are a captain, four lieutenants, one quartermaster sergeant, four sergeants, four corporals, one saddler, one farrier, one bugler, one trumpeter, and not more than 100, nor less than 40, privates.

All officers take rank from the date of their commissions, except when they are of the same date, and then by lot. The captains, and all other inferior officers of the militia, are chosen by the companies; but field and general officers by the council and assembly, and all are commissioned by the governor. The brigade and regimental staff officers, are commissioned by him on certificates of their appointment by the officers making them; non-commissioned officers and musicians, are appointed by the captains and subalterns. The uniform is that worn by officers of the United States.

The commanding officers of each regiment, independent battalion, and squadron, are required to convene their respective officers twice a year; and at one of such meetings, the orderly sergeants; and at the meeting not attended by the non-commissioned officers, may direct the attendance of one of the companies under their command, for the purpose of military improvement. The attendance of such company is in lieu of company training, and absence is punishable as in other cases of neglect of military service. And the non-commissioned officers attending such drill, is entitled to fifty cents per day.

The militia meet three times, annually, for improvement in discipline and martial exercise; once by companies or troops, on the 3d Monday in April; once by battalion or squadron, and once by regiment or independent battalion. The fine for non-attendance on days of exercise, absence from roll call, or leaving parade without permission, is, on a field officer, eight dollars; every other commissioned officer, four dollars; on every non-commissioned officer and private, two dollars per day; and for appearance on parade without appropriate arms, fifty cents, where the soldier is able to provide them. When called into active service, every militiaman must appear fully equipped, with every article required by act of congress, under penalty, if an officer, of ten dollars; and if a private, two dollars. No militiaman having a substitute in actual service, is thereby excused from duty on parade days. But no militiaman is finable more than two dollars in one year, for neglect of duty, if he have attained thirty-five years; provided, that when he shall attend at any one of the days required by law, and perform military duty, he shall be fined one dollar for every other day's absence therefrom. And when the brigade board shall disband any company, its officers may be exempted from military duty.

Delinquents are marked at roll call by the orderly sergeant, and reported to the company court, composed of the officers of the company or troop, of which the officer first in rank is president. Such court is empowered, to hear and decide on, the excuse of delinquents reported, and the president is required to make return within ten days, to the commanding officer of the battalion, of all delinquents, and the sum imposed on each. The battalion court of appeal, consists of the commanding officer of the battalion, the surgeon, or surgeon's mate, and the senior captain, or, in his default, of the captain next in rank ; and is empowered to hear excuses on appeal, and to remit fines ; and in case of permanent inability, by certificate, to discharge from military duty. The president of this court, makes returns of delinquents and the fines imposed, to the battalion and brigade paymasters. Failure to attend such court by its members, or the president to make return, is punishable, in the first case, by a fine of ten, and in the second, by a fine not exceeding thirty, nor less than fifteen, dollars.

The battalion paymaster, on receipt of the return, and such fines as may have been collected by the battalion commandant, after efforts to collect, and after the first Monday in September, delivers the list of delinquents to a justice of the peace, who issues execution against them, as in case of taxation ; the constable being required to levy the same on the goods of the delinquent, or in default of goods, to commit him to prison, until payment, &c. But the brigade board, or any three of them, may discharge delinquent unable to pay. If, upon levy and sale, there be a balance in the hands of the constable which the delinquent will not receive, he pays it to the paymaster of the battalion, to be accounted for in his settlement with the brigade board, and certifies the same to the judge advocate, or brigade board. The fines and penalties imposed on minors, are payable by the parent, guardian, or master.

The battalion paymaster returns to the brigade board the list of delinquent commissioned officers certified by the orderly ; keeps a journal of their proceedings ; an account of fines and the modes of their payment, whether voluntary or involuntary, and of such as may not be recovered, with the reason thereof ; all which is submitted to the brigade board. The battalion and brigade paymasters are appointed by such board, and give bond with sureties, the first in five hundred, and the second in two thousand dollars, conditioned for the faithful performance of their duties ; to which effect, they, also, make oath before the county clerk. The brigade paymaster receives all vouchers and returns, and keeps distinct accounts of the monies arising from fines and forfeitures in the several regiments and battalions in the brigade, and of monies received and paid by him, subject to the examination of the brigade board ; collects the fines imposed by the board on delinquent officers, and, in case of non-payment for sixty days, puts the list into the hands of a justice of the peace, which is then proceeded upon as above stated.

The brigade board is composed of the brigadier general, brigade major and commandants of regiments, independent battalions, and squadrons of the respective brigades ; a majority of whom form a quorum, meeting annually on the third Monday in December, at a place of their own appointment, within the brigade. The officer of first grade and seniority presides, and the board has power : To compel the attendance of its members by fine, not exceeding twenty dollars—to arrange the regiments, battalions, squadrons, troops, and companies, as they may deem expedient—to authorize the formation of new uniform companies, and to attach them to such battalion or regiment as they may deem proper—to draw orders on the brigade paymaster for lawful expenses—to make a reasonable compensation to the brigade and battalion paymasters for their services ; adjust their accounts, remove them in case of malfeasance, and to appoint a successor who in case of brigade paymaster shall prosecute his predecessor for monies of the brigade in his hands—and also the battalion paymasters who may be in arrears—to allow adjutants for extra services—to compensate brigade judge advocates—to assess fines on delinquent officers, returned by the brigade major or battalion paymaster—to preserve order at their meetings by imposition of fines not exceeding ten dollars, upon transgressors, and to erect a covering for the protection of field artillery—to keep an account of all sums by them received from their several battalion paymasters, and disbursements, with an account of the expenses of the militia system, and the appropriations made for arms, &c.—and make reports thereof, annually, to the legislature.

The judge advocate is appointed by the brigade board, of which he is *ex officio* clerk, and is required to attend its meetings and record its proceedings.

The adjutant general distributes all orders of the commander in chief, to the several corps, attends public reviews, if required, when the commander in chief reviews the troops,—obeys all orders from him, executing or perfecting the military system established by law,—furnishes blank forms of the different returns directed by the commander in chief,—receives from the several officers returns of all militia under their command, together with reports of the state of the arms, ammunition, &c. from which he reports proper abstracts to the commander in chief, who lays them before the legislature. He annually reports all the militia of the State to the president of the United States—Keeps a record of all orders, returns names of commissioned officers, and proceedings relative to the details of the military force ordered out by the commander in chief upon requisitions of the president or Congress of the United States, in cases of invasion, or other emergency—Records all certificates of election of officers before commissioned by the commander in chief—and lays his accounts, annually, before the legislature, who appropriate, annually, one hundred dollars for his services.

The brigade inspectors attend the brigade, regimental and independent battalion meetings of the militia composing their several brigades, during the time of their being under arms, to inspect their arms, &c.—makes returns, annually, to the adjutant general of the militia of his brigade, reporting particularly the name of the reviewing officer, the state of the arms, &c. and every thing which, in his judgment, may advance good order and military discipline. He receives for ordinary duty, thirty dollars per annum, and for extra duty, such allowance as the brigade board may direct; and is subject to a fine of fifty dollars for malfeasance, and the forfeiture of his annual salary, unless he produce the acknowledgment of the adjutant general for his returns. In the absence of the brigade inspector, the commanding officer appoints some one to perform his duties.

Company officers report their acceptance of office to the commanding officer of the battalion, within ten days after notice of their election, otherwise the election is deemed void. Resignations are made to the brigade commander; and where vacancy happens in the company, by death, removal or resignation, such commander directs his warrant to the battalion commandant, to hold an election to supply the vacancy.

Persons enrolled in a uniform company are, upon the certificate of the commanding officer, excused from service in the militia : but such certificate may not be given until such persons have appeared in uniform, under penalty of ten dollars upon the officer.

The majors are charged with organizing the several companies under their respective commands. Where the militiamen of any company or district, fail to choose officers, the major may appoint a sergeant, to take command of the company until proper officers are duly qualified; and to constitute his company court, such sergeant may appoint persons from the list of the company, who may elect one of their number president.

No officer or private, on his way to, or return from, militia service, may be charged toll or ferriage, and refusal to permit his passage is punishable by fine of eight dollars; nor can he be arrested on civil process on any legal day for training, nor can his arms, &c. be levied on and sold under execution.

The commander in chief may, in case of invasion or other emergency, order out any proportion of the militia of the State, to march to any part thereof, and continue so long as he may think necessary, not exceeding two months. In such case, substitutes may be received for any person called on to do a tour of duty, but no substitute is admissible at ordinary training, under penalty on the officer, of ten dollars. Horses of militiamen, taken into service, are registered and appraised, and their value paid to the owner, in case the horse be killed or taken by the enemy. The accounts of the quartermaster, for rations or ammunition, must be approved by the commanding officer of the regiment or independent battalion, and by the governor, before payment at the treasury.

Courts martial are appointed, for the trial of officers above the rank of field officers, by the commander in chief,—for field officers, by the major generals, in their respective divisions,—for captains and subaltern commissioned officers, by the brigadier generals, each in his own brigade. And the commandant of regiments and independent battalions may institute a regimental court martial whenever they shall find it necessary. Officers appointing such court must, in all cases, approve or disapprove its sentence, and may mitigate or remit the punishment, except where the

I

offence is of a personal nature, when the sentence is conclusive. And such officer may, in case of emergency, appoint a judge advocate, *pro tempore.*

The regimental court martial is composed of five members, the president of whom shall not be under the rank of captain. The general court martial consists of thirteen commissioned officers, not under the rank of captain, the senior of whom is president. The concurrence of two-thirds of the court is necessary, in every sentence for inflicting punishment; and each member, with the judge advocate, swears to determine the case according to the evidence, that he will not divulge the sentence until it have been approved or disapproved; and will at no time, discover the vote or opinion of any member, unless required to give evidence thereof in a court of justice.

The expense of a court martial, trying an officer of the general staff, is payable from militia fines in the State treasury; trying an officer above the grade of major, by the paymaster of the brigade; trying a major, or inferior officer, by the battalion paymaster. Members of courts martial receive $1 50 per day, and witnesses fifty cents—payable on certificates of the judge advocate.

Commissioned officers guilty of unofficer-like conduct, may be cashiered by the court, or punished by fine, not exceeding fifty dollars. The commanding officer of a regiment, battalion, or squadron, failing to give orders for assembling his command, as directed by his brigadier, or in case of invasion, may be cashiered, and punished by a fine not exceeding one hundred dollars: and a commissioned officer of a company, guilty of like offence, under the orders of the commandant of the regiment, &c., is subject to like punishment; and a non-commissioned officer, to a fine not exceeding thirty dollars. The commanding officer of a company, &c., failing to return a list of persons, notified to perform a tour of duty, to the colonel, &c., may be cashiered, or fined in a sum not exceeding one hundred dollars.

Non-commissioned officers, or privates, appearing drunk upon parade, disobeying orders, using reproachful or abusive language to officers, quarrelling or promoting quarrels among fellow-soldiers, may be disarmed and put under arrest, until the company be dismissed, and be fined by court martial, not exceeding eight dollars. A militiaman deserting whilst on a tour of duty, may be fined not exceeding one hundred dollars, and imprisoned not more than two months; and if a non-commissioned officer, shall be degraded to the ranks. Non-commissioned officer, or private, bringing on parade, or discharging, within a mile thereof, any loaded fire arms, on the day assigned for improvement or inspection, without permission from a commissioned officer, is subject to a fine of one dollar.

When ordered out for improvement or inspection, the militia are under military discipline, from the rising to the setting of the sun, and none, during such time, may be arrested on civil process: on days of exercise they may be detained under arms, on duty, in the field, six hours; but not more than three hours without time being allowed to refresh themselves. The retailing of spirituous liquors, on, or within a mile of the parade, is prohibited under a penalty of forfeiture of such liquors. The rules of discipline are such as may be established by Congress for disciplining the regular troops of the United States.

By-standers at any muster, molesting or insulting, by abusive words or behaviour, any officer or soldier, while on duty, may be put under guard, and kept at the discretion of the commanding officer, until sundown; and if guilty of like misconduct, before a court martial, may be fined not exceeding twenty dollars, and costs of prosecution.

Fines imposed by courts martial, are certified by the judge advocate to the brigade board, and are collected by the brigade paymaster, in the manner above directed. The surplus money in the hands of the brigade paymaster, is appropriated to the purchase of arms, accoutrements, colours, instruments of music, and the preservation of arms (the arms being subject to the order of the commander in chief, in case of invasion, insurrection, or war). And the judge advocate is required, after the annual meeting of the brigade board, to transmit to the adjutant general, a statement of the disbursements, and arms, &c., to be laid by him before the legislature. The commandants of regiments, independent battalions, and squadrons, account to the brigade board for the monies received by them for teaching music, and other purposes.

The commander in chief, or of brigade, when the militia may be called into actual service, may receive uniform companies from any brigade in the State as volunteers, who having served their tour, are exempted from draft, until their battalions, regiment, or brigade shall have performed like service; and their brigade is accredited for the number so volunteering. Due authority is given to the commander in chief for organizing companies on the sea-board when necessary for its protection: and he may furnish any uniform company with arms, the property of the State; the officers giving bond for keeping them in repair, and returning them when required. Uniform companies are attached to the battalion within the bounds of which a majority of the company resides.

Any person desirous to be exempt from militia duty, is required, on or before the first of April, annually, to report himself to the commanding officer of the company, in the bounds of which he may reside. Such officer returns the list of exempts to the township collector, on or before the twentieth of June, annually, who taxes each, the sum of five dollars, in addition to his other taxes; designating it in his duplicate, delivered to the township collector; and he, also, furnishes the collector of the county, on or before the first of December, annually, two certified abstracts of the names of such exempts. The township collector pays to the county collector, such taxes, and his certificate of the death, insolvency, or absconding of the exempt, is a sufficient voucher against the tax; and the county collector pays to the State treasurer, the exempt taxes, with other State taxes, and the treasurer carries them to the credit of the school fund.

The commanders of the respective companies enrol all persons within their bounds liable to perform militia duty, not returned as exempts, and fine them for non-attendance on days of parade, according to law, under the penalty of thirty dollars for omission. But exempts may be classed as enrolled militia when called into actual service. And due provision is made by law for classifyng the militia for actual service when required.

The following is the state of the militia, apparent from the last return of the adjutant general, viz: Commander in chief, 4 aids-de-camp; 1 quartermaster general, 4 deputies; 1 adjutant general, 4 deputies; 4 major generals, each having two aids; 13 brigades and brigadiers, and the independent battalion of Cape May county.

BRIGADE STAFF, consisting of 13 brigade majors and one adjutant, 13 paymasters, 11 quartermasters, 6 surgeons, 13 judges advocate.

CAVALRY :—1 brigadier general, 4 colonels, 9 majors, 31 captains, 63 lieutenants, 25 cornets, 86 sergeants, 73 corporals, 11 saddlers, 10 farriers, 36 trumpeters, and 1673 privates, making an aggregate of 1810. CAVALRY ARMS: sabres 734, pairs of pistols 609, holsters 733, cartridges 376, cartridge-boxes 359, horses, saddles, and bridles, each, 963.

ARTILLERY :—30 captains, 54 lieutenants, 93 sergeants, 75 corporals, 40 bombardiers, 68 gunners, 36 drummers, 25 fifers, 1802 privates,—total 1886. *Ordnance apparatus and equipments :* 18 six pounders, 8 four pounders, 1 two pounder, 1 swivel, 18 tumbrels and wagons, 25 ramrods and screws, 16 port-fire stocks, 33 dragropes, 14 handspikes, 159 muskets, 19 bayonets, 329 swords, 39 cartouche boxes, 23 powder horns and wires, and 43 knapsacks.

RIFLE CORPS :—17 captains, 44 lieutenants, 48 sergeants, 16 corporals, 22 drummers, 16 fifers, 12 buglers, 1052 privates,—total 1115. *Arms and equipments :* 54 swords, 336 rifles, 132 fusees, 117 muskets, 17 powder horns and pouches.

INFANTRY :—Colonels 47, majors 96, adjutants 58, paymasters 98, quartermasters 48, surgeons 47, surgeon's mates 37, drum majors 20, fife majors 21, sergeant-majors 33, captains 406, lieutenants 397, ensigns 327, sergeants 1065, corporals 664, drummers 329, fifers 263, privates 28,882,—aggregate 30,456. *Arms and equipments :* swords 796, espontoons 57, muskets 8268, bayonets 3565, iron ram rods 5084, firelocks, other than muskets, 3373, cartridge boxes 1293.

RECAPITULATION.

COUNTIES.	Commander in chief, Suite, and General Staff.	Division and Brigade General and staff officers.	Cavalry.	Artillery.	Rifle.	Infantry.	Total in each Brigade.	Total in each Division.
Burlington, -			46	44		3288	3378	
Gloucester, -			37	81		1948	2066	
Salem, - -			88	152	120	1508	1868	
Cumberland, -			45	187		1746	1978	
Cape May, -				124		424	548—	9838
Bergen, - -			93	153	21	2074	2341	
Essex, - -			250	422	51	4283	5006	
Morris, - -			155	123	227	2369	2874—	10,221
Middlesex, -			238	93	37	1443	1811	
Monmouth, -			124	50	213	3292	3679	
Somerset, - -			158	107	93	1304	1662—	7152
Hunterdon, -			327			2584	2911	
Warren, - -			77	198	142	1883	2300	
Sussex, - -			172	152	211	2310	2845—	8056
Grand total	15	78	1810	1886	1115	30,456	35,267	35,267

III. The judiciary, as established under the colonial government, was recognised by the constitution, in the general clause continuing the laws existing at the time of its adoption, and in that, limiting the tenure of office of the judges. Some modifications and enlargement of jurisdiction have, however, since been made; and the judiciary power is now vested in a Court of Appeals, Court of Chancery, Supreme and Circuit Courts, Courts of Oyer and Terminer, and General Jail Delivery: Courts of Common Pleas, Quarter Sessions and Orphan's Court, and Courts for the trial of small causes, holden by Justices of the Peace. These institutions will be best viewed, passing from those of the lowest to those of the highest order; and attempting an outline of the constitution of each.

The courts for the trial of small causes or Justices' Courts, now depend upon the act of 12th of February, 1818, and its supplements. By these, every suit of a civil nature, at law, including suits for penalties, where the matter in dispute does not exceed the value of one hundred dollars, is cognizable before a justice of the peace of any county, who holds a court of record, endowed with the usual powers of such courts. From this jurisdiction, however, are excepted, actions of replevin, slander, trespass for assault, battery, or imprisonment, and actions wherein the title to real estate may come in question. The territorial jurisdiction of the justice is coextensive with his county, and his process is confined to it, except in the case of the *subpœna ad testificandum*, which may run into other counties. The constables of the several townships of the county are the ministerial officers of the court, who execute its process, tested on the day it is issued, and signed and sealed, by the justice.

The initiatory process is summons or warrant. The first is required when the defendant is a freeholder, and resident of the county where issued, and in cases where defendant cannot be held to bail; and may be used on all occasions, at the election of plaintiff; the warrant may issue against persons not freeholders, or against freeholders about to abscond from the county. The summons is returnable in not less than five, nor more than fifteen days from its date; and must be served at least five days before the day given therein for appearance, personally, upon the defendant, or by a copy left at his dwelling. The warrant is returnable forthwith. Upon arrest the defendant either gives bond, with freehold surety, to the constable for his appearance at a stated day, not more than eight from the service, or is carried before the justice, where he enters into recognisance with like security, conditioned for his appearance, or is committed to prison to await the time of hearing, which must not be more than three days from the return of the warrant; or he is held by the constable, until the plaintiff be notified and have time to proceed to trial.

The amount of the sum demanded is endorsed upon the writ, with the costs, and may be paid to the constable in full discharge of the debt and arrest.

On the appearance of the parties, the trial is had, or the hearing is adjourned, by the justice himself, or on cause shown by either party, not longer than fifteen days: but if the defendant do not appear, judgment may be rendered by default; and by consent of parties may be entered, without process, for any sum within the jurisdiction of the justice.

After appearance of defendant, and plea entered, and before inquiry into the merits of the cause by the justice, either party may demand a trial by jury; upon which, where the sum claimed does not exceed sixteen dollars, six jurymen, and where over sixteen dollars, twelve jurymen may be summoned. The costs of the jury of twelve, when finding for the applicant, above five, and not exceeding twenty-five dollars, are paid, in part by him; but if finding for him, five dollars, or under, then the whole costs are paid by the applicant; the costs of the jury of six, finding in favour of the applicant, under five dollars, are wholly payable by him.

By consent, and at request of the parties, the justice may enter rules of reference of the matters in difference to such persons as shall be nominated by the parties.

Upon judgment rendered before the justice, no execution can issue against a female, when the debt is under two dollars. Where the debtor is a freeholder, and when sued by summons, he is to be taken as such, unless the presumption be disproved, or when a sufficient freeholder of the county shall join with him in confession of judgment to the adverse party, stay of execution may be had, where the judgment is over five, and under fifteen dollars, for one month; when over fifteen and under sixty dollars, for three months, and when over sixty dollars, for six months.

The execution continues in force for one year from the time it is issued; but may be renewed upon *scire facias*, and judgment thereon, and takes priority from the time of levy made, and the surplus proceeds of sale under the first execution are applicable to the satisfaction of others, in successive order. The levy is made on the goods and chattels of defendant; and if another claim property in the goods levied upon, the constable stays the sale for ten days, unless indemnified by plaintiff; during which, the claimant, on application to a justice, may have his rights tried by a jury of six men, and if the application be not made within that time, the claim is deemed abandoned. The verdict, if against the claimant, protects the constable in making sale of the goods. For want of goods whereon to levy, the body of the defendant is liable to imprisonment until the debt and costs be paid, or until delivered by due course of law: and where there are no personal effects an action may be brought in the Common Pleas, on the judgment before the justice, in order to reach the real estate.

From the judgment of the justice, on default, on absence or confession of defendant, or when the matter in dispute does not exceed three dollars in value, there is no appeal. In other cases, an appeal lies by either party to the Common Pleas to be holden next after rendition of judgment; the appellant giving bond, with surety, to the other party conditioned for the prosecution of his appeal. The justice determining the cause is excluded from sitting upon it in the appellate court.

The judgment of the justice may, also, be revised by the Supreme Court, by certiorari (but not by writ of error) issued within eighteen months from the rendition. Any justice is authorized, in cases in a Justice's Court, to take the deposition of infirm, sick, or going witnesses, and to issue commission for the examination of witnesses.

The justices (among whom are to be esteemed the mayor, recorder, and aldermen of any city, borough, or town corporate, within their respective territorial jurisdictions) are chosen by the legislature in joint meeting, for the term of five years, and may be reappointed for such terms, indefinitely, and dismissed upon impeachment by the assembly, and conviction by the council. Such justices are, by the act of 1794, conservators of the peace, and as such, are charged and empowered to cause the laws to be observed, and to apprehend and punish offenders as the laws may direct. They exercise also many ministerial duties, as notaries in certain cases; and act as substitutes for the coroner, &c. &c. As the Justices' Court is that which disposes of the major part of the disputes among the citizens, we have occupied more space in relation to it than we shall give to the courts of higher order.

The Court of Quarter Sessions, in each county, is composed of the justices of the county, or any three of them; and is a court of record, having cognisance of all indictable offences perpetrated in the county: and authority by its precepts to the sheriff, to summon grand and special juries, and to do all necessary things relative thereto, as directed by law; sending, however, all indictments found for treason, murder, manslaughter, sodomy, rape, polygamy, arson, burglary, robbery, forgery, perjury, and subornation of perjury, to be tried in the Supreme Court, or Court of Oyer and Terminer. To this court the several justices of the county send their recognisances for keeping the peace or good behaviour, and the examination of offenders, taken before them; and generally return to it the recognisances of witnesses and of bail in criminal cases. It has cognisance of cases of bastardy; may grant tavern licenses, the sums payable for which, not less than $10 nor more than $70, pertain to the county treasury; may recommend to the governor persons for license as pedlars; may hear appeals from the order of justices, between master and servant, and in pauper cases, and from conviction, by justices, under the acts for suppressing vice and immorality, &c.; and has, generally, the powers of a court of record, relative to the subjects of its jurisdiction.

The Common Pleas consist of judges appointed by the legislature, in joint meeting, who hold their offices for five years. The number in each county is unlimited, and varies from time to time. Any one of the judges may hold the court. They choose their own president for a year, and receive no salary or compensation, but certain bench fees, divided among them, rarely amounting to their expenses at the court. Their territorial jurisdiction is only coextensive with the county, but they may issue subpœnas for witnesses throughout the State. The court has unlimited original jurisdiction, at common law, in all personal actions where the freehold does not come in question, with some restriction as to costs, in cases cognisable before a justice. Its proceedings may be revised on writ of error to the Supreme Court.

The judges of the Court of Common Pleas, in the several counties, or any three of them, constitute the Orphans' Court; which is a court of record, and is holden four times a year, in the same week with the Courts of Quarter Sessions, and at such other times as the judges may deem proper. This court is empowered: to determine all controversies respecting the existence of wills, the fairness of inventories, the right of administration and guardianship, the allowance of the accounts of executors, administrators, guardians, or trustees, audited and stated by the surrogate; to award process to bring before them all persons interested, or witnesses, in any pending cause; or who, as executors, administrators, guardians, trustees, or otherwise, are accountable for any property belonging to an orphan, or person under age. And the ordinary, his register, and surrogates, are required to transmit into this court, upon application, copies of all bonds, inventories, accounts, &c., relating to estates of orphans, &c. Where insufficient surety has been taken on granting letters of administration, or guardianship, this court has power to require administrators or guardians to give further security; and upon refusal, or malfeasance in their trust, to dismiss them and substitute others: and where an executrix having minors of her own, or is concerned for other minors, or is like to marry without securing the minors' estates; or where an executor, guardian, or other trustee of minors' estates is like to prove insolvent, refuses or neglects to account for such estates, to order that he give security to those for whom he is concerned, by mortgage or bond, in such sum as the court may deem proper; conditioned for the performance of their respective trusts: and, where the surety in bond given by an administrator or guardian, alleges that such officer is wasting or mismanaging the estate, whereby the complainant is liable to damage, the court may compel such officer to render an account, and if the malfeasance be apparent, may, on pain of dismissal, compel him to give separate security to his surety for the faithful performance of duty: and where there are two or more acting executors, guardians, or administrators, the court may, from time to time, on the application of any one of them, and sufficient reason shown, order the executor, &c., to account with his coexecutor, &c., and compel him to give separate security to such executor, &c., and on refusal, to authorize such coexecutor, &c., to sue for the assets in the hands of the executors, &c., refusing.

The court has also authority, to make partition of the lands of an intestate, among his heirs, when any of them are under the age of twenty-one years ; and also of the lands devised to two or more devisees, under such age, where the bounds of each devisee's share is unascertained ; and to appoint commissioners for the admeasurement of dower. But where the lands of such intestate or devisor lie in two or more counties, the duty of partition devolves upon the surrogate general. The court may order sale of lands for the payment of debts when the personalty is exhausted, either upon application of the executor, administrator, or creditor ; or the sale of lands of orphans, when necessary for their maintenance and education ; and direct the fulfilment of contracts for the conveyance of real estate, made by the testator or intestate, in his life time : and may also compel creditors of the estates of decedents, to render their accounts, within a stated time, under penalty of being barred of their actions. And in case the estate prove insolvent, may direct distribution of proceeds among creditors ; and where the debts are paid, may divide the balance among the representatives of decedent.

This court has jurisdiction, also, in the settlement of the accounts of assignees, under the assignment of a debtor for the benefit of creditors.

By the 8th article of the constitution the governor is *ex officio* ordinary, or surrogate general. One deputy or surrogate, in each county, is appointed by the legislature, for five years, whose power is confined within the same, and whose duty is—to take the depositions to wills, (ten days after death of testator) administrations, inventories, and administration bonds, in cases of intestacy, and issue thereon letters testamentary and of administration ; but where doubts arise on the face of the will, or a caveat be put in against proving it, or disputes happen respecting the existence of a will, the fairness of an inventory, or the right of administration, he is to issue citations to all persons concerned, to appear at the next Orphans' Court, of the county, where the cause is determined in a summary way, subject to an appeal to the Prerogative Court, to which all other proceedings of the surrogate may, also, be carried directly by appeal : To record all wills and inventories proven before him, or the Orphans' Court, with the proofs ; all letters of guardianship and letters testamentary by him granted, a copy of which, under his hand and seal, is evidence in any court of the State. He transmits to the register of the Prerogative Court, on the first Mondays of February, May, August, and November, annually, all wills and inventories proved by him, and a return of all letters of administration granted during the preceding three months, to be filed in the register's office. Files all administration and guardianship bonds, and other writings, required by law, in conducting the business of his office : Gives bond for the faithful performance of his duties, with sureties in the sum of two thousand dollars : Audits and states the accounts of executors and administrators, exhibited to him, and report the same to the Orphans' Court, giving at least two months' notice of his intention, in at least five of the most public places of the county, as near as may be, to the place of residence of the parties concerned. He is required to keep up in his office, at all times, in some conspicuous place, a true list of all fees lawfully demandable by him as surrogate, or as clerk of the Orphans' Court ; and he is punishable for extortion by fine.

The jurisdiction of the ordinary or surrogate general extends only to the granting of probate of wills, letters of administration, letters of guardianship and the hearing and finally determining all disputes that may arise thereon. For the last purpose, he holds, at stated periods, a Prerogative Court, at the times and places for holding the Court of Chancery, where he hears, and finally determines, all causes that come before him, either directly or by appeal from any of the surrogates or from the Orphans' Court. Of this court the secretary of state is register, and is required to record the names of the testators of all wills he may receive, in alphabetical order, with the year in which they were proved, and to file such wills in his office, the wills of each year and county to be put by themselves ; and in like manner to record the names of all intestates, and all inventories in manner aforesaid ; and transcripts of any will or testament registered by him are receivable in evidence in all courts of the commonwealth.

Supreme and Circuit Courts.—The first consists of a chief justice and two associates, and holds, annually, at Trenton, four terms, commencing on the last Tuesday of February, the second of May, the first of September, and the second of November, by the chief justice or any one of the justices. Issues in this court, determinable by jury, are tried in the county where the lands in question lie, or the cause of action arises; unless upon motion upon behalf of the State, when the State is party, or where the amount in dispute is three thousand dollars, and either party order the trial at bar, which he may do, receiving only the costs of a Circuit Court if he do not recover that sum. Transitory actions, at the discretion of the court, are tried in the county in which the cause of action arose; and trials by foreign juries may be had where the court deem it proper. The court has original jurisdiction in all cases without regard to amount, but the party recovering not more than two hundred dollars, exclusive of costs, is not entitled to costs, unless the freehold, inheritance or title to real estate may come in question, or the suit be removed into this court by the defendant. But no suit may be removed from an inferior court by *habeas corpus* unless the value of the matter in controversy exceed two hundred dollars. It has power to appoint commissioners of bail, and to make rules for justifying such bail; to try treason committed out of the State; to review proceedings of justices in cases of landlords and tenants; to authorize the filing of an information in the nature of a *quo warranto;* to make partition of land and tenements between jointtenants and tenants in common; to appoint commissioners to ascertain county lines; to entertain prosecutions against vessels seized for engaging in the slave trade; to issue writs of dower, and admeasurement of dower, &c.; and writs of error in all cases to the Common Pleas, and to determine thereon, and also to determine causes removed hither by certiorari from the Orphans' Court: to appoint viewers of roads in certain cases, and to receive and determine on their report.

The chief justice, or one of his associates, twice in a year, holds a Circuit Court in every county except in that of Cape May, for the trial of issues which have been joined in, or brought into the Supreme Court, and which may be triable in the county: but the same judge does not hold the court twice in succession in the same county, unless on special occasions; and the clerks of the Common Pleas, in the several counties, are clerks of the Circuit Courts, and of the Courts of Oyer and Terminer and General Jail Delivery.

The Court of Oyer and Terminer is holden semi-annually, in each county, except that of Cape May, where it is holden annually only, by one of the justices of the Supreme Court, and the judges of the Courts of Common Pleas, or any three of them. It has cognisance of all crimes and offences within the county; and authority to deliver the jails of the prisoners therein. Its process runs into all the counties of the State, and it may direct that indictments found in it for offences indictable in the Quarter Sessions be sent to the sessions for trial.

The Supreme Court has original jurisdiction in criminal cases, and appellate jurisdiction from the Court of Oyer and Terminer, &c.

The governor is, by the constitution, chancellor of the State, and holds at Trenton, annually, four stated terms on the third Tuesday of January, the first in April, the second in July, and the second in October, and such stated terms as he may from time to time appoint. If the court be not opened at any of the said terms, the process returnable, and the suits pending therein, are continued, of course, until the court shall sit. This court is considered as always open for the granting of injunctions, writs of *ne excat* to prevent the departure of defendants from the State, and other writs and process in vacation. The chancellor may call to his assistance the chief justice or other justice of the Supreme Court, or one or more masters of chancery, to advise with on the hearing of a cause, argument, or motion; or he may send any matter of law to the Supreme Court for its opinion; or if a matter of fact render the intervention of a jury necessary, he may send an issue for trial to such court. The masters in chancery are appointed by the chancellor, and the clerk of the court formerly named by him, is now, by virtue of the act of 14th February, 1831, appointed by the legislature in joint meeting, and continues in office five years.

In addition to the subjects of jurisdiction abovementioned, we may add here, that of foreclosure of mortgages as a prominent one. But the jurisdiction of this court is extensive and complex, embracing those many subjects on which the law cannot justly operate, by reason of its generality, and is not defined by the statutory law. A knowledge of it can be obtained, therefore, only from the thousand volumes of English and American law, and it must remain a mystery to all but the erudite student.

To the Supreme and Chancery Courts a reporter is attached, whose duty is, to report and publish their decisions.

The governor and council, seven of whom make a quorum, constitute the court of appeals in the last resort, in causes of law or equity removed from the Supreme

Court, or from Chancery, after final judgment; and possess the power of granting pardons to criminals after condemnation, in all cases of offence. This court holds annually at Trenton, two terms; one commencing on the third Tuesday in May, and the other on the first Tuesday of November; but, if the legislature be elsewhere in session at either of the said terms, the court is holden where the legislature may be; and the governor, with the advice of the council, or three of them, may hold another term, at Trenton, annually. The secretary of state is the clerk of the court. The members of council, sitting as judges, receive the same pay and mileage, as when sitting in council; and the clerk, as when acting as clerk of council. If a sufficient number of members do not attend the court, on the first day of term, it may adjourn from day to day, or until the next term, and all proceedings therein are continued, of course.

Compensation of Officers. The compensation of the chancellor, judges of the Common Pleas, Orphans' Courts, Quarter Sessions, and justices, and of the clerks, sheriffs, coroners and constables, engaged therein, secretary of state, attorney general and deputies, is by fees, respectively, allotted to them by law.

The chief, and other justices of the Supreme Court, are allowed a per diem compensation for attending the Circuit Courts, in addition to their annual salaries, and certain fees on law proceedings, and an allowance for travelling expenses, which may increase their compensation on the whole to $1,300 or $1,400 per annum. The statutes regulating fees are perpetual; but those which fix salaries are annual; and thus the chief officers of State are kept dependent upon the legislature. The act of 2d Nov. 1832, allotted for the then next succeeding year, to the governor, at the rate of $2,000; chief justice, $1,200; associate justice of Supreme Court, $1,100; treasurer, $1,000; law reporter and chancery reporter, each $200; attorney general, $80; quartermaster general, $100; adjutant general, $100. All of which are payable, on warrants signed by the governor or vice president. The salary ceases on the removal of the officer by death or otherwise.

The same act, allotted to the vice president of council and speaker of assembly, $3 50; and to every member of council and assembly, $3 per day; and $3 for every twenty miles of travel to and from the seat of government; to the secretary of council and clerk of assembly, each $3 50 per diem; and eight cents per sheet of 100 words, for recording minutes, and the like for copy for the printer, and per sheet to engrossing clerk. To the sergeant at arms and door keepers, $2 per day.

IV. Having, as fully as our limits will permit, pourtrayed the physical and political condition of the State, it remains, to complete our view, that we trace an outline of the provisions which exist for religious, moral, and intellectual improvement. The principal religious associations are the Presbyterian, Baptist, Methodist, Dutch Reformed, Quaker, and Catholic. Beside these, there are several other Christian denominations, such as Universalists, *Chris-ti-ans*, &c. &c., but the number of members pertaining to them, are inconsiderable. We have sought to give the condition of each from their records, and where such documents were not accessible, from other authentic sources.

The Synod of the Presbyterian Church of New Jersey, comprises the Presbyteries of Newark, Elizabethtown, New Brunswick, Newton, and Susquehanna. But we do not note the latter. The reader will observe, that in the following table, P. attached to a minister's name, denotes that he is pastor of some church, and P. attached to a church, that it has a pastor. W. C. stands for, *without charge;* S. S. for stated supply; O. S. for occasional supply; V. for vacant; *Presb.* for Presbytery; *Prest.* for president of some college; *Prof.* for professor in some college or theological seminary; *Miss.* for missionary; *Chap.* for chaplain to the navy or some public station; *Ch.* for church; *Cong.* for congregational. The expense of each church will not exceed $600.

K

MINISTERS AND LICENTIATES.	NAMES OF CHURCHES.	Com. added on examina.	Com. added on certific.	Total of Communicants.	Total of Baptisms.	Missionary Funds raised.	Funds for Commissioners.	Education Funds raised.	Fund of the Contingent Assembly.	POST-OFFICE ADDRESS.
Presbytery of Newark.										
Stephen Grover, P.	Caldwell, P.	34		291	19		2 12	5 28	2 12	Caldwell, N. J.
Asa Hillyer, D. D. P.	1st Church, Orange, P.	13	7	439	46		2 53	5 54	2 53	Orange, N. J.
Cyrus Gildersleeve, S. S.	South Orange, S. S.		4	41	13		1 13		1 13	Bloomfield, N. J.
Aaron Condit, W. C.										Hanover, N. J.
Noah Crane, W. C.										
Samuel Fisher, D. D. P.	Patterson, P.	28		294	28		5 50	12 00	5 50	Paterson, N. J.
Barnabas King, P.	Rockaway, P.	18	7	233	38		3 25		3 25	Rockaway, N. J.
Humphrey M. Perrine, W. C.										
John Ford, P.	Parsippany, P.	15		223	9		3 38	5 00	3 38	Parsippany, N. J.
Gideon N. Judd, P.	Bloomfield, P.	76	8	404	36			10 52		Bloomfield, N. J.
Edward Allen, Teacher.										Harmony Vale, N. J.
Enos A. Osborn, P.	Succasunna, P.	20		87	19		4 60	1 75	4 60	Succasunna, N. J.
Philip C. Hay, P.	2d Church, Newark, P.	21		370	23			4 56		
Jacob Tuttle, P.	New Milford, P.	2	17	114	6		3 00	7 25	3 00	Deckertown, N. J.
Peter Kanouse, P.	Wantage, P.			400						Augusta, N. J.
Nathaniel Conkling, S. S.	Frankford, S. S.	37	17	417	31		7 17	12 75	7 17	Newark, N. J.
Baxter Dickinson, P.	3d Church, Newark, P.		22	414	18		9 78	30 01	9 78	Do.
William T. Hamilton, P.	1st Church, Newark, P.	34	33	164	20		2 27	6 03	2 27	Orange, N. J.
George Pierson, P.	2d Church, Orange, P.	4	3	78	7		1 02		1 02	Harmony Vale, N. J.
Elias R. Fairchild, S. S.	North Hardiston, S. S.									
Sylvester Graham, W. C.										
Baker Johnson, P.	Caldwell, P.	5	2	274	10		2 17	5 12	2 17	Hanover, N. J.
William Toby, S. S.	Hanover, S. S.	36	2	97	14					
Thomas Smith, Miss.	Hardiston, V.			150						
Moses Jewell, W. C.	Newfoundland, S. S.			12						
Licentiates.										
Albert Pierson.	Stony Brook, V.			35						
Festus Hanks.	Berkshire Valley, V.			25			1 62		1 62	
Abraham De Witte.	4th Church, Newark, S. S.			9						
	Camptown, S. S.									
	Jersey City, V.									

African Church, Newark, V.	24									
Totals, 28	350	122	12 / 4582	337		$49 55	$105 81	$49 52	
Presbytery of Elizabethtown.										
Stephen Thompson, P.	Connecticut Farms, P.	6	2	122	4		$1 50	$50 00	$1 50	Union, N. J.
John M'Dowell, D.D. P.	1st Ch. Elizabethtown, P.	38	4	576	51	$236 00	10 25	500 00	10 25	Elizabethtown, N. J.
Jacob Briant, W. C.	Mount Freedom, V.			70						Mount Freedom, N. J.
Alexander G. Fraser, P.	Chatham, P.	1	2	175	6		1 22	5 00	1 22	Bottle Hill, N. J.
David Magie, P.	2d Ch. Elizabethtown, P.	34	6	184	24	150 00	6 00	110 00	6 00	Elizabethtown, N. J.
Abraham Williamson, P.	Chester, P.			105			1 65	9 06	1 65	Chester, N. J.
William B. Barton, P.	Woodbridge, P.	24	3	166	14		2 50	12 00	2 50	Woodbridge, N. J.
James B. Hyndshaw, P.	New Providence, P.	13	3	127	12	12 00	2 00	3 50	2 00	New Providence, N. J.
Holloway W. Hunt, P.	2d Church, Woodbridge, P.	41	9	205	28	8 15	4 50	8 56	4 50	Metuchin, N. J.
Lewis Bond, P.	Plainfield, P.	34	10	98	33	19 13	1 25	2 25	1 25	Plainfield, N. J.
Daniel H. Johnson, P.	Mendham, P.			257			3 25	39 00	3 25	Mendham, N. J.
Alfred Chester, W. C.										Morristown, N. J.
Joseph M. Ogden, P.	Chatham Village, P.	20	6	103	27		2 31	4 00	2 31	Chatham Village, N. J.
Charles Hoover, P.	Morristown, P.			659						Morristown, N. J.
James M. Hunting, P.	Westfield, P.	7	1	268	21	150 00	3 91		3 91	Westfield, N. J.
Thomas L. Janeway, P.	Rahway, P.	46	14	199	36		1 42	10 00	1 42	Rahway, N. J.
Horace Doolittle, P.	Springfield, P.	1	2	204	10	47 00	1 50	2 20	1 50	Springfield, N. J.
	Perth Amboy, S. S.	7	2	37	1					
Licentiates.										
John T. Halsey.										
Arthur Granger.										
Isaac Todd.										
Augustus O. B. Ogden.										
Totals, 21	17	272	64	3555	267	$622 28	$43 26	$755 57	$43 26	
Presbytery of New Brunswick.										
Samuel Miller, D. D. Prof.										
Arch. Alexander, D. D. Prof.										
George S. Woodhull, P.	Princeton, P.	36	6	250	38	$114 25	$7 50		$7 50	Princeton, N. J. / Do.
David Comfort, P.	Kingston, P.	51	1	189	48		9 75		5 50	Kingston, N. J. / Princeton, N. J.
James Carnahan, D. D. Prest.										
Isaac V. Brown, W. C.	Freehold, V.		2				4 50	4 50	4 50	Lawrenceville, N. J.
Eli F. Cooley, P.	1st Church, Trenton, P.	6		143	7	52 32	2 43		2 05	Trenton, N. J.

MINISTERS AND LICENTIATES.	NAMES OF CHURCHES.	Com. added on examina.	Com. added on certific.	Total of Communicants.	Total of Baptisms.	Missionary Funds raised.	Funds for Commissioners.	Education Funds raised.	Contingent Fund of the Assembly.	POST-OFFICE ADDRESS.
Presbytery of New Brunswick.										
Symmes C. Henry, P.	Cranbury, P.	8	1	403	23	$27 56	$5 00	$15 00	$5 00	Cranbury, N. J.
Ravaud K. Rodgers, P.	Boundbrook, P.	42	7	272	27	100 00	5 00	50 00	5 40	Boundbrook, N. J.
Henry Perkins, P.	Allentown & Nottingham, P.	12	3	175	11	40 75	5 00	18 00	2 00	Allentown, N. J.
Peter O. Studdiford, P.	Solebury, P.	1		81	3	5 00	2 00		2 00	Lambertsville, N. J.
	Lambertsville, P.	5	2	53	2	5 00	2 00	37 00		
Charles Hodge, Prof.										Princeton, N. J.
Charles S. Stewart, Chap.										
Joseph H. Jones, P.	New Brunswick, P.	34	10	260	30	308 40	12 31	40 00	12 31	New Brunswick, N. J.
Jared D. Fyler, W. C.										
Benjamin Ogden, P.	Pennington, P.	19	6	202	17	20 63	5 00	3 00		Pennington, N. J.
William H. Woodhull, P.	2d Ch. Upper Freehold, P.									Hightstown, N. J.
James W. Alexander, P.	Trenton City, P.	10		298	14	175 00				Trenton, N. J.
Clifford S. Armes, S. S.	Middletown Point, S. S.			50		10 00		30 00		Middletown Point, N. J.
Peter J. Gulick, Miss.										
John Maclean, Vice-President.	Dutch Neck, V.									Princeton, N. J.
Robert Baird, Agent.	Lawrence, P.	20	4	140	19	8 00	4 00	11 86		Philadelphia, Pa.
Henry Axtell, P.	Shrewsbury, S. S.	6	2	44	7	45 79		18 85		Lawrenceville, N. J.
James W. Woodward, S. S.	1st Church, Howell, V.									Shrewsbury, N. J.
Albert B. Dod, Prof.										Princeton, N. J.
Licentiates.										
Theodore Gallaudette.										
Alexander N. Cunningham.										
James W. Blythe.										
John S. Rice.										
Sidney S. M'Roberts.										
Thomas Martin.										
Rezeau Brown.										
John B. Pinney.										
Sloan M'Intire.										
William A. Holiday.										

George B. Bishop.
James Bucknall.

Totals, 37	19	259	44	2560	246	$912 70	$64 49	$228 21	$42 21
Presbytery of Neaton.									
Holloway W. Hunt, Sr. P.									Perryville, N. J.
Bethlehem, P. and Alexandria, P.		6	2	133	14				
William B. Sloan, P. — Greenwich, P.		2	1	79	12	$ 2 50	$ 1 50		Bloomsbury, N. J.
Joseph Campbell, P. — Hacketstown, P.		53		192	33	34 10			Hacketstown, N. J.
Jacob Kirkpatrick, P. — Amwell United 1st, P.		52	1	311	30				Ringoes, N. J.
Amwell 2d, P.		5		132	8				
Joseph L. Shafer, P. — Newton, P.		75	4	112	49	23 11	5 50	$17 50	$ 3 67 — Newton, N. J.
Jacob R. Castner, P. — Mansfield, P.		19	1	289	24	25 00	3 00	5 00	5 00 — Asbury, N. J.
John F. Clark, P. — Flemington, P.		2	2	166	6	25 00	2 00	5 00	4 00 — Flemington, N. J.
Amwell 1st, P.		9	2	117		1 75	3 00		
Jehiel Talmage, P. — Knowlton, P.		11	1	68	13				Centreville, N. J.
John C. Vandervoort, P. — Baskingridge, P.		33	10	109			2 00	1 58	Baskingridge, N. J.
Benjamin I. Lowe, P. — Hardwick, P.		9		432	7				Johnsonborough, N. J.
Marksborough, P.		1		120	8				
William W. Blauvelt, P. — Lamington, P.		36	1	65	17	17 75	2 00	2 00	1 50 — Germantown, N. J.
Mantius S. Hutton, P. — German Valley, P.				209	27	96 25	1 52		Washington, N. J.
Fox Hill, P.				74					
Isaac N. Candee, S. S. — Oxford, W. S.				30			5 00	5 00	11 00 — Belvidere, N. J.
James G. Force, Miss. — Pleasant Grove, V.				150	12				
Lower Mount Bethel, V.									Schooley's Mount. N. J.
Harmony.									
Licentiates.									
James Wyckoff, Miss. — Scott's Mountain, V.		11	1	30	12				
George M'Lin, S. S. — Clinton, S. S.									Clinton, N. J.
Kingwood.									
Stillwater.									
Totals, 16	25	322	25	2818	260	$225 46	$25 02	$36 08	$25 17

The Baptists in New Jersey have sixty-one churches, whose location and condition, in some measure, appears from the following table. Their general affairs are directed by a state convention, which assembles, annually, on the first Wednesday of November, at such place as may be fixed at the prior meeting. It maintains six missionaries, and its funds, in 1832, amounted to $1143 74. The cost of maintaining each church, including the funds raised for all kinds of ecclesiastical purposes, is estimated at $300, making in the whole, $18,300.

STATISTICAL TABLES OF ASSOCIATIONS AND CHURCHES.

NEW JERSEY ASSOCIATION.—"There is a healthful action in this body. Sabbath schools, tracts, temperance and missionary operations, are encouraged to a very laudible extent by the churches; and in many of them seasons of refreshing have been enjoyed during the year past. There is an efficient body of ministers belonging to the association, most of them in the prime of manhood."

CHURCHES.	MINISTERS.	POST OFFICES.	Bap.	Total	Consti.
Cohansey, -	H. Smalley, *W. Sheppard,* -	Roadstown, -	55	188	1900
Cape May, -	Samuel Smith, - - -	Cape May, -	7	80	1712
Salem, - -	Charles J. Hopkins, - -	Salem, - -	5	141	1755
Dividing Creek,	Thomas Brooks, - - -	Dividing Creek,	5	55	1762
Tuckahoe, -	William Clark, - - -	Tuckahoe, -		20	
Pemberton, -	Clarence W. Mulford, -	Pemberton, -	28	170	1764
Pittsgrove, -	William Bacon, - - -	Pittsgrove, -	4	34	1771
Upper Freehold,	James M. Challiss, - -	Imlaytown, -	16	196	1766
Manahawkin, -	C. C. Park, - - -	Manahawkin, -	5	25	1770
Jacobstown, -	—*Ezekiel Sexton,* - -	New Egypt, -	6	62	1785
West Creek,	— - - - -	- - -	4	33	1792
Burlington, -	— G. Allen, P. Powell, J. Boozer,	Burlington, -	1	77	1801
Mount Holly, -	J. Sheppard, J. Maylin, -	Mount Holly,	7	92	1801
	J. E. Welsh, *E. W. Dickerson,*				
Evesham, -	— - - - -	Evesham, -	12	58	1803
Trenton and Lamberton, -	Morgan J. Rhees, - -	Trenton, - -	20	159	1805
Williamsburg,	— - - - -	Princeton, -	2	38	1805
Port Elizabeth,	— - - - -	Millville, - -	2	11	1805
Haddonfield, -	John Sisty, *S. Hervey,*	Haddonfield, -	2	54	1818
Canton, - -	E. M. Barker; J. P. Thompson,	Canton, - -	12	64	1811
Bordentown, -	— - - - -	Bordentown,		36	1821
Woodstown, -	— - - - -	- - -	11	43	1821
2d Cohansey,	J. C. Harrison, - -	Bridgetown, -	5	74	
Allowaystown,	— - - - -	Allowaystown, -	3	50	1830
2d Cape May, -	Ambrose Garrett, - -	Cape May, -		42	1828
Churches 24.	Ministers 24.	Totals	213	1802	

NEW YORK ASSOCIATION.

CHURCHES.	MINISTERS.	CLERKS.	POST OFFICES.	Bapt.	Total	Consti.
Middletown, -	— - -	- -	Middletown, -	14	132	1688
Piscataway, -	— - -	- -	New Brunswick,	18	129	1689
Scotch Plains,	John Rogers,	- -	Scotch Plains,	18	126	1747
	E. *Frost,* - -					
Morristown, -	P. C. Broome,	- -	Morristown, -	1	39	1752
Mount Bethel,	M. R. Cox, -	- -	- -	22	83	1767
Lyon's Farms,	P. Sparks, -	- -	- -	14	58	1769
	J. Wilcox, -					
Northfield, -	A. Elliott, -	- -	- -	2	72	1785
Samptown, -	L. Lathrop, -	- -	- -	30	133	1792
Newark, - -	Daniel Dodge,	- -	Newark, -	8	120	1801
Randolph, -	—M. Quin, sup.	- -	- -		20	1802
New Brunswick,	G. S. Webb, -	P. P. Runyon,	New Brunswick,	29	111	1816
Perth Amboy,	Jacob Sloper,	- -	- -	1	35	1818
Plainfield, -	D. T. Hill, -	D. Dunn, -	Plainfield, -	24	113	1818
Paterson, -	D. D. Lewis, -	- -	Paterson, -	1	48	1825
Churches 15.	Ministers 14.			Totals	190	1319

WARWICK ASSOCIATION.

CHURCHES.	MINISTERS.	CLERKS.	POST OFFICES.	Bap.	Total	Consti.
1st Wantage,	Tim. Jackson,	H. Martin, -	Deckertown,		245	1756
2d Wantage,	A. Harding, -	Israel Dillison,	- -		39	1797
Newfoundland,	— - -	I. Dean, - -	Newfoundland,	1	27	
Hardiston, -	Henry Ball, -	T. Beardsley,	- -	4	63	
1st Newton, -	T. Teasdale, -	J. B. Maxwell,	Newton, - -	23	50	
Hamburg, -	John Teasdale,	I. H. Wood,	Hamburg, -	11	88	
Churches 6.	Ministers 4.		Totals	39	512	

CENTRAL ASSOCIATION.

CHURCHES.	MINISTERS.	POST OFFICES.	Bap.	Total	Consti.
1st Hopewell, -	John Boggs, - -	Hopewell, -	7	172	1715
Hightstown, -	John Seger, - -	Hightstown, -	5	220	1745
Amwell, - -	C. Bartolett, Thos. Burrass,	- -	23	164	1798
	Wm. Pollard, E. Burrass,				
2d Hopewell, -	C. Suydam, - -	- -	1	48	1803
Squan, - -	— - - -	Manasquam, -		40	
Nottingham Square,	— - - -	Trenton, - -		115	
Sandy Ridge, -	Joseph Wright, -	- -	7	79	
Lambertsville, -	D. B. Stout, -	Lambertsville, -	4	27	
Oxford, - -	— - - -	- -	18	30	1831
Washington, -	J. C. Goble, - -	South River, -	27	129	
Churches 10.	Ministers 10.	Totals	92	1024	

HUDSON RIVER ASSOCIATION.

2d Newark, -	P. L. Platt, - -	Newark, - -	15	33	1831

PHILADELPHIA ASSOCIATION.

Kingwood, -	Wm. Curtis, A. Williamson,	Kingwood, -	7	198	1742
	W. R. Robinson, -				

CENTRAL UNION ASSOCIATION.

Camden, - -	—A. Smith, C. Sexton,	Camden, -		33	1818

UNASSOCIATED CHURCHES.

Schooly's Mountain,	—Michael Quin, -	Schooly's Mountain,	4	14	1832
Hackensack, -	Henry Tonkin, - -	Hackensack, -		8	1832

SUMMARY VIEW.

ASSOCIATIONS.	Chs.	Va. Ch.	Or. Min.	Lic's.	Bapt'd.	Total.	Consti.	MEETINGS IN 1833.
New Jersey, -	24	9	21	3	213	1802	1811	Upper Freehold, Sept. 24.
Central, - -	10	3	9	1	92	1024		Washington, Oct. 16.
New York, -	15	3	13	1	190	1319	1791	1st. Ch. N. Y. city, May 28.
Warwick, - -	6	1	4		39	512	1791	Orange, N. Y. June 11.
Hudson River,	1		1		15	33	1815	Oliver Street Church, June 19.
Philadelphia, -	1		1	2	7	198	1707	Spruce Street Church, Oct. 1.
Central Union,	1		2			33	1832	Second Street Church, May 28.
Unassociated chs.	3	1	2		4	60		
Totals	61	17	53	7	560	3981		

The clergymen report, that during the years 1831 and 1832, 1000 persons have been baptized in the State, and that a spirit of enlightened liberality is diffusing itself among the churches.

In addition to what is done for the objects of the convention, from two to three hundred dollars are annually raised for foreign missions.

The Methodist Episcopal Church, in New Jersey, is divided into three districts, each under the charge of a presiding elder, always a minister, appointed by the bishop, and changed at least once in four years. Each district is divided into circuits and stations; thus, the district of West Jersey, comprehending Burlington county, and the country south thereof, contains eight circuits and three stations, and supernumeraries included, twenty-three ministers; the district of East Jersey, including the country as far north as Flemington and Belleville, four circuits and ten stations, and twenty-three ministers; and Asbury district, comprehending the remainder of the State, eight circuits, three stations, and eighteen ministers.

Circuits are formed of territories of greater or less dimensions, including several churches, under the charge of one pastor, aided, commonly, by one or more assistants, who serve the churches in rotation. Stations consist, generally, of one church, but occasionally, of more, confided to the care of one pastor, who, sometimes, where there are more churches than one, has an assistant. The circuits and stations depend, in their government, upon the annual conference of Philadelphia, and upon the quarterly conferences held in them respectively. Disputes among the members of any church, may be considered, in the first instance, by a committee of their church, from whose decision an appeal lies to the quarterly conference, composed of the pastor, local preachers, exhorters, stewards, and class leaders, at whose head is the presiding elder of the district; and its determination is conclusive, unless one of the parties be a minister; in such case, he may appeal to the annual conference; and if he be a travelling minister, from the annual, to the general, conference.

The whole number of clergymen of this denomination, in the State, is sixty-four; the cost of whose maintenance, including donations of every character, together with the expenses of maintaining the churches, is estimated at about $412 each, per annum; which, distributed among the whole number of members, (15,467,) gives an average charge of $1 77, annually, upon each member. And the annual cost of establishing and repairing churches, is stated at twenty-five cents, each member; so that the whole average annual charge, for religious instruction, upon each member of the Methodist Church, may be set down at about two dollars.

The following table shows the circuits and stations of the several districts, with the number of communicants and clergymen, in each, for the year 1832.

WEST JERSEY DISTRICT.	Mem's.	Min's.	EAST JERSEY DISTRICT.	Mem's.	Min's.	ASBURY DISTRICT.	Mem's.	Min's.
Burlington,	424	2	New Brunswick and) Somerville,)	268	2	Kingswood,	170	1
Pemberton,	878	4				Asbury,	698	2
Tuckerton,	848	2	Freehold,	678	4	Belvidere and Warrent.	167	4
Bargaintown,	989	2	Trenton,	360	1	Newton and Hamburg,	937	4
Cumberland,	894	2	Crosswicks,	539	2	Milford,	50	
Bridgeton,	357	1	Pennington,	156	1	Haverstraw,	210	1
Gloucester,	955	2	Plainfield,	32	1	Paterson,	420	1
Salem,	1160	5	Rahway,	152	1	Essex,	445	2
Camden,	713	2	Elizabethtown,	136	1	Morristown,	178	1
Presiding Elder,		1	Woodbridge,	75	1	New Providence,	150	1
	7218	23	Bloomfield and Orange,	450	2		4425	18
			Belleville,	160	1		3924	23
			Newark,	779	2		7218	23
			Somerset Mission,	106	4		15,567	64
			Bergen Neck, do.	33	1			
			Presiding Elder,		1			
				3924	23			

The condition of the Episcopalian Church is drawn from the report of the general convention of the Protestant Episcopal Church, in the United States of America, held in the city of New York, October 1832, and from the report of the 50th annual convention of the church in the diocese of New Jersey, held at Camden in May 1833. From these it appears that during the year, ending October 1832, there were three persons admitted to the order of the priesthood, and one to that of deacon: That there have been eleven institutions within the last three years; that eight clergymen have been received in the diocese, and there were therein eighteen resident, all presbyters: That the number of Episcopal families is 340; of communicants, 900; baptisms reported, 517; persons confirmed,168; candidates for the ministry, 2; and congregations, 33; located and supplied, as mentioned in the following list.

NAME.	PLACE.	INCUMBENTS.
Christ,	New Brunswick,	J. Croes.
St. Matthew's,	Jersey City,	E. D. Barry, D. D.
St. Paul's,	Paterson,	R. Williston, Minister.
Trinity,	Newark,	M. H. Henderson.
Christ Chapel,	Belleville,	(Vacant.)
St. John's,	Elizabethtown,	B. G. Noble.
St. Mark's,	Orange,	B. Holmes.
St. Peter's,	Morristown,	H. R. Peters.
Christ,	Newton,	C. Dunn.
St. Luke's,	Hope,	P. L. Jaques, dea. M'y.
St. James's,	Knowlton,	P. L. Jaques, dea. M's.
St John's,	Johnsonsburgh,	P. L. Jaques, dea. M'y.
St. Peter's,	Spotswood,	J. M. Ward.
St. Peter's,	Freehold,	J. M. Ward, Minister.
Christ,	Shrewsbury,	H. Finch.
Christ,	Middletown,	H. Finch.
St. Peter's,	Perth Amboy,	J. Chapman.
St. James's,	Piscataway,	W. Douglass, Minister.
Trinity,	Woodbridge,	W. Douglass, Missionary.
St. Thomas's,	Alexandria,	W. Douglass, Missionary.
St. Michael's,	Trenton,	F. Beasley, D. D.
Trinity,	Princeton,	(Just organized.)
St. Mary's,	Burlington,	C. H. Wharton, D. D.
St. Andrew's,	Mount Holly,	G. Y. Morehouse.
St. Mary's,	Colestown,	(Vacant.)
St. Paul's,	Camden,	(Vacant.)
St. Peter's,	Berkeley,	(Vacant.)
Trinity,	Swedesborough,	N. Nash, Rector Elect.
St. Thomas's,	Glassborough,	(Vacant.)
St. John's,	Chew's Landing,	(Vacant.)
St. Stephen's,	Mullica Hill,	(Vacant.)
St. John's,	Salem,	H. M. Mason.
St. George's,	Penn's Neck,	H. M. Mason.

It also appears, that the Sunday schools flourish, and are gradually connecting themselves with the diocesan Sunday school society; that the missionary fund amounts to $4,500, which contributes to aid, most materially, in reviving and supporting old and decayed, as well as new congregations; the episcopal fund, to $2,049.33; that the fund for the relief of widows and children of deceased clergymen, has of late years rapidly increased, and now amounts to almost $15,000; and that the Episcopal Society for the promotion of Christian Knowledge and Piety pursues the even and noiseless tenor of its way, doing good by the distribution of Bibles, prayer books, tracts, and aiding the missionary fund, and candidates for orders. Its permanent fund exceeds $1,500. Six hundred dollars per annum is estimated as the annual expense of each church.

The want of full parochial reports renders it impracticable to give an accurate statement of the actual condition of the respective churches.

The Reformed Dutch Church of New Jersey consists of three classes, attached to the particular synod of New York, the condition of which is apparent from the annexed tables. We are unable to furnish a detailed account of the cost to the members of maintaining this church, but we are instructed, from good authority, that $650 will amply cover all the expenses of each church. There are 36 churches, and consequently the whole charge, about $23,400, annually, including theological and missionary contributions.

L

CLASSIS OF NEW BRUNSWICK.

CHURCHES.	PASTORS.	No. of Families	Total of the Congregation	In communion per last Report	Rc'd On Certificate	Rc'd On Confession	Dismissed	Suspended	Died	Total in Communion	Infants	Adults
New Brunswick,	Samuel B. Howe,				20	24	5		2	345	25	3
Six Mile Run,	Vacant,											
Hillsborough,	J. L. Zabriskie,	130		279	8	14	9		8	284	26	4
Raritan,	A. Messler,	310	1700		7	12	8		11	355	16	
Bedminster,	Isaac M. Fisher,											
North Branch,	A. D. Wilson,											
Rockaway,	Jacob I. Shultz,	78	508	101		9	1		1	108	17	2
Lebanon,	Do.	110	600	100	1	3	3		1	100	12	1
Spotswood,	Henry L. Rice,	208	1160			15	1			115	21	5
Freehold,	S. A. Van Vranken,											
Middletown,	J. T. Beekman,	110	600	125		17				142	8	12
Minisink,	C. C. Eltinge,					90	2	2	2	190	11	25
Mahakkamak,	Do.				1	29		2	3	130	4	5
Walpack,	Vacant,											

CLASSIS OF BERGEN.

CHURCHES.	PASTORS.	No. of Families	Total of the Congregation	In communion per last Report	Rc'd On Certificate	Rc'd On Confession	Dismissed	Suspended	Died	Total in Communion	Infants	Adults
Bergen,	B. C. Taylor,	185	1050	195	2	12	1		10	198	24	2
Hackensack,	J. V. C. Romeyn,	90		98								
E. Neighbourhood,*	Philip Duryea,	100			12	16	1	1	8	71	32	
Belville,	Gustavus Abeel,	120		118	9	21	1		2	145	30	
Fairfield,	Henry A. Raymond,	170	1000	133		2	1		2	132	18	
Pompton Plains,	James R. Talmage,	170	1060	108		6				114	25	
Pompton,	Isaac S. Demund,	130		100	2	11	1	1		111	8	1
Montville,	Frederic F. Cornell,	100	500	50	3	17			1	70	10	1
Ponds,	Z. H. Kuypers,	65	353	46		16	1			65	19	
Preakness,	Do.	55	251	48						53	10	
Wyckoff,	Do.	78	457	62						67	15	
Bergen Neck,	Ira C. Boice,	64	384	35	1	5			2	39	7	
Jersey City,	Vacant,	56	254	63	2	1	2		3	61	9	
Schraalenberg,	Vacant,	166		157								
Stonehouse Plains,	Vacant,											

Minister without charge—Rev. John Duryea.

* N. B. The Report from the Church at English Neighbourhood is for four years.

CLASSIS OF PARAMUS.

CHURCHES.	PASTORS.	No. of Families	Total of the Congregation	In communion per last Report	Rc'd On Certificate	Rc'd On Confession	Dismissed	Suspended	Died	Total in Communion	Infants	Adults
Tappan,	N. Lansing,	161	617	150	1	13	4		5	155	34	3
Clarkstown,	Alex. H. Warner,	159	714		3	3			5	160	11	
Saddle river and }	Stephen Goetchius,	147	611	248	1	5	3	2	3	250	16	
Pasgack }	Do.	72	225	51						51	8	
Paramus & 1st Ref. }	W. Eltinge,	170	1065	286		10		3	2	291	25	
D. C. of Totowa, }	Do.	130	765	112						121	23	2
Warwick,	J. I. Christie,				2	5	7		1		3	1
2d Ref. D.C. Totowa,	Isaac D. Cole,	100	450	11	5	4				90	23	
Aquackinunck,	Wm. R. Bogardus,	200	1068	119	3	42			2	160	29	2
West New-Hamp- }	J. Wynkoop,											
stead & Ramapo, }	Do.											

The Quakers, or Society of Friends, as is well known, have been divided into two great parts, each claiming to hold the ancient doctrines of the church. As these parts do not concur in the account of their former or present condition, we have deemed it proper to publish the statement of each. Both parties claim the venerated name of " Friends," but we are compelled to distinguish them by the titles they give to each other. The first of the following statements is given by the *Hicksite*, and the second by the *Orthodox* party.

1st. "Friends' meetings in New Jersey, and members.—Burlington quarterly meeting, before the division, was composed of five monthly meetings, eighteen meetings for worship, and 1849 members.

Burlington quarterly meeting of Friends, since the division, is composed of four monthly meetings, fourteen meetings for worship, and 1049 members.

And that of the Orthodox Friends, four monthly meetings, thirteen meetings for worship, and 800 members.

Haddonfield quarterly meeting, before the division, was composed of five monthly meetings, ten meetings for worship, 1686 members.—Haddonfield quarterly meetings of Friends, since the division, is composed of four monthly meetings, six meetings for worship, 859 members. That of the Orthodox Friends consists of five monthly meetings, nine meetings for worship, and 827 members.

Salem quarterly meeting, before the division, was composed of five monthly meetings, ten meetings for worship, 1536 members.—Salem quarterly meeting of Friends, since the division, is composed of five monthly meetings, ten meetings for worship, and 1238 members. And that of the Orthodox Friends, three monthly meetings, four meetings for worship, and 298 members.

Shrewsbury quarterly meeting, before the division, was composed of four monthly meetings, eight meetings for worship, and 925 members.—Shrewsbury quarterly meeting of Friends, since the division, is composed of four monthly meetings, eight meetings for worship, and 750 members. And that of the Orthodox Friends, of two monthly meetings, three meetings for worship, and 175 members. About 6000 members, in New Jersey, in all."

2d. " The following statement of the number of members in the Society of Friends previous to the late division, and also of the two portions into which it has been separated, is made out from authentic sources, and a careful examination of the state of the respective meetings.

At the time of the separation, there were in the state of New Jersey four quarterly meetings, nineteen monthly meetings, and forty-six meetings for divine worship. Friends now hold five quarterly meetings, fourteen monthly meetings, and twenty-nine meetings for divine worship.

The quarterly meetings are as follow:—Burlington quarterly consisted, before the separation, of five monthly meetings, and eighteen meetings for worship, comprising two thousand one hundred and twenty-five members. Since the separation, it has four monthly meetings, twelve meetings for worship, and one thousand one hundred and eighty-eight members. The Hicksites, in this quarter, are nine hundred and thirty-seven in number, and hold four monthly meetings.

Haddonfield quarterly meeting, both before and since the separation, consisted of five monthly meetings, and ten meetings for worship, embracing one thousand seven hundred and eighty-eight members, of whom six hundred and forty-four went with the Hicksites, and forty-seven remained undivided, leaving one thousand and ninety-seven Friends. The Hicksites, in this quarter, hold four monthly meetings.

Salem quarterly meeting, before the division, had five monthly meetings, and ten meetings for worship, including one thousand six hundred and three members. Since the separation, Friends hold four meetings for worship, and three monthly meetings, embracing four hundred and fifty-four members. The Hicksites have one thousand one hundred and forty-five members, and hold five monthly meetings.

Shrewsbury and Rahway quarterly meeting, at the time of the separation, was composed of four monthly meetings, eight meetings for worship, and eight hundred and eighty-eight members. Friends now hold two monthly meetings, and three meetings for worship, including two hundred and thirty-three members. The Hicksites, in this quarter, are six hundred and fourteen in number, and hold four monthly meetings. There were forty-one members who did not side with either party."

```
The whole number of Friends in New Jersey is,  - - - - - - - -  2,972
                          Hicksites,  - - - - - - - - - - - - -  3,344
                          Neutrals,   - - - - - - - - - - - -       81
                                                                  ─────
      Total,  - - - - - - - - - - - - - - - - - - - - - -        6,404
                                                                  ─────
```

See Foster's Report, vol. II. p. p. 388 and 395.

Of the forty-five meeting houses in which meetings of Friends were held previous to the separation, there are now *five* in the exclusive possession of Friends—*fifteen* which are occupied by Friends and Hicksites, jointly,—and *twenty-five* in the exclusive possession of the Hicksites."

RECAPITULATION.

Thus it appears that the Presbyterians have 85 churches.

```
                      Baptists,  - - -  61  do.
                      Methodists,  - -  64  ministers.
                      Episcopalians,  -  33  churches.
                      Dutch Reformed,   36  do.
                      Quakers,  - - -   67  meetings.
      Other denominations, conjectural,  10
                                         ───
      Total number,  - - - - - - -      356
                                         ───
```

In this summary, we have given, we believe correctly, the number of churches of each denomination, save that of the Methodist, which has many more churches than ministers; but we have not been able to ascertain the number of churches, although we have taken much pains for that purpose. In the circuits, there are commonly not less than two churches or congregations to a minister; but in such cases the congregations consist of few members. Many of the churches have no pastors. The Quakers, it is well known, have none; and of the 289 churches which remain in the list after deducting their meeting houses, we consider that 39 may continue constantly vacant. We have then 250 churches whose maintenance may be deemed a steady charge upon the people.

In the maintenance of the churches, we include all the expenditures for religious purposes, comprehending the sums conventionally paid to the pastors, the donations of every kind, made directly to them or for their use, the amount expended in the erection and repair of churches, and in aids to bible missionary and tract societies; and we, upon consultation with distinguished clergymen of various denominations, set down as an average expenditure for each church, the sum of $480 per annum, which, multiplied by 250 churches, make the actual charge of $120,000, upon the state for all the expenses of religion, and which we consider sufficiently liberal to cover the expenses of the Society of Friends for the like purpose. The Quakers, have no salaried clergy; and the expenses of their association consist of the very small sums requisite to keep their meeting houses and grave yards inrepair, and the contributions for the support and education of their poor members. Demands of this kind are rare and occasional, only; and the interest of funds vested for schools, by Friends, has been employed in the education of the poor children of other denominations.

In addition to the 356 churches of all denominations, which the State contains, the inhabitants have exemplified their disposition to sustain and improve their moral condition, by the establishment of bible societies, missionary societies, Sunday school unions, and temperance societies. In every county there are bible societies, in most, considerable sums are collected for the missionary cause, and almost every thickly settled neighbourhood has its Sunday school. Temperance societies, in many districts, have effectually bruised the head of the *worm of the still.*

The cultivation of literature and science has, until of late years, been too little regarded; but not less, than in the adjacent and more wealthy states. Yet in the higher departments the "College of New Jersey," at Princeton, has for more than eighty years maintained a reputation unsurpassed in the Union; Rutger's College, at New Brunswick, has, for several years, been in successful operation; academies have been established in most of the county towns and large villages; and common schools are every where seen in populous districts. The "School Fund," which has lately been established, will rapidly increase, and will, at no distant day, furnish means to teach the rudiments of science to the whole population. We proceed to give a more particular notice of the colleges and the school fund.

The "College of New Jersey" was first incorporated in the year 1746, and in 1748 obtained, through the aid of Governor Belcher, an ample and liberal charter from George II., which, after the revolution, was confirmed by the legislature of this State. The institution was located, first, at Elizabethtown, under the direction of the Rev. Jonathan Dickenson. Upon his death, in 1748, it was removed to Newark, and the Rev. Aaron Burr became its president. In the year 1756, it was permanently established at Princeton, whither president Burr removed with his pupils, and where for nearly eighty years it has maintained a high and unvarying reputation, as a seat of literature and science; and, with occasional diminution of numbers, has continued to command a large share of public confidence and patronage.

The present number of under graduates (1833) is one hundred and forty-four. The faculty consists of a president, seven professors, and three tutors.

Provision is made for imparting instruction in the Greek, Latin, French, Spanish, German, Italian, and English languages; in mathematics, (the study of which is pursued to an extent, not excelled by any college in the country,) in natural philosophy, in chemistry, and the various branches of natural history; in belles lettres, in mental and moral philosophy, in logic, political economy, natural theology, the evidences of christianity, and the exposition of the holy scriptures; in anatomy and physiology, in architecture, and civil engineering. The libraries of the college, and two literary societies connected with it, contain about twelve thousand volumes. The college has a very valuable philosophical and chemical apparatus, a museum of natural history, a small anatomical museum, and a mineralogical cabinet.

The principal edifice, called Nassau Hall, is one hundred and seventy-six feet long, fifty wide, and four stories high, and is used chiefly for the lodging of students: another building, erected for the same purpose in 1833, is one hundred and twelve feet in length, and four stories high. There are two other buildings, each sixty-sixfeet in length, by thirty-six in breadth, and three stories high. One of them contains the library and recitation rooms; the other the refectory, museum, and chemical laboratory.

There are also, at Princeton, several other literary institutions, (see Princeton,) among which, the theological seminary claims the first place.

This school was founded by the General Assembly of the Presbyterian Church of the United States, and is under its control and patronage. The plan of the institution was formed in 1811, and carried into effect in May, 1812, by the appointment of trustees, and a professor of didactic and polemical theology. The latter was inaugurated, and entered upon his duties, with three students only, on the 12th August following. In May, of 1813, a professor of ecclesiastical history was named, and ten years afterwards, the plan was completed by the nomination of a professor of oriental and biblical literature.

The edifice for the use of the seminary, commenced in 1813 and rendered habitable in the autumn of 1817, is of stone, one hundred and fifty feet long, fifty wide, and four stories high, including the basement; and is regarded as a model of economical, neat, and tasteful architecture. Besides the apartments for the library, recitations, refectory, and the steward, there are accommodations for eighty students.

This institution is conducted on very liberal principles; for, though founded and supported by the Presbyterian church, and primarily intended to promote the training of a pious and learned ministry for that church, students of all Christian denominations are admitted into a full participation of its benefits, upon equal terms. It is wholly unconnected with the college, but enjoys, by contract, the free use of the college library.

The funds of the institution, though considerable, are yet inadequate to the full support of its officers. The endowment of four professorships has been commenced, but none is fully completed. Twenty-three scholarships have been founded, by as many benevolent individuals, and maintain that number of poor and pious youth, in a course of theological study. There are, here, two public libraries; one called after the Rev. Ashbel Green, D. D. L. L. D., one of the most ardent and liberal of its contributors; and the other presented by the synod of the Associate Reformed Church, and named the "Mason Library," in honour of the Rev. John M. Mason, D. D. by whose exertions, chiefly, it was collected. The former contains six, and the latter four thousand volumes.

The course of study is extended through three years. The first is devoted to the Hebrew language, exegetical study of the scriptures, biblical criticism, biblical antiquities, introduction to the study of the scriptures, mental and moral science, evidences of natural and revealed religion, sacred chronology, and biblical history. The *second* to the continued exegetical study of the Hebrew and Greek scriptures, and to didactic theology and ecclesiastical history. The *third* to polemic theology, church government, pastoral theology, composition and delivery of sermons. The classes are distinguished, numerically, into *First, Second and Third.* The members of the first, or highest class, are required to exhibit original compositions, once in two weeks; those of the second class, once in three weeks; and those of the third class, once in four weeks.

There are three vacations in each year. The first of six weeks, from the first Thursday of May; the second of six weeks, from the last Wednesday of September; and the third of two weeks, in the month of Feb., at the discretion of the professors. Board may be obtained at various prices, from $1 25 to $1 75 per week; firewood from $4 to $6 per annum; washing, $7; each student pays to the seminary $10 per annum, towards the general expense fund; but there is no charge for tuition, use of library, &c. The number of students on the catalogue of the institution for the current year (1833) is 132.

Rutgers' College, located at New Brunswick, was chartered by George III. in 1770, and was called Queen's College, in honour of his consort. The present name was substituted by the legislature of the State, in 1825, at request of the trustees, in honour of Col. Henry Rutgers, of New York, to whom the institution is indebted for liberal pecuniary benefactions. The charter was originally granted to such Protestants as had adopted the constitution of the reformed churches in the Netherlands, as revised by the national synod of Dordrecht, in the years 1618 and 1619. That synod, composed of distinguished delegates from almost all denominations of Protestant Europe, formed one of the most august ecclesiastical assemblies of modern times. Their doctrines as embodied in the confession of faith and catechisms of the Reformed Dutch Church in America, substantially comports. with the 39 articles of the church of England, and entirely with the doctrines of the Presbyterian church in the United States; and the government of the church is strictly Presbyterian. This denomination of Christians is established chiefly in New York, New Jersey, and Pennsylvania. In the city of New York, alone, it has twelve churches, in which divine worship has long been exclusively conducted in the English language.

Dr. Jacob R. Hardenburg, an American, was appointed first president of the college, in 1789; he was distinguished by a powerful mind, great piety and industry, and success in the ministry. He died in 1792.

The Theological College of the Reformed Dutch Church is established here, and intimately blended with the literary institution. At a meeting in New York, Oct. 1771, of *Coetus* and *Conferentie,* until then, contending parties in the church, peace was restored, and a plan laid for the organization of this, the first theological school in America. Its completion, however, was delayed by the revolutionary war, until 1784, when the Rev. Dr. John H. Livingston, was chosen professor of didactic and polemical theology, who performed the duties of this office, in New York, in connexion with his pastoral services. In 1807, by a covenant between the trustees and the synod, the professorate was united with the college; of which, in 1810, Dr. Livingston was chosen president, on the death of Dr. Ira Condict. The duties of the literary institution were at this time suspended, for want of funds. Dr. Livingston died, 20th January, 1825, in the 79th year of his age, the 55th of his ministry, and the 41st of his professorial labours.

At a general synod, convened at Albany, in February, 1825, the Rev. Philip Milledoler, D. D., was chosen professor of didactic and polemical theology; and in the September following, was elected, by the trustees, president of the college, and professor of the evidences of christianity and moral philosophy. At the same time a plan was matured for reviving the literary institution; by which, one of the theological professors must always be chosen president of the college, and each of such professors must hold a professorship therein, and be a member of its faculty.

The effect of this amalgamation of theology and literature, is said to have been highly favourable to the moral character of the institution, and not to have imparted to it a sectarian influence.

The college edifice, of dark red freestone, is a handsome spacious building, surmounted by a cupola. It is reared on an eminence near the town, a site of great beauty, presented to the institution by the honourable James Parker, of Amboy. The views from thence, embracing great variety of scenery, of mountain and valley, forest and river, are delightfully picturesque, and the country is as healthy as it is lovely. The institution may be considered in a flourishing condition. The number of students in September, 1833, was eighty, with the prospect of much increase during the session. The charge for board and tuition is about $125 per annum. The students board in respectable private families, under the supervision of the faculty, where their habits, morals, and manners are duly regarded. The number of students in theology has varied from sixteen to thirty. There are three libraries; that of the college is large and valuable, and those pertaining to the Peithesopian and Philoclean Societies, are respectable. The cabinet of minerals is considerable, and increasing; and the philosophical and chemical apparatus extensive.

The faculty (in 1833) consists of the Rev. *Philip Milledoler*, D. D., president, professor of moral philosophy and didactic and polemical theology; the Rev. *Jacob J. Janeway*, D. D. vice president and professor of rhetoric, evidences of christianity, political economy, &c.; the Rev. *James S. Cannon*, D. D., professor of metaphysics and philosophy of the human mind, of ecclesiastical history, church government, and pastoral theology; *Theodore Strong*, A. A. S., C. A. S., professor of mathematics and natural philosophy; the Rev. *Alexander M'Clelland*, D. D., professor of oriental and biblical literature; *Lewis Black*, M. D., professor of chemistry and natural history; *John D. Ogilby*, A. M., professor of languages; and *Frederic Ogilby*, A. B., assistant instructer of languages.

The grammar school attached to the college, and under the immediate inspection of the trustees and faculty, is committed to the rectorship of the Rev. *Cornelius D. Westbrook*, D. D., assisted by *Isaac A. Blauvelt*, A. M., an alumnus of the college.

The location of this college equidistant from Philadelphia and New York, the healthfulness and beauty of the adjacent country, the excellent morals which prevail in the city as in the college, the high character and capability of the professors, and the cheapness of tuition and subsistence, give this institution strong claims to the attention of the public.

The first step towards the establishment of the school fund of this State, commenced with the act of 9th February, 1816, which directed the treasurerto invest in the public six per cent. stocks of the United States, the sum of $15,000, arising from the payment of the funded debt, and from the dividends on the stock held by the State in the Trenton Bank; and at the end of every year, to invest the interest on the capital, in the same manner.

On the 12th February of the succeeding year, the "Act to create a fund for free schools" was passed, setting apart the stock and its accumulations vested under the act of 1816; the dividends on the stock held by the State, in the Cumberland Bank, and in the Newark Turnpike Company, the proceeds of the sale of a house and lot, in New Brunswick, the property of the State, and one-tenth part of all monies, thereafter raised by tax for State use; and the treasurer was instructed to vest these as they came to his hands, in the public stocks of the United States. By the act of 12th February, 1818, the governor, vice-president of council, speaker of assembly, the attorney general, and secretary of state, for the time being, were appointed "Trustees for the support of Free Schools;" and the treasurer was directed to transfer to them the school funds, to be by them applied in the mode to be prescribed by the State, reserving to the legislature the authority to change the existing fund, and to dissolve the trust at pleasure; and requiring an account of the fund to be annually laid before the legislature. This act made the following additions to the fund.—The balance of the old six per cent. stock, due 12th February, 1817, with the interest and reimbursement thereof since 9th Feb., 1816; the three per cent. stock of the U. States, belonging to the State on the 12th February, 1817; the shares of the State in the Trenton and Cumberland Banks, with the dividends since 9th February, 1816; all monies receivable from the foregoing items, future appropriations, and such gifts and grants, bequests and devises, as should be made for the purposes contemplated by the act; and one-tenth part of the State tax for the year 1817. The last appropriation, being, specifically, one-tenth of the tax, has been construed as repealing the general appropriation on the tax under the act of 1817.

The fund thus augmented and transferred to the trustees amounted to $113,238 78, and consisted of the following sums:—

1st. Six per cent. stock U. States, purchased under the law of 1816,	$15,000 00
2d. Six per cent. stock United States, purchased under act 1817,	16,224 15
3d. Stock in Newark Turnpike Company, - - - -	12,500 00
4th. Three per cent. stock of United States, - - - -	7,009 12

5th. Interest, and reimbursement, of the principal of the deferred six
 per cent. stock of United States, - - - - - 7,810 73
6th. Twelve hundred'shares Trenton Bank stock, - - - 36,000 00
7th. Forty shares in the Cumberland Bank, - - - - 2,000 00
8th. Interest and dividends from the several stocks since 9th Feb. 1816, 10,429 66
9th. Cash and one-tenth of State tax for 1817, - - - - 6,265 12
Since 1818, there have been added to the principal of the fund the following
items by legislative appropriation :—
1st. Proceeds of sale of the State House in Jersey City, - - $4,907 64
2d. Twenty-two shares in Sussex Bank, - - - - - 1000 00
3d. Donation from William J. Bell & Co. - - - - 23 15
4th. Bonus of People's Bank at Paterson, recd. 26th Sept. 1825, 4,000 00
5th. Bonus from Monmouth Bank, 9th June, 1825, - - - 800 00
6th. Sale of part of a lot in Trenton, - - - - - 1,061 00
7th. Under the act 28th December, 1824, one-tenth of State tax, and
 tax on Monmouth bank for the year 1826, - - - 2,200 00
 Same, 1827, - - - - - - - - - 2,200 00
 Same, 1828, - - - - - - - - - 3,200 00
8th. Under the act 5th March, 1828, repealing act of 28th December.
 1824, and in lieu of one-tenth of the State tax, giving all the tax
 from banking, insurance and other incorporated companies, which,
 in the year 1829, amounted to - - - - 11,709 58
And estimated to produce, annually, $10,000.

                  $31,101 37

Making whole amount of appropriations by legislature, in 1830, $144,240 15

In the management of the fund, great advantage has arisen from the act of 18th
Feb. 1829, directing the investment of the annual income in advance, by which the
trustees were empowered, to invest on or before the first of March, annually, an
amount equal to the estimated receipts of the fund during the year, to be advanced
by the State treasurer, and to be replaced by him as the monies accruing from the
fund shall be received; thus enabling the trustees to invest at one time all the income of the year.

The sources of income of the school fund, are now, the dividends on the various
stock which the trustees hold, and which, in October 1832, amounted to $228,611 75.
And the annual tax of half per cent. upon the dividends of the several bank and insurance companies of the State, which amounts annually to near $11,000.

The first expenditure which has been directed out of the fund, was by the " act
establishing common schools," passed 21st February, 1829, appropriating annually
$20,000 from the income of the fund, for the establishment and maintenance of
schools. This act was altered and amended by the act of 1st March, 1830. But both
acts were repealed by that of 16th February, 1831, by which the system of common
schools is now regulated. That act appropriates $20,000 annually, from the in-
come of the school fund, to the establishment and maintenance of such schools; and
directs, in case such annual income shall not have been received in full on the first
Monday of April, or shall be insufficient to cover the appropriation, the trustees to
draw from the State treasury for the deficiency; such amount to be replaced from
the annual receipts of the school fund. The act further provides, that the trustees
shall apportion the sum, so appropriated, among the several counties, in the ratio of
their taxes paid for the support of government, and shall file a list of such apportionment with the treasurer, that he may notify the collectors of the several counties, to
draw for the same ; that the boards of chosen freeholders, of the respective counties, shall at their annual meetings, apportion among the several townships, the monies received by the collectors, in the ratio of the county tax paid by the several
townships, a list of which apportionments, the clerk of the freeholders is required, to
file, to deliver a copy thereof, to the county collector, and to notify the collectors
of the several townships of the amounts so apportioned, suce collectors report such
amounts to the inhabitants, at their next annual town meeting ; that may, (and they
are recommended so to do,) at such meetings, raise, by tax or otherwise, such additional sum for the same object, as they may deem proper ; and may authorize the
township collector, to draw on the county collector, for the amount apportioned, and

may apply the sum received from the State, to schooling the indigent poor of the township, if they so elect; that the inhabitants at their town meetings, annually, shall choose, as other town officers are chosen, three or more persons, who shall constitute the school committee, and whose duty is to recognise and ascertain the number of common schools within their respective townships; that the patrons, supporters, or proprietors of the several common schools in the respective townships, be authorized to organize such schools, by the appointment of a board of trustees, in such form, and consisting of such number, as they may deem proper; and any board of trustees so organized shall transmit to the school committee, of the proper township, a certificate of its organization, and shall thereon be recognised by the committee as entitled to an apportionment of the monies assigned to such township from the school fund.   And such trustees are required to render to the school committees, on or before the first Monday of April, annually, a statement of the average number of scholars resident in the township, taught in such school during each quarter of the preceding year, and where from convenience, scholars from an adjoining township attend such school, to report their number &c. to the school committee of such adjoining township; to visit and inspect the affairs of their respective schools, to apply the monies received, at discretion, for their benefit, and at the end of every year, to exhibit to the school committee, a correct account of the expenditure of such monies; that the school committees, at or before the end of their term of service, shall apportion the whole of the monies assigned to their respective townships, and raised therein, among such common schools, in the ratio of the number of scholars reported to them, respectively, during the preceding year; or where any township may elect to appropriate such funds exclusively to the education of the poor, to apportion the same among the several schools, in proportion to the number of poor children taught; and shall draw in favour of the boards of trustees respectively, for the amount of their several dividends, on the town collector; and shall on or before the first Wednesday of May, yearly, transmit to the clerk of the board of chosen freeholders of their respective counties, a written statement, embracing the number of common schools duly organized within their respective townships, the number of scholars taught therein, the amount of the monies received by them from the township collector, and raised by the township, and the manner in which the same has been applied; that such clerk shall condense such statements into a report, in writing, and transmit the same to the trustees of the school fund, to be laid before the legislature, in a condensed form.   No compensation is allowed under this act.

It will be observed, that in framing this system, no attempt has been made to coerce the respective townships into raising monies, in addition to their allotted share of the sum appropriated from the school fund; but, in accordance with the spirit of the government of the State, which considers the townships as integral corporations, whose inhabitants are competent to judge of their wants, and possess the means to supply them, the legislature has, we think, wisely left with each township, the liberty to tax itself for the purposes of education, as to it may seem meet; whilst it has promptly offered all the aid which it has to bestow.   It is possible, that learning may advance less rapidly, than if urged by a forced culture; but we are not sure, that the happiness of the people will be less promoted.   We would not be understood to mean that literature is not a source of happiness; but it is not the only one. He who is compelled to a diet which is unacceptable to his appetite, will not boast of his enjoyment; and we have no difficulty in determining, which is the most hospitable host, he who forces manna upon the revolting stomach of his guest, or he, who, placing the dish before him, permits him to eat at pleasure, whilst he expatiates upon its agreeable and nourishing properties.   None, properly instructed, would reject the joys of paradise; but, were paradise a prison, we should long to leap its crystal walls.   Emulation, we think, will soon be awakened among the townships of each county, and among the counties, upon this all-important subject; and although the sum of $20,000 is a small one to distribute among a population of 330,000 souls, it will have one excellent effect; it will turn, periodically, the attention of the people to the means of mental improvement, will set them to compare their condition with that of their neighbours, and when inferior, to improve it. For it may be taken as a truism, that when the people are at liberty to consider and improve their condition, they will, when dissatisfied, amend it.

Among the provisions for enlightening the public mind, we may justly include those for publishing the laws, not only of the State, but also of the general government. The act of 7th June, 1820, directs: 1st, That the secretary of state shall cause the laws of the State to be published immediately after the passing thereof, in one of the public newspapers, of the city of Trenton; and that they shall also be published in a pamphlet form, together with the votes and proceedings of assembly, the journals of council, and minutes of joint meetings, and delivered by the printer within sixty days from the rising of the legislature, to the State treasurer, who shall distribute them in the following manner, at the expense of the State, viz:—to himself, two copies; to the governor, for himself, three copies, and also to be forwarded by him, and presented to the secretary of state of the United States, four copies; to the executive of each state, and territory of the United States, for the use of the executives and legislatures, three copies; to each of the senators, and representatives of this State, in congress, one copy; to the president of the American Antiquarian Society, one copy; to the justices of the Supreme Court, the attorney general, secretary of state, clerk of council, assembly, Courts of Chancery and Supreme Court, each one copy; to the clerk of the council, for the use of council and assembly, sixty copies; and the remainder among the several counties in the ratio they contribute to the support of the government, directed to the county collector. The county collector, retaining a copy for himself, transmits, at the expense of the county, one set of the laws and proceedings, to each of the following officers:—the judges and clerk of the Common Pleas, the justices of the peace, the magistrates of corporate towns, the sheriff, surrogate, clerk of the board of chosen freeholders, and the representatives of the county in the legislature, and each incorporated library company; and divides the remainder among the several townships of the county, transmitting equal proportions to the clerk of each township, who, retaining one copy for the use of the township, causes the residue to be distributed among the officers of the township, giving preference in the following order:—to the assessor, collector, chosen freeholders, and overseers of the poor, each one set.

The laws of the United States, apportioned to this State by Congress, are distributed by the treasurer, at the expense of the State; to himself, to the governor, attorney general, justices of Supreme Court, secretary of state, members of the legislature, each one set; to the clerk of council, and the clerk of the assembly, four sets; to the librarians of Princeton college, and to the two library societies in the college, each one set; and the remainder, among the counties in proportion to their quota of State taxes, to be transmitted to the collectors, and by them distributed to the clerk and judges of the court of Common Pleas, each one set, and to every public library one set; and the residue, as may be directed by the board of chosen freeholders.

Reports of the decisions of the Supreme and Chancery Courts are annually prepared by officers appointed by the legislature for a term of five years, who receive a compensation of $200 per annum. Such reports are printed, and distributed, annually, with the pamphlet laws.

Lastly, and certainly not least, among the agents of moral improvement, we must rank the periodical journals of the State. The commonwealth partakes largely in the benefits flowing from the press, in the cities of Philadelphia and New York, and we therefore might suppose would not extensively encourage newspapers within her own boundaries; yet she has not less than thirty-one weekly papers, engaged in sowing broadcast the germs of literature and science. Of these useful auxiliaries we annex the following table.

NEWSPAPERS.	EDITORS.	WHERE PUBLISHED.
Bergen County Courier,		Jersey City, Bergen Co.
Sussex Register,	Hall,	Newton, Sussex Co.
N. J. Herald,	Grant Fitch,	Do. do.
Belvidere Apollo,	Franklin Ferguson,	Belvidere, Warren Co.
Warren Journal,	Fitch & Co.	Do. do.
Palladium of Liberty,	John R. Eyres,	Morristown, Morris Co.
Jerseyman,	Robbins,	Do. do.
Rahway Advocate,	Thomas Green,	Rahway, Middlesex.
Fredonian,	Randolph and Carman,	New Brunswick, do.
Times,		Do. do.
Sentinel of Freedom,	George Bush & Co.	Newark, Essex.
Daily Advertiser,		Do. do.
Newark Monitor,	S. L. B. Baldwin,	Do. do.
Do. Eagle,	Bartlett and Crowell,	Do. do.

Princeton Courier,	Baker and Connolly,	Princeton, Somerset.
American System,	J. Robinson & Co.	Do. do.
Somerset Messenger,	Gore and Allison,	Somerville, do.
State Gazette,	George Sherman,	Trenton, Hunterdon.
National Union,	E. B. Adams,	Do. do.
Emporium,	Joseph Justice,	Do. do.
Hunterdon Gazette,	Chas. George,	Flemington, do.
Monmouth Enquirer,	John J. Bartleson,	Freehold, Monmouth,
Burlington Herald,	Joseph Pugh,	Mount Holly, Burlington.
Mount Holly Mirror,	Nathan Palmer,	Do. do.
Camden Mail,	Sickler and Ham,	Camden, Gloucester.
National Republican,	Josiah Harrison,	Do. do.
Village Herald,	Joseph Sailor,	Woodbury, do.
Salem Statesman,	H. H. Elwell,	Salem, Salem.
Do. Messenger,	Elijah Brooks,	Do. do.
Washington Whig,	Nelson and Powers,	Bridgeton, Cumberland.
Bridgeton Observer,	F. Pierson,	Do. do.

GAZETTEER OF NEW JERSEY.

—••••◉◉●••••—

ACQ

Absecum, post town of Galloway t-ship, Gloucester co., 50 miles S. E. from Woodbury, 95 from Trenton, and 105 from W. C., upon Absecum creek, about two miles above Absecum bay, contains a tavern, store, and 8 or 10 dwellings, surrounded by sand, and pine forest.

Absecum Creek rises by several branches, on the line between Galloway and Egg Harbour t-ship, Gloucester co., and flows S. E., by a course of 8 or 9 miles, into Absecum bay. It gives motion to several saw mills.

Absecum Bay, a salt marsh lake, Gloucester co., on the line of Egg Harbour and Galloway t-ship, circular in form, and about 2 miles in diameter, communicating with Reed's bay, and by a broad channel, called Absecum Inlet, 4 miles in length, with the ocean.

Absecum Beach, on the Atlantic Ocean; extends, eastwardly, from Great Egg Harbour Inlet, about 9 miles to Absecum Inlet; broken, however, by a narrow inlet, near midway between its extremities.

Ackerman's Run, small stream, 2 miles long, flowing to the Passaic River, about 3 miles below Paterson, from Saddle River t-ship, Bergen co.

Acquackanonck, t-ship, Essex co., bounded on the N. W., N. E. and E. by the Passaic river, which forms a semi-ellipsis, N. by Paterson t-ship, and S. by Bloomfield and Caldwell t-ships; centrally distant, N. from Newark, 10 miles; greatest length, E. and W. 7, breadth N. and S. 6½ miles; area about 14,000 acres. Mountainous on the W., rolling on the E.; soil red shale, and where well cultivated, productive. Acquackanonck, Little Falls, and Weasel are

ALA

villages, of the t-ship; the two first, post towns. Acquackanonck, on the Passaic river, distant 5 miles S. E. of Paterson, is at the head of tide water, and consequently the outport of Paterson. Pop. in 1830, about 1,300. In 1832, the t-ship contained 300 taxables, 125 householders, 47 single men, 7 merchants, 6 grist mills, 2 cotton factories, 5 saw mills, 1 paper mill, 13 tan vats, one printing and bleaching establishment, 1 woollen factory, 345 horses and mules, and 766 neat cattle above 3 years of age; and it paid state tax, $230 62 cents; county, $607 37 c.; poor, $500; and road, $700. Aquackanouck town is a p-t, 8 miles N. E. of Newark, 224 from W. C., 58 from Trenton, 10 from New York, to which there is a turnpike and rail road. It contains 3 taverns, 6 stores, about 80 dwellings, and a Dutch Reformed church; has six sloops trading with New York. A small stream, which may be termed the Fourth river, runs near the town, and gives motion to several mills. Blatchley's mineral spring lies about 1½ miles W. of the town. This is the depot of lumber for the neighbourhood.

Alamuche, p-t. of Independence t-ship, Warren co., on the eastern part of the t-ship; by the post route 228 miles N. E. of W. C., and 65 from Trenton, and 17 from Belvidere the C. T.; seated on a small tributary of Pequest creek, and near a lake of the same name, contains a grist and saw mill, a grain distillery, a store, tavern, and 12 or 15 dwellings. It is surrounded by a limestone soil of excellent quality, well cultivated.

Alamuche Lake is one of the many mountain ponds which characterize this country, and which are, in many cases, reservoirs formed in limestone rock. This is about a mile in diameter, and sends forth a tributary to the Pequest creek.

Alamuche Mountain is one of the chain of hills which bounds the valley of the Musconetcong creek in Warren county.

Alberson's Brook, a tributary of Spruce Run, a fork of the south branch of the Raritan river, rises at the south foot of the Musconetcong mountain, and flows easterly by a course of 7 or 8 miles to its recipient.

Alexandria, p-t. of Alexandria t-ship, Hunterdon co., on the bank of the Delaware river, at the junction of Nischisakawick creek with that stream, 11 miles W. of Flemington, 35 N. of Trenton, 189 from W. C.; contains a tavern, store, grist mill, and 8 or 10 dwellings, a Presbyterian and an Episcopalian church.

Alexandria t-ship, Hunterdon co., bounded on the N. E. by Bethlehem t-ship, N. W. by the Musconetcong creek, which separates it from Warren co., and S. W. by the river Delaware; centrally distant, N. E. from Flemington, 12 miles; greatest length, E. and W., 12 miles; breadth, N. and S., 9 miles; area 33,000 acres. Surface on the N., mountainous, the Musconetcong mountain running N. W. across the t-ship. Soil, on the S. E., red shale; at the foot of the mountain, grey limestone; and on the mountain, clay, sand and loam. It is drained, S. W. by the Nischisakawick, the Hakehokake, and other small mill streams. Alexandria, Milford, Mount Pleasant, and Pittstown are p-towns of the t-ship. Pop., in 1830, 3,042. In 1832, the t-ship contained 10 saw mills, 7 grist mills, 4 oil mills, 4 ferries and toll bridges, 6 distilleries, 8 stores, 861 horses, 1287 neat cattle above the age of 3 years; and it paid poor tax, $1000; road tax, $800; and state and county tax, $1413 48 cents.

Allentown, p-t. of Upper Freehold t-ship, Monmouth co., near the western line of the county, between Doctor creek and Indian run, on the road

from Bordentown to Freehold, 8 miles from the former and 18 from the latter, 177 from W. C., and 11 from Trenton; contains from 75 to 80 dwellings; 1 Presbyterian church, with cupola and bell, handsomely situated on the hill on the west; an academy, 2 schools, 1 Methodist Church, grist mill, saw mill, and tilt mill, on Doctor creek, and saw mill on Indian run; below which, at a short distance west of the town, is a cotton manufactory. This is a compact pleasant village, with some very good frame and brick houses; but the lands around are sandy, and not of the best quality. A considerable business is done in the town.

Alexsocken Creek, a small mill stream of Amwell t-ship, Hunterdon co., which flows westerly into the Delaware river, by a course of 5 or 6 miles, about a mile above Lambertville.

Alloways Creek, Salem co., rises in the N. W. angle of Pittsgrove t-ship, and flows by a S. W. course of more than 20 miles, through Upper and Lower Alloways, and Elsinborough t-ships, to the Delaware river, below Reedy island. It is navigable above Allowaystown, in Upper Alloways t-ship, a distance of about twelve miles from the mouth, for wood shallops; along its margin for about 10 miles, are some excellent banked meadows.

Allowaystown, p-t. of Upper Alloways t-ship, Salem co., about 7 miles E. of Salem, 177 N. E. from W. C., and 71 S. from Trenton; contains from 70 to 80 dwellings, 2 taverns, 4 or 5 stores, 1 Methodist, and 1 Baptist church. The Messrs. Reeves, have here 2 very powerful saw mills, engaged principally in cutting ship timber, and a valuable grist mill, on the Alloways creek. They employ from 75 to 100 horses in drawing timber &c., to their works.

Alloways Creek, Upper, t-ship, Salem co., bounded N. E. by Pittsgrove t-ship, S. E. by Deerfield, Hopewell, and Stow creek t-ships, Cumberland co.; S. W. by Lower

Alloways creek t-ship, and N. W. by Elsinborough and Mannington t-ships; centrally distant, S. E. from Salem 7 miles. Greatest length E. and W. 10½, breadth N. and S. 9 miles. Area, about 34,000 acres; of which more than 10,000 are unimproved. Soil upon the N. E., stiff clay and loam; on the S. E. sand and gravelly loam, with rolling surface. The forest known as the "Barrens," runs here, producing much white oak and pine wood for market, which finds its way to Philadelphia, by Alloways creek. By the census of 1830, the township contained 2136 inhabitants, and by the assessor's abstract of 1832, 415 taxables, 5 grist mills, 10 saw mills, 2 carding machines, 1 fulling mill, 2 distilleries, 416 horses and mules, and 854 neat cattle, upwards of 3 years old; and it paid t-ship tax, $400; county tax, $834 10; State tax, $218 74. The t-ship is drained by Alloways creek, which runs centrally through it, by a S. W. course, and by Stow creek, which forms part of the southern boundary. Allowaystown and Quinton's Bridge, are villages and post-towns of the t-ship. Guineatown is a name given to a few negro huts, on the northern boundary. Friesburg, lies near the south line.

Alloways Creek, Lower, t-ship, Salem co., bounded N. by Elsinborough, Salem and Upper Alloways creek t-ships; on the E. by Upper Alloways creek t-ship; on the S. by Stow creek, which divides it from Stow creek and Greenwich t-ships, of Cumberland co., on the W. by the river Delaware; centrally distant, S. from Salem, 9 miles; greatest length N. and S. 12 miles; breadth E. and W. 9 miles; area, about 30,000 acres; surface level; soil on the W. for more than half the t-ship, marsh meadow, much of which is embanked; and on the E. a deep clay and loam well cultivated. It is drained by Alloways creek on the N., and Stow creek on the S., and by Hope creek, Deep creek, and

Muddy creek, small streams which flow into the Delaware, from the marsh between them. Pop. of the t-ship by census of 1830, 1222. By the assessor's abstract of 1832, it contained 260 taxables, 3 stores, 2. grist mills, 2 distilleries, 255 horses and mules, and 881 neat cattle above 3 years old. It has 3 schools, 1 Methodist, and 1 Friend's meeting house.

Amboy. See *South Amboy, Perth Amboy.*

Amwell t-ship, Hunterdon co., bounded N. by Lebanon t-ship, N. E. by Readington t-ship, E. by Hillsborough t-ship, of Somerset co., S. E. by Hopewell t-ship, and S. W. by the river Delaware, and N. W. by Ringwood t-ship. Greatest length N. and S. 16; breadth E. and W. 15 miles; area, 77,000 acres; surface hilly on the N. W. and S. E.; on the first, there being a clay ridge well timbered and productive, and on the latter, a chain of trap hills, rough, broken, and barren. The intervening space is undulating valley, of red shale, which, where covered with sufficient soil, is grateful for the care bestowed upon it, producing particularly fine crops of grass. The t-ship is drained on the N. E. by the south branch of the Raritan, on the N. W. by the Laokatong and Wickhechecoke creeks; S. W. by the Alexsocken and Smith's creeks, on the S. by Stony brook, flowing easterly to the Raritan river. Pop. in 1830, 7385; in 1832, the t-ship contained 2 Presbyterian churches, 4 stores, 8 fisheries, 15 saw mills, 21 grist mills, 3 oil mills, 2 ferries and toll bridges, 88 tan vats, 12 distilleries, 4 carding machines, 2 fulling mills; and it paid poor tax, $1200; road tax, $2500; State and county tax, $3722 62. Flemington, Sergeantsville, Ringoes, Prallsville, Lambertsville, are p-ts. of the t-ship.

Anderson, p-t. of Mansfield t-ship, Warren co., on the turnpike road leading from Philipsburg to Schooley's mountain, and between the Morris canal and Musconetcong creek, within a mile of either; distant by the post route from W. C. 205, from Trenton 49, and from Belvidere, the co. town, E. 11 miles; 16 miles from Easton, and 25 from Morristown; contains 2 stores and 15 dwellings; situate in a fertile limestone valley. Lands valued at $50 the acre.

Andover p-t., Newton t-ship, Sussex co., on the south angle of the t-ship on the Newton turnpike road, distant by the post-route from W. C. 228, from Trenton 65, and from Newton 5 miles.

Andover Forge, Byram t-ship, Sussex co., on the N. bank of the Musconetcong river, at the junction of Lubber run with that stream, and within 2 miles of the Morris canal, is situate in a very narrow valley, and has around it a store, saw mill, and some 6 or 8 dwellings.

Anthony, hamlet on Schooley's mountain, Lebanon t-ship, Hunterdon co., 18 miles N. E. of Flemington, on Spruce run; contains a saw mill, and some half dozen dwellings.

Arneystown, p-t. of Hanover t-ship, Burlington co., near the eastern line; 13 miles N. E. of Mount Holly, 175 from W. C., 11 from Trenton S. E., and 8 E. from Bordentown; contains a store, tavern, 15 dwellings, and a large meeting house pertaining to "Friends," surrounded by a country of fertile loam.

Arthur's Kill. See *Staten Island Sound.*

Artles' Brook, tributary of the north branch of the Raritan river, Bedminster t-ship, Somerset co., unites with its recipient after a S. course of five miles.

Asbury, p-t. of Mansfield t-ship, Warren co., in the S. W. angle of the t-ship near the Musconetcong creek, by post-route 199 miles from W. C., and 40 from Trenton, 11 miles S. E. from Belvidere; lying in a deep and narrow valley on a soil of rich limestone, contains a Methodist church, 2 grist mills, 1 saw mill, an oil mill, a woollen factory, 1 tavern, 3 stores, and about thirty dwellings.

Assiscunk Creek, Burlington co.,

rises on the line between Mansfield and Springfield t-ships, and flows westward about 14 miles, forming, for the greater part of that distance, the boundary between the t-ships, uniting with the Delaware river, between the city of Burlington and the point of Burlington island. It has one or two mills upon it.

Atquatqua Creek, branch of the Atsion river, rising on, and forming part of the S. W. boundary of Burlington co. It may be deemed the main stem of the river under another name.

Atsion, p-t. and furnace, on the Atsion river, partly in Galloway t-ship, Gloucester co., and partly in Washington t-ship, Burlington, co., 9 miles above the head of navigation, 12 miles from Medford, 17 from Mount Holly, on the road leading to Tuckerton, and 57 from Trenton. Besides the furnace, there are here, a forge, grist mill, and three saw mills. The furnace makes from 800 to 900 tons of castings, and the forge from 150 to 200 tons of bar iron annually. This estate, belonging to Samuel Richards, Esq., embraces what was formerly called Hampton furnace and forge, and West's mill, and contains about 60,000 acres of land. There are about 100 men employed here, and between 6 and 700 persons depending for subsistence upon the works.

Atsion River, main stem of Little Egg Harbour river, forming in part, the boundary between Gloucester and Burlington cos. It bears this name for about 14 miles above Pleasant Mills, and is formed by the union of the Atquatqua and Tuscomusco creeks. Atsion furnace is on the north side of the river, in Burlington co.

Augusta, p-t. of Frankford t-ship, Sussex co., distant by post-route from W. C. 233, from Trenton 75, and from Newton 7 miles, contains 7 or 8 dwellings and a Presbyterian church.

Babcock's Creek, Hamilton t-ship, Gloucester co., rises by 4 branches, viz: North, East, Main, and Jack Pudding, which, uniting near May's landing, flow westerly into the Great Egg Harbour river at that village.

Back Creek, Fairfield t-ship, Cumberland co., flows about 6 miles into Nautuxet cove, Delaware bay.

Back Water, branch of Maurice river, Millville t-ship, Cumberland co., has a westerly course to its recipient, of about 7 miles.

Bacon Creek, a tributary of Pequest creek, Independence t-ship, Warren co., having a westerly course of 2 or 3 miles.

Bacon's Neck, a strip of rich land, in Greenwich t-ship, Cumberland co., between Cohansey and Store creeks.

Back Neck, a strip of land of Fairfield t-ship, Cumberland co., comprehended by the bend of Cohansey creek and Cohansey cove.

Bambo Creek, small tributary of the Lamington river, rising in Chester t-ship, Morris co., and flowing by a southerly course of about 4 miles, to its recipient in Bedminster t-ship, Somerset co.

Baptisttown, Middletown t-ship, Hunterdon co. See *Holmdel*.

Baptisttown, p-t. Ringwood t-ship, Hunterdon co., 9 miles W. of Flemington, 33 N. of Trenton, and 187 from W. C., contains a tavern, a store, 8 or 10 dwellings, and a Baptist church. There is a Presbyterian church within a mile of the town. The surrounding country is level, with soil of red shale, of good quality, and carefully cultivated.

Bargaintown, Egg Harbour t-ship, Gloucester co., p-t., on Cedar Swamp creek, 4 miles from Great Egg Harbour bay, 45 S. E. from Woodbury, 90 from Trenton, and 200 by postroute from W. C., contains 2 taverns, 1 store, a grist mill, Methodist church, and about 30 dwellings.

Barnegat Bay, Monmouth co., extends N. from Barnegat Inlet to Metetecunk river, the distance of 20 miles, varying in breadth from 1 to 4 miles. It is separated from the ocean by Island Beach and Squam Beach, narrow strips of land no where exceeding a mile in width. It receives the waters of Metetecunk river, Kettle creek, Toms' river, Cedar creek, and Forked river. The inlet from the ocean is over a mile wide. By act of assembly, 21 Feb. 1833, authority was given to a company, by a canal, to connect the head of this bay with Manasquan Inlet, by which much time and space will be saved to vessels bound thence to New York. The capital proposed for this undertaking is $5000.

Barnegat, p-t. of Stafford t-ship, Monmouth co., near Barnegat Inlet, 36 miles S. from Freehold, 78 S. E. from Trenton, and 202 N. E. from W. C., contains about 50 dwellings, 3 taverns, 4 stores, on a sandy soil, surrounded by pine forest.

Barnesborough, village, of Greenwich t-ship, Gloucester co., 6 miles S. W. from Woodbury, contains a store, tavern, and 12 or 15 dwellings. It lies on the edge of the pines.

Barrentown, Freehold t-ship, Monmouth co., on the road from Freehold to Middletown, 4 miles from the one, and 10 from the other, contains some 6 or 7 dwellings, in a poor sandy country.

Baskingridge, p-t. of Bernard t-ship, Somerset co., 11 miles N. E. of Somerville, 213 from W. C., and 47 from Trenton, beautifully situated in a high, rich, well cultivated, and healthy country; contains a Presbyterian church, an academy for young gentlemen, in much repute, formerly under the care of Drs. Brownlee and Findlay. The residence and estate of General Lord Sterling were near this town.

Bass River Hotel, p-o., Little Egg Harbour t-ship, Burlington co., 183 miles N. E. from W. C., and 71 S. E. from Trenton.

Batsto River, Washington t-ship, Burlington co., a large branch of Little Egg Harbour river, which rises in Northampton t-ship, and flows by a southerly course of 16 miles, to the Atsion river, below Pleasant Mills; the united streams form the Little Egg Harbour river. Batsto Furnace is on the former within 2 miles of their junction, and near the head of the stream, are Hampton Furnace and Forge, now in ruins.

Batsto Furnace is about 8 miles above Gloucester Furnace, about 30 miles S. E. from Woodbury, and one from Pleasant Mills. There are made here 850 tons of iron, chiefly castings, giving employment to 60 or 70 men, and maintaining altogether near 400 persons. There are here also, a grist and saw mill, and from 50 to 60,000 acres of land appurtenant to the works

Bear Fort Mountain, near the W. boundary of Pompton t-ship, Bergen co. It is broken through by Woodruff's Gap, from which runs a branch of Belcher's creek, and by which passes the Ringwood and Long Pond turnpike road. The whole length of the range of hills in this t-ship is about 11 miles.

Bear Brook, western branch of Pequest creek, rises in Hunt's Pond, Green t-ship, Sussex co., and flows S. W., through the S. E. angle of Hardwick t-ship, Warren co., and joins the main stream, in the Great Meadows, Independence t-ship, having a course of about 10 miles.

Bear Swamp, a noted swamp of Downe t-ship, Cumberland co., near Nantuxet or Newport, through which flows the Oronoken creek. The timber upon it is chiefly oak and poplar.

Bear Swamp, Burlington co., near the west boundary of Northampton t-ship, about 2 miles in length by 1 in breadth.

Beasley's Point, Upper t-ship, Cape May co., on Great Egg Harbour Bay. There are here, upon a neck of land, between the salt marshes, of about 1 mile wide, 2 taverns, and several farm houses. where visiters to the shore may find agreeable accommodations.

Beatty's Town, on the N. E. angle of Mansfield t-ship, Warren co., on the bank of the Musconetcong creek, and at the west foot of Schooley's Mountain, within 2 miles of the mine-ral spring, and 16 E. of Belvidere. The Morris Canal is distant 2 miles from it on the north. The village contains 1 store, 1 tavern, a grist and saw mill, a school, and from 15 to 20 dwellings. The land around it is limestone, of excellent quality, and valued, in large farms, at 50 dollars the acre.

Beaver Brook, tributary of the Rockaway river, Pequannock t-ship, Morris county, flows by a S. W. course of 8 miles through a hilly country, giving motion to several forges.

Beaver Brook, Warren co., rises by two branches, one in Hardwick t-ship, from Glover's Pond, the other in Knowlton t-ship, from Rice's Pond, which unite in Oxford t-ship, near to, and south, from the village of Hope, and thence join the Pequest creek, about 3 miles from its mouth, having a course of about 14 miles.

Beaver Run, Galloway t-ship, Gloucester co., a tributary of Nacote creek, flowing to its recipient below Gravelly Landing.

Beaver Dam Run, a tributary of the south branch of Rancocus creek, which flows to its recipient, by a north course of about 4 miles, at Vincenttown.

Beaver Branch, of Wading river, rises in Little Egg Harbour t-ship, and flows westerly by a course of about 6 miles, to its recipient, about a mile below Bodine's bridge and mill.

Beden's Brook, a mill stream, rises in the Nashanic mountain, Hopewell t-ship, Hunterdon co., and flows E. about 8 miles, through Montgomery t-ship, Somerset co., to the Millstone river, receiving several tributaries by the way.

Bedminster Township, Somerset co., bounded N. by Washington, Chester, and Mendham t-ships, Morris co.; E. by the north branch of the Raritan, dividing it from Bernard t-ship; S. by Bridgewater t-ship, from which it is divided by Chamber's brook and Lamington river; and W. by Lamington river, forming the boundary between it and Tewksbury

N

and Readington t-ships, Hunterdon co.; Centrally distant, N. W. from Somerville, 8 miles; greatest length, N. and S., 8 miles; breadth, E. and W., 4½ miles; area, 19,300 acres; surface, hilly; soil, lime, clay, and red shale; generally well cultivated and fertile. Pepack, Little Cross Roads, Pluckemin, Lamington, and Cross Roads, are villages; the three first, p-ts. of the t-ship. Pepack and Artle's brooks are tributaries of the N. branch, flowing through the t-ship. Pop. in 1830, 1453. In 1832, the t-ship contained about 300 taxables, 60 householders, whose ratables did not exceed $30, 40 single men, 8 merchants, 6 saw mills, 6 grist mills, 19 tan vats, 3 distilleries, 499 horses and mules, and 818 neat cattle, 3 years old and upwards; and paid state tax, $242 48; county tax, 626 30. There is a Dutch Reformed church in the t-ship.

Belcher Creek rises near the centre of Pompton t-ship, Bergen co., and flows northerly about 7 miles, to mingle its waters with those of Long Pond, or Greenwood lake.

Belle Mount, a circular hill in the N. W. angle of Hopewell t-ship, Hunterdon co., on the shore of the Delaware river, between which and an oval hill on the south, flows Smith's creek.

Belvidere, p-t., and seat of justice of Warren co., situate on the river Delaware, in Oxford t-ship, at the junction of the Pequest creek, with that stream; by the post road, 210 miles from W. C., and 54 from Trenton, 69 from Philadelphia, 13 from Easton, 70 from New York, and 19 from Schooley's mountain springs. The town is built on an alluvial flat, based on limestone, and extends for about half a mile, on both sides of the creek, over which there are 2 bridges for carriages, and 1 for foot passengers. The town, which rapidly increases, contains a spacious court house, of brick, with offices attached, and a prison in the basement story; the doors of which, to the honour of the county, are commonly unclosed, and its chambers tenantless, save by the idle warder; a very large and neat Presbyterian church, a Methodist church, an academy, in which the classics are taught; a common school, 2 grist mills, 2 saw mills, a clover mill, 6 stores, 3 taverns, a turning lathe, driven by water, and an extensive tannery; a bank, chartered in 1829, with a capital of $50,000, but which may be extended; a county bible society, a county Sunday school union, auxiliary to the great charity established at Philadelphia; tract and temperance societies; 2 resident clergymen, 3 lawyers, and 2 physicians; 2 weekly journals, viz: The Apollo, edited by Franklin Ferguson; and the Warren Journal, by James J. Browne; and above 80 dwellings, most of which are neat and commodious, and many of brick and stone; among which, the residence of Dr. Green deserves particular notice, as well from its size and finish as from its beautiful and commanding situation. A very extensive business is done here, in general merchandise, in flour and lumber, the saw mills being abundantly supplied with timber from the Delaware. The Pequest creek having a large volume of water, and a rapid fall, affords very advantageous mill sites. Within 144 chains from the mouth of the creek the available fall is 49 feet 64-100, equal to 768 horse power, the whole of which is the property of Garret D. Wall, Esq., who offers mill seats for sale here on advantageous terms. But in addition to this great power derived from the creek, the Delaware river, within 2 miles of the town, offers a still greater, where the whole volume of that stream may be employed. A company has been incorporated, with a capital of $20,000, for erecting a bridge across the river at or near this place, for which three sites have been proposed. 1st. At the Foul Rift, where the channel is 170 yards wide. 2d. The mouth of the Pequest, where it is 205 yards. 3d. At the Deep Eddy, above the creek, where the channel is divided by Butz's island, and the stream, on the Jersey side, is 127 yards, the island 86 yards, and the remaining water 23 yards. The proposed rail road through New Jersey, from Elizabethtown, is designed to cross the Delaware here, and to connect with the Delaware and Susquehanna rail road.

Belleville, p-t. of Bloomfield t-ship, Essex co., beautifully situated on the right bank of the Raritan river, $3\frac{1}{2}$ miles N. E. from Newark, 218 from W. C., 52 from Trenton, and 9 from New York. The margin of the river, here, has width sufficient for a road or street, and for dwellings with spacious lots on both its sides, from which the gently sloping hill, clad in rich verdure, has a very pleasant appearance. Including North Belleville the town is considered as extending 3 miles along the river, and in that distance contains a handsome Dutch Reformed church, having a very large congregation, 1 Methodist and 1 Episcopalian church, 2 large schools for boys, a school for girls, under the superintendence of a lady, a boarding school for males and females, under the care of the Rev. Mr. Lathrop; 2 public houses, one a very large and well finished hotel, kept by Mr. Chandler, where many summer boarders may be accommodated, in this delightful retreat, from the bustle and noise of the great neighbouring city; 6 stores, and about 200 dwellings. Two streams, which flow into the Passaic, at about 3 miles distance from each other, and which, within 2 miles of their course have, respectively, a fall much over an hundred feet, render this place as interesting for its manufactures as for its beauty. There are here 1 brass rolling mill and button manufactory, belonging to Messrs. Stevens, Thomas, and Fuller, occasionally engaged in copper coinage for Brazil; the copper founderies and rolling mills of Messrs. Isaacs, and of Hendricks and brothers; the calico print works of Mr. Andrew Gray, the silk printing establishment of Messrs. Duncan and Cunningham; the Brittania metal factory of the Messrs. Lee; the lamp factory of Stephens and Dougherty, and the grist mill of Mr. Kindsland. These works are estimated to produce, annually, manufactured articles worth two millions of dollars. Two thousand tons of merchandise are supposed to be transported to and from the wharves of Belleville annually.

Belleville, p-o., Sussex co., 241 miles N. E. from W. C., and 75 from Trenton.

Ben Davis' Point, W. Cape of Nantuxet cove, in the Delaware bay, and in Fairfield t-ship, Cumberland co.

Bergen County, was established with its present boundaries, by the act of 21 January, 1709-10, which directed "That on the eastern division, the county shall begin at Constable's Hook, and so run up along the bay and Hudson river, to the partition point between N. Jersey and the province of N. York, and along that line between the provinces, and the division line of the eastern and western division of this province, to Pequanock river; thence by such river and the Passaic river, to the Sound; thence by the Sound to Constable's Hook, where it began." Bounded N. E. by Orange and Rockland co., N. Y.; E. by N. Y. bay and North river; S. by the strait, which connects N. Y. bay with Newark bay, S. W. by Essex and Morris co., and N. W. by Sussex co. It is shaped like an I. Greatest width N. W. and S. E. 32 miles; greatest breadth N. E. and S. W. 28 miles. Area 267,500 acres, or about 418 square miles.

S. E. of the Ramapo mountain, the county consists of the old red sandstone formation, which appears under the form of red shale, and of massive stone, well adapted to buildings; large quarries of which, have been worked on the Passaic near Belleville, and at other places. This formation is in places, covered with trap rock, which in the Closter mountain, assumes a columnar form, in the palisades, 400 feet high, on the North river; and the same form is visible in the continuation of the First and Second mountains across the Passaic at Paterson and

Little Falls. In the Ramapo mountain, and upon the N. W. of it, the primitive formation prevails, and the large township of Pompton is broken into ridges and knolls, of considerable elevation. Limestone is found in the valleys, here, and magnetic iron ore in the hills. The great vein of such ore, which is first discoverable in the White Hills of New Hampshire, may be traced through this county.

The surface of the country W. of the Saddle river, is hilly, with broad and fertile valleys. The left bank of that river, is also high ground, and a very fine valley lies between it and the Closter mountain, which is drained by the Hackensack river. The southern part of the valley is low, and admits the tide to the town of Hackensack, 20 miles from the sound. In this distance, there is a body of salt marsh and valuable cedar swamp. The northern part of the valley and its banks, on the Saddle river, the Passaic and the Hudson, are divided into small well cultivated farms, whose neat, cleanly, and cheerful appearance, declare the thrift and content of their owners. There are few spots in New Jersey presenting more pleasing attractions than this country above the Hackensack, and on the highlands on each side of the river. The houses, generally, built in the ancient Dutch cottage form, of one full story, with its projecting pent houses, and dormitories within the slopes of the roof, are sometimes large, always painted white, and surrounded with verdant lawns, shrubbery, and well cultivated gardens. And we may here remark, that the taste for horticulture and ornamental shrubberies, appears more general in the central and northern parts of New Jersey, than in the southern parts, or in the state of Pennsylvania.

Extensive deposits of copper are found on the banks of the Passaic, in Lodi t-ship, about 1 mile S. E. of Belleville.

The county is well watered, having, beside the rivers on its boundaries, Ringwood, Ramapo, and Saddle rivers; all of which, rising in New York, flow S. to the Passaic; each having considerable tributaries, which though short, are by their rapid falls made available for hydraulic purposes. Ringwood river receives a considerable accesion to its waters, from Long pond or Greenwood lake, in a high and narrow valley between a ridge of the Wawayanda mountains and Sterling mountain. The lake is nearly 5 miles long, but only about a mile of its length is within the state of New Jersey. It pours forth its tribute through Long Pond river.

Hohokus Brook is a rapid stream of Franklin t-ship, which, after having, in a course of 9 miles, given motion to many mills, unites with the Saddle river. The Hackensack, also rising in New York, has an independent course to Newark bay, and receives several tributaries from either hand.

In this county, the first settlements of the state by Europeans were made. The Hollanders were here the pioneers of civilization, aided probably by some Danes or Norwegians, who adopted the name of Bergen from the capitol of Norway. Their descendants occupy the lands of their ancestors, and retain much of their primitive habits and virtues, their industry, cleanliness, and love of flowers; for the latter is a taste so pure and delightful, that we dare to rank it among the virtues. New York is much indebted to the Dutch gardeners for her supplies of flowers and vegetables.

After the country was reduced under the English rule, in 1764, English settlers came in considerable numbers from Long Island and Barbadoes. They were not so numerous, however, as immediately to lose their character of strangers, and they resided chiefly in the "*English Neighbourhood*," and at New Barbadoes.

In 1830, the population of the county was 22,412, divided as follows: white males 10,299, white females 9634, free coloured males 1061, females 834, male slaves 306, female slaves 280. Of these, there were aliens 213; deaf and dumb whites 10, blacks 3; blind, whites 12, blacks 5. The provisions for moral instruction are the religious societies, consisting of the German Reformed, Episcopalian, Presbyterian, Baptist, and Methodist; a county bible society, Sunday schools, and temperance societies; academies in the larger villages, and common schools in every populous vicinity.

The chief towns are Jersey City, Hoboken, Bergen, Hackensack, the seat of justice, Closter, New Milford, New Prospect, Godwinsville, New Manchester, Ryerson's, Ramapo, Boardville, Ringwood, Stralenberg, Old Bridge, New Bridge, New Durham, English Neighbourhood, Communipaw, and Pamrepaw.

In 1832, the county contained 5796 taxables, 1262 householders, whose rateables did not exceed 30 dollars, 533 single men, 75 merchants, 7 fisheries, 84 run of stones for grinding grain, 16 cotton factories, 5 woollen factories, 10 carding machines, 4 furnaces and 16 forges, 93 saw mills, 3 paper mills, 4 fulling mills, 127 tan vats, 13 distilleries, 1 flint glass, and 1 china manufactory, both extensive; 1 printing, dyeing and bleaching establishment, and 4025 horses and mules, and 10,188 neat cattle above 3 years of age; and it paid state tax $2631 43, county tax $5000, poor tax $2500, school tax $100, road tax $6000.

The county is extensively agricultural, raising a large surplus of grain and esculent vegetables for its manufacturing population, and for the New York market.

The improved means for transporting its produce to market, are beside the ordinary country roads, nine turnpikes and two rail-roads, exclusive of that made by Mr. Stephens along the North river. The turnpikes are, two from Jersey City to Newark, one from Hoboken to Paterson, one from Hoboken to Hackensack, one from Hackensack to Paterson, one from New Prospect to the Ramapo works, in the State of New York, the Ringwood and Long Pond road, the Newark and Pompton, and the Paterson and Hamburg. These have been made, and others have been authorized by law. A rail-road has been completed from Jersey City to Paterson, and another is now being made from the Hudson river through Newark, Elizabethtown, Rahway and Woodbridge, to New Brunswick.

The courts of the county are holden at Hackensack; the common pleas, orphans' and general quarter sessions, on the following Tuesdays, viz. 4th January, 4th March, 2d August, 4th October; and the circuit courts, on the Tuesdays of 4th March and 4th October.

Bergen sends 1 member to the legislative council, and 3 to the assembly.

The following notice of the country embraced by this county, taken from Smith's History of New Jersey, will be interesting to its present inhabitants. "Near the mouth of the bay, upon the side of Overprook creek, adjacent to Hackensack river, several of the rich valleys were then, (1680,) settled by the Dutch; and near Snake hill was a fine plantation, owned by Pinhorne and Eickbe, for half of which, Pinhorne is said to have paid £500. There were other settlements upon Hackensack river, and on a creek near it, Sarah Kiersted, of New York, had a tract given her by an old Indian sachem, for services in interpreting between the Indians and Dutch, and on which several families were settled; John Berrie had a large plantation, 2 or 3 miles above, where he then lived, and had considerable improvements; as had also near him, his son-in-law, *Smith*, and one Baker, from Barbadoes. On the west side of the creek, opposite to Berrie, were other plantations; but none more northerly. There was a considerable settlement upon Bergen point, then called Constable Hook, and first improved by Edsall, in Nicoll's time. Other small plantations were improved along Bergen neck, to the east, between the point and a large village of 20 families (*Communipaw*). Further along lived 16 or 18 families, and opposite New York about 40 families were seated. Southward from this, a few families settled together, at a place called Duke's farm; and further up the country was a place called Hobuck, formerly owned by a Dutch merchant, who, in the Indian wars with the Dutch, had his wife, children and servants murdered by the Indians, and his house and stock destroyed by them; but it was now settled again, and a mill erected there. Along the river side to the N. were lands settled by William Lawrence, Samuel Edsall, and Capt. Beinfield; and at Haversham, near the Highlands, governor Carteret had taken up two large tracts; one for himself, the other for Andrew Campyne, and Co.,

which were now but little improved. The plantations on both sides of the neck, to its utmost extent, as also those at Hackensack, were under the jurisdiction of Bergentown, situate about the middle of the neck; where was a court held by selectmen or overseers, consisting of 4 or more in number, as the people thought best, chose annually to try small causes, as had been the practice in all the rest of the towns at first; 2 courts of sessions were held here yearly, from which, if the cause exceeded £20, the party might appeal to the governor, council, and court of deputies or assembly."

" *Bergen*, a compact town which had been fortified against the Indians, contained about 70 families; its inhabitants were chiefly Dutch, some of whom had been settled there upwards of 40 years."

STATISTICAL TABLE OF BERGEN COUNTY.

Townships, &c.	Length.	Breadth.	Area.	Surface.	Population. 1810	1820	1830
Barbadoes, New,	7	4	11,500	level,	2835	2592	1693
Bergen,	13	4	20,000	part hilly,	2690	3137	4651
Franklin,	10	9	45,000	hilly, rolling,	2839	2968	3449
Hackensack,	9	2½	24,000	hill and valley,	1918	2076	2200
Harrington,	9½	7	34,000	do. do.	2087	2296	2581
Lodi,	10	5	22,000	flat,			1356
Pompton,	14	12	70,000	mountainous,	2060	2818	3085
Saddle River,	10	8	41,000	do.	2174	2291	3397
			267,500		16,603	18,178	22,412

Bergen, village, of Bergen t-ship, Bergen co., about 16 miles S. of Hackensack, and 3 west of Jersey city, upon the summit of Bergen ridge, and equidistant between the turnpike roads leading to Newark, contains a Dutch Reformed church, and some twenty or thirty houses. This town was settled about 1616, probably by Danes, who accompanied the Hollanders.

Bergen t-ship, Bergen co., is bounded N. by Hackensack t-ship, E. by Hudson river and New York bay, S. by the strait called Kill Van Kuhl, W. by the Hackensack river and Newark bay; greatest length N. and S. 13, breadth 4 miles; area, 20,000 acres. Surface hilly on the N. E., on the W. and S. level. Soil, red shale and marsh. A large body of the latter, with Cedar swamp, lies on the Hackensack river, extending from the head of Newark bay, through the t-ship. The t-ship is intersected by several turnpike roads running in various directions. New Durham, Weehawk, Hoboken, Jersey City, Bergen, Communipaw, and Pamrepaw, are towns of the t-ship. There are post-offices at Jersey City and Hoboken. Population in 1830, 4651.

In 1832, there were in the t-ship 1167 taxables, 366 householders, whose ratable estate does not exceed 30 dollars, 191 single men, 22 merchants, 2 grist mills, 1 saw mill, 3 ferries, 1 toll bridge, 10 tan vats, 1 grain distillery, 1 glass and 1 china manufactory, and 1 woollen manufactory, 446 horses and mules, and 1287 neat cattle above the age of three years. The t-ship paid state tax, $422 74; county, $613 36; poor, $800; road, $1500.

Berkely. (See *Sandtown.*)

Berkshire Valley, the S. W. part of Longwood valley, Jefferson t-ship, Morris co., W. of Greenpond mountain, 12 miles N. W. from Morristown, 237 from W. C., and 71 from Trenton. A wild and rocky spot, through which runs a branch of the Rockaway river, giving motion to several forges, &c. There is also a post-office and a Presbyterian church here.

Bernard t-ship, Somerset co., bounded N. by Mendham t-ship, Morris co.; E. by the Passaic river, dividing it from Morris t-ship, of the said county; S. E. by Warren t-ship, S. W. by Bridgewater t-ship, and W. by Bedminster t-ship. Centrally, distant N. E. from Somerville, 7 miles; greatest length, N. and S. 9; breadth, E. and W. 7 miles; area, 25,000 acres; surface hilly, and in great part mountainous; soil on hills, clay and loom; in the valleys, limestone; well cultivated by wealthy farmers. The north branch of the Raritan flows on the western boundary, and receives from the t-ship Mine brook and smaller tributaries. Dead run flows to the Passaic, on the S. E. line. Baskingridge, Liberty Corner, Logtown and Vealtown, are villages of the t-ship; the two first post-towns. Population in 1830, 2062. In 1832, the t-ship contained about 400 taxables, 68 householders, whose ratable estate did not exceed 30 dollars, 34 single men, 5 stores, 8 saw mills, 3 grist mills, 1 fulling mill, 5 distilleries, 461 horses and mules, and 1105 neat cattle 3 years old and upwards,

and paid state tax, $306 70; county tax, $695 50.

Berry's Creek, a marsh creek of Lodi t-ship, Bergen co., has a southerly course of about 4 miles.

Bethany Hole Run, small tributary of Hains' creek, Evesham t-ship, Burlington co., flows by a course of about 3 miles into the dam of Taunton furnace.

Bethel, mount and church, Mansfield t-ship, Warren co., 12 miles E. of the town of Belvidere.

Bethlehem t-ship, Hunterdon co., bounded N. W. by the Musconetcong river, which divides it from Warren co., N. E. by Lebanon t-ship, S. E. by Ringwood, and S. W. by Alexandria. Centrally distant N. W. from Flemington, 13 miles; greatest length E. and W. 9 miles, breadth N. and S. 9 miles; area 25,000 acres; surface mountainous on the north, elsewhere hilly; soil, clay, red shale, and loam, with a vein of limestone on the cast foot of the Musconetcong mountain; drained chiefly by Alberson's brook, a tributary of Spruce run, and some small tributaries of Musconetcong creek. Charleston, Bloomsbury, Hickory, Pattenburg, are villages of the t-ship—Vansyckles and Perryville, post-towns. Population in 1830, 2032. In 1832, the t-ship contained a Presbyterian church, 3 stores, 3 saw mills, 5 grist mills, 1 oil mill, 25 tan vats, 5 distilleries, 480 horses and mules, and 820 neat cattle above the age of 3 years; and paid poor tax, $900; road tax, $700; county and state tax, $791 68.

Bevens, p-o., of Sussex co., named after the postmaster, James C. Bevens, 241 miles N. E. from W. C., and 83 from Trenton.

Billingsport, more properly written Byllingsport, named after Edward Bylling, a merchant of England, the purchaser of Lord Berkeley's undivided moiety of the province. It lies upon the river Delaware below the mouth of Mantua creek, and 12 miles below Camden, and was rendered famous by the fort erected here during the revolutionary war, for defence of the channel of the river, remains of which are still visible. It contains a tavern and ferry, and some half dozen dwellings.

Birmingham, small hamlet of Trenton t-ship, Hunterdon co. 5 miles N. W. from the city of Trenton, contains a tavern and some half dozen dwellings.

Birmingham, formerly called New Mills, village, on the north branch of the Rancocus creek, Northampton t-ship, Burlington co., 4 miles S. E. of Mount Holly, contains a cotton manufactory, a grist mill, saw mill, fulling mill, a cupola furnace, and from 15 to 20 dwellings. Shreve's calico printing works are within two miles of the village, upon the same stream.

Black Creek, Vernon t-ship, Sussex co., rises on the S. E. foot of the Pochuck mountain, flows northwardly, about 5 miles to the Warwick creek.

Blackwoodtown, village of Gloucester co., upon the main branch of Big Timber creek, near the head of navigation; 8 or 9 miles from its mouth, 5 miles S. E. of Woodbury, and 11 miles from Camden; contains 1 Presbyterian and large Methodist church, an extensive woollen manufactory chiefly employed on kerseynette, belonging to Newkirk and Co., 3 stores, 1 tavern, and about 50 dwellings; a 2 horse stage plies daily between this town and Camden.

Black's Creek, S. W. boundary of Chesterfield t-ship, rising by several branches in Hanover t-ship, flowing W. and N. W. about 8 miles to the river Delaware, below Bordentown. The Amboy rail-road crosses its mouth over a wooden bridge. Bacon's run is a branch of the stream, and part of the aforesaid boundary; the creek drives several mills.

Black Horse. (See *Columbus*.)

Black Run, tributary of the S. branch of Toms' river, Dover t-ship, Monmouth co.

Black Brook, tributary of the Passaic river, rises at the N. E. base of Long hill, Chatham t-ship, Morris

co., flows westerly along the hill, by a course of 7 or 8 miles to its recipient in Morris t-ship.

Blackley's Mineral Spring, Acquackanonk t-ship, Essex co., 10 miles N. W. from New York, 4 S. E. from Paterson; formerly much frequented as a useful chalybeate.

Blackwood Meadow Brook, a small tributary of the Passaic river, flowing W. to its recipient in the N. W. angle of Livingston t-ship, Essex co.

Black River, is the name given to the Lamington river, above Potter's Falls. It rises by 2 small branches, on the borders of Roxbury and Randolph t-ships, flows under this name a S. W. course of about 16 miles, to the falls at the point of junction, between Hunterdon, Somerset and Morris co., draining a valley of considerable extent, and in parts very fertile.

Black River, or *Cooper's Mills*, is also the name of a small village on the above stream, situate in Chester t-ship, Morris co., on the turnpike road leading from Morristown to Easton, 14 miles N. W. from the former; contains 1 grist mill, 2 saw mills, a store, and 6 or 8 dwellings; it is a place of considerable business; the country around it is hilly, and not very fertile.

Blackwells, hamlet of Hillsborough t-ship, Somerset co., on the left bank of the Millstone river, 6½ miles S. of Somerville, pleasantly situated, in a fertile country; contains a large grist mill, fulling mill, store, and several dwellings; a bridge crosses the Millstone river here.

Black Point, at the confluence of the Shrewsbury and Nevisink rivers, Shrewsbury t-ship, Monmouth co.

Blazing Star Ferry, over Staten Island Sound, on the road from Woodbury to Staten Island, about 7 miles N. E. from Amboy; the post-route to New York, formerly lay by this ferry.

Bloomfield t-ship, Essex county, bounded N. by Acquackanonck t-sp, E. by the Passaic river, which divides it from Bergen co., E. by Newark t-ship, S. and S. W. by Orange, and W. by Caldwell. Centrally distant N. from Newark, 6 miles; greatest length 5, breadth 4½ miles; area, 14,000 acres; surface hilly; mountainous on the west; on the eastern boundary, the ground rises gradually from the river, and offers beautiful sites for country seats, many of which are thus occupied. It is drained by two streams which rise near the foot of the mountain, and flow by tortuous courses to the river, known as the Second and Third rivers. The first has a length scarce exceeding 6 miles, and the last, which forms a semi-ellipsis, and rises in the notch in Acquackanonck t-ship, may be double that length. These streams are the source of the wealth of the t-ship, and have converted it almost wholly into a manufacturing village. The soil is based on red sandstone, in which are exhaustless quarries of fine building stone, vast quantities of which have been sent to New York, and other places. The villages of the t-ship are Belleville, Bloomfield, Spring Garden, and Speertown. At the two first are post-offices. Pop. in 1830, 4309; in 1832, the t-ship contained 500 taxables, 206 householders, whose ratable estate did not exceed $30; 82 single men, 17 merchants, 6 grist mills, 2 cotton manufactories, 5 saw mills, 4 rolling mills for copper, 3 paper mills, 1 paint factory, 2 calico printing and bleaching works, 1 very extensive; 40 tan vats, 3 woollen factories, and several very extensive shoe factories; 387 horses and mules, and 862 neat cattle above three years old. And the t-ship paid state tax $754 50; county $238 37; poor $1200; and road $1200. The annual value of manufactured products, probably exceed 2½ millions of dollars.

Bloomfield, p-t. of the above t-ship, 3½ miles N. of Newark, extending for near 3 miles in a N. W. direction, and including what was formerly known as West Bloomfield. The chief part of the town lies upon the old road, but part of it on the turn-

pike; it contains about 1600 inhabitants, above 250 dwellings, 2 hotels, an academy, boarding school, 4 large common schools, 12 stores, 1 Presbyterian church, 2 Methodist churches; a very extensive trade is carried on here in tanning, currying, and shoemaking, and the following manufactories are considered as annexed to the town: 2 woollen factories, 1 mahogany saw mill, 1 cotton mill, 1 rolling mill, 1 calico printing work, 2 saw mills for ordinary work, 1 paper mill, and 1 grist mill.

Bloomingdale, village on the Pequannock creek, Pompton t-ship, Bergen co., 20 miles N. W. from Hackensack, upon the Paterson and Hamburg turnpike road; contains 1 forge, a saw mill, grist mill, machine factory, bark mill, 1 tavern, 2 stores, and some 8 or 10 dwellings; the country around it is mountainous and barren.

Bloomsbury, p-t. of Greenwich t-ship, Warren co., on the turnpike road from Somerville to Philipsburg, and on both sides of the Musconetcong creek, part of the town being in Hunterdon co.; by the post-route 198 miles from W. C., 49 from Trenton, and 14 S. from Belvidere, 18 miles N. W. from Flemington; contains 1 grist mill, 1 oil mill, a cotton manufactory, 2 taverns, 1 store, and from 30 to 40 dwellings; the soil of the valley around it is rich limestone.

Bloomsbury, village of Nottingham t-ship, Burlington co., a suburb of the city of Trenton, below the Assunpink creek, and at the head of the sloop navigation of the river. The bridge across the Delaware runs from the centre of the village; there are here a Presbyterian meeting, several taverns and stores, steam-boat landings and wharves, with about 150 dwellings and 900 inhabitants. The race-way of the Trenton water power company, will pass through the village. (See *Trenton*.)

Blue Ball, village of Howell t-ship, Monmouth co., 4 miles S. from Freehold; contains a tavern and store, 10 or 12 dwellings, 1 Presbyterian and

O

1 Methodist church. The soil here has been so greatly improved by marl, that lands which 15 years since would not bring $20 the acre, now command $50.

Blue Anchor, tavern and hamlet of Gloucester t-ship, Gloucester co., in the heart of the pine forest, about 25 miles S. E. from Camden.

Boonton, manufacturing village of Hanover t-ship, Morris co., on the N. side of Rockaway river, 9 miles N. of Morristown, situate on the side of a high hill, at the entrance of a dark, narrow, rocky valley; contains the works of the East Jersey Iron Manufacturing Company, consisting of an extensive rolling mill, a blast furnace and foundery, 3 stores, and about 40 dwellings, a school house and a handsome church. In forcing the Trowbridge mountain here, the stream has formed a rapid and a picturesque cascade of about 30 feet fall, and this circumstance has made the site a very advantageous one for hydraulic works. The Morris canal ascends from the valley by an inclined plane 800 feet long, having a lift of 80 feet, which is passed over in from 12 to 15 minutes. Pop. between 300 and 400, principally English; the village was founded in 1828, and is one of the most romantic spots in the state.

Bonhamtown, Woodbridge t-ship, Middlesex co., 5 miles N. E. from New Brunswick, on the turnpike road leading thence to Woodbridge, from which it is distant 6 miles; contains 10 or 12 dwellings, 2 taverns, 1 store and school house; surrounded by a gravelly and poor soil.

Boardville, on Ringwood river, and on the Ringwood and Longwood turnpike road in Pompton t-ship, Bergen co., 21 miles N. W. from Hackensack; contains a Dutch Reformed church, a forge, distillery, a school house, and several farm houses. The narrow valley in which it lies is rich and well cultivated.

Bordentown, borough and p-t., of Chesterfield t-ship, Burlington co., situate on the bank of the Delaware river, at the junction of the Cross-wick's creek with that stream, 11 miles N. W. from Mount Holly, 170 N. E. from W. C., 30 from Philadelphia, 10 from Burlington, and 7 S. E. from Trenton; contains about 1000 inhabitants, 200 dwellings, a Quaker meeting house, a Baptist and a Methodist church, 5 stores and 5 taverns, and is surrounded by a fertile and well cultivated country of sandy loam. The Camden and Amboy rail-road passes through the town, by a viaduct beneath its principal streets; and stages run from the town, daily, to Trenton, Princeton, New Brunswick, Long Branch, New Egypt, Mount Holly, &c. &c., and 4 steam-boats, to Bristol, Burlington, and Philadelphia.

This town was founded by Mr. Joseph Borden, an early settler here, and a distinguished citizen of the state, and has borne his name for nearly a century. It was incorporated 9th December, 1825. Its site is perhaps the most beautiful on the Delaware, and the village is alike remarkable for its healthiness and cleanliness, and the neatness of its dwellings. Built upon a plain 65 feet above the surface of the river, and from which there is a descent upon three sides, its streets, speedily drained after the rain, are dry; and lined by umbrageous trees, furnish always an agreeable promenade during the summer season. From the brow of the hill, there is a delightful view of the majestic Delaware, pursuing for miles its tranquil course through the rich country which it laves. The beauty of this scene is greatest in the autumn, when the thousand varied and brilliant tints of the forest trees are contrasted with the deep azure of the sky, and the limpid blue of the mirror like waters. The attractions of the scene determined Joseph Buonaparte, Count de Surveilliers, in his choice of a residence in this country; and this distinguished exile, who has filled two thrones, and has pretensions based on popular suffrage to a third, has dwelt here many years in philosophic retirement. He has in the vicinity about 1500 acres of land, part of which possessed natural beauty, which his taste and wealth have been employed to embellish. At the expense of some hundred thousand dollars, he has converted a wild and impoverished tract, into a park of surpassing beauty, blending the charms of woodland and plantation scenery, with a delightful water prospect. The present buildings, plain but commodious, are on the site of the offices of his original and more splendid mansion, which was destroyed by fire, together with some rare pictures from the pencils of the first masters, whose merit made them invaluable. With characteristic liberality, the Count has opened his grounds to the public, but we regret to perceive, that he has been ungratefully repaid, by the defacement of his ornamental structures, and mutilation of his statues.

Bordentown is much resorted to by the citizens of Philadelphia during the hot months, who find excellent entertainment in the large commodious public houses, and in private and more retired mansions. Few places near the city are more desirable as a summer residence, which is now rendered uncommonly convenient to citizens by the almost hourly means of communicating with Philadelphia and New York. The benefit of these advantageous circumstances to the town, becomes apparent in its increase, many new houses having been built in 1832 and 1833. The outlet lock of the Delaware and Raritan canal is in front of the town, which will in all probability become a depot, for much produce of the surrounding country destined for the New York or Philadelphia market. Under these prospects the value of property here, we are told, has risen 50 per cent. within two years.

Borden's Run, an arm of the S. branch of Toms' river, Upper Freehold t-ship, Monmouth co., flows E. about 7 miles through the S. E. angle of the t-ship.

Bottle Hill, p-t., Chatham t-ship, Morris co., on the turnpike road from Elizabethtown to Morristown, 13 miles from the one, and 4½ from the other; 223 N. E. from W. C. and 57 from Trenton; contains a tavern, three stores, a Presbyterian church, an academy, and above 40 dwellings, generally very neat; the surrounding country gently undulating, and well cultivated.

Bound Brook, p-t., of Bridgewater t-ship, Somerset co., on the S. W. boundary of the county, at the confluence of the Green Brook with the Raritan river. A part of the village is in Piscataway t-ship, of the adjoining county of Middlesex, on the turnpike road from New Brunswick to Somerville, 7 miles from the one, and 4 from the other. The town, including Middle Brook, extends a mile from Green Brook to Middle Brook, and contains a large and neat Presbyterian church, an academy, 3 taverns, 4 stores, a large grist mill, &c., and about 50 dwellings. There is a bridge over the river here. The surrounding country is fertile. The Delaware and Raritan canal runs near the town.

Bound Brook, small stream rising in Newark t-ship, and running S. E. through the marsh, into Newark bay, forming the boundary between Elizabeth and Newark t-ships.

Bound Brook. (See *Green Brook*.)

Bowentown, Hopewell t-ship, Cumberland co., a small hamlet, of some half dozen houses, midway on the road from Bridgetown to Road's town, about 2½ miles from each.

Branchville, p-t., of Frankford t-ship, Sussex co., on the Morris turnpike road, by the mail route, 235 miles from Washington city, 77 from Trenton, 7 from Newton, and 2 from Augusta. There are several mills here upon a branch of the Paulinskill, within the space of two miles.

Bread and Cheese Run, tributary of the south branch of Rancocus creek, Northampton t-ship, Burlington co., unites with that stream 8 or 10 miles below its source.

Brigantine Inlet, Old, formerly

through Brigantine Beach, on the Atlantic, now closed.

Brigantine Beach, on the Atlantic ocean, Galloway t-ship, Gloucester co., extends from Quarter's Inlet, eastwardly, to Old Brigantine Inlet, about 6 miles, by about a half a mile in width. Several salt works have been established here.

Bricksborough, village, of Maurice t-ship, Cumberland co., upon the left bank of Maurice river, 12 miles from its mouth, within 2 of Port Elizabeth, and 14 of Bridgeton, contains from 12 to 15 dwellings. It lies at the confluence of Muskee run, with the river.

Bridgeport, small hamlet of Washington t-ship, Burlington co., upon the left bank of Wading river, 29 miles S. E. from Mount Holly, and 5 from the confluence of Wading with the Little Egg Harbour river, contains a tavern, store, and some 4 or 5 dwellings, in sandy, pine country. The river is navigable above the town.

Bridgeton, p-t. and seat of justice of Cumberland co., upon the Cohansey creek, 20 miles from its mouth, 175 N. E. from W. C., and sixty S. of Trenton. The town is built on both sides of the creek, over which is a wooden drawbridge, from whence it has its name. It formerly bore that of Cohansey. It contains a courthouse of brick, in the centre of a street, upon the W. bank of the creek, a prison of stone, and public offices, on the E., a Presbyterian, a Baptist, and a Methodist church; a bank with an authorized capital of $200,000, of which $50,000 have been paid in; a public library, a Masonic lodge, an academy, a woollen manufactory, a grist mill, an extensive rolling mill, foundery, and nail factory. It exports lumber, flour, grain, nails, and iron castings. Thirty schooners and sloops, of from 50 to 80 tons burthen, sail from the port, which is one of entry and delivery. The collection district of Bridgeton comprehends the counties of Gloucester, Salem, Cumberland, and Cape May; excepting such parts of Gloucester and Cape May, as are included in the district of Egg Harbour. The collector resides at Bridgeton.—250 licenses issued from his office in the year 1832. The country around is a sandy loam, rich and productive in wheat, corn, and rye. The most remarkable object, here, is the iron works of Messrs. Reeves and Whitaker, which occupy a number of stone buildings on the W. side of the creek, above the bridge, and are driven by a water power of 15 feet head and fall. They were originally built in 1815, but were consumed by fire in 1822, and rebuilt and enlarged in the same year. The rolling mill is capable of manufacturing into hoop and round iron, from blooms, 25,000 tons per annum. The nail factory contains 29 nail machines, competent to make 1500 tons of nails annually; and the foundery will make 250 tons of castings, from a cupola furnace, with anthracite coal. These works give employment to 125 men and boys, who receive their wages, monthly, in cash, to the amount of $30,000 per annum; and yield the means of support to nearly 500 persons. Two vessels are constantly employed in bringing coal to the works from Richmond, and one in the intercourse with the city of Philadelphia. There are some very good houses in the town, which has quite an air of business.

Bridgeville, small hamlet of Oxford t-ship, Warren co., 4 miles E. of Belvidere, the county town.

Bridgewater t-ship, Somerset co., bounded N. by Bedminster and Bernard t-ships, N. E. by Warren t-ship, S. E. by Greenbrook, dividing it from Piscataway t-ship, Middlesex co., S. by the Raritan river, separating it from Franklin and Hillsborough t-ships, and S. W. by Readington t-ship, Hunterdon co. Greatest length N. E. and S. W. 13 miles; breadth E. and W. 11 miles; area, about 35,000 acres; surface, on the N. E., mountainous, elsewhere level, or gently undulating; soil, generally, red shale, and well cultivated in grain and grass. The N. branch of the Raritan unites with the Lamington river, on the N.

boundary, and flows thence, S. to meet the S. branch, about 4 miles W. from Somerville; the latter river receives from the W., Holland and Campbell's Brooks; Middle Brook crosses the E. part of the t-ship to the main branch of the Raritan, about 5 miles E. of Somerville. Somerville, the county town, North Branch, Bound Brook, and Middle Brook, are villages, the three first named, post-towns. Popu- in 1830, 3549. In 1832 the t-ship contained about 700 taxables, 152 householders, whose ratable estate did not exceed 30 dollars, 93 single men, 17 stores, 5 saw mills, and 3 grist mills, 3 fulling mills, 29 tan vats, 4 distilleries for cider, 6 carding ma- chines, 858 horses and mules, and 1570 neat cattle, 3 years old and up- wards; and paid state tax, $464 96; county, $1145 32.

Broadway, village, of Mansfield t-ship, near the S. W. boundary line, Warren co., on the turnpike road from Philipsburg to Schooley's moun- tain, about 10 miles from the former, and 14 from the latter, contains a store and tavern, 2 grist mills, 1 saw mill, and 10 or 12 dwellings. It lies in the valley of the Pohatcong creek, upon a soil of fertile limestone.

Broad Oyster Creek, Downe t-ship, Cumberland co., flows from Orano- ken creek, through the salt marsh, into the Delaware bay.

Brooklyn, hamlet, of Piscataway t-ship, Middlesex co., on Dismal Brook, 6 miles N. E. from New Brunswick, contains a grist mill, saw mill, and some 8 or 10 dwellings.

Brown's Point, on the Raritan bay, at the mouth of Middletown creek, Middletown t-ship, Monmouth co., 5 miles S. E. from Perth Amboy, 14 miles N. E. from Freehold. There are here, a good landing, 2 taverns, 3 stores, and 12 or 15 dwellings; sur- rounding country, flat and sandy, but made productive by marl.

Brunswick, North, t-ship, of Mid- dlesex co., bounded N. by the river Raritan, E. by South Amboy t-ship, S. by South Brunswick, and W. by Franklin t-ship, Somerset co. Great-

est length E. and W. 9 miles; breadth N. and S. 7 miles; area, 23,000 acres, of which 5000 are unimproved; surface level; soil red shale and sandy loam, drained on the N. by the Rari- tan, N. E. by South river, centrally by Lawrence's Brook, and N. W. by Six Mile run and its branches. The Princeton and Brunswick, and the Trenton and Brunswick turnpike roads run along and through the t-ship; the first on the W. boundary of the t-ship and county. New Bruns- wick, the seat of justice of the county, Washington, Six Mile Run, and Old Bridge, are villages, and the three first, post-towns of the t-ship. Population in 1830, 5274. In 1832 the t-ship contained about 1050 taxables, whose ratable estates did not exceed 30 dol- lars, 111 single men, 47 stores, 1 saw mill, 4 run of stones for grain, 1 plaster mill, 3 carding machines and fulling mills, 90 tan vats, 4 distilleries for cider, 593 horses and mules, and 831 neat cattle, above the age of 3 years; and it paid state tax, $456 84; county, $561 76; road, $200; poor, $1250.

Brunswick, South, t-ship, of Mid- dlesex co., bounded on the N. E. by North Brunswick, E. by South Am- boy, S. by East and West Windsor, and W. and N. W. by Franklin t-ship, Somerset co. Centrally distant from New Brunswick S. W. 12 miles; greatest length N. and S. 10; breadth E. and W. 7 miles; area, about 36,000 acres; surface, generally, level, with some hills on the west; soil sandy loam and red shale; in places ex- tremely well cultivated and produc- tive; drained N. E. by Lawrence's Brook, S. W. by Millstone river and its tributaries, Cranberry Brook, Devil's Brook, Heathcoat's Brook. Kingston, and Cranberry, are post- towns, lying partly in the t-ship; and Plainsborough Cross Roads and Ma- plestown are hamlets of the t-ship. Population 2557, in 1830. In 1832 the t-ship contained 527 taxables, whose ratables did not exceed 30 dol- lars; 32 single men, 10 merchants, 7 saw mills, 8 run of stones for grist, 5 tan vats, 10 distilleries for cider, 755 horses and mules, and 1275 neat cattle; and it paid state tax, $438 79; county, $539 49; poor, $700.

Buck Pond, Pompton t-ship, Bergen co., near Bear Fort mountain, covers about 150 acres, and sends a small tributary to the Pequannock creek.

Buckshutem, hamlet, near the confluence of Buckshutem creek with Maurice river, Milleville t-ship, Cumberland co., 3 miles from Port Elizabeth; contains 8 or 10 dwellings, a grist and saw mill, and store.

Buckshutem Creek, tributary of Maurice river, Cumberland co., rises by 2 branches, one on the line between Milleville and Fairfield t-ships; the other on the line between Fairfield and Downe t-ships, and the main stream divides Milleville from Downe. It is a fine mill stream.

Buddstown, hamlet, Northampton t-ship, Burlington co., on Stop the Jade creek, a tributary of the south branch of the Rancocus; contains a tavern, store, and saw mill, on the edge of the pines.

Budd's Pond, small lake of Roxbury t-ship, Morris co., on the summit of Schooley's mountain, 17 miles N. W. of Morristown, and 7 from the mineral spring, from which the visiters resort hither, for amusement, in boating and fishing.

Bull's Creek, small tributary of Little Egg Harbour river. Sooy's mill is near its mouth.

Bull's Island, in the Delaware river, 23 miles above Trenton, near Saxtonville. The feeder of the Delaware and Raritan canal communicates with the Delaware here.

Burlington County : the first recognition we find of the bounds of this co. is in the act of Assembly, 1694, but its limits were more definitely settled by the act 21st Jan. 1710, declaring, that the line of partition between Burlington and Gloucester counties begins at the mouth of Pensauken, otherwise, Cropwell creek; thence up the same to the fork; thence along the southernmost branch thereof, sometimes called

Cole Branch, until it comes to the head thereof; thence by a straight line to the southernmost branch of Little Egg Harbour river; thence down the said branch and river, to the mouth thereof; thence to the next inlet, on the S. side of Little Egg Harbour's most southerly inlet; thence along the sea coast, to the line of partition between East and West Jersey; thence on such line, by Maidenhead and Hopewell, to the northernmost bounds of Amwell t-ship; thence to the river Delaware, and by the river, to the first mentioned station. This surface has been reduced by the act which established Hunterdon county, March, 1714, making the Assunpink creek the N. boundary of the county. It is now bounded N. by Hunterdon co., E. by Monmouth co., S. E. by the Atlantic ocean, S. W. by Gloucester co., and N. W. by the Delaware river. Central latitude, 39° 50′; longitude E. from W. C., 2° 18′; greatest length, N. W. and S. E. 54; breadth, E. and W., 31 miles; area, 553,000 acres, or near 833 square miles.

Except immediately on the border of the Assunpink creek, where some primitive rock appears, the whole of this county is alluvial, composed of sand, gravel, loam and clay, variously blended. It would seem that the diluvian of the mountainous country above has been spread by the Delaware river, over the northwestern border of the county, for some 12 or 14 miles from the present bank, forming with the aggregations from the sea a very fertile loam, which, manured with stable dung, ashes, or marl, produces abundant crops of rye, corn, oats, beans, peas, grass, and potatoes. Strips of sand occur in this loamy belt, and sometimes masses of stiff clay, which were probably once washed by the tides of the ocean. East of the belt of loam, is a mass of sand overlaying clay, and extending, for near 40 miles, to the marshes, which border the sea shore. In this sandy district, there are occasionally spots where the clay, approaching the surface, mingles with the sand, and forms tolerable soil, producing oak; and in low grounds, where marl is near the surface, some natural meadow, easily brought to produce the reclaimed grasses. But the great wealth of this portion of the county is the pine timber, with which it is covered, and which is cut into valuable lumber, or fed to the furnace of the iron foundery or steamboat. Bog ore is found in many places; marl generally through the western part of the county, and possibly may be turned up every where, by digging sufficiently deep. In the marl pits, animal reliques, such as shells, bones, and also petrified vegetables, are frequent. But the most extraordinary relic, yet discovered in these deposits, is a piece of wrought copper bolt, about an inch square, and two inches long, bearing the marks of tools, taken about 10 years since, from a marl pit, 10 feet below the surface, and within a short distance of Mount Holly, on the farm of Mr. Thomas Howell. Of the time when, and the means by which such a deposit was made, it is scarce possible to form a plausible conjecture.

The waters of the county flow, either N. W. to the Delaware river, or S. W. to the Atlantic ocean. The former consist of the Assunpink, Crosswick's, Black's, Craft's, Assiscunk, Rancocus, and Pensauken creeks, and their tributaries; the latter of the Wading and Mullica rivers, and their branches. The dividing ridge between these streams runs nearly parallel with the Delaware, and at about 20 miles distant from it. The streams are generally crooked, and sluggish; and the larger are navigable for 10 or 15 miles from their mouths. In Springfield t-ship, on the farm of Mr. James Shreve, is a well, whose water petrifies wood. Blocks of hickory, cut into the form of hones, have been converted into stone, in 5 years, by immersion therein.

The chief villages, and post-towns of the county are, Arneytown, Atsion, Bass River Hotel, Bordentown, Burlington, Columbus, Crosswicks, Evesham, Jacksonville, Jobstown, Juliustown, Medford, Moorestown, Mount Holly, the seat of justice, Pemberton, Recklesstown, Tuckerton, Vincenton, Wrightstown, &c. &c.

The county contained, by the report of the assessors of 1832, 123,524 acres of unimproved land, which might, with propriety, be nearly doubled; 14,210 neat cattle, 6055 horses over the age of three years, 19 stud horses, 3256 householders, with taxable property not exceeding $30 in value; 1095 single men, 86 merchants, 16 fisheries, 48 saw mills, 91 grist mills, 4 furnaces, 3 forges, 2 paper mills, one extensive, and of the most approved construction; 1 calico printing factory, 7 fulling mills, 4 cotton factories, 1 plaster mill, 350 tan vats, 11 carding machines, 35 distilleries for cider, 29 coaches and chariots, 6 phaetons and chaises, 8 four horse and 19 two horse stages, 392 dearborns, 977 covered wagons, 206 chairs and curricles, and paid state tax, $4607 12; county tax, $15,000; and township tax, $13,450.

The population of the county, in 1830, was 31,705; of whom 14,710 were white males; 15,033 white females; free coloured males, 869; free coloured females, 901; male slaves, 77; female slaves, 115; 174 aliens; 12 white, deaf and dumb; 7 white, and 3 blacks, blind. The county sends 5 members to the Assembly, and one to the Council.

STATISTICAL TABLE OF BURLINGTON COUNTY.

Townships, &c.	Length.	Breadth.	Area.	Surface generally level.	Population. 1810	1820	1830
Burlington,	7	7	9,702		2419	2758	2670
Chester,	7	6	22,000		1839	2253	2333
Chesterfield,	8	6	16,000		1839	2087	2386
Egg Harbour, Little,	20	10	76,800		913	1102	1490
Hanover,	16	13	44,000		2536	2642	2859
Mansfield,	10	6½	21,000		1810	1957	2083
Evesham,	15	10	67,000		3445	3977	4239
Northampton,	33	18	135,000		4171	4833	5516
Nottingham,	10	7	25,000		2615	3633	3900
Springfield,	10	6	18,000		1500	1568	1534
Washington,	20	19	112,000		1273	1225	1315
Willingboro'.	6	4	7,500			787	782
			553,002		24,360	28,822	31,107

Burlington t-ship, Burlington co., bounded N. E. by Mansfield and Springfield t-ships, S. E. by Northampton, S. W. by Willingboro', and N. W. by the River Delaware. Centrally distant N. W. from Mount Holly, 6 miles; length N. and S. 7; breadth E. and W. 7 miles; area, 9702 acres; surface, level; soil, sandy loam, very well cultivated, and abundantly productive, in grass, corn, wheat, and garden vegetables, and fruits; drained by the Assiscunk creek on the north, and a branch of the Rancocus on the south. Burlington city is in the t-ship. Population in 1830, 2670. In 1832 the t-ship contained, including the city, 575 taxables, 145 single men, 6 stores, 2 fisheries, 2 grist mills, 1 ferry, 34 tan vats, 1 distillery for cider, 14 coaches and chariots, 2 two horse stages, 27 dearborns, 57 covered wagons, 9 chairs and curricles, and 30 gigs and sulkies; and it paid state tax, $373 45; county tax, $1292 16; and t-ship tax, $1000.

Burlington Island, in the river Delaware, above the city of Burlington, and opposite the town of Bristol, originally termed Matenicunk, and also Chygoes island. (See *Burlington City*.)

Burlington Collection District comprehends that part of West Jersey lying on the eastward and northward of Gloucester, and all the waters thereof within the jurisdiction of the state. Burlington city is the port of entry, and Lamberton a port of delivery only; the collector resides at the latter.

Burlington City, of Burlington t-ship, Burlington co., 20 miles N. E. from Philadelphia, 158 from W. C., and 12 S. W. from Trenton, upon the river Delaware, and opposite to the town of Bristol; contains about 300 dwellings, and 1800 inhabitants; one Episcopal, 1 Baptist, and 2 Methodist churches, one of which are for coloured people, and 1 Friend's meeting house; 1 large and commodious boarding school for girls, beautifully situate on the river bank, and 1 large boarding school for boys; the former under the direction of S. R. Gummere, and the latter of John Gummere; a free school maintained chiefly from the rents of Matenicunk or Chygoes island, lying near the town, and which was given to it for that purpose by the proprietaries, by act of Assembly, 28th September, 1682. This island contains about 300 acres, and yields a rent of about $1000 annually. There are here also a boarding school endowed by the "Society of Friends;" five common schools for white, and one for coloured children.

The town is laid out upon 9 streets running N. and S., and 4 E. and W. The lots are generally deep, admitting of spacious gardens, in which much and excellent fruit is produced, among which grapes of various kinds are common. Upon the main street, the houses are closely built, but in other parts of the town they are wide asunder, and surrounded by gardens, orchards, and grass lots. Many of the buildings are very neat and commodious, and occupied as country seats by citizens of Philadelphia— those on the river bank, below the town, are beautifully situated, with a fine verdant velvet sward to the water's edge, giving them a perpetual air of freshness and coolness, most desirable in the summer months. There are here, also, a public library, several fire companies, a beneficial society, a distinguished nursery of fruit trees, 7 considerable stores, 5 taverns, 3 practising attorneys, 3 physicians, and extensive manufactories of shoes, employing near 300 hands. Burlington was laid out as a town in the year 1677, by the first purchasers from Lord Berkeley, and was incorporated by the proprietary government, including the island only, in 1693, and subsequently by Governor Cosby. The present incorporation is by act of the state legislature, 21st December, 1784, constituting the town and port of Burlington, of the length of 3 miles on the Delaware, and such part of the river and islands opposite thereto, within the jurisdiction of the state, and extending from the river at right angles one mile into the county, "*the city of Burlington;*" and authorizing its government, by a mayor, recorder, and 3 aldermen, annually elective, with power to hold a commercial court monthly. Prior to May, 1676, the site of this town was holden by 4 Dutch families, one of whom kept a public house for the entertainment of travellers passing to and from the settlements on the west shores of the Delaware, and New York. The river here is about a mile wide, the harbour pretty good,

but the town has no commerce. A great portion of the city is isolated by a creek, over which there are several bridges; the tide has been stopped out, and the marshes, which it formerly covered, are good meadows. The town is deemed healthy. Four steam-boats pass this town, to and from Philadelphia, daily.

Burnt Cabin Brook, principal branch of the Rockaway river, rises in Greenpond, in the valley between Greenpond mountain and Copperas mountain. It has a S. W. course of about 8 miles, before it unites with the main stream.

Burnt Meadow Brook, small tributary of Ringwood river, Pompton t-ship, Bergen co., into which it flows eastwardly by a course of about 6 miles.

Bustleton, hamlet, of Mansfield t-ship, Burlington co., 7 miles N. W. from Mount Holly, and 4 from Burlington city; contains a Friends' meeting house, and some half dozen farm houses, surrounded by a well cultivated country of fertile sandy loam.

Butcher's Forge, on Metetecunk river, on the line between Howell and Dover t-ships, Monmouth co., at the head of navigation, 18 miles S. E. from Freehold. There are here a forge, a grist mill, a tavern, 2 stores, and 15 or 20 dwellings. The mill pond is the largest in the state, having a length of nearly 3 miles, by nearly half a mile in breadth. Wood from the surrounding forest is boated on it to the furnace.

Byram t-ship, Sussex co., bounded N. W. by Newton t-ship; E. by Hardiston t-ship, and by Jefferson t-ship, Morris co.; S. by Roxbury t-ship, of the same co., and W. by Green t-ship, of Sussex co. Centrally distant S. E. from Newton 8 miles; greatest length N. and S. 10 miles, breadth E. and W. 8 miles; area, 21,760; surface mountainous, the t-ship being wholly covered by the South mountain. The t-ship is drained chiefly by Lubber run, which receives the waters of Lion pond, Hopatcong lake upon the E., and by Musconetcong river,

P

which courses the whole of the southern boundary. It is crossed N. W. by the Morris and Newton turnpike road. By the census of 1830 it contained 958 inhabitants; and in 1832 187 taxables, 5 stores, 5 saw mills, 10 forge fires, 6 tan vats, 1 distillery, 123 horses and mules, and 497 neat cattle, over the age of 3 years. Andover, Lockwood, Columbia, and Stanhope, are the names of the forges within the t-ship; Brooklyn forge lies on the S. E. boundary. The Morris canal touches the south boundary of the t-ship at Stanhope. The t-ship is noted for its iron and other minerals.

Cabbagetown, hamlet, of Upper Freehold t-ship, Monmouth co., on the line between that county and Middlesex, 17 miles from Freehold, and 12 from Trenton, contains some half dozen dwellings, a wheelwright, smith and joiner's shop.

Calais, Randolph t-ship, Morris co., on the road from Morristown to Stanhope forge, 6 miles N. W. from the former; contains a Presbyterian church, store, tavern, and 12 or 15 dwellings.

Caldwell t-ship, Essex co., bounded on the W. and N. by the Passaic river, which separates it from Hanover t-ship, Morris co., E. by Acquackanonck and Bloomfield t-ships, S. by Orange and Livingston t-ships. Centrally distant N. E. from Newark 10 miles; greatest length E. and W. 7; breadth N. and S. 6; area, 16,500 acres; surface mountainous on the E., elsewhere rolling, except in the valley of the river; drained, or rather watered, by Deep and Green brooks; soil red shale and alluvion; towns, Caldwell, Fairfield, and Franklin; the first a post-town; population in 1830, 2001. In 1832 the t-ship contained 325 taxables, 36 single men, 8 merchants, 3 grist mills, 1 cotton manufactory, 3 saw mills, 12 tan vats, 1 woollen factory, 325 horses and mules, and 1001 neat cattle, over the age of 3 years: and it paid state tax, $201 06; county, $526 06; poor, $600; road, $1327.

Caldwell, p-t. of preceding t-ship,

Essex co., 10 miles N. E. from Newark, 225 from W. C., and 59 from Trenton, contains a tavern, 3 stores, a grist and saw mill on Pine Brook, about 30 dwellings, and 2 Presbyterian churches. The country around it is deep clay loam.

Camden, city and t-ship, of Gloucester co., on the river Delaware, opposite to the city of Philadelphia, and port of entry and delivery of Bridgeton collection district, 8 miles N. W. from Woodbury, 137 N. E. from W. C., and 31 S. from Trenton. The site upon which it stands, was taken up between the years 1681 and 1685, in several parcels, by Messrs. Cooper, Runyon and Morris. The city was incorporated by acts 13 Feb. and 1 March, 1828, and 9 Feb. 1831; and as a t-ship by act Nov. 28, 1831. Its bounds by these acts are as follow: Beginning at the Pennsylvania line in the Delaware, opposite the mouth of a small run of water below Kaighnton, and running E. to the mouth of said run; thence by the same, crossing the public road to Woodbury, from the Camden academy; thence N. by the E. side of said road, to the road from Kaighnton to Cooper's creek bridge; thence by the E. side of the last mentioned road, and the S. side of the causey and bridge, to the middle of Cooper's creek; thence by the middle of the creek to the Delaware; thence due N. to the middle of the channel, between Petty's island and the Jersey shore; thence down the channel to the nearest point on the line between the states of Pennsylvania and New Jersey; thence by said line to the place of beginning. The district has a length of 2¼ miles on the river, by about 1¼ in breadth to the bridge over Cooper's creek. But a small portion only, of this area, is built upon: the greatest portion is employed in tillage, chiefly of fruit and early vegetables, for the Philadelphia market, to which the soil is admirably adapted; and a considerable part is still in woods, yielding shade and recreation to the inhabitants of the great city, in the hot season. The district is divided into 3 distinct villages, separated by vacant grounds from half a mile to nearly a mile in extent. That, opposite to the Northern Liberties, is known as Cooper's Point, at which there is an extensive ferry establishment, tavern, store, livery stable, and a dozen dwellings. The lower village, nearly opposite to the Navy Yard, is called Kaighnton or Kaighn's Point, from the family of that name, which settled on it in 1696, and whose descendants, still residents on, and owners of the greater part of the adjoining property, laid out town lots here, and established the ferry to Philadelphia in 1809. It contains 35 dwellings, a store, school house, 2 taverns, a tannery, an extensive smithery and manufactory of steel springs for carriages. The central and largest part of the city was originally called Camden, about the year 1772, when first divided into town lots, by the then proprietor, Jacob Cooper, and is nearly equidistant between the two Points, and opposite to the central part of Philadelphia. The land at Cooper's Point, and extensive adjacent tracts, were taken up in 1687, by William Cooper, one of the first and distinguished emigrants to the province, after the sale by Lord Berkeley to Byllinge; the whole of which is, at this time, not only possessed by his descendants, but actually, by descendants bearing the name of Cooper; no portion of it, at any time, having, in the space of 146 years, been aliened by the family.

At the period of incorporation, 1828, the population of the district was 1143; in 1830 it had increased to 1987, and now, Sept. 1833, by a census made for this work, amounts to 2341; of whom 417 are heads of families, or housekeepers, 1237 males, 1104 females, 78 widows, and 105 people of colour. It contains 364 dwelling houses, and 60 other buildings used for manufactories, stores, and schools, a Baptist, a Methodist, and a Quaker meeting house, a courthouse, or town hall, where the city sessions are holden, quarterly, by the mayor, recorder, and aldermen, for the trial of minor offences, and a prison connected therewith; an academy, at which are taught the rudiments of a common English education; "the State Bank at Camden," with a capital of $300,000 dollars; a turpentine, a patent leather, and a tinware manufactory; 2 tanneries, a steam saw mill and steam grist mill, 2 saddlers and harnessmakers, other than those connected with the coachmakers; 6 coachmakers, whose business exceeds in value $60,000, annually, and whose work, much of which is exported, is remarkable at once, for cheapness, lightness, strength, and beauty of finish; 8 smitheries, connected with 2 of which are manufactories of steel springs; a white or silver smith, a clock and watchmaker's shop, a comb manufactory, a trunk manufactory, 2 bakeries, 2 cooper's shops, 2 druggist's shops, 12 stores, 5 lumber yards, 5 livery stables, 9 taverns, including the ferry houses, 2 cabinetmaker's shops, 2 tailor's shops, 11 master carpenters, 4 master stone and brick masons, 2 painters and glaziers, a gold and silver plater, 2 printing offices, from each of which a weekly newspaper is issued, and 3 physicians and 6 lawyers.

There are here also several handsome public gardens, much frequented by the Philadelphians, who have ready access to them by the steam ferry boats constantly passing the river. Of these useful vessels, there are at present eight belonging to the five ferry establishments, including those at Cooper's and Kaighn's Points; employing a capital of $60,000, exclusive of the real estate, such as wharves, ferry houses, &c. valued at $100,000. The gross income from which, is estimated at not less than $80,000 per annum. The boats adapted for carriages and passengers cross, in from 5 to 15 minutes, according to the state of the tide; and are impelled by steam engines of from 15 to 20 horse power.

The ship channel is on the Philadelphia side of the river. The water on the New Jersey side is too shoal for vessels of the largest size to ascend higher than Kaighn's Point, where it is sufficiently deep for those of any tonnage. Brigs and schooners of 150 tons come to the central parts of Camden at high tide, and unload at the wharves. Efforts are making to convert this into a port of entry, and to annex it to the Philadelphia collection district.

Campbell's Brook rises at the foot of the mountain in Readington t-ship, Hunterdon co., and flows by a S. E. course of about 7 miles to the south branch of the Raritan river, in Bridgewater t-ship, Somerset co.

Camptown, Orange t-ship, Essex co., 3½ miles S. W. from Newark, contains within a circle of a mile and a half in diameter, 75 dwellings, a free church of stone, of three stories, the first used as an academy, the second as a church, open to all denominations of Christians, and the third a masonic lodge; a Presbyterian church, 1 tavern, 3 stores, 1 saw mill, and 1 grist mill, upon Elizabeth river. The lands here vary in value, according to quality, from 50 to $100 the acre. The name is derived from the circumstance that the American army had a camp in the vicinity during the revolution.

Canoe Brook, small tributary of the Passaic river, Livingston and Springfield t-ships, Essex co., has a westerly course of three miles.

Cape May County, by the act of Assembly, 21st of January, 1710, begins at the mouth of a small creek, on the west side of Stipson's island, called Jecak's creek, and continues thence by the said creek, as high as the tide floweth; thence, along the bounds (of what was then Salem county, now Cumberland,) to the southernmost main branch of Great Egg Harbour river; thence down the said river to the sea; thence along the sea coast to Delaware bay, and so up the said bay to the place of beginning. It is, therefore, bounded on the north by Cumberland county, E. and S. by the Atlantic ocean, and W.

by Delaware bay. Its greatest length, N. E. and S. W. is 30 miles; greatest breadth E. and W., 15 miles; form semi-oval: area 252 square miles, or about 161,000 acres. Central lat. 39° 10'; long. 2° 7' E. from W. C.

This county is wholly of alluvial formation. Upon the coast, from the mouth of Great Egg Harbour bay, and for some miles on the Delaware bay, above the capes, is a sand beach: on the east, this beach, from a half mile to two miles in width, is covered with grass which affords pasture for neat cattle and sheep. It is broken by several inlets, by which the sea penetrates the marshes, and forms lagunes or salt water lakes, in several places, two miles in diameter, connected by various channels. The marsh has an average width of about four miles; a similar marsh extends along the N. W. part of the county, on the bay, widening as it advances northward. The Tuckahoe river, on the north, divides this from Gloucester co., receiving from Cape May co. Cedar Swamp creek, which interlocks with Dennis' creek, the latter emptying into the Delaware bay. Both streams flow through an extensive cedar swamp, stretching for 17 miles across the county. Several other, but inconsiderable streams, flow westerly into the Delaware bay. The *fast land* of the county is composed of clay based on sand, generally covered with oak forest, from which large quantities of timber and cord wood are annually sent to the Philadelphia and New York markets. The greater portion of the inhabitants are settled on the east and west margins of this fast land, along which run the main roads of the county. The forest land, when cleared, becomes arable, and, with due cultivation, produces good crops of corn and rye. The farms are generally large, running from the roads landward. Some cleared and cultivated tracts are interspersed with the forest. The wealth of the county is in its timber.

The name of this county is derived from Cornelius Jacobse Mey, a navigator in the service of the Dutch West India Company, who visited the Delaware bay in 1623, for the purpose of colonization, but the settlements, if any were made here by him, were soon abandoned. In 1630 a purchase of land, extending along the bay for sixteen miles, and sixteen inward, was made of the Indians, by the Dutch governor of New Amsterdam, Van Twiller, for the Sieurs Goodyn and Blomaert, directors of the West India Company; but we do not learn that these lands were immediately peopled by Europeans. From the records of the court of this county, it appears probable that some English settlers were established here at an early period, from New England, and we may conjecture that they were colonists from New Haven, some of whose descendants may yet remain in the county.

The county is divided into 4 t-ships; its pop. in 1830, was 4396 souls; being about 20 to the square mile; of whom 2400 were white males, 2308 white females, 118 free coloured males, 107 free coloured females, 3 slaves; among these were 1 deaf and dumb, but there were none blind nor alien.

The seat of justice is centrally situated at Middletown, where there are a frame court house, brick fire proof offices, and a stone prison; the other public buildings of the county, consist of an Episcopalian church, 2 Baptist do., 2 Methodist do.

At an early period of its history the inhabitants were engaged in the whale fishery; at present, their chief support is derived from the timber and cord wood trade, raising of cattle, and supplying the market with oysters, clams, fish, &c. At Cape Island, a considerable revenue is derived from the company who visit the sea shore during the hot weather. By the assessor's report for 1832, the county contained but 20,244 acres of improved land, a little more than one-eighth part of its area; 669 householders, 8 grist mills, the chief part of which are moved by wind, 16 saw mills, 29 stores, 679 horses, and 2093 neat cattle over 3 years of age; and paid for t-ship purposes $324 60; for state purposes $646 01, and $2000 for county uses.

By the act of 8th March, 1797, it sends 1 member to the assembly, and by the constitution, 1 member to council.

The court of common pleas and quarter sessions for Cape May co., sit on the 1st Tuesdays of February, the last of May, the 1st of August, and the 4th of October; and the circuit courts on the last Tuesday of May, annually, at Middletown.

This portion of the state has not generally been holden in due estimation. If its inhabitants be not numerous, they are generally as independent as any others in the state, and enjoy as abundantly the comforts of life. They are hospitable, and respectable for the propriety of their manners, and are blessed, usually, with excellent health. Until lately they have known little, practically, of those necessary evils of social life, the physician and the lawyer. Morse assures us, that their women possessed the power not only of sweetening life, but of defending and prolonging it, being competent to cure most of the diseases which attack it. We learn, however, that their practice in the latter particular, has lately been contested; that one or more physicians have crept in, but we rejoice to hear that they find little employment. We learn also, that the county, like Ireland, refusing nourishment to noxious animals, no lawyer can subsist in it.

STATISTICAL TABLE OF CAPE MAY COUNTY.

Townships.	Length.	Breadth.	Area.	Surface.	Population.		
					1810	1820	1830
Upper,	12½	11½	37,000		1664	2107	1067
Dennis,	14	8½	43,500				1508
Middle,	12	10	60,000		1106	1157	1366
Lower,	8	8	21,000		862	1001	995
			161,500			4265	4936

Cape May Court House, p-t. and seat of justice of Cape May co., centrally situate in Middle t-ship, 104 miles N. E. from W. C., and 102 S. from Trenton, 34 S. E. from Bridgeton, and 74 from Philadelphia; contains a court house of wood, a jail of stone, fire-proof offices of brick, 2 taverns, 8 or 10 dwellings, and a Baptist church of brick. Lat. 39° N. long. 2° 8′ E. from W. C.; it is called Middletown, in the post-office lists.

Cape May, the most southern point of N. J., and the eastern cape of the Delaware bay, formed by the bay and the Atlantic ocean; lat. 38° 56′, long. 2° 18′ E. from W. C.; a light house stands upon the point. The name of this cape should have been written Mey, since it has its name from Cornelius Jacobse Mey, a distinguished navigator, who visited the Delaware in 1623, in the employ of the Dutch West India Company. He gave his Christian name, Cornelius, to the west cape of the bay.

Cape May Island, beach of the Atlantic ocean, near the southern point of the state, in Lower t-ship, Cape May co., 104 miles by post-route from Philadelphia, 115 from Trenton, and 117 from W. C.; it is a noted and much frequented watering place, the season at which commences about the first of July, and continues until the middle of August, or 1st September. There are here six boarding houses, three of which are very large; the sea bathing is convenient and excellent, the beach affords pleasant drives, and there is excellent fishing in the adjacent waters. There is a post-office here.

Carllsburg, hamlet of Deerfield t-ship, Cumberland co., between 3 and 4 miles N. E. of Bridgeton.

Carpenter's Landing, post-town of Greenwich t-ship, Gloucester co., upon Mantua creek, at the head of sloop navigation, 3 miles S. W. from Woodbury; 7 miles by the creek from the Delaware; 42 miles from Trenton, and 148 from W. C. It is a place of considerable trade, in lumber, cord wood, &c., and contains 1 tavern, 2 stores, 30 dwellings, and 1 Methodist church.

Cat-tail, hamlet, of Upper Freehold t-ship, Monmouth co., on Cat-tail creek, on the line between Middlesex and Monmouth cos., 16 miles S. W. from Freehold, and 28 S. E. from Trenton.

Cedar Bridge, hamlet, Stafford t-ship, Monmouth co., upon the Oswego, or E. branch of Wading river, 33 miles S. of Freehold, contains a saw mill, 2 taverns, and several dwellings, surrounded by pine forest.

Cedar Creek, Stafford t-ship, Monmouth co., flows S. W. about 6 miles, into Little Egg Harbour bay, 2 miles below the mouth of Manahocking creek.

Cedar Creek, Dover t-ship, Monmouth co., rises by several branches, and flows eastwardly about 16 miles to the Atlantic ocean. The village of Williamsburg is seated upon it, near the head of tide water, and contains 10 or 12 dwellings, 2 taverns, 2 stores. Goodluck is a thickly settled neighbourhood, a short distance on the S. W. The country on the E. is salt marsh; elsewhere, sandy, and covered with pine forest.

Cedar Creek, Fairfield t-ship, Cumberland co., rises in the t-ship, and flows westerly through it for about 10 miles, giving motion to several mills, and emptying into Nantuxet cove, Delaware bay. It is navigable about 4 miles to Cedarville.

Cedar Pond, small lake of about 100 acres, Pompton t-ship, Bergen co., sends forth a portion of its waters to supply the stream of Clinton forges.

Cedar Swamp Creek, Upper t-ship, Cape May co., rises in the t-ship by 2 branches, and flows N. E. 8 miles, into Tuckahoe river. Its course is through an extensive cedar swamp.

Cedar Swamp Creek, of Egg Harbour t-ship, Gloucester co., a mill stream, which flows S. W., by Bargaintown, about 7 or 8 miles, into Great Egg Harbour bay.

Cedarville, p-t. of Fairfield t-ship, Cumberland co., pleasantly situated, on Cedar creek, at the head of navigation, about 4 miles from the mouth of the creek, 7 S. from Bridgeton, 183, by post route, N. E. from W. C., and 77 S. from Trenton; contains about 60 dwellings, a store, and tavern, grist and saw mill, and an extensive button manufactory. The country about it is sandy and poor; but the lots in the village are carefully cultivated and productive. Trade, wood and lumber. Inhabitants, 375.

Cedarville, of Caldwell t-ship, Essex co., upon Peekman's run, about 2 miles above its confluence with the Passaic river. There are here several small mills, such as grist mill, saw mill, and cotton factory.

Centreville, p-t. of Pittsgrove t-ship, Salem co., upon Muddy run, and upon the line dividing Salem from Cumberland co., 17 miles S. E. from Salem town, and 75 S. from Trenton; contains some 12 or 15 dwellings, tavern, store, and school house.

Centreville, East Windsor t-ship, Middlesex co., upon the turnpike road from Bordentown to Cranberry, 9 miles from the former, and 18 miles S. W. from New Brunswick, contains a tavern and several dwellings.

Centreville, small village, of

Knowlton t-ship, Warren co., on the road leading from Hope to Knowlton mills and Columbia; about 4 miles from the first and last, and 10 N. E. from Belvidere; contains a tavern, store, smith shop, Presbyterian church, and several dwellings.

Centreville Post-Office, Hunterdon co.; by post route, 189 miles from W. C., and 30 from Trenton.

Chambers' Brook, tributary of the north branch of the Raritan, and S. E. boundary of Bedminster t-ship, Somerset co., rises in the mountain on the E., and flows S. W., about 4 miles to its recipient.

Chambers' Mill Branch, a small stream, rising in the centre of Montague t-ship, Sussex co., and flowing westerly, about 5 miles, into the river Delaware. It gives motion to several mills near its mouth.

Change Water, furnace, on the Musconetcong creek, in Mansfield t-ship, Warren co., 3 miles from the village of Mansfield, and 10 S. E. from Belvidere, the county town.

Charlottesburg, the name of a furnace, formerly on the Pequannock creek, Pompton t-ship, Bergen co., now in ruins.

Charleston, small village, in the N. E. part of Bethlehem t-ship, Hunterdon co., on the Musconetcong mountain, 13 miles N. of Flemington.

Charleston, hamlet, of Kingwood t-ship, Hunterdon co., 10 miles W. of Flemington; contains a tavern, store, and several dwellings.

Chatham t-ship, Morris co., bounded north by Hanover t-ship; E. and S. E. by the Passaic river, which separates it from Livingston, Springfield and New Providence t-ships, Sussex co.; W. and S. by Morris t-ship. Centrally distant, S. E. from Morristown, 6 miles; greatest length, N. and S. 9 miles, breadth, E. and W. 5 miles; area, 14,400; surface undulating, except on the south, which is covered by Long Hill. Black Brook rises in the t-ship and flows W. to the Passaic river, through Morris t-ship. Bottle Hill, Chatham, and Columbia are villages of the t-ship, the first two post-towns; population in 1830, 1865. In 1832 there were in the t-ship 340 taxables, 40 single men, 9 stores, 3 saw mills, and 5 grist mills, 5 distilleries, 1 fulling mill, 1 carding engine, 254 horses and mules, and 1015 neat cattle, under 3 years old; and the t-ship paid state tax, $248 35; county tax, $556 04; poor tax, $600; road tax, $600. The turnpike roads from Elizabethtown and Newark cross this t-ship to Morristown.

Chatham, p-t. of Chatham t-ship, Morris co., on the road from Elizabethtown to Morristown, 10 miles from the one, and 7½ from the other; 220 N. E. from W. C., and 54 from Trenton; contains 1 Presbyterian and 1 Methodist church, an academy, 3 stores, 2 taverns, a grist mill and saw mill, and between 40 and 50 dwellings. A thriving village, with neat dwellings, surrounded by a pleasant, well cultivated country, watered by the Passaic river, which flows through the town.

Cheapside, agricultural village, of Livingston t-ship, Essex co., on the turnpike road from Newark to Morristown, 10 miles W. of the former.

Cheesequake's Creek, with several branches flowing into the Raritan bay, about 3 miles below Amboy, Middlesex co., drains a swamp of considerable extent.

Chesnut Neck, strip of fast land, lying between Little Egg Harbour river and Nacote creek, Galloway t-ship, Gloucester co.

Chesnut Run, small branch of the Assunpink creek, Upper Freehold t-ship, Monmouth co.

Chester t-ship, Morris co., bounded N. by Roxbury t-ship, N. E. by Randolph t-ship, E. by Mendham t-ship, S. by Bedminster t-ship, Somerset co., and W. by Washington t-ship. Centrally distant W. from Morristown 12 miles; greatest length N. and S. 9, breadth E. and W. 6 miles; area, 18000 acres; surface rolling; soil on the N. loam, on the S. grey limestone, under good cultivation; drained on the W. by the Black

river, and on the E. by tributaries of the N. branch of the Raritan river; population in 1830, 1338. In 1832 the t-ship contained 324 taxables, whose ratables did not exceed $30; 23 single men, 3 stores, 5 saw mills, and 2 grist mills, 4 distilleries, 1 forge, 2 fulling mills, and 311 horses and mules, and 669 neat cattle, above 3 years of age; and paid the following taxes: state, $193 14; county, $432 43; poor $400; road, $400.

Chester t-ship, Burlington co., bounded N. E. by the Rancocus creek, S. E. by Evesham t-ship, S. W. by Pensauken creek, which divides it from Gloucester co., Waterford t-ship, and N. W. by the river Delaware. Centrally distant S. W. from Mount Holly 9 miles; greatest length 7, breadth 6 miles; area, 22,000 acres; surface level; soil sand and sandy loam, of good quality, generally, well cultivated, and productive of grass, grain, vegetables, and fruits. Beside the streams already mentioned, the t-ship is drained by the N. branch of Pensauken creek, by Pompeston creek, and Swede's branch, the last two emptying immediately into the Delaware. All are mill streams. The Rancocus Drawbridge, Westfield, and Moorestown, are villages of the t-ship, the last a post-town; population in 1830, 2333. In 1832 the t-ship contained taxables 524, householders 205, whose ratables did not exceed $30; single men 96, stores 8, fisheries 5, grist mills 3, saw mills 6, tan vats 27, carding machines 2, distilleries for cider 3, coaches and chariots 7, two horse stages 2, dearborns 52, covered wagons 90, chairs and curricles 30, gigs and sulkies 22, neat cattle 1060, and horses and mules 570, over 3 years of age; and it paid state tax, $336 38; county, $1173 91; and road tax, $1100.

Chester, p-t. of Chester t-ship, Morris co., on the turnpike road leading from Morristown to Easton, 13 miles N. W. from the former, 50 N. E. from Trenton, and 216 from W. C.; at the foot of a low isolated mountain, which covers it on the north; it extends along the road for more than a mile, and contains 1 Presbyterian, and 1 Congregational church, 2 taverns, 3 stores, and about 30 dwellings, and lies upon, or near, a vein of grey limestone.

Chesterfield t-ship, Burlington co., bounded N. W. and N. by Crosswick's creek, which divides it from Nottingham t-ship, S. E. by Hànover t-ship, S. W. by Bacon's run and Black's creek, and W. by the river Delaware. Centrally distant N. E. from Mount Holly 12 miles; greatest length N. and S. 8 miles; greatest breadth E. and W. 6 miles; surface level; soil, generally, sandy, mixed with clay and loam; drained by the creeks mentioned, which flow to the Delaware river, the bank of which is here considerably elevated, giving a picturesque appearance to the country, especially at and near Bordentown. Bordentown and Recklesstown are the post-towns, and only villages of the t-ship; population in 1830, 2386. In 1832 the t-ship contained 554 taxables, whose ratables did not exceed $30; 75 single men, 1030 neat cattle, and 510 horses, above 3 years old; 10 stores, 1 saw mill, 2 grist mills, 40 tan vats, 6 distilleries for cider, 2 coaches and chariots, 3 phaetons and chaises, 7 four horse stages, 10 two horse stages, 41 dearborns, 58 covered wagons, 8 chairs and curricles, 17 gigs and sulkies; and it paid state tax, $346 49; county tax, $1216 32 and t-ship tax, $1000.

Chew's Landing, p-t. of Gloucester t-ship, Gloucester co., upon the N. branch of Big Timber creek, at the head of navigation, 9 miles S. E. from Camden, and 6 N. E. from Woodbury, 41 S. E. from Trenton, and 149 N. E. from W. C. It is a place of considerable business in lumber and cord wood, and contains 2 stores, 2 taverns, 2 grist mills, and between 30 and 40 dwellings, 1 Episcopal and 1 Methodist church.

Clarkesburg, hamlet, of Upper Freehold t-ship, Monmouth co., on the road from Wrightsville to Free-

hold court-house, 12 miles from the latter, and 20 from Trenton; contains some half dozen dwellings, store and tavern.

Clarkesborough, p-t. of Greenwich t-ship, Gloucester co., 5 miles S. W. from Woodbury, 44 from Trenton, and 150 from W. C.; contains a store, tavern, and from 25 to 30 dwellings; and within 2 miles S. W. there is a Friend's meeting house.

Clarkesville, (formerly called Sodom) p-t. of Lebanon t-ship, Hunterdon co., on Spruce run, and on the Musconetcong mountain, on the western line of the t-ship, 14 miles N. of Flemington, 37 from Trenton; contains 1 tavern and store, 2 saw mills, 2 grist mills, and 6 or 8 dwellings; the surface is very rough and stony, but parts are productive; iron abounds in the mountain, and plumbago is also found in several places upon it, near the village.

Clarkesville, small hamlet, of West Windsor t-ship, Middlesex co., on the straight turnpike road from Trenton to Brunswick, 7 miles N. E. from the one, and 18 S. W. from the other; contains 2 taverns, and 6 or 8 dwellings; soil good, and country pleasant around it.

Clementon, village, of Gloucester t-ship, Gloucester co., on a branch of Big Timber creek, 5 miles above Chew's landing, 10 miles S. E. of Woodbury, and 13 from Camden; contained formerly some glass works, at present 1 tavern, store, grist and saw mills, and some 12 or 15 dwellings; marl abounds in the vicinity, and is advantageously used upon the soil.

Clinton, formerly called Hunt's Mills, p-t., of Hunterdon co., on the south branch of Raritan river, at the point of junction of Lebanon, Bethlehem, and Kingwood t-ships, lying partly in each, and on the turnpike road leading from Somerville to Easton; about 20 miles from the former, and 17 from the latter; 10 miles N. E. from Flemington, 33 from Trenton, and 210 from W. C. The town is built in a valley surrounded on all

Q

sides by hills, which on the N. N. E. and N. W., approach closely to it, but are more distant on the south. It contains 1 Presbyterian church, 1 common English, and a Sunday school, 2 large grist mills, 2 runs of stones each, an oil mill, at which from 8000 to 10,000 bushels of flaxseed are annually manufactured, a woollen manufactory, with fulling mill and cards for country work, 3 stores, 3 taverns, and 35 dwellings. The fall used at the water-works here, is 8½ feet only, but a very great power may be obtained, the stream having a very rapid descent, and large volume. The surrounding country is very fertile, and carefully tilled, being enriched by lime made from a grey stone, which in a broad vein skirts the Musconetcong mountain, and which rises in cliffs at the village, nearly 100 feet high. The average product in wheat here, is rated at 18 bushels the acre, and from the best farms 25 bushels the acre are obtained. Iron ore, and plumbago, abound in the neighbouring mountain, and the inhabitants look for increased prosperity from a rail-road contemplated to be made through their town, leading from Elizabethtown to Belvidere. The town lies 177 feet above tide water. By act of 19th February, 1833, authority was given to incorporate a company for any species of manufacture here, with a capital of $120,000.

Clinton Forge, Pompton t-ship, Bergen co., on a small stream flowing from Hanks, Cedar, and Buck ponds, and emptying into Pequannock creek, 28 miles N. W. from Hackensack.

Clonmell Creek, small stream of Greenwich t-ship, Gloucester co., flowing by a course of 2 or 3 miles into the Delaware river, opposite to Little Tinicum island.

Closter, village, of Hackensack t-ship, Bergen co., 4½ miles N. E. of Hackensack town, near the W. foot of the Palisade Hills, surrounded by a soil of rich loam, contains a tavern, a store, and from 12 to 15 dwellings.

Closter Mountain, part of the Ber-

gen ridge, Bergen co., Hackensack and Harrington t-ships, forming the right bank of the North river, and the Palisades. Its formation is trap, resting upon red and grey sandstone. Height about 400 feet; the eastern side precipitous, the west gently declining; thickly settled and well cultivated; the top generally covered with wood.

Clove River. (See *Deep Clove River*.)

Clove Church, on the bank of Clove river, Wantage t-ship, Sussex co.

Cohansey River, rises in Upper Alloways creek t-ship, Salem co., its head waters interlocking with those of Alloways creek. It flows, thence, by a due S. course of 15 miles, by Bridgeton, forming the division line between Deerfield and Hopewell t-ships, Cumberland co., into Fairfield t-ship; turning, thence, westerly, it runs about 8 miles to the town of Greenwich, and thence by a meandering course S. W. of 7 or 8 miles, it unites with the Delaware bay. The river is banked in, above Greenwich, to which place it is navigable for large brigs and schooners; vessels of 80 tons burthen ascend to Bridgeton, 20 miles from the mouth. Above Bridgeton the stream is not navigable, but affords a very valuable water power, which is used at the town for driving a rolling and slitting mill, nail factory, and gristmill, &c. &c. (See *Bridgeton*.)

Cohansey Cove, bay of the Cohansey creek, Fairfield t-ship, Cumberland co., an inlet from the Delaware bay.

Cold Spring Inlet, Lower t-ship, Cape May co., between Two Mile Beach, and Poverty Beach, upon the Atlantic sea-board. It is less than half a mile in width. It has its name from a spring about 3 or 4 miles inland, which sends its tribute to the ocean by this passage.

Cold Spring, p-t., of Lower t-ship, Cape May co. Centrally situated on the road to Cape May Island, 9 miles S. from Cape May court-house, 112 from Trenton, and 117 N. E. from W. C.; contains 1 tavern, 2 stores, from 15 to 20 dwellings, and an Episcopal church. It derives its name from a remarkble spring near it, which rises in the marsh, and is overflowed at every tide.

Cold Brook, small tributary of Lamington river, flowing into it S. W. from Tewkesbury t-ship, Hunterdon co., by a course of about 4 miles, giving motion to a mill near its mouth.

Cold Branch, tributary of Hospitality creek, an arm of the Great Egg Harbour river, Hamilton t-ship, Gloucester co.

Colestown, hamlet, of Evesham t-ship, Burlington co., 12 miles S. W. of Mount Holly, and 3 from Moorestown; contains an Episcopal church and several dwellings.

Collard Branch, of the west arm of Wading river, rises in Northampton t-ship, Burlington co., and flows S. W. about 8 miles, to its recipient, in Washington t-ship, at the head of the mill pond of Martha furnace.

Colt's Neck, p-t., Shrewsbury t-ship, Monmouth co., 6 miles N. E. of Freehold, 206 from W. C., and 41 from Trenton; contains from 15 to 20 dwellings, 1 tavern, 2 stores, 3 grist mills, 2 saw mills, a place of considerable business, on a soil of red and fertile sand.

Columbia, village, of Chatham t-ship, Morris co., on the turnpike road from Newark to Morristown, 13 miles from the one, and 4 from the other; contains 1 store, 1 tavern, and 5 or 6 dwellings, in a level pleasant country.

Columbia Forge, on Lubber run, centrally situate in Byram t-ship, Sussex co.

Columbia, p-t. and village, of Knowlton t-ship, on the Delaware river, near the mouth of Paulinskill, distant 253 miles from W. C., 94 from Trenton, and 10 from Belvidere; contains 2 taverns, a store, a Presbyterian church, a glass house, a saw mill, and 20 dwellings. The town is prettily situated on a high

bank of the river, and surrounded by a limestone soil, tolerably well cultivated. A company was incorporated by act of 12th February, 1833, with authority to employ $100,000 in the conduct of the glass works here.

Columbia, p-t., of Hopewell t-ship, Hunterdon co., on the turnpike road from New Brunswick to Lambertville, 10 miles S. E. from Flemington, 17 N. from Trenton, formerly called Hopewell Meeting House; contains 1 Baptist meeting, 2 taverns, 1 store, and 10 or 12 dwellings.

Columbus, or Black Horse, p-t., of Mansfield t-ship, Burlington co., 7 miles N. E. of Mount Holly, 5 S. E. from Bordentown, 13 from Trenton, and 163 from W. C.; contains a tavern, store, and about 30 dwellings, surrounded by a fertile country.

Communipaw, village, on New York bay, 2 miles S. of Jersey city, Bergen t-ship, Bergen co., one of the earliest settlements of the Dutch, and remarkable for the tenacious adherence of its inhabitants to their primitive costume and manners; some 15 or 20 dwellings, whose inhabitants are chiefly agriculturists.

Congassa Run, tributary of the S. branch of Toms' river, Dover t-ship, Monmouth co.

Cooper's Creek, Gloucester co., rises by two branches, the N. near the E. boundary of the county, and the S. on, and forming, the line between Waterford and Newton and Gloucester t-ships, uniting N. of Haddonfield, above which the stream is not navigable. There are mills on both branches near their sources.

Cooperstown, Willingboro' t-ship, Burlington co., 7 miles N. W. from Mount Holly, and 3 S. W. from Burlington; contains a Friends' meeting house, tavern, store, and 8 or 10 dwellings.

Copperas Mountain, Pequannock t-ship, Morris co., on the S. W. side of Greenpond valley, thus named on account of the large quantity of the sulphate of iron found here, and which was formerly made into the copperas of commerce.

Corson's Inlet, a passage of the sea, through the beach, to the lagunes and marshes of Upper t-ship, Cape May co., about half a mile in width.

Coursenville, p-t. of Stillwater t-ship, Sussex co., distant by post-route from W. C. 239 miles, from Trenton 81 miles, and from Newton, S. W., five miles; contains a store and some half dozen dwellings; adjacent country, slate.

Cove, small village of Upper Penn's-neck t-ship, Salem co., about 12 or 13 miles N. of Salem, and 2 S. of Penn's Grove, on the river Delaware; contains 8 dwellings, a tavern and store.

Cox Hall Creek, small stream of Lower t-ship, Cape May co., flowing into the Delaware bay.

Crabtown, Howell t-ship, Monmouth co.; contains 10 or 12 dwellings, 2 taverns, and a store.

Craft's Creek, Mansfield t-ship, Burlington co.; rises near the eastern border of the t-ship, and flows W. and N. W. about 9 miles to the river Delaware, opposite the lower point of Newbold's island. By act of assembly passed 11th February, 1833, authority was given to make a rail or Macadamized road from the mouth of this creek to the neighbourhood of New Lisbon, a distance of 13 miles 39 chains.

Cranberry p-t., lying partly in South Brunswick t-ship, and partly in South Amboy t-ship, Middlesex co., on the turnpike road leading from Bordentown to South Amboy, 16 miles from the former, 185 from W. C., and 15 from Trenton; pleasantly situated in a level country, and light sandy soil; contains a Presbyterian church with cupola and bell, an academy, a grist mill, 2 tanneries, 3 taverns, 2 stores, and from 60 to 80 dwellings. Cranberry brook, tributary of the Millstone river, flows through the town.

Cranberry Inlet, formerly from the ocean to Barnegat Bay, between Island beach and Squam beach.

Crane's Gap, in the first mountain, Bloomfield t-ship, Essex co., through which passes the turnpike road from Newark to Rockaway.

Craven's Ferry, p-o., Salem co.

Cropwell, village of Evesham t-sp, Burlington co., near the western boundary, 11 miles S. W. of Mount Holly; contains a tavern, store, 12 or 15 dwellings, and a Quaker meeting house; soil, sandy loam.

Cross Keys, hamlet of Trenton t-ship, Hunterdon co., on the road from Trenton to Pennington; contains 4 or 5 dwellings.

Cross Creeks, name given to small tributaries of Back creek, Fairfield t-ship, Cumberland co., near the Delaware bay, which intersect each other.

Cross Roads, Bedminster t-ship, Somerset co., between 7 and 8 miles N. W. of Somerville, on Artle's brook, in a level, fertile, limestone country; contains a store, tavern, and 5 or 6 dwellings.

Cross Roads, hamlet of South Brunswick t-ship, Middlesex co., 9 miles S. W. from New Brunswick; contains 2 taverns, a store, and several dwellings; soil, light and sandy.

Cross Roads, hamlet of Evesham t-ship, Burlington co., 8 miles S. from Mount Holly; contains a tavern, a store, a Methodist church, and 8 or 10 dwellings; soil, sandy loam.

Crosswick's Creek, the Indian name of which is said to be *Clossweeksunk, a separation*, rises by two branches, the north in Hanover t-ship, Burlington co., near Wrightstown; and the south in Upper Freehold, Monmouth co., uniting in the latter t-ship and county near New Egypt, thence running northerly and north westerly across Chesterfield t-ship, Burlington co., to the River Delaware, at Bordentown. It is a steady and serviceable mill-stream, whose course is semicircular, and in length about 25 miles; it is navigable to Grove Mill, about 6 miles from the mouth; marl is frequently found on its banks.

Crosswicks, p-t. of Chesterfield t-ship, Burlington co., on the high southern bank of Crosswick's creek, 4 miles E. from Bordentown, 14 N. E. from Mount Holly, 174 from W. C., and 8 S. E. from Trenton; contains from 40 to 50 dwellings, a very large Quaker meeting house and school, 4 taverns, 5 or 6 stores, a saw mill and grist mill; the village is pleasantly situated in a fertile country, whose soil is sandy loam; near the town is a bed of iron ore, from which considerable quantities are taken to the furnaces in the lower part of the county.

Culver's Pond, Frankford t-ship, Sussex co., at the foot of the Blue mountain; one of the western sources of the Paulinskill.

Culver's Gap, in the Blue mountain, between Sandistone and Frankford t-ships, Sussex co., through which the turnpike road from Milford passes; distant from Newton N. W. 10 miles.

Cumberland County, was taken altogether from Salem, by the act of 19th January, 1748, with the following boundaries. Beginning at the mouth of Stow creek, thence up the creek to John Buck's mills, leaving the mills in this county; thence up Stow creek branch to the house of Hugh Dunn, leaving such house within the new county; thence by a straight line to Nathan Shaw's house, also within the new county; thence by a N. E. course, intersecting the Pilesgrove line; thence leaving Pilesgrove, in Salem co., along such line till it intersects the line dividing the counties of Gloucester and Salem; thence S. E. down the Gloucester line to the boundaries of Cape May co.; thence by such county to the Delaware bay, and up the bay to the place of beginning. By the same act, the county was divided into six precincts or townships, viz. Greenwich, Hopewell, Stow creek, Fairfield, Deerfield, and Maurice river; to which Milleville, taken from Maurice river and Fairfield t-ships, in 1801, and Downe t-ship, have been since added. The county is bounded by the Delaware bay on the S. S. W.,

Salem co. N. W., Gloucester N. E., and Cape May co. on the S. E. Its greatest length is about 30 miles N. and S., and breadth 30 miles E. and W.; area, 524 square miles, or 33,500 acres; central lat. 39° 20′ N.; Long. 2° E. from W. C.

Geologically considered, Cumberland co. belongs to the belt of diluvial and alluvial formation, which extends along the continent of North America, from Long Island to the Gulf of Mexico, and contains in place, the deposits of greenish blue marl, intermixed with shells, similar to those found in the limestone and grauwacke of the transition, and abundantly in the secondary horizontal limestone and sandstone, with beds of bog iron ore, and ochre. The elevated ridges between the streams, are crowned in places with sandstone and puddingstone cemented with iron ore. The marl beds yet developed, lie chiefly on Stow creek, and the iron ore in Greenwich t-ship. The marl is used for manure with much advantage upon the lighter soils, and its use is daily extending. The surface of the country is generally flat; the soil south of Cohansey creek is generally sandy. A salt marsh extends along the Delaware bay, in breadth from half a mile to two miles, adjoining which, eastwardly, is a strip of clay and loam, having an average width of about a mile, tolerably fertile and covered with farms. A prolific marsh borders the creeks, which are embanked, at various distances from their mouths, and employed for grazing cattle. The northern part of the county, particularly, that portion of it lying north and west of the Cohansey creek, is composed of clay and sandy loam, on which considerable quantities of wheat, oats and corn, are grown. The timber above Cohansey, consists of white oak, black and red oak, and hickory, which also characterize the clay and loam of the western belt. Below Cohansey, it is generally pine; forests of which cover the greater portion of the eastern part of the county, which, having been generally once, at least, cut over, are now in various stages of growth.

The principal streams are Stow creek on the N. W. boundary; Cohansey creek in the N. W. section, Maurice river running centrally through the co., and Tuckahoe river upon the east.

The chief towns are Bridgeton, the seat of justice, Greenwich, Deerfield, Roadstown, Millville, Port Elizabeth, Nantuxet, or Newport, Dividing Creek, Mauricetown, Bricksboro', Dorchester, Leesburg, and Marshallville, or Cumberland Works, Cedarville, and Fairton.

There are in the county 2 furnaces, one at Millville, and the other above Port Elizabeth, on the Manamuskin creek; and three extensive glass manufactories, one at Millville, one at Port Elizabeth, and the third at Marshallville. At the last place, and on Maurice river, there is considerable ship building, in vessels of from 50 to 100 tons burthen. Large quantities of grain are exported from Bridgeton, and timber and cordwood from every creek of the county.

The religious sects are Episcopalians, Presbyterians, Baptists, Methodists, and Quakers.

A county Bible society holds its meetings at Bridgeton, and temperance societies have been established with great success in the townships. The provisions for education consist of an academy at Bridgeton, another at Port Elizabeth, and common schools in the several towns and townships.

The inhabitants of the county are derived chiefly from English, Swiss, and German settlers; and it is probable, from several circumstances, that a colony of Puritans, from Newhaven, was settled near the margin of the Delaware so early as 1640, some of whose descendants may yet remain.

By the census of 1830, the population amounted to 14,093, of whom 6723 were white males; 6582 white females; 2 female slaves; 431 free coloured males; 355 free coloured females; of which 27 were aliens, 4 deaf and dumb, and 7 blind.

By the abstract of the assessors, there were, in 1832, in the county, 2742 taxables, 774 householders, whose ratables did not exceed $30; 33 single men; 54 storekeepers, or merchants; two fisheries, 1 woollen manufactory, 1 cupola furnace, 2 blast furnaces, 44 runs of stones for grinding grain, 21 saw mills, 1 forge, 1 rolling and slitting mill, 1 fulling mill, 6 tanneries, 4 glass manufactories, 4 distilleries for cider, 2053 horses, 5713 neat cattle, above the age of 3 years, and 9 stud horses.

By the act of 3d November, 1814, the county sends 3 members to the Assembly, 1 member to Council.

The courts of common pleas and general quarter sessions, are holden annually at Bridgeton, on the third Tuesday of February, the fourth Tuesday of September, the first Tuesday of June, and the last Tuesday of Nov. The circuit court is holden at the same place on the first Tuesday of June, and last Tuesday of November, annually.

STATISTICAL TABLE OF CUMBERLAND COUNTY.

Townships.	Length.	Breadth.	Area.	Surface generally level.	Population. 1810	1820	1830
Deerfield,	11	9	34,000		1889	1903	2417
Downe,	14	11½	58,240		1501	1749	1923
Fairfield,	15	8	46,720		2279	1869	1812
Greenwich,	7	6	13,440		858	890	912
Hopewell,	10	6	20,000		1987	1952	1953
Maurice River,	19	11	79,360		2085	2411	2724
Milleville,	16	16	73,500		1032	1010	1561
Stow Creek,	7	6	10,240		1039	884	791
			335,460		12,670	12,668	14,093

Cumberland Furnace, on Mana-muskin creek, Maurice river t-ship, about 5 miles above Port Elizabeth, and 17 east of Bridgeton.

Cumberland Works, (See *Mar-shallville*.)

Daretown, Pittsgrove t-ship, Salem co., near the N. W. boundary, on the head waters of Salem river, 13 miles, a little N. of E. from Salemtown; contains 12 or 14 dwellings, 2 stores, one Presbyterian, and one Methodist church.

Dead River, a tributary of the Passaic river, rising by several branches in the Mine mountain of Bernard t-ship, Somerset co., and flowing E. to its recipient, along the N. base of Stony Hill; including Harrison's brook, its longest branch, its length may be about 9 miles.

Dayton's Bridge, post-office, Salem county.

Danville, post-office, Warren co.

Deal, small hamlet, and watering place, 220 miles N. E. from W. C., and 64 from Trenton, on Poplar Swamp creek, about a mile from the sea, in Shrewsbury t-ship, Monmouth co., 16 miles E. from Freehold, and 3 S. of Long Branch boarding houses. There are several boarding houses at this place, where from 50 to 100 persons may be comfortably accommodated.

Deckertown, p-t., of Wantage t-ship, Sussex co., at the intersection of the Newton and Bolton, with the Paterson and Hamburg turnpike

road; 244 miles from W. C., 86 from Trenton, and 14 from Newton. The town contains a grist mill, a Presbyterian church, 4 stores, 2 taverns, and from 15 to 20 dwellings, and lies in a rich limestone country.

Deep Brook, Caldwell t-ship, Essex co., rises in the Second mountain, and flows N. to the Passaic river, having a semicircular course of 3 or 4 miles, and receiving a small tributary, called Green Brook.

Deep Creek, Lower Alloways creek t-ship, Salem co., rises in that t-ship, and flows S. W., a meandering course, through the meadows and marshes for 7 or 8 miles, to the Delaware. It is not navigable.

Deep Creek, Shrewsbury t-ship, Monmouth co., makes in from the ocean, between 1 and 2 miles; less than a mile above Shark inlet.

Deep Clove River, a tributary of Wallkill river; rises at the east foot of the mountain, in Wantage t-ship, and flows S. E. by a course of 12 miles, to its recipient; receiving from the S. W. the Papakating creek, a short distance below Deckertown. There are several mills on both these streams.

Deep, or *Great Run*, a tributary of the Great Egg Harbour river, Hamilton t-ship, Gloucester co., into which it flows from the west, about a mile below Weymouth furnace.

Deep Run, tributary of South river, rises in Upper Freehold t-ship, Monmouth co., and flows by a N. W.

course of between 8 and 9 miles, to its recipient, in South Amboy t-ship, Middlesex co., a mill stream.

Deerfield Township, Cumberland co., bounded N. E. by Pittsgrove t-ship, N. W. by Upper Alloways creek t-ship, Salem co.; S. by Fairfield and Millville t-ships, and W. by Hopewell t-ship, Cumberland co. Greatest length, N. and S. 11 miles, breadth, E. and W. 9 miles; area, 34,000 acres. Surface, level; soil, clay, gravel and sand, and not remarkable for fertility, but improving under the application of marl. It is drained by the Cohansey creek, which runs southward along its western boundary, and by Muddy run, a branch of Maurice river, which flows on the S. E. line. Population in 1830, 2,417: In 1832, there were in the t-ship, taxables, 305; 2 Presbyterian, 1 Baptist and 1 Methodist church; 1 academy and several schools; 118 householders, whose ratables did not exceed $30; 11 stores; 9 pairs of stones for grinding grain; one woollen manufactory; 2 saw mills; 1 fulling mill; 316 horses, and 560 neat cattle, above the age of 3 years; and the township paid for township purposes, $500, and for county and state tax, $835 25. Bridgeton, Deerfield and Carllsburg are towns of this t-ship.

Deerfield Street, post town of Deerfield t-ship, Cumberland co., 7 miles N. of Bridgeton; 165 miles N. E. of Washington city, and 63 S. from Trenton; contains from 20 to 25 dwellings, occupied chiefly by agriculturists, 1 tavern, 1 store, and a Presbyterian church.

Dell's Brook, small branch of the Rockaway river, flowing eastwardly about 5 miles through Pleasant valley, Randolph t-ship, Morris co.

Delaware River and *Bay*, called by the Indians, *Poutaxat, Marisqueton, Makeriskitton, Makeriskkiskon, Lenape-Wihittuck* (stream of the Lenape,) by the Dutch, *Zuydt* or South river, Charles river, and Nassau river, and by the Swedes, *New Swedeland stream*, one of the most considerable in N. America, rises by two princi-

pal branches, in the state of New York. The northernmost, the *Mohawk* or *Cooquago*, issues from Lake Utsaemthe lat. 42° 45', takes a S. W. course, and turning S. E. crosses the Pennsylvania line in lat. 42°. Seven miles below this point it receives the *Popachton* branch, which rises in the Katskill mountain, from the S. E. It touches the N. W. corner of N. Jersey, in lat. 41° 24', at Carpenter's Point, at the mouth of the Nevisink or Mackackomack river. The course of the current, above and below the Blue mountain, is crooked; and is through a mountainous country, until it leaves the Water Gap. The Delaware Water Gap is one of the greatest natural curiosities of the state. It would seem, from the quantity of alluvial lands, above the mountain, that at some remote period, a dam of great height, here, impeded the progress of the river. Had the dam been half as high as the mountain, it would have turned the water into the North river. It may have had an elevation of 150 or 200 feet, forming a lake of more than 50 miles in length; extending over the Minisink settlements. It has been conjectured that this dam was engulphed by some great convulsion of the earth; and the opinion is supposed to be sustained by the extraordinary depth of the channel in several places of its passage through the mountain. An hundred years ago the boatmen reported, that they could not reach the bottom with their longest lines; and even now we are informed that the bottom in these places cannot be attained with two plough lines attached to each other. But we see nothing in these appearances that renders it necessary to resort to the conjecture, that an earthquake was employed to open an adequate passage for the river, and that it performed its office with such accuracy, and economy of power, as to do no more than was indispensable, and to leave the rugged and lofty wall, 1600 feet high, rising almost precipitously from the water's edge, unbroken. The distance through the mountain is about two miles. The rock presents a great variety of strata, in which granitic rock, slate, grauwacke and the old sandstone alternate. The sandstone is, at one place, at least, and probably at others, so soft as to disintegrate rapidly. At the place referred to, the water has scooped out a basin from the hill of many acres in extent, which are now under cultivation. Before the bed of the river was broken down, there must have been a cataract here, higher than that of Niagara. Supposing the waters to have been poured over the precipice upon a bed of soft or disjointed stones, very deep excavations must have been made, which the great mass of waters, in seasons of freshet, would continue to preserve. It is probable that so much of the mountain as forms the present bed of the river was, throughout, of soft or very friable material. The stream has obviously sought the most practicable passage; and to attain it, has formed an almost right-angled course through the mountain. Whatever may have been the resistance, the conquest has been complete, and it now flows through the deep ravine in calm and silent majesty, without a ripple to tell of its whereabout; and occasionally resting in motionless pools, of from two to three hundred yards wide, as if to reflect the picturesque scenery which surrounds and hangs over it.

The lovers of diversified nature cannot visit this spot without high gratification. The " Gap," the break, in the almost unvarying line of the Kittatinny mountain is visible at nearly as great a distance as the mountain itself. As we approach it from the S. E., the ground rises rapidly, almost precipitously, differing in this particular, as do all the mountain ranges of our country, from the N. W. declivity, whose descent is long and gradual. At the entrance, the sides of the mountain, close to the water's edge, leave scarce room for a road, overhung by immense masses of rock,

threatening destruction to the traveller beneath. The passage, however, widens as we proceed, and the scenery assumes a less imposing character. Verdant isles stud the bosom of the stream, and contrast beautifully with the rocky and wood-clad eminences, which now have a more rounded form. These islands are rich, and bear the most luxurious harvests. About two-thirds of the way through the mountain from the Jersey shore, may be seen, most advantageously, near Dutotsburg, on the Pennsylvania bank, the pretty cascade formed by Cherry creek, which precipitates its waters in foam and spray, over a declivity of more than 50 feet.

" The sunbow's rays still arch
The torrent with the many hues of heav'n,
And roll the sheeted silver's waving column
O'er the crags headlong perpendicular,
And fling its lines of foaming light along,
And to and fro, like the pale courser's tail,
The giant steed, to be bestrode by Death,
As told in the Apocalypse."—BYRON.

On the top of the mountain, 2 miles from the " Gap," is a large chalybeate spring, which deposits much ferruginous ochre, similar to that of the Paint spring of Freehold t-ship, Monmouth co.; and, also, a deep lake, near a mile in circumference, well stored with fish. The margin of the river, above the mountain, is narrow, but very fertile; and, on the Pennsylvania side, abounds in lime. A road follows each bank through the mountain. That on the Jersey shore, rough, but safe, was made in the year 1830, by the aid of a donation of $2000 from the state. Before its completion, we are told, that the inhabitants, north of the mountain, made their way over the precipices by means of ladders of ropes.

We know no more admirable spot for a summer retreat than at the foot of the mountain, on the north side of the Gap. Here might be enjoyed the charms of diversified and always delightful scenery; a revivifying breeze, which follows the river through the sinuosities of its valley— fine rides on its banks, into the rich

R

limestone country of the Wallpack; renovated vigour from the bracing mineral fountain; fine fishing upon the lake, the river and mountain brooks, of which the richest spoil is the gilded perch and speckled trout ; and the more manly exercise of shooting, the country abounding in game. A good house established at Brotzmanville, upon the prattling stream, which there makes the air musical, and which might be used with great convenience for baths, and other purposes, we think would be much encouraged, provided the road through the mountain be kept in good order.

From New Jersey, the principal tributaries to the Delaware, above tide water, are Flatkill, Paulinskill, Pequest, Musconetcong, Laokatong, the Wickhechecoke, and the Assunpink ; below tide, the Crosswicks, Rancocus, Cooper's, Oldman's, Salem, Stow, and Cohansey creeks, and Maurice river. At Easton, the Delaware receives, from Pennsylvania, the Lehigh river. From the South mountain, below Easton, to the tide water at Trenton, the river has a S. W. course of about 60 miles, in which there are 25 noted rapids, with an aggregate fall of 165 feet. But the navigation has been improved, and is safe at the ordinary height of the water. From Easton to Bristol, the Delaware division of the Pennsylvania canal has been completed, and in connexion with the Lehigh canal, affords advantageous communication with the coal mines, and the valley of the Lehigh river. Two surveys have been made for a canal along the valley of the Delaware from Easton to Carpenter's Point.

The Delaware and Raritan canal receives its water by a feeder, which taps the river on the left bank, about 23 miles above Trenton. The Morris canal enters the river below Phillipsburg, and opposite to Easton.

At Camden, opposite Philadelphia, the river is divided into two channels, by Petty's and Smith's islands. The western, near the centre of Philadelphia, is 900 feet wide, with a mean depth of 30 feet; the eastern is 2100 feet wide, with a mean depth of 9 feet; the whole area equal to 46,350 feet, affording a commodious and safe harbour, to which ships of the line may ascend.

At the head of the bay, at Delaware City, and opposite to Fort Delaware, which commands the passage of the river; the Delaware and Chesapeake canal, 14 miles in length, connects this with the Chesapeake bay, and its many tributary rivers. This point is distant from Camden 45 miles, and the bay extends, thence, 75 miles to the ocean, with a width varying from 3 to 30 miles, occupying an area of 630,000 acres. Its navigation is difficult and dangerous, being infested with shoals, which often prove destructive. It opens into the Atlantic, between Cape Henlopen, on the S. E., and Cape May, on the N. E., which are about 20 miles apart. The length of the bay and river, to the head of tide, at Trenton, is 155 miles. A 74 gun ship may ascend to Philadelphia, 120 miles; sloops, to Trenton falls; boats, of 8 or 10 tons, 100 miles above them; and canoes 150 miles higher.

Below Port Penn, 70 miles from the sea, the bay affords no safe harbourage; nor is there S. of New York, for several hundred miles, any place, where a vessel, during the rudest season of the year, when approach to the coast is most dangerous, may seek protection against the elements. The losses from this cause have induced the national government to form an artificial port, or breakwater, at the entrance of the bay. The law for this purpose was enacted, in 1828-9, and the work is in steady progression, and will be speedily completed. The anchorage ground, or roadstead, is formed by a cove in the southern shore, directly west of Cape Henlopen; and the seaward end rests on an extensive shoal, called the Shears; the tail of which makes out from the shore about 5 miles up the bay, near Broadkill creek; whence it extends eastward, and terminates at a point, about 2 miles to the N. of the shore, at the cape. The breakwater consists of an isolated dyke, or wall of stone; the transversal section of which is a trapezium, the base resting on the bottom, and the summit line forming the top of the work. The other sides represent the inner and outer slopes of the work; that to the seaward being the greater. The inward slope is 45°, the top horizontal, 22 feet in breadth, and raised 5½ feet above the highest spring tides; the outward, or sea slope, is 39 feet in altitude, on a base of 105¾ feet; both these dimensions being measured, in relation to a horizontal plane, passing by a point 27 feet below the lowest spring tides. The base bears to the altitude nearly the same ratio as similar lines in the profiles of the Cherbourg and Plymouth breakwaters. The opening or entrance from the ocean is 650 yards wide, between the north part of the cape and east end of the breakwater, and will be accessible by all winds from the sea. The *Breakwater*, proper, is a dyke in a straight line from E. S. E. to W. N. W., 1200 yards in length. At the distance of 350 yards from the upper or western end, that space forming the upper entrance, a similar dyke, 500 yards long, is projected in a direct line W. by S. ½ S., forming an angle of 146° 15' with the breakwater. This part of the work is designed as an icebreaker.

The whole length of the two dykes will be 1700 yards, and they will contain, when finished, 900,000 cubic yards of basalt and granite rock, weighing from a quarter of a ton to three tons, and upwards. The depth of water, at low tide, is from 4 to six fathoms, over a surface of 7 tenths of a square mile. Although unfinished, this magnificent work has already proved its utility, saving many vessels and many valuable lives.

There are five bridges erected over the Delaware river, viz. at Trenton, at Lambertville, at Prallsville, at Philipsburg, and at Columbia. Authority has also been given to erect a bridge over the river at Philadelphia, and another opposite Taylorsville. The Delaware and Hudson canal crosses the river by means of a dam, constructed below the mouth of the Lackawaxan.

Den Brook, mill stream and tributary of the Rockaway river, rises in Randolph t-ship, Morris co., and flows by a course N. E., about 8 miles along the N. W. base of Trowbridge mountain, to its recipient near Danville.

Dennis's Creek t-ship, Cape May co., bounded N. E. by Upper t-ship, S. E. by the Atlantic ocean, S. by Middle t-ship, S. W. by Delaware Bay, W. and N. W. by Maurice River t-ship, Cumberland co. Centrally distant from Cape May courthouse N. 9 miles; greatest length E. and W. 14 miles; breadth N. and S. 8½ miles; area, 43,500 acres. Dennis's creek runs on the S. W. border, through a very extensive cedar swamp, and the northern part of the t-ship consists of sandy plains; the population in 1830 was 1508. In 1832 the t-ship contained about 300 taxables, 198 householders, whose ratables did not exceed $30; 3 grist mills, 7 saw mills, 2 carding machines, 8 stores, and 185 horses, 503 head of neat cattle, over 3 years of age; it paid t-ship tax, $94 27; state tax, 162 75; and county tax, $503 54. Part of Ludlam's beach fronts the ocean, between which and Leaming's beach, the tide rushes in over the marshes and lagunes which border the eastern boundary for a breadth of about 2 miles. Dennis's Creek is the post-town. There are 2 churches in the t-ship.

Dennis's Creek, p-t. of Dennis's Creek t-ship, Cape May co., at the head of the navigation of Dennis's creek, 6 or 7 miles from the Delaware bay, 7 miles N. from Cape May court-house, 194 from W. C., and 97 from Trenton; contains from 30 to 40 dwellings, 2 taverns, 3 stores, and a tide grist mill. The town is built on both sides of the creek, extending each way, about half a mile. Ship building and trade in lumber are carried on extensively here. The country around it, above the marsh, is of sandy loam.

Denn's Branch, of Stow creek, a small tributary of Stow creek, Salem co., flowing westerly into its recipient by a course of 3 or 4 miles.

Denville, p-t. of Hanover t-ship, Morris co., on the right bank of the Rockaway river, 7 miles N. of Morristown, 231 N. E. from W. C., and 65 from Trenton; contains a store, tavern, cider distillery, and 6 or 8 dwellings.

Devil's Brook, small tributary of the Millstone river, in South Brunswick t-ship, Middlesex co., flowing S. W. about 5 miles to the river.

Deptford t-ship, Gloucester co., bounded N. E. by Gloucester t-ship, S. E. by Hamilton t-ship, S. W. by Greenwich t-ship, and N. W. by the river Delaware. Greatest length N. W. and S. E. 25, and breadth 7 miles; area, 57,600 acres; surface level; soil sandy: in the northern part, grass, vegetables, and fruit are successfully cultivated; the southern is chiefly pine forest, valuable for timber and cord wood. It is drained northward by Big Timber creek; Mantua creek on the west boundary; and southward by Innskeeps, Squankum, and Faraway, branches of the Great Egg Harbour river. Iron ore, and some chalybeate waters are found within 2 miles of Woodbury. Woodbury, the seat of justice for the county, Malaga, and Glassborough, are post-towns of the t-ship; population in 1830, 3599. In 1832 the township contained 449 householders, whose ratables did not exceed $30 in value, 19 stores, 8 fisheries, 6 grist mills, 1 cotton and 1 woollen manufactory, 1 carding machine, 9 saw mills, 1 ferry, 1 distillery, 1 glass factory, 1389 neat cattle, and 672 horses and mules above the age of 3 years.

Dickerson, the seat of the Hon. Mahlon Dickerson, former Governor of New Jersey, and representative of that state in the United States Senate, and the site of one of the most extensive and valuable iron mines in the state; ten miles N. W. from Morristown, Randolph t-ship, Morris county, upon the northern part, or continuation of Schooley's mountain.

Dillon's Landing, Dover t-ship, Monmouth co., on the north side of Toms' river bay, about 2 miles from its confluence with Barnegat bay.

Dividing Creek, Downe t-ship, Cumberland co., rises centrally in the t-ship, and flows southerly by a very crooked course of 10 or 12 miles, into Maurice creek cove, in Delaware bay. It is navigable to the village of Dividing Creek.

Dividing Creek, p-t. of Downe t-ship, Cumberland co., about 17 miles S. of Bridgeton, 86 from Trenton, and 192 N. E. from W. C.; contains from 25 to 30 dwellings, a store, tavern, and grist mill.

Dogtown, a mountain hamlet, on the line separating Amwell from Kingwood t-ship, Hunterdon co., 5 miles N. W. from Flemington; contains a tavern, a wheelwright shop, and two or three cottages.

Doctor's Creek, branch of the Crosswicks, rises near Clarkeville, in the eastern part of Upper Freehold t-ship, Monmouth co., and flows by a west course of about 14 miles, by Imlaystown and Allentown, to its recipient near the Sand Hills in Nottingham t-ship, Burlington co., turning several mills by the way.

Dorchester, village, of Maurice river t-ship, Cumberland co., on the left bank of the river, about 10 miles from the Delaware bay, and 20 S. E. from Bridgeton; contains between 30 and 40 dwellings, 1 tavern, and 2 stores. The soil about it is sandy.

Dorson's Brook, tributary of the north branch of Raritan river, Mendham t-ship, Morris co., having a course on and near the west t-ship line of about 4 or 5 miles.

Dover t-ship, Monmouth co., bounded N. by Howell and Freehold t-ships, E. by the Atlantic Ocean, S. by Stafford t-ship, S. W. by Northampton and Hanover t-ships, Burlington co., and N. W. by Upper Freehold. Centrally distant S. from Freehold, 24 miles; greatest length E. and W. 22; breadth N. and S. 17 miles; area, including Barnegat bay, and the Atlantic beach, 200,000 acres. It extends from the Atlantic Ocean to the western line of the county. Surface generally level, but there are some hills in the south, at the head of Forked river, called Forked River mountains; soil, generally sand or light gravel, covered with pine forest, whence enormous quantities of timber and cord wood are taken for the New York market, and for the supply of iron works in the t-ship. It is drained E. by Toms' river and its several branches, Cedar creek, and Forked river; on the W. by some branches of the Rancocus. Toms' river, Cedar creek, and Goodluck, are villages; the two first post-towns of the t-ship. Population in 1830, 2898. In 1832, the t-ship contained about 550 taxables, 201 householders, whose ratables did not exceed 30 dollars, 72 single men, 9 stores, 7 saw mills, 2 grist mills, 3 blast furnaces, 350 horses and mules, and 925 neat cattle, 3 years old and upwards; and paid in state and county taxes, $1265 06.

Dover, p-t. of Randolph t-ship, Morris co., on the Rockaway river, 8 miles N. W. from Morristown, 233 N. E. from W. C., and 67 from Trenton; the mountains recede here, and form a small plain, on which the town is built, on several streets and on both sides of the river, which is passed by one, perhaps more bridges. It contains 3 large rolling and slitting mills, boring and turning engines, a cupola furnace or foundery, and saw mill, the property of the heirs of the late Mr. M'Farlane, of New York, a factory of machinery, owned by W. Ford, a bank with an actual capital of $50,000 and the right to extend it to $150,000, an academy, used also as a church, and about 30 dwellings; much business has formerly been done here; the Morris canal descends into the valley by an inclined plane and 4

locks; a valuable iron mine, known as "Jackson's," near the town, is extensively worked, and governor Dickerson's mine is about 3 miles distant.

Downe t-ship, Cumberland co., bounded N. by Fairfield and Milleville t-ship, E. by Maurice river, S. and W. by the Delaware. Centrally distant, S. E. from Bridgeton, 14 miles; greatest length E. and W. 14, breadth N. and S. 12 miles; area, 58,240 acres; surface, level; soil, marsh upon the bay and Maurice river; loam for a narrow strip of about a mile in width, adjoining the marsh, the remainder sandy. Maurice river follows the whole of the east boundary; Nantuxet creek the north-west, between which flows Dividing, Oranoken, Fishing, Broad, Oyster, and Fortescue creeks. Population in 1830, 1923; in 1832, there were in the t-ship, taxables, 310, householders 93, whose ratables did not exceed $30; stores 6, grist mills 5, saw mills 2, carding machine 1; 120 horses, 901 cattle above the age of 3 years; Mauricetown, Newport, Dividing Creek, Port Norris, and Buckshutem, are villages of the t-ship, of which the three first are post-towns.

Double Pond, a sheet of water in the Wawayanda mountain, Sussex co., which sends forth northwardly a small stream called Double Pond creek, which unites with Warwick creek, in the state of New York.

Drakestown, Morris co., on the line dividing Washington from Roxbury t-ship, on the road from Morristown to Hackettstown, 15 miles from the former and three from the latter, and upon Schooley's mountain; contains a store, and from 12 to 15 dwellings.

Drakesville, Roxbury t-ship, Morris co., on the turnpike road leading from Morristown by Stanhope furnace, 12 miles N. E. from the former, and upon the Morris canal; contains a tavern, a store, and from 12 to 15 dwellings. The country on the S. and S. E. is level, sandy, and poor; on the N. hilly and rough, but improving by the use of lime.

Drowned Lands, on the line separating Wantage from Vernon t-ships, Sussex co., and extending thence into Orange co., of New York. This is a morass of unusual extent for the northern states, and celebrated for the yearly inundation to which it is subject, and the malaria which it occasions during the autumn. It is twenty miles long, and varies in breadth from 1 to 5 miles. Through it flows the Wallkill, with a current scarce perceptible, to whose waters, when swelled by the spring freshets, it owes its annual submergence. It is composed of an accumulation of vegetable matter, whose surface is imperfectly converted into soil, abounding with carbonaceous substance, empyreumatic oil, and gallic acid, and covered in midsummer with rank and luxuriant vegetation. The ditches, made in several places, in forming roads across it, disclose peat of excellent quality. This equivocal lake encircles several islands, the largest of which contains 200 acres of excellent land, well cultivated; the smaller ones are uninhabited, and generally covered with wood, among which the beautiful flowering shrub, *Rhododendron Maximum*, laurelled leaved rose tree, grows abundantly. The rocks on the island, and upon the borders of the morass, indicate that it reposes on blue cherty limestone; but in one place, at least the island near Woodville, primitive limestone, the rock of the neighbouring country appears. No successful effort has yet been made to drain this vast swamp, which is abandoned as pasturing ground to cattle on the subsidence of the spring inundation, for a few weeks only, and is for the rest of the year a desolate waste.

Dry Branch, tributary of Paulin's creek, Knowlton t-p. Warren co.

Duck Island, in the Delaware river, above Bordentown, in Nottingham township, Burlington county. It is somewhat more than a mile in length.

Dunker Pond, south of Bear Fort mountain, Pompton t-ship, Bergen co., sends forth a small tributary to the Pequannock creek.

Dunks's Ferry, a noted and long established ferry on the Delaware river, Willingboro' t-ship, Burlington co., 4 miles below the city of Burlington.

Dyer's Creek, a small marsh stream of Middle t-ship, Cape May co., which flows into the Delaware, after a course of 3 or 4 miles.

Dutch Neck, village of W. Windsor t-ship, Middlesex co., 18 miles S. W. from Trenton; contains a tavern and 3 or 4 stores; soil, gravelly and poor.

East Creek, mill stream of Dennis t-ship, Cape May co., flowing about 7 miles S. W. into the Delaware bay.

East Windsor. (See *Windsor, East*.)

Eayrstown, village of Northampton t-ship, Burlington co., on the S. branch of Rancocus creek, near the junction of Haines' creek with that stream, and at the head of tide, between 3 and 4 miles S. W. from Mount Holly; contains a cotton factory, a grist mill, saw mill, fulling mill, 1 tavern, 1 store, and 12 or 15 dwellings; soil, sandy loam, fertile and well cultivated.

Edinburgh, W. Windsor t-ship, Middlesex co., on the Assunpink creek, 18 miles S. W. from N. B., and 8 miles E. of Trenton; contains a Presbyterian church of wood, 1 store, 1 tavern, a grist mill, and 12 or 14 dwellings; soil, sandy and light.

Eaton, p-t. of Shrewsbury t-ship, Monmouth co., 2 miles S. from Shrewsburytown, upon Shrewsbury river, 11 miles from Freehold, 48 from Trenton, and 213 from W. C., on a branch of Swimming river, 1½ miles above navigable water; contains about 30 dwellings, 5 or 6 stores, 2 taverns, a grist mill, and an academy, in a pleasant and fertile country.

Edgepeling, a tributary of Atsion river, rising in Evesham t-ship, Burlington co., and flowing by a southerly course of 8 or 9 miles, to its recipient in Washington t-ship.

Egg Harbour, Little, t-ship, Burlington co., bounded N. by Oswego, or east branch of Wading river, which separates it from Northampton t-ship, S. E. by Stafford t-ship, Monmouth co., S. by Little Egg Harbour river and bay, and W. by Washington t-ship. Centrally distant from Mount Holly, S. E. 35 miles; greatest length N. and S. 20 miles; breadth E. and W. 10 miles; area, 76,800 acres, including bays and inlets; surface, level; soil, gravel and sand. The northern part of the township, called the Plains, is of the former, covered with low pines and scrub oaks, forming an excellent covert for deer and grouse, which find abundant food in the mast produced by the latter. The southern part of the t-ship is sandy, covered with forest. It is drained chiefly by branches of Little Egg Harbour river, of which Bass river is here the chief. Tuckerton, upon Shorl's mill branch, is the posttown. Population in 1830, 1490. In 1832, the t-ship contained 150 householders, whose ratables did not exceed $30; 347 taxables, 51 single men, 6 stores, 4 saw mills, 3 grist mills, 1 two horse stage, 7 dearborns, 36 covered wagons, 10 gigs and sulkies, 640 neat cattle, 170 horses and mules; and it paid state tax, $127 48; county tax, $444; road tax, $300.

Egg Harbour Bay, Little, partly in Little Egg Harbour t-ship, Burlington co., and partly in Stafford t-ship, Monmouth co.; extends about 14 miles in length, and from 2 to 4 in breadth, from Little Egg Harbour inlet to Barnegat inlet, and contains many islands, the haunts of ducks, geese, and sea-fowl.

Egg Harbour, Little, or *Mullica's River*, rises by several branches in Burlington and Gloucester cos.; the chief of which are Batsto river, near Burlington, Atsion river, on the boundary between the two counties, Mechescalaxin and Nesochcaque, which unite near Pleasant Mills, 25 miles

from the sea. Half way below this point, Wading and Bass rivers blend with the main stream, which is navigable, for sloops, to Batsto furnace, 25 miles. The Little Egg Harbour bay and inlet, and Great bay, form a sheet of salt water, separated from the ocean by Brigantine, Tucker's and Long beaches, the communication with which, from the sea, is chiefly by the New inlet, which admits vessels of from 15 to 18 feet draught, many of which, during the late war, entered and discharged valuable cargoes. The Old inlet, to the north from Tucker's island, is now little used, except for vessels of very light burden. The collection district of Little Egg Harbour, comprehends the shores, waters, bays, rivers and creeks, from Barnegat inlet to Brigantine inlet, both inclusively. Tuckerton is the sole port of entry, at which the collector resides.

Egg Harbour River, Great, rises in Gloucester t-ship, Gloucester co., by Inskeep's branch, and flows a S. E. course through Deptford, Hamilton, Weymouth, and Egg Harbour t-ships, to the ocean, about 45 miles; receiving in its way several, but not very considerable tributaries, on either hand, and draining a wide extent of sandy soil and pine forest. It is navigable for sloops of considerable burden, above May's Landing, more than 25 miles; and from this point flows through a continued marsh. Large quantities of wood, coal, and lumber, are annually exported from this river.

Great Egg Harbour bay is entered by Great Egg Harbour inlet, between Absecum and Peck's beaches. The bay is about five miles long, and has a very irregular breadth, varying from half a mile to 4 miles. The inlet, at its mouth, is more than a mile in width, and communicates with the bay by several channels.

Egg Harbour t-ship, Gloucester co., bounded N. E. by Absecum creek, bay, and inlet, which separate it from Galloway t-ship; S. E. by the Atlantic ocean; S. W. by Great Egg Harbour inlet, bay, and river, and N.

W. by Hamilton t-ship. Centrally distant from Woodbury S. E. 48 miles; greatest length E. and W. 12; breadth N. and S. 12 miles; area, 85,000 acres, including beaches, bays, and rivers; surface level; marsh several miles in width, within the beach; sandy elsewhere, and, generally, covered with pine forest. Bargaintown and Somers' Point are post-towns of the t-ship; population in 1830, 2510. In 1832 the t-ship contained 122 householders, whose ratables did not exceed $30; 5 stores, 2 grist mills, 1 carding machine, 6 saw mills, 510 neat cattle, and 260 horses and mules; and paid county taxes, $307 59½; poor tax, $153 90; road tax, $800.

Great Egg Harbour, collection district, comprehends the river of Great Egg Harbour, together with all the inlets, bays, sounds, rivers, and creeks, along the sea coast, from Brigantine inlet to Cape May.

Egg Island, Downe t-ship, Cumberland co., Delaware bay, off the western point of Maurice Cove, of a triangular form, extending about half a mile upon each side.

Egg Island, false, a point of Downe t-ship, about 4 miles higher up the bay, than the foregoing, and which, from similarity of configuration, is often mistaken for it.

Egg Islands, Barnegat bay, Dover t-ship, Monmouth co., about 3 miles below the mouth of Toms' bay, each near a mile in length.

Eight Mile Branch, of Cedar creek, Dover t-ship, Monmouth co., rises west of the Forked mountains, and flows eastwardly to its recipient.

Elizabethtown, and t-ship, Essex co., thus named after Lady Elizabeth Carteret, the wife and executrix of Sir George Carteret. The town lies upon Elizabeth creek, 1½ miles W. from a point of fast land, running through the marsh to Staten Island Sound, and on the turnpike road and rail-road, from New Brunswick to New York, 17 miles by the post road from the former, and 15 from the latter; 42 from Trenton, and 210 from W. C.; pleasantly situated, in a level and fertile country, of clay loam; contains 400 dwellings, 3 handsome churches of brick, one belonging to the Episcopalians, and two to the Presbyterians, the first congregation of whom, is, probably, as old as the town itself; and 1 Methodist church, of wood. There were two churches in this town, in 1748, which the Swedish traveller, Kalm, preferred to any in Philadelphia: 2 temperance societies, having together 450 members, whose beneficial influence is said to be extensively felt, there not being a distillery in the t-ship, and all the respectable farmers conducting their labours without the stimulus of ardent spirit; a bank called the "*State Bank at Elizabeth*," with an authorized capital of $200,000, of which $132,924, have been paid in, conducted reputably and profitably; 5 taverns in the town and two at the Point; 9 stores, at none of which is ardent spirit sold; 1 book store, 2 boarding schools for girls, at which there are about 100 pupils from various parts of the country; 1 classical boarding school for boys, containing 40 boarders, under the care of the Reverend Mr. Halsey, all of which are in high repute; 2 public libraries, one religious, the other miscellaneous, called the Elizabethtown Apprentices' Library, much and advantageously used; 1 printing office, from which is issued the newspaper called the New Jersey Journal, originally founded by the venerable judge Hallock, at Chatham, in 1779, removed to this town in 1786, and conducted by him for nearly half a century; an oil mill, large grist and saw mill, 2 large saw mills for cutting mahogany, with circular saws for veneers; 2 large oil cloth manufactories, belonging to the same company; 2 earthenware, and 1 earthen and stoneware potteries; flax works, which break and dress 2 tons per day, driven by steam; a rope, twine, and cotton bagging factory, also driven by steam, and employing 20 hands; 2 tin, sheet iron, and stove factories, 1 clock manufactory, and 1 shears manufactory, moved by steam; 2 carriage makers, 2 tanneries, one of which dresses oil, morocco, and alum, leather; 1 iron foundery for making malleable castings, connected with which is a steam engine factory, and machine shop, worked by steam; and a book bindery.

The town or t-ship is bounded N. by Newark t-ship, E. by Newark bay and Staten Island Sound, S. by Rahway, and W. by Union t-ships; greatest length N. E. and S. W. 5 miles; breadth, 3½ miles; area, 10,000 acres; soil, red shale, clay, loam, and marsh; from the last of which, large quantities of grass are cut, chiefly for manure. The soil is of excellent quality, and repays the labour of the husbandman abundantly. Bound Brook runs on the north, and Morss Brook on the south boundary. There are 470 dwellings in the t-ship, and the population was, in 1830, 3455. In 1832, the t-ship contained 550 taxables, 235 householders, whose ratable estate did not exceed 30 dollars, 83 single men, 22 merchants, 289 horses and mules, 579 neat cattle over 3 years of age; and it paid in 1833, state tax, $313 13; county, $819 17; road, $800; poor, $900. The t-ship has a house and farm of 50 acres, upon which its poor are kept.

This town was the first English settlement made in the state. The land was purchased for a company called the Elizabethtown Associates, from the Indians in 1664. These Associates, 74 in number, were originally from Jamaica, Long Island. They held adversely to Berkeley and Carteret, the grantees of the Duke of York; and their pertinacious adherence to the right, real, or supposed, obtained under the Indian grant, was cause of disturbance and commotion, not only during the government of the proprietaries, but for many years of the royal administration. During the revolution, the town suffered much from its contiguity to New York. On the 21st January, 1780, the first

Presbyterian church was burned by the British, and in the following November, its minister, the Rev. James Caldwell, was shot.

Elizabethtown is a desirable residence, whether health, business, or pleasure, be in view. The excellent order and morals which prevail here, the advantages derived from its schools, the short distance from New York, to which the inhabitants, three times a day, have access, by steamboats from the Point, and at other times by stages; the rail-road now being constructed through the town, and that to be made by Somerville to Belvidere, cannot fail to increase its population, and the price of its lands. The town is built upon streets uncommonly wide, and has many very handsome buildings, surrounded by large well improved lots. The t-ship was originally incorporated by Governor Philip Carteret, about the same time as its neighbour Woodbridge, by a most liberal charter; and subsequently, 28th November, 1789, by act of Assembly, with bounds including parts of the present adjacent townships. Its area has been greatly diminished by various acts. The corporate officers of the "Borough of Elizabeth" are a mayor, deputy mayor, recorder, seven aldermen or assistants, a sheriff, coroner, treasurer, clerk, high constable, and seven constables. It has power to regulate general police, markets, roads, &c., and has a court of common pleas and general sessions, holden 4 times annually, with a jurisdiction like to, and exclusive of, that of the county courts. At Elizabethtown Point there was formerly a ferry by which passengers, from and to New York, crossed to Staten Island.

Ellisburg, small hamlet, of Waterford t-ship, Gloucester co., 6 miles S. E. from Camden, 9 miles N. E. from Woodbury, and 2 from Haddonfield; contains a tavern, store, smith shop, and several dwellings.

Elsinborough, t-ship, Salem co., bounded N. by Salem creek, and Salem t-ship, E. by Lower Alloways t-ship, S. by Alloways creek; and W. by the Delaware river. Centrally distant from the town of Salem, 3 miles; greatest length N. and S. 6 miles; breadth E. and W. 4 miles; area, about 8000 acres; surface, level; soil, rich loam and marsh meadow, highly cultivated. The t-ship is drained by Alloways creek on the south, and Salem creek on the north. Population in 1830, 503. In 1832, the t-ship contained 56 householders, whose ratables did not exceed 30 dollars, 117 taxables, 118 horses and mules, and 547 neat cattle, above the age of 3 years.

Empty Box Run, Upper Freehold t-ship, Monmouth co., a small branch of the Assunpink creek.

Englishtown, p-t., of Freehold t-ship, Monmouth co., upon Matchaponix creek, near the N. W. boundary of the t-ship and county; contains a grist mill, 2 taverns, 2 stores, and about 30 dwellings, surrounded by a light sandy soil.

English Neighbourhood, pleasant village, of Hackensack t-ship, Bergen co., 5 miles S. E. from Hackensacktown, and 5½ from Hoboken, on the turnpike road to Hackensack; contains a post-office, a Dutch Reformed church, and a church of Chris-ti-ans, 3 taverns, 2 stores, and from 15 to 20 dwellings. This village is at a convenient distance from New York, by a good road, which, through a pleasant country, affords a very agreeable drive on a summer's afternoon, to the business-worn citizens.

English Creek, a smart mill stream, of Egg Harbour t-ship, Gloucester co., which flows by a S. W. course of 4 or 5 miles, into the Great Egg Harbour river, about 5 miles from the bay.

English Creek, a tributary of the Hackensack river, which rises, and has its course, in Hackensack t-ship, Bergen co.; and almost the whole of its length of 7 miles is through a cedar swamp. This creek formed the defence of the garrison of 3000, who retreated from Fort Lee, attacked by Lord Cornwallis, 18th November, 1776.

Essex County, had its boundaries fixed by act 21st January, 1709-10, commencing at the mouth of Rahway river, where it falls into the Staten Island Sound; thence up the river to Robeson's branch; thence west to the line between the former eastern and western divisions of the colony; thence by the same line, to Pequannock river, where it meets the Passaic river; thence down the Passaic to the Bay and Sound; thence down the Sound to the place of beginning. These limits were modified by the act of 4th November, 1741, annexing part of the county to Somerset. Essex is now bounded W. N. and E. by the Passaic river, which separates it, W. and N. W. from Morris co., N. and E. from Bergen co., S. E. by Newark bay and Long Island Sound, S. by Middlesex co., and S. W. by Somerset co. Greatest length N. and S. 28 miles, breadth E. and W. 19 miles; area in acres, 154,680, or 241¼ square miles. Central lat. 40° 45' N.; long. 2° 45' E. from W. C.

Geologically considered, this county will be classed with the secondary or transition formation, as the old red sandstone shall be determined to belong to either. The whole seems based upon this substratum. It is crossed, however, diagonally from S. W. to N. E., by 2 mountain ridges, entering New Providence and Westfield t-ships from Somerset county, which extend for 25 miles, unbroken by any stream of water, to the Passaic, at Paterson. These are known by the local names of First and Second Mountains, and the latter by that of Short Hills. These ridges, from 1 to 2 miles asunder, are of trap formation, and in some points assume, particularly at the Great and Little Falls, on the Passaic, a columnar character and appearances of the action of fire in their cellular form, which support the igneous origin of that rock. These hills, generally covered with wood, send forth tributaries to the cardinal points of the compass, and their rocky basis have caused the beautiful cataracts of the Passaic Falls.

The great river of the county is the Passaic, whose main stream encompasses it on all sides, save the south, and receives, with few exceptions, all the other streams. On the west of the mountains, these tributaries are Deep, Pine, Black Rock, Meadow, and River Canoe, brooks; on the east, Second and Third rivers, and several inconsiderable streams. Peckman's river runs northward, in the valley between the mountains, emptying into the Passaic, about 2 miles below the Little Falls. The Rahway river, which rises in the same valley, and whose source is not a mile south of the former, runs by an opposite course into Staten Island Sound. Green brook, which rises in the Short Hills, has a southwest course to the Raritan, on the line below Somerset and Middlesex counties. On the east side of the mountains, there are 2 noted chalybeate springs; one in Acquackanonck, and the other in Orange township.

The soil of the county is generally of red shale, except where formed of the *debris* of the mountains. The first is almost every where well cultivated, and in many places highly productive in grain and grass; and, as a large proportion of the population is employed in manufactures, an advantageous market is produced at the door of the farmer for all his productions; consequently, the whole country, almost without exception, has the air of growing wealth and present enjoyment. A large portion of the surface of the county, on each side of the mountains is level, but some of it, hilly.

The principal towns are on the east of the mountain; Newark, the seat of justice; Paterson, Weasel, Acquackanonck, Bloomfield, Belleville, Orange, South Orange, Camptown, Springfield, Elizabethtown, Rahway, Westfield, Scotch Plains, Plainfield, &c.

Four turnpike roads cross the county, north-westerly, leading from Elizabethtown, Newark, and Jersey City, respectively.

In the north part of the county, a considerable portion of the agricultural population is of Dutch descent, whilst the south has been peopled from English sources, and principally from Long Island and New England. The inhabitants have the love of order, decorum, industry, and thrift of their ancestors.

In 1830, the census gave an aggregate of 41,911 souls, of whom 20,242 were white males; 19,502 white females; 921 free coloured males; 1018 free coloured females; 107 male slaves; 111 female slaves. There were 1176 aliens; whites, deaf and dumb 27, and 22 blind; and 1 coloured person blind.

In 1832, the county contained 7710 taxables, 3370 householders, whose ratable estates did not exceed $30; 1412 single men, 306 merchants, 42 grist mills, 22 cotton, and 13 woollen manufactories, 41 saw mills, 5 furnaces, 5 carding machines, 19 paper mills, 1 fulling mill, 223 tan vats, 3 bleaching and printing establishments for cotton, &c., and 5 distilleries. Besides these sources of trade, a very large business is done in the manufacture of shoes and hats for foreign markets.

In the same year, the county paid state tax, $3822 04, county tax, $10,000, poor tax, $10,570, road tax, $10,204.

The means for moral improvement consist of many religious institutions, such as churches pertaining to Episcopalians, Presbyterians, Methodists, Baptists, and Dutch Reformed—bible, missionary, and temperance societies; academies in the principal towns, at which the languages and the higher branches of an English education are taught, and common and Sunday schools, in every vicinity.

STATISTICAL TABLE OF ESSEX COUNTY

Townships, &c.	Length.	Breadth.	Area.	Surface.	Population.		
					1810.	1820.	1830.
Acquackanonck,	7	6½	14,000	hilly,	2023	3338	7710
Bloomfield,	5	4½	14,000	do.		3085	4309
Caldwell,	7	6	16,500	do.	2235	2020	2004
Elizabeth,	5	3½	10,000	do.	2977	3515	3455
Livingston,	5	4½	13,000	do.		1056	1150
Newark,	7	6	12,000	level,	8008	6507	10,953
New Providence,	6	2½	7680	pt. hill, pt. valley,	756	768	910
Orange,	7	5	14,000	hilly, rolling,	2266	2830	3887
Rahway,	8	4½	10,000	level,	1779	1945	1983
Springfield,	6	5	13,500	hilly,	2360	1804	1653
Union,	5½	5	12,000	level,	1428	1567	1405
Westfield,	7	6	18,000	pt. hilly pt. level,	2152	2358	2492
			154,680		25,984	30,793	41,911

Etna, furnace and forge, and grist and saw mills, on Tuckahoe creek, Weymouth t-ship, Gloucester co., about 15 miles from the sea.

Everittstown, Alexandria t-ship, Hunterdon co., 11 miles N. W. of Flemington, upon the Nischisakawick creek, contains 1 tavern, a grist mill, a Methodist church, and several dwellings.

Evesham t-ship, Burlington co., bounded on the N. E. and E. by Northampton t-ship, S. E. by Washington t-ship, S. W. by Waterford t-ship, Gloucester co., and on the N. W. by Chester t-ship. Centrally distant S. W. from Mount Holly 8 miles; greatest length N. and S. 15 miles; breadth 10 miles; area, 67,000 acres; surface, generally level; soil, sand and sandy loam; the north-western portion pretty well cultivated and productive. The south branch of the Rancocus forms, in part, the N. E. boundary; Haines' creek, and several other tributaries, are on the E.; and on the S. the t-ship is drained by the head waters of the Little Egg Harbour river. Evesham, Medford, Colestown, Lumberton, Fostertown, Evesham Cross Roads, Bodine, Cropwell, &c. are the villages of the t-ship, the two first are post-towns; population in 1830, 4239. In 1832 the t-ship contained taxables 850, householders 366, whose ratables did not exceed $30, single men 90, stores 9, saw mills 12, grist mills 7, fulling mills 2, distilleries for cider 4, phaetons and chaises 3, two horse stages 1, dearborns 40, covered wagons 221, chairs and curricles 39, gigs and sulkies 11, 2303 neat cattle, and 1016 horses and mules, above 3 years old; and it paid state tax, $607 21; county tax, $2119 15; and t-ship tax, $1500.

Evesham, p-t., Evesham t-ship, Burlington co., 8 miles S. W. from Mount Holly, and 4 miles S. E. from Moorestown, 34 from Trenton, and 147 from W. C.; contains a Quaker meeting house and several dwellings.

Evesham Cross Roads, Evesham t-ship, Burlington co., 6 miles S. W. from Mount Holly.

Ewing's Neck, on the Delaware bay, between Tarkiln creek and Maurice river t-ship, Cumberland co.

Factory Branch, of Cedar creek, small stream of Dover t-ship, Monmouth co.

Fairfield t-ship, Cumberland co., is bounded on the N. by Deerfield, Hopewell, and Greenwich t-ships, from the two last of which, it is separated by the Cohansey creek; E. by Milleville t-ship, and S. by Downe t-ship and the Delaware bay. Centrally distant S. from Bridgeton 7 miles; greatest length E. and W. 15 miles; breadth 8 miles; area, 46,720 acres; surface, level; soil, with the exception of a strip of marsh and upland on the bay, the latter of which is clay and loam, is of sand. The t-ship is drained on the north line by the Cohansey creek, on the south line by Nantuxet creek, and intermediately, by several small streams, of which Cedar creek is the most considerable; all of which flow westward; eastward it sends forth some small tributaries to Maurice river; population in 1830, 1812. In 1832 there were in the t-ship 410 taxables, 105 householders, whose ratables did not exceed in value $30; 9 stores, 6 run of stones for grinding grain; 2 saw mills, 1 tannery, 310 horses, and 1188 neat cattle, above 3 years old; and it paid road tax, $100; county and state tax, $868 55. Cedarville and Fairton are post-towns of the t-ship. There are in the t-ship a Presbyterian and Methodist church.

Fairfield, small village, in the northern part of Caldwell t-ship, Essex co.; contains a Dutch Reformed church, and some 8 or 10 dwellings, distant 11 miles north west from Newark.

Fairton, p-t. of Fairfield t-ship, Cumberland co., in the fork formed by Mill creek and Rattle Snake run, which unite and flow into Cohansey creek; distant about 4 miles S. of Bridgeton, 179 N. E. from W. C., and 73 S. from Trenton; contains from 30 to 40 dwellings, 2 stores, a Methodist church, and about 200 inhabitants. There is also a Presbyterian church near the town. Marl has been lately discovered here on the estate of Michael Swing, the use of which adds much to the fertility of the lands.

Fairview, or *Quakertown*, p-t. of Kingwood t-ship, Hunterdon co., 7 miles N. W. of Flemington, 29 from Trenton, and 188 from W. C.; contains a Quaker meeting house, 2 stores, a tavern, and some 12 or 15 dwellings, and several mechanics' shops. The soil here is a stiff clay,

which is becoming fertile by the use of lime.

Faraway Branch, small tributary of Hospitality creek, an arm of the Great Egg Harbour river, in Franklin and Deptford t-ships, Gloucester co.

Fenwicke Creek, Mannington t-sp. Salem co., named after John Fenwicke, the first Quaker settler in this country, rises by two branches, one of which, and the main stem, form the eastern and northen boundary of Salem t-ship, separating it from Mannington. The greatest length of the stream may be 6 miles. It empties into Salem creek, at the town of Salem, where it is crossed by a neat covered bridge, to which it is navigable.

Finesville, small village on the Musconetcong creek, a mile above its mouth, and 19 miles S. W. from Belvidere, the county town, and 8 from Easton; lies in a very narrow but fertile valley; contains a grist mill, saw mill, and oil mill, a woollen manufactory, 1 tavern, 1 store, and from 15 to 20 dwellings.

Finn's Point, a noted point on the Delaware, of Lower Penn's Neck t-ship, Salem co., about 4 miles above Salem creek, and 1 above Fort Delaware. It has its name from the first landing or residence of the Finn's here.

Fishing Creek, a small stream of Downe t-ship, which flows from Oranoken creek, through the salt marsh, into the Delaware bay.

Fishing Creek, S. W. boundary of Middle t-ship, Cape May co., flows westerly 4 or 5 miles to the Delaware bay. It gives name to a post-office; distant 109 miles from W. C., and 112 from Trenton.

Five Mile Beach, between Hereford and Turtle Gut inlets, partly in Middle and partly in Lower t-ship, Cape May co., of a wedge-like form, having in its greatest width about a mile.

Flaggtown, p-t., of Hillsborough t-ship, Somerset co., 6 miles S. W. from Somerville; contains 1 tavern, and about a dozen houses. It is 191 miles N. E. from W. C., and 25 from Trenton.

Flanders, p-t., of Roxbury t-ship, Morris co., in the valley of the south branch of the Raritan river, and in a fertile country, at the east foot of Schooley's mountain; 13 miles N. W. of Morristown, 54 N. E. from Trenton, and 220 from W. C.; contains a grist and saw mill, a Methodist church, a school, 2 taverns, 2 stores, and from 20 to 25 dwellings.

Flatkill, Big and Little, creeks, of Sussex co., both of which rise in Montague t-ship, and unite near the southern boundary of Sandistone t-ship; thence the stream flows S. W. into the river Delaware, at the Walpack Bend. The course of the main stream is parallel with the Blue mountain from its source, and for the length of 25 miles, in which it receives some inconsiderable and innominate tributaries from the mountain.

Flat Brookville, post-office, Sandystone t-ship, Sussex co., 247 miles N. E. from W. C., and 89 from Trenton.

Flemington, p-t., of Hunterdon co., situate at the northern extremity of the valley, lying between Rock mountain and Mount Carmel, and near the S. E. foot of the latter, and 2 miles E. of the south branch of the Raritan river, 23 miles N. from Trenton, 45 from Philadelphia, and 182 from W. C., 25 N. W. from Brunswick, and 25 S. E. from Easton; the two last are the principal markets for this portion of the country. The surface for many miles south and east is gently undulating; the valley between the mountains extending about 8 miles; the soil is of red shale, underlaid by the old red sandstone formation, and if not generous in spontaneous production, is grateful for the careful cultivation it receives, yielding abundance of grass, wheat, rye, oats, Indian corn, and flax; of the last, many farmers sow from 12 to 15 acres, for the product of which they find a ready market at Philadelphia. The town is also famed for excellent cheese, made at the extensive dairy of Mr.

Capner. Much attention is also given here to raising horses, of which the breeds are greatly admired, and eagerly sought for. The town contains 50 dwellings, and about 300 inhabitants; a very neat Presbyterian church, of stone, built about 35 years since; a Methodist church, of brick, a neat building; and a Baptist church, of wood; two schools, one of which is an incorporated academy, and 3 sunday schools; a public library, under the care of a company also incorporated; a court-house, of stone, rough-cast, having a Grecian front, with columns of the Ionic order. The basement story of this building is used as the county prison: the second, contains an uncommonly large and well disposed room for the court: the third, a grand jury room; and other apartments. From the cupola, which surmounts the structure, there is a delightful prospect of the valley, bounded by mountains on the S. and S. W., but almost unlimited on the S. E., and of the hill, which rises by a graceful and gentle slope on the N. and N. W., ornamented with well cultivated farms to its very summit. The houses, built upon one street, are neat and comfortable, with small court yards in front, redolent with flowers, aromatic shrubs and creeping vines. The county offices, detached from the court-house, are of brick and fire-proof. There are here, 5 lawyers, 2 physicians; a journal, published weekly, called the Hunterdon Gazette, edited by Mr. Charles George; a fire engine, with an incorporated fire association. The name of the place is from its founder, Mr. Fleming, who resided here before the revolution. A valuable deposit of copper is said to have been lately found here.

Fork Bridge, over Maurice river, about 2 miles below the village of Malaga, on the line between Gloucester, Salem and Cumberland counties. It takes its name from the fork of the river above it. There are here two mills and several dwellings.

Forked River, Dover t-ship, Monmouth co., rises at the foot of the Forked river mountains, and flows E., about 10 miles, to the Atlantic ocean.

Forked River Mountains, two considerable sand hills in the southern part of Dover t-ship, Monmouth county.

Forstertown, Evesham t-ship, Burlington co., 6 miles S. of Mount Holly, is a cluster of some 8 or 10 farm houses, upon an excellent soil of sandy loam, highly cultivated.

Fortescue Creek, Downe t-ship, Cumberland co., flows from the Oranoken creek, through the salt marsh into the Delaware bay.

Fort Lee, on the North river, and in Hackensack t-ship, Bergen co., about 5 miles E. of Hackensack town. This was a noted post during the revolutionary war, commanding in common with Fort Washington, on the New York side, the navigation of the river. Both forts were strongly garrisoned by the American troops, and bridled the English forces in New York, after the battle of Long Island. Possession of them was unfortunately holden after their insufficiency to prevent the passage up the river by the British vessels had been experimentally proven. The capture of Fort Washington lost the Americans 3000 men, and the like number in Fort Lee were saved from the same fate only by the timely abandonment of the works, by order of Gen. Greene, on the 18th November, 1776. A metallic vein was worked near this fort, at the commencement of the American war, under the impression that it contained gold. But it has been determined by Dr. Torrey, that the ore is pyritous and green carbonate of copper, in a matrix of quartz and siliceous and calcareous breccia, dipping under green sandstone.

Frankford t-ship, Sussex co., bounded N. by Wantage; E. by Hardiston; S. by Newton, and W. by Sandiston t-ship. Centrally distant, N. from Newton, 8 miles; greatest length, 11; breadth, 8 miles;

area, 28,800 acres. The surface of the t-ship is hilly towards the west; the boundary on that side running on the Blue mountain. The remainder consists of valley lands. At the foot of the mountain, Long pond and Culver's pond, are the principal sources of Paulinskill creek, which flows S. W. towards the Delaware. On the N. the t-ship is drained by the Papakating creek, a tributary of the Wallkill river. Two turnpike roads, that from Morristown to the Delaware, opposite Milford, running north-west, and the Newton and Bolton, running north-east, cross the township. Augusta and Branchville are post towns, lying on the former. Population in 1830, 1996. Taxables in 1832, 370. There were in the t-ship, in 1832, 110 householders, whose ratables did exceed $30; 6 stores, 14 run of stones for grinding grain, 2 carding machines; 1 fulling mill, 460 horses and mules, and 1540 neat cattle, above three years old; 48 tan vats, 5 distilleries. The t-ship paid state and county tax, $812 70; poor tax, $900; road tax, $800. Lime and slate alternate in several veins or beds, in the township. Their soils are fertile.

Franklin t-ship, Somerset co., bounded N. by Bridgewater t-ship and river; N. E. by Raritan river, separating it from Piscataway t-ship, Middlesex co.; S. E. by North and South Brunswick t-ships, of that county; and S. W. and W. by Millstone river, dividing it from Montgomery and Hillsborough t-ships, Somerset co. Centrally distant, S. E., from Somerville, 7 miles. Greatest length, N. E. and S. W., 13; breadth, E. and W., 8 miles; area, about 30,000 acres. Surface on the S. W., hilly, elsewhere gently undulating. Drained by the Millstone and Raritan rivers, and by several tributaries, of which Six Mile Run is the chief. Griggstown is a village of the t-ship; near it, at the foot of Rocky hill, is a deposit of copper ore, not wrought. Part of Kingston and Six Mile Run villages are within the east boundary, on the Princeton and New Brunswick turnpike. Population in 1830, 3352. In 1832, there were 716 taxables; 67 householders, whose ratables did not exceed $30, and 58 single men, 10 stores, 4 saw mills, 4 grist mills, 13 tan-vats, 2 distilleries, 862 horses, and mules, and 1335 neat cattle above the age of three years; and it paid, state tax, $709 30; county, $996 11.

Franklin t-ship, Bergen co., bounded N. by Rockland co., state of New York; E. by Saddle river, which divides it from Harrington t-ship; S. by Saddle river t-ship, and W. by Pompton. Centrally distant, N. W. from Hackensack, 13 miles; greatest length, N. and S. 10 miles; breadth, E. and W. 9 miles; area, above 45,000 acres. There are elevated grounds on the E. and W.; on the W. lies the Ramapo mountain. The greater part of the township is valley, with undulating surface and diluvial soil, of gravel, loam and sand, poured over a sandstone base; generally well cultivated and productive; and a large portion of the produce is consumed at the numerous manufactories of the township. It is drained by the Ramapo river, coursing the base of the Ramapo mountain, in the N. W. angle, and by Saddle river on the east boundary, with their tributaries. Population in 1830, 3449. In 1832, the t-ship contained 862 taxables, 83 householders, whose ratables did not exceed $30; 7 merchants, 18 grist mills, 13 cotton mills, 25 saw mills, 3 paper mills, 1 woollen factory, 1 furnace, 2 fulling mills, 22 tan vats, 4 distilleries, 803 horses, and 1780 mules, above 3 years old; and it paid state tax, $370 51, county tax, $753 25, poor, $500, roads, $2000. In Franklin there are 4 Dutch Reformed, 2 Seceders, and 2 Methodist churches.

Franklin, t-ship, Gloucester co., bounded N. E. by Deptford t-ship, S. E. by Hamilton, S. W. by Millville t-ship, Cumberland co., and Pittsgrove t-ship, Salem co., and N.

W. by Greenwich and Woolwich t-ships. Centrally distant, S. E. from Woodbury, 15 miles, greatest length 16 miles; breadth, 7 miles; area, 72,000 acres; surface, level; soil, sandy, and generally covered with pine forest. It is drained northward by the head waters of Raccoon creek, S. W. by the sources of Maurice river, and S. E. by branches of the Great Egg Harbour river. Glassboro', Malaga, Little Ease, and Union, are villages of the t-ship; at the two first are post-offices. There are iron works at Union. Population in 1830, 1574. In 1832, the t-ship contained 276 householders, whose ratables did not exceed $30; 4 stores, 2 grist mills, 9 saw mills, 1 distillery, 3 glass factories; and paid county tax, $392 72, poor tax, $196 33, and road tax, $1000.

Franklin Furnace, and village, Hardiston t-ship, Sussex co., in the valley of the Wallkill river, 11 miles N. E. of Newton, contains 2 forges of 2 fires each, a cupola furnace, a blast furnace not now in operation, a woollen manufactory for the manufacture of broad cloth, a grist and saw mill, a school house, and a new stone Baptist church, and 24 dwellings. Dr. Samuel Fowler is the chief proprietor here, and is alike distinguished for his hospitality and his pursuit of mineralogy. He has a cabinet of minerals richly meriting notice, and the country around him is considered as one of the most interesting mineral localities of the United States. The manufactures of this place seek a market at New York, or at Dover and Rockaway.

Franklin, small village of Caldwell t-ship, Essex co., 11 miles N. W. of Newark.

Freehold, Upper, t-ship of, Monmouth co., bounded N. and N. W. by East Windsor t-ship, Middlesex co., E. by Lower Freehold, S. and S. E. by Dover t-ship, and W. and S. W. by Northampton t-ship, Burlington co. Centrally distant S. W. from Freehold, the county town, 15 miles. Greatest length N. W. and S. E. 16;

breadth 10 miles; area, about 90,000 acres; surface, level; soil, clay, sandy loam, and sand. The western part of the t-ship contains some excellent lands, abundantly productive in rye, corn, oats, and grass; wheat is not a certain crop, and is not extensively cultivated. The south-eastern part of the t-ship is covered with pine forest. Population in 1830, 4862. In 1832, the t-ship contained about 900 taxables, 253 householders, whose ratables did not exceed $30; 80 single men, 20 stores, 12 saw mills, 15 run of stones for grain, 1 fulling mill, 3 carding machines, 50 tan vats, 16 distilleries for cider, 1036 horses and mules, 2438 neat cattle, 3 years old and upward; and paid state and county taxes to the amount of $3669 33. The t-ship is remarkable for the large quantities of pork which it annually sends to market. It is drained on the N. E. by the Millstone river, on the S. E. by the head waters of Toms' river, N. W. by Crosswick's creek and its tributaries, Lakaway and Doctor's creeks, and by branches of the Assunpink; and S. W. by the tributaries of the Rancocus. Wrights-ville, Imlaystown, Allentown, Var-minton, Prospertown, and Hernes-town, are villages of the t-ship.

Freehold, Lower, t-ship, Mon-mouth co., bounded N. E. by Mid-dletown t-ship, E. by Shrewsbury and Howell, S. by Dover, S. W. by Upper Freehold, and N. W. by South Amboy t-ships, Middlesex co. Great-est length N. E. and S. W. 23 miles; greatest breadth 11 miles; area, 104,000 acres; surface, level; soil, sand and sandy loam, not more than half of which is in cultivation, being barren, or covered with pine forest. There are, however, some very good farms, which produce abundance of rye, corn, &c. Pork is also a staple product. Englishtown and Freehold are villages and post-towns. The t-ship is drained by the Millstone ri-ver on the N. W.; Matchaponix brook, a tributary of the South river, on the north; by branches of the Swimming river on the N. E., and

by arms of the Manasquan and the Metetecunk on the S. E., and by Toms' river on the south. Popula-tion in 1830, 5481. In 1832, the t-ship contained about 1100 taxables, 203 householders, whose ratables did not exceed $30, 71 single men, 11 stores, 11 saw mills, 16 run of grist mill stones, 2 fulling mills, 4 carding machines, 16 tan vats, 14 distilleries for cider, 1245 horses and mules, and 2569 neat cattle, 3 years old and upwards; and it paid state and county tax, $3563 86.

Freehold, or *Monmouth*, post-town of Freehold t-ship, and seat of justice of Monmouth co., about 4 miles W. of the east boundary of the t-ship, 201 miles N. E. from W. C., and 36 S. E. from Trenton, situate upon a level soil of sandy loam, which is fast improving under the present mode of culture. The town, though long stationary, is now thriving, and contains from 35 to 40 dwell-ings, a court house, prison, and public offices, an Episcopal, a Me-thodist, a Presbyterian, Dutch Re-formed, and a Baptist church, 3 ta-verns, 5 or 6 stores, 4 practising at-tornies, 2 physicians, an academy and printing office. This place is noted in the revolutionary history, on account of the battle of Monmouth, which was fought near it.

Friesburg, a small German settle-ment of Upper Alloways Creek t-ship, near the south-east boundary, 12 miles S. E. from Salem, and 5 from Allowaystown; contains 1 ta-vern, a Dutch Reformed church, and a school.

Fredon, post-office, Sussex co., 232 miles N. E. from W. C., and 74 from Trenton.

Galloway t-ship, Gloucester co., bounded on the N. E. by Atsion ri-ver, and Mullica or Little Egg Har-bour river, and Great Bay, which separate it from Burlington co., S. E. by the Atlantic ocean, S. W. by Hamilton and Egg Harbour t-ships, and N. W. by Gloucester and Here-ford t-ships. Centrally distant S. W. from Woodbury, 35 miles; greatest length, **33**; breadth, 10 miles; area, 147,000 acres; surface level, and soil sandy. The sea coast is girded by Brigantine beach, within which, for a depth of seven miles, is a space covered with lagunes and salt meadows. Among the small lakes, Absecum, Reed's and Grass bays, are the most considerable. The remainder of the township is chiefly covered with pine forest, through which flow many streams of water, tributary to Little Egg Harbour river. Pleasant Mills, Leed's Point, Gloucester Furnace, Absecum and Smith's Landing, are villages of the township. Population, in 1830, 2960; and in 1820, only 1895, presenting an instance of the greatest increase in the state. In 1832, there were in the township, as reported by the assessor, 165 householders, whose ratables did not exceed $30, 7 stores, 3 grist mills, 1 cotton manufactory, 1 blast furnace, 5 saw mills, 375 neat cattle, and 205 horses and mules over three years of age.

Georgetown, hamlet of Mansfield t-ship, Burlington co., near the N. E. boundary line, 6 miles S. E. from Bordentown, and 9 N. E. from Mount Holly.

Georgia, a small hamlet of Freehold t-ship, Monmouth co., 5 miles S. from Freehold town.

German Valley, Washington t-sp, Morris county, and in Schooley's mountain. It is about 10 miles long, varying, in width, from one to two miles. The soil is grey limestone throughout, and is well cultivated, and highly productive. The inhabitants are of German descent, and retain the industrious and thrifty habits of their ancestors. The valley is drained by the south branch of the Raritan river, and is crossed by the turnpike road from Morristown to Easton, which passes through the post town of Washington, lying in the vale. There is a Presbyterian church here.

Gibson's Creek, small tributary flowing eastwardly into the Great Egg Harbour river, Weymouth t-ship, Gloucester co.

Glassboro', p-t. of Franklin t-ship, Gloucester co., 14 miles S. E. from Woodbury, 22 from Camden, 49 from Trenton, and 155 from W. C.; contains an Episcopal and Methodist church, 2 glass houses or factories which make hollow ware, belonging to Messrs. Stangeer & Co., 1 tavern, 2 stores, and about 30 dwellings.

Gloucester County, was first laid off in 1677, forming one of the only two counties of West Jersey; and its boundaries were fixed by the act of 21st of January, 1709–10: beginning at the mouth of Pensaukin creek; thence, running up the same to the fork thereof; thence along the bounds of Burlington co., to the sea; thence along the sea coast to Great Egg Harbour river; thence up said river to the fork thereof; thence up the southernmost and greatest branch of the same to the head thereof; thence upon a direct line to the head of Old Man's creek; thence down the same to the Delaware river; thence up Delaware river to the place of beginning. It is, therefore, bounded N. W. by the Delaware river, N. E. by Burlington co., S. E. by the Atlantic ocean, and S. W. by the counties of Cumberland and Salem. Greatest length, from Absecum inlet, on the S. E. to Red Bank, on the N. W. 55 miles: greatest breadth, from the head of the Great Egg Harbour bay, to Tuckahoe river, 30 miles; area, 1114 square miles, or 713,000 acres. Central lat. 39° 40', N. long. from W. C. 2° 10', E.

The whole county pertains to the alluvial formation. Along the shores of the Delaware, and for several miles inward, a black or dark green mud is raised even from a depth of forty feet, in which reeds and other vegetables, the evidences of river alluvion, are distinctly visible. The remaining part of the county seems to have been gained from the sea; and beds of shells, whole and in a state of disintegration, are found, at various depths, in many places. The green earth, or marl, in which these are imbedded together with the shells, are used with great advantage upon the soil, especially in the cultivation of grass, clover particularly. Bog iron ore is found near Woodbury, and exported for manufacture.

The surface is uniformly level, except where worn down by the streams, and the soil sandy; having, on the N. W. an admixture of loam or clay, in many places. S. E. of a line drawn about 7 miles from the Delaware river, N. E. across the county, the country is universally sandy and covered by a pine forest, generally, (but with occasional cleared patches of greater or less extent,) from which large quantities of timber and cord wood are taken for market. Along the coast, within the beach, is a strip of marsh of an average width of four miles, in which are lagunes, the chief of which are Grass, Reed's, Absecum, and Lake's bays.

The county is drained southwardly by Maurice river, which flows from it, through Cumberland county, into the Delaware bay; by Tuckahoe river, forming the line between it and Cumberland; by Great and Little Egg Harbour rivers, which rise far north in the county, and empty into the Atlantic; the latter, throughout its whole course, forming the boundary between Gloucester and Burlington counties. All these streams are navigable some miles from the sea, and afford great facilities in transporting the lumber and cord wood, the most valuable products of this region, to market. Their inlets, and the small bays on the coast, abound with oysters and clams, the fishing for which gives subsistence to many of the inhabitants. These rivers have also many tributaries, which intersect the forest in almost every direction. The streams on the N. W. are Oldman's, Raccoon, Little Timber, Repaupo, Clonmell, Mantua, Big Timber, Newton, Cooper's and Pensauken creeks, most of which are navigable for a short distance, and furnish outlets for an amazing quantity of fruit and garden truck and firewood, for the sup-

ply of the Philadelphia market, and other towns on the western side of the river.

The post towns of the township are, Absecum, Bargaintown, Camden, an incorporated city, Carpenter's Landing, Chew's Landing, Clarkesboro', Glassboro', Gloucester Furnace, Gravelly Landing, Haddonfield, Hammonton, Jackson Glassworks, Leeds' Point, Longacoming, Malaga, May's Landing, Mullica Hill, Pleasant Mills, Smith's Landing, Somers' Point, Stephens' Creek, Sweedsboro, Tuckahoe, and Woodbury, the seat of justice of the county.

There are several academies for teaching the higher branches of education; and primary schools in most of the agricultural neighbourhoods. There are also established, Sunday schools, in most, if not all, of the populous villages; a county bible society, various tract societies, and many temperance associations; which have almost rendered the immoderate use of ardent spirits infamous.

In 1832, by the report of the assessors, the county contained 3075 householders, whose ratables did not exceed $30 in value; 978 single men, 102 stores, 21 fisheries, 45 grist mills, 2 cotton and 2 woollen manufactories, 4 carding machines, 4 blast furnaces, 3 forges, 63 saw mills, 4 fulling mills, 8 ferries, 9 tan yards, 29 distilleries, 7 glass factories, 2 four horse stage wagons, 967 covered wagons with fixed tops, 204 riding chairs, gigs, sulkies, and pleasure carriages, 4 two horse stage wagons, 31 dearborns with steel, iron, or wooden springs; and it paid county tax, $10,000; poor tax, $5000; and road tax, $15,000; state tax, ——

By the census of 1830 Gloucester co. contained 28,431 inhabitants, of whom 13,916 were white males; 12,962 white females; 14 female slaves; 835 free coloured males; 714 free coloured females. Of these there were deaf and dumb, under 14 years, 64; above 14 and under 30, 73; above 25 years, 80; blind, 205 white, 22 black; aliens 3365.

There is a county poor house established upon a farm near Blackwoodstown, but in Deptford t-ship, containing more than 200 acres of land.

The following extract from the records of this county, presents singular features of the polity of the early settlers. It would seem that the inhabitants of the county deemed themselves a body politic, a democratic commonwealth, with full power of legislation, in which the courts participated, prescribing the punishment for each offence, as it was proven before them.

Gloucester, the 28th May, 1686.

By the proprietors, freeholders, and inhabitants of the third and fourth tenths, (alias county of Gloucester) then agreed as follows:

Inprimus. That a court be held for the jurisdiction and limits of the aforesaid tenths, or county, one time at Axwamus, alias Gloucester, and at another time at Red Bank.

Item. That there be four courts, for the jurisdiction aforesaid, held in one year, at the days and times hereafter mentioned, viz: upon the first day of the first month, upon the first day of the fourth month, and the first day of the seventh month, and upon the first day of the tenth month.

Item. That the first court shall be held at Gloucester aforesaid, upon the first day of September next.

Item. That all warrants and summons shall be drawn by the clerk of the court, and signed by the justice, and so delivered to the sheriff or his deputy to execute.

Item. That the body of each warrant, &c., shall contain or intimate the nature of the action.

Item. That a copy of the declaration be given along with the warrant, by the clerk of the court, that so the deft. may have the longer time to consider the same, and prepare his answer.

Item. That all summons and warrants, &c., shall be served, and declarations given, at least ten days before the court.

Item. That the sheriff shall give the jury summons six days before the court be held, in which they are to appear.

Item. That all persons within the jurisdiction aforesaid, bring into the next court the marks of their hogs, and other cattle, in order to be approved and recorded.

Rex vs. *Wilkes.* } Indict. at Gloucester Ct. N. J. 10 Sept. 1686, for stealing goods of Dennis Lins, from a house in Philadelphia. Dft. pleads guilty, but was tried by jury. Verdict guilty, and that prisoner ought to make pay't. to the prosecutor of the sum of sixteen pounds. Sentence. The bench appoints that said Wilkes shall pay the aforesaid Lins, £16 by way of servitude, viz: if he will be bound by indentures to the prosecutor, then to serve him the term of four years, but if he condescended not thereto, then the court awarded that he should be a servant, and so abide for the term of five years. And so be accommodated in the time of his servitude, by his master, with meat, drink, clothes, washing, and lodging, according to the customs of the country, and fit for such a servant.

In 1832 the county was divided into 12 t-ships as in the following table, to which Camden is now to be added.

STATISTICAL TABLE OF GLOUCESTER COUNTY.

Townships, &c.	Length.	Breadth.	Area.	Population. 1810.	1820.	1830.
Deptford,	25	7	57,600	2978	3281	3599
Egg Harbour,	12	12	85,000	1830	1635	2510
Galloway,	32	10	147,000	1648	1895	2960
Gloucester,	20	8	60,000	1726	2059	2332
Greenwich,	15	7	35,840	2859	2699	2657
Newton,	6	4	9,000	1951	2497	3298
Franklin,	16	7	72,000		1137	1574
Hamilton,	18	11	106,880		877	1424
Waterford,	25	8	50,000	2105	2447	3088
Weymouth,	12	10	50,000	1029	781	1270
Woolwich,	16	7	40,000	3063	3113	3033
Gloucestertown, (area included in Gloucester township.)					662	686
			713,320	19,189	23,089	28,431

Gloucester, t-ship, Gloucester co., bounded N. by Gloucestertown, N. E. by Hereford t-ship, S. E. by Hamilton, and S. W. and W. by Deptford t-ship. Centrally distant S. E. from Woodbury, 10 miles; greatest length N. W. and S. E. 20; breadth 8 miles E. and W.; area, about 60,000 acres; surface, level; soil, sand more or less mixed with loam, and in the northern part cultivated in vegetables and fruit, the southern being chiefly pine forest, valuable for timber and fuel. It is drained northward by Cooper's creek on the eastern, and Big Timber creek on the western boundary, southward by Inskeep's branch of the Great Egg Harbour river. Chew's Landing, Longacoming, Clementon, Blackwoodtown, Tansborough, and New Freedom, are villages of the t-ship; the two first post-towns. Population in 1830, 2232. In 1832, there were in the t-ship, including Gloucestertown, 781 householders, whose ratables did not exceed $30 in value; 11 stores, 5 grist mills, 9 saw mills, 2 tanneries, and 1 glass factory; and it paid county tax, $799 78; poor tax, $400 73; road tax, $1000.

Gloucestertown, small t-ship of Gloucester co., bounded N. by Newton, E. and S. E. by Gloucester t-ship, S. W. by Big Timber creek, which separates it from Deptford t-ship, and W. by the river Delaware. Centrally distant N. E. from Woodbury 4 miles; greatest length E. and W. 4; breadth N. and S. 3 miles.

Gloucester, small town of Gloucester t-ship, Gloucester co., on the Delaware river opposite Gloucester point; contains a fishery, a ferry from which a team-boat plies, about 20 dwellings, 1 store, and 1 tavern.

Gloucester, post-town and furnace of Galloway t-ship, Gloucester co., upon Landing creek, a branch of the Mullica or Little Egg Harbour river, 36 miles S. E. from Woodbury, 71 from Trenton, and 179 from W. C.; contains a furnace, grist and saw mill, a store, tavern, and a number of dwellings, chiefly for the accommodation of the workmen, of whom there are about 60, constantly employed, whose families may amount to 300 persons. The furnace makes annually about 800 tons of iron, chiefly castings, and has annexed to it about 25,000 acres of land.

Glover's Pond, Hardwick t-ship, Warren co., the extreme source of Beaver brook.

Godwinsville, Franklin t-ship, Bergen co., upon Goffle brook, 8 miles N. W. from Hackensack; contains 1 tavern, 2 stores, 7 cotton mills, having together 5000 spindles, and from

45 to 50 dwellings; soil around it red shale, fertile and well cultivated.

Goffle Brook, rises in Franklin t-ship, Bergen co., about a mile and a half E. of Hohokus, and flows by a southerly course of 5 miles through Saddle river t-ship, to the Passaic. It is a rapid, steady stream, and gives motion to several cotton mills at Godwinsville. About 1½ miles above its mouth, is the small hamlet called Goffle, containing 5 or 6 farm dwellings.

Goodwater Run, small tributary of Batsto river, Washington t-ship, Burlington co., uniting with the river at the head of Batsto furnace pond.

Good Luck, town, or more properly neighbourhood, of Dover t-ship, Monmouth co., a little S. W. of Cedar creek or Williamsburgh, separated from Barnegat bay by a strip of salt marsh, and surrounded by a pine forest and sandy soil.

Good Luck Point, Dover t-ship, Monmouth co., on the S. side of Toms' bay, at its junction with Barnegat bay.

Goose Creek, Dover t-ship, Monmouth co., puts in from Barnegat bay, 2 miles N. of Toms' bay.

Goose Pond, on the sea shore of Shrewsbury t-ship, Monmouth co., about 2 miles above the south boundary of the t-ship.

Goshen, village of Upper Freehold t-ship, Monmouth co., and near the head of Toms' river, 13 miles S. of Monmouth Court House, 23 S. E. from Trenton; contains 1 tavern, 2 stores, 10 or 12 dwellings, a grist and saw mill, and Methodist meeting; country around, sandy and flat; timber, pine.

Goshen Creek, mill-stream of Middle t-ship, Cape May co., rises in the northern part of the t-ship, and flows westerly into the Delaware bay, by a course of 5 or 6 miles; it is navigable for about 3 miles to the landing, for the small village of Goshen. A channel through the marshes, communicates between this stream and Dennis creek.

Goshen, post-town of Cape May

co., in Middle t-ship, near the head of navigation of Goshen creek, about 5 miles N. W. from Cape May courthouse, 198 N. E. from W. C., and 101 S. from Trenton; contains a tavern, 2 stores, a steam saw mill, and 12 or 15 dwellings, and a school house, in which religious meetings are held.

Grant Pond, on the Pochuck mountain, Vernon t-ship, Sussex co., a source of a tributary to Warwick creek.

Grass Bay, a salt marsh lake, about 5 miles long, and one wide, in Galloway t-ship, Gloucester co., communicating by several channels with Reed's bay and with the ocean.

Grass Pond, Green t-ship, Sussex co., one of the sources of the Bear branch of Pequest creek.

Gratitude, p-t., Sussex co., 221 miles N. E. from W. C., and 68 from Trenton.

Gravel Hill, village and p-t. of Knowlton t-ship, Warren co., in the valley of the Paulinskill, near the east line of the t-ship, distant by post road from W. C. 243 miles, from Trenton 85, and from Belvidere N. E. 15 miles; contains a large grist mill, tavern, store, tannery, and 6 or 8 dwellings; soil limestone.

Gravelly Landing, p-t. of Galloway t-ship, Gloucester co., 40 miles S. E. from Woodbury, 79 from Trenton, and 187 N. E. from W. C., on Nacote creek; contains a tavern, store, and 10 or 12 dwellings.

Gravelly Run, small tributary of Great Egg Harbour river, flowing westerly from Egg Harbour t-ship to its recipient, 2 miles below May's Landing.

Great Meadows, a large body of 6 or 8000 acres of meadow land, in Independence t-ship, Warren co., watered by the Pequest creek.

Great Brook, Morris t-ship, Morris co., rises at the head of Spring valley, and flows by a semicircular course of 8 or 9 miles, partly through the t-ship of Chatham, to the Passaic river, on the S. W. part of Morris t-ship.

Green Brook, or *Bound Brook*, a

considerable tributary of the Raritan river, rising in a narrow valley between New Providence and Westfield t-ships, Essex co., and thence flowing by a S. W. course of about 16 miles, skirting the semicircular mountain of Somerset co., to its recipient at Bound Brook. It is a mill stream of considerable power.

Green Brook, village, on Green brook above described, in Piscataway t-ship, Middlesex co., 8 miles from New Brunswick, 6½ from Somerville; contains a mill, a school house, 2 stores, and 15 dwellings. The country on the south and east, level and fertile, valued at $50 the acre; on the north mountainous.

Green Creek, small stream of Middle t-ship, Cape May co., which by a course of 2 or 3 miles, flows into the Delaware bay. It gives name to a post-office near it, distant 106 miles from W. C., and 109 from Trenton.

Green Pond, Valley, and *Mountain*; the first a beautiful sheet of water, 3 miles in length and 1 in breadth, embosomed in the valley to which it gives name, between the Copperas and Green Pond mountains, Pequannock t-ship, Morris co. The pond is much resorted to for its fish, and its beautiful scenery, where nature is yet unsubdued, and the red deer still roam at will. The valley is drained by the Burnt Cabin brook, a principal branch of the Rockaway river. Green Pond mountain, which has its name also from the same source, extends about 13 miles from the Rockaway to the Pequannock creek; it is a high, narrow, and stony granitic ridge, and lies on the boundary between Pequannock and Jefferson t-ships.

Greene t-ship, Sussex co., bounded N. E. and E. by Newton and Byram t-ships, S. by Roxbury t-ship, Morris co., W. by Independence and Hardwicke t-ships, of the same county, and N. W. by Stillwater t-ship, of Sussex co. Centrally distant S. W. from Newton 7 miles; greatest length N. and S. 9 miles; breadth E. and W. 4 miles; area, 14,080 acres; sur-

face on the south mountainous, elsewhere hilly. It is drained by tributaries of the Pequest creek, which flow through it to the southwest. Hunt's and Grass ponds are noted sheets of water in the t-ship; Greenville near the centre is the post-town. By the census of 1830 the t-ship contained 801 inhabitants, and in 1832 150 taxables, 23 householders, whose ratables did not exceed $30, 1 store, 2 grist mills, 1 saw mill, 150 horses and mules, and 400 neat cattle 3 years old and upwards, 12 tan vats; and paid a state and county tax of $279 60; poor tax, 200; and road tax, $400. The mountain on the S. E. is composed of grey rock; the basis of the soil, in the remainder of the t-ship, is limestone and slate, the former prevailing.

Green Bank, settlement on the left bank of Mullica river, Washington t-ship, Burlington co., about 10 miles by the river from its union with Great bay. There are here, 2 taverns, 2 stores, and 12 or 15 dwellings, within a space of 2 miles. The shore is clean and high; the soil sandy loam, of tolerable quality and well cultivated.

Greenville, p-t. and village, of Greene t-ship, Sussex co., by the post route, 222 miles N. E. of W. C., 69 from Trenton, and 8 S. W. from Newton; contains a store, tannery, and 10 or 12 dwellings, and is surrounded by a rich limestone country.

Green Village, Chatham t-ship, Morris co., 3½ miles S. E. from Morristown; contains some 5 or 6 dwellings, situated in a pleasant fertile country.

Greenwich t-ship, Gloucester co., bounded on the N. E. by Deptford t-ship, S. E. by Franklin, S. W. by Woolwich t-ships, and N. W. by the river Delaware. Centrally distant S. W. from Woodbury 7 miles; greatest length 15 miles; greatest breadth 7 miles; area, 35,840 acres; surface level; soil sandy. It is drained N. W. by Mantua on the N. E., and by Repaupo creek on the S. W. boundary; Clonmell and Crab creeks are small intermediate streams; and on the S. W. by Raccoon creek. Byllingsport, Paulsboro', Sandtown, Clarkesboro', Carpenter's Landing, Barnsboro', and Mullica Hill, are villages of the t-ship; population in 1830, 2557. In 1832 the t-ship contained 306 householders, whose ratables did not exceed $30 in value; 9 stores, 3 fisheries, 5 grist mills, 1 woollen manufactory, 5 saw mills, 1 ferry, 2 tan yards, 1054 neat cattle, and 549 horses and mules, under 3 years of age; and paid county tax, $1491 85; poor tax, $745 92; road tax, $1100.

Greenwich, t-ship of Cumberland co., bounded N. by Newport creek, which divides it from Stow Creek t-ship, E. by Hopewell t-ship, S. by Cohansey creek, which divides it from Fairfield t-ship and the river Delaware, and W. by Stow creek, which separates it from Lower Alloway's Creek t-ship. Centrally distant W. from Bridgeton, 8 miles; greatest length N. and S. 7 miles; breadth E. and W. 6 miles; area, 13,440 acres; surface, level; soil, generally of clay and deep rich loam, and well cultivated. Beside the streams named, the t-ship is drained by Mill creek on its south-east boundary, and by Pine Mount creek; Greenwich is the village and post-town. Population of the t-ship in 1830, 912. In 1832, it contained 205 taxables, 72 householders, whose ratables did not exceed in value $30; 5 stores, none of which sell ardent spirits, 3 grist mills, 1 carding machine, 1 tannery, 1 distillery for cider, and 148 horses and 484 neat cattle 3 years old and upwards.

Greenwich, post-town of the above t-ship, on the Cohansey creek, 6 miles from the mouth, and 6 S. W. from Bridgeton, by post-route 195 N. E. from W. C., and 81 from Trenton; contains between 40 and 50 dwellings of stone, frame, and brick; 1 tavern, 3 stores, and a large grist and merchant mill, 2 Quaker meeting houses, 1 Methodist church, a temperance society, counting more than 200 members; the soil clay

and rich loam, well cultivated, and very productive in wheat, oats, rye, and corn.

Greenwich, t-ship, Warren co., bounded N. by Oxford t-ship, N. E. by Mansfield, S. E. by the Musconetcong creek, which separates it from Hunterdon co., and W. by the river Delaware. Centrally distant S. from Belvidere, the county town, 10 miles; greatest length N. and S. 13 miles; breadth E. and W. 11 miles; area, 38,000 acres; surface hilly, the South Mountain covering the t-ship. Drained by Lopatcong, Pohatcong, and Musconetcong creeks, all which flow S. W. through the t-ship to the Delaware river. The turnpike road from Somerville runs N. W. and that from Schooley's mountain W. through the t-ship to Philipsburg, on the Delaware, opposite to Easton. Below that town the Morris canal commences, and runs across the t-ship. The population in 1830, was 4486. Taxables in 1832, 830; at that time the t-ship contained 266 householders, whose ratables did not exceed $30 in value; 9 stores, 17 run of stones for grinding grain, 1 fishery, 2 carding machines, 1 cotton factory, 3 oil mills, 1 fulling mill, 3 distilleries, 930 horses and mules, and 1265 neat cattle over 3 years of age. Although this t-ship be very mountainous, it is one of the most productive, not only of the county, but of the state. Whilst the mountains assume a granitic character, the valleys are every where underlaid with limestone, and their soils fertile. The valleys of the Musconetcong, the Pohatcong, and Lopatcong, and even the small vales through which their tributaries wander, are highly cultivated and improved, and there are farmers who send to market from one thousand to three thousand bushels of wheat, annually, beside other agricultural productions. The most interesting minerals yet discovered in the t-ship, are marble, steatite or soapstone, and iron.

Greenwood, forest, east of the Wawayanda mountain, and west of Bear

Fort Mountain, on the borders of Vernon and Pompton t-ships, and Sussex and Bergen counties; extending N. and S. 14 miles into the state of New York.

Griggstown, Franklin t-ship, Somerset co., on the right bank of the Millstone river, and on the Delaware and Raritan canal, 5 miles below Kingston, and 9 south of Somerville; contains a tavern, store, and some half dozen dwellings. A grist mill formerly here has been torn down, being in the route of the canal, which follows the bank of the river. A copper mine near this place has been wrought, but not with success.

Groveville, village of Nottingham t-ship, Burlington co., in a bend of the Crosswick's creek, about 6 miles S. E. of Trenton, and 4 N. E. from Bordentown; contains a large woollen manufactory, grist and saw mill, and 10 or 12 houses. The creek is navigable from the Delaware to the village, a distance of more than six miles.

Guineatown, a small hamlet of Upper Alloways Creek t-ship, near its northern boundary; contains 8 or 10 dwellings, chiefly inhabited by negroes.

Gum Branch, an arm of the south branch of Toms' river, flows easterly about 4 miles through the S. E. part of Upper Freehold t-ship, Monmouth county.

Hackensack t-ship, Bergen co., bounded N. by Harrington, E. and S. E. by Hudson's river, S. by Bergen t-ship, S. W. by Lodi, and N. W. by New Barbadoes. Centrally distant from Hackensacktown, 2½ miles E.; greatest length N. and S. 9 miles; breadth E. and W. 5 miles; area, 24,000 acres; surface on the E. hilly, on the W. level; soil red shale, with some marsh on the Hackensack river and English creek, generally well cultivated and productive. It is drained S. by the Hackensack and by English creek, and N. by other tributaries of the river. There are four bridges over the Hackensack, connecting this with New Barbadoes t-ship, viz. one at New Milford, at Old Bridge, at New Bridge, and one at Hackensacktown; these, with Strahlenburg, Closter, Fort Lee, Mount Clinton, and English Neighbourhood, are the most noted places of the t-ship. The frontier on the North river, is marked by the perpendicular trap rocks, known as the Palisades. Population in 1830, 2200. In 1832 the t-ship contained 535 taxables, 94 householders, whose ratables did not exceed $30 in value, 56 single men, 7 merchants, 11 grist mills, 4 fisheries, 11 saw mills, 2 fulling mills, 1 ferry, over the Hudson, 8 tan vats, 460 horses, and 1170 neat cattle, above 3 years old; and the t-ship paid the following taxes: state, $303 61; county, $615 38; poor, $300; road, $1000.

Hackensack River, rises by two branches in Rockland co., state of New York; one in the Hightorn mountain, a spur of the Ramapo; and the other from a pond, in the high bank of the Hudson river, opposite to Sing Sing. These unite below Clarkestown, and thence pursue their way southwardly, through that county into Bergen co., and thence to Newark bay. Its whole length by meanders of the stream, may be from 35 to 40 miles. Until it meets the tide at Hackensacktown, it is a fine mill stream. Below that town it flows through a marsh to the bay. Sloops ascend to the town.

Hackensack, post and county town of Bergen co., on the right bank of the Hackensack river, 15 miles from its mouth, 12 from New York, 63 from Trenton, and 229 from W. C. It is a pleasant and neat town, stretching through the meadows, on the river, for about a mile in length; containing about 150 dwellings and 1000 inhabitants, principally of Dutch extraction; three churches, viz. one Dutch Reformed, and two formed of seceders from that church: two academies, one boarding school for females, ten stores, three taverns, two paint factories, one coach maker, two tanneries, several hatters, three smiths, and four or five cordwainers. The county court house is a neat and

U

spacious brick edifice; the offices of the surrogate and county clerk are of the same material, and fire proof. Considerable business is done here with the adjacent country, and several sloops ply between the town and New York, carrying from it wood, lumber and agricultural products. The Weehawk Bank, originally established at Weehawk, on the North river, was removed here in 1825, and then received the name of the Washington Bank. Its authorized capital is $200,000, of which $93,460 have been paid in. A good turnpike road runs from Hoboken to Hackensack, and thence to Paterson. Hackensack was the scene of considerable military operations during the revolutionary war.

Hackettstown, p-t., Independent t-ship, Warren co., lying between the Morris canal and Musconetcong river, which are here about one mile distant from each other. The village is by the post road, 215 miles N. E. from W. C., 59 from Trenton, and 15 E. from Belvidere, the county town, and 6 from Belmont Spring, Schooley's mountain; contains 5 large stores, 2 taverns, and from 30 to 40 dwellings of wood and brick, 1 Presbyterian and 1 Methodist church, an academy, in which the classics are taught, 2 common schools, 1 resident Presbyterian clergyman, and 3 physicians, 2 large flour mills, a woollen manufactory and a clover mill. The town is built upon cross streets; is surrounded by a fertile limestone country, where farms sell at from 50 to 75 dollars the acre. This vicinity is rapidly improving by means of the Morris canal.

Haddonfield, p-t., of Newton t-ship, Gloucester co., near the west bank of Cooper's creek, 6 miles S. E. from Camden, 9 N. E. from Woodbury, 144 from W. C., and 36 S. from Trenton; contains 100 dwellings, a Quaker meeting and Baptist church, 2 schools, a public library, 2 fire companies, and 2 fire engines, 7 stores, 2 taverns, 2 grist mills, a woollen manufactory and 2 tanneries. This is a very pleasant town, built upon both sides of a wide road, along which it extends for more than a half mile. The houses are of brick and wood, many of them neat and commodious, and surrounded by gardens, orchards, and grass lots. This was a place of some note, bearing its present name, prior to 1713. The house erected by Elizabeth Haddon, of brick and boards, brought from England, in style which must then have been deemed magnificent, has upon it " 1713, Haddonfield," formed of the arch brick. For many years the town has undergone little change, but a disposition to build has lately been awakened. The soil of the surrounding country is of excellent quality, being fertile sandy loam, and is highly productive of corn, vegetables, fruits and grass, which, with its vicinity to market, occasions it to be much sought after, and at high prices; whole farms selling at from 60 to 100 dolls. the acre.

Hagerstown, a small hamlet, of Elsinborough t-ship, Salem co., on the road leading from Salem to Hancock's bridge, about 4 miles S. of the former, contains 10 or 12 cottages, inhabited chiefly by negroes.

Haines' Creek, a considerable tributary of the Rancocus creek, rising by several branches in Evesham t-ship, Burlington co., on all of which there are mills. It flows N. E. by a course of about 14 miles to its recipient, near Eayrstown.

Hakehokake Creek, rises in Alexandria t-ship, Hunterdon co., and flows S. W. by a course of 6 or 7 miles, to the Delaware river, three miles above the town of Alexandria, passing by Mount Pleasant, and giving motion to several mills.

Hall's Pond, small basin of water, in Newton t-ship, Sussex co., 3 miles S. E. of the town of Newton.

Hamburg, p-t., of Vernon t-ship, Sussex co., in the S. W. angle of the t-ship, within 1½ miles of the west foot of the Wallkill mountains, near the E. bank of the Wallkill river, and near the Pochuck turnpike road.

Distant, by post route from W. C., 248, from Trenton, 90, and from Newton, 14 miles; contains a church common to Baptists and Presbyterians, 2 taverns, 4 stores, 2 grist mills, and two saw mills, and 15 or 20 dwellings. This is a thriving village, and the water power on the river offers strong inducements to settlers.

Hamburg, or *Wallkill Mountains*, a local name given to the chain of hills on the South mountain, extending N. E. across the townships of Byram and Hardiston, and interlocking with Wawayanda and Pochuck mountain, in Vernon t-ship; about 25 miles in length.

Hamilton t-ship, Gloucester co., bounded N. E. by Galloway t-ship, S. E. by Egg Harbour and Weymouth t-ships, S. W. by Maurice river and Milleville t-ships, of Cumberland co., and N. W. by Franklin, Deptford and Gloucester t-ships. Centrally distant, S. E. from Woodbury, 30 miles; greatest length, N. and S., 18 miles; breadth, E. and W., 11 miles; area, 106,880 acres. Surface level, and soil sandy, covered generally with pine forest, and drained, southwardly, by Great Egg Harbour river, which runs centrally through it, receiving several small tributaries on either hand. Hamilton and May's Landing are villages of the township; the latter a post town. Population in 1830, 1424. In 1832, the township contained 115 householders, whose ratables did not exceed $30; 7 stores, 2 grist mills, 1 blast furnace, 6 saw mills, 1 forge with 4 fires, 135 neat cattle, and 171 horses and mules, above the age of three years; and paid county tax, $209 62; poor tax, $104 74¼; road tax, $800. The assessor returns but 670 acres of improved land.

Hamilton Village. (See *May's Landing.*)

Hammonton Post Office, Gloucester co., by post-route, 167 miles from W. C., and 59 from Trenton.

Hancock's Bridge, Lower Alloways Creek t-ship, Salem co., over the Alloways creek. There is a post-town here, which contains between 30 and 40 dwellings, a Friend's meeting house, a tavern, and 2 stores. Distant 5 miles S. of Salem, 174 N. E. from W. C., 54 S. from Trenton: the soil immediately about the town is of rich clay, and marsh meadow, banked and productive.

Hank's Pond, covers about 300 acres, in Pompton t-ship, Bergen co., near Clinton forges, to which it pays a tribute of its waters.

Hanover t-ship, Burlington co., bounded N. E. by Upper Freehold and Dover t-ships, Monmouth co., S. by the North and Pole Bridge branches of the Rancocus creek, which separate it from Northampton t-ship, W. and N. W. by Springfield, Mansfield, and Chesterfield t-ships. Centrally distant N. E. from Mount Holly, 12 miles; greatest length N. W. and S. E. 16 miles; greatest breadth, 13 miles; area, 44,000 acres; surface, generally level; soil, sandy loam and sand, and in the S. E. part covered with pine forest. Drained N. E. by tributaries of the Crosswick's creek, on the N. W. by Black's creek, and on the S. by the north branch of the Rancocus, upon which, near the S. W. angle of the t-ship, is the County Poor House. Arney'stown, Shelltown, Jacobstown, Wrightstown, and Scrabbletown, are villages of the t-ship; at the first of which there is a post-office. Population in 1830, 2859. In 1832, the t-ship contained 530 taxables, 298 householders, whose ratables did not exceed $30 in value; 77 single men, 10 merchants, 5 saw mills, 5 grist mills; 1 furnace, called Hanover; 20 tan vats, 1 carding machine, 7 distilleries for cider, 1 two horse stage, 36 dearborns, 85 covered wagons, 5 chairs and curricles, 13 gigs and sulkies, and paid state tax, $392 14; county tax, $1369 19; and township tax, $500.

Hanover t-ship, Morris co., bounded N. by Pequannock t-ship, E. by Livingston t-ship, Essex co., S. E. by Chatham t-ship, S. by Morris, and W. by Randolph t-ships. Centrally distant N. from Morristown, 5 miles; greatest length E. and W. 12; breadth N. and S. 9 miles; area, 35,000 acres; surface on the N. W. hilly, Trowbridge mountain there crossing the t-ship; on the E. and S. E. level; soil, clay, loam and gravel. The Rockaway river forms its northern boundary, running into the Passaic, which on the east divides the t-ship from Essex county. The Whippany and Parsipany rivers also flow through it, uniting about a mile before they commingle with the Rockaway. Population in 1830, 3718. In 1832, the t-ship contained 700 taxables, 173 householders, whose ratables did not exceed $30 in value; 79 single men, 14 stores, 7 saw mills, 7 grist mills, 29 tan vats, 9 distilleries, 3 paper mills, 5 forges, 2 rolling and slitting mills, 2 fulling mills, 2 carding machines, 4 cotton manufactories, 621 horses and mules, and 2080 cattle above 3 years old; and paid state tax, $548 98; county, $1229 08; poor, $1000; road tax, 1000. This t-ship is not remarkable for the extent of its agricultural produce, the soil not being of the best quality, yet it is generally well cultivated. It contains, however, many and various manufactories, and abundant water power for others.

Hanover, post-town of preceding t-ship, on the turnpike road from Newark to Milford, 7 miles E. from Morristown, 225 from W. C., and 59 from Trenton; contains a Presbyterian church and half a dozen dwellings, situate on the plain near the bank of the Passaic.

Hanover Neck post-office, Morris co., 227 miles N. E. from W. C., and 61 from Trenton, by post-route.

Hardinsville p-o., Gloucester co.

Hardiston t-sp, Sussex co., bounded N. by Wantage t-ship, N. E. by Vernon, S. E. by Bergen and Morris counties, and W. by Newton and Frankford t-ships. Greatest length 13½ miles; breadth 9 miles; area, 41,960 acres; surface mountainous, covered principally by the Hamburg or Wallkill mountains. Pimple Hill

is also a distinguished eminence. The t-ship is drained chiefly by the Wallkill river, which flows northward, centrally through it, and Pequannock creek, which flows through the eastern angle. Norman's Pond, and White Ponds, are basins which send forth tributaries to the river. Population in 1830, 2588. Taxables in 1832, 450. There were in the t-ship in 1832, 2 Presbyterian churches, 171 householders, whose ratables did not exceed $30 in value; 8 storekeepers, 13 pairs of stones for grinding grain, 2 carding machines, 7 mill saws, 1 furnace, 13 forge fires, 1 fulling mill, 407 horses and mules, and 1437 neat cattle above the age of 3 years; 37 tan vats, 9 distilleries. The t-ship paid state and county tax, $915; poor tax, $500; and road tax, $1200. Sparta and Monroe are post-towns of the t-ship; there is a third post-office at Harmony Vale, in the N. W. angle of the t-ship. The Hamburg or Wallkill mountain, which has an unbroken course through the t-ship, contains an inexhaustible mass of zinc and iron ores, and the t-ship generally is considered as one of the most interesting mineral localities in the United States.

Hardwick t-ship, Warren co., bounded E. by Stillwater and Green t-ships, of Sussex co., S. by Independence t-ship, W. by Knowlton, and N. by Pahaquarry t-ships. Centrally distant N. E. from Belvidere, 15 miles; greatest length N. and S. 11; breadth E. and W. 8 miles; area, 24,320 acres. Population in 1830, 1962. There were in the t-ship in 1832, 82 householders, whose ratable estates did not exceed $30 in value; 5 stores, 13 pairs of stones for grain, 2 carding machines, 1 wool factory, 5 saw mills, 56 tan vats, 4 distilleries; and it paid a state and county tax of $967 59. The surface of the t-ship is generally hilly, and is drained south-westerly by Paulinskill, Beaver brook, and Bear branch of the Pequest creek, and also by some limestone sinks; Marksboro', Lawrenceville, Johnsonburg, and Shiloh, are post-towns of the t-ship. Lime and slate alternate in the t-ship, as in Knowlton; the ridges being of the latter, and the valleys of the former; both are productive, except where the slate rock approaches too near the surface. White Pond in this t-ship, about a mile north of Marksboro', is a great natural curiosity. (See *Marksboro'*.)

Harlingen, p-t., Montgomery t-sp. Somerset co., 9 miles S. W. from Somerville, 185 from W. C., and 19 from Trenton; contains a Dutch Reformed church, a store, tavern, and 4 or 5 dwellings, in a fertile country of red shale.

Harmony, post-office and Presbyterian church, of Greenwich t-ship, Warren co., by the post route, distant from W. C. 200, from Trenton 60, and from Belvidere, 8 miles.

Harmony Vale, p-t., in the N. W. angle of Hardistone t-ship, Sussex co., 240 miles from W. C., 82 from Trenton, and 10 from Newton; contains some 10 or 12 dwellings, and a Presbyterian church.

Harrington t-ship, Bergen co., bounded N. by Rockland co., New York, E. by the Hudson river, S. by New Barbadoes and Hackensack t-ships, and W. by Franklin t-ship. Centrally distant from the town of Hackensack N. 7 miles; greatest length 9½; breadth 7 miles; area, 34,000 acres; surface level, except near the bank of the North river, along which runs the Closter mountains, 400 feet high, forming the Palisades; soil loam, well cultivated and fertile. It is watered by the Hackensack river, flowing southerly and centrally through it, receiving the Paskack brook, which, rising in New York, seeks its recipient near the centre of the t-ship; and by Saddle river, which, rising also in New York, flows along the western boundary; population in 1830, 2581. In 1832 there were 776 taxables, 152 householders, whose ratables did not exceed $30 in value, 46 single men, 10 stores, 20 grist mills, 3 cotton manufactories, 2 furnaces, 23 saw mills, and 685

horses, and 1332 neat cattle, over 3 years of age, 1 fulling mill, 26 tan vats, 2 woollen factories; and it paid state tax, $432 57; county, $910 92.

Harrison's Brook, branch of the Dead river, a tributary of the Passaic, rises in the Mine mountain near Vealtown, and flows S. 5 miles to its recipient, about a mile below Liberty Corner.

Heathcote's Brook, tributary of Millstone river, rising near the Sand Hills, and flowing westerly about 5 miles, to its recipient, near Kingston.

Herberton, town of Hopewell t-sp. Hunterdon co., 11 miles S. of Flemington, 11 N. from Trenton; contains some half dozen dwellings, a Baptist church, store, and tavern; the country around it is hilly, with soil of red shale, well cultivated. The t-ship poor-house, on a farm of 140 acres, is near it, where the average number of 30 paupers are annually maintained by their own labour.

Hereford Inlet, Middle t-ship, Cape May co., a passage of between one and two miles wide, between Leaming's and Five Mile beach, through which the sea enters the lagunes and marshes upon the Atlantic coast.

Hickory, small hamlet of Bethlehem t-ship, Hunterdon co., 12 miles N. W. of Flemington, at the south foot of the Musconetcong mountain, and on the line dividing Bethlehem from Alexandria t-ship.

Hightstown, p-t. of East Windsor t-ship, Middlesex co., on the turnpike road from Bordentown to Cranberry, and on Rocky brook, 13 miles from Bordentown, 183 from W. C., and 18 from Trenton; contains a Baptist and Presbyterian church, 3 taverns, 2 stores, a grist and saw mill, and from 30 to 40 dwellings. The rail-road from Bordentown to Amboy passes through the town, and a line of stages runs thence to Princeton, &c.

Hillsborough t-ship, Somerset co., bounded N. by the main stem, and south branch of Raritan river, which separates it from Bridgewater, E. by Millstone river, dividing it from Franklin, S. by Montgomery, and W. by

Amwell t-ship, Hunterdon co. Centrally distant S. W. from Somerville 5 miles; greatest length E. and W. 10; breadth N. and S. 7 miles; area, about 36,000 acres; surface on the west hilly, the Neshanie or Rock mountain extending over it; the soil clay and loam: on the east level and gently undulating; soil red shale. The whole t-ship is well cultivated. Besides the streams on the boundaries, the only considerable one is Roy's brook, flowing into the Millstone. Flaggtown, Millstone, Neshanie, Koughstown, and Blackwells, are the villages of the t-ship; the two first post-towns. Population in 1830, 2878. In 1832 the t-ship contained about 560 taxables, 95 householders, whose ratables did not exceed $30 in value, 58 single men, 9 stores, 8 saw mills, 8 grist mills, 1 fulling mill, 10 tan vats, 4 distilleries, 2 carding machines, 939 horses and mules, and 1638 neat cattle, of 3 years old and upwards; and paid state tax, $382 92; county, $1182 53. There is a Dutch Reformed church in the t-ship.

Hoboken, village of Bergen t-ship, Bergen co., on the North river, opposite to the city of New York, built chiefly on one street, and contains about 1 hundred dwellings, 3 licensed taverns, many unlicensed houses of entertainment, 4 or 5 stores, and several livery stables and gardens, and between 6 and 7 hundred inhabitants. It is remarkable, however, chiefly as a place of resort, for the citizens of New York, during the hot days of the summer; the bank of the river is high, and the invigorating sea breeze may be enjoyed at almost all hours when the sun is above the horizon. The liberality of Mr. Stevens, who is an extensive landholder here, has opened many attractions to visiters, in the walks along the river bank, over his grounds; and in the beautiful fields studded with clumps of trees, and variegated by shady woods, the business-worn Yorker finds a momentary relaxation and enjoyment in the " Elysian fields;" and the gastronomes, whether of the corporation of New Amstel, or invited guests, find a less rural, though not a more sensual pleasure, in the feast of Turtle grove. The value of the groves of Hoboken to the inhabitants of N. York, is inappreciated and inappreciable. They are the source of health to thousands.— Several steam-boats ply constantly between this town and New York.

Holland's Brook, tributary of the south branch of the Raritan river, rises in Readington t-ship, Hunterdon co., and flows by a S. E. course of about 7 miles, to its recipient in Bridgewater t-ship, Somerset co.

Holmdel or *Baptistown*, p-t. of Middletown t-ship, Monmouth co., 7 miles N. E. from Freehold, 219 from W. C., and 53 E. from Trenton; contains an academy, a Baptist church, 2 stores, 8 dwellings, lying in a highly improved country, producing rye, corn, grass, &c.

Hog Island, in Little Egg Harbour river, Galloway t-ship, Gloucester co.

Hohokus Brook, rises and has its course S. E. 9 miles in Franklin t-ship, Bergen co. It is a rapid wild stream, studded with mills, and gives name to the village of

Hohokus, village, situate on the turnpike road leading thence to the Sterling mountain, N. Y., 9 miles from Hackensack; contains a tavern, store, cotton mill, and several dwellings.

Hope Creek, a small stream of 4 or 5 miles in length, which rises in, and flows through, the meadows and marshes of Lower Alloway's Creek t-ship, Salem co. It is not navigable.

Hope, p-t., on the line dividing Knowlton from Oxford t-ship, on a branch of Beaver brook, 212 miles from W. C., and 59 from Trenton, and 10 N. E. from Belvidere; contains a grist mill and saw mill, 6 stores, 2 taverns, and about 30 dwellings, an Episcopal and Methodist church. The soil around it is limestone, and well cultivated. This was originally a Moravian settlement.

Hopewell t-ship, of Cumberland co., bounded E. by Deerfield, S. E. and S. by Fairfield, W. by Greenwich and

Stow Creek t-ships, and N. by Hopewell t-ship, of Salem co. Greatest length 10, breadth 6 miles; area, 20,000 acres; surface rolling; soil clay loam. Cohansey creek bounds the t-ship on the east and south, and Mount's creek and Mill creek, its tributaries, are on and near the S. W. boundary. Population in 1830, 1953. In 1832 there were in the t-ship 468 taxables, 1 Seventh-day Baptist, and 1 Methodist church, 112 householders, whose ratables did not exceed $30 in value, 4 stores, 5 run stones for grinding grain, 1 cupola furnace, 1 rolling and slitting mill, 3 tanneries, 2 distilleries for cider; and the t-ship paid for road tax, $500; and for county and state tax, $1052 87. Part of the town of Bridgeton is on the eastern boundary, and Shiloh and Roadstown are on the west. Bowentown lies midway on the road between the first and the last.

Hopewell t-ship, Hunterdon co., bounded N. by Amwell t-ship, E. by Montgomery t-ship, of Somerset co., S. E. by Lawrence t-ship, S. by Trenton t-ship, and W. by the river Delaware. Centrally distant S. from Flemington 12 miles; greatest length E. and W. 12; breadth N. and S. 10 miles; area, 36,000 acres; surface on the north hilly, a chain of low, trap mountains extending across it; and on the south level, and abundantly productive; soil red shale, loam, and gravel. It is drained on the west by Smith's and Jacob's creeks, and east by Stony brook. Population in 1830, 3151. In 1832 the t-ship contained 70 houses and lots, 11 stores, 5 fisheries, 6 saw mills, 8 grist mills, 2 oil mills, 17 tan vats, 1 distillery, 1 carding machine, 1 fulling mill, 863 horses and mules, and 1078 neat cattle, over 3 years of age; and paid poor tax, $300; road tax, $1200; state, $1722 84. Pennington and Woodsville are post-towns, and Hebertown and Columbia, villages of the t-ship.

Hopper's or *Ramapotown*, on the Ramapo river, east foot of the Ramapo mountain, 16 miles N. W. from

Hackensack; contains a tavern, and some 6 or 8 dwellings.

Hornerstown, hamlet, on Marl Ridge, Upper Freehold t-ship, Monmouth co., 20 miles S. W. of Freehold court-house, and 15 S. E. from Trenton; contains several dwellings, a grist mill, and saw mill, and fulling mill, upon the Lahaway creek, a branch of the Crosswicks. The soil on the north side of the creek is deep, rich loam; and on the south, barren sand. There is here a great deposit of valuable marl.

Hospitality, branch of the Great Egg Harbour river, rises in Deptford t-ship, Gloucester co., and flows S. E. to the river at Pennypot Mill, in Hamilton t-ship, about 14 miles from its source, receiving from the west, Faraway, Lake, and Cold branches.

Howell township, Monmouth co., bounded N. by Shrewsbury, E. by the Atlantic ocean, S. by Dover t-ship, and W. by Freehold t-ship. Centrally distant S. E. from Freehold 11 miles; greatest length E. and W. 13; breadth N. and S. 11 miles; area, 70,000 acres; surface level; soil sand, sandy loam, and clay; drained by Shark, Manasquan, and Metetecunk rivers, which flow east to the ocean; the first on the north, and the last on the south boundary. Manasquan, Squankum, and Howell's Furnace, are post-towns of the t-ship. Population in 1830, 4141. In 1832 there were in the t-ship about 800 taxables, 122 householders, whose ratables did not exceed $30, and 42 single men, 11 stores, 10 saw mills, 5 grist mills, 2 fulling mills, 4 carding machines, 26 tan vats, 2 distilleries, 1 furnace in operation, 365 horses and mules, and 1400 neat cattle, 3 years old and upwards.

Howell Furnace, p-t., Howell t-ship, Monmouth co., 12 miles S. E. of Freehold, 47 from Trenton, and 212 N. E. from W. C., on the left bank of the Manasquan river. The manufacture of iron is extensively carried on here, and for the accommodation of the workmen, there are from 40 to 50 dwellings, and a store.

A company was incorporated for conducting the works, the stock of which, we understand, is now in great part, if not wholly, the property of Mr. James P. Sairs of New York.

Hughesville, village, on the Musconetcong creek, about 5 miles from its mouth, 15 miles S. of Belvidere, and 6 S. E. from Philipsville, in Greenwich t-ship, Warren co., and in a narrow and deep valley; it contains a tavern, a store, a school and from 15 to 20 dwellings. Lead or zinc ore is said to be found in the mountain north of the town; but most probably the latter, as the hill is part of the range of the Hamburg or Wallkill mountains, in which that mineral abounds.

Hunterdon County, was taken from Burlington, by act of Assembly 13th March, 1714, and received its name from governor Hunter. It has been since modified by the erection of Somerset, Morris and Warren cos., and is now bounded N. E. by Morris, E. by Somerset, S. E. by Middlesex, S. by Burlington, S. W. and W. by the river Delaware, and N. W. by the Musconetcong river, which separates it from Warren co. Greatest length N. and S. 43 miles; breadth 26 miles; area, 324,572 acres, or about 507 square miles. Central lat. 40° 3′ N.; long. 2° 5′ E. from W. C.

This county borders S. on the great eastern alluvial formation. The primitive rock is first found in it at the falls of the Delaware river, near Trenton, and may be traced from the respective banks N. E. and S. W. It has in Jersey, however, a narrow breadth, being overlaid by a belt of the old red sandstone which stretches across the country for about 20 miles to the low mountain ridge north of Flemington. About 12 miles north of Trenton, this formation is broken by a chain of trap hills which cross the Delaware below New Hope, and are known in this county by the name of Rocky mountain, &c.; but this chain has the sandstone for its base. Between it and the chain north of Flemington, lies a fertile valley of red sandstone. With the hills north of Flemington, the primitive formation is again visible, but the valleys which intersect them discover secondary limestone, particularly at New Germantown, Clinton, &c. in the German valley, and in the valley of the Musconetcong.

The surface of the county S. and S. E. of Flemington, with the exception of the Rocky hills of which we have spoken, may be deemed level; on the north of Flemington it is mountainous; the ridges, however, are low and well cultivated to the summits. Many of them, particularly those N. and W. of Flemington, produce abundance of excellent ship timber. The red shale of the sandstone formation, is generally susceptible of beneficial cultivation, and is grateful to the careful husbandman. The limestone valleys may be made whatever the cultivator pleases, provided he bounds his wishes by the latitude and climate. And by the use of lime, the cold clay of the primitive hills may be converted into most productive soil. On the whole, this county may be considered one of the finest and most opulent of the state. It is tolerably well watered by streams, part of which seek the Raritan, whilst others flow to the Delaware river: of the first, proceeding from the north, are Spruce run, the main south branch of the Raritan, Lamington river, Rockaway creek, Neshanie creek, and Stony brook: of the second are the Musconetcong river, Hakehokake, Nischisakawick Lackatong, Wickechecoke, Alexsocken, Smith, Jacob's, and Assunpink creeks. The towns of the county are Alexandria, Baptistown, Centreville, Clarksville, Clinton, Flemington, Hepborn's, Hopewell Meeting, Fairview, Lambertsville, Lawrenceville, Lebanon, Mattison's Corner, Milford, Mount Pleasant, New Germantown, New Hampton, Pennington, Pennyville, Pittstown, Potterstown, Prallsville, Quakertown, Ringoes, Sergeantsville, TRENTON, Vansyckle's, White

House, Woodsville, &c., all of which are post-towns. There are beside these, some small hamlets of little note. The county contained in 1832, by the assessor's abstract, 86 merchants, 17 fisheries, 71 saw mills, 80 grist mills, 13 oil mills, 9 ferries and toll bridges, 524 tan vats, 5 distilleries for grain, 58 for cider; 1 cotton manufactory, 17 carding machines, 10 fulling mills, 50 stud horses, 7538 horses and mules, and 12,492 neat cattle, over 3 years of age; and it paid poor tax, $6850; road tax, $8300; county tax, $14,535 84; and state tax, $4146 76.

For the dissemination of moral and religious instruction, there are in the county Bible and tract societies, Sunday schools and temperance societies, in almost all thickly settled neighbourhoods; and the people generally, are remarkable for their sober and orderly deportment.

The population of the county, derived principally from English and German sources, by the census of 1830, amounted to 31,060, of whom 14,465 were white males; 14,653 white females; 869 free coloured males, and 901 free coloured females; 77 male, and 95 female slaves; 34 deaf and dumb, all white; 19 white, and 2 blacks, blind; 210 aliens.

STATISTICAL TABLE OF HUNTERDON COUNTY.

Townships.	Length.	Breadth.	Area.	Surface.	Population.		
					1810.	1820.	1830.
Alexandria,	12	9	33,000	mount's. hilly.	2271	2619	3042
Amwell,	16	15	77,000	p't hilly, p't level.	5777	6749	7385
Bethlehem,	9	9	25,000	mountainous.	1738	2002	2032
Kingwood,	17	7	35,312	hilly.	2605	2786	2898
Hopewell,	12	10	36,000	p't level, p't hilly.	2565	2881	3151
Lawrence,	8	6	13,093	level.		1354	1430
Lebanon,	15	7	42,000	mountainous.	2409	2817	3436
Readington,	12	7½	29,558	generally level.	1797	1964	2102
Tewkesbury,	8	6½	23,000	mountainous.	1308	1499	1659
Trenton,	7	5	10,609	level.	3002	3942	3925
			324,572		23,472	28,604	31,060

Hunt's Pond, a small basin on the N. W. line of Greene t-ship, Sussex co., supplies the Bear branch of Pequest creek.

Hunt's Mills. (See *Clinton.*)

Hurricane Brook, a tributary of the south branch of Toms' river, Dover t-ship, Monmouth co., which unites with Black run, in the mill pond of Dover furnace.

Imlaytown, post-town of Upper Freehold t-ship, Monmouth co., 3 miles E. of Allentown, 180 N. E. from W. C., and 14 miles S. E. from Trenton; contains 12 or 15 dwellings, a grist and saw mill, tannery, 1 tavern, 1 store, wheelwright and smith shop. The surrounding country is gently undulating; soil, clay, and sandy loam, generally well cultivated and productive.

Imlaydale, pleasant hamlet on the Musconetcong creek, Mansfield t-ship, Warren co., 4 miles S. of the village of Mansfield, and within 1 of New Hampton, in the adjacent county of Hunterdon, and 12 miles S. E. of Belvidere; contains a mill, a store, and 3 dwellings.

Independence t-ship, Warren co., bounded N. by Hardwick t-ship, E. by Green t-ship, Sussex co., S E. by Roxbury t-ship, Morris co., S. W. by Mansfield, and W. by Oxford t-ship. Centrally distant N. E. from Belvidere, the county town, 14 miles; greatest length 9 miles N. and S.; breadth E. and W. 8½; area, 29,440

x

acres; surface hilly on the E. and W., but a valley runs centrally N. E. and S. W. through the t-ship which is drained by the Pequest creek, and on which there is a large body of meadow land. Bacon creek is a small tributary of the Pequest, which unites with it above the village of Vienna. The Musconetcong river forms the S. E. boundary, and in its valley, parallel therewith, runs the Morris canal. Alamuche, Hackets-town, and Vienna, are post-towns of the t-ship; there is a Quaker meet-ing house in the N. E. part of the t-ship. There were in the t-ship in 1830, 2126 inhabitants; in 1832, 429 taxables, 10,000 acres of im-proved land, 414 horses and mules, and 1066 neat cattle, over 3 years of age; 146 householders, whose ra-tables did not exceed $30; 8 stores, 11 pairs of stones for grinding grain, 6 saw mills, 21 tan vats, 4 distille-ries; and it paid in t-ship taxes for the poor and roads, $900; and in county and state tax, $880 95. This ranks among the most valuable precincts of the state. The valleys are of fertile limestone, and the hill sides have been subjected to cultivation to a very great extent. The ridges which cross the t-ship from the S. W. to the N. E. are metalliferous, and upon the " *Jenny Jump*," in the N. W., a gold mine is said to exist. Preparations have ostensibly been made for smelt-ing the ore, but the " wise ones" have little confidence in the undertaking, and consider the mineral discovered, if any, to be pyrites or fool's gold.

Inskeep's Mill, at the junction of the N. E. branch of Great Egg Har-bour river, called Inskeep's branch, with the Squankum branch of said river, near the south border of Dept-ford t-ship, Gloucester county, about 33 miles from Camden.

Island Beach, Delaware t-ship, Monmouth co., extends N. 12 miles on the Atlantic ocean and Barnegat bay, from Barnegat inlet to what was formerly Cranberry inlet; it no where exceeds half a mile in breadth.

Indian Branch, a principal tribu-

tary of the north branch of the Rari-tan river, rising in Randolph t-ship, Morris co., on the N. W. foot of Trowbridge mountain, and flowing S. W. through Mendham t-ship, giving motion to several mills in its course.

Indian Run, branch of Doctor's creek, on the N. W. boundary of Upper Freehold t-ship, Monmouth co., flows S. W. by a course of about 2 miles, to its recipient, west of Allen-town, giving motion to a saw mill.

Inskeep's Branch, or rather the main stem of the Great Egg Harbour river, above Inskeep's Mill, about 30 miles from the mouth of the river, rises in Gloucester t-ship, Gloucester co., and flows a S. E. course of 12 or 14 miles, to the mill, receiving Four Mile Branch and Squankum Branch.

Jacksonville, on the line between Lebanon and Tewkesbury t-ships, Hunterdon co., about 11 miles N. of Flemington, and on the turnpike road from Somerville to Easton; contains a tavern, store, grist mill, and 2 or 3 dwellings.

Jacksonville, formerly called Im-lay's Mills, on Rocky brook, a branch of the Millstone, in Upper Freehold t-ship, Monmouth co., 10 miles E. from Freehold; contains a grist and saw mill, 2 stores, 7 dwellings, and a Presbyterian church. There is a large body of good bog ore at a short distance north of the town, and some indications of extensive mining opera-tions, said to have been carried on near it, many years since, in pursuit of copper.

Jacksonville, post-office, Burling-ton co., 160 miles N. E. of W. C., and 17 S. of Trenton.

Jackson Glass Works, post-office, Gloucester co., by post route 156 miles from W. C., and 48 from Tren-ton.

Jacobstown, Hanover t-ship, Bur-lington co., near the Great Monmouth Road, 12 miles N. E. from Mount Holly, and 9 miles S. E. of Borden-town; contains 2 taverns, a store, and some 12 or 15 dwellings.

Jake's Brook, small tributary of

Toms' river, or rather of Toms' bay, with which it unites, below the village of Toms' River.

Jefferson, village, Orange t-ship, Sussex co., 6 miles W. from Newark, at the foot of the First mountain; contains about 30 dwellings, a Baptist church, and school house.

Jefferson t-ship, Morris co., bounded N. W. by Hardistone t-ship, Sussex co., N. E. by Pompton t-ship, Essex co., S. E. by Pequannock t-ship, and S. W. by Roxbury t-ship, Morris co., and by Byram t-ship, Sussex co. Centrally distant N. W. from Morristown 15 miles; greatest length 14, breadth 3½ miles; area 25,000 acres. The whole surface is covered with mountains, save a deep and narrow valley, the lower part of which is called Berkshire, and the upper Longwood, valley, bounded on the N. W. by the Hamburg mountain, and on the S. E. by Green Pond mountain. Through this valley flows the main branch of the Rockaway river, which has its source in the Hamburg mountain near the county line; and which, in its course through the vale, gives activity to a dozen forges and other mill works. On the top of the Hamburg mountain, near the S. W. line of the t-ship, lies Hurd's pond and Hopatcong lake. The first receives a small stream which has a S. W. course of 4 or 5 miles, and pours its waters into the second. Hurd's pond is about 1½ mile in length, by 1 mile in breadth; and the lake is between 3 and 4 miles long, and about a mile broad, covering about 3000 acres. These waters are remarkable, as well for their place, as their use; being at the summit level of the Morris canal, and employed as its feeders. They are the source also of that fine stream, the Musconetcong creek, and are much celebrated for their fish. The mountain is rough and broken, and the descent into Berkshire valley is wildly picturesque: of which character Longwood also partakes. The base of the whole t-ship is granitic rock, which breaks through the surface in every direction, in rude and

heavy masses. From a soil thus constituted, little fertility is expected; but the product of the mountain, in wood and iron, is very valuable. The population in 1830, was 1551. In 1832 the t-ship contained 250 taxables, 127 householders, whose ratables did not exceed $30 in value, 6 stores, 2 grist, 9 saw mills, 3 distilleries, and 18 forges, 206 horses and mules, and 598 neat cattle, over 3 years of age; and paid state tax, $139 79; county, $312 97; poor, $600; and road, $1000.

Jenny Jump, a noted eminence in the northern part of Oxford t-ship, Warren co., extending N. E. and S. W. for about 10 miles, and into Independence t-ship.

Jersey City, lies on a point of land projecting into the Hudson river, opposite to the city of New York, distant therefrom, 1 mile, 1 chain, 47 links, in Bergen t-ship, Bergen co., 13 miles S. of Hackensack, 224 miles N. E. from W. C., 58 from Trenton, and 8 from Newark. It was first incorporated Jan. 28, 1820, comprising " All that portion of the t-ship of Bergen, owned by the Jersey Associates, formerly called Powles Hook, constituted and surrounded by a certain ditch, as the boundary line between the Jersey Associates and the lands of Cornelius Van Vorst, dec'd, on the W. and N. W., and by the middle of the Hudson river, and the bay surrounding all the other parts of the same." By the act of Assembly the municipal government is vested in seven selectmen, who are *ex officio*, conservators of the peace, a president chosen by the board, a treasurer, secretary, city marshal, &c. The town is commodiously laid out into lots, 25 feet by 100, distributed into 45 blocks, each 2 acres, with broad streets, and contains many good buildings. The whole number of dwellings may be 200, and the inhabitants about 1500. There are here, an Episcopalian church of wood, and a new church of stone being erected, and a Dutch Reformed church, 2 select schools, and an academy, owned by the public; the Morris Canal Banking Company, authorized to have a capital not exceeding one million of dollars, of which, $40,000 only, have been paid in; 20 licensed stores, 5 taverns, a public garden on the bay, called the Thatched Cottage Garden; a wind mill, an extensive pottery, at which large quantities of delfware are made, in form and finish scare inferior to the best Liverpool ware; a flint glass manufactory, employing from 80 to 100 hands, at $750 the week wages, yielding an annual product of near $100,000, of the best plain and cut glass ware. Both these large manufactories are conducted by incorporated companies. There are 2 turnpike roads running from this city to Newark, a rail-road to Paterson, and another through Newark to Brunswick; and a basin in this town is proposed to be the eastern termination of the Morris canal, now completed to Newark. Three lines of stages run from Jersey City, to Newark, twice each day. Two steam-boats, belonging to the Associates of the Jersey Company, cross to New York every 15 minutes. This company was chartered in 1804, for the sole purpose of purchasing the place from Cornelius Van Vorst, the former proprietor.

The city is a port of entry, annexed to the collection district of New York, together with all that part of the state of New Jersey, which lies north and east of Elizabethtown and Staten Island. An assistant collector resides at Jersey, who may enter and clear vessels as the collector of New York may do, acting in conformity, however, with such instructions as he may receive from the collector of New York. There is a surveyor also at this port.

Jobsville, or *Wilkinsville*, named after the proprietor, Deptford t-ship, Gloucester co., near the mouth of Woodbury creek, between 3 and 4 miles W. from Woodbury; contains some half dozen dwellings.

Jobstown, p-t. of Springfield t-ship, on the Great Monmouth road, 6 miles N. E. from Mount Holly, 169 from W. C., and 23 S. E. from Trenton; contains a tavern, a store, and 8 or 10 dwellings, surrounded by excellent farms. The proposed rail-road or Macadamized road from the mouth of Craft's creek to Lisbon, is designed to pass by this village.

Johnsonburg, p-t. and village of Hardwick t-ship, Warren co.; centrally situate in the t-ship, by post route, 218 miles N. E. of W. C., 65 from Trenton, and 16 from Belvidere; contains an Episcopal and a Presbyterian church, a church belonging to the sect of *Christ-i-ans*, 2 taverns, 2 stores, many mechanic shops, a grist mill, and from 25 to 30 dwellings. The surrounding soil is of fertile limestone, and well cultivated. A small tributary of the Bear branch of Pequest creek, flows through it, and gives motion to the mill of the town.

Jones' Island, Fairfield t-ship, Cumberland co., formed by Cedar creek, Nantuxet creek, and their tributaries, and by Nantuxet Cove.

Jugtown, small village, in a valley of the Musconetcong mountain, and on the road from Somerville to Philipsburg, about 12 miles N. W. from Flemington; contains a tavern, mill, and some half dozen dwellings.

Juliustown, p-t. of Springfield t-sp, Burlington co., 6 miles N. E. of Mount Holly, 163 from W. C., and 25 S. E. from Trenton; contains 1 tavern, 2 stores, and from 20 to 30 dwellings. A rail, or Macadamized road, from the mouth of Craft's creek to Lisbon, is designed to pass by this village.

Jumping Brook, one of the sources of Crosswick's creek, Freehold t-ship, Monmouth co., which, after a west course of about 4 miles, unites with South Run, and forms the creek. It is a mill stream.

Kettle Run, small tributary of Haines' creek, Evesham t-ship, Burlington co., unites with the main stream at Taunton furnace.

Kettle Creek, Dover t-ship, Monmouth co., rises by two branches, north and south, which flow east, the first about 6, and the second about 4 miles. Their union forms an arm of Barnegat bay. There is a post-office in the neighbourhood, named after the creek, about 65 miles from Trenton.

Kill Van Kuhl, the narrow strait between Staten island and the south shore of Bergen co., connecting New York bay with Newark bay, and in length about 5 miles.

Kingston, p-t., on the turnpike road from Princeton to Brunswick, 13 miles from the latter, 180 from W. C., and 13 from Trenton, and on the line separating South Brunswick t-ship, Middlesex co., from Franklin t-ship, Somerset co., so that part of the town lies in each county, and half way between Philadelphia and New York. There are here a Presbyterian church, an academy, 3 taverns, 4 stores, a large grist mill, saw mill, and woollen factory, driven by the Millstone river, which runs through the town. The Delaware and Raritan canal also passes through it, with a lock at this place. There are here also, about 40 dwellings. The soil around the town is of sandy loam, upon red sandstone, fertile, and in a high state of cultivation, and valued, in farms, at $60 the acre. This place was once remarkable for the number of stages which passed through it, for New York and Philadelphia, the passengers in which, commonly dined at the hotel of Mr. P. Withington. Before the completion of the Bordentown and Amboy rail road, 49 stages, loaded with passengers, between the two cities, have halted here at the same time; when more than 400 harnessed horses were seen standing in front of the inn. Mr. Withington has lately made a very large fish pond on his lands, well stocked with trout, and other fish of the country, with which he can, at any time, supply his table in a few minutes.

Kingwood t-ship, Hunterdon co., bounded N. E. by Lebanon, S. E. by Amwell, W. by the Delaware river, and N. W. by Bethlehem t-ship. Centrally distant W. from Flemington 7 miles; greatest length N. E. and S.

W. 17, breadth E. and W. 7 miles; area, 35,312 acres; surface, hilly and rolling; soil, red shale, clay, and loam; in many places fertile and well cultivated. The tract known as the Great Swamp, extends on the top of the mountain into this t-ship, and is alike remarkable for its fine timber and extraordinary fertility. The t-p. is drained southwardly by the Laokatong creek. Baptisttown, Fairview, Dogtown, Charleston, and Milltown, are villages and hamlets of the t-ship; at the first there is a post-office, and there is another office bearing the name of the t-ship. Population in 1830, 2898. In 1832 there were in the t-ship 4 stores, 7 saw mills, 7 grist mills, and 1 oil mill, 7 distilleries, 2 carding machines, 733 horses and mules, and 1347 neat cattle, above the age of 3 years; and the t-ship paid state and county tax, $1323 75.

Kinseyville, p-t. of Lower Penn's Neck t-ship, Salem co., on the Delaware river, opposite to the town of Newcastle, 170 miles from W. C., 58 from Trenton, and 7 from Salem. It is named after James Kinsey, the proprietor, and contains 4 or 5 dwellings, 2 taverns, store, and ferry to Newcastle.

Kirkland's Creek, through the salt marsh of Lodi t-ship, Bergen co.; near its head is a saw mill. The length of the creek is about 3 miles.

Kline's Mills, post-office, Somerset co., by post route 206 miles N. E. from W. C., and 40 from Trenton.

Knowlton, t-ship, Warren co., bounded N. by Pahaquarry t-ship, E. by Hardwick t-ship, S. by Oxford t-ship, and W. by the Delaware river. Centrally distant N. E. from Belvidere, 10 miles; greatest length 10 miles, breadth 10 miles; area 44,800 acres. The Blue mountain lies upon the northern boundary, and the Delaware makes its way through it at the celebrated Water Gap, at the N. W. point of the t-ship. The t-ship is every where hilly, and is said to derive its name from its knolls. It is centrally drained by Paulinskill, and its branches; on the south-east by

Beaver brook, and north-east by the Shawpocussing creek. Gravel Hill, Sodom, Columbia, Centreville, Hope, and Ramsaysburg, are villages and post towns of the t-ship. Population in 1830, 2827; taxables in 1832, 630. There were in the t-ship, in 1832, 132 householders, whose ratables did not exceed $30, 13 pairs of stones for grinding grain, 7 saw mills, 10 tan vats, 4 distilleries, 1 glass manufactory, 744 horses and mules, and 1390 neat cattle over three years of age; and the t-ship paid $1300 for t-ship use, and $1550 for state and county purposes. Slate and lime alternate throughout the t-ship; the hills are commonly of the one, and the valleys of the other.

A slate quarry above Columbia is extensively wrought, from whence excellent roof and writing slates are taken. There is 1 Presbyterian and 1 Episcopalian church in the t-ship.

Knowlton, post town and village of the above t-ship, on Paulinskill, 2 miles from its mouth, and by the post route 217 from W. C., 64 from Trenton, and 10 from Belvidere; contains 1 tavern, 1 store, a large grist and saw mill, a clover mill, and 6 or 7 dwellings. The country around is hilly, soil limestone.

Koughstown, village, on the line between the t-ship of Hillsborough, in Somerset co., and the t-ship of Amwell, in Hunterdon co. 5 miles S. E. of Flemington, contains a tavern and some 4 or 5 dwellings.

Koughstown, small village on the line dividing Hillsborough t-ship, Somerset co; from Amwell t-ship, Hunterdon co., 11 miles S. W. from Somerville, and 4 miles S. E. from Flemington; contains a tavern, store, Dutch Reformed church, and several dwellings, pleasantly situated upon soil of red shale, in the valley of the Neshanie creek.

Krokaevall, small mill stream of Saddle river t-ship, Bergen co., rising on the N. border, and flowing by a course of about 5 miles, to the Passaic river, a mile above the great Falls.

Lafayette, post town of Newton t-ship, near the north line of the t-ship, on the Union Turnpike Road, distant by the post route 233 miles from W. C., 75 from Trenton, and 5 miles from Newton; contains 1 tavern, 1 store, a cupola furnace, a grist mill, with 4 run of stones, driven by the Paulinskill, a Baptist church, and some 10 or 12 dwellings. The prevailing soil around it is limestone, in excellent cultivation.

Lahaway Creek, Upper Freehold, t-ship, Monmouth co., rises near the E. boundary, and flows S. W. about 9 miles, to the Crosswicks creek, below Hornerstown, giving motion to some mills at that place and at Prospertown.

Lake Branch, of Hospitality creek, an arm of the Great Egg Harbour river, Franklin and Hamilton t-ships, Gloucester co.

Lake's Bay, in the salt marsh, on the Atlantic ocean, Egg Harbour t-ship, Gloucester co., communicates by several inlets with the ocean; is about 3 miles long and a mile and a half wide.

Lambertsville, post town of Amwell t-ship, Hunterdon co., 11 miles S. W. from Flemington, 16 N. from Trenton, and 170 from W. C.; a thriving, pleasant village, on the bank of the Delaware river, opposite to the town of New Hope, containing 1 Baptist and 1 Presbyterian church, 2 schools, one of which is a boarding school, under the care of the Rev. Mr. Studdiford, and more than 30 dwellings, many of which are neat and commodious. A turnpike road runs from the town to New Brunswick, and a fine bridge is thrown over the river by a joint stock company, with a capital of $160,000, incorporated in 1812, by the Legislatures of Pennsylvania and New Jersey; built in 1814. It is supported on 9 stone piers; length between the abutments 1050 feet, width 33 feet, elevation above the water 21 feet; roofed. The company for some time employed a portion of its capital in banking operations.

Lamington River, tributary of the north branch of the Raritan, rises in Duck pond, Roxbury t-ship, Morris co., and flows thence by a S. W. and S. course of 34 miles, uniting with its recipient in Bedminster t-ship, Somerset co. It is a large and rapid mill stream, on which there are many mills, particularly at Potter's Falls; in the north part of its course it bears the name of Black river.

Lamington, village of Bedminster t-ship, Somerset co., on the road from Somerville to Philipsburg, 10 miles N. W. of the former; contains a Presbyterian church, a tavern, and 3 or 4 dwellings, situate in a pleasant fertile country.

Landing Creek, Galloway t-ship, Gloucester co., rises on the S. W. line of the t-ship, and flows about 9 miles eastwardly, to the Little Egg Harbour river; Gloucester furnace lies upon it. It has two branches, Indian Cabin branch, and Elisha's creek.

Laokatong Creek, a fine mill stream of Kingwood t-ship, Hunterdon co., rises in the t-ship and flows S. W. 10 or 12 miles into the river Delaware; it gives motion in its course to several mills.

Lawrenceville, Knowlton t-ship, Warren co., on both banks of the Paulinskill, 15 miles N. E. of Belvidere, and 3 miles W. of Marksboro'; contains a store and tavern, and 10 or 12 scattering dwellings. The country around it is hilly; the soil slate on the left, and limestone on the right side of the creek.

Lawrence t-ship, Hunterdon co., bounded N. W. by Hopewell, N. E. by Montgomery t-ship, Somerset co., and West Windsor t-ship, Monmouth co., S. E. by Nottingham t-ship, of Burlington co., and S. W. by Trenton t-ship. Centrally distant from Trenton N. E. 6 miles; greatest length 8, breadth 6 miles; area, by assessor's return, 13,093 acres; surface, rolling; soil, loam and clay, generally well cultivated; drained southward by some branches of the Assunpink creek, and northward by

Stony brook: Lawrenceville is the post-town, and only village of the t-ship. Population in 1330, 1430. In 1832, there were in the t-ship 1 store, 2 saw mills, 3 grist mills, 8 tan vats, 339 horses and mules, and 710 neat cattle, above the age of 3 years; and it paid poor tax, $500; road tax, $400; state and county tax, $726 80. Two turnpike roads from Trenton to Brunswick run north-easterly through the t-ship, one of which leads by Princeton.

Lawrenceville, post-town of Lawrence t-ship, Hunterdon co., 6 miles N. E. from Trenton, 18 S. E. from Flemington, 172 from W. C., situate on a level and fertile plain, well cultivated in grain and grass, and contains 1 Presbyterian church, 1 tavern, 1 store, a flourishing boarding school and academy, under the care of Mr. Philips.

Lawrenceville, town of Hardwick t-ship, Warren co., near the western t-ship line, 82 miles N. E. from Trenton, and 15 from Belvidere.

Lawrence's Brook, rises in South Brunswick t-ship, Middlesex co., and flows N. E. through New Brunswick t-ship, by a course of about 12 miles to the Raritan river, near 3 miles below New Brunswick.

Leaming's, or *Seven Mile Beach*, Middle t-ship, Cape May co., extending from Townsend's inlet to Hereford inlet, having an average width of half a mile.

Lebanon Branch, of Maurice river, rises in Deerfield t-ship, Cumberland co., and flows eastwardly to the river, about 2 miles above the town of Milleville; it is a mill stream, and has a tributary called Chatfield run.

Lebanon t-ship, Hunterdon co., bounded N. E. by Washington t-ship, Morris co., E. by Readington and Tewkesbury t-ships, S. by Kingwood t-ship, W. by Bethlehem, N. W. by Musconetcong creek, which divides it from Mansfield t-ship, Warren co. Greatest length N. and S. 15 miles; breadth E. and W. 7 miles; area, 42,000 acres; surface mountainous, and generally hilly; soil, clay and loam on the hills, with grey limestone in the valleys; in parts rich and well cultivated. The Musconetcong mountain and its spurs cover the greater part of the northern part, and there are some high hills on the S. E., encircling Round Valley. It is drained by Spruce run and the south branch of Raritan river, the latter forming part of the eastern and the southeastern boundary, and crossing the t-ship from Morris county. The turnpike road from Somerville to Philipsburg, runs westerly through the township, by the towns of Lebanon and Clinton. New Hampton and Sodom, or Clarkesville, are post-towns of the t-ship. Population in 1830, 3436. The t-ship contained in 1832, 13 saw mills, 16 grist mills, 2 oil mills, 87 tan vats, 1 distillery for grain, 11 distilleries for cider, 2 carding machines, 2 fulling mills, 886 horses, and 1540 neat cattle, above the age of 3 years; and it paid poor tax, $1100; road tax, 800; and county and state tax, $1585 36.

Lebanon, post-town of Lebanon t-ship, Hunterdon co., centrally situated, upon the turnpike road leading from Somerville to Philipsburg; 11 miles N. of Flemington, 47 from Trenton, and 211 from W. C.; contains 1 tavern, 1 store, and several dwellings. There is a Dutch Reformed church in the neighbourhood.

Leed's Point, post-town, Galloway t-ship, Gloucester co., 44 miles S. E. from Woodbury, 83 from Trenton, and 191 N. E. from W. C.; contains a store, tavern, and some 4 or 5 houses.

Leesburg, village of Maurice River t-ship, Cumberland co., on the left bank of Maurice river, about 5 miles from its mouth, and 20 S. E. of Bridgetown; contains 15 or 20 houses, 1 store, 1 tavern, and a Methodist church. There is a considerable quantity of ship building here, such as sloops, schooners, &c., and much trade in lumber and wood. The soil in the village and country immediately around, is very productive; it

is one of the oldest settlements upon the river.

Libertyville, p-t., of Wantage t-sp, Sussex co., on the turnpike road leading to Milford, Pennsylvania, about 3 miles E. of the Blue mountain.

Liberty Corner, p-t., Bernard t-sp, Somerset co., 7 miles N. E. of Somerville, 209 from W. C., and 43 from Trenton, near Harrison's brook; contains a tavern, store, and about 20 dwellings, inhabited by intelligent, respectable families, in a fertile and well cultivated valley.

Lion Pond, a source of Lubber run, Byram t-ship, Sussex co., lying near the centre of the t-ship.

Lisbon, small village of Hanover t-ship, Burlington co., in the forks of the Slab Bridge branch, and the north branch of the Rancocus creek; contains a grist mill, saw mill, store, tavern, and 10 or 12 dwellings. A railroad or Macadamized road, is about to be made from this village to the mouth of Craft's creek, upon the Delaware, about 15 miles, in order to bring to market a quantity of excellent pine wood, which grows in the vicinity.

Little Beach, Burlington co., Little Egg Harbour t-ship, between Little Egg Harbour, New Inlet, and Old Brigantine Inlet.

Little Ease, village of Franklin t-ship, Gloucester co., 20 miles S. E. of Woodbury, upon the head waters of Maurice river; contains a tavern, store, saw mill, and some half dozen dwellings; soil, sandy.

Little Egg Harbour River. (See *Egg Harbour River, Little.*)

Little Falls, of the Passaic, name of the manufacturing village and post-town which has grown up here; (See article *Passaic*) and which contains, on the right bank of the creek, 2 saw and 1 grist mill, 2 cotton mills, one of a thousand, and another of fourteen hundred spindles, a turning mill, a woollen carpet manufactory, 4 stores, 3 taverns, a school house, used also as a church, and 47 dwellings. On the left bank there is a saw mill and turning mill. This is an admirable position for mill works of all kinds. The whole river may be used under a head of 33 feet, 10 of which only are now employed to drive the few works above named, and which would give motion to a much larger quantity. The proprietors of this desirable site, Messrs. Ezekiel and Isaac Miller, and the heirs of Samuel Bridges, offer mill seats for sale on very advantageous terms, and the rights of the former gentlemen to the right bank, with half the water power, have been holden at $50,000 only. The place from its elevation is very healthy; land in the neighbourhood sells at from 30 to 60 dollars the acre, and town lots, 100 feet deep, at 2 dollars the foot, front, in fee simple. The town is 226 miles N. E. from W. C., 60 from Trenton, 10 from Newark, 4 from Paterson, and 5½ from Acquackanonck Landing. It has also the advantage of the Morris canal, which crosses the river by an aqueduct below the falls.

Lamberton. See *Trenton.*

Little Pond, a small basin of water in Newton t-ship, Sussex co., distant about 4 miles west of the town of Newton, which supplies, in part, a small tributary of Paulinskill.

Little Pond, on the sea shore, Shrewsbury t-ship, Monmouth co., about 3 miles north of the south boundary of the t-ship.

Little ⋈ Roads, p-t., Bedminster t-ship, Somerset co., 9 miles N. W. from Somerville, 209 from W. C., and 43 from Trenton; contains a tavern, store, and 5 or 6 dwellings, in the valley of the north branch of the Raritan.

Littletown, p-t., Hanover t-ship, Morris co., on the turnpike road from Newark to Milford, 5 miles north of Morristown, 224 from W. C., and 59 from Trenton; contains 1 tavern, 1 store, and 4 or 5 dwellings.

Livingston, t-ship, Essex co., bounded N. by Caldwell, E. by Orange, S. by Springfield, and W. by the Passaic river, which divides it from Morris co. Centrally distant, N. W. from Newark, 9 miles; great-est length, N. and S. 5 miles; breadth E. and W. 4½ miles, area 13,000 acres; surface on the east, mountainous, elsewhere rolling, except near the river, where it is level. It is drained on the N. by the Black Rock Meadow brook, and on the S. by Canoe creek, which flow to the Passaic by short courses, not exceeding three miles. Towns, Centreville, Livingston, post-town, Northfield, Squiretown, and Cheapside. Population in 1830, 1150. In 1832, the t-ship contained 200 taxables, 65 householders, whose ratables did not exceed $30; 52 single men, 5 merchants, 1 saw mill, 1 woollen factory, 166 horses and mules, and 637 neat cattle under three years of age; and it paid state tax, $120 03; county tax, $314 04; poor tax, $350; and road tax, $525.

Livingston, small village, and post town of preceding t-ship, on the turnpike road from Newark to Dover, 10 miles N. W. from the former, 225 N. E. from W. C., and 59 from Trenton; contains a tavern, store, and some 8 or 10 dwellings.

Lockwood, forge and post-office; on Lubber run, Byram t-ship, Sussex co.; distant by post route 224 miles from W. C., 61 from Trenton, and 9 south from Newton.

Lodi, t-ship, Bergen co., bounded N. by New Barbadoes t-ship, E. and S. E. by Hackensack river, which separates it from Bergen t-ship, and W. and S. W. by the Passaic river, dividing it from Essex co. Centrally distant, S. W. from Hackensacktown, 5 miles. Greatest length 10, greatest breadth E. and W. 5 miles; area 22,000 acres; surface level. More than half the t-ship consists of salt marsh and cedar swamp. On the N. E. there are about 4000 acres of arable land, and on the west a strip running the whole length of the t-ship, and varying from 1 to 2 miles in width. These are of red shale, with a margin of alluvial, on the Passaic, well cultivated, and productive. Along the latter river are strewed many handsome country seats, and

Y

about a mile S. E. of Belleville lies the well known Schuyler copper mine. Population of t-ship, in 1830, 1356. In 1832 it contained 527 taxables, 57 householders, whose ratables did not exceed $30; 21 single men, 1 store, 5 grist mills, 4 saw mills, 2 toll bridges, and 291 horses and mules, and 931 neat cattle, above the age of 3 years. And it paid state tax, $208 87; county $427 69; poor, $400; road, $500. There are several creeks through the marsh, such as Berry's, Kirkland's, and Saw-mill creeks.

Logtown, small hamlet of Lower Alloway's creek t-ship, Salem co., 7 miles S. of Salem-town, and 2 from Hancock's bridge.

Logansville, 6 miles S. W. of Morristown, Morris t-ship, Morris co., a fine settlement on Primrose creek, called after the owner, who has a large estate here.

Logtown, on Mine mountain, Bernard t-ship, Somerset co., at the head of Mine brook, 12 miles N. of Somerville, contains a mill and 3 or 4 dwellings.

Longacoming, p-t. of Gloucester co., on the line dividing the t-ship of Gloucester and Waterford, 14 miles S. E. from Woodbury, 45 from Trenton, and 153 N. E. from Washington; surrounded by pine forest, soil sandy, and naturally barren, but improving by the application of marl. The village contains from 20 to 30 dwellings, 2 taverns, 2 stores, and a Methodist church.

Long Beach, upon the Atlantic ocean, Stafford t-ship, Monmouth co., extending about 11 miles from the inlet to Little Egg Harbour bay, to Barnegat inlet. There are several houses on this beach, one of which was erected by a Philadelphia company, for the accommodation of themselves and friends in sea-bathing.

Long Branch, mill stream and tributary of Shrewsbury river, Shrewsbury t-ship, Monmouth co.; has a course of about 4 miles N. W. There is a small village of 12 or 15 houses, 1 tavern, and 2 stores, east of this stream, and between it and the Atlantic, to which the name of Long Branch is given.

Long Branch, well known and much frequented sea-bathing place, on the Atlantic ocean, 75 miles from Philadelphia, and 45 from New York, in Shrewsbury t-ship, and Monmouth co., which has its name from the stream and hamlet above. The inducements to the invalid, the idle, and the hunters of pleasure, to spend a portion of the hot season here, are many. Good accommodations, obliging hosts, a clean and high shore, with a gently shelving beach, a fine prospect seaward, enlivened by the countless vessels passing to and from New York, excellent fishing on the banks, 3 or 4 miles at sea, good gunning, and the great attraction of all watering places, much, and changing and fashionable company. During the season, a regular line of stages runs from Philadelphia, and a steamboat from New York, to the boarding houses here, of which there are several; Wardell's, Renshaw's, and Sear's are the most frequented. Many respectable farmers also receive boarders, who, in the quiet of rural life, enjoy in comfort and ease, their season of relaxation, perhaps more fully than those at the public hotels. Along the beach at Long Branch is a strip of fertile black sand, several miles in length, and exceeding more than a mile in width. The land adjacent to the ocean rises perpendicularly from the beach, near 20 feet. The boarding houses are 20 rods from the water, with lawns in the intermediate space. The high banks are formed by strata of sand, clay, and sea mud.

Long Bridge, over Pequest creek, Independence t-ship, Union co., at the head of the Great Meadows, 16 miles N. E. from Belvidere. There is a hamlet here of 6 or 8 dwellings, and the neighbourhood is settled by members of the society of Friends, who have a meeting house within 2 miles of the Bridge. The soil of the vicinity is limestone, naturally fertile, and susceptible of improvement, as may be supposed from the character of its cultivators; for "Friends" of all vanities, dislike most, vain labour.

Long Pond, a small sheet of water in the Blue mountains, in Walpack t-ship, Sussex co., whence Vancamp creek has its source.

Long Pond, Frankford t-ship, Sussex co., at the east foot of the Blue mountain, the extreme S. W. source of the W. branch of Paulinskill.

Long Pond, Newton t-ship, Sussex co., five miles S. E. of Newton.

Long Pond, or *Greenwood Lake*, crosses the state boundary from Orange co., New York, into Pompton t-ship, Bergen co.; it is about 4½ miles long by near a mile wide, but only a mile of its length is within this state. It sends forth a stream called Long Pond river, which empties into Ringwood river, near Boardville.

Long Pond, Shrewsbury t-ship, Monmouth co., upon the sea-shore, 6 miles S. of Long Branch Boarding Houses, communicates with the sea by a narrow inlet.

Longwood Valley, Jefferson t-ship, Morris co., lying between the Hamburg and Greenpond mountains, extending longitudinally N. E. and S. W. about 10 miles; narrow, deep, and stony, with soil not very fertile; it is drained S. W. by a principal branch of the Rockaway river, on which are several forges for making iron, the ore and fuel for which are supplied abundantly by the adjacent hills; Berkshire Valley is the name given to the S. W. portion of this vale. The scenery here is wild, rude, and picturesque. Newfoundland is the post-office of Longwood Valley.

Lopatcong Creek, rises in the southern part of Oxford t-ship, Warren co., and flows thence by a S. W. course of 9 or 10 miles through Greenwich t-ship, to the river Delaware, 3 or 4 miles below Philipsburg, giving motion to several mills in its course, and draining a fertile valley of primitive limestone.

Lower t-ship, Cape May co., bounded N. by Middle t-ship, E. and S. by the Atlantic ocean, and W. by the Delaware bay. It is the most southern t-ship of the state, nearly one-half consists of sea beach and salt marsh, and the remainder of clay, covered with oak forest. Centrally distant from Cape May Court House, S. 9 miles; length N. and S. 8, breadth 8 miles; area, 21,000 acres, Pond creek, New England creek, and Cox Hall creek, are short streams, which flow westerly into the Delaware bay. Cape May, Cape May island, and the Cape May light-house, are in the t-ship. Population in 1830, 995. In 1832, there were in the t-ship about 200 taxables, 91 householders, whose ratables did not exceed $30; 3 grist mills, 7 stores, 136 horses, 380 neat cattle, over 3 years of age; it paid t-ship tax, $51 92; state tax, $129; county tax, $399 38.

Ludlam's Beach, extends upon the ocean about 6 miles from Carson's to Townsend's inlet, partly in Middle, and partly in Dennis t-ship, Cape May co.

Lumberton, town of Northampton t-ship, Burlington co., on the south branch of Rancocus creek, 3 miles S. W. from Mount Holly; contains 2 stores, 2 taverns, a steel furnace, and from 25 to 30 dwellings, surrounded by very good farms.

Mackepin Pond, Pompton t-ship, Bergen co., about 2 miles in length, by half a mile in breadth; lies among the mountains, and sends forth a small tributary to the Pequannock creek.

Malaga, p-t. of Franklin t-ship, Gloucester co., 23 miles S. E. from Woodbury, at the angle of junction of Salem, Cumberland and Gloucester counties; on the head waters of Maurice river, 58 miles S. from Trenton, and N. E. 164 from W. C.; contains 1 tavern, 2 stores, a glass manufactory, employed on window glass, 30 dwellings and a grist mill.

Mamapaque Brook, an arm of the south branch of Toms' river, Dover t-ship, Monmouth co.

Manahocking River, Stafford

t-ship, Monmouth co., flows S. E. about 9 miles into Little Egg Harbour bay, giving motion to a mill, at the town of Manahocking.

Manahocking, p-t. of Stafford t-ship, Monmouth co., 38 miles S. E. of Freehold, 73 from Trenton, and 197 N. E. from W, C., upon the creek of the same name, about 4 miles from Little Egg Harbour bay, contains a saw and grist mill, 2 taverns, several stores, and from 20 to 30 dwellings, a Friends' meeting house, a Baptist and a Methodist church. There is a considerable trade carried on here in wood and lumber, and cedar rails, supplied by the swamps of the neighbourhood.

Manalapan Brook, or *South River*, rises in Upper Freehold t-ship, Monmouth co., near Paint Island spring, and flows by a devious, but generally, N. E. course, through South Amboy t-ship, (forming in part the line between it and South Brunswick) a distance of about 28 or 30 miles, to the Raritan river, about 4 miles below New Brunswick, receiving from the south, several considerable tributaries. When the passage to New York was made by the town of Washington on this river, a canal, of about a mile in length, was cut through the marshes, that by turning the river into it the steam-boat might avoid some detours of the Raritan, and shorten her course. The project, we believe, was not successfully executed.

Manaway Creek, Milleville t-ship, Cumberland co., a tributary of Maurice river.

Manantico Creek, a considerable branch of Maurice river, rising near the S. W. border of Gloucester co., and flowing S. W. about 14 miles, uniting with the river about two miles above Port Elizabeth; it turns several mills; it receives two tributaries, Berryman's and Panther branches.

Manasquan River, mill stream of Monmouth co., rises by several small branches in Freehold t-ship, which unite on the boundary line between Freehold and Howell townships;

thence the river flows by a S. E. direction 18 miles through the latter township to the ocean, by Manasquan inlet. The tide water of the river, about 3 miles above the mouth, is crossed by Squan bridge.

Mannington t-ship, Salem co., bounded N. by Salem river, which divides it from Upper Penn's Neck creek, and Pilesgrove township, E. by Pilesgrove, S. by Upper Alloways township, and Salem township, and W. by Salem river, which here separates it from Lower Penn's Neck township. Centrally distant N. E. from Salem, 6 miles; length N. and S. 9; breadth E. and W. 8 miles; area, about 90,000 acres, of which more than 18,000 are improved; surface, level; soil, heavy rich loam, well cultivated in wheat and grass. The township is drained by Salem river, bounding it on the N. and W. and by Mannington creek, which has its whole course within it, and is a tributary of the former. Near the village of Mannington Hill, which is the post-town of the township, is a noted nursery of fruit and ornamental trees, planted by Mr. Samuel Reeves, who sold from it during the year 1832, 15,000 peach trees alone. The poor-house of the county lies near the eastern line of the township, in which from 80 to 120 paupers are annually relieved. Population, in 1830, 1726. In 1832, there were in the township 1 Methodist and 1 Baptist church, 102 householders, whose ratables did not exceed $30; 1 store, 2 distilleries, 353 taxable inhabitants; and the township paid for, township purposes, $1000; for county purposes, $1085 34; and state tax, $339 64.

Mannington Hill, p-t., and small village of Mannington t-ship, Salem co. Centrally situate in the township, upon Mannington creek. It contains 6 or 8 houses and a store. It is about 175 miles from W. C., 60 from Trenton, and 5 N. E. of Salem.

Mannington Creek, a small tributary of Salem river, which rising on the S. W. border of Mannington township, Salem county, flows westerly by a meandering course of 8 miles to its recipient. It is not a mill stream, but along its banks are some valuable meadows.

Mansfield t-ship, Warren co., bounded N. E. by Independence, S. E. by the Musconetcong river, which separates it from Morris and Hunterdon cos., S. W. by Greenwich t-ship, and N. W. by Oxford t-ship. Centrally distant from Belvidere, the county town, 9 miles; greatest length on the river 15 miles; breadth 6½ miles; area, 33,000 acres; surface, mountainous; drained by the Musconetcong and Pohatcong creeks, which, divided by a chain of lofty hills, run parallel to each other, but at a distance of nearly 4 miles apart. There is a mineral spring, a chalybeate, in the S. W. part of the t-ship, much frequented. Population in 1830, 3303. In 1832 there were 800 taxables, 169 householders, whose ratable estates did not exeeed $30; 11 stores, 12 pairs of stones for grinding grain, 8 carding machines, 5 saw mills, 1 furnace, 1 fulling mill, 36 tan vats, 7 distilleries, 862 horses and mules, and 1407 neat cattle in the t-ship; and the t-ship paid $1200 road and poor tax; and $1659 42 state and county tax. The Morris canal winds through the hills the whole length of the t-ship. This is one of the richest t-ships of the state, having a large proportion of valley land underlaid with limestone. Large quantities of wheat are raised, and some farmers sell as many as 3000 bushels annually. Iron ore abounds in the hills, and silver *is said* to have been discovered near the spring, but most probably this is iron pyrites.

Mansfield, small village of Mansfield t-ship, Burlington co.; centrally situated in the t-ship 8 miles N. of Mount Holly, and 4 miles S. of Bordentown; contains a Friends' meeting house and 4 or 5 dwellings.

Mansfield or *Washington*, p-t. of Mansfield t-ship, Warren co., founded in 1811, on the turnpike road leading from Philipsburg to Schooley's mountain; by the post route 202 miles from W. C., and 46 from Trenton, and 8½ miles S. E. of Belvidere, the county town, 30 from Morristown, 12 from Easton, and 3 miles from Musconetcong creek; contains 1 tavern, 2 stores, from 35 to 40 dwellings, 1 Methodist and 1 Presbyterian church, and 1 school. Iron ore abounds in Scott's mountain north of the village. Around the town the soil is limestone, fertile and well cultivated, and valued at from 20 to 50 dollars the acre. The town is supplied with excellent water from a spring on the south, which is distributed by 4 public fountains.

Mansfield t-ship, Burlington co., bounded N. E. by Chesterfield t-ship, S. by Springfield, W. by Burlington t-ship, and N. W. by the river Delaware. Centrally distant from Mount Holly N. 7 miles; greatest length E. and W. 10 miles; breadth N. and S. 6½ miles; area, about 21,000 acres; surface, level; soil, various, sand, loam, and clay; generally well cultivated, and productive. It is drained north-westerly by Black's, Craft's, and Assiscunk creeks, all of which flow to the Delaware river. Along the river are some noted clay banks, from which clay is taken for the manufacture of fire bricks, and for other purposes requiring great resistance to heat. The towns are White Hill, Georgetown, Mansfield, Bustletown, Columbus or Black Horse, the last of which is a post-town. Population in 1830, 2083. In 1832 the t-ship contained 432 taxables, 216 householders, whose ratables did not exceed $30; 65 single men, 1390 neat cattle, and 548 horses and mules, above 3 years old, 4 stores, 2 saw mills, 3 grist mills, 1 fishery, 1 furnace, 1 fulling mill, 31 tan vats, 1 carding machine, 5 distilleries of cider, 4 coaches and chariots, 3 phaetons and chaises, 49 dearborns, and 84 covered wagons, 3 chairs and curricles, and 18 gigs and sulkies; and it paid state tax, $345 88; county tax, $1212 38; and t-ship tax, $1100.

Mantua Creek, Gloucester co.,

rises on, and forms the line between Deptford and Greenwich t-ships, and flows N. W. by a course of 15 miles to the Delaware river, above Maiden island. It is navigable for sloops 7 or 8 miles to Carpenter's Landing, above which it gives motion to several mills.

Maple Island Creek, sets in from Newark bay about 1½ or 2 miles into the salt marsh, on the S. E. of Newarktown.

Mapletown, hamlet on Millstone river, a short distance above the mouth of Stony Brook, 2 miles S. E. of Princeton, 15 from New Brunswick; contains a fine grist and saw mill, and fulling mill, and 4 or 5 dwellings. North of the hamlet on the river, are some excellent quarries of freestone; a fine grey, with portions of red, standstone, streaked with small veins of quartz. It works well under the hammer, and has been used in the erection of the locks of the Delaware and Raritan canal.

Mare Run, small tributary of the Great Egg Harbour river, flowing from the west to its recipient, in Hamilton t-ship, Gloucester co., about 3 miles above May's Landing.

Marksboro', p-t. and village of Hardwick t-ship, Warren co.; centrally situate in the t-ship, and by post route distant from W. C. 240, from Trenton 82, from Belvidere 15 miles, 10 from Newton, and 12 from Columbia, and on the south bank of the Paulinskill; contains a Presbyterian church, a grist mill, a cotton manufactory making 1500 lbs. of yarn per week, a clover mill, 1 lawyer, 1 physician, and about 20 dwellings. The town itself lies on a slate ridge, which is fertile and well cultivated, but the soil on the north side of the creek is secondary limestone; the most valuable slate lands rate, at about $30, and the lime, at about $40 the acre. The celebrated White Pond lies about 1 mile north of the town. Its shores and bottom are covered with vast quantities of snail shells, and its waters afford abundance of white perch and other fish.

Marshs'bog, town of Howell t-ship, Monmouth co., 9 miles S. E. of Freehold; contains 2 taverns, 2 stores, and 10 or 12 dwellings; the surrounding country is sterile, but there is considerable business done in the village.

Marshallville, or *Cumberland Works*, on Tuckahoe creek, Maurice Creek t-ship, Cumberland co., at the eastern extremity of the co., 28 miles S. E. of Bridgeton; contains from 30 to 40 houses, some extensive glass works belonging to Randall Marshall, Esq., at which much window glass is manufactured, 1 tavern, and 2 stores. There is much ship building carried on here in vessels of from 50 to 100 tons; soil, sandy.

Martha Furnace, Washington t-ship, Burlington co., on the Oswego branch of Wading river, about 4 miles above the head of navigation; there are here also a grist and saw mill. The furnace makes about 750 tons of iron castings annually, and employs about 60 hands, who, with their families, make a population of near 400 souls, requiring from 40 to 50 dwellings; there are about 30,000 acres of land appurtenant to these works.

Martinsville post-office, Somerset co., 203 miles N. E. from W. C., and 37 from Trenton.

Matchaponix Brook, fine mill stream, which has its source in Upper Freehold t-ship, Monmouth co., and flows about 10 miles N. W. by Englishtown, through South Amboy t-ship, to its recipient, the South river, near Spotswood.

Matouchin, p-t. of Woodbridge t-ship, Middlesex co., at the intersection of the turnpike roads leading, one from New Brunswick to Elizabethtown, and the other from Perth Amboy towards Bound Brook, 5 miles from New Brunswick, 6 miles from Perth Amboy, 31 from Trenton, and 198 from W. C.; contains a Presbyterian church, store, 2 taverns, and 10 or 12 dwellings, surrounded by a fertile country of red shale.

Mattison's Corner, post-office Hunterdon co., by post-route 185 miles from W. C., and 26 from Trenton.

Mauricetown, p-t. on Maurice river, 10 or 12 miles from its mouth, 87 miles S. of Trenton, 18 from Bridgeton, and 184 from W. C.; contains some 20 dwellings, store, tavern, an academy, and Methodist church. The town is handsomely situated upon a high belt of rich land, and some of the dwellings are of brick, very neat and pleasant, and surrounded by valuable meadows.

Maurice River t-ship, Cumberland co., bounded N. by Hamilton t-ship, Gloucester co., E. by Weymouth t-ship, of same co., S. by Upper and Dennis t-ships, of Cape May co., and by the Delaware bay, and W. by Maurice river, from its source to its mouth, separating it from Downe and Milleville t-ships, Cumberland co. Centrally distant S. E. from Bridgeton, 20 miles; greatest length 19, breadth 11 miles; area, 79,360 acres; surface, level; soil, generally sandy except along the margin of the creeks, where loam and clay prevail. It is drained E. by Tuckahoe creek and its tributaries, and S. by Tarkill creek. Population in 1830, 2724. In 1832, there were in the t-ship 525 taxables, 117 householders, whose ratables did not exceed $30 ; 11 stores, 6 pairs of stones for grinding grain, 1 blast furnace and forge, 6 saw mills, 2 glass manufactories, 1 at Port Elizabeth, and the other at Marshallville, or Cumberland Works, 295 horses, and 1810 neat cattle, above 3 years old; there are some very valuable meadows on Maurice river, commencing 5 miles from the mouth, and extending nearly to Milleville, 15 miles. Port Elizabeth, Bricksboro', Dorchester, Leesburg, and Marshallville, are villages of the t-ship; all, except the last, upon or near the east bank of Maurice river, and the last upon Tuckahoe creek.

Maurice River, Prince, rises by several small branches in Deptford and Franklin t-ships, Gloucester co., which uniting above Fork Bridge on the line between the S. E. boundary of Salem co. and Cumberland co., form a considerable stream, which there gives motion to several mills. About 8 miles below this point, the river receives from Salem co. a large tributary, called Muddy run, above the head of the dam of the Milleville works. From this dam, which checks the whole river, a canal of near 3 miles in length, supplies the works at Milleville. From this town the river is navigable for 20 miles to the bay, for vessels of 80 or 100 tons, and to within 5 miles of its mouth, its shores are lined with valuable embanked meadows. It receives in its course a number of considerable tributaries, on either hand. The oysters taken at the mouth of this river, are famed for their excellent quality.

Maul's Bridge, over the Maurice river, between Salem and Cumberland counties.

May's Landing, p-t. of Hamilton t-ship, Gloucester co., upon the Great Egg Harbour river, at the head of sloop navigation, 16 miles from the sea, 35 miles S. E. from Woodbury, 73 from Trenton, and 181 N. E. from W. C.; built on both sides of the river, including the village of Hamilton, and contains 3 taverns, 4 stores, a Methodist church, and 25 or 30 dwellings; a considerable trade in cord-wood, lumber, and ship building, is carried on at this place.

Mead's Basin, post-office, Bergen co., 240 miles from W. C., and 74 from Trenton, N. E.

Meekendam Creek, small tributary of Little Egg Harbour river, uniting with it about 4 miles below Pleasant Mills.

Mechescalaxin Creek, tributary of Atsion river, rises in Hereford t-ship, Gloucester co., and by a course of 13 miles S. E., unites with Atsion river, near Pleasant Mills, in Galloway t-ship.

Medford, p-t. Evsham t-ship, Burlington co., on Haines' creek, 7 miles S. W. from Mount Holly, 16 miles E. from Camden, 29 S. E. from Trenton, and 154 N. E. from W. C.;

contains a large Quaker meeting house, 2 taverns, 4 stores, and from 30 to 40 dwellings, surrounded by a pleasant fertile country.

Mendham t-ship, Morris co., bounded N. by Randolph, E. by Morris, S. by Bernard, and Bedminster t-ships, of Somerset co., and W. by Chester co. Centrally distant, W. from Morristown, 7 miles; greatest length, E. and W. 6; breadth, N. and S. 4½ miles; area, 14,000 acres; surface generally hilly, and on the N. mountainous; soil clay, loam and grey limestone; the last fertile and well cultivated; drained southwardly, by arms of the north branch of the Raritan, and E. by Whippany river. Mendham is the post-town. Population in 1830, 1314. In 1832, the township contained 270 taxables, 48 householders, whose ratables did not exceed $30; 30 single men, 5 stores, 4 saw mills, 3 grist mills, 1 cotton manufactory, 2 fulling mills, 2 wool carding machines, 26 tan vats, 7 distilleries and 1 forge, 273 horses and 686 neat cattle, above the age of three years; and paid state tax, $176 03; county tax, 394 12; poor tax, $250; road tax, $800. Sulphur was reported to be found, in this township, in large quantities, during the revolutionary war.

Mendham, p-t. of the preceding township, on the Morris and Easton turnpike-road, 6 miles W. of the former, 221 N. E. from W. C., and 55 from Trenton; contains a Presbyterian church, a boarding school for boys, in much repute, under the care of Mr. Fairchild, 1 grist mill, 1 tavern, three stores, and between 40 and 50 dwellings. Circumjacent country rolling, soil limestone, well cultivated and fertile.

Merritt's Branch of Pohatcong Creek, rises in Oxford t-ship, Warren co. and flows S. through Greenwich township, to its recipient, having a course of about 7 miles.

Metetecunk River, Monmouth co., rises by two branches, the N. and S. in Freehold township, and flowing S. E. about 16 miles, uniting in the pond of Butcher's works, on the line of Dover and Howell townships, about 4 miles above the north end of Barnegat bay, into which the river empties. Each branch gives motion to several mills. The main river is navigable to Butcher's works.

Middle t-ship, Cape May co., bounded N. by Dennis' creek t-ship, E. by the Atlantic ocean, S. by Lower t-ship, and W. by the Delaware bay; greatest length, N. and S. 12, breadth, 10 miles; area, 60,000 acres; surface, level; soil, sand and marsh; Dennis' creek runs on the N. W. border of the township; Leaming's and Seven Mile beaches lie on the Atlantic, between which, is Hereford's inlet, admitting the sea to the marshes and lagunes, which extend westerly, for about four miles. On the bay there is also, a strip of marsh from half a mile to two miles in width, through which flow Goshen, Dyer's, Green and Fishing creeks. The interval land between the marshes, is a stiff clay, covered with oak forest, through which are interspersed some arable lands. The population is chiefly seated along the edge of the marshes, and consisted, in 1830, of 1366 souls. In 1832, the township contained about 320 taxables, 207 householders, whose ratables did not exceed $30; 1 grist mill, 3 saw mills, 218 horses, 650 neat cattle over 3 years of age, 8 stores, and paid township taxes, $101 3; county do. $630 47; and state tax, $203 53. There are two villages in the township; one at Cape May Court House, and the other called Goshen.

Middle Run, Weymouth t-ship, Gloucester co., a marsh creek, which empties into Great Egg Harbour bay.

Middlebrook, Warren and Bridgewater t-ships, Somerset co., rises in and flows through a mountain valley by a S. W. and S. course of about 9 miles, and emptying into the Raritan near the village of Middlebrook in the latter township.

Middlebrook, village. See *Bound Brook*.

Middlesex co., was first erected by an act of Assembly under the proprietary government in 1682. Its boundaries have been settled by the acts of 1709, 1713 and 1790. It is now bounded N. by Essex county; N. E. by Arthur's Kill or Staten Island Sound; E. by Raritan bay; S. E. by Monmouth county; S. W. by Burlington, and Huntingdon counties; and W. and N. W. by Somerset county; greatest length, N. E. and S. W. 35 miles; greatest breadth, 17 miles; area, in acres, 21,700, or about 339 square miles. Central lat. 40° 25' N.; long. from W. C. 2° 34' east.

Geologically considered, the county is based upon the primitive and old red sandstone formations. The former is, in many places, covered by the latter, and appears most conspicuously in the S. W. portion of the county. The red and grey freestone from the quarries of West Windsor township, S. E. of Princeton, and the redstone near New Brunswick, and in many other parts of the county, are admirably adapted for, and have been extensively used in building; the former especially in the locks of the Delaware and Raritan canal. The sand of this stone is mingled in various portions with other constituents of the soil, forming in some places, deep sand, in others, loam, of diverse consistence, from the light sandy, to the heavy clay. Generally, however, the soil is of improvable quality, and is in many places highly cultivated. The surface is as various as the soil; on the S. E. it is generally level, and on the N. and N. E. is undulating, but cannot any where be deemed hilly; except at the sand hills, a few miles E. of Kingston.

Copper ore is found in the red sandstone near New Brunswick. Mines were opened and worked many years ago, but all operations therein have long been suspended.

The river Raritan divides the county into two unequal parts, flowing by a general but serpentine easterly course of 12 or 14 miles through it, into the Raritan bay; receiving from the south, Lawrence's brook and the South river, whose many branches water the country on the S. E.; and from the N. some inconsiderable tributaries. The Millstone river crosses the S. W. portion of the county in a N. W. direction, and is divided from the Assunpink creek, by a neck of land from four to five miles wide. The one, bending to the north, seeks the Raritan river, in Somerset county; and the other turning to the S. W. runs to the Delaware, on the line between Burlington and Hunterdon counties. The Rahway river courses the N. E. line, and Greenbrook the N. W. boundary, both of which receive tribute from the county. The bay of the Raritan affords an excellent harbour, communicating at all times by a single tide, with the ocean; and by Staten Island Sound, with the bay of New York.

Perth Amboy was originally the seat of justice of the county, which has long since been removed to the city of New Brunswick.

Besides these cities, the county contains the following towns, viz. Bridgetown, Samptown, Brooklyn, New Market, New Durham, Woodbridge, Matouchin, Bonhamtown, Piscataway, Washington, Old Bridge, Spotswood, Kingston, Princeton, Williamsburg, Cranberry, Hightstown, Millford, Edinburg, Centreville, &c.

A turnpike road from Trenton runs by Princeton, along the western boundary of the county, to New Brunswick; and thence a like road passes to New York; a second runs from Trenton, by a straight line, N. W., to New Brunswick; and a third from Bordentown to Amboy, which last two places are also connected by the Bordentown and Amboy rail-road. The New Jersey rail-road, now in progress, will unite the cities of Jersey and New Brunswick. The Delaware and Raritan canal runs a very considerable distance through the county, and communicates with the Raritan at New Brunswick.

The population, by the census of 1830, was 23,157: of whom 10,523 were white males; 10,487 white females; 904 free coloured males; 914 free coloured females; 130 male slaves; 179 female slaves; 174 aliens; 12 whites, deaf and dumb, 7 blind, and 3 blacks blind.

The business of the county is chiefly agricultural, but considerable trade is carried on from New Brunswick. In 1832 the county contained about 4500 taxables, 841 householders, whose ratables did not exceed $30; 477 single men, 99 stores, 20 saw mills, 42 run of stones for grinding grain, 2 plaster mills, 2 woollen factories, 7 carding machines, 39 distilleries, and 3684 horses and mules, and 7675 neat cattle over 3 years of age; and it paid state tax, $3253 26; county, $4000; poor, $5850; road, 3600.

The provisions for moral improvement, in the county, consist of the following religious associations: viz.

Presbyterian, Episcopalian, Baptist, Seventh-day Baptist, Dutch Reformed, and Methodist; one college, and one theological institution belonging to Presbyterians, several academies and boarding schools, at Princeton; a college and theological seminary pertaining to the Dutch Reformed, a grammar school, and other schools, at New Brunswick; two academies at Rahway, and common schools, at which the rudiments of an English education are given in every populous vicinity; a county bible society, Sunday schools, in almost every village, and temperance societies which are spreading over the county.

The public buildings in addition to the churches and seats of literature, consist of the court-house, public offices, and prison, at New Brunswick.

The following are post-towns of the county: Amboy, Cranberry, Hightstown, Kingston, New Brunswick, New Market, Rahway, Six Mile Run, South or Washington, Spotswood, and Woodbridge.

STATISTICAL TABLE OF MIDDLESEX COUNTY.

Townships, &c.	Length.	Breadth.	Area.	Surface.	Population.		
					1810.	1820.	1830.
Perth Amboy,			2,577	rolling.	815	798	879
South Amboy,	18	6	64,000	partly rolling.	3071	3406	3782
North Brunswick,	9	7	23,000	level.	3980	4275	5274
South Brunswick,	10	7	36,000	do.	2332	2489	2557
East Windsor,	12	6	24,000	do.	1747	1710	1903
West Windsor,	7	5	19,000	do.	1714	1918	2129
Piscataway,	9	7½	27,000	do.	2475	2648	2664
Woodbridge,	9	9	24,000	do.	4247	4226	3969
			219,577		20,381	21,470	23,157

Middletown t-ship, Monmouth co., bounded N. by Raritan bay and Sandy Hook, E. by the Atlantic ocean, S. by Shrewsbury t-ship, and W. by South Amboy t-ship, Middlesex co. Centrally distant N. E. from Freehold 10 miles; greatest length E. and W. 16, breadth N. and S. 10 miles; area, 50,000 acres; surface, on the east and centre, hilly, elsewhere, level; soil, loam, sand, and clay, not naturally of the first quality, but highly improved, in places, by the use of marl, which has become common. Sandy Hook bay runs south into the t-ship from the Raritan, and is bounded on the S. W. by the promontory of the highlands of Nevisink, and on the E. by the sand beach, forming Sandy Hook, running 6 miles north from Shrewsbury Inlet; upon the north point of which stands Sandy Hook Light-house. The t-ship is drained on the S. E., S. and S. W. by Swimming and Nevisink rivers; on the N. W. by Middletown creek; N. by Waycake, and N. E. by Watson's and Shoal Harbour creeks. Middletown, Middletown Point, Baptisttown, or Holmdel and Mount Pleasant are villages, the two first post-towns, of the t-ship. Population in 1830, 5128. In 1832 the t-ship contained about 1000 taxables, 277 householders, whose ratables did not exceed $30; 169 single men, 27 stores, 5 saw mills, 13 run of stones for grinding grain, 1 fulling mill, 36 tan vats, 11 distilleries, 956 horses and mules, and 2286 neat cattle, above 3 years of age; and paid state and county taxes, $2620 20. Good lands will bring in this t-ship an average price of $60 the acre.

In 1682 Middletown contained about 100 families; several thousand acres had been collected for the town, and many thousand for out-plantations. John Browne, Richard Hartshorne, and Nicholas Davis, had well improved settlements here; and a court of sessions was holden twice or thrice a year, for Middletown, Piscataway and their jurisdictions.

Middletown, post-town of Middletown t-ship, Monmouth co., 13 miles N. E. from Freehold, 56 from Trenton, and 221 from W. C., situate in a rolling and fertile country, based on marl; contains an Episcopal, a Dutch Reformed, and a Baptist church, 2 stores, 2 taverns, and from 20 to 25 dwellings, among which, there are several very neat and commodious.

Middletown Point, port of delivery of Perth Amboy district, and post-town of Middletown t-ship, Monmouth co., upon Middletown creek, about 3 miles from the Raritan bay, 11 miles N. of Freehold, 47 N. E. from Trenton, and 213 from W. C.; lies on a bank elevated about 50 feet above the stream, fronting a marsh on the opposite side; contains a Presbyterian church, from 75 to 100 dwellings, many of which are very good buildings, 8 or 10 stores, 4 taverns, and a grist mill. This is the market of an extensive country, and large quantities of pork, rye, corn, cord wood, and garden truck, are thence sent to New York. The soil immediately around the town is sandy. There is a bank here, incorporated in 1830, with a capital of $50,000, of which $10,000 only were paid in, in 1833.

Middleville, Orange t-ship, Essex co., 5 miles S. W. of Newark, contains a tavern, a store, a grist mill, saw mill, and Universalist church.

Mill Brook, a small stream of Montague t-ship, Sussex co., flowing N. E., a course of about 6 miles, to the Nevisink river, in the state of New York, about 1 mile north of the boundary, giving motion to several grist, and other mills.

Mill Creek, a tributary of Cohansey creek, flowing southward into it, and forming the S. W. boundary of Greenwich t-ship, Salem co.; length between 3 and 4 miles.

Mill Creek, another tributary of Cohansey creek, rising in Fairfield t-ship, Cumberland co., and flowing S. W. about 4 miles, by the village of Fairton, to its recipient, giving motion to two mills.

Millford, E. Windsor t-ship, Middlesex co., on Rocky Brook, 17 miles S. W. from New Brunswick, on Rocky Brook; contains a Presbyterian church, a grist mill, and some 10 or 12 farm houses, and dwellings of mechanics. Soil light, and not productive.

Millford, village of Alexandria t-ship, Hunterdon co., on the river Delaware, at the confluence of a small creek with that stream, 13 miles N. W. from Flemington, and 40 from Trenton; contains a tavern, store, grist mill, 2 saw mills, and from 15 to 20 dwellings, a Presbyterian church, and a church of Unitarians, which styles itself *Christian*, and which admits females to participate in the ministry. This is a place of considerable business, particularly in the lumber trade.

Millhill, village of Nottingham t-ship, Burlington co., on the S. side of the Assunpink creek; contains 2 cotton manufactories, several taverns and stores, a market house, and about 80 dwellings. (See *Trenton*, of which it is a suburb.)

Millington, post-office, Somerset co., 219 miles N. E. from W. C., and 48 from Trenton.

Millstone River, rises near Paint Island spring, Upper Freehold t-ship, Monmouth co., and flows thence by a N. course of about 5 miles, to the line between Monmouth and Middlesex cos.; thence N. W. 13 or 14 miles, through Middlesex to the mouth of Stony Brook, thence N. E. by Kingston, into Somerset co., 16 miles to the river Raritan. It is a strong and rapid stream, receiving the waters of an extensive country, including that drained by Stony Brook; and runs, in many places, through very narrow valleys, and consequently is subject to sudden and great overflows. The Delaware and Raritan canal enters the valley of this river, with Stony Brook, and follows it to the Raritan. The whole length of the Millstone may be about 35 miles, by comparative courses.

Millstone, post-town of Hillsborough t-ship, Somerset co., on the left bank of the Millstone river, 194 miles N. E. of W. C., 28 from Trenton, 5 S. of Somerville; contains 2 taverns, 3 stores, a Dutch Reformed church, and between 30 and 40 dwellings, in a level, fertile, red shale country. Some of the dwellings are very neat and commodious.

Milltown, a small village in the southern part of Kingwood t-ship, Hunterdon co., on the Laokatong creek, 10 miles S. W. from Flemington; contains a mill, store, and 8 or 10 dwellings.

Millville t-ship Cumberland co., bounded N. by Gloucester and Salem cos., and by Deptford t-ship, S. E. by Maurice River t-ship, S. by Downe, and W. by Fairfield t-ships. Cen-

trally distant E. from Bridgeton, 12 miles; length N. and S. 16 miles; breadth E. and W. 15; area, 73,000 acres; surface, level; soil sandy, and generally not very productive. It is drained by Maurice river and its tributaries, of which Manantico creek is here the chief. Millville and Buckshutem, are towns of the t-ship; the first a post-town. Population in 1830, 1561. In 1832, there were in the t-ship 349 taxables, 136 householders, whose ratables did not exceed $30; 7 stores, 6 run of stones for grinding grain, 1 carding machine, 1 blast furnace, 8 saw mills, 2 glass manufactories; and it paid road tax, $800, and county and state tax, $553 58.

Millville, p-t. of Millville t-ship, Cumberland co., on the left bank of Maurice river, 20 miles from its mouth, 11 miles S. E. of Bridgeton, 79 from Trenton, and 176 N. E. from W. C.; contains about 60 dwellings, 2 taverns, 4 or 5 stores, a furnace belonging to Mr. D. C. Wood, and extensive glass works belonging to Messrs. Burgin and Pearsall; consisting of 2 factories, 1 containing an 8, and the other a 7 pot furnace, employed chiefly in the manufacture of bottles, demijohns, carboys, and the various kinds of vials used by druggists and apothecaries, giving employment to from 75 to 100 workmen. The town lies near the head of sloop navigation.

Milton, post-town of Morris co., 242 miles N. E. from W. C., and 79 from Trenton, and 15 N. of Somerville.

Minisink Island, formed by the Delaware river, and making the extreme S. W. part of Montague t-ship, Sussex co.

Mine Mountain, composed of trap rock, Bernard t-ship, Somerset co., extends from the north branch of the Raritan, 6 miles to the Passaic river, and is intersected by tributaries of the respective rivers; the chief of which is

Mine Brook, rising near Logtown, on the summit of the mountain, and running 6 miles S. W. to the north branch of the Raritan. It is a mill stream of great fall, and studded with mills.

Miry Run, tributary of the Assunpink creek, rises in East Windsor t-ship, Middlesex co., and flows N. W. through Nottingham t-ship, Burlington co., by a course of 8 miles, giving motion to several mills.

Miry Run, small stream of Egg Harbour t-ship, Gloucester co., flowing westerly about 3 miles to the Great Egg Harbour river, having a mill at its mouth.

Monroe, p-t. Hardiston t-ship, Sussex co., at the cross-roads N. W. of Pimple Hill, 236 miles from W. C., 78 from Trenton, and 9 from Newton; contains a mill, store, and several dwellings. It is surrounded by soil of primitive limestone.

Monroe, village of Hanover t-ship, Morris co., near the Whippany river, 3 miles N. E. of Morristown; contains a store, 5 or 6 dwellings, and an extensive paper mill. It is surrounded by soil of loam and gravel, well cultivated.

Monmouth County; the bounds of this county were established by the Acts of 21st January, 1709-10, and 15th march, 1713-14; and it is now limited on the N. by Raritan bay; E. and S. E. by the Atlantic ocean; S. W. and W. by Burlington co.; and N. W. by Middlesex; greatest length 65, breadth 33 miles; area, 665,000 acres, or about 1030 square miles. Central lat. 40° 5′ N., long. from W. C. 2° 42′ E. The whole country belongs to the alluvial formation, and consists of clay mingled with sand, gravel, and in low places vegetable mould. In many parts there are large beds of marl, varying in quality from that composed almost altogether of shells, already highly indurated, to that of blue clay and sand, in which the shells are finely broken and sparsely strewed. In the N. part of the county, marl is generally used as manure, and with the greatest advantage. It has restored many tracts of worn-out land to fertility, and preserved much more from exhaustion and abandonment.

The surface of the county, except in Middletown t-ship, is generally level, and a large portion of it covered with pine forest; N. of Manasquan inlet the sea-coast is high, bold, and clean; S. of that channel commences a series of sand beaches, formed into islands, by Barnegat and Little Egg Harbour inlets, having a width, varying from half a mile to a mile, and which extend in this county to Little Egg Harbour inlet, a distance, southwardly of full 40 miles. Behind the beach, a bayou, continues, nominally divided into two, under the names of Little Egg Harbour, and Barnegat bays, which also varies much in width, being from ½ a mile to 4 miles broad; with a broad border of salt marsh, on the west.

The county is well watered, by many small streams, most of which flow E., to the ocean. The principal of these are Manasquan, Metetecunk, Kettle, Cedar, Oyster, Manahocking, and Westecunk creeks, Nevisink, Shrewsbury, Toms', and Forked rivers. From the N. the Millstone and South rivers flow to the Raritan, and the W. sends forth the Assunpink, the Crosswick's, and the Rancocus, tributaries of the Delaware.

The post-towns of the county are, Allentown, Barnegat, Cedar Creek, Colts' Neck, Eatontown, Englishtown, Freehold, the seat of justice, Holmdel, Howel Furnace, Manohocking, Manasquan, Middletown, Middletown Point, New Egypt, Shrewsbury, Squankum, and Toms' River. There are several other less considerable villages.

The business of the county is chiefly agricultural, but many persons are employed in cutting and sawing timber, and in preparing and carying cord wood to market, large quantities of which are sent from Toms' river, and large quantities of the finest pork are annually raised for exportation. Iron is also made in the central parts of the county, at Phœnix, Dover, and other furnaces. The population, originally composed of a few Dutch, and some New England men, who removed from Long Island, prior to, and about, the year 1664, amounted in 1830, to 29,233: of whom there were, white free males, 13,900; free white females, 13,304; male slaves 97; female slaves, 130; free coloured males, 1794; free coloured females, 978. There were also, 19 deaf and dumb, and 14 blind, of the whites; 1 deaf and dumb, and 1 blind, of the coloured population.

By returns of the assessors of 1832, there were in the county, about 6000 taxables, 1385 householders, whose ratables did not exceed $30; 603 single men, 103 stores, 52 saw mills, 67 run of stones for grinding grain, 6 fulling mills, 17 carding machines, 5 furnaces, 238 tan vats, 46 distilleries for cider, 4942 horses and mules, and 12,068 neat cattle, over the age of 3 years; and it paid county and state taxes, $15,492 80.

STATISTICAL TABLE OF MONMOUTH COUNTY.

Townships, &c.	Length.	Breadth.	Area.	Surface.	Population.		
					1810.	1820.	1830.
Dover,	24	22	200,000	level.	1882	1916	2898
Upper Freehold,	16	10	90,000	do.	3843	4541	4826
Lower Freehold,	23	11	104,000	do.	4784	5146	5481
Howell,	13	11	70,000	do.	2780	3354	4141
Middletown,	16	10	50,000	part hilly.	3849	4369	5128
Shrewsbury,	13	13	64,000	do.	3773	4284	4700
Stafford,	18	12	87,000	do.	1239	1428	2059
			665,000		22,150	25,038	29,233

Montague, N. W. t-ship of Sussex co., bounded on the N. E. by the state of New York, S. E. by the Blue mountains, S. W. by Sandistone t-ship, and on the N. W. by the river Delaware. Centrally distant from Newton, 16 miles; greatest length 8½, breadth 7½ miles; area, 21,620 acres; surface on the S. E. mountainous, on the N. W. line, river alluvion. Population in 1830, 990. There were in the t-ship in 1832, 85 householders, whose ratables did not exceed $30; 6 store keepers, 3 pair of mill stones, 3 saw mills, 208 horses and mules above 3 years old, 843 neat cattle, above that age; 11 tan vats, 1 distillery. The t-ship paid a school tax of $150; state and county tax, $364 89; poor tax, 100; and road tax, $500. It is drained N. E. by Mill brook, W. by Chamber's Mill brook, and S. W. by Big and Little Flat Kills. There is a post-office here, bearing the name of the t-ship;

distant 245 miles from W. C., 87 from Trenton, and 17 from Newton. Two turnpike roads run through the t-ship, and unite at the Delaware, opposite Milford bridge; this bridge, completed in 1826, cost $20,000. Between the Blue mountain and Delaware river, the space is six miles, through which runs a vein of transition limestone, bordered by an extensive river flat. The soil is fertile and well cultivated, producing much wheat. The t-ship was originally settled by the Dutch, some years prior to 1680.

Montgomery t-ship, Somerset co., bounded N. by Hillsborough, E. and S. E. by Millstone river, which separates it from Franklin t-ship, W. by Lawrence and Hopewell t-ships, Hunterdon co. Centrally distant S. W. from Somerville 12 miles; greatest length N. and S. 8, breadth E. and W. 8 miles; area, 36,500 acres; surface, hilly; soil, clay, sandy loam, and red shale. Beden's Brook and its tributaries, Rock, Pike, and No-pipe Brooks flow eastwardly through the t-ship to the Millstone river, and Stony Brook crosses the S. W. angle. Rock mountain or the Nashanic, forms the N. W. angle, and Rocky hill spreads itself over the south. Princeton, the northern side of the main street, Rocky Hill, Stoutsville, Harlingen, and Plainville, are towns of the t-ship. Population in 1830, 2834. In 1832 the t-ship contained about 600 taxables, 170 householders, whose ratables did not exceed $30; and 66 single men, 15 stores, 5 saw mills, 5 grist mills, 1 fulling mill, 54 tan vats, 5 distilleries, 743 horses and mules, 1295 neat cattle, 3 years old and upwards; and paid state tax, $352 72; county tax, $900 94.

Montville, village of Pequannock t-ship, Morris co., lying in a deep valley, through which passes the Morris canal, by two inclined planes; the town lies between 10 and 11 miles N. E. from Morristown, and contains a grist mill, saw mill, 2 stores, 1 tavern, and from 10 to 15 dwellings, and a Dutch Reformed church.

Moorestown, p-t., Chester t-ship, Burlington co., on the great road from Camden to Monmouth, 10 miles from the former, and 8 S. W. of Mount Holly, 30 miles from Trenton, and 147 from W. C. This is a very pleasant town, situated on a fertile plain of sandy loam, extremely well cultivated, near the north branch of Pensauken creek; contains a large Quaker meeting house, a Methodist church, a school, 3 taverns, 4 or 5 stores, and between 50 and 60 dwellings, most of which are neat and commodious, some large and elegant. The town has communication by stages, daily, with Camden and Mount Holly.

Morris County, was taken from Hunterdon, by act of Assembly of 15th March, 1738-9, directing that the portion of "said county lying to the northward and eastward of a well known place, being a fall of water, in part of the north branch of the Raritan, called in the Indian language Allamatonck, to the north-eastward of the north-east end of the lands called the New Jersey Society Lands, along the line thereof, crossing the south branch of the said river, and extending westerly to a certain tree marked with the letters L M, standing on the north side of a brook emptying itself into the said south branch, by an old Indian path to the northward of a line to be run north-west from the said tree to a branch of Delaware river called Musconetcong, and so down the said branch to Delaware river." It was named from Lewis Morris, then Governor of the province. These ample limits were contracted by the erection of Sussex county, 8th June, 1753, from which Warren was subsequently taken. Morris county is now bounded on the N. W. by Sussex, N. E. by Bergen, E. and S. E. by Essex, S. by Somerset, S. W. by Hunterdon, and W. by Warren. Greatest length N. E. and S. W. about 30 miles; breadth 27 miles; area, 292,900 acres; central latitude 40° 53' N.; longitude 2° 28'' E. from W. C.

The county is divided between the transition and primitive formations, two-thirds of it on the south being of the latter, but even in it, the primitive appears in the hills as in the Trowbridge mountain, and the ridge on the north-west of Morristown. The transition also appears in the range most generally primitive, as in the grau-wacke of the Copperas mountain, and the grey limestone at its southern base; a bed of which, probably, underlays the country from Potter's Falls on the S. W., to Charlottesburg on the N. E., upon Pequannock creek. Trap rocks are scattered over the county in various places, as in the Pompton Hills, Long Hill, and elsewhere.

The northern portion of the county is mountainous and divided into several ridges, whose continuity is broken as they extend south and east. Schooley's, or the Hamburg mountain, which is a continuation of the Musconetcong, continues in an unbroken mass across the county, varying from three to six miles in width. On the north-east, longitudinal divisions are formed by the branches of Rockaway river, in the Green Pond and Copperas mountains; whilst Pequannock t-ship is covered with short ridges and rounded knolls. The Trowbridge mountain is a considerable eminence near the centre of the county, varying in breadth from one to three miles, and having a length of fifteen miles. South and east of this ridge the county is level, or at most, undulating with a soil in which red shale predominates; it may be deemed the valley of the Passaic. On the south-east border of the county, however, rises another hill, around whose western extremity the Passaic turns, to follow its base north-eastwardly.

The county is rich in iron ore, and we believe that the great bed of red oxide of zinc, found in the Hamburg mountain near Sparta, in the adjacent county, extends into this. Iron ore is indeed here very abundant. and is chiefly of the magnetic character. The great bed first worked in Franconia, near the White Hills in New Hampshire, extends in the direction of the stratification, into this county, and which is said by Mr. M'Clure, to lose itself near Blackwater; but which most probably extends indefinitely S. W.; since iron of the same character is abundant near the spring at Schooley's mountain. The mine of the Hon. Mr. Dickerson, on the head waters of the Black river, is one of the best and most extensively wrought of the district. (See Randolph t-ship.)

The county is abundantly watered; a line drawn almost due south and north from the village of Mendham, to Drakesville, determines the course of the streams east and west. Thus the Rockaway with its tributaries, the Parcippany and Whippany rivers, seek the first; whilst the tributaries of the north and south branches of the Raritan river, have a westerly inclination. The Passaic river has its source in a swamp near the village of Mendham, and forms a natural boundary between this and the county of Somerset on the south, and the county of Essex on the S. E., receiving the Rockaway west of the village of Franklin, and the Pequannock, or Pompton river, north of the village of Fairfield. The last stream forms the N. E. boundary of the county, separating it from Bergen.

The chief villages and post-towns of the county are Berkshire Valley, Bottle Hill, Chatham, Chester, Denville, Dover, Flanders, Hanover, Hanover Neck, Littleton, Mendham, Milton, Montville, Morristown, the seat of justice, Mount Freedom, Newfoundland, New Vernon, Parsippany, Pompton, Powerville, Rockaway, Schooley's Mountain, Stockholm, Suckasunny, Washington, &c.

The provisions for moral improvement in the county, consist in churches of the Presbyterians, the Dutch Reformed, the Methodists, and the Episcopalians; a county Bible Society, a county Sunday school union, and several Sunday schools and temperance societies in various parts of the county; several academies in the larger villages, where the rudiments of the classics and mathematics are taught, and common English schools in almost every vicinity.

By the census of 1830, the population consisted of 23,666 souls, of whom 10,719 were white males; 1108 white females; 77 male slaves; 88 female slaves; 438 free coloured males; 364 coloured free females: and of whom there were 20 whites, and 4 blacks, deaf and dumb; 11 whites, and 1 black, blind; and 497 aliens.

In 1832, the county contained 4836 taxables, 1083 householders, whose ratables did not exceed $30 in value; 528 single men, 83 stores, 71 saw mills, 56 grist mills, 215 tan vats, 53 distilleries, 5 paper mills, 5 four horse stages, 43 forges and 2 furnaces, 9 rolling and slitting mills,

12 fulling mills, 11 carding machines, 1 plaster mill and 6 cotton mills, 4056 horses and mules, and 11,821 neat cattle, above 3 years old; and it paid state tax, $3171 23; county tax, $7100; poor tax, $10,900.

The courts of common pleas, orphans' court, and quarter sessions, are holden at Morristown, on the following Tuesdays; 3d December, 3d March, 1st July, and 4th September; and the circuit courts, on the 3d Tuesdays in March, and 4th of September.

This county abounds with copper, iron, zinc, plumbago, copperas, manganese, ochres of various colours, excellent brick clay, freestone, limestone, precious marbles, oil stone, &c. &c. With such metallic resources, the pioneers in the settlement of this portion of New Jersey, were rather manufacturers than agriculturists; and the narrow valleys of the mountain region, which contain many and excellent mill seats, were only partially tilled for the subsistence of wood cutters and bloomers. The forge was uniformly the precursor of the farm. The iron master occupied large tracts of land, which, when stripped of timber, were subdivided among agricultural successors, operating on the smallest scale. As the country was cleared, the makers of iron gradually retired to the remote, rough, and almost inaccessible regions, where the cost of transportation of the ores, and of the metal to market, rendered their operations very unprofitable. Relief in this respect will be obtained from the completion of the Morris canal, which has been created in a great measure with that view.

A region abounding so much in metallic ores, necessarily produces mineral springs; but that of Schooley's mountain, is the only one which has yet attained celebrity. A few years since, the county was famed for its apple orchards, its cider, and apple whiskey; of the last, large quantities were annually made for market. The annual average product of the Morris orchards was estimated at 800,000 bushels. But a succession of bad crops, for some years, has discouraged the cultivation. Few new orchards are planted, and the old ones are frequently neglected. Attempts have been made to cultivate the foreign grape upon the hill sides, but without success, the frosts proving too severe. It is possible that some indigenous qualities might be planted with profit.

STATISTICAL TABLE OF MORRIS COUNTY.

Townships.	Length.	Breadth.	Area.	Surface.	Population.		
					1810.	1820.	1830.
Chatham,	9	5	13,400	various.	2019	1832	1865
Chester,	9	6½	18,000	rolling.	1175	1212	1338
Jefferson,	14	3	25,000	mountainous.	1281	1231	1551
Hanover,	12	9½	35,000	various.	3843	3503	3718
Mendham,	6	4½	14,000	do.	1277	1326	1314
Morris,	13	6	33,000	hilly.	3753	3524	3536
Pequannock,	16	11	74,000	mountainous.	3853	3820	4451
Roxbury,	12	10	35,000	do.	1563	1792	2262
Randolph,	7	5	18,000	do.	1271	1252	1443
Washington,	8	7½	27,500	do.	1793	1876	2188
			292,900		21,828	21,368	23,666

2 A

Morris t-ship, Morris co., bounded N. and N. E. by Hanover t-ship; E. by Chatham; S. E. by New Providence t-ship, of Bergen co.; S. and S. W. by Somerset co.; and W. by Mendham and Randolph t-ships, Morris co. Greatest length N. and S. 13 miles; breadth E. and W. 6 miles; surface, on the north, centre, and south, hilly; elsewhere, generally rolling, with occasional plains; soil, clay and sandy loam; drained on the W. and S. by the Passaic river (and its tributaries) which courses its boundary; and on the N. E. by the Whippany river. The Elizabethtown and Morris, Newark and Morris, Morris and Easton, Morris and Milford turnpike roads cross the t-ship. Morristown, Logansville, New Vernon, Morris's Plains, are villages of the t-ship. Morristown is the seat of justice for the county. Population in 1830, 3536. In 1832 there were in the t-ship 780 taxables, 21 stores, 6 saw mills, 4 grist mills, 11 distilleries, 1 paper mill, 1 fulling mill, 1 carding machine, and 546 horses, and 1674 neat cattle, above the age of 3 years. The t-ship paid state tax, 558 85; county tax, 1251 19; poor tax, $600; and road tax, $2000.

Morristown, Morris t-ship, post-town and seat of justice of Morris co., on the Whippany river, by post-route 221 miles N. E. of W. C., 71 from Trenton, 17 from Newark and Elizabethtown, and 26 from New York; pleasantly seated on a high plain, built upon several streets, with a large area or public ground in the centre of the town; on which, front the Presbyterian church, many of the best houses, and most of the places of business. The town contains 1 Presbyterian, 1 Episcopalian, 1 Baptist, and 1 Methodist church; an academy in which the classics and mathematics are taught; a very large and handsome court-house, newly built of brick, with the prison in the basement story; a grist mill, saw mill, and 2 paper mills; a bank with a capital of $50,000, which may be extended to $100,000, incorporated by

act of 28th January, 1812, and continued by act 19th February, 1820; 5 taverns, 18 stores, 4 practising attorneys, and 3 physicians, 2 printing offices, from each of which a weekly newspaper is issued, viz. The Jerseyman and The Palladium of Liberty; a county bible society, Sunday school union, and temperance societies. This is a beautiful town. The houses are generally well built, neatly painted, surrounded with garden plots, and impress upon the visiter the conviction, that comfort at least, reigns here. The town is supplied by water from a fine spring a mile and a half distant, and distributed by subterraneous pipes. A stage runs to Elizabethtown daily; one every other day to Easton and Jersey City, and one to Oswego in New York, three times a week. It was a noted station of the American army during the revolutionary war, and the ruins of a small fort, overgrown by stately trees, still crown the hill which commands the town.

Morris Plains, hamlet and level land, lying S. E. of Trowbridge mountain, with a tolerable soil of sandy loam, watered by a branch of Whippany river. The hamlet is on the line between Morris and Hanover t-ships, 2 miles north of Morristown, and contains a half dozen dwellings.

Moses' Pond, small sheet of water on the Pochuck mountain, Vernon t-ship, Sussex co., which sends forth westerly, an inconsiderable tributary to the Wallkill river.

Mount Bethel, hamlet, on Stony Hill, Warren t-ship, Somerset co., 7 miles N. E. of Somerville; contains a Baptist church, tavern, store, and 4 or 5 dwellings.

Mount Carmel, a mountain hamlet of Amwell t-ship, Hunterdon co., 3 miles N. W. from Flemington; contains a tavern and some 4 or 5 dwellings, and a store. The soil around it is clay, cold, and at present not very productive, but it is improvable by the use of lime.

Mount Clinton, a village laid out on the Palisade rocks on the North river, in Hackensack t-ship, Bergen co., 5 miles N. E. of Hackensack-town.

Mount's Creek, a small tributary of the Cohansey river, near the S. W. border of Hopewell t-ship, Salem county.

Mount Ephraim, village, of Gloucester t-ship, Gloucester co., 5 miles S. E. from Camden, and the same distance N. E. of Woodbury; contains a store, tavern, and some 20 or 30 dwellings. The hill from which it has its name is, for this country, elevated, and affords an extensive view of the vicinity, even to the Delaware.

Mount Freedom, p-t., Morris co., 227 miles N. E. from W. C., and 61 from Trenton; contains a Presbyterian church, and some 10 or 12 dwellings.

Mount Holly, p-t., Northampton t-ship, and seat of justice of Burlington co., on the road from Camden to Freehold, and at the head of tide and navigation, on the north branch of Rancocus creek, 20 miles N. E. from the city of Camden, 6 S. E. from Burlington, 21 from Trenton, 156 from W. C., and 18 from Philadelphia, has its present name from a mount of sand and sandstone near it, and some holly trees about its base. It was formerly called Bridgetown; and this name was recognised in a charter for a library company here, so early as 1765. At the period of the revolutionary war, the town contained 200 dwellings, and at present, 1833, has not more than 230; many of which are good brick buildings, erected on 7 streets. It contains a court-house of brick, about 40 by 60 ft., two stories high, with cupola and bell; a stone prison, 1 Episcopal, 1 Methodist, 1 Baptist churches, and 2 Quaker meeting houses; 1 boarding school for young ladies, 4 day schools, 5 taverns, 8 stores, 1 grist mill, 1 saw mill, 1 fulling mill, woollen factory, plaster mill, and a paper mill, of the latest and most improved construction, where paper of fine quality is made by machinery, and from 40 to 50 hands are employed.—10,000 reams of paper may be manufactured in this mill yearly. The country around is flat; soil, sandy loam, generally of good quality, well cultivated, and worth from 40 to 120 dollars the acre, in extensive farms; corn, rye, and oats, are the chief products. A bank was established here in 1816, with authority to possess capital to the amount of $200,000; of which $100,000 only have been paid in. There run from the village, 2 stages twice a day to Burlington, 1 to Camden, 1 to Trenton, 1 to Pemberton, 1 to Vincenttown, 1 to New Egypt; and 2 to Manahocking, triweekly. There are 2 newspapers printed here, weekly; viz. the Herald, and New Jersey Mail.

Mount Misery, hamlet of Northampton t-ship, Burlington co., 15 miles S. E. from Mount Holly, in the pine forest; contains a tavern, saw mill, and 4 or 5 dwellings.

Mount Pleasant, p-t., Alexandria t-ship, Hunterdon co., 9 miles N. W. from Flemington, 43 from Trenton, and 196 from W. C., on the Hakehokake creek; contains a church, grist mill, store, and some half dozen dwellings.

Mount Pleasant, small village and forge, Pequannock t-ship, Morris co., on the t-ship road leading from Morristown, N. W. 10 miles; there are here a grist mill, and some half dozen houses, and very valuable iron mines, extensively wrought.

Mount Pleasant, village of Middletown t-ship, Monmouth co., on Middletown creek, 10 miles N. of Freehold; contains from 12 to 15 dwellings, a grist mill, a tavern and store. The ground around it is sandy, but high; elevated at least 50 feet above the waters.

Muddy Creek, a small marsh stream of Lower Alloways Creek t-ship, Salem co., which has a course of a mile or two; and empties into the Delaware, between Stow and Deep creeks.

Muddy Run, a branch of the Morris river, running near to, and forming in part, the S. W. boundary of

Pittsgrove t-ship, and the line between Salem and Cumberland cos.

Mud Pond, a small basin in the Wallkill mountains, Vernon t-ship, Sussex co., which sends forth a tributary to the Wallkill river.

Mullica Hill, p-t. and village of Gloucester co., on the line separating Greenwich from Woolwich t-ships, and on Raccoon creek, 7 miles S. E. from Woodbury, and 5 E. from Swedesboro'; 47 S. from Trenton, and 153 N. E. from W. C.; contains a Friends' meeting house, an Episcopal church, 2 taverns, 2 stores, and between 50 and 60 dwellings. The country around the village is much improved by the use of marl which abounds here, and in some places is found in an indurated state, assuming the character of limestone.

Musconetcong Creek, or *River,* issues from the Hopatcong pond, or lake, in Jefferson t-ship, Morris co.; and flows by a course S. W. and nearly straight, through a longitudinal valley of the South mountains, for nearly forty miles. This valley is bounded S. E. by the Musconetcong and Schooley's mountains, and on the N. W. by a southern continuation of the Hamburg hills; it is narrow and deep, and has throughout its whole length a limestone base. The stream has a large volume, and gives motion to a very great number of mills for various purposes.

Musketoe Cove, an arm of Barnegat bay, Dover t-ship, Monmouth co., which makes about two miles inward through the marsh, between Toms' bay and Kettle creek.

Nacote Creek, a tributary of Little Egg Harbour river, rises by two branches, Clark's mill, and Moss branch, which unite at Wrangleboro', in Galloway t-ship, Gloucester co.; the whole length of the stream is about 9 miles.

Nantuxet Creek, said to be more properly called *Antuxet,* Cumberland co., rises on the boundary line between Fairfield and Downe t-ships, and flows along the boundary, about 9 miles to Nantuxet cove, in the Delaware; it is navigable near four miles to Nantuxet, or Newport Landing.

Nantuxet Village. (See *Newport.*)

Nantuxet Cove, inlet to Nantuxet creek, from the Delaware bay.

Nashanic Creek, a tributary of the south branch of the Raritan river, rises by several branches at the foot of a range of hills on the N. W. line of Amwell t-ship, Hunterdon co., and flows by an easterly course to its recipient in Hillsborough t-ship, Somerset co., giving motion to several mills. It is a large stream, and with its several tributaries drains the easterly part of the wide valley between the Nashanic or Rock mountain, and Mount Carmel.

Nashanic Mountain, or *Rock Mountain,* part of the chain of trap hills which extends from below Lambertsville, on the Delaware, to the Raritan river, near Somerville: it is the largest and most prominent of the chain; is about 11 miles long and about 3 miles over at its widest part. Rock brook, a tributary of Beden's brook, almost passes through it.

Nashanic, small stream on the N. W. foot of the Nashanic mountain, 7 miles S. W. from Somerville; contains a Dutch Reformed church, a store and tavern, and 10 or 12 dwellings; soil, clay, sandy loam, and red shale.

Nesochcaque Creek, tributary of Atsion river, rises by several branches in Gloucester, Hereford, and Galloway t-ships, Gloucester co., and unites with the river, at Pleasant Mills, in the last named t-ship.

Nevisink Hills, on the Atlantic coast, and extending across the northern part of the county of Monmouth. Adjacent to the ocean these hills are between 300 and 400 feet high. They consist in the higher strata of sandy earth, coloured by oxide of iron, and imbedding reddish brown sand and pudding stone, cemented by iron, resting on banks of oyster shells and other marine relics, blended with clay and sea mud. A small portion of these hills only, is cultivated, being rough, broken and generally covered with wood. (See *Introductory Chapter*, fol. 1 and 2.)

Nevisink or *Carpenter's Point*, a small neck of land formed by the Delaware and Nevisink rivers, at the extreme northern point of the state.

Nevisink River, called above tide water Swimming river, rises by several branches in Freehold, Shrewsbury, and Middletown t-ships, Monmouth co. The main stream flows about 13 miles to the salt water estuary or arm of Sandy Hook bay; which is about 5 miles long, to the S. E. base of the Nevisink hills, varying in breadth from ¾ to 1½. Swimming river and its north and south branches are mill streams, on which are several mills. The Nevisink is separated from the Shrewsbury river, by a neck of land about 2 miles in breadth.

Newark, p-t., and seat of justice, Newark t-ship, Essex co., on the right bank of the Passaic river, between 4 and 5 miles by the course of the stream from Newark bay, 9 miles a little N. of W. from New York, 215 N. E. from W. C., and 49 from Trenton; stands upon a plain of fertile loam, resting on old red sandstone, bounded westward by rising ground which was probably the primitive bank of the river. Lat. 40° 44' N., long. 2° 44' E. from W. C. This is, perhaps, the most flourishing town of the state. In 1830 its population, t-ship included, amounted to 10,953, and in November, 1833, it is ascertained to be nearly 15,000; the increase having been greater during the last three years than in the ten preceding. There are 1712 dwellings, of which 1518 are wooden, and 194 stone and brick. 109 dwellings were built in 1832, and as many in 1833; many of them large and elegant. The town is remarkable for its manufactures, with which it supplies the market throughout the United States; and in which the great proportion of the inhabitants are engaged. The principal of these are saddlery and harness, carriages, shoes,

and hats. Sixteen extensive manufactories of saddlery and harness, employ 272 hands, and a capital of $217,300, yielding an annual product of $346,280, and paying wages $70,000 annually. These are independent of the coachmakers who make their own saddlery and harness. Ten carriage manufactories have 779 workmen, an aggregate capital of $202,500, and produce $593,000 annually. These establishments, generally, do all their work, including plating, lamp making, &c. Eighteen shoe manufactories engage 1075 hands, to whom they pay $175,000 yearly wages; have a capital of $300,000, whose annual product is estimated at $607,450: they cut up annually, $400,000 worth of leather. The amount of sales of boots and shoes, in 1832, was $900,000; the balance, over the product of the town, having been procured abroad, in order to supply the orders. This large amount is exclusive of the manufacture for home consumption, which, it is supposed, employs 225 additional hands. Nine hat manufactories employ 487 hands, a capital of $106,000; pay $142,000 in yearly wages, and make an annual return of $551,700. Thirteen tanneries employ 103 hands, a capital of $78,000, and return annually, $503,000. Beside these prominent manufactories, there are others of less, though great consideration.— Thus, there are two soap and candle manufactories, with a capital of $21,000, whose gross product is $165,000; 7 iron and brass founderies, employing 125 men; 2 extensive founderies of malleable iron, employing 60 men; 2 coach spring factories, employing 50 hands; besides 2 others connected with the carriage-making establishments; 5 tin, sheet iron, and stove factories; 1 hardware manufactory, employing 50 workmen; and 2 patent leather manufactories. There are, also, more than 350 tailors engaged in making garments for the home and southern markets; 140 carpenters, 26 sash and blind makers, 100 masons, 60 cabinetmakers, 51 coach lace weavers, 25 chairmakers, 42 trunkmakers, 9 looking glass manufacturers, 12 stone and marble cutters, 10 iron turners, 50 jewellers, and many other species of handicrafts, of which we are unable to give particular details, such as smitheries, wagon-making, manufactories of saddle trees, watches and clocks, segars, silver plating; planes, locks, guns, whips, brushes, coopering, ploughs, pumps, &c.; with the usual number of butchers, bakers, confectioners, painters, glaziers, book binders, &c. &c.

There are here also, 2 breweries, 2 grist mills, 1 extensive steam saw mill, 5 saw mills driven by horses, 1 distillery, 2 rope walks, 1 pottery, and 2 dyeing establishments.

Four printing offices employing 22 hands, from which 3 weekly and 1 daily newspapers are issued; 40 schools with 1669 scholars; and about 1500 scholars receive instruction in the Sunday schools; 4 Presbyterian churches with large congregations, beside a small Presbyterian congregation of coloured persons. The first Presbyterian church was founded in 1787, by the Rev. Alexander M'Whorter, D. D., who presided over the congregation from 1759 until his death in 1807, nearly a half a century; public worship was first offered in it 1st Jan. 1794: The second Presbyterian church in 1808; the third, in 1824; and the fourth, in 1831, 1832. One Episcopal church, with a large and increasing congregation, which was commenced about 1734, by Col. Isaiah Ogden and others, who left the Congregationalists in consequence of the rigour with which his conduct, in saving his grain in a wet harvest, by labouring on the Sabbath, was condemned. The present house for worship was erected in 1808, on a site occupied by a first and older building: Two Baptist churches; the congregation of the first was constituted in 1801, and the church built in 1804, was rebuilt in 1810; the second church was constructed in 1833: 1 Dutch Reformed congregation, recently organized, with a settled minister: 2 large Methodist Episcopal churches; the first congregation was organized in 1806, and the first chapel built in 1810; the second chapel was built in 1832: 1 Primitive Methodist church, and 1 African Episcopal Methodist chapel, built in 1810: a Roman Catholic church, built in 1824. Of these churches the first and second Presbyterian, the Episcopal and the Catholic, are of stone; the third Presbyterian, of brick; the others of wood: the fourth Presbyterian, second Baptist, and second Methodist Episcopal churches are remarkably large, and some of them have great architectural beauty.

Beside the churches, the only public building of the town, of much importance, is the court-house and prison, of brick, under the same roof—in which the keepers' apartments and cells of the prisoners are on the ground floor; the court room, jury rooms, and sheriff's office, on the second; and the apartment for insolvents on the third. The offices of the clerk and surrogate are also in the same building. An election in 1807 for determining the location of the court-house, is still remembered by the inhabitants, as the most exciting recorded in their annals. The contest was between Newark and Day's Hill. By a construction given to the state constitution, the women were then suffered to vote, and they seem to have been so delighted with this privilege of exercising their wills, that they were unwilling to circumscribe it within the legal limit; many ladies voting, we are told, 7 or 8 times, under various disguises.

Of literary institutions in addition to the schools, we may name an apprentices' library, a circulating library, and the mechanics' association for literary and scientific improvement, which possesses a valuable library and philosophical apparatus. It is to the credit of the town, that the New Jersey college was located here for several years subsequent to 1747, under the charge of its second president, the Rev. Aaron Burr, father of the ex-vice President of the United States; who was in 1736, called to the pastoral charge of the first Presbyterian church, and was highly distinguished for his learning, energy, and public spirit, which contributed much to the growth and prosperity of the town.

The commerce of Newark, already considerable, rapidly increases. It is a port of delivery, and efforts are used to make it a port of entry. It employs 65 vessels, averaging 100 tons, in the coasting trade; 8 or 9 of which are constantly engaged in transporting hither various building materials. The Morris canal, which runs through the town, gives it many advantages for internal trade, for which purpose 25 canal boats are supplied by the inhabitants. The facilities for communication with New York, render the town a suburb of that great city. A steam-boat plies twice a day between the two places, carrying an average of 75 passengers each trip, each way; two lines of stages communicate between them almost hourly, conveying at least 800 passengers a week; and this communication will be still more frequent and facile, when the New Jersey Rail-road, now rapidly progressing, shall have been completed. The Directors of the Rail-road Company have not only run the road through part of the town, but have opened a splendid avenue of 120 feet wide, by its side, and propose to cross the Passaic river, about the centre of the town, upon a wooden bridge on stone abutments, which will give an additional trait of beauty to the place.

There are three banks here, viz. "*The Newark Banking and Insurance Company,*" incorporated in 1804, with an authorized capital of $800,000, of which $350,000 have been paid in; "*The State Bank at Newark,*" incorporated in 1812, with an authorized capital of $400,000, of which $280,000 have been paid in; and "*The Mechanics Bank at New-*ark," incorporated in 1831, with an authorized capital of $250,000, of which $200,000 have been paid in. During the year 1833, the business of the town, manufacturing and commercial, has greatly increased, and consequently the demand for banking capital; to meet which, one of the banks has called in a further instalment, and another has availed itself of the privilege given by charter, to double its capital. The rise in the value of real estate, the sure indication of prosperity, has been astonishingly great—a remarkable instance of which is given us in November, 1833; where a property was sold at public auction for $10,000, which but five years, previously, was purchased by the late vendor for $60! A whaling and sealing company has been incorporated, (October, 1833) which is vigorously prosecuting its object.

The town is laid out upon broad streets, and has a great and salubrious ornament, in the greens or commons, which are shaded by noble trees, and bounded by the principal avenues. It is abundantly supplied with wholesome water, by a joint stock company, from a fine and steady spring, about a mile distant; and seven miles of iron pipes have already been laid for the accommodation of the inhabitants. The present style of building, copied from that of the great cities, is costly, elegant, and commodious. Granite basement stories, in the places of business, admit of convenient stores, whilst lofty edifices give accommodation to families. Houses designed for private residence are now generally of brick, neat, and frequently splendid.

We close this interesting account of this thriving town, for which we are indebted to a committee* of the Young Men's Society, &c., with a brief historical notice, much of which has been abstracted from the town records.

* Consisting of Messrs. A. Armstrong, C. H. Halsey, S. H. Pennington, D. A. Hays, and J. B. Congar.

Soon after the arrival of Governor Carteret, in 1665, he published in New England, and elsewhere, the "Concessions" of the proprietaries, and invited settlers to the new colony. The first fruit of this measure was the settlement of Elizabethtown. In the succeeding year, agents were despatched from Guilford, Brandford, and Milford, in Connecticut, to survey the country, and to ascertain the state of the Indians who inhabited it. Upon their favourable report, particularly, of that district "beyond the marshes lying to the north of Elizabethtown," they were empowered to contract for a township, to select a proper site for a town, and to make arrangements for an immediate settlement. Thirty families from the above named towns and New Haven, embarked in the same year, and after a passage, as long and tedious as a voyage in the present time across the Atlantic, arrived in the Passaic river. Their landing was opposed by the Hackensack tribe of Indians, who claimed the soil which the governor had granted to the emigrants, and insisted on a full compensation therefor, previous to its settlement. The governor not being able to remove this obstacle, the discouraged voyagers prepared to return; but were at length, by the solicitation of the governor and others, induced to hold a council with the Indians, from whom they eventually purchased a tract of country on the west side of the Passaic river, extending from *Woquakick* (or Bound) creek, on the south, to its fountain head; and thence westerly about seven miles to the ridge of the Great mountain, called by the Indians (*Wacchung*); thence by the said ridge north to the line of Acquackanonck t-ship; thence east by that line to the mouth of (*Yantokah*) Third river; thence down the Passaic river and bay to the place of beginning. These limits formed the original t-ship of Newark, comprehending the present t-ship of that name, and the t-ships of Springfield, Livingston, Orange, Bloomfield,

and Caldwell. The price of this purchase was £130 New England currency, 12 Indian blankets, and 12 Indian guns. The title thus derived from the aborigines, was subsequently set up against that of the proprietaries, and was the source of much litigation and forcible contention, which for many years disturbed the peace of East Jersey.

The settlers at first segregated themselves according to the towns whence they came; but the sense of mutual danger soon induced a change in this respect. On the 21st May, 1666, delegates from the several towns resolved to form one t-ship, to provide rules for its government, and "to be of one heart and hand, in endeavouring to carry on their spiritual concernments, as well as their civil and town affairs, according to God and godly government." And for the more speedy accomplishment of their desires, "a committee of eleven were appointed to order and settle the concernments of the people of the place." These rules had a full proportion of the puritanical spirit of the people who made them, and of that religious intolerance which was the distinguishing trait of the inhabitants of Massachusetts, whence they were originally derived; contrasting strongly with the liberality of the "Concessions" of Berkeley and Carteret, to which these emigrants were indebted for the very soil on which they had alighted. "No person could become a freeman or burgess of their town, or vote in its elections, but such as was a member of some one of the Congregational churches:—nor be chosen to the magistracy, nor to any other military or civil office. "But all others admitted to be planters, were allowed to inherit and to enjoy all other privileges, save those above excepted." With a singular disregard of the rights of the proprietaries of New Jersey, and apparently with a resolution of disclaiming all fealty towards them, and of depending on their Indian grants, they, also, resolved "to be ruled by such officers as the town should annually choose from among themselves, and to be governed by the same laws as they had, in the places from whence they came." At this period, (1667,) there were 65 efficient men in the settlement, beside women and children.

At the first distribution of land, each man took by lot six acres as a *homestead ;* and as the families from each of the several original towns, had established themselves at short distances from those of other towns, the allotments were made to them in their respective quarters of the new settlement. Seven individuals, selected for the purpose, assessed on each settler his portion of the general purchase money. The lands were eventually divided into three ranges ; each range into lots, and parcelled by lottery ; first setting apart certain portions, called tradesmen's lots ; one of which was to be given to the first of every trade, who should settle permanently in the place ; reserving also, the present *Upper Green* of the town for a market place, and the *Lower Green* for a military parade ; and that part of the town in and adjacent to Market street, where the tanneries now are, then a swamp, for a public watering place for cattle. This last portion having been sold by the town, is altogether in possession of individual owners.

In 1767, the Rev. Abraham Pierson, the first minister, commenced his official duties here. He is said to have been "episcopally ordained" at Newark, in South Britain, and to have named this town after that of his ordination ; by which name it was sometimes called abroad, but was known at others by that of Milford. In the next year, the first "meeting house," 26 feet wide, 34 long, and 13 between the joists, was erected ; the town voting £30, and directing that every individual should perform such labour as a committee of five might require, towards its completion.

Robert Treat, and Jasper Crane,

were chosen the first magistrates, in 1668 ; and representatives to the first assembly of New Jersey, convened at Elizabethtown, 26th May, of the same year ; by which the first state tax, £12 sterling, of which the proportion of Newark was 40*s.*, was laid. Mr. Treat was also chosen first recorder or town clerk ; and after a residence here of many years, returned to Connecticut, where he became governor, and died. The town also established a court of judicature, holding annually one session, on the last Wednesday of February, and another on the 2d Wednesday of September ; having cognizance of all causes within its limits. On the 24th May, 1669, the first selectmen, five in number, were chosen. The number was subsequently increased to seven, who continued to administer affairs until 1736, when the present township officers were created by law. And in this year Indian hostility appears to have displayed itself in petty robberies and depredations, the increase of which, in 1675, induced the townsmen to fortify their church as a place of refuge, in case of general attack, and to take proper measures of watch and ward.

On the 23d October, 1676, a warrant was granted by the Governor, for 200 acres of land and meadow, for parsonage ground, and also, for so much as was necessary for landing places, school house, town house, market place, &c.; and in 1696, a patent from the proprietaries to the town, covered all the lots, in various parts of the township, called "Parsonage Lands;" which have been since divided, with some difficulty and contention, among five churches ; viz. the three Presbyterian, and the Episcopal, at Newark, and the First Presbyterian church, at Orange.

In 1721, the first freestone was quarried for market ; and this article, celebrated for its excellent quality, has long been exported in great quantities.

At the commencement of the revolutionary war, the town was much divided upon the questions agitating the country; and on the Declaration of Independence, by the State, several families, among whom was Mr. Brown, pastor of the Episcopal church, who had ministered from its foundation, joined the royalists in New York. From its vicinage to that strong hold of the enemy, the town suffered greatly, by his visitations, made by regular troops and marauders. On the night of the 25th of January, 1780, a regiment of 500 men, commanded by Colonel Lumm, came from New York, *following the river on the ice,* and burned the academy, then standing on the upper green. This was a stone building, two stories high, with apartments for the teacher. On the same night another British party, unknown to the first, fired the Presbyterian church, at Elizabethtown, the light from which affrighted the incendiaries at Newark, and caused their hasty retreat. They carried away with them Joseph Heddens, Esq., an active whig, who had zealously opposed their previous depredations; dragging him from a sick bed, and compelling him to follow, with no other than his night clothing. The party returned by the route by which they came; and a soldier, more humane than his fellows, gave Mr. H. a blanket, a short time before they reached Paules Hook. At this place Mr. H. was confined in a sugar house, where he perished in a few days, in consequence of the sufferings from that dreadful night.

The prosperity of this enterprising and industrious town, is deservedly great; and being founded on the indispensable manufactures of the country, will necessarily progress with the general population, and with such increased momentum as the highly stimulated spirit of its inhabitants will not fail to give it.

Newark, t-ship, Essex co., bound on the N. by Bloomfield t-ship; N. E. by the Passaic river, which separates it from Bergen co.; E. by Newark bay; S. by Elizabeth and Union

t-ships; and W. by Orange t-ship. Greatest length, E. and W. 7 miles; breadth, N. and S. 6 miles; area, about 12,000 acres; surface level; soil marsh and red shale; a large proportion of this t-ship lying N. of Boundbrook, and E. of the turnpike road from Elizabethtown to Newark, is salt marsh; the remainder consists of well improved land. Population, in 1830, including the town of Newark, 10,953. In 1832, there were 2500 taxables, 1114 householders, whose ratables did not exceed $30; 527 single men, 95 merchants, 4 grist mills, 3 saw mills, 3 furnaces, 1 fulling-mill, 26 tan vats, 1 wool factory, and 1 distillery. The t-ship paid in state tax, $933 72; county, $2443 92; poor tax, $2500; road tax, $500.

Newark Bay, a large sheet of water, of 7 miles in length, and 2 in breadth, between Bergen and Essex cos., and separated from the New York, by a strip of land one mile wide, but communicating therewith, by the Kill-van-Kuhl. The Passaic and Hackensack rivers debouch in this bay. Its easterly shore is bold and clean, but its westerly, has a broad margin of salt marsh.

New Barbadoes, t-ship, Bergen co., bounded N. by Harrington; E. and S. E. by Hackensack; S. W. by Lodi, and W. by Saddle river t-ships. Greatest length, N. and S. 7; breadth, E. and W. 4 miles; area, 11,500 acres; surface generally level, but towards the N. there is some undulating ground; soil, sandy loam, and red shale, extremely well cultivated, and productive in grass and vegetables for the New York market. The farms are generally small, and remarkable for their neatness. Most of the dwellings are built in the simple Dutch cottage style, with a single story, high gable ends, and projecting pent-houses. The t-ship is drained on the E. boundary, by the Hackensack river, on which are the post-towns of New Milford, and the hamlets of Old and New Bridge; and on the W. line, by Saddle river. The town of Hackensack, the county seat of justice, lies in the S. E. angle. Population in 1830, 1693. In 1832, there were in the t-ship, 440 taxables, 85 householders, whose ratables did not exceed $30; 40 single men, 15 merchants, 5 grist mills, 5 saw mills, 2 carding machines, 1 fulling mill, 1 wool factory, 28 tan vats, 315 horses, and 548 neat cattle, under 3 years old; and paid taxes, state, $188 90; county, $339 97; poor, $500; school, $100; road, $1000.

New Bargaintown, Howell t-ship, Monmouth co., upon Manasquan river, 9 miles S. E. of Freehold; contains a grist mill, and some half dozen dwellings, surrounded by a sandy soil, and pine forest.

Newbold's Island, in the Delaware river, about 2 miles below Bordentown, and ½ a mile from White Hill, in Mansfield t-ship, Burlington co.; has a fertile alluvial soil, and a fine fishery.

New Bridge, hamlet, of Hackensack t-ship, Bergen co., on the Hackensack river, 2 miles above Hackensack town; contains a grist and saw mill, a store, tavern, and 10 or 12 dwellings. Surrounding country, level; soil, fertile loam.

New Brunswick, p-t. and city, and seat of justice for Middlesex co., lying on the right bank of the river Raritan, 15 miles from the head of the bay at Amboy, 40 miles by water and 25 by land S. W. from New York, 26 N. E. from Trenton. The city is partly in North Brunswick t-ship, Middlesex co., and partly in Franklin t-ship, Somerset co., the post-road or Albany street forming the line between the t-ships and counties.

At the close of the seventeenth century, the place where the city now stands, was covered with woods, and called after the name of its proprietor, " *Prigmore's Swamp.*" The first inhabitant, of whom any account is preserved, was one Daniel Cooper, who resided where the post-road crossed the river, and kept the ferry which afterwards, in 1713, when the county line was drawn, was called Inian's Ferry. This ferry was granted by the proprietors, 2d Nov. 1697, for the lives of Inian and wife, and the survivor, at a rent of 5 shillings sterling per annum. One of the first houses is said to be still standing, at the foot of Town lane; and some other buildings, erected at an early period, may be distinguished by their antique structure, in Burnet and Albany streets. The first inhabitants of European origin, were from Long Island. About 1730 several Dutch families emigrated from Albany, bringing with them their building materials, in imitation of their ancestors, who imported their bricks, tiles, &c. from Holland. Some of them built their houses upon the present post-road, which thence acquired the name of Albany street; though originally it was called French street, in honour of Philip French, Esq. who held a large tract of land on the north side of it. About this time the name of New Brunswick was given to the place, which had, hitherto, been distinguished as " The River."

The city was incorporated in 1784, and is now divided into five wards. The old market, called Coenties' market, was of ancient date, and stood in Commerce Square; the present was built in 1811. The court-house was erected in 1793; the bridge, originally, in 1796, and was rebuilt by a joint stock company in 1811, at the cost of $86,687. It is a wooden structure about 1000 feet in length, divided into two carriage ways by a wood partition, and rests on eleven stone piers and abutments.

A portion of the town lying immediately on the river, is low, and the streets are narrow, crooked, and lined principally with small frame houses, extending for near half a mile from the bridge to the landings for steamboats. Albany street is a broad, well paved thoroughfare, ornamented with some excellent buildings, and the streets upon the upper shelving bank, are generally wide, and the houses neat and commodious; many of them expensively built, and surrounded by gardens. The streets generally, are paved with boulders. Those unpaved are, in the rainy season, scarcely passable, the red sandy loam of the soil, being easily wrought into deep paste. From the top of the hill or bank, especially from the site of Rutgers' college, there is a wide prospect of miles, terminating on the north by the Green Brook mountains, and on the east by the Raritan bay.

The tide in the river extends to Raritan Landing, about two miles above the town; but immediately above the bridge, at the town, the river is fordable. At this point the ice, when broken up in the spring, sometimes lodging, forms a dam, which raising the water many feet above its usual level, causes it to overflow the lower streets. The Delaware and Raritan canal has its outlet here, by a lock of 12 feet lift, into a basin 200 feet wide, made in the bed of the river, and extending a mile and a quarter in front of the town, where vessels of 200 tons burden may lie. From the canal a very important hydraulic power will be obtained, under a fall of 14 feet, with all the water of the Raritan river, and all the surplus water of the canal. Consequently, New Brunswick may, at no distant period, claim consideration among the manufacturing towns of the United States.

The city contains between 5 and 6000 inhabitants, about 750 dwellings, 120 large stores, among which are 12 extensive grain stores; 20 taverns, 12 practising attorneys, and 8 physicians; 1 Methodist church, built in 1811, and another belonging to blacks of the same denomination: A Dutch Reformed church, the present house being the third pertaining to that profession; the first was built on the corner of Schuremem and Burnet streets, before the year 1717; the second, on the site of the present, between the years 1750 and 1783, during the ministry of the Rev. Johannes Leydt; and the present, commenced in 1812, was completed in 1828, by the construction of a brick stuccoed steeple—a Presbyterian congregation occupying their second house for worship; their first was built before, or during the ministry of the Rev. Gilbert Tennent, who became their pastor in 1726, in Burnet street, below Lyell's Brook; and was wantonly destroyed by the British soldiers in 1776 or 1777; the present edifice was erected in 1784;—The Episcopal church, called Christ church, was built in 1743, the steeple in 1773; but the latter was burned to the stone basement in 1802, and rebuilt in the same year: the Baptist church was erected in 1810, and a small Catholic chapel in 1832. There are in the town a college called Rutgers' college, and grammar school connected with it; 2 academies; an extensive boarding and day school for young ladies; a Lancasterian school, incorporated and endowed with about $4000, and several common schools.

The town has an extensive trade. The enterprising inhabitants have opened a ready communication with Easton and the valley of the Delaware, by the Jersey turnpike road; and have made it the depot of the produce from a large tract of fertile country; its business will be greatly increased by the trade of the Delaware and Raritan canal. There are now 12 sloops employed in its commerce, and 300,000 bushels of Indian corn, and 50,000 bushels of rye are annually exported. Two lines of stages connected with steam-boats here and at Lamberton, on the Delaware, run daily from the town, and stages depart hence daily to various parts of the country; and communication is had four times, daily, by steam-boats, with New York. There are now two banks established here: the State Bank incorporated in 1812, with an authorized capital of $400,000 of which 88,000 have been called in; and the New Brunswick Bank, incorporated in 1807, with a capital of $200,000, 90,000 of which have been paid.

There is a vein of copper ore adjacent to the town, which was formerly very extensively wrought, but which has been for many years abandoned. For an account of this mine, see prefatory chapter, page 10.

New Durham, village on the turnpike-road leading from Hoboken to Hackensack, Bergen t-ship, Bergen co., 3 miles from the one and seven from the other; contains 2 taverns, a store, and some 10 or 12 dwellings.

New Durham, small village of Piscataway t-ship, Middlesex co., 5 miles east of north from New Brunswick, and on the turnpike road leading from Perth Amboy toward Bound Brook; contains a tavern, store, and some half dozen dwellings.

New Egypt, p-t. of Upper Freehold t-ship, Monmouth co., on the Crosswicks creek, 23 miles S. W. from Monmouth Court House, 170 N. E. from W. C., and 16 miles S. E. from Trenton ; contains about 20 dwellings, 2 taverns, 2 or 3 stores, valuable grist and saw mills, and a Methodist church within a mile of the town. The country around it is level; soil, of clay and sand. The name is derived from the excellent market the mills formerly afforded for corn.

New England, village of Fairfield t-ship, Cumberland co., near Cohansey creek, 5 miles S. of Bridgeton; contains some 12 or 15 dwellings, scattered along the road within the space of a mile; near it is a Methodist church.

New England Creek, a small stream of Lower t-ship, Cape May co., flowing into the Delaware bay.

New Freedom, small village of Gloucester t-ship, Gloucester co., on the road from Camden to Great Egg Harbour river, 18 miles S. E. from the former, and 14 from the latter; contains a Methodist meeting, a glass manufactory, a tavern and store, and some 12 or 15 dwellings. It is in the midst of the pines, on Inskeep's branch of Great Egg Harbour river.

Newfoundland, is the post-office of Longwood Valley, 17 miles N. W. from Morristown, 245 N. E. from W. C., and 79 from Trenton; there is a Presbyterian church here.

New Germantown, p-t. of Tewkesbury t-ship, Hunterdon co., on the turnpike-road leading from Lamington to Schooley's mountain, 14 miles N. E. from Flemington, 45 from Trenton, and 211 from W. C.; contains about 30 dwellings, 1 tavern, 3 stores, 1 Lutheran, 1 Methodist, and a Presbyterian, church and an academy. The town lies near the foot of a spur of the Musconetcong mountain, and is surrounded by a rich and highly cultivated limestone soil, in which there are masses of brescia or pudding limestone, which are perhaps equal in beauty, to that in the capitol at Washington.

New Hampton, p-t. of Lebanon t-ship, Hunterdon co., in the N. W. angle on the S. side of Musconetcong creek, and on the turnpike leading to Oxford Furnace, 18 miles N. W. from Flemington, 41 from Trenton, and 200 from W. C.; contains 1 grist mill, 1 saw mill, 2 stores, 3 taverns, and from 20 to 25 dwellings.

New Hamburg, post-office, Bergen co.

New Market, village of Amwell t-ship, Hunterdon co., 8 miles S. of Flemington; contains a tavern and store, 6 or 8 dwellings. Snydertown, a small hamlet, divided from it by a branch of Stony creek, contains a grist mill, and 2 or 3 dwellings; the surrounding country is hilly, stony, and poor.

New Market, formerly called *Quibbletown,* village of Piscataway t-ship, Middlesex co., 7 miles N. of New Brunswick, on the left bank of Cedar creek; contains a grist mill, a tavern, a store, and some 20 dwellings, in a fertile country of red shale.

New Milford, village of Hackensack t-ship, Bergen co., in the extreme N. W. angle of the t-ship, 4 miles N. of Hackensacktown, upon the Hackensack river; contains 2 mills, some half dozen dwellings, a store and tavern; surrounding country, level; soil, sandy loam, with red shale, well cultivated and fertile.

New Mills. (See *Pemberton.*)

Newport Creek, rises on the confines of Stow creek and Greenwich t-ships, Cumberland co., and flows westerly about 6 miles into Stow creek, forming the south boundary of the first, and north boundary of the second t-ship.

Newport, or *Nantuxet,* said to be more properly called " *Antuxet,*" p-t. of Dover t-ship, Cumberland co., on the Nantuxet creek, 5 miles above its mouth, 10 miles S. from Bridgeton, 187 N. E. from W. C., and 81 S. of Trenton ; contains from 20 to 30 houses, 1 tavern and store. This place is noted as having been the resort of refugees and tories during the revolution.

New Prospect, p-t. of Franklin t-ship, on the Hohokus creek, 241 miles N. E. from W. C., 74 from Trenton, and 11 N. W. from Hackensack ; very pleasantly situated upon high ground, on a fertile soil, and in the centre of a thriving manufacturing settlement ; what may appropriately be called the town, contains 2 taverns, 1 store, 2 paper mills, 2 grist mills, and chair manufactory, with lathes running by water, and several dwellings.

New Providence t-ship, Essex co., bounded N. E. by Springfield t-ship ; E. by Westfield ; S. by Warren t-ships, Somerset co. ; and W. and N. W. by the Passaic river ; which separates it from Morris co. Centrally distant S. W. from Newark, 13 miles ; greatest length 6, breadth 2½ miles ; area, 7680 acres ; surface hilly, on the west mountainous ; soil, clay loam, and red shale ; carbonate of lime is found on the east, near Green Brook, in which are metallic appearances supposed to be gold and silver, but are perhaps only the deceptive pyrites of iron or copper. Population in 1830, 910. In 1832, the t-ship contained 195 taxables, 45 householders, whose ratables did not exceed $30 ; 29 single men, 3 merchants, 3 grist mills, 5 saw mills, 1 paper mill, 13 tan vats, 147 horses, and 503 neat cattle, above 3 years old ;

and it paid state tax, $97 43 ; county, $254 92 ; poor, 300 ; road, $702.

New Providence, p-t. of preceding t-ship, 13 miles S. W. of Newark, 218 N. E. from W. C., and 52 from Trenton ; contains a Presbyterian and Methodist church, a tavern, store, and several dwellings.

Newton t-ship, Gloucester county, bounded N. by the city of Camden ; N. E. by Cooper's creek, which separates it from Waterford t-ship ; S. E. by Gloucester t-ship ; S. W. by Gloucestertown t-ship ; and W. by the river Delaware. Centrally distant N. E. from Woodbury 6 miles ; greatest length E. and W. 6, breadth N. and S. less than 4 miles ; area, 9000 acres ; surface, level ; soil, sandy ; timber, chiefly yellow pine ; the cultivated land employed principally in raising vegetables and fruit for market. Besides Cooper's creek on the N. W., it has Newton creek on the S. W., which being stopped out, makes some valuable meadows.— Haddonfield and Rowantown are villages of the t-ship, the first a post-town. Population in 1830, including, we presume, the city of Camden, 3298. In 1832 the t-ship contained 199 householders, whose ratables did not exceed $30 ; 6 stores, 2 fisheries, 3 grist mills, 1 saw mill, 1 fulling mill, 1 tan yard, 2 distilleries, 643 neat cattle, and 287 horses and mules above 3 years of age. The t-ship paid county tax, $532 44 ; poor tax, $266 47 ; road tax, $700.

Newton Creek, Newton t-ship, Gloucester co., rises on the south border of the t-ship, and flows N. W. about 5 miles, to the river Delaware. The influx of the tide to the creek is stopped by dam and sluice, by which some valuable meadows are gained along its banks.

Newton or *Pine Creek,* Galloway t-ship, Gloucester co., a tributary of Little Egg Harbour river.

Newton t-ship, Sussex co., bounded N. by Frankford t-ship ; E. by Hardiston t-ship ; S. E. by Byram t-ship ; S. W. by Green t-ship ; W. by Stillwater, and N. W. by Sandistone t-ships. Greatest length N. and S. 12, breadth E. and W. 10 miles; area, 65,920 acres; surface, hilly on the N. W. and S. E.; centrally, level. It is watered chiefly by the Paulinskill, which flows S. W. through it, towards the Delaware. (See *Paulinskill*.) The Newton and Bolton turnpike road runs centrally through the t-ship, and through the town of Newton; and the turnpike road by Sparta to Milford, through the N. E. angle, on which lies the post-town of Lafayette. Population of the t-ship in 1830, 3464; taxables in 1832, 530. There were in the t-ship in 1832, 140 householders, whose ratables did not exceed $30; 14 stores, 14 run of stones for grinding grain, 6 carding machines, 3 fulling mills, 650 horses and mules, and 1330 neat cattle, above the age of 3 years; 4 tan vats, 8 distilleries. The t-ship paid in 1832, state and county tax, $1156 05; poor tax, $400; road tax, $1200.

Newton, borough, county, and post-town, Newton t-ship, Sussex co., on the Newton and Bolton turnpike road, distant by the post-route 228 miles from W. C., and 75 from Trenton, 60 from New York, 40 from Easton, and 100 from Philadelphia. The town lies upon the slope of a gentle hill, of mingled slate and limestone, at whose foot a spring sends forth the first waters of the Paulinskill, the chief river of the county, whose volume is swelled by the tribute from Moore's Pond, covering 8 or 10 acres, distant about 1 mile S. E. from Newton. There are several streets, and a large common or public lot, fronts the court-house and prison, and on which the public offices are erected. It contains about 130 dwellings, and 900 inhabitants, 4 taverns, 8 extensive stores, 2 printing offices, at each of which a weekly journal is published, viz. the New Jersey Herald, by Mr. Fitch, and the Sussex Register, by Mr. Hall; a very large and commodious Presbyterian church, an Episcopal church, with a valuable glebe farm of 200 acres, near the town; and a Methodist church; 2 seminaries, in which the classics are taught—one of which is incorporated as an academy; 6 common schools, 3 Sunday schools, a public library, a lyceum for the promotion of the study of letters and science; a bank with a capital of $100,000, established in a handsome building, specially erected for it. The court-house is a low and ancient looking stone building, finished in 1765, having the prison in the basement story. There are in the town 4 practising attorneys, 4 physicians, and 2 resident clergymen. Some of the dwellings are very neat: the place has an air of business, and there is in fact a very considerable trade carried on with the surrounding country. In healthiness of situation, by the report of the inhabitants, it cannot be excelled.

New Village, p-t., of Greenwich t-ship, Warren co., on the turnpike road from Schooley's mountain to Philipsburg, and on the Morris canal, by the post-route 196 miles from W. C., 52 from Trenton, and 10 miles from Belvidere, the county town; contains 1 store, 1 tavern, and 10 or 12 dwellings. It is surrounded by a fertile limestone country.

New Vernon, p-t., of Morris t-ship, Morris co., 4 miles S. W. from Morristown, 217 N. E. from W. C., and 51 from Trenton; contains a store, an academy, and 4 dwellings.

Nischisakawick Creek, rises in Alexandria t-ship, Hunterdon co., and flows S. W. into the Delaware river, by a course of 7 or 8 miles, at the town of Alexandria.

Norman's Pond, small lake of Hardistone t-ship, Sussex co., on the Hamburg or Wallkill mountain, near the town of Sparta, a principal source of the Wallkill river. The stream from the pond gives motion to a forge immediately on issuing from the lake.

Northampton t-ship, Burlington co., bounded N. E. by Springfield and Hanover t-ships; E. by Monmouth co.; S. by Little Egg Harbour and Washington t-ships; W. by Evesham and Chester t-ships; and

N. W. by Willingboro' and Burlington t-ships. Greatest length N. W. and S. E. 33 miles; breadth E. and W. 18 miles; area, 135,000 acres; surface, generally level; soil, sand and sandy loam; the portion on the north-west of the t-ship well cultivated and productive; southern and easterly parts chiefly pine and oak forests. It is drained north-west by the north and south branches of the Rancocus creek, and southerly by tributaries of the Little Egg Harbour river. Mount Holly, the county town, New Mills, or Pemberton, Vincenttown, Eayrstown, Buddstown, Tabernacle, &c., are villages of the t-ship. Population in 1830, 5516. In 1832, the t-ship contained 1000 taxables, 654 householders, whose ratables did not exceed $30; 183 single men, 2371 cattle, and 1005 horses and mules; 13 stores, 7 saw mills, and 9 grist mills, 2 forges, 1 paper mill, 2 fulling mills, 1 cotton factory, 1 plaster mill, 50 tan vats, 3 carding machines, 6 distilleries for cider, 1 four horse stage, 2 two horse stages, 60 dearborns, 154 covered wagons, 4 chairs and curricles, 43 gigs and sulkies; and paid state tax, $675 87; county tax, $2359 50; t-ship tax, $3900.

North Branch, or *Bailes'*, p-t., of Bridgewater t-ship, Somerset co., on the turnpike road from Somerville to Easton, 4 miles from the former and 29 from the latter, 203 N. E. from W. C., and 29 from Trenton, upon the north branch of the Raritan river, in a level, fertile country; contains a large grist mill and fulling mill, a tavern, 2 stores, and about 20 dwellings. There is a Dutch Reformed church in the neighbourhood.

North Brunswick. (See *Brunswick, North*.)

Northfield, small village of Livingston t-ship, Essex co., 8 miles W. of Newark; contains a Baptist church, store, and 3 or 4 dwellings.

No Pipe Brook, tributary of Beden's brook, rises by two branches in the Nashanic mountain, on the confines of Montgomery and Hillsborough t-ships, Somerset co., which flow S. E. about 5 or 6 miles to their recipient.

Notch, The, a pass over the First, or Newark mountain, Acquackanonck t-ship, Essex co., through which the road leads from Acquackanoncktown to the Little Falls of the Passaic, distant 7 miles from the former.

Nottingham t-ship, Burlington co., bounded N. W. by the Assunpink creek, which divides it from Trenton and Lawrence t-ships, Hunterdon co.; N. E. by East and West Windsor t-ships, of Middlesex co.; S. by the Crosswicks creek, and S. W. by the river Delaware. Centrally distant N. E. from Mount Holly, 17 miles; greatest length N. and S. 10 miles; greatest breadth, 7 miles; area, 25,000 acres; surface generally level, varied only by the abrasion of the streams, which have worn their courses through deep and narrow valleys; soil, various; along the banks of the river and creeks, there is some stiff clay; sandy loam and sand characterize the remainder. Much of the t-ship, with due care, is susceptible of beneficial cultivation, and is productive in wheat, rye, corn, oats, and grass; the latter being much aided by the use of marl, which is abundant. The streams are the Assunpink, on the north, with its tributaries, Miry and Pond runs, and the Crosswicks, on the south, which receives a small stream from the t-ship. The villages are Sandtown, Nottingham Square, Mill Hill, Bloomsbury, Lamberton, and the Sand Hills. Population in 1830, 3900. In 1832, there were in the t-ship 960 taxables, 430 householders, whose ratables did not exceed $30; 165 single men, 11 merchants, 5 fisheries, 4 saw mills, 19 pair of grist mill stones, 1 paper mill, 1 fulling mill, 3 cotton manufactories, 75 tan vats, 2 carding machines, 5 distilleries for cider, 3 four horse stages, 3 two horse stages, 37 dearborns, 37 covered wagons, 50 chairs and curricles, and 2 gigs and sulkies; 1032 cattle, and 604 horses and mules over 3 years of age; the t-ship paid state tax, $486 87; county tax, $1702 05; township tax, $1900.

Nottingham Square, village of Nottingham t-ship, Burlington co., on the road from Trenton to Allentown, 6 miles E. of the former, on a sandy plain; contains 1 Presbyterian, and 1 Baptist church, a store, a tavern, and from 8 to 12 dwellings.

Obhonon, an arm of the south branch of Toms' river, Dover t-ship, Monmouth co.

Ogdensburg, village of Hardiston t-ship, Sussex co., about 75 miles N. E. from Trenton, and about 9 miles from Newton, in the valley of the Wallkill river; contains 21 dwellings, a small store, and saw mill, scattered along the road within the distance of a mile. There are some good lands in the narrow valley here, but the sides of the mountain are broken and stony.

Old Bridge, hamlet of Hackensack t-ship, Bergen co., on the Hackensack river, 4 miles N. of Hackensack town; contains a store, tavern, and 10 or 12 dwellings; country level; soil, fertile loam, well cultivated.

Old Bridge, hamlet of North Brunswick t-ship, Middlesex co., on South river, and on the turnpike-road from Bordentown to South Amboy, 6 miles S. E. from New Brunswick; contains a tavern, and some half dozen dwelling houses; surrounded by a sandy and light soil.

Old Man's Creek, rises in Gloucester co., Franklin t-ship, about 3 miles E. of a point on the Salem co. line; from which line it runs N. W., forming the boundary between Gloucester and Salem cos. for about 25 miles, following the meanderings of the creek to the river Delaware. It is a crooked stream flowing through a flat country, and has considerable tracts of banked meadow on its margin, as high as Pedricktown, to which place wood shallops ascend.

Ong's Hat, hamlet of Northampton t-ship, Burlington co., 10 miles S. E. of Mount Holly.

Orange t-ship, Essex co., bounded N. W. by Caldwell; N. E. by Bloomfield; E. and S. E. by Newark; S. by Union; S. W. by Springfield; and W. by Livingston. Centrally distant, N. W., from Newark, 4½ miles; greatest length, N. and S., 7; breadth, E. and W., 5 miles; surface, on the west, hilly; the First and Second mountains crossing it here; elsewhere rolling; soil, red shale, generally well cultivated; area, about 14,000 acres. Orange, the post town, South Orange, Camptown, Middleville and Jefferson village, are towns of the township. It is drained N. E. by Second river, and S. W. by branches of the Rahway. Population in 1830, 3887; in 1832, there were in the township, 625 taxables, 172 householders, whose ratables did not exceed $30 in value, 76 single men, 15 merchants, 3 grist mills, 2 saw mills, 40 tan vats, 362 horses and mules, and 1099 neat cattle, above the age of three years; and it paid state tax, $298 19; county, 780 20; poor, $600; road, $1050.

Orange, is a straggling village of the preceding township, and a post-town, extending about 3 miles along the turnpike road, from Newark to Dover; and distant about 3 miles N. W. from the former; 219 N. E. from W. C., and 53 from Trenton; contains 1 Episcopal, 2 Presbyterian, and 1 Methodist churches, 2 taverns, 10 stores, 2 saw mills and a bark mill, from 200 to 230 dwellings, many of them very neat and commodious. A large trade is carried on here in the manufacture of leather, shoes and hats. The country about it is level, red shale, and carefully cultivated. A chalybeate spring near the town is much resorted to.

Orange, South, a village of the same township, lies on the turnpike-road from Newark to Morristown, 5 miles W. of the first; it contains about 30 dwellings, a tavern and store, a paper mill and a Presbyterian church; the lands around it are also rich and well farmed.

2 C

Oranoken Creek, Downe t-ship, Cumberland co., rises in the township, and flows S. W. 12 or 14 miles, into Maurice River Cove, sending forth several small streams, laterally to the west, which have their mouths higher up in the bay.

Oswego, east branch of Wading river. (See *Wading River*.)

Oxford t-ship, Warren co., bounded N. W. by Knowlton; E. by Hardwick and Independence; S. E. by Mansfield; S. by Greenwich t-ships, and W. by the Delaware river. Greatest length, N. E. and S. W., 16 miles; breadth, N. W. and S. E., 5½ miles; area, 42,000 acres. Drained chiefly by the Pequest creek and its tributary, Beaver Brook. Population in 1830, 3665; taxables, in 1832, 800. In 1832, the township contained 254 householders, whose ratables did not exceed $30 in value, 17 stores, 18 pair of stones for grinding grain, 1 carding machine, 7 saw mills, 3 furnaces, 10 tan vats, 4 distilleries, and 862 horses and mules, and 1407 neat cattle; and it paid tax for township use, $1200, and for state and county purposes, $2229 02. Belvidere, the county town, lies on the Delaware river, in this township, and Bridgeville, Oxford and Concord are small villages from 3 to 4 miles distant from it. The surface of the township is much broken, and it possesses a great variety of soil and cultivation. The mountains, which are composed of granitic rock and crowned with wood, cover a considerable portion of it, and are cultivated wherever the hopes of reward will justify the labour. The valleys of limestone are very productive; and large quantities of wheat are grown for market. Greenpond is a small lake 1½ mile long by ¾ of a mile wide, on the S. E. declivity of Jenny Jump mountain; mountain and bog ore abound, and manganese on the Delaware below Foul Rift. The towns are Belvidere, the seat of justice of the county, Bridgeville, Oxford, Concord, and Roxburg.

Oxford, small hamlet of Oxford t-ship, Warren co., three miles S. E. of Belvidere, the county town; contains a Presbyterian church, a tavern, 1 grist and 1 clover mill, and 10 or 12 dwellings.

Oxford Furnace, and village, on a branch of the Pequest creek, near the E. line of Oxford township, and five miles E. of Belvidere, the seat of justice, at the N. W. foot of Scott's mountain. This mountain vale is a very ancient site for the manufacture of iron, a furnace having been erected here more than seventy years since by the ancestor of the present owners, Messrs. Robison; but it had been out of blast for more than 20 years, when Messrs. Henry and Jordon, of Pennsylvania, undertook to renew operations. These gentlemen have obtained a lease of the furnace, with 2000 acres of woodland, and have rebuilt the works. Abundance of excellent iron ore is found in the mountain a few hundred yards from the furnace; and the lessees have sunk several shafts, and are now working a vein of magnetic ore about 13 feet thick, enclosed by walls of rotten mica. This ore is very rich and easily smelted. Old excavations are visible in many places, and shafts have recently been discovered more than 100 feet deep, and drifts exceeding 120 yards in length. The rock of Scott's mountain is primitive, and its constituents are found separately in masses, and also variously combined with each other, with hornblende and with iron of various species, forming granite, sienite, &c. The whole range of hills, of which Scott's mountain is part, forms a very interesting study for the mineralogist and geologist.

Oyster Creek, Stafford t-ship, Monmouth co., flows N. E. about 10 miles, and empties into Barnegat bay, on the line separating Stafford from Dover township.

Pacak Creek rises in the Wawayanda mountains, Vernon t-ship, Sussex co., and by a southerly course, of about seven miles, unites with the Pequannock creek, in Hardistone township.

Pahaquarry, N. W. t-ship of Warren co., bounded N. E. by Walpack t-ship; S. E., by Hardwick and Knowlton t-ships; S. W. and W. by the river Delaware. It lies wholly between the Blue mountain and the river; is centrally distant, N. from Belvidere, 15 miles. Greatest length, N. E. and S. W., 13 miles; breadth, 2½ miles; area, 12,800 acres; surface, mountain and river bottom. Population by census of 1830, 258. In 1832, it contained 13 householders, whose ratables did not exceed $30 in value; but no store, and but one grist mill, 4 mill saws, 59 horses and mules, and 121 neat cattle above the age of three years, and paid a state and county tax of $109 61. Vancamp brook flows southerly through the N. W. part of the township. Pahaquarry is the name given to a small cluster of houses, situate in the northern part of the township. The Water Gap, by which the Delaware flows through the Blue mountain, is on the southwestern boundary of the township. Brotzmanville is the post-office. A road has lately been made through the Gap, and partly cut out of the mountain at the expense of the state. Before it was made, even foot passengers were unable to follow the river through the Gap on the Jersey side without the aid of rope ladders to assist them over the precipitous rocks. The narrow margin above the river, which nowhere exceeds the breadth of the fourth of a mile, is fertile. Upon the Pennsylvania side this margin is wider and underlaid with limestone.

Paint Island Spring, on the boundary between Upper and Lower Freehold t-ships, Monmouth co., 5 miles E. of Wrightsville, and near the source of Toms' river. This is a large chalybeate spring whose waters hold so great a quantity of the super carbonate of iron, blended with the black oxyde of iron in solution, that they leave a very extensive deposit of this mineral. By exposure to the air an atom of carbonic acid escapes, the oxyde takes another atom of oxygen from the atmosphere, and is precipitated in the form of oxy-carbonat, an insoluble powder of a yellow colour. The colour may be converted into a beautiful brown by heating the yellow ochre sufficiently to expel its carbonic acid, leaving behind the second oxide of iron. The heat of boiling water is sufficient for this purpose; and the ore so changed has most of the properties of umber. A manufacture of this paint has given name to the spring. It is esteemed by the neighbours for medicinal qualities, and *pic nic* parties are made here frequently in the summer. It was also formerly known as Lawrence's spring, but is now, we believe, the property of Samuel G. Wright, Esq.

Pamrepau, small scattering settlement, in Bergen t-ship, Bergen co., on New York bay, about 5 miles below Jersey City, occupied by descendants of the original Dutch settlers.

Panther Pond, on the N. W. of Byram t-ship, Sussex co., one of the eastern sources of the Pequest creek.

Papaking Creek, rises in Frankford t-ship, Sussex co., and flows, N. E. by a course of about 10 miles, to Deep Clove creek, below Deckertown, Wantage t-ship; giving motion to several mills.

Paramus, small hamlet, on the Saddle River, and on the boundary of Harrington and Franklin t-ships, Bergen co.; contains a church, a tavern, a mill and several dwellings, about 7 miles N. W. from Hackensack.

Parcipany, p-t. of Hanover t-ship, on the turnpike road from Franklin to Mount Pleasant, 7 miles N. of Morristown, 229 N. E. from W. C., and 63 from Trenton, on the Parcipany river; contains 2 grist mills, 2 stores, 2 taverns, a Presbyterian, and a Methodist church, an academy, and from 15 to 20 dwellings. The soil around it, is sandy loam, well cultivated.

Parcipany Creek, rises by two branches, in the Trowbridge mountain, Hanover t-ship, Morris co.; and flows by a S. E. course of about 8 or 9 miles, into the Whippany river, about a mile above its junction, with the Rockaway, giving motion to several mills.

Parvin's Run, Fairfield t-ship, Cumberland co., a tributary of the Cohansey creek, which joins its recipient, 2 miles S. of Bridgeton; notable as part of the boundary between Deerfield and Fairfield t-ships.

Parvin's Branch, of Maurice river, rises in Millville t-ship, Cumberland co., and flows eastwardly to the head of the Pond, of Millville works.

Paskack Brook, tributary of Hackensack river, rises in Rockland co., New York, and flows by a course, S. and S. E., of about 12 miles, to its recipient, in Harrington t-ship, Bergen co., giving motion to many mills.

Passaic River. This stream is endowed with a very singular character. Rising in, and flowing through a mountainous country, it is the most crooked, sluggish, and longest of the state; and yet presents the two most profound cataracts, and the greatest hydraulic force. Its extreme source is near Mendham, Morris co., where its head waters interlock with those of the north branch of the Raritan: thence it flows a little E. of S. about 10 miles; in which distance, it has considerable fall—turns several mills, and forms the boundary between Somerset and Morris cos.; thence turned by Stony Hill, of the former co., at the N. base of which it receives Dead river, it assumes a N. E. course, by the foot of Long Hill, dividing Morris from Essex county. On this line, for 20 miles, it steals its way, partly through a narrow vale, and partly through a broad valley, with scarce a ripple or a murmur to indicate its course; and consequently, with few mill-works of any kind. At the S. W. point of the Horse-Shoe

mountain, it receives the Rockaway river, which having had for many miles, a rapid, spirited, and useful course, assumes the torpor of its recipient; and spreads itself as if seeking rest, after its hurried flow and mighty labours. Collecting its waters, the united stream meanders along the curve of the Horse-Shoe, about 8 miles, when deflected by the north-eastern point, it inclines to the Second mountain, still preserving its monotonous and sluggish character. But, in its way through this mountain, that character is suddenly changed for high and admirable energy. By two perpendicular leaps, and a rocky rapid, it descends, at the Little Fall, 51 feet in the distance of a half mile, into the valley N. of the First mountain. The first fall has comparatively a gentle, and certainly, a very beautiful appearance. It is 10 feet deep, and more than an hundred yards broad, and has been artificially formed into a broad angle opening down the stream, over which the whole river, but now still and lifeless, as a sea of glass, is precipitated, in two broad and dense sheets, which are shaken by the shock into clouds of foam, and scarce recover their liquid form, until they encounter the second precipice. This has a depth of 16 feet, over which the flood, confined, in ordinary seasons, to a very limited bed, pours in a deep mass, with tremendous force, covering itself with a perpetual halo of spray, and then hastening rapidly away, beneath the bold and lofty arch of the aqueduct of the Morris canal, as if regretting, and gladly seeking, its broken quiet. The aqueduct, a beautiful piece of architecture, formed of cut stone, with a span of 80 feet, and height of 50 feet, adds an admirable feature to the scene; the whole of which, including the basaltic columnar walls of the ravine, erected upon their broad bases of red sandstone, is best seen from the rocky brink of the river, which may be descended to, from either bank, but more commodiously from the left.

Between the Little and the Great Falls, a distance of 5½ miles, the river is broken by some inconsiderable ripples, which afford sufficient fall for mills, but do not much disturb the placidity of its course; but before the great leap, it is again composed into a steady calm, as if concentrated for a new and more vigorous effort. Ere it reaches the perpendicular pitch, it rolls over the artificial dam, erected by the Passaic Manufacturing Company, and a low ledge of rocks; and then pours itself in one unbroken column, 50 feet in altitude, into a deep and narrow chasm, of about 60 feet in width; through which it dashes, foams and roars, into a broad and still basin, which it has excavated for itself. From this it rushes impetuously, by a rapid descent of 20 feet, beneath the level of Paterson plain, curbed by walls of trap-rock and sandstone, whose loose and disjointed character, has enabled the stream to excavate its passage through the deep chasm.

From Paterson to the port of Acquackanonck, 10 miles, where the river meets the tide, its course is again sweetly still; and the tide waters of no river can present a more charming scene. The shore spreading like an amphitheatre upon either side, is covered with verdure, and studded with dwellings, and other monuments of successful industry, which give it the appearance of a highway, through a thrifty village; whilst the clear and quiet waters tempt the spectator to venture upon their bosom. Few rivers possess more attraction than the Passaic, between Paterson and Newark, above the marshes; nor are the charms of its beautiful scenery diminished, by the sport which the stream offers, to the patient follower of Isaac Walton, in the finny tribe, with which it is stored. From Acquackanonck to the head of Newark bay, the distance may be 15 miles, and thus the whole course of the river is about 70 miles, in passing through which, it has looked to every quarter of the compass, save the west.

Paterson. This thriving manufacturing town is one of the creations of the genius of Alexander Hamilton, the true father of the system of domestic industry, now cherished as the American system. In the early part of the year 1791, on the recommendation, and by the active and influential exertions of this distinguished and patriotic statesman, a number of public spirited individuals of New York, New Jersey, and Pennsylvania, associated themselves for establishing useful manufactures, by the subscription of a capital of more than $200,000. The number of shares originally subscribed was 5000, at $100 the share; but 2267 shares only, were fully paid up. The general object of the company was to lay the foundation of a great emporium of manufactures for all articles not prohibited by law. Their immediate object was the manufacture of cotton cloths; and the attempt is highly characteristic of the enterprising spirit of our countrymen. At this period, the improvements of Arkwright in cotton machinery, though perfected, were not very extensively used, even in England, and were absolutely unknown in all other countries. In America no cotton had been spun by machinery. Having resolved to establish themselves in New Jersey, the "contributors" were incorporated by the legislature on 22d Nov. 1791, by an act authorizing a capital stock of one million of dollars, with the right to acquire and hold property to the amount of four millions, and the power to improve the navigation of the rivers, make canals for the trade with the principal site of their works, and to raise by way of lottery, the sum of one hundred thousand dollars. The act of incorporation, which was drawn, or revised by Mr. Hamilton, also gave a city charter, with jurisdiction over a tract of six square miles. The society was organized at New Brunswick, on the last Monday of November, 1791, by the choice of its first board of directors, composed of William Duer, John Dewhurst, Benjamin Walker, Nicholas Low, Royal Flint, Elisha Boudinot, John Bayard, John Neilson, Archibald Mercer, Thomas Lowring, George Lewis, More Furman, and Alex. M'Comb. William Duer was chosen the first governor of the company. We give these names, because they are illustrated by the present flourishing condition of the society, the result of their labours.

Mr. Hamilton, who was not a stockholder of the company, and whose disinterested exertions in its behalf, were prompted by higher motives than pecuniary gratification, had, previously to the act of incorporation, at the request of the company, engaged English and Scotch artizans and manufacturers of cotton machinery and cotton goods, to establish their business here. After its organization, the society advertised their desire to purchase a suitable site for their city, with the requisite water power, in any part of New Jersey. They received proposals from the West Jersey Associates, from South River, Perth Amboy, Millstone, Bull's Falls, the Little Falls of the Passaic, and from the inhabitants of the Great Falls of that river; and in May, 1792, they selected, with admirable judgment, the last place, as the principal site of their proposed operations; giving to their town the name of Paterson, after governor William Paterson, who had signed their charter. At this period there were not more than ten houses here.

At a meeting of the directors, at the Godwin hotel, on the 4th July, 1792, appropriations were made for building factories, machine shops, and shops for calico printing and weaving; and a race-way was directed to be made, for bringing the water from above the falls to the proposed mills. Unfortunately, the direction of these works was given to Major L'Enfan, a French engineer, not more celebrated for the grandeur of his conceptions, than his recklessness of

expense; and whose magnificent projects commonly perished in the waste of means provided for their attainment. He immediately commenced the race-way and canal, designing to unite the Upper Passaic with the Lower, at the head of tide, near the present village of Acquackanonck, by a plan better adapted to the resources of a great empire than to those of a private company.

In January, 1793, Peter Colt, Esq. of Hartford, then comptroller of the state of Connecticut, was appointed "general superintendent of the affairs of the company, with full powers to manage the concerns of the society, as if they were his own individual property," Major L'Enfan being retained, however, as engineer; but he, after having spent, uselessly, a large sum of money, resigned his office in the following September. Mr. Colt, thus in sole charge of the works, completed the race-way, conducting the water to the first factory erected by the society. The canal to tide water, had been abandoned before the departure of the engineer.

The factory, 90 feet long by 40 wide, and 4 stories high, was finished in 1794, when cotton yarn was spun in the mill; but yarn had been spun in the preceding year, by machinery moved by oxen. In 1794, also, calico shawls and other cotton goods were printed; the bleached and unbleached muslins being purchased in New York. In the same year the society gave their attention to the culture of the silk worm, and directed the superintendent to plant the mulberry tree for this purpose. In April of this year, also, the society, at the instance of Mr. Colt, employed a teacher to instruct, gratuitously, on the Sabbath, the children employed in the factory, and others. This was probably the first Sunday school established in New Jersey.

Notwithstanding their untoward commencement, and the many discouragements attending their progress, the directors persevered in their enterprise; and during the years

1795, and 1796, much yarn of various sizes was spun, and several species of cotton fabrics were made. But, at length satisfied that it was hopeless to contend, successfully, longer with an adverse current, they resolved, July, 1796, to abandon the manufacture, and discharged their workmen. This result was produced by a combination of causes. Nearly $50,000 had been lost, by the failure of the parties to certain bills of exchange purchased by the company, to buy in England plain cloths for printing; large sums had been wasted by the engineer; and the machinists and manufacturers imported, were presumptuous, and ignorant of many branches of the business they engaged to conduct; and more than all, the whole attempt was premature. No pioneer had led the way, and no experience existed in the country, relative to any subject of the enterprise. Beside, had the country been in a measure prepared for manufactures, the acquisition of the carrying trade, which our merchants were then making, was turning public enterprise into other channels. The ruin of the company under these circumstances, cannot now be cause of astonishment. But to this catastrophe the children of Mr. Colt, now deeply interested in the operations of the company, have the just and proud satisfaction to know, that their parent was in no way auxiliary. On closing their concerns, the directors unanimously returned him their thanks "for his industry, care and prudence, in the management of their affairs, since he had been employed in their service; fully sensible that the failure of the objects of the society was from causes not in his power, or that of any other man, to prevent."

The cotton mill of the company was subsequently leased to individuals, who continued to spin candle wick and coarse yarn until 1807, when it was accidentally burned down, and was never rebuilt. The admirable water-power of the company, was not however wholly unem-

ployed. In 1801, a mill seat was leased to Mr. Charles Kinsey, and Israel Crane; in 1807, a second, and 1811, a third, to other persons; and between 1812, and 1814, several others were sold or leased. In 1814, Mr. Roswell L. Colt, the present enterprising governor of the society, purchased, at a depreciated price, a large proportion of the shares, and reanimated the association. From this period, the growth of Paterson has been steady, except during the 3 or 4 years which followed the peace of 1815.

The advantages derivable from the great fall in the river here, have been improved with much judgment. A dam of $4\frac{1}{2}$ feet high, strongly framed and bolted to the rock in the bed of the river above the falls, turns the stream through a canal excavated in the trap rock of the bank, into a basin; whence, through strong guard-gates, it supplies in succession three canals on separate planes, each below the other; giving to the mills on each, a head and fall of about 22 feet. By means of the guard-gate, the volume of water is regulated at pleasure, and a uniform height preserved; avoiding the inconvenience of back-water. The expense of maintaining the dam, canals, and main sluice-gates, and of regulating the water, is borne by the company; who have expended, in raising the main embankment, and constructing the feeder from the river and new upper canal, and for works to supply water to the third tier of mills, the sum of $40,000.

The advantages which Paterson possesses for a manufacturing town, are obvious. An abundant and steady supply of water; a healthy, pleasant, and fruitful country, supplying its markets fully with excellent meats and vegetables—Its proximity to New York, where it obtains the raw material, and sale for manufactured goods; and with which it is connected by the sloop navigation of the Passaic, by the Morris canal, by a turnpike-road, and by a rail-road, render it one of the most desirable sites in the

Union. The transportation of merchandise to and from New York, has heretofore cost from two, to two and a half dollars the ton; but will be reduced on the rail-road to one dollar.

A water-power, consisting of as much water as may be drawn through an aperture one foot square, or of 144 square inches, with a lot for buildings, having 100 feet on the front and rear, was let in the first instance at a rent of $75 per annum; in the second, at $100; in the third, at $160; and the price has been advanced from time to time, to $200, $250, $300, $400, and $500 rent, per annum. At present, the terms of the company for such power and lot, are—rent of $500 per annum, on a lease of 21 years; renewable every 21 years at the same rent, on the payment of a fine of $500, or an absolute right in fee simple for the sum of $10,000. Lots for dwellings, &c., may be obtained at from $150, to $1000 each. In good situations, the ordinary price is about 5 or 6 hundred dollars for 25 feet in front, by 100 in depth.

The city of Paterson is incorporated pursuant to 26th and 27th sections of the act of 22d November, 1791, and the plot, lies partly in the county of Bergen, and partly in the county of Essex, on both sides of the river, and covers 36 square miles, and is governed by a mayor, recorder, common council, &c. It is 15 miles N. from Newark, and 18 N. W. from New York, 61 N. E. from Trenton, 91 from Philadelphia, and 227 from W. C. The following statistics of the town are derived from a very valuable memoir prepared by the Rev. Dr. Fisher, pastor of the First Presbyterian church there, in 1832. The number of dwellings are 765, stores, &c. 76, families 1586, consisting of 4515 males, and 4570 females, of whom 3949 were under 16 years of age, and 250 were coloured persons. During the year ending 4th July, 1832, the number of births was 321, and of deaths 170; excess of births

151. This population is divided into 14 religious denominations, strongly illustrating the diversity of religious opinion in thickly settled districts of the United States, and the harmony which may prevail among the worshippers of the Deity, where lust of temporal dominion cannot be gratified. There were here of heads of families, Presbyterians 384, Reformed Dutch 323, Roman Catholics 288, Methodists 269, Episcopalians 149, Baptists 86, Reformed Presbyterians 35, Dutch Seceders 6, Lutherans 6, Friends 2, Christian Baptist 1, Universalists 2, Unitarians 2, Deists 4; and there were 11 persons who either professed no religion, or whose sentiments were unknown. There are 9 houses for religious worship, viz: Presbyterian 1, Reformed Dutch 2, Roman Catholic 1, Methodist 1, Episcopal 1, Reformed Presbyterian 1, Baptist 1, True Reformed Dutch 1; the eight first of which had, each, its settled minister. The provision for education in the town, consisted of 20 pay schools, 13 for males and 7 for females, having scholars 384; a free school supported by the town for poor children, having 188 pupils; an infant school under the direction and patronage of a society of ladies, selected from the different religious denominations, in which poor children between the ages of 3 and 8 years, are gratuitously instructed, without regard to the religious professions of their parents. At this school, there was 173 pupils, making the whole number of children thus instructed, weekly, 1195. Seven Sabbath schools taught 1531 scholars, a large proportion of whom attended no other schools.

There is here also, a philosophical society composed of young gentlemen, who have associated for literary improvement, and have collected a respectable library; and a mechanics' society, incorporated by the legislature, for advancement in science and the mechanic arts, which has laid the foundation of a library and a collection of philosophical apparatus.

In 1832 the town contained 163 widows, in whose families there were 834 souls, the greater portion of whom, now maintained by the manufacturing establishments, would, otherwise, have been dependant upon public or private charity, for support.

There were, at this time, 12 blacksmiths, besides those immediately connected with the machine shops—in these 22 fires, and 37 hands are employed; 34 shoemakers, employing 183 hands; 13 tailors and tailoresses, employing 70 hands; 9 milliners, employing 34 hands; 3 bookstores; 1 bindery; 1 circulating library, of 1300 volumes; 1 incorporated library company, with a library of 250 volumes; 1 bank, viz. "The People's Bank of Paterson"—Alex. Carrick, president, and James Nazro, cashier; 10 physicians; 6 licensed attorneys; 2 commissioners; 3 masters in chancery, and 5 notaries; 3 judges of the county courts, and 10 justices of the peace; 2 printing offices, from which are issued 2 weekly papers, viz. the "Paterson Intelligencer," printed by David Burnett, the proprietor, and published on Wednesday; and the "Paterson Courier," printed by A. S. Gould, the proprietor, and published on Tuesday: 1 post-office, Moses E. De Witt, post-master; 10 licensed taverns; 40 grocery and provision stores; and 51 grogshops, where little else but ardent spirits is sold; 1 dry good, hardware, crockery, and grocery store; 2 dry good and crockery stores; 14 fancy dry good stores; 2 hardware stores; 1 fancy chair store; 1 fancy chair and looking-glass store; 1 apothecary and paint store, and 4 medicine stores; 5 shoe stores; 1 corset, millinery, and fancy store; 2 hat stores, and 1 hatter, employing 4 hands; 1 poor-house, 21 paupers; 2 breweries; 1 file cutter; 1 girth manufacturer, and 4 looms; 1 reed maker; 4 bakeries; 2 carpet weavers; 1 manufactory of fine ingrained carpets, employing 7 looms and 12 hands; 1 gun and locksmith, &c.; 2 coopers,

employing 11 hands; 1 sizing establishment; 3 dyeing establishments, separate from the factories, and 8 hands; 1 umbrellamaker; 1 chair bottomer; several heddlemakers; 2 tobacconists, 9 hands; 2 watchmakers, jewellers and silversmiths; 4 cabinetmakers, 35 hands; 1 candle and 2 soap factories; 2 barbers; 3 lottery offices; 1 tanner and currier, 33 vats and 9 hands; 3 hay scales, Bull's patent; 4 painters and glaziers, 22 hands; 1 Masonic hall; 1 auction mart; 1 counterpane weaver; 1 marble yard, 6 hands; 1 freestone yard, 5 hands; 7 slaughter-houses, and 9 butchers; 4 livery stables; 7 wheelwrights and 19 hands; 2 saddle and harnessmakers, and trimmers, 10 hands; 8 confectionery and toy shops; 2 copper, tin, and sheet iron manufactories, and 24 hands; 2 large and commodious market-houses, and the market is well supplied with meat, fish, and vegetables of the various kinds; 1 museum, fitted up with taste; 1 hoe factory, 4 hands; 1 sashmaker, 2 hands; 4 public engines for extinguishing fires, and 7 private ones—2 moveable and 5 attached to the factories; 15 master carpenters, employing 122 hands; 8 master masons, employing 174 hands; 1 public dispensary, incorporated by act of the legislature.

Paterson contains 1 saw mill, with 2 saw carriages and 2 saws; 1 grist mill, with 2 run of stones; 4 turning and bobbin factories, employing 43 hands; 2 bleaching establishments, employing 18 hands; 5 millwright establishments, employing 59 hands; 1 manufactory of cotton wadding, where wadding of a superior quality is manufactured; 4 machine factories, employing 404 hands. In the last the manufacture of cotton and other machinery is brought to a high state of perfection. In that of Messrs. Plunket and Thompson, are employed between 60 and 70 hands, and being recently established, it contains the latest improvements in their art, and produces machinery of superior quality.

Attached to the works of Godwin, Clark, and Co., and of Rogers, Ketchum, and Grosvenor, are two extensive brass and iron founderies, where mill shafts, wheels, and the various parts of cotton machinery, &c. are cast: 20 manufactories of cotton; in these are 40,501 spindles in operation; they employ 1646 hands, and use annually 3,360,272 lbs. of raw cotton.

The Phenix Manufacturing Company, in addition to their cotton establishment, have 1616 spindles, employed in spinning flax; the flax annually consumed is 493,000 lbs., giving employment to 196 hands. This flax is manufactured into duck and bagging.

In the cotton establishment of John Colt, Esq. were manufactured in 1831, 460,000 yards of cotton duck: A sattinet factory, with a dyeing establishment annexed, employs 1322 spindles, 75 hands, 23 power looms, and 13 hand looms; consuming, annually, 105,000 lbs. of wool.

The power looms in operation in all the factories were 311, hand looms 14. In the village and out of the factories, there were only 50 hand looms.

Total number of power and hand looms 374. Total spindles 43,439. Total cotton, wool, and flax annually consumed is 3,958,272 lbs. Total hands employed in all the establishments 2543: a large proportion of whom are children.

A button factory, employing 28 hands. In this factory are made steel buttons, clasps, ornaments, and a variety of other articles of iron and steel: A gilt button manufactory, employing 20 hands, and manufacturing at the rate 9000 groce of buttons a year. The average price of these buttons is about $4 50 a groce. Annual produce $40,000. The buttons manufactured at this establishment, as it respects perfection of workmanship and elegance of finish, in the opinion of competent judges, are not surpassed by any gilt buttons imported from Europe.

The large four story brick factory of Rogers, Ketchum, and Grosvenor, besides the room occupied by the machinists, is capable of containing 5000 cotton spindles, with the machines for preparation.

One large three storied paper mill.

In the establishment of Messrs. Collet and Smith, were manufactured in 1831, 900 pieces of nankeen, of a superior quality, from nankeen cotton, raised by Governor Forsyth of Georgia.

That part of the village of Paterson, situated on the north side of the Passaic river, usually called New Manchester, had

	dwellings,	families.	souls.
In 1824,	31	48	289
1827,	66	115	625
1829,	89	154	852
1832,	114	217	1214

In the whole village of Paterson, in 1824, there were,

		814 families,	&	4787 souls.
In 1825,	849	do.		5084 do.
1827,	1046	do.		6236 do.
1829,	1220	do.		7033 do.
1832,	1568	do.		9085 do.

The spindles in operation in 1825, were 19,036; in 1827, 25,998; in 1829, 30,295; and in 1832, 43,439.

The raw material consumed in 1827, was,

Cotton,	1,843,100 lbs.
Flax,	620,000
Total,	2,463,100 lbs.

In 1829, Cotton,	2,179,600 lbs.
Flax,	600,000
Total,	2,779,600 lbs.

In 1832, Cotton,	3,360,272 lbs.
Flax,	493,000
Wool,	105,000
Total,	3,958,272 lbs.

In consequence of the great improvement in cotton machinery, yarn of a much finer thread is spun; consequently, the consumption of the raw material has not increased in proportion to the increased number of spindles.

In 1827, there were employed in all the manufacturing establishments, 1453 hands, and the annual amount of wages paid to them, as ascertained from the pay lists of the manufacturers, was $221,123. In 1829, there were employed, 1879 hands; annual wages, $285,453; in 1832, there were employed, 2543 hands; annual amount of wages, $367,003.

The salutary influence of this thriving town, is sensibly felt throughout the whole of the N. E. section of the state. The agriculturist has participated, in no small degree, in its prosperity. His lands have greatly increased in marketable value, and his physical and moral condition has been in all respects improved. If wise, he will maintain this source of present enjoyment to himself, and of future happiness to his posterity, with a zeal becoming its value.

Pattenbury, small village of Bethlehem t-ship, at the S. foot of Musconetcong mountain, on Alberson's brook, 12 miles N. W. of Flemington, Hunterdon county, contains a grist mill, a store, 6 dwellings. Soil, red shale, through or near which a vein of limestone probably passes.

Paulinskill, creek of Sussex and Warren counties, which rises by two branches; the easterly one from a pond on the south of Pimple hill, in Hardiston t-ship, and flowing thence N. W., through Newton township, into Frankford township; the westerly one, from Long and Culver's ponds, at the foot of the Blue mountain, in Frankford, in which township the branches unite near the town of Augusta, and flow thence by a south-west course of 22 or 23 miles, to the Delaware river: the whole length of the stream, by its eastern branch, may be 35 miles. It gives motion to many mills, and flows through a very fertile country of lime and slate formations, separating them for a considerable part of its course.

Paulsboro', town of Greenwich t-ship, Gloucester co., near Mantua creek, 4 miles W. of Woodbury; contains a tavern, store, 10 or 12 dwellings, and a Methodist church.

Paxton's Island, in the Delaware river, Amwell t-ship, Hunterdon co.

Peck's Beach, on the coast of the Atlantic ocean, in Upper t-ship, Cape May co., extends about 10 miles, from Corson's to Egg Harbour inlet.

Pedricktown, p-t. of Upper Penn's Creek t-ship, Salem co., lying on Oldman's creek, about 8 or 9 miles from its mouth; contains between 20 and 30 dwellings, 1 Friends' meeting house, 1 tavern, 2 stores, 1 school; and is inhabited by agriculturists and mechanics. The soil around it is a sandy loam and well cultivated, by means of the marl found in the neighbourhood. The *Palma Christi,* or castor bean, is extensively produced here, and about 1500 galls. of oil manufactured annually. The town is distant, 16 miles N. E. from W. C.; 54 S. from Trenton, and 14 or 15 N. from Salem.

Pemberton, or *New Mills,* p-t. of Northampton t-ship, Burlington co., on the north branch of the Rancocus creek, 6 miles above Mount Holly, 13 from Burlington, 27 from Trenton, and 162 from W. C.; contains a grist mill, saw mill, fulling mill, a cotton manufactory, a cupola furnace, 1 Methodist and 1 Baptist church, a school house, 2 taverns, 5 stores, and about 100 dwellings. This is a thriving town, growing rapidly by reason of its manufactures.

Pennington, p-t. of Hopewell t-ship, Hunterdon co. Centrally situated, 8 miles N. of Trenton; 174 from W. C., and 15 S. from Flemington; in a level country of red shale, fertile and well cultivated; contains 1 Methodist and 1 Presbyterian church, both good buildings of brick, the latter having a cupola and bell, 3 taverns, as many stores, and about 30 dwellings, a public library and an academy. This is a very neat and pleasant village, surrounded by wealthy and liberal farmers.

Penn's Grove, small hamlet and ferry, on the Delaware river, in Upper Penn's Neck t-ship, Salem co., distant about 15 miles N. of Salem; there are here 6 or 8 dwellings, a tavern and store. The Wilmington and Philadelphia steam boat touches here daily, to receive and land passengers, and a 4 horse stage runs daily between the ferry and the town of Salem.

Penn's Neck, (see *Williamsburg*,) lies in the angle formed by the Stony Brook and Millstone river, West Windsor township, Middlesex county, about a mile S. E. of Princeton.

Penn's Neck, Lower, t-ship, of Salem co, bounded N. by Upper Penn's Neck; E. and S. E. by Salem river, which divides it from Mannington; and S. W. and W. by the river Delaware. Centrally distant, N. W. of Salem, 5 miles; greatest length, 9; breadth, 6 miles; area, 12,645 acres; surface, level; soil, partly rich clay loam, partly sandy loam, and partly excellent marsh meadow. Products, wheat, rye, corn and vegetables for market. Population in 1830, 994. In 1832, the township contained 228 taxables; 73 householders, whose ratables did not exceed $30 in value; 4 school houses, an Episcopal, a Presbyterian and a Methodist church, 2 taverns, 2 stores, 2 fisheries; and it paid township tax, $300; county tax, $722 76; state tax, $226 50.

A canal, of two miles in length, near the northern boundary, cut through a dead level, unites the Salem river with the Delaware at about 12 miles above the mouth of the former, saving to vessels from this point, a circular navigation of 25 miles. Kinseyville is a small village on the Delaware, at which there is a ferry.

Penn's Neck, Upper, t-ship, Salem co., bounded N. and E. by Woolwich t-ship, Gloucester co.; S. E. by Piles Grove t-ship, Salem co.; S. by Mannington t-ship; S. W. by Lower Penn's Neck; and W. by the river Delaware. Centrally distant from Salem, 10; greatest length, 9;

breadth, 7½ miles; surface level; soil light sandy loam; generally cultivated with rye and Indian corn; area, 21,053 acres. There are, in the township, 1 Friends' and 1 Methodist meeting, 5 schools, 5 taverns, 6 stores, 1 grist and 1 saw mill, 1 ferry, 1 distillery. In 1832, there were 340 horses and mules, and 900 neat cattle, over three years of age; 117 householders, whose ratables did not exceed $30; 330 taxable inhabitants. In 1830, the population by census, was 1638. In 1832, the township paid township tax, $400; county tax, $738 20; state tax, $230 75.

A valuable bed of shell marl lies in the township, near Pedricktown; the extent of which has not yet been explored. Large quantities have been dug and used with great advantage in this and the neighbouring townships. It is found most useful on the light and sandy soils, in the culture of grass and grain, when applied in quantities of 10 or 12 two horse wagon loads to the acre. In opening the pits a bed of oyster and other shells, at irregular distances from the surface, from three to twenty feet, presents itself. This bed is about three feet thick. Beneath it is a mass of undiscovered depth, composed of black earth and shells, known as gunpowder marl, but it is not in as much repute as the stratum of shells. These shells, when exposed to the air, disintegrate rapidly. The marl is sold at about 50 cts. the wagon load. More than an acre of this bed has been already excavated.

Pennypot, name of a small tributary of the Great Egg Harbour river, and also of a tavern and mill, near the junction of Hospitality branch, with the main stream, in Hamilton t-ship, Gloucester co.

Pensaukin Creek, rises by two branches, one in the N. part of Evesham t-ship, and the other on the line between that t-ship, in Burlington co., and Waterford t-ship, of Gloucester co., uniting about four miles above the mouth, and flowing into the Delaware, three miles above Petty's island. It is a mill stream, navigable for 5 or 6 miles, and forms part of the boundary line between Burlington and Gloucester counties.

Pepack Creek, mill stream, and tributary of the N. branch of the Raritan; rises in Chester t-ship, Morris co., and flows to its recipient, by a southerly course of about 7 miles, in Bedminster t-ship, Somerset co.

Pepack, p-t., of Bedminster t-ship, Somerset co., 11 miles N. W. from Somerville, 212 from W. C., and 46 from Trenton; contains a tavern, store, grist mill, and some 10 or 12 dwellings, in a fertile limestone country.

Pequannock, t-ship, Morris co., bounded N. E. by the Pequannock creek, which separates it from Pompton t-ship, Bergen co.; E. by Pompton river, dividing it from Saddle river t-ship, of the same co.; S. E. by Caldwell t-ship, Essex co.; S. by Hanover and Randolph t-ships, and W. by Jefferson t-ship. Centrally distant, N. from Morristown, 10 miles. Greatest length, E. and W. 16, breadth, 11 miles; area, 74,000 acres. The surface of the t-ship is hilly, being covered with mountain ridges and knolls. On the northern boundary, is Green Pond mountain, girding a narrow valley, through which flows the Burnt Meadow branch of the Rockaway river, and bounded southward, by Mount Hope, and Copperas mountain. Between these and the next ridge, is a wider valley, drained by the Beaver Branch of the same river, and south of this, innominate knolls and ridges make valleys, through which run minor tributaries of the river. The soil of the t-ship is generally loam and clay, but grey limestone is found in the valley, S. of Copperas mountain, and probably in other places. Iron abounds in the hills in the N. W., and is of excellent quality, from which many iron works in the neighbourhood are supplied. From the sulphate of iron in the Copperas mountain, much copperas was formerly made. Green Pond is a large sheet of water, nearly 3 miles long, by a half-mile in width; in the vale between Green Pond and Copperas mountain, much resorted to for boating and fishing; and the wild scenery around it is much admired. The valley is inhabited sparsely, by persons dependant upon the iron works. Pompton plains, on the east border of the t-ship, are level and sandy, but densely inhabited, and tolerably cultivated. Pompton, Montville, Powerville, &c., are post-towns of the t-ship. Population in 1830, 4451. In 1832, the t-ship contained 129 householders, whose ratables did not exceed $30 in value, 132 single men, 1050 taxables, 8 stores, 9 saw mills, 5 grist mills, 37 tan vats, 2 distilleries, 30 chairs and sulkies, 14 forges for making iron, 1 furnace, 1 four horse stage, 4 rolling and slitting mills, 1 fulling mill, 690 horses and mules, and 2265 neat cattle, above the age of 3 years; and it paid state tax, $574; county tax, $1285 10; poor tax, $800; road tax, $3000. The Newark and Milford turnpike road crosses the western, and the Newark and Hamburg, and Paterson and Hamburg, turnpike roads, cross the eastern end of the t-ship, and the Morris canal runs through the southern part, and for some distance along the valley of the Rockaway river.

Pequannock Creek, rises in the Wallkill and Wawayanda mountains, in Sussex co., and flows by a southeast and south course, of about 27 miles, to the Passaic river; forming the boundary between Morris and Bergen cos. Below Pompton village it takes the name of Pompton river. It has a rapid current, through a narrow valley, and considerable volume; and is, therefore, an excellent mill stream.

Pequest Creek, rises by two branches, in the eastern part of Sussex co., which unite in Independence t-ship, Warren co., and flow thence by a S. W. course, through Oxford t-ship, to the Delaware river, at the town of Belvidere. Its whole length is about

30 miles. This is a large and rapid stream, affording abundant water-power, and draining, by the main stem and branches, an extensive valley of primitive limestone. (See *Belvidere*.)

Perryville, small p-town of Bethlem t-ship, Hunterdon co., on the turnpike road from Somerville to Philipsburg, about 10 miles N. of Flemington, 35 from Trenton, and 194 from W. C.

Perth Amboy City, p-t., t-ship, and port of entry of Middlesex co., at the head of the Raritan bay, and at the confluence of the Raritan river with the Arthur Kill, or Staten Island Sound. It lies 14 miles from the sea, at Sandy Hook, 25 miles by the Sound from New York, 15 by the river, and 10 by land, from New Brunswick; 36 by post-route from Trenton, 65 by rail-road from Philadelphia, and 212 from W. C. The port, large and safe, and one of the best on the continent, is easily approached from the sea by a broad estuary, having generally 12 feet water, and in the main channel from 24 to 26 feet.

This advantageous site for a town, was early noticed by the agents of the East Jersey proprietors; in the language of deputy governor Lawrie, in 1684, "there being no such place in all England, for conveniency and pleasant situation." The place was known to the aborigines as *Ambo*, the Point; and was greatly resorted to by them on account of its fish and oysters, the latter of which are yet abundant here. The relics of Indian festivities, are still visible in the large quantities of oyster shells which mingle with, and enrich portions of the soil. The name of Perth was given to it in honour of James, Earl of Perth, one of the 24 proprietaries; and it was called by that name only in the instructions of the proprietaries, until 1698, when we, for the first time, in the instructions to the deputy governor, Basse, find the name of "Perth Amboy."

The town was laid out into 150 lots, by Samuel Groome, one of the proprietaries, and surveyor general, as early as 1683. In the following year, Gawn Lawrie, a proprietary and deputy governor, added large tracts for out-lots. The town plot was designed to contain 1500 acres; and lots were sold at 20 pounds, with condition that the purchasers should each build a house 30 feet long, by 18 feet wide. Lawrie contracted at this time for the erection of several houses for the proprietaries, and one 60 feet long and 18 wide, for the governor. He was directed to make the town the seat of government and the chief mart of the province, and to incorporate the inhabitants by charter, with the necessary privileges and jurisdiction of a city.

This was a favourite spot with the East Jersey proprietaries, who used many efforts to render it the site of a large city, but it was overshadowed by New York, and their exertions were in vain. After the surrender of the proprietary governments to the crown, the general assembly and the supreme court of the province, assembled at this place and Burlington, alternately.

The city was incorporated under the proprietary and royal governments, but its present charter embracing the provisions of the prior ones, is under the act of 21st December, 1784, and gives the following boundaries. "Beginning at the meeting of the waters of the Raritan river with those of the Sound, at that part of Staten Island from the main to the southward of the flat or shoal that runs off from Cole Point; thence up the Sound, on the eastern bank of the channel as the same runs to Woodbridge creek; thence up the creek to the mouth of the stream on which Cutler's mill stands; thence up said creek to a lane leading to a line between George Herriott and Grace Innsley; thence by said lane to the road leading from Amboy to New Brunswick; thence by said road south to a lane leading to Florida Landing; thence by said lane to the north corner of the farm late of Samuel Neville; thence by the line of the same to Raritan river, and across the same to the south bank of the channel thereof; and thence to the place of beginning." The government of the city is under a mayor, recorder, three aldermen, who are justices of the peace, ex-officio, and appointed by the legislature for seven years; and six common councilmen, sheriff, coroner, and sergeant-at-mace, and township officers, elected annually by the people. The mayor, recorder, and aldermen, have power to grant tavern licenses, and to hold a court of record, having jurisdiction of all causes of a commercial nature, wherein the matter in dispute shall have arisen within the corporation, and subsists between foreigner and foreigner, or between foreigner and citizen of the United States. And to induce the settlement of merchants here the port was declared *free*, and they exempt from taxation for 25 years. The township contains 2577 acres of land, of alluvial formation, consisting of clay, sand loam, and gravel, in which, at various depths, are found organic remains. It is elevated above the tide some 40 or 50 feet, and is undulating in its surface. The population, which is principally gathered near the point, there not being more than 20 dwellings separated from the town, amounted in 1830, to 879. The township in 1832, contained about 140 dwellings, 78 householders, whose ratable estates did not exceed $30 in value; 39 single men, 10 storekeepers or traders, 5 taverns, an Episcopal, Presbyterian, and a Baptist church, 1 school for boys, another for girls, and a third established under the school fund of the state. St. Peter's the Episcopal church, was founded probably about the year 1685. In July 30th, 1718, it was incorporated by George I; and William Eier, and John Barclay, were appointed the first church wardens, and Thomas Gordon Esq.,

John Rudyard, Robert King, and John Stevens, the first vestrymen. The church is indebted to Thomas Gordon, George Willocks, and Margaretta Willocks, his wife, and major John Harrison, for considerable endowments, upon which its prosperity is based. There is an extensive pottery of excellent stone-ware in the town in which the clay from South Amboy is chiefly, if not solely used. But the chief business of the city is the oyster fishery. The shell-fish are abundant in the bay, and the bottom is so favourable to their growth, that large numbers are transplanted thither, not only from the river above, but also from Virginia. A capital of more than $40,000 is said to be thus employed, yielding an annual profit of more than $20,000. The state of New Jersey has leased about 250 acres of land, covered with water, here, in small lots, of a few acres each, whose tenants rear oysters upon them. But the state of New York, claiming exclusive right of property, in the soil under water, to the line of low-water mark, on the shore of the state; conflicting claims have induced vexatious disputes, and even alarming riots, which have prevented the quiet enjoyment of the tenants, and the collection of rents. In 1832, the city paid poor tax, $350; county tax, $135 87; and state tax, $110 56.

From its agreeable position, vicinity to the ocean, and sea-water baths, Perth Amboy is a pleasant residence during the hot months, and is much visited for recreation, by the citizens of New York. Some years since, a very large and commodious hotel, called Brighton, was erected for their accommodation; but, at that period, there was not sufficient support to sustain it, and Brighton-house is now a handsome country-seat.

The destiny of this town, long obscured, notwithstanding its fine port, and pleasant and healthy position, is probably about to receive a favourable change, through the agency of the Delaware and Raritan canal, and the rail-roads to Philadelphia. The ready transportation of merchandise, by these means, may convert this into an out-port of Philadelphia.

The collection district of Perth Amboy, comprehends all that part of East New Jersey, (that part excepted which is included in the district of Little Egg Harbour) south of Eliza-bethtown, together with all the waters thereof, within the jurisdiction of the state. The towns of New Brunswick, and Middletown Point, are ports of delivery only. The collector resides at Amboy, and a surveyor at New Brunswick.

Peter's Beach, on the Altantic ocean, Galloway t-ship, Gloucester co., at the mouth of Absecum inlet, and between it and Quarter inlet.

Philipsburg, town of Greenwich t-ship, Warren co., on the left bank of the Delaware river, opposite the borough of Easton, in Pennsylvania, 14 miles below the town of Belvidere, and about 60 above Trenton. Con-tains about 20 dwellings, 4 stores, and 2 taverns. The Morris canal communicates with the Delaware here, opposite to, and a short distance below, the basin of the Lehigh canal. A bridge of wood of three arches, covered, 600 feet long, and 24 feet wide, over the Delaware, which cost $80,000, connects Philipsburg with Easton.

Pike Brook, tributary of No-Pipe Brook, rises in the Nashanic moun-tain, Montgomery t-ship, Somerset co., and flows S. E. about 5 miles to its recipient.

Pilesgrove, t-ship, Salem co., bounded, N. E. by Woolwich t-ship, Gloucester co., from which it is di-vided by Oldman's creek; S. E. by Pittsgrove t-ship; S. W. by Upper Alloways, and Mannington t-ships, and N. W. by Upper Penn's Neck t-ship. Centrally distant, N. E. from Salem, 10 miles. Greatest length 9, breadth 6½ miles; area, about 24,000 acres; of which, little more than 1000 may be unimproved. Surface, level; soil, stiff clay and deep loam, well cultivated in wheat, rye, oats, and corn. The Salem creek flows N. W. through the t-ship, and gives motion to a woollen factory, and several mills. Population in 1830, 2150. In the year 1832, there were in the t-ship, 128 householders, whose ratables did not exceed $30; 3 grist mills, 3 saw mills, 4 tan yards, 2 distilleries for cider, 553 horses and mules, and 966 head of neat cattle, above the age of 3 years. Sharptown and Woods-town are villages and post-towns of the t-ship. Near the latter are some valuable marl beds. There are 1 Quaker, 1 Baptist, and 1 African Methodist church in the t-ship.

Pimple Hill, a noted eminence of Hardiston t-ship, Sussex co., near the eastern line of the t-ship.

Pine Brook, Caldwell t-ship, Essex co., rises in the Second mountain, and flows W. to the Passaic river, by a course of about 3 miles. It is a mill stream.

Pine Mount Creek, Greenwich t-ship, Salem co., rises on the E. line of the t-ship, and flows southward, some 3 or 4 miles, when dividing into two branches, in opposite directions, it isolates an eminence covered with pines, and bounded southward by the Cohansey river, of which the creek is a tributary.

Piscataway, t-ship, Middlesex co., bounded N. by Westfield t-ship; E. by Woodbridge; S. and S. W. by the Raritan river, and N. W. by Green Brook, separating it from War-ren t-ship, Somerset co. Centrally distant, N. from New Brunswick, 5 miles. Greatest length, N. and S. 9 miles; breadth, E. and W. 7½ miles; area, 27,000 acres. Green Brook receives from the t-ship two tributa-ries, Amherst and Cedar Brooks. New Market, post-town; Samptown, Green Brook, Brooklyn, New Durham, Pis-cataway, and Raritan Landing, are villages of the t-ship. Population in 1830, 3969. In 1832, the t-ship contained an Episcopalian church, 695 taxables, 85 householders, whose ratables did not exceed $30 in value; 91 single men, 10 stores, 2 saw mills, 6 grist mills, 1 plaster mill, 4 distilleries, 709 horses and mules, and 1501 neat cattle, above the age of 3 years; and it paid state tax, $495 91; county tax, $609 72; poor tax, $1400; road tax, $1000. The surface of the t-ship is level, soil of loam, clay, and red shale, generally very well cultivated.

Piscataway, village of the above t-ship, 3 miles E. from New Brunswick, and 1 N. from the Raritan river, on the turnpike road from New Brunswick to Woodbridge; contains an Episcopal church, a store, tavern, and some 10 or 12 dwellings, in a tolerably fertile country. This was an old Indian village, and is remarkable for having been the seat of justice for Middlesex and Somerset cos., so early as the year 1683. At that period, the courts were holden sometimes at this place, and sometimes at Woodbridge.

Piscot Brook, a small tributary of the south branch of the Raritan river, rises in Round valley, in the S. E. angle of Lebanon t-ship, Hunterdon co.

Pittsgrove, t-ship, Salem co., bounded N. E. by Franklin and Woolwich t-ships, of Gloucester co.; S. E. by Millville t-ship, of Cumberland co.; S. W. by Upper Deerfield t-ship, of Cumberland, and by Upper Alloway's Creek t-ships, of Salem co. Centrally distant, E. from Salem, 16 miles. Greatest length, 15, breadth, 7 miles; area, about 44,000 acres, of which 26,000 acres are unimproved. Population in 1830, 2216. Surface, partly undulating, and partly level; the soil is chiefly sandy and gravelly loam. A proportion on the N. W. part, is forest, of pine and white oak timber, which has been much cut over, and is known as the *Barrens*. It is drained on the S. E. and S. W. by branches of Maurice run, and on the N. W. by the head waters of Salem and Oldman's creeks. Daretown, Centreville, and Pittstown, are villages of the t-ship; the last two of which are post-towns. There were in 1832, in the t-ship, 1 Presbyterian, 1 Baptist, and 3 Methodist churches; 161 householders, whose ratables did not exceed $30 in value; 510 taxables, 6 stores, 2 grist mills, 5 saw mills, 2 fulling mills, 1 large tan yard, 5 cider distilleries, 525 horses and mules, and 933 neat cattle, above 3 years of age. The t-ship paid tax for t-ship purposes, $300; county, $921 92; state tax, $294 42. By the act of 19th Nov., 1821, and its supplement, 19th Nov., 1823, a township called Centreville, was taken from this, but was returned to it, by act 18th Feb., 1829.

Pittstown, p-t., of Salem co.; centrally situate in Pittsgrove t-ship, 16 miles E. of Salem; 180 N. E. of W. C., and 74 S. from Trenton; contains 15 dwellings, 2 taverns, and 2 stores, a grist mill, saw mill, school house, and masonic hall. The soil around it, light and sandy.

Pittstown, Alexandria t-ship, Hunterdon co., on the line of Kingwood t-ship, and on a tributary of the S. branch of the Raritan river, 8 miles N. W. of Flemington, 31 from Trenton, and 190 from W. C.; contains 1 tavern, 1 store, a grist mill, and between 15 and 20 dwellings. The soil around it is clay, cold and poor; surface hilly.

Plainfield, a large and thriving village of Westfield t-ship, Essex co., on Green Brook, the line between that and Somerset co. 211 miles N. E. from W. C., 65 from Philadelphia, 45 from Trenton, 20 S. W. from Newark, 16 from Elizabethtown, 25 from New York, and 11 N. E. from New Brunswick;—on a plain of very level land, between 2 and 3 miles wide, and about 11 long; contains 1 Presbyterian, 1 Baptist, and 1 Methodist church, 2 Friends' meeting houses, (Hicksite and Orthodox) 2 grist mills, 1 saw mill, 4 stores, 3 schools, 2 clergymen, 1 lawyer, 2 physicians, 2 taverns, 4 stores, 13 master hatters, who manufacture about $75,000 worth of hats annually; 5 master tailors, employing 70 hands, who work for the southern market; a fire engine, and company, a mutual insurance company, esta-

2 E

blished in 1832, which in a few months, executed policies to the amount of more than $150,000; and 120 dwellings; a ladies' library, an apprentices' library. A four-horse mail stage, to New York, three times a week, and as often to Philadelphia, on alternate days, runs through the village. The country around the town is rich, well cultivated, and healthy; the water good, and the society moral and religious, and ambitious of improvement. The neighbouring mountain, about a mile N. of the town, affords an abundant supply of cheap fuel, and screens the valley from the violence of the N. and N. W. winds; and gives a very pleasing prospect to the S. and E., over a space of 30 miles.

Plainsborough, hamlet of South Brunswick t-ship, Middlesex co., 14 miles S. W. of New Brunswick, 14 S. E. from Trenton; contains a tavern, store, and 8 or 10 dwellings. Soil, light, gravelly and sterile.

Plainville, Montgomery t-ship, Somerset co., 8 miles S. W. from Somerville; contains a tavern, store, and 4 or 5 dwellings.

Pleasant Grove, on Schooley's mountain, Washington t-ship, Morris co., on the turnpike road from Morristown to Easton, 21 miles from the former, and 20 from the latter; contains a tavern, store, and several dwellings, and a very neat stone church, belonging to Presbyterians. The surrounding country is pleasant, and is improving much by the use of lime; the soil is a stiff clay.

Pleasant Mills, p-t. of Galloway t-ship, Gloucester co., on the Atsion river, 30 miles S. E. from Woodbury, 65 from Trenton, and 173 from W. C.; contains a tavern, 2 stores, a glass factory, belonging to Messrs. Coffan & Co., a cotton factory, with 3000 spindles, and from 20 to 30 dwellings.

Pleasant Valley, of the South mountain, Mansfield t-ship, Warren co., through which runs a small tributary of the Pohatcong creek. The soil here, as in other valleys of the t-ship, is of primitive limestone. There is a small hamlet in the valley, at which there is a grist mill, and several dwellings, upon the turnpike road to Easton.

Pleasant Valley, Randolph t-ship, Morris co., through which flows Dell's brook. The sides of the vale are of gentle ascent; part of the land good, and well cultivated.

Pluckemin, p-t. of Bedminster t-ship, Somerset co., 6 miles N. W. from Somerville, at the foot of Basking Ridge, 205 miles N. E. from W. C., and 39 from Trenton; contains 1 tavern, 2 stores, and from 25 to 30 dwellings.

Pochuck Mountain, on the W. side of Vernon t-ship, Sussex co., extends about 8 miles northwardly. Along its eastern foot runs the Pochuck turnpike road, leading from Hamburg towards the state of New York. The mountain is composed of primitive rock, of which hornblende is a principal constituent. Its base is surrounded with primitive limestone.

Pohatcong Creek, Warren co., rises near the N. E. boundary of Mansfield t-ship, and flows S. W. through that and Greenwich t-ships, by a course of three or four and twenty miles to the Delaware river, 8 or 9 miles below Philipsburg. This fine stream flows through and drains a wide and fertile valley of primitive limestone, which is very well cultivated, and produces large quantities of wheat. There is a fine view of the valley from the south-eastern acclivity of Scott's Mountain, on the road to Oxford furnace; the creek runs somewhat parallel with the Musconetcong, both following the range of the mountains, and at their mouths are scarce two miles asunder.

Point Comfort, west cape of Sandy Hook bay, Middleton t-ship, Monmouth co., projecting into the Raritan bay, 8 miles S. E. of Perth Amboy, and about an equal distance from Sandy Hook light-house.

Pole Tavern, a noted tavern and cluster of houses in Pitsgrove t-ship, about 4 miles N. W. of Pittstown, and 14 E. of Salem.

Pompeston Creek, mill stream of Chester t-ship, Burlington co., flowing by a N. W. course of about 5 miles, and emptying into the Delaware river, nearly opposite to the mouth of the Pennepack creek.

Pompton t-ship, Bergen co., bounded N. by Orange co., New York; E. by Franklin t-ship; S. by Pequannock and Jefferson t-ships, Morris co.; and W. by Hardiston and Vernon t-ships, Sussex co. Centrally distant N. W. from Hackensack, 23 miles; greatest length E. and W. 14 miles; breadth N. and S. 12 miles; area, about 70,000 acres, of which about 55,000 are unimproved, and much of it covered with forest; surface, very hilly; the Ramapo mountain, extending over the eastern boundary, and Bear Foot mountain along the western; the intervening space is broken into knolls of various sizes and shapes. The soil is generally clay and loam, but some primitive limestone appears near Mackepin lake. In these hills is found an extensive deposit of iron, in the same vein which runs through Schooley's mountain. Ringwood river bathes the western base of the Ramapo mountain; Long Pond or Greenwood lake, which crosses the northern boundary from New York, sends a tributary to it called Long Pond river. Dunker, Buck, Cedar, Hanks, and Mackepin ponds, in the south-west part of the t-ship, give their surplus waters to the Pequannock, which, under the name of Pompton river, flows along the southern boundary; Long House creek flows northerly through the north-west angle. Population in 1830, 3085. In 1832, the t-ship contained 750 taxables, 229 householders, whose ratables did not exceed $30; 79 single men, 6 stores, 15 grist mills 14 saw mills, 16 forge fires, 2 fulling mills, 20 tan vats, 2 distilleries, 519 horses and mules, and 1816 neat cattle over 3 years of age; and paid state tax, $340 13; county, $649 17.

The Morris canal crosses the Pompton river about 2 miles above its mouth in this t-ship, by a wooden aqueduct 236 feet long, supported by 9 stone piers.

Pompton Plain, lies between the Pompton mountain and the Preakness hills, and is nearly 20 miles in circumference, with a variable breadth seldom exceeding four miles. It is a fresh water alluvion, and strata of gravel, sand, and clay, without rocks in place, are uniformly found here wherever wells have been dug. It was, probably, at some remote period, the bed of a lake. The Pequannock, Ringwood, and Ramapo rivers, uniting at the head of the Plain, form the Pompton river, which flows along its eastern side to the Passaic, about 8 miles. The southern, and much of the western part of the plain is marshy, and embraces about 1500 acres of peat ground, the fuel from which, so far as can be determined by a ditch running four miles through it, appears to be good. In the southern part of the plain, good granular argillaceous oxide of iron, or pea ore is raised from a space of about 200 acres. There is a straggling village upon the plain, comprising a Dutch Reformed church, a tavern, 3 stores, an academy, and about 30 dwellings: and at the head of the plain is

Pompton, p-t., 18 miles N. E. of Morristown, 236 from W. C., and 70 from Trenton; containing a tavern, store, grist mill, and 12 or 15 dwellings, and a Dutch Reformed church. (See *Ryersons*.)

Pompton Mountain, an angular hill, of Pequannock t-ship, Morris co., bounding the Pompton plains, W. and N. W. The sides of the angle are respectively about 4 miles long.

Pond Creek, Downe t-ship, Cumberland co., a short inlet to the marsh on the W. side of Maurice river cove.

Pond Creek, a small stream flowing from Lower t-ship, Cape May co., into the Delaware bay, near 2 miles N. of the Light-house.

Pond Run, small tributary of the

Assunpink creek, Nottingham t-ship, Burlington co., unites with its recipient, after a N. W. course of about 5 miles.

Ponds; name given to a neighbourhood of the S. W. part of Franklin t-ship, Bergen co.; so called, possibly, from a small lake. There is a German Reformed church here, also called Ponds.

Port Elizabeth, p-t. of Maurice river t-ship, Cumberland co., upon the Manamuskin creek, near its confluence with the Maurice river, about 14 miles from the Delaware bay, 16 S. E. from Bridgeton, 85 from Trenton, and 182 from W. C.; contains from 80 to 100 dwellings, 1 tavern, 4 stores, a Baptist church, an academy—a commodious building; some large glass works, managed by a company of Germans, under the firm of Getz, Zinger, and Co., at which large quantities of window glass and hollow ware are made. The hands of this establishment speak the German language altogether, and are remarkable for their cultivation of music. A considerable lumber trade is carried on from the town, and some ship building is done there. The town is 16 miles from the Delaware bay, by the sinuosities of Maurice river, and 8 by land. The river is navigable for vessels of 120 tons. There are 4 grist, and 3 saw mills within 3 miles of the town. Much business is done here in wood, lumber, and rails. The town is built on good land, and is surrounded by very valuable meadows, worth $100 the acre.

Port Norris, landing and storehouse, with a tavern, store, and 6 or 8 dwellings, on the west side of Maurice river, about 10 miles from the mouth, 5 miles from Dividing Creek village, and 22 from Bridgeton.

Pottersville, p-t. of Hunterdon co., on the line separating Readington from Tewkesbury t-ship, and on the turnpike road leading from Somerville to Philipsburg, 10 miles N. E. from Flemington, 43 miles from Trenton, and 211 from W. C.; con-

tains a tavern, store, and a few dwellings.

Potter's Falls, on the Lamington river, at the angle of junction of Hunterdon, Morris, and Somerset cos.

Poverty Beach, on the Atlantic ocean, immediately north of Cape May Island, Lower t-ship, Cape May co., extends about three miles in length by half a mile in breadth.

Powershon, small village of Bloomfield t-ship, Essex co., 5 miles north of Newark; contains a school house and several dwellings. The poorhouse of the t-ship is in the valley near it.

Powerville, p-t. of Pequannock t-ship, Morris co., in the valley of the Rockaway river, 10 miles N. E. from Morristown, 234 from W. C., and 68 from Trenton; contains a tavern, 2 stores, a forge, a grist and saw mill, and from 10 to 15 dwellings. Country around rough and sterile.

Prallsville, p-t. of Amwell t-ship, Hunterdon co., on the river Delaware, 10 miles S. W. from Flemington, 20 N. from Trenton, and 174 from W. C.; contains 1 store, 1 tavern, some 6 or 8 dwellings, and a grist mill, at the mouth of the Wickhechecoke creek. There is a fine bridge here over the Delaware, erected on stone piers, by an incorporated company. The surrounding country is hilly.

Preakness Mountain, a distinguished hill of Saddle River t-ship, Bergen co., commencing about three miles N. W. from Paterson, and running in a semicircular direction several miles. It is formed by sandstone surmounted by trap rock, and embosoms an extensive valley.

Preakness Brook, Saddle River t-ship, Bergen co., which, after a south course of about 6 miles, flows into the Passaic river, about 2 miles above the Little Falls. Preakness Dutch Reformed church, is in the valley of this stream, near its source.

Primrose Creek, tributary of the Passaic river, Morris t-ship, Morris co., has a course of about six miles from its source to its recipient.

Prospect Plains, level tract of country extending between Cranberry Brook and Manalapan Brook, with a light sandy soil, in South Amboy t-ship, Middlesex co.

Princeton, p-t. and borough, partly in Montgomery t-ship, Somerset co., and partly in Windsor t-ship, Middlesex co., on the main road between New York and Philadelphia, 50 miles from the one, and 40 from the other, 11 from Trenton, 25 from New Brunswick, and 177 from W. C.; situated in a very pleasant country of red shale and alluvion, and remarkable for the salubrity of its climate, the beauty of its villas, and the neatness, generally, of its buildings. It was incorporated as a borough in 1813, and contains about 185 dwelling houses, and at least 1100 inhabitants, exclusive of the youth connected with the public institutions, of whom there are, at present, (1833) about 350.

The Delaware and Raritan canal runs within a half mile of the borough, and has already contributed, in no small degree, to its prosperity. The office of the company is established here.

Besides the buildings belonging to the literary institutions, (for these see pages 84, 85,) there are in Princeton, a Presbyterian church, an Episcopal church, and two other houses for public worship, belonging to the Presbyterian society; one of which is for the use of the coloured population. The literary institutions of Princeton are a college, a theological seminary, three classical schools, two schools for the instruction of young ladies, and three or four common schools; all independent of each other.

The name of Princeton is associated, not only with the literary reputation of our country, but also with her struggle for independence; since, in the immediate vicinity of this place, was fought the memorable battle of January 3d, 1777, in which the British army was routed by the Americans, under the command of General Washington, and in which the lamented Mercer was mortally wounded. A large painting commemorative of these events, is suspended in the chapel of the college.

Quarter's Inlet, from the Atlantic ocean to Reed's bay, between Brigantine beach on the east, and Peter's beach on the west, Galloway t-ship, Gloucester co.

Quaker Bridge, over Batsto river, Washington t-ship, Burlington co., 6 miles S. E. of Shamong village, and 4 from Atsion Furnace. There is a tavern here.

Quakertown. (See *Fairview*.)

Quinton's Bridge, small village and p-t. on Alloways creek, in Upper Alloways t-ship, Salem co., 5 miles S. E. of Sâlem, 174 N. E. from W. C., and 68 S. from Trenton; contains some 12 or 15 dwellings, 1 tavern, and 2 stores. It is a landing at which much wood is delivered for the Philadelphia market. The bridge is noted in the county for a massacre of some militia, by a party of British troops, while on a foraging party, during the occupancy of Philadelphia by Sir William Howe, in the revolutionary war.

Raccoon Creek, rises in Franklin t-ship, Gloucester co., and flows thence N. W. through Woolwich t-ship, by a course of 17 miles to the River Delaware, opposite to Shiver's island. It is navigable for sloops 7 or 8 miles to Swedesborough, and for boats to Mullica Hill, 5 miles further.

Rahway River, called by the aborigines Rahawack, *anglicé*, Man's River, rises in the valley between First and Second mountains, Orange t-ship, Essex co., and flows thence S. W. and S. to Springfield, where it receives several considerable tributaries; thence by a south course of about 8 miles it passes by Rahway village, where it meets the tide; and thence by a south-east course of about 5 miles, dividing Middlesex from Essex co., it unites with Staten Island Sound, 9 or 10 miles N. E. of Perth Amboy. It is navigable to Rahway village for vessels of 80 tons burden, and receives at the village the Middle or Robinson's branch, and the South branch. Upon these branches there are severable valuable mill seats, and on the main branch between Springfield and tide-water, there are 20 mills employed in grinding grain, sawing lumber, and manufacturing paper, cotton, and wool. On the river, there is some of the best brick clay of the United States; and the manufacture of bricks was, at one period, so great here, as to employ steadily about 40 sloops in their transport to New York. Owing to the scarcity of fuel, this manufacture has declined.

Rahway, p-t., including what was formerly called Bridgetown, lies upon the Rahway river, at the head of tide, five miles from its mouth, partly in Woodbridge t-ship, Middlesex co., and partly in Rahway t-ship, Essex co.; distant N. E. 205 miles from W. C., 39 from Trenton, 11 from Brunswick S. W., 10 from Newark, 18 from Jersey City, and 8 from Amboy; consists of four detached villages, Rahway Proper, north of Robinson's branch, Union, Bridgetown, and Leesville, on the south. This diversity of names is productive of some irregularity in the transit of letters to the town, and has induced a wish to change the name; and some of the inhabitants propose to substitute that of " *Athens*." There are here, about 350 dwellings, containing, it is said, 3000 inhabitants, mostly of New England origin ; this would give a greater average number of inhabitants to a house, than in any other district of the state; an elegant Presbyterian church erected in 1831, a Methodist, Baptist, and an African Episcopal church, and two Quaker meeting houses pertaining to the Orthodox and Hicksite parties, respectively. The citizens, with enterprise and liberality worthy of high commendation, have established, under the general incorporation law of the state, a library company, and a Sunday school association, which has erected a commodious house, sup-

posed to be the first designed expressly and exclusively for Sunday schools in the world; and a second Sunday school house is about to be built by the Methodists here. A joint stock company have reared the " *Athenian Academy*," a noble building 68 feet long by 36 wide, two stories high ; the upper used as a lecture room; costing 5000 dollars, and which was opened for literary exercises 12th August, 1833, by a neat and exciting address from the president of the trustees of the institution, Mr. Robert Lee. The tutors of this seminary have fixed salaries, and are thus relieved from the anxiety and distraction of mind arising from uncertain and precarious compensation. But we may observe also, that the stimulus to exertion and the attainment of excellence, has been in a great measure thereby removed. The professors in the schools of Germany, certainly inferior to none in the world, are supported by their pupils, whose number depends on the reputation of the teachers. Perhaps the best mode of compensation, is that which, providing certain subsistence, leaves merit to find its own reward from popular favour. " The Athenian Academy", had 106 pupils in the first week of its existence. Besides this institution, Rahway has six common public schools, and a very large and commodious literary institution, built and directed by Mr. Samuel Oliver. There are also in the village a bank, called the " Farmers and Mechanics," incorporated in 1828, with an authorized capital of $200,000, of which 60,000 have been paid in ; a fire engine, a mutual insurance company, and a printing office ; from which issues a weekly paper, called the Rahway Advocate ; 25 stores, 4 taverns, (and be it remembered, 10 schools,) a large building called " The Taurino Factory," originally designed for the manufacture of coarse cloth and carpets from cow's hair, but about to be employed in the colouring and printing of silk ; the " Mammoth Saw Mill," said to be the largest in the state; belonging to Mr. Joseph O. Lufberry, and for the supply of which, there was in the river, in September, 1833, more than $30,000 worth of pine and oak timber; a steam-boat company, whose operations will probably be superseded by the Jersey rail-road now making; 5 lumber and coal yards, 1 soap and candle manufactory, 3 bakeries, 2 watchmakers, 4 millinery shops, and extensive manufactories of hats, boots, shoes, carriages, cabinet furniture, and clothing for export; clock, earthenware, coach-lace, plated ware for carriages, &c. &c. On the Rahway river, some distance above the town, are extensive cotton bleaching and printing works, employing about 100 hands. The amount of capital vested in manufactures here and in the neighbourhood, is estimated at 356,000 dollars, and the surplus product of the town and its vicinity, at from 1,000,000 to 1,200,000 annually. Thriving as this place certainly is, new stimulus will be given to its activity by the rail-road now being made from "Jersey City" to New Brunswick, which will pass through the village, and thus bring it within an hour's journey of New York. The town has now communication thrice daily with New York, by stages and steam-boats via Elizabethtown Point, and also by other conveyances.

The soil, for many miles around the town, is well adapted to grass and grain, consisting of a fertile loam resting on sand, gravel and red shale, and much hay and grain are annually sent to market. In 1830, the population of Woodbridge township was 3909, and of Rahway township, 1983, making in the two townships in which the village lies, 5952 souls. It is said, the population of these townships, now, 1833, amounts to 10,000; but, though the increase is certainly great, we fear it has been overrated.

We insert *verbatim*, the following remark, which needs no comment, made by a highly respectable inhabitant of the town. "Leesville, at the southern part of the town, takes its name from a family named Lee, who have long resided there, and furnished our most enterprising and public spirited citizens; and as merchants and manufacturers, were the first to lead the way to our extensive trade with the southern states, and who have, by their industry and perseverance, liberality and enlightened views in other respects, greatly added to the prosperity of the town."

Rahway t-ship, Essex co., bounded N. W. by Union, and N. E. by Elizabeth t-ship; E. by Staten Island Sound; S. by Woodbridge t-ship, Middlesex co.; and W. by Westfield t-ship. Centrally distant, S. W. from Newark, 9 miles. Greatest length, E. and W., 8; breadth, N. and S., 4½ miles; area, 10,000 acres; surface, level; soil, red shale and well cultivated. Drained by the Rahway river, which runs S. centrally through the township, and bounds it on the S. E.; by Robinson's brook, a tributary of that stream; and by Moss's creek, which, after a crooked course of about 7 miles, empties into the Sound, on the N. E. boundary. Rahway post-town, is the only village of the township, and one-half of that is in the adjoining county. Population in 1830, 1983. In 1832, there were in the township, 375 taxables, 177 householders, whose ratables did not exceed $30; 117 single men, 5 merchants, 6 grist mills, 4 saw mills, 1 paper mill, 1 printing and bleaching establishment, 254 horses and mules, and 711 neat cattle, over 3 years of age; and it paid state tax, $212 98; county, $557 25; poor, $600; road, $400.

Ramapo River, rises in the recesses of Sterling mountain, Orange co., New York; and flows thence by a S. course, dividing the Ramapo mountain, to the boundary between that state and New Jersey, 14 miles; thence, deflecting S. W. it follows the base of the mountain, 13 miles to Pompton river, about 2 miles below Ryerson's, forming in part, the boundary between Franklin and Pompton townships. It is a fine mill stream, receiving several small tributaries from the east, which also move mills.

Ramapo Mountain, Bergen co., is a high hill of angular form, with its base upon Ramapo river, in the state of New York, and enclosed by that river on the east, and Ringwood river on the west; partly in Pompton and partly in Franklin townships. Its breadth, at the base, is about 5 miles, and its length about 10. Its height under 1000 feet, composed of primitive rock, and covered with wood.

Ramsaysburg, p-t. of Knowlton t-ship, Warren co., on the bank of the Delaware, 215 miles N. E. from W. C., and 59 from Trenton, and 5 miles N. from Belvidere. Contains a tavern, store, an Episcopal church, and some half dozen dwellings.

Rancocus Creek, rises by two branches; the north, on the western border of Monmouth county, flowing a little north of west, about 28 miles, passing by the town of Mount Holly, to which place it is navigable; the south branch, composed of several streams, which have their source in Burlington county, and flow northwestward, uniting at Eayrstown, and thence running by Lumberton, to the junction with the north branch, four miles below that town. This branch is navigable to Eayrstown. The united streams continue a N. W. course for about 7 miles, to the Delaware. The wood, timber, and produce of a large extent of country find their way to market by this stream.

Randolph t-ship, Morris co., bounded N. by Rockaway river, which separates it from Pequannock t-ship; E. by Hanover and Morris t-ships; S. by Mendham; S. E. by Chester, and W. by Roxbury t-ships. Centrally distant, N. W., from Morristown, 7 miles; greatest length, 7; breadth, 5 miles; area, 18,000 acres; surface, mountainous—Schooley's mountain, filling the northern part, and Trowbridge mountain crossing

the southern. In the valley, between them, rises and flows Den branch of Rockaway river. Black river has one of its sources in the northern mountain, near the seat of the honourable Mahlon Dickerson, Esq., near which also rises Dell's brook, a tributary of the Rockaway, flowing eastward through Pleasant valley. The great bed of magnetic iron ore which may be traced in the direction of the stratification from the White Hills, in New Hampshire, terminates in this township near the Black river, upon its western boundary. On this bed the mine of Mr. Dickerson is remarkable for the abundance and excellent quality of its product, and the skill with which it is wrought; and the ore is transported in wagons and by the Morris canal, to the furnaces and forges, not only of this county, but of the neighbouring counties and states. This mine has been wrought many years. Shafts have been sunk to the depth of 70 feet, and drifts driven more than 120 feet. There is carbonate of lime mingled with the iron, which renders any other flux unnecessary in smelting. In 1830, the population of the township was 1443 souls; and in 1832, the township contained 324 taxables, 78 householders, whose ratables did not exceed $30; 40 single men, 5 stores, 6 saw and 4 grist mills, 1 furnace, 1 forge, 1 oil mill, 1 fulling mill, 1 carding machine, 35 tan vats, 250 horses, and 770 neat cattle over three years of age, 4 distilleries; and it paid state tax, $156 70; county tax, $350 82; poor tax, $800; road tax, $800.

Raritan River, is formed by three great branches, the North, the South, and the Millstone river. (For a description of the last, see article *Millstone River*.) The North Branch rises in the valley N. of Trowbridge mountain, in Randolph t-ship, Morris co., and flows S. through that and Somerset co., to the main branch in Bridgewater t-ship, of the latter, about 4 miles W. of Somerville, receiving in its course, Black or Lamington river, a stream longer and larger than itself, and several smaller tributaries. Passing through a mountainous country, it is a rapid stream, with a pretty direct course, and gives motion to several mills. The South Branch has its source in Budd's pond or lake, on the summit of Schooley's mountain, and within three miles, becomes an efficient mill stream, turning several water works. It flows by a S. W. course, through the chain of hills of the South mountain to Clinton; thence deflects easterly through the same chain, passing within a mile and a half of Flemington, to the western boundary of Somerset co.; thence turned to the N. W. by the Nashanic mountain, it receives the North Branch, and by an easterly course, traverses that county to the eastern boundary: flowing within two miles of Somerville, and receiving the Millstone river from the south, about three miles from that town. From Bound Brook it reassumes a S. E. course, and forms the boundary between Somerset and Middlesex counties, to New Brunswick; thence through the latter county by a winding course in the salt marsh, it meets the ocean at Perth Amboy. From this point the Raritan bay extends to the lighthouse on Sandy Hook, 14 miles. The length of the river is from Amboy to New Brunswick, by the windings 15 miles; from New Brunswick to the mouth of the Millstone 10; from the mouth of the Millstone to the mouth of the North Branch 7; and from thence to its source, 42 miles; in all 74 miles. It may be navigated by small boats beyond Bound Brook; but we believe this is never attempted above New Brunswick. To that town, sloops, schooners, and steam-boats of considerable burden ascend. The Delaware and Raritan canal enters the valley of the river at the mouth of the Millstone, and terminates at New Brunswick. Immediately above Brunswick the river may be forded at low water, when below the town a 20 gun ship may securely ride. In high tide, however, sloops may pass a mile above the ford. The bridge opposite the city, near 1000 feet in length, wide enough for two carriages to pass abreast, with a foot way, built of wood, on 11 stone piers beside the abutments, was first completed in 1796; and rebuilt by a joint stock company, in 1811.

Raritan Bay, extends from the mouth of Raritan river, at Perth Amboy eastward, 14 miles to the ocean, at Sandy Hook, and is about 2 miles wide at Amboy Point, but increases in width between Sandy Hook and the Narrows at Fort Richmond on Staten Island. There are two channels through the bay. The northern carries from 24 to 28 feet water to Amboy; the southern about 12 feet. The bay abounds with oysters, and the lands beneath the water, claimed by the state, are in part divided into small lots, and granted on rent (badly paid) to the fishermen. More than 250 acres have been thus leased, on which oysters are planted from time to time, whose increase gives large annual profits to those concerned in the fishery. (See *Perth Amboy.*)

Raritan Landing, on the left bank of the Raritan river, at the head of tide water, and two miles above New Brunswick, in Piscataway township, Middlesex co. This is a place of considerable business; contains some 20 dwellings, 2 stores and a tavern, chiefly on the primitive bank of the river, which is here high, and having between it and the water, a broad bottom of rich alluvial land. There is a wooden bridge here across the river.

Rattle Snake Run, branch of Mill creek, Fairfield t-ship, Cumberland co., uniting with its recipient at the village of Fairton.

Readington t-ship, Hunterdon co., bounded N. by Tewkesbury t-ship; E. by Bridgewater t-ship, Somerset co.; S. and S. W. by Amwell t-ship; W. by Kingwood, and N. W. by Bethlehem t-ship. Centrally distant N. E. from Flemington 8 miles; length N. and S. 12 miles; breadth

E. and W. 7½ miles; surface, hilly, except on the S. E. where it is level; soil, red shale, clay, and loam. The South Branch of the Raritan river, flows on the S. W., S., and S. E. of the t-ship, and receives from it Campbell's and Holland's Brooks. The northern part is drained by Rockaway creek and its branches. Population in 1830, 2102. In 1832 there were in the t-ship 7 merchants, 5 saw mills, 7 grist mills, 6 distilleries, 2 carding machines, and 2 fulling mills, 705 horses and mules, 1200 neat cattle over 3 years of age. The t-ship paid state and county taxes, $1323 75. White House and Potterstown are post-towns of the t-ship.

Recklesstown, p-t. of Chesterfield t-ship, Burlington co., 12 miles N. E. of Mount Holly, 5 S. E. from Bordentown, 11 from Trenton, and 177 from W. C.; contains a tavern, store, and 10 or 12 dwellings, in a very fertile country of sandy loam.

Red Bank, p-t. of Shrewsbury t-ship, Monmouth co., on the south shore of the Nevisink river, 46 miles E. from Trenton, 13 miles N. E. from Freehold, 3 N. from Shrewsbury; contains within a circle of a mile in diameter about 100 dwellings, 3 taverns and 4 stores. The surrounding country is fertile and pleasant; a steam-boat runs between it and New York, and many persons from that city spend the hot weather of summer here; finding very agreeable entertainment in the families of respectable farmers, in visits to the sea shore, in fishing, and other rural sports. A bridge near 300 feet in length, resting on wooden piers, has been thrown across the river here, at the expense of the county.

Red Bank, on the Delaware river, between Big Timber and Woodbury creeks, named from the colour of the earth of which it is composed; remarkable for a fort called Mercer, erected here during the revolutionary war, and its brave and successful defence by Col. Green, against a detachment from the British army, commanded by Count Donop, on the 22d

Oct. 1777; in which the Count and many officers were made prisoners, and a lieutenant colonel, 3 captains, 4 lieutenants, and 70 privates were killed. In commemoration of this event, a monument of handsome grey marble has been reared, bearing the following inscription.

THIS MONUMENT
was erected on the 22d October, 1829,
To transmit to posterity, a grateful remembrance of the
Patriotism and Gallantry of
Lieut. Col. Christopher Green, who with
400 men, conquered the Hessian army
of 2000 troops, then in the British
service, at the Red Bank, on
the 22d October, 1777.
Among the wounded was found their
commander,
COUNT DONOP,
who died of his wounds, and whose body
is interred near the spot where he fell.
A number of the
New Jersey and Pennsylvania
volunteers,
Being desirous to perpetuate the memory
of the distinguished officers and soldiers, who fought and bled in
the glorious struggle for
American Independence,
HAVE
Erected this Monument, on the 22d day
of October, Anno Domini, 1829.

Red Lion, hamlet of Northampton t-ship, Burlington co., 9 miles S. W. from Mount Holly.

Reed's Bay, a salt marsh lake of Galloway t-ship, Gloucester co., about 2 miles in length, and 1 in breadth, communicating with Absecum bay, and with the ocean, by a channel flowing through Absecum inlet.

Repaupo Creek, Gloucester co., rises on the line separating Greenwich from Woolwich t-ship, and flows N. W. 7 or 8 miles, to the Delaware river, opposite to Chester Island.

Rice's Pond, Knowlton t-ship, Warren co., source of Beaver Brook, which flows thence to Pequest creek, by a S. W. course of 10 miles, turning several mills in its course.

Ringwood River, rises in Sterling pond, Sterling mountain, state of New York, and runs by a southerly course of 16 miles, through Pompton t-ship, Bergen co., to the Pequannock creek, forming with it Pompton river. It is a rapid mill stream, and receives several tributaries, which also turn mills.

Ringwood, village, on the above stream, and within a mile and a half of the state line; contains a blast furnace, a forge, a store, and three dwellings beside those for the workmen at the iron works. Surrounding country, mountainous and barren; distant 24 miles from Hackensack.

Ringoestown, p-t. of Amwell t-ship, Hunterdon co., 6 miles S. of Flemington, 17 N. of Trenton, and 176 N. E. from W. C.; contains 1 tavern, 3 stores, 1 Presbyterian church, an academy, and 26 dwellings, saddlery, and smith shop, cotton and woollen factory, and grist mill. This is a delightful village, lying in the valley immediately at the foot of the Rock mountain, and upon a soil of loam, composed of red shale and clay, very deep, and highly cultivated in grain and grass. Lands immediately round the village, readily bring $100 the acre, and those more distant in the valley, $50 the acre.

Roadstown, p-t. of Cumberland co., on the line dividing Stow Creek and Hopewell t-ships, 5 miles W. of Bridgeton, 179 N. E. of W. C., and 73 by post-route from Trenton; contains 20 dwellings, 1 tavern, 2 stores, and a large Baptist church of brick. The town is peopled principally by the cultivators of the soil; the soil is good loam, and improving by the use of marl.

Robinhood, branch of Maurice river, a small tributary, flowing from the east into the river, about 2 miles below Maul's bridge.

Robin's, branch of Batsto river, rises in Northampton t-ship, Burlington co., and flows S. W. about 10 miles, to its recipient in Washington t-ship. It is a mill stream.

Robinson's Brook, tributary of Rahway river, rises on the S. W. border of Rahway t-ship, and flows E. by a course of about 6 miles, to its recipient at Bridgetown or Rahway.

Rockaway river, Morris co., rises by two principal branches in the mountains of Pequannock and Jefferson t-ships; the one flowing through Longwood valley, and the other through Green Pond valley, and commingling about a mile S. E. of Mount Pleasant. The united streams, thence, flow through a deep and rapid channel, by a very serpentine course of about 20 miles, to the Passaic river. The volume and fall of this stream adapt it admirably to hydraulic purposes, and there are many mills upon it, principally for working of iron, as at Dover, Rockaway village, Boonton, &c.

Rockaway Valley, of Hanover and Pequannock t-ships, Morris co., north of Trowbridge mountain; a narrow vale crossed by the Rockaway river.

Rockaway, p-t. of Morris co., on both banks of the Rockaway river, 8 miles N. of Morristown, 229 N. E. from W. C., and 63 from Trenton; contains 1 rolling mill, 2 forges, 1 grist and saw mill, 4 stores, 1 tavern, a Presbyterian or Dutch Reformed church, and from 20 to 25 dwellings. The Morris canal passes through the village.

Rocky Hill, one of the chain of trap rock hills, which extend from the Delaware, below Lambertsville, N. E. across the state, in Amwell t-ship, Hunterdon co., and in Montgomery t-ship, Somerset co., about 2 miles N. of Princeton. The surface of this hill is rugged; soil, deep clay, covered with heavy timber. It extends E. and W. about 6 miles, to the Millstone river, which seems to have forced a passage through it.

Rocky Hill, p-t., Montgomery t-ship, Somerset co., at the N. E. base of Rocky hill, on the Millstone river, and turnpike road from New Brunswick to Lambertsville, 12 miles S. W. of Somerville, 185 N. E. from W. C., and 14 from Trenton; contains a grist and saw mill, a woollen manufactory, 2 stores, 2 taverns, and 12 or 15 dwellings.

Rockaway Creek, Hunterdon co., rises by two branches; one from the northern part of Tewkesbury t-ship, and the other from the western border of Readington t-ship, uniting in the latter t-ship, and thence flowing into Lamington river, or the north branch of the Raritan. By its longest arm the stream has a course of 12 miles. It is a fine, rapid mill stream.

Rock Brook, tributary of Beden's Brook, rises in the Nashanic mountain, Amwell t-ship, Hunterdon co., and by a S. E. course of about 6 miles, unites with its recipient near the centre of Montgomery t-ship, Somerset co.

Rock Mountain, fills the S. E. angle of Amwell t-ship, and the N. E. angle of Hopewell t-ship, Hunterdon co., and extends N. E. into Somerset co., having a length of about 10 miles, with a very irregular breadth. On the north it sends forth tributaries to the south branch of the Raritan river, and on the south to the Millstone river. The hill is of trap rock, imposed on old, red sandstone.

Rocksbury, village of Oxford t-sp, Warren co., 5 miles S. of Belvidere, upon the road leading to Philipsburg; contains a tavern, store, 2 grist and 1 oil mill, an air furnace for small castings, and from 15 to 20 dwellings.

Rocktown, small hamlet, of Amwell t-ship, Hunterdon co., 7 miles S. of Flemington; contains 1 tavern, 1 store, and some 2 or 3 dwellings. It lies in the pass through the Rock mountain, and is named from the abundance of large rocks around it.

Rocky Brook, a tributary of Millstone river, rises in Upper Freehold t-ship, Monmouth co., above Imlay's mill, and flows by a N. W. course through East Windsor t-ship, Middlesex co., about 9 miles to its recipient, on the boundary of South Brunswick t-ship, passing through Hightstown, and turning several mills.

Rotten Pond, covering about 150 acres, on the boundary between Franklin and Pompton t-ships, Bergen co., and on the Ramapo mountain.

Round Valley, in the S. E. angle of Lebanon t-ship, Hunterdon co., nearly surrounded by mountains; drained by Piscot Brook, a tributary

of the south branch of the Raritan river.

Rowandtown, small village of Newton t-ship, Gloucester co., on the road from Camden to Haddonfield, about 4 miles from the former, and 2 from the latter; contains some 6 or 8 dwellings, and several mechanics; surrounded by a country of sandy loam.

Roxbury t-ship, Morris co., bounded N. and W. by the Hopatcong lake and Musconetcong river, which separates it from Warren and Sussex counties; N. E. by Jefferson t-ship; E. by Randolph; S. E. by Chester; and S. W. by Washington t-ships. Centrally distant from Morristown N. W. 14 miles; greatest length N. and S. 12, breadth E. and W. 10 miles; area, 35,840 acres; surface, generally mountainous; but the Sucka-sunny Plains extend some miles in length, by two or three in breadth. Schooley's mountain fills the greater portion of its area. On its summit lies Budd's Pond, two miles in length by one in breadth, whence flows a tributary of the south branch of the Raritan river; the main stream of which has its source in a small pond, two miles north of Drakesville, in this t-ship. Black river forms, in part, its eastern boundary. On the mountain the soil is clay and loam, but limestone is even there mixed with the granitic rock, and is found in the valley on the S. W. Flanders, Sucka-sunny, Drakestown, and Drakesville, are villages of the t-ship; at the two first of which are post-offices. Population in 1830, 2262. In 1832 the t-ship contained 410 taxables, 92 householders, whose ratables did not exceed $30 in value; 44 single men, 4 stores, 9 saw, 10 grist, and 2 fulling mills, 16 tan vats, 8 distilleries, 15 chairs and sulkies; and it paid state tax, $261 07; county tax, $584 51; poor tax, $300; and road tax, $800.

Roxbury. (See *Rocksbury*.)

Ryersons, a village at and near the junction of Ringwood and Pequannock rivers, in the S. E. angle of Pompton t-ship. There are here

1 tavern, 3 grist mills, a carding machine, a furnace, and store, a Dutch Reformed church, an academy, and from 15 to 20 dwellings; surrounded by a rich and productive country. The post-office is at Pompton, on the right side of the river, in Morris co.

Roy's Brook, a tributary of the Millstone river, rising at the S. E. foot of Nashanic mountain, and flowing by a devious, but generally, N. E. course of about 7 or 8 miles, to its recipient, below Rogers' mill.

Saddle River, rises in the state of New York, 3 or 4 miles beyond the northern boundary of this state, and flows thence, southwardly, about 18 miles, through Bergen co., forming the boundary between Franklin and Harrington t-ships, Saddle River, and New Barbadoes, and Lodi t-ships, to its recipient, the Passaic river, about a mile above Acquackanonck. It has a rapid course, and considerable volume, and mills are strung thickly along its banks. The valley through which it flows is broad, and shows evidence in the gravel, and boulders, and water-worn hills, that at some day, a much larger volume of water ran through it.

Saddle River t-ship. The t-ship and river both have their name from the shape of the former, which receives from the Passaic river the shape of a saddle. It is bounded N. by Franklin t-ship; E. by Saddle river, separating it from Harrington, New Barbadoes, and Lodi t-ships; S. by the Passaic river; and W. by Pompton river, which divides it from Morris co., and by Pompton t-ship. Centrally distant N. W. from Hackensacktown 8 miles: greatest length E. and W. 10 miles; breadth N. and S. 8 miles; area, 41,000 acres, of which, about 17,000 are improved: the surface is generally hilly, the First and Second mountains of Essex co., crossing the Passaic and continuing through it. On the east, however, between the Passaic and Saddle rivers, there is a neck of low and level land; soil, red shale and loam; the valleys fertile and well cultivated,

and the hills well wooded. Through the valleys flow several small brooks, such as Singack, Preakness, Krokaevall, Goffle, and Ackerman's Brooks. Goffle, and New Manchester, a part of Paterson City, are the chief villages of the t-ship. Population in 1830, 3397. In 1832 there were 741 taxables, 496 householders, whose ratables did not exceed $30 in value; 80 single men, 7 stores, 8 grist mills, 1 cotton manufactory, 1 furnace, 10 saw mills, 13 tan vats, 2 distilleries, 1 wool factory, 506 horses and mules, and 1324 neat cattle over 3 years of age; and it paid state tax, $364 10; and county tax, $690 26.

Salem County has its name from its chief town and seat of justice, Salem, founded by John Fenwicke, in the year 1675. By the act for ascertaining the bounds of all the counties in the province, passed 21st January, 1710, the following were the boundaries given to it: " Beginning at the mouth of a creek on the west side of Stipson's island, called Jecak's creek, now West creek; thence by said creek as high as the tide floweth; thence by a direct line to the mouth of a small creek at Tuckahoe, where it comes into the southernmost main branch of the fork of the Great Egg Harbour river; thence up the said branch to the head thereof; thence along the bounds of Gloucester county to the river Delaware, and thence by the river and bay to the place of beginning; and thus it included the whole of Cumberland county. The latter county was taken from it by the act of 19th Jan. 1748; and the boundaries then established, confirmed by the act of 7th Dec. 1763, by which the southern boundary of Salem county was then fixed as follows: Commencing at the middle of the mouth of Stow creek; thence by the same, opposite to the mills formerly of John Brick; thence up the middle of Stow creek branch opposite the house of Hugh Dunn; thence by a direct line to said house, leaving it in Cumberland county; and thence by a straight line N. 51° 15' E. 94 chains, to the house of Aziel Pierson, leaving that also in Cumberland county; thence N. E. by a line intersecting the line of Pilesgrove t-ship, 305 chains; thence by Pilesgrove line S. 47° E. to the middle of Maurice river, below the mouth of Muddy run; thence up the middle of said river to the foot of Scotland branch; thence up the middle of said branch to Gloucester line." The county is, therefore, now bounded by the Delaware bay and river on the S. W., W., and N. W.; by Gloucester co. on the N. E; and Cumberland co, on the S. E. Greatest length N. and S. about 30 miles; breadth E. and W. 26 miles; area, 320 square miles, or 204,936 acres; central lat. 39° 33'; long. from W. C. 1° 50' E.

The surface of the county is generally flat. Its soil, in the northern and western parts, clay and loam, mixed more or less with sand, and generally productive, in wheat, grass, oats, &c. In the south-eastern parts, the soil is sandy and gravelly, and less fertile, but yielding much timber and cord wood of oak and pine, which succeed alternately when a clearing is made. This is particularly the case with a strip of about 20 miles long, extending across Lower and Upper Alloways Creek and Pittsgrove t-ships, denominated the *Barrens*. The county is well watered, having Oldman's creek on its northern boundary, Salem and Alloways creeks running through it centrally, and Stow creek on the southern limits.

The county consists of alluvial and diluvial formation, the washings of the ocean and the primitive strata, being very irregularly mingled, and beds of stiff clay, loam, and gravel, are interspersed with white sea sand. From two to twenty feet below the surface, in several places, there is found a species of greenish blue marl, as at Pedricktown and Woodstown, which is used as manure. In it there are shells, as the ammonite, belemnite, ovulite, ostrea, terebratula, &c. similar to those found in the limestone

and grauwacke of the transition; and in the horizontal limestone and sandstone. We have not heard of any bog iron ore in the county, though it probably exists; but sandstone and puddingstone, cemented with iron ore, are not uncommon.

Salem, Woodstown, Sharptown, Sculltown, Pedricktown, Daretown, Pittstown, Allowaystown, Friesburg, Canton, Hancock's Bridge, and Quinton's Bridge, are villages of the co.

The county was originally settled by Dutch and Swedes; and subsequently by the English, companions of John Fenwicke, who landed here in 1675; and it derived its principal inhabitants from the same source. Some Dutch fixed themselves at, and gave name to, Friesburg, in Upper Alloways Creek t-ship. The population by the census of 1830, amounted to 14,155, of whom, 6443 were white males; 6300 white females; 1 slave; 673 free coloured males, and 638 free coloured females. There were also in the county, 6 whites, deaf and dumb; 7 blind, and 27 aliens; and in 1832, taxables, 3092; 1103 householders, whose ratables did not exceed $30; 47 storekeepers, 6 fisheries, 13 grist mills, 19 saw mills, 2 carding machines with spinning machines for wool, 6 fulling mills, 7 tanneries, 15 distilleries, 19 stud horses, 3103 horses and mules, 7300 neat cattle, over 3 years of age; and the county paid for t-ship purposes, $5076; for county purposes, $7000; and state tax, $2156 60.

There were in the county 7 Friends' meeting houses, 6 Methodist, 5 Baptist, 1 Seven-day Baptist, 2 Episcopalian, 2 Presbyterian, and 2 African Methodist churches; 1 academy at Salemtown, and sufficient other schools there, and in every t-ship, to teach the rudiments of an English education.

The other public buildings of the county consist of a large court-house, with fire proof offices detached, of brick; a stone prison, a large poorhouse, with a farm annexed, and two buildings erected for masonic halls.

The trade of the county consists of wheat, rye, Indian corn, oats, and garden vegetables for market, lumber, and cord wood. Considerable quantities of grain are annually exported from Salem to the Eastern states. The courts of common pleas and general quarter sessions of the peace, for the county, are annually holden at Salem, on the first Tuesdays of March and December, the second Tuesday of June, and the third Tuesday of September; and the circuit court, on the second Tuesday of June and the first Tuesday of September. The county, by virtue of the constitution, elects one member of council, and three members of the Assembly.

STATISTICAL TABLE OF SALEM COUNTY.

Townships.	Length.	Breadth.	Area.	Surface.	Population.		
					1810.	1820.	1830.
Upper Alloways Creek,	10½	9	34,000	p't level, rolling.	1921	2194	2136
Lower Alloways Creek,	12	9	30,000	level.	1182	1217	1222
Elsinborough,	6	4	8000	do.	517	505	503
Mannington,	9	8	20,000	do.	1664	1732	1726
Upper Penn's Neck,	9	7½	21,053	do.	1638	1861	1638
Lower Penn's Neck,	9	6	12,645	do.	1163	1158	994
Pilesgrove,	9	6½	24,000	do.	1756	2012	2150
Pittsgrove,	15	7	44,000	p't level, p't roll.	1991	2040	2216
Salem,	2	2	1238	level.	929	1303	1570
			204,936		12,761	14,022	14,155

Salem t-ship and post-town, and seat of justice of Salem county, situate 171 miles N. E. of W. C., 65 S. of Trenton, and 34 S. E. from Philadelphia; lat. 39° 32′; long. from W. C. 1° 35′. The t-ship is of circular form, and is nearly surrounded by water, having on the N. W. the Salem creek, on the N. E. and E. Fenwicke's creek, a tributary of that stream, and on the W. another small tributary of the same stream. The town is distant from the Delaware, by the creek, 3½ miles. The t-ship is about 2 miles in diameter, and contains 1238 acres of well improved land, of a rich sandy loam, divided into town lots and 12 farms. The town contains about 250 dwellings; a fine court-house, about 60 by 40 feet, of brick, with brick fire proof offices adjacent; 1 Episcopalian, 1 Methodist, 1 Presbyterian, 1 Baptist, 1 African Methodist, and 2 Quaker (one being orthodox and the other Hicksite) churches; 1 building of brick, of gothic architecture, designed for a masonic hall, but which is now appropriated to other purposes, the lodge being extinct; a bank with capital paid in of $75,000; a stone jail with yard, surrounded by a high stone wall, both of small dimensions; 1 market house, 2 fire engines, 2 public libraries, 1 academy, and 5 daily schools for teaching the rudiments of an English education; 5 Sunday schools, 2 printing offices, at each of which is printed a weekly newspaper, called, respectively, "*The Salem Messenger,*" and "*The American Statesman;*" 21 stores, 2 hotels, 7 physicians, 5 lawyers, 3 lumber yards, 1 steam mill which grinds much grain, 1 horse mill, 5 apothecaries' stores, 1 livery stable. A steamboat leaves the town daily, for Delaware City and Newcastle, to meet the morning steam-boat from Philadelphia; 1 four horse stage runs daily to Philadelphia, another to Pennsgrove, on the Delaware, to meet the Wilmington steam-boat for Philadelphia; a two horse daily line to Bridgetown, and a two horse line to Centerville, once a week. The creek at the town, is 152 yards wide, over which is a wooden bridge, resting on wooden piers, with a draw for the passage of vessels. Over Fenwicke creek, a short distance above its junction with Salem creek, is another wooden bridge, a neat structure, roofed. Vessels of 50 tons may approach the town safely, but the bar at the mouth of the creek prevents the entry of vessels drawing more than eight feet water. Large quantities of wheat, rye, oats, and corn, are exported from this place to the eastern states. The streets of the town are wide—footways paved, and bordered with trees; the houses of frame and brick, the former painted white, are surrounded with gardens and grass lots, and adorned with flowers, giving to the place, a cheerful and healthy appearance, surpassed by few villages in the United States. The t-ship contained in 1830, 1570 inhabitants: in 1832, 267 householders, whose ratables did not exceed $30 in value; and 397 taxables, 2 tan yards, 1 distillery; and it paid taxes for t-ship purposes, $426; county use, $738 25; and state use, $233 35.

The site of the town of Salem was the first spot visited, and we believe, the first settled, by the English emigrants to West Jersey. Soon after the sale by Lord Berkeley of one moiety of the province, to Edward Byllinge, John Fenwicke, the agent of the latter set sail, (in 1675) to visit the new purchase in a ship from London, called the Griffith. After a short passage, he landed at this pleasant spot, which, from its aspect of peace, he called Salem. He brought with him two daughters, and several servants, two of which, Samuel Hedge and John Adams, afterwards married his daughters. Other passengers were, Edward Champness, Edward and Samuel Wade, John Smith, Samuel Nichols, Richard Guy, Richard Noble, Richard Hancock, John Pledger, Hypolite Lefever, and John Matlock, and others, who were masters of families.

Salem Creek, Salem co., rises in Pittsgrove t-ship, and flows N. W. through that and Pilesgrove t-ship, by Woodstown and Sharptown, about 17 miles to the S. W. angle of Upper Penn's Neck t-ship; thence turning S. and S. W., it divides Mannington and Lower Penn's Neck t-ships, and passing by Salem, empties into the Delaware river, 3½ miles below that town. There is a bar at the mouth, on which at high tide there are eight feet water. Vessels of 50 tons approach the town safely; but within the bar, there is water, it is said, for vessels of 300 tons burden. The whole length of the creek may be about 30 miles, and it is navigable for shallops nearly half that distance. A short canal of 3 or 4 miles, through Upper and Lower Penn's Neck t-ships, unites the creek with the Delaware, saving a distance to the craft which navigate the creek, of about 20 miles.

Samptown, Piscataway t-ship, Middlesex co., about 8 miles N. from New Brunswick, on the left bank of Cedar creek; contains a Baptist church, 10 or 12 houses, tavern and store, in a tolerably fertile country of red shale.

Sand Hills, small hamlet of Nottingham t-ship, Burlington co. There is a tavern, and 12 or 15 dwellings here; the turnpike road, and the Camden and Amboy rail-road, run near it. The carriages from and for Trenton meet the rail-road cars here. Distance from Trenton, about 5, and from Bordentown, 3 miles.

Sand Hills, noted hills in the N. W. part of South Brunswick t-ship, Middlesex co., covering an area of about 4 miles by 2; about 7 miles W. from Brunswick.

Sandy Hook, Sandy Hook bay: the first is a sandy beach, extending northward, from Old Shrewsbury inlet, and the S. point of the highlands of Nevisink, 6 miles, of an irregular width, varying from half a mile to a mile, forming the eastern boundary of the bay. The bay sets in from the Raritan bay, southwards, and is about 7 miles wide, between Point

Comfort, the western cape, and the point of the Hook. Its depth to the S. point of the Nevisink hills, which form the coast for about 6 miles, is about 6 miles. The western shore encroaches, eastwardly, upon the water until it is narrowed to three-quarters of a mile.

Sand Pond, a small sheet of water, in Walfkill mountains, Vernon t-ship, Sussex co., which sends forth a small tributary to the Wallkill river.

Sand Pond, the source of Stout's brook, on the N. line of Hardwick t-ship.

Sandtown, or *Berkely*, village of Greenwich t-ship, Gloucester co., on Mantua creek, 4 miles S. W. from Woodbury; contains a store, tavern, 12 or 15 dwellings, and an Episcopal church.

Sandtown, Nottingham t-ship, Burlington co., on the road from Trenton to Cranberry, about 5 miles E. of the former, on a sandy plain; contains a tavern, smithery, and some half-dozen dwellings.

Sandistone t-ship, Sussex co., bounded on the N. E. by Montague t-ship; S. E. by the Blue mountain, which divides it from Newton, Frankford, and Wantage t-ships; S. W. by Walpack t-ship; and W. by the Delaware river; centrally distant, N. W. from Newton, 12 miles; greatest length, $8\frac{1}{2}$, breadth, 7 miles; area, 19,320 acres; surface on the E. mountainous, and on the W. river alluvion. Population in 1830, 1097. There were in the t-ship in 1832, 65 householders, whose ratables did not exceed $30; taxable inhabitants, 240; 4 merchants or traders, 5 pair of stones for grinding grain, 1 carding machine, 4 saw mills, 204 horses and mules, and 841 neat cattle over 3 years; 13 tan vats, 1 distillery. The t-ship paid state and county tax, $426 77; poor tax, $100; road tax, $500. It is watered by the Big and Little Flat Kill creeks, and their tributaries, and by the river Delaware. The Morristown and Milford turnpike road crosses it north-westwardly, on which lies the post-office, dis-

tant 241 miles from W. C., 83 from Trenton, and 13 from Newton. Between the Blue mountain and the Delaware, there is a rich flat, increasing from two to six miles in width, through which runs a bed of transition limestone, girded by an alluvial belt. This flat produces excellent crops of wheat. The t-ship was originally settled by Dutch, whilst that people held possession of New York.

Sandy New, small hamlet of Middletown t-ship, Monmouth co., 9 miles N. E. of Freehold; contains a tavern, and some 3 or 4 dwellings, in a fine fertile country.

Sargeantsville, p-t. of Amwell t-ship, Hunterdon co., 6 miles S. W. from Flemington, 23 N. from Trenton, and 177 N. E. from W. C.; contains a tavern, store, and some 6 or 8 dwellings. Surrounding country hilly and poor; lands rated at $20 per acre. Near this village, on a farm of 150 acres, Mr. R. Rittenhouse has established the Mantua Manual Labour Institute, with accommodations for about 30 students, and the purpose to increase them as they may be required. At this institute are taught the Greek and Latin languages, and all other branches of learning, taught at similar institutions. About three hours every day, Saturday and Sunday excepted, are employed in manual labour, by the students, for which they receive reasonable compensation. The charge for tuition, board, washing, lodging, candles, and fuel, is $25 per quarter.

Saw Mill Creek, a marsh stream about 2 miles in length, in Lodi t-sp, Bergen co.

Saxtonville, small hamlet of Amwell t-ship, Hunterdon co., on the river Delaware, 12 miles S. W. from Flemington; contains some 3 or 4 dwellings; named from the proprietor.

Schooley's Mountain, Schugl's Hills, form part of the central granitic chain, which extends in a N. E. and S. W. direction, across the state of New Jersey, from the Delaware to the Hudson river. The name, Schooley's Mountain, derived from a family formerly owning a considerable portion of its soil, is applied chiefly, to that portion of the chain which crosses the N. W. part of Morris county. The height of the mountain above its base, has been determined by geometrical measurement, to be more than 600 feet; and a calculation, made by approximation, on the falls of water, on the different mill dams along the rapid channel of the Musconetcong river, to its junction with the Delaware, and on the descent, thence to Trenton, gives to that base an elevation of 500 feet above tide; making the height of the mountain, above the level of the ocean, somewhat more than 1100 feet.

From the top of the mountain a turnpike road runs northward to Sussex, another westward to Easton, a third eastward to New York, and a fourth southward towards Trenton. The mineral spring near the top has given much celebrity to this region. It is said to have been known to the aborigines, and to have been employed by them as a remedy, which, with characteristic selfishness, they would have concealed from the whites. The latter, however, have resorted to it, since the settlement of the country. Remarkable cures have been ascribed to it, and some persons have habitually frequented it, season after season, on account of the benefit they have derived from the use of its waters. It is situated in Washington t-ship, Morris co., 19 miles N. W. of Morristown, 50 from New York, 70 N. E. from Philadelphia, 56 from Trenton, and 213 from W. C.

The spring is, in strictness, a rill which issues from a perpendicular rock, having an eastern exposure, between 40 and 50 feet above the level of a brook, which gurgles over the stones, and foams down the rocks in the channels beneath. A small wooden trough is adapted to the fissure, so as to convey the water to a platform where the visiters assemble, and to the structure containing the baths. The temperature of the water is 56° F. being 6° warmer than the spring water nearer the summit. The fountain emits about 30 gallons per hour; which quantity does not vary with any change of season or weather. The water, like other chalybeates, leaves a deposit of oxidized iron, as it flows, which discolours the troughs, baths, and even the drinking vessels. The bare taste and appearance shows that it is a chalybeate; and it is strongly characterized by the peculiar astringency and savour of ferruginous impregnations. Though remarkably clear when first taken, the water becomes turbid upon standing for some time in the open air, and after a long interval, an irridescent pellicle forms on its surface. Ochre and other indications of iron are dispersed extensively through the surrounding rocks and soil. Iron ore is so plentiful in the vicinity that furnaces are worked, both in the eastern and western district of the chain, and much of the ore is magnetic. Grey limestone is found at the base of the hills and along the valleys. The analysis of the water, by Dr. M'Nevin of New York, has given the following result:

Vegetable extract 92, muriate of soda 43, muriate of lime 2.40, muriate of magnesia 50, carbonate of lime 7.99, sulphate of lime 65, carbonate of magnesia 40, silex 80, carbonated oxide of iron 2, loss 41—total 16.50.

The iron from the mineral water is very easily separated. Exposure to the atmosphere induces metallic precipitation; and transportation to a distance, even in corked bottles, produces a like effect; and when thus freed from its iron, the water may be used in making tea. The heat of ebullition, also, seems to separate the ferruginous ingredient, and to prevent any dusky or black tint; for if an infusion of green tea be mixed with water fresh from the spring, a dark and disagreeable hue is instantly produced. The carbonic acid which this water contains, is altogether in a state of combination, and hence it never occasions flatulence or spasm in the weakest stomach, whilst it gradually strengthens the digestive powers.—This chalybeate is considered by medical men, as one of the purest of this, or any other country, and as beneficial, in most cases of chronic disease, and general debility, and especially in cases of calculus in the bladder or kidneys.

To those in pursuit of health or pleasure, this region presents equal attraction. A short journey brings the patient from the level of tide water to a very desirable elevation, which tempers the summer's heat, and braces the relaxed frame. The plain on the top of the mountain, affords very pleasant rides amid ever changing and delightful scenery, in which cheering views of improved and profitable agriculture are blended with the velvet plain, the craggy hill, and shadowy vale. Thus the invalid has every incentive to exercise, by the highest gratification from his exertions. To him who seeks relaxation from the cares of business, or to change sedentary occupation and feebleness for activity and vigour, the excellent society which assembles here during the summer months, the abundant sport in fowling and fishing, and the delightful scenery, hold forth strong inducements; to which, we would be unjust not to add the excellent fare, cheerful attention, and comfortable accommodation given to visiters at the three hotels, and several farm houses in the vicinity of the spring. Belmont Hall, kept by Mr. G. Bowne, situate on the highest part of the mountain, shadowed and embowered by various fruit, forest, and ornamental trees, is a fine building, 50 feet square and three stories high, with very extensive wings; and the Heath House of Mr. E. Marsh, less showy, but not less commodious or pleasant, afford the visiter all the means of enjoyment usual at watering places; whilst their distance from the fountain, (about ¾ of a mile) by adding the benefits of exercise, does not diminish the salubrious effects of

the water. There is, however, a third house, immediately at the spring, where such visiters as desire to be near it, can be accommodated. The season commences here on the 1st of June, and continues during the hot weather.

For the man of science, the mineral region, and geological formation of the country, possesses much interest. It abounds with iron and other minerals. The first, in a mine opened within gun-shot of the Heath House, is highly magnetic; so much so, indeed, as to render the use of iron tools about it very inconvenient. The following extraordinary circumstances we give on the authority of Mr. Marsh. The tools, by continued use, become so strongly magnetized, that in boring the rock, the workman is unable, after striking the auger with his hammer, to separate them in the usual mode of wielding the hammer, and is compelled to resort to a lateral or rotatory motion for this purpose; and the crowbar has been known to sustain, in suspension, all the other tools of the mine, in weight equal to a hundred pounds. These facts are supported by the assurance of General Dickenson, that the magnetic attraction of the tools, used in his mine, adds much to the fatigue of the workmen; and that it is of ordinary occurrence for the hammer to lift the auger from the hole during the process of boring.

Besides the houses for public entertainment, at and near the springs, there are several others, which, with a church and school house built by Mr. Marsh, with the aid of the visiters, and a post-office, give the neighbourhood a village-like appearance. And, among the attractions of the mountain, we must not forbear to mention the fishing and boating on Budd's Pond, a beautiful sheet of water, two miles in length by one in breadth, at seven miles distance from the spring. This little mountain lake of great depth and clear as crystal, abounds with perch, sun, pike, and other fish.

Scotch Plains, p-t. of Westfield

t-ship, Essex county, 14 miles from Newark, Somerville, New Brunswick, Morristown, Elizabethtown Point, and Amboy; 214 miles N. E. from W. C., and 48 from Trenton, on the road from Springfield to Somerville; contains, within the diameter of a mile, 1 Baptist church, an academy, 1 tavern, 2 stores, 3 grist mills, 2 saw mills, 1 oil mill, 1 straw paper mill, and about 70 dwellings. The surface of the adjacent country is level, except on the W. and N. W. which is mountainous; soil, clay loam, well cultivated, and productive, and valued, in farms, at $40 the acre. Within 2 miles of the village, a bed of carbonate of lime has been lately discovered, in which are metallic appearances supposed to be gold and silver, but which are, probably, only deceptive pyrites.

Scott's Mountain, lying in Greenwich, Oxford, and Mansfield t-ships, Warren co., forms part of the chain of the South mountain, of which this portion covers much of the area of the three t-ships above named. The height of the mountain here may be from 700 to 800 feet above tide, and it is composed of granitic rock, based on, or breaking through limestone. It abounds with iron of several varieties, which, for near a century, has been extensively worked, near Oxford furnace; where Messrs. Henry and Jordan are, now, extensively engaged in the iron manufacture. The mountain is generally well wooded, and the valleys fruitful.

Scrabbletown, hamlet of Hanover t-ship, Burlington co., 10 miles E. from Mount Holly, and 12 S. E. from Bordentown; contains a tavern, and 6 or 8 cottages, in a poor, sandy, pine country.

Sculltown, a village of Upper Penn's Neck t-ship, Salem co., on Oldman's Creek, at the head of navigation; containing from 20 to 30 dwellings, a tavern, and 2 or 3 stores. It is about 12 miles N. E. of Salem.

Secaucas, island in the Cedar swamp, of the Hackensack river, in Bergen t-ship, Bergen co. It is near

4 miles long by half a mile wide; terminating in a very distinguished elevation, called Snake-hill. The island is crossed by the turnpike and rail-road from Hoboken to Paterson.

Serepta, a post-office, Warren co.

Seven Causeways, noted union of 7 roads, near the junction of 4 mile branch, with Inskeep's branch of the Great Egg Harbour river, 25 miles S. E. from Camden, on the line of Deptford and Gloucester t-sps, Gloucester co.

Shabacung Island, formed by the Delaware river, and part of the t-ship of Montague, Sussex co., near the remote N. end of the state.

Shark River, mill stream, rises in Shrewsbury t-ship, Monmouth co., and flows along the boundary, between that and Howell t-ship, about 6 miles, into a broad estuary, and thence about 3 miles through Shark inlet, into the Atlantic ocean.

Sharptown, p-t. and village of Pilesgrove t-ship, Salem co., on Salem creek, between 3 and 4 miles below Woodstown, and 8 or 9 miles N. E. from Salem, 162 from W. C., and 56 S. from Trenton; contains between 40 and 50 dwellings, 1 tavern, 2 stores, 1 grist mill, and one school house, used occasionally as a church. The surrounding country is level and fertile.

Shawpocussing Creek, small tributary of the Delaware river, which rises in Knowlton t-ship, Warren co., at the foot of the Blue mountain, and flows S. W. to its recipient, having a course of five miles.

Shelltown, on the line between Hanover t-ship, Burlington co., and Upper Freehold t-ship, Monmouth co., on a small branch of the Crosswicks creek; contains some half-dozen dwellings. There is a Friends' meeting house near it, in Monmouth county.

Shiloh, p-t. in the S. W. angle of Hardwick t-ship, Warren co., 12 miles N. E. of Belvidere, and 60 miles from Trenton.

Shiloh, hamlet of Cumberland co., on the line dividing Hopewell from

Stow Creek t-ship, about 5 miles N. W. of Bridgeton; contains 8 or 10 dwellings, and a Seventh-day Baptist church. The country around it is of light loam, but in an improving condition.

Shipetaukin, small branch of the Assunpink creek, rising in Lawrence t-ship, Hunterdon co., and flowing S. by a course of 5 or 6 miles to its recipient, through an extensive body of meadow land.

Shoal Harbour Creek, small stream at the N. W. foot of the Nevisink hills; runs about a mile and a half N. E. into Sandy Hook bay.

Shrewsbury Inlet, Old, was opened in 1778, from the ocean into the estuary formed by the Nevisink and Shrewsbury rivers, Monmouth co.; was closed by the moving of the sands in 1810, but was reopened in 1830. Vessels now pass through it.

Shrewsbury River, so called, is a continuation of Sandy Hook bay, Shrewsbury t-ship, Monmouth co., which receives from the t-ship, Shrewsbury river proper, a small stream of 6 or 7 miles long, Long Branch, and several other tributaries. This arm of the bay, from the mouth of the Nevisink river, is about 5 miles long, with an average breadth of a mile and a half, and has a considerable quantity of salt marsh on its borders. It is separated from the Nevisink by a high neck of land, 2 miles wide.

Shrewsbury, p-t. of Shrewsbury t-sp., Monmouth co., between Shrewsbury and Nevisink rivers, 12 miles E. from Freehold, 50 S. E. from Trenton, and 215 N. E. from W. C.; contains 12 or 15 dwellings, an Episcopalian and Presbyterian church, 1 tavern, and 2 stores. Soil, sandy and light.

Shrewsbury t-ship, Monmouth co., bounded N. by Middletown t-ship; E. by the Atlantic ocean; S. by Howell t-ship, and W. by Freehold. Centrally distant 7 miles E. from Freehold; length N. and S. 13, breadth E. and W. 13 miles; area, 64,000 acres; drained on the N. E.

by the Nevisink and Shrewsbury rivers, and their tributaries; E. by White Pond, and Deal creeks, and S. E. by Shark river; surface level; soil, clay and sandy loam, on marl, of good quality on Swimming river, and its tributaries; on the S. of these, sandy, poor, and covered with pine. On the E., along the shore near and below the Long Branch boarding-houses, is a very fertile black sand. The sea shore in this t-ship, is generally high and bold, and without marsh. The celebrated Long Branch boarding houses, so named from their vicinity to a long branch of Shrewsbury river, are in this township. Population in 1830, 4700. In 1832 the t-ship contained about 900 taxables; 265 householders, whose ratables did not exceed $30; and 150 single men; 21 stores, 5 saw mills, 12 run of stones, for grinding grain, 1 carding machine, 60 tan vats, 730 horses and mules, 1650 neat cattle, 3 years old and upwards; and paid state and county tax, $2144 69. Shrewsbury, Eatontown, Colts Neck, Long Branch, and Tinton's Falls, are villages and post-towns of the t-ship.

Several thousand acres in this t-ship were settled in 1682, and the inhabitants were then computed at 400. Lewis Morris of Barbadoes, the brother of Richard Morris, the first settler at Morrisania, New York, and uncle of Lewis Morris, subsequently governor of New Jersey, had iron works and other considerable improvements here.

Singack, small tributary of Preakness brook, Saddle River t-ship, Bergen co.

Six Mile Run, village and stream. The first, a post-town on the Princeton and Brunswick turnpike, (and on the line between New Brunswick t-ship, Middlesex co., and Franklin t-ship, Somerset co.,) 12 miles from the one, and 4 from the other, 189 from W. C., and 23 from Trenton; contains a Dutch Reformed church, 2 taverns, 1 store, and from 10 to 12 dwellings. Soil, red shale, level, and well cultivated.—The stream flows from North Brunswick, through Franklin t-ship, by a W. course of about 6 miles, to the Raritan river.

Slabtown, hamlet of Springfield t-ship, Burlington co., on the road from Mount Holly to Bordentown, 4 miles N. of the former; contains a Friends' meeting house, and 10 or 12 dwellings, 1 store, and 2 taverns.

Slab Cabin Branch, of the Rancocus creek, rises in Monmouth co., and flows a S. W. course of 10 miles, to its recipient, the North Branch of that creek, on the south boundary of Hanover t-ship, Burlington co. Hanover furnace lies upon it, and it turns several mills.

Slab Cabin Brook, Dover t-ship, Monmouth co., a small stream about 3 miles in length, which flows into the south side of Toms' Bay.

Sleepy Creek, a tributary of Atsion river, rises in Hereford t-ship, and flows by a S. E. course of about 6 miles, to its recipient, in Galloway t-ship, Gloucester co.

Smith's Creek, a small mill stream, which rises near Herbertstown, in Hopewell t-ship, Hunterdon co., and flows S. W. by a course of 6 miles, to the river Delaware, at the foot of Belle Mount.

Smithville, village of Galloway t-ship, Gloucester co., 42 miles S. E. of Woodbury, and 2 miles E. from Leed's Point; contains a tavern, store, Methodist meeting house, and 10 or 12 dwellings; surrounded by pines, and near the salt marsh.

Snake Hill, a noted eminence of Secaucus Island, in the marsh on Hackensack river, and a very prominent object from the road, between Jersey City and Newark. Its formation is of trap rock, on sandstone base.

Snover's Brook, rises in Sucker Pond, Stillwater t-ship, Sussex co., and flows by a S. W. course of about 8 or 9 miles through the north part of Hardwicke t-ship, into Paulinskill, on the northern part of Hamilton t-sp, Warren co.

Snuffletown, a small village of San-

distone t-ship, Sussex co., at the east foot of the Wallkill mountain, and in the valley of the Pacake creek, on the Paterson and Hamburg turnpike road, about 15 miles N. E. of Newton; contains a Methodist meeting house, a store, tavern, and tannery, and 6 or 8 dwellings.

Sodom, p-t. of Knowlton t-ship, Warren co., on Paulinskill, 12 miles N. of Belvidere, 4 E. from Columbia; contains a grist and saw mill, tavern, store, and some half-dozen dwellings. Some smelting works have lately been erected here, said to be for precious metals, discovered in the Jenny Jump mountain.

Sodom, Lebanon t-ship, Hunterdon co. (See *Clarkesville.*)

Somerset County, was taken from Middlesex, by an act of the proprietaries in 1688. Its bounds were subsequently modified by the legislative acts of 1709, 1713, and 1741. It is now bounded on the N. and N. E. by Morris co.; on the E. by Essex and Middlesex; on the S. E. by Middlesex; and on the S. W. and N. W. by Hunterdon co.: greatest length N. and S. 28 miles; breadth E. and W. 20 miles; area, 189,800 acres, or about 297 square miles: central lat. 40° 34'; long. 2° 15' from W. C.

The whole county lies within the transition formation, if the old red sandstone be included within it. Hills of trap rock, upon the sandstone base, are scattered over it, as at Rock Hill, near the southern boundary, Rocky, or Nashanic mountain on the S. W., and Stony Hill N. of Somerville. The ridges N. of the last, contain grauwacke, and the valleys transition limestone, generally of a grey colour. The surface of the county is various: the N. W. section being mountainous; the S. and S. W. hilly, whilst the centre and S. E., the valley of the Raritan, is either level, or gently undulating. The soil varies with the surface: that of the hills is generally of clay and stiff loam, whilst that of the plains is a sandy loam, formed of the red shale; and the mountain vales, as we have already observed, are of limestone. All are, however, fertile under proper culture, and the county may vie with her neighbours of Hunterdon, Essex, and Middlesex, in the variety and quantity of agricultural products.

The county is well watered. It is cut into two, almost equal parts, by the main stem and south branch of the Raritan river, which receives the north branch, flowing southward and centrally through the northern section, and the Millstone river, flowing northward and centrally through the southern section; and it is thus by these three streams, divided into four parts, intersected by smaller brooks and creeks, in almost every direction. The Delaware and Raritan canal enters the county at Kingston, with the Millstone river, and follows that stream to its junction with the Raritan, 3 miles S. E. of Somerville, whence it pursues the valley of the last stream to Brunswick.

Copper ore has been discovered in considerable veins in the first range of hills, N. E. from Somerville; and mines have been opened in at least two places; the first within 2, and the second within 6 miles of the town. Attempts have been made to work both, but every effort has hitherto been unsuccessful: and yet the ore is said to contain not only a very valuable proportion of copper, but to be worth working on account of the gold which it yields. Public opinion attributes these failures more to the want of adequate capital to sustain the expense of the first steps in mining, than to the want of skill, or poverty of ore. It is said, also, that particles of gold and silver have been discovered in a gangue of carbonate of lime, on Green Brook, N. of the Scotch Plains.

A turnpike road from Brunswick, enters the county by a bridge over Bound Brook, and passes through Somerville, to North Branch, and thence to Philipsburg, opposite to Easton. From North Branch a turnpike road runs northward over Schooley's mountain to Hacketstown, in Warren co.; and a rail-road is in contemplation, through Somerville to Belvidere.

The post-towns of the county are Baskingridge, Bound Brook, Flaggtown, Harlingen, Kline's Mills, Lesser Cross-Roads, Liberty Corner, Martinsville, Millington, Millstone, North Branch, Peapack, Pluckemin, Princeton, Rocky Hill, Somerville, the county town, and Warren.

The county was early settled by the Dutch, whose industrious habits soon rendered it remarkable for its fruitfulness, and it became soon one of the most thickly settled of the province. By the census of 1830, the population amounted to 17,689 souls, of whom 7665 were white males, 7717 white females; 945 free coloured males, 914 free coloured females; 214 male slaves, 234 female slaves. Among these there were 118 aliens; deaf and dumb, 14 whites—blind, whites, 17, coloured, 3.

In 1832, there were in the co., 3500 taxables; 668 householders, whose ratables did not exceed $30; 391 single men, 68 merchants; 44 saw mills, 64 grist mills, or run of stones for grinding grain, 8 fulling mills, 211 tan vats, 28 distilleries, 11 carding machines, 4621 horses and mules, and 8634 neat cattle, above the age of 3 years; and it paid in state tax, $2642 86, and in county tax, $6000.

The courts for the county are holden at Somerville; the common pleas, orphan's court, and general quarter sessions, on the following Tuesdays: viz. last in January, 3d in April, 3d in June, and 1st in October; and the circuit courts on the 3d Tuesday in April, and the 1st in October.

STATISTICAL TABLE OF SOMERSET COUNTY.

Townships.	Length.	Breadth.	Area.	Surface.	Population. 1810	Population. 1820	Population. 1830
Bedminster,	8	4½	19,300	hilly,	1312	1393	1453
Bernard,	9	7	25,000	mountainous,	1879	2063	2062
Bridgewater,	13	11	35,000	level,	2906	3147	3549
Franklin,	13	8	30,000	do. [level,	2539	3071	3352
Hillsborough,	10	7	36,000	part hilly, part	2456	2885	2878
Montgomery,	8	8	26,500	hilly,	2282	2495	2834
Warren,	8	4	18,000	mountainous,	1354	1452	1561
			189,800		14,728	16,506	17,689

Somers' Point, p-t. and port of entry for Great Egg Harbour district, upon the Great Egg Harbour bay, about 43 miles S. E. from Woodbury, 88 from Trenton, and by post-route 196 from W. C. There is a tavern and boarding house here, and several farm houses. It is much resorted to for sea bathing in summer, and gunning in the fall season.

Somerville, p-t. and seat of justice, of Somerset co., situate about a mile N. of the Raritan river, on the turnpike road from New Brunswick to Philipsburg, 11 miles N. W. from the former, 33 S. E. from the latter, or from Easton, 28 N. E. from Trenton, and 199 from W. C. It lies upon a high well cultivated plain of red shale, about 2 miles south of a ridge of the South mountains; in which are some noted copper mines. It contains a Dutch Reformed church, a Methodist meeting, an academy where the classics and mathematics are taught, a boarding school for young ladies, 3 taverns well kept, and 7 stores, 1 large grist mill, 5 practising attorneys, 4 physicians, and 1 resident clergyman, 600 inhabitants, and about 100 dwellings. The court-house and other public buildings, are large and commodious, and many of the private dwellings are very neat; and the town is a healthy, pleasant, and desirable place of residence. The proposed rail road from Elizabethtown to the Delaware, at Belvidere, is designed to pass through it.

South Amboy, p-t. of South Amboy t-ship, Middlesex co., at the head of the Raritan bay and mouth of the Raritan river, 15 miles below New Brunswick, and 35 N. E. from Trenton; contains a hotel and some 15 or 20 dwellings, and an extensive manufactory of stone ware, made from clay obtained in the vicinity. This clay is of excellent quality, and much of it is exported to various parts of the country. It is used in the manufacture of delf ware at Jersey City, and in the fabrication of china at Philadelphia. The beds extend in the hills for several miles around the point. The turnpike road from Bordentown, and the Camden and Amboy rail road terminate here. There is a safe harbour here for vessels, and deep water at the landing.

South Amboy t-ship, Middlesex co., bounded N. by the Raritan river; N. E. by the Raritan bay; S. E. by Middletown and Upper Freehold t-ships, of Monmouth co.; S. W. by Millstone river; and N. W. by North Brunswick and South Brunswick t-ships. Centrally distant S. E. from New Brunswick 9 miles: greatest length N. E. and S. W. 18, and breadth 6 miles; area, 64,000 acres; surface, flat; soil, sandy; drained on the S. W. by the Millstone, and on the N. E. by South river and its tributaries, Tenant's run, Deep run, Matchaponix brook, and Manalapan creek. The turnpike and rail road from Bordentown to Amboy run through the t-ship. Upon the former lie the post-towns of Cranberry and Spotswood, and South Amboy. Population in 1830, 3782.

South River. (See *Manalapan Brook.*)

South Brunswick. (See *Brunswick, South.*)

Sparta, p-t. of Hardistone t-ship, Sussex co., at the west foot of the Wallkill mountain, 236 miles N. E. of W. C., 78 from Trenton, and 8 from Newton, on the Union turnpike road, in the valley, and near the source of the Wallkill river. This is a pleasant village, having some very good houses, a neat Presbyterian church with cupola, a school house, 2 grist mills, 2 saw mills, 4 forges for making iron, in which there are, together, 6 fires; 1 tavern, 3 stores, and from 35 to 40 dwellings. Iron and zinc ores are abundant in the neighbourhood; but only a small portion of the first is used in making iron here; the chief part being carted from the mines in Morris co., at the cost of $2 50 the ton. The zinc ore is not worked. The soil in the valley is limestone, and tolerably well cultivated.

Speertown, agricultural village of Bloomfield t-ship, Sussex co., 7 miles N. of Newark, near the foot of the First mountain; contains from 20 to 30 dwellings, 1 tavern, 1 store, a Dutch Reformed church, and school; surrounded by a country of red shale, carefully cultivated.

Spottswood, thriving p-t. of South Amboy t-ship, Middlesex co., on the turnpike road and rail road from Bordentown to South Amboy, about 25 miles from the former, 202 from W. C., and 26 from Trenton, and on the South river; contains a large gristmill, a fine Presbyterian church of wood, a Dutch Reformed church, 1 tavern, 2 stores, 2 tobacco manufactories, and about 30 dwellings.

Spruce Run, Lebanon t-ship, Hunterdon co., flows S. W. through the north part of the t-ship, and along the west boundary, and is a branch of the Raritan river.

2 H

Springfield t-ship, Essex county, bounded N. by Livingston t-ship; E. by Orange and Union t-ships; S. by Westfield and New Providence t-ships; and W. by the Passaic river, which divides it from Chatham t-ship, Morris co. Centrally distant W. from Newark 8 miles : greatest length N. and S. 6, breadth E. and W. 5 miles; area, 13,500 acres; surface, generally hilly; soil, clay loam and red shale. It is washed on the eastern boundary by the Rahway river, which receives several tributaries from the t-ship. Springfield the post-town; Vauxhall and part of Chatham are villages of the t-ship. The pretensions of Springfield, as an agricultural t-ship, are not high, but it claims consideration for its paper manufactories. Population in 1830, 1653. In 1832 there were 365 taxables, 97 householders, whose ratables did not exceed $30; 93 single men, 7 merchants, 1 grist mill, 3 carding machines, 12 paper mills, 6 tan vats, 1 woollen manufactory, 1 distillery, 220 horses and mules, and 818 neat cattle, above the age of 3 years. It paid state tax, 198 96; county, $520 56; poor, $500; road, $8.

Springfield p-t. of the preceding t-ship, on the turnpike road from Elizabethtown to Morristown, 7 miles W. from the one, and 10 E. from the other, 216 N. E. from W. C., and 50 from Trenton, and upon the Rahway river, at the foot of the First mountain; contains about 200 dwellings, some of which are neat structures; 1 Presbyterian church, with cupola and bell; 1 Methodist church, 3 taverns, 5 stores, 2 grist mills, 1 saw mill, and 10 paper mills. The surface of the country around it, is rugged, and the soil, a stiff cold clay, unproductive; and farms are not averaged at more than 20 dollars the acre.

Springfield, t-ship, Burlington co., bounded N. by Chesterfield, and Mansfield t-ships; S. E. by Hanover t-ship; S. W. by Northampton t-ship, and W. and N. W. by Burlington t-ship; centrally distant N. E. from Mount Holly, 5 miles; greatest length, E. and W. 10 miles; breadth, N. and S. 6 miles; area, 18,000 acres; surface level; soil, sand and sandy loam, well cultivated, and productive; drained, N. by the Assiscunk creek, which forms the northern boundary, and its branches, and S. by the tributaries of the north branch of the Rancocus creek. Slabtown, Jobstown, and Juliustown, are villages of the t-ship, at the two last of which, are post-offices. The population, a great portion of which are Friends, was, in 1830, 1531. In 1832, the t-ship contained, 3 Friends' meeting houses, 147 householders, whose ratables did not exceed $30, in value; 61 single men, 330 taxables; 3 stores, 14 tan vats, 1 distillery for cider, 31 dearborns, 100 covered wagons, 17 chairs, 11 gigs and curricles, 1975 neat cattle, and 507 horses and mules, over 3 years of age; and paid state tax, $388 85; county tax, $1358 29; and township tax, $500.

Spring Garden, or *North Belleville*, Bloomfield t-ship, Essex co., upon the Third river, and about a mile W. of the Passaic river; contains from 50 to 70 dwellings, a cotton manufactory, a school, and a Methodist church. (See *Belleville*.)

Spring Mills, village of Alexandria t-ship, Hunterdon co., 13 miles N. W. from Flemington, on a small stream, which empties into the Delaware; contains a grist mill, and several dwellings.

Springtown, small village of Schooley's mountain, on the Somerville and Easton turnpike road, 18 miles W. of Morristown, and 3 miles E. of the mineral spring; contains some 6 or 8 dwellings.

Spring Valley, hamlet of Morris t-ship, Morris co., 4 miles S. E. of Morristown; contains a tavern, and some half-dozen dwellings.

Squan Beach, extends from Old Cranberry inlet, N. 10 miles to Manasquan inlet, dividing for part of that distance, Barnegat bay, from the At-

lantic ocean. It no where exceeds half a mile in width.

Squan, a vicinage in the S. E. part of Howell t-ship, Monmouth co., between Manasquan and Metetecunk rivers. It is much frequented for sea-bathing; and comfortable accommodations are found at the farm-houses, of which there are several where boarders are received.

Squankum, p-t. of Howell t-ship, Monmouth co., 10 miles S. E. from Freehold, 44 from Trenton, and 209 N. E. from W. C.; contains a Friends' meeting house, a grist mill, and fulling mill, 2 taverns, 1 store, and 12 or 15 dwellings, surrounded by pine forest, and sandy soil.

Squankum, tavern, and creek; the creek is a tributary of Inskeep's branch of the Great Egg Harbour river, Deptford t-ship, Gloucester county.

Stafford t-ship, Monmouth co., bounded on the N. by Dover t-ship; E. and S. E. by the Atlantic ocean; S. W. by Little Egg Harbour t-ship; and W. by Northampton t-ship, Burlington co. Centrally distant S. from Freehold, 38 miles; greatest length, N. and S. 18 miles, breadth 12 miles; area, 87,000 acres; surface level; soil, sand, gravel, and marsh. On the E. front of the t-ship, Long Beach extends upon the ocean, about 11 miles, with an average breadth of about 1 mile, separating Little Egg Harbour bay from the sea. The bay varies from 2 to 3 miles in width, and between it and the fast land, there is a body of salt marsh of like width, through which flow several creeks; the principal are Manahocking, Gunning, Cedar, and Westecunk. Barnegat, Manahocking, Cedar Bridge, and Westecunk, are villages; the two first post-towns of the t-ship. Population in 1830, 2059. In 1832 the county contained about 400 taxables; 64 householders, whose ratables did not exceed $30; 30 single men; 4 stores, 2 saw mills, 1 grist mill, 1 furnace, 210 horses and mules, and 802 neat cattle, above 3 years of age.

Stanhope, forge, and post-town, on the Musconetcong river, and on the Morris canal, on the S. boundary of Byram t-ship, Sussex co., by the post route, 222 miles from W. C., 59 from Trenton, 11 S. of Newton, and 16 N. W. of Morristown; contains a grist mill, 3 forges, 2 taverns, 2 stores, and from 20 to 30 dwellings, and one large school house. The creek has here been led from its bed, by which means a fine waterfall of 30 feet, available for mill purposes, has been obtained;.an inclined plane of the canal at this place, surmounts an elevation of 76 feet. This thriving little town was founded by Mr. Silas Dickenson; and is surrounded by an excellent soil of limestone.

Staten Island Sound, or *Arthur-Kill*, the strait which divides Staten Island from New Jersey. It has a devious, but general N. E. course, from the head of Raritan bay, and including the *Kill-van-Kuhl*, extends to New York bay, a distance of about 18 miles, having a breadth, commonly much under, and no where exceeding half a mile. It is the ordinary passage of the steamboats which ply between Brunswick, Amboy, and New York. As the tide flows from, and into both bays, from and into this strait, the navigator never has a current with him through its whole length. The channel is skirted on both sides by an agreeable country. That of New Jersey is the more level, and that of Staten Island the more variegated and picturesque. For several miles from New York bay, the shore of the island is so closely covered with houses, as to have the appearance of a continued street.

Steddam's Neck, a strip of land lying in the N. W. angle of Greenwich t-ship, formed by the junction of Newport and Stow creeks.

Steelman's Creek, small tributary, flowing eastwardly into the Great Egg Harbour river, Weymouth t-ship, Gloucester co.

Stephen's Creek, Weymouth t-ship, Gloucester co., tributary of Great Egg Harbour river, having an easterly course of 8 or 9 miles. Two miles from its mouth, is a village and post-town which bears its name; 39 miles S. E. from Woodbury, 78 from Trenton, and 106 N. E. from W. C. It contains a grist and saw mill, tavern, store, and 6 or 8 dwellings.

Stewartsville, p-t. of Greenwich t-ship, Warren co., centrally situate in the t-ship, on Merritt's branch of Pohatcong creek, 10 miles S. E. of Belvidere; contains a tavern, a store, and 10 or 12 dwellings; surrounded by a fertile limestone country, and lying about a mile south of the Morris canal, and about 5 miles east from Easton, Pennsylvania.

Still Valley, of Greenwich t-ship, Warren co., lying between Lopatcong and Pohatcong creeks, and extending N. E. from the river Delaware. This is a rich valley of limestone land, thickly settled, and highly productive in wheat. There is a post-office here named after the valley, on the turnpike road, between 4 and 5 miles from Easton, Pennsylvania.

Stillwater t-ship, Sussex co., bounded N. E. by Newton t-ship; S. E. by Greene t-ship; S. W. by Hardwick t-ship, Warren co.; and N. W. by Walpack t-ship. Centrally distant from Newton, E. 7 miles; greatest length N. and S. 10 miles; breadth E. and W. 7 miles; area, 28,160 acres; surface hilly, on the N. W. mountainous. It is drained by Paulinskill, which crosses it centrally, and receives a tributary from Swartwout's pond in the t-ship. Population in 1830, 1381. Taxables in 1832, 230. Stillwater and Coursenville are post-offices of the t-ship, which contained, in 1832, 40 householders, whose ratables did not exceed $30, 4 run of stones for grinding grain, 4 stores, 6 saw mills, 277 horses and mules, and 692 neat cattle above three years of age, 1 distillery, 64 tan vats. It paid state and county tax, $378 85; poor tax, $200; road tax, $600. S. E. of the Paulinskill, the soil is slate; N. W.

of the creek, lime, slate, and grey rock, and is generally fertile.

Stillwater, p-t. of the above t-ship, by the post-route, 236 miles from W. C., 78 from Trenton, and 7 S. W. from Newton; contains a tavern, store, a grist and oil mill, a Presbyterian church, formerly Dutch Reformed, and 8 or 10 dwellings. The soil around it is limestone, well cultivated.

Stipson's Island, a neck of fast land, near the west boundary of Dennis t-ship, Cape May co., projecting into the marshes, having a length of about 3 miles.

Stockholm, post-office and forge of Jefferson t-ship, Morris co., upon the Pequannock creek, at the N. E. end of the Greenpond mountain, 18 miles N. W. of Morristown, 249 N. E. from W. C., and 83 from Trenton.

Stockingtown, a small hamlet of 6 or 8 dwellings, of Upper Alloways Creek t-ship, Salem co., about 9 miles E. of Salem t-ship, and 3 from Allowaystown.

Stone House Brook, branch of the Pompton river, rising in Pequannock t-ship, and flowing by a course of 6 miles N. W. to its recipient, giving motion to some forges.

Stony Brook, Pequannock t-ship, Morris co., small tributary of the Rockaway river, which flows by several branches, in length from 4 to 5 miles, through Rockaway valley.

Stony Hill, extends from the north branch of the river Raritan, in Bernard and Bridgewater t-ships, through Warren t-ship, in Somerset co., into Essex co., in the form of a crescent; formed of trap rock, on old red sandstone base. Under this name the mountain, following its curve, is about 12 miles long.

Stop-the-Jade Creek, tributary of the S. branch of the Rancocus creek, Northampton t-ship, Burlington co.; unites with the latter at Vincenttown, after a westerly course of 9 miles.— A mill stream.

Stout's Branch, of Paulin's creek, rises in Sand Pond, Hardwick t-ship, Warren co., at the foot of the Blue mountain, and flows by a southerly course of 7 or 8 miles, to its recipient.

Stoutsville, on the line dividing Montgomery t-ship, Somerset co., from Hopewell t-ship, Hunterdon co., and on the turnpike road from Brunswick to Lambertsville, 13 miles S. W. from Somerville; contains a tavern, and 6 or 8 dwellings, in a fertile, pleasant valley.

Stow Creek t-ship, Cumberland co., bounded N. and W. by Stow creek, which divides it from Salem co.; E. by Hopewell t-ship, and S. by Greenwich t-ship. Centrally distant, N. W. from Bridgeton, 7 miles; greatest length, E. and W. 7; breadth, N. and S. 6 miles; area, 10,240 acres; surface, partly level, partly rolling; soil, clay, loam, sand, and gravel. Population in 1830, 791. In 1832, the t-ship contained 170 taxables, 21 householders, whose ratables did not exceed $30; 4 grist mills, 1 saw mill, 198 horses and 557 cattle, above the age of 3 years, 1 store; and paid road tax, $200; state and county, $437 81. Newport creek forms the boundary between this and Greenwich t-ship.

Stow Creek, rises on the confines of Salem and Cumberland cos., and Hopewell and Upper Alloways Creek t-ships, and by a S. W. and S. course, forms the line between these counties, by the meanders of the creek; 25 miles to the Delaware bay. It is navigable for sloops, about 18 miles, and has some good banked meadow on its borders, for the distance of 9 miles, commencing 9 miles from its mouth.

Straw, hamlet of Greenwich t-ship, Warren co., about 5 miles S. E. of Philipsburg, and 12 miles S. of Belvidere; contains 3 or 4 dwellings only.

Stralenberg, hamlet, Hackensack t-ship, Bergen co., about 5 miles N. E. of Hackensacktown; contains 1 Dutch Reformed, and 1 Seceder's church, some 8 or 10 dwellings, a store and tavern; surrounded by a pleasant, level country, of fertile loam, well cultivated.

Stretch's Point, on Stow creek, Lower Alloways Creek t-ship, Salem co., about 7 miles from the mouth of the creek.

Suckasunny, the name of a village and plain; the latter extending in width from 2½ to 3 miles, and in length about 6 miles; is sandy and not very fertile, and is drained by Black, or Lamington river. On the N. E. of this plain, terminates the great vein of iron which has continued a S. W. course from the White Hills in New Hampshire.

The village and post-town is situate on the Morristown and Easton turnpike road, 11 miles N. W. from the former, 63 N. E. from Trenton, and 226 from W. C.; contains a Presbyterian church, a store and tavern, and some 12 or 15 dwellings.

Sucker Pond, a small basin of water, at the east foot of the Blue mountain, in Stillwater t-ship, Sussex co.

Sussex County, was taken from Morris, by act of Assembly, 8th June, 1753, with bounds which included the present county of Warren. Warren was erected by act of 20th Nov. 1824; and Sussex is now bounded S. by the Musconetcong river and Hopatcong pond; thence by a line running N. E. dividing it from Morris and Bergen counties, to the line of the state of New York; thence along that line N. W., to the Delaware river, at the mouth of the Nevisink, or Macacomac river; thence by the river, to the mouth of the Flatkill; and thence by a line S. E., separating it from Warren co., to the Musconetcong river, somewhat more than a mile below Andover furnace. Its form approaches an oblong, with a mean length of 26, and breadth of 22 miles; area, about 572 square miles, or 366,000 acres: central lat. 41° 8' N.; long. 2° 15' from W. C.

The county is divided geologically by the primitive and transition formations. The former passing N. E. by Sparta, and including within its limits, the Hamburg or Wallkill, and the Wawayanda mountains. These

mountains abound with a variety of minerals, of which iron and zinc are the most considerable. The country between these hills and the Blue mountain is rolling; nay, hilly; in which, ridges of slate, alternate with valleys of limestone; and is highly fertile, and every where well cultivated. The Blue, or Kittatinny mountain, is skirted on the east by grey rock, which bears great resemblance to the primitive, and certainly contains little evidence of recombination. The mountain itself appears to be composed partly of similar rock, of a bluish green and red sandstone, the colours of which are singularly and intimately blended. Upon the N. W. the mountain is bounded by a broad strip of grey limestone.

A dividing ridge running from Blue mountain, in Frankford t-ship, north of Culver's Pond, through the S. E. angle of that t-ship, on towards Sparta, gives a determination to the waters of the county, sending part N. E. towards the Hudson, and part towards the Delaware river. Thus all the waters of the eastern portion pour from the hills north and south, into the valley of the Wallkill, where the flatness of the surface causes them to spread over a considerable space, and occasions an extensive marsh along the borders of that stream, greatly enlarged within the bounds of the state of New York. The western portion of the county is drained chiefly by the Paulinskill, flowing by a deep and rapid course, through this and Warren county, to its recipient near Columbia.

The face of the country is dotted with large ponds, or small lakes, some of which are on the highest hills. Swartwout's and Culver's ponds are the largest—the first being 3 miles in length, by 1 in breadth, and the other 2 miles in length, by the same breadth. But the most remarkable are the White Ponds, which have been so called, from the appearance of their shores and bottoms, covered with shells of the snail, in very extensive masses. Two of these lie on the line between Newton and Hardiston townships.

The agriculture of the county is in a state of progressive improvement, and is now very productive. The limestone lands yield large crops of wheat, and the slate, where the rock does not come too near to the surface, is scarce less fertile. Lime is not yet much employed as manure, but its use is growing, and will doubtlessly be extensive, when its benefits shall be generally known. Wheat, rye, oats, corn, and iron, are staple products.

The principal towns and post offices, are Newton, the county town, Deckertown, Hamburg, Ogdensburg, Sparta, Andover, Greenville, Stillwater, Branchville, Augusta, and Lafayette. Benville, Coursenville, Flatbrookville, Fredon, Gratitude, Harmony, Hamburg, Lafayette, Libertyville, Lockwood, Monroe, Montague, Sandystone, Stanhope, Vernon, Walpack, and Wantage.

By returns of the assessors, for the year 1832, there were 1075 householders, 58 merchants, shopkeepers, and traders, 87 run of stones for grinding grain, 18 carding machines, 3 iron furnaces, 55 saw mills, 28 forge fires, 7 fulling mills, 3875 horses and mules, 13,070 neat cattle 3 years old and upwards, 6 ferries and toll bridges, 227 tan vats, 36 distilleries, and 101,887 acres of improved land. The amount of state and county tax, was $7500 95; poor tax, $3300; road tax, $8600.

By the census of 1830, the population of the county amounted to 20,346 souls, of whom 10,240 were white males; 9654 white females; 206 free coloured males; 195 free coloured females; 21 male, and 30 female slaves. Of these inhabitants, 89 were aliens; 6 deaf and dumb; 14 blind.

The provision for moral improvement in the county, consist of 2 classical seminaries at Newton, 6 common schools in that town, and others in sufficient numbers for the wants of the people throughout the county; a Lyceum for the cultivation of letters and science, and a public library at Newton; a county Bible society, a county Sunday school union, and district Sunday schools and temperance societies.

The county elects 1 member to the legislative council, and 2 to the Assembly. The courts of common pleas, orphans', and quarter sessions, are holden at Newton, on the last Tuesday of January, the 4th Tuesday of May, the 3d of August, and the 4th of November; and the circuit courts, and sessions of oyer and terminer and general jail delivery, are holden on the 4th Tuesdays of May, and November.

STATISTICAL TABLE OF SUSSEX COUNTY.

Townships.	Length.	Breadth.	Area.	Surface.	Population. 1810.	1820.	1830.
Byram,	10	8	21,760	mountainous.	591	672	958
Frankfort,	11	8½	28,800	valley.	1637	2008	1996
Green,	9	4	14,080	p't hilly, p't level.			801
Hardiston,	13	9	41,960	mountainous.	1702	2160	2588
Montague,	8½	7½	21,620	moun. & riv. flat.	661	964	990
Newton,	12	10	65,920	hilly, p't level.	2082	2743	3464
Sandistone,	8½	7	19,320	moun. & riv. flat.	703	1945	1097
Stillwater,	10	7	28,160	moun. level.			1381
Walpack,	10	4	15,360	moun. & riv. flat.	591	822	660
Wantage,	11	8½	42,880	do. do.	2969	3307	4034
Vernon,	11	10	52,480	mountainous.	1708	2096	2377
			352,300		12,644	16,617	20,346

We have already, in our introductory chapter, noted generally the geological and mineralogical character of this county. But the reader will be gratified with the following special notice from Dr. Samuel Fowler, whose intimate knowledge of the subject, renders the account highly valuable.

Perhaps in no quarter of the globe is there so much found to interest the mineralogist, as in the white crystalline calcareous valley, commencing at Mounts Adam and Eve, in the county of Orange, and state of New York, about three miles from the line of the state of New Jersey, and continuing thence, through Vernon, Hamburg, Franklin, Sterling, Sparta and Byram, a distance of about twenty-five miles, in the county of Sussex, and state of New Jersey. This limestone is highly crystalline, containing no organic remains, and is the great imbedding matrix of all the curious and interesting minerals found in this valley. When burned, it produces lime of a superior quality. A considerable quantity of this stone is burned into lime near Hamburg, and when carted to the towns below, as Patterson, Newark, &c. is sold for one dollar per bushel. It is principally used in masonry, for whitewashing, cornice work, and wall of a fine hard finish, and is considered superior to the best Rhode Island lime. Some varieties, particularly the granular, furnish a beautiful marble; it is often white, with a slight tinge of yellow, resembling the Parian marble from the island of Paros; at other times clouded, black, sometimes veined, black, and at other times arborescent.

Franklinite; a new metalliferous combination, containing, according to Berthier, of oxide of zinc 17, of iron 66, and manganese 16, is very abundant; indeed it appears inexhaustible. It commences about half a mile north-east of Franklin furnace, and extends two miles southwest of Sparta, a distance of nine miles. It is accompanied in this whole distance by the red oxide of zinc, mutually enveloping each other. The greatest quantity appears to be at Franklin furnace. The bed here, is about 100 feet high above the adjoining land, on the west side of it, and from ten to forty feet wide. Various attempts have been made to work this ore in a blast furnace, but without success. It frequently congeals in the hearth, before time is allowed to get it out in a liquid state, in consequence of a combination of the iron with manganese. All this difficulty I apprehend might be overcome, if a method could be discovered of smelt-

ing iron ore in a blast furnace with anthracite coal; as the Franklinite requires a greater degree of heat to cause it to retain its liquid state, than can be obtained by the use of charcoal. It occurs in grains imbedded in the white carbonate of lime, and detached in concretions of various sizes, from that of a pin's head to a hickory nut; also, in regular octahedral crystals, emarginated on the angles, small at Franklin, but very perfect, with brilliant faces. At Sterling, the crystals are large and perfect. I have one from that place that measures sixteen inches around the common base.

Red Oxide of Zinc.—At Sterling, three miles from Franklin, a mountain mass of this formation presents itself about 200 feet high. Here, as Mr. Nuttall truly observes, the red oxide of zinc forms as it were a paste, in which the crystals of Franklinite are thickly imbedded; in fact a metalliferous porphyry. This appears to be the best adapted for manufacturing purposes. The Franklinite imbedded in the zinc ore here, is highly magnetic, and may be all separated by magnetic cylinders, recently brought into use to separate the earthy portion of magnetic iron ore. It was long since observed, that this ore is well adapted for the manufacture of the best brass, and may be employed without any previous preparation. It is reduced without any difficulty to a metallic state, and may be made to furnish the sulphate of zinc (white vitriol).

It is remarked by Professor Bull, "that this ore, from its abundance, and the many uses to which it may be applied, promises to be a valuable acquisition to the manufacturing interest of the United States." Berthier found it to contain oxide of zinc 88, red oxide of manganese 12.

Magnetic Iron Ore. On the west side of the Franklinite, and often within a few feet of it, appears an abundance of magnetic iron ore, usually accompanied by hornblende rock. In some places it soon runs into the Franklinite, which destroys its usefulness; and the largest beds are combined with plumbago, which renders it unprofitable to work in a blooming forge, but valuable in a blast furnace. On the Franklin or Warwick mountain, about four miles east of the furnace, are numerous beds of iron ore, from which many thousand tons have been taken; and which still contain a large quantity of the best quality of ore, either for a blooming forge or blast furnace. Iron pyrites occur here, both in the valley and on the mountain, of a proper quality to manufacture sulphate of iron—(copperas.) It also occurs crystallized, in cubes, in octahedrons, and dodecahedrons, frequently perfect, and highly splendid.

The other minerals found in this district are numerous, rare, interesting, and several of them new, and not found in any other place, but better calculated to instruct the naturalist and adorn his cabinet, than for any particular uses to which they have as yet been applied. A catalogue of which I have subjoined, designating the minerals as they occur in each township.

In Byram t-ship, considered the south western extremity of the white carbonate of lime.

1. Spinelle, colour reddish brown, green, and black, in octahedral crystals, associated with orange coloured brucite.

2. Brucite of various shades, from that of a straw colour, to a dark orange, and nearly black.

3. Grey hornblende in six-sided prisms, with diedral summits.

In the Township of Hardiston.

At Sparta:

1. Brucite of a beautiful honey colour— the finest we have is found here.

2. Augite in six-sided prisms, colour brownish green.

At Sterling:

1. Spinelle, black, green, and grey, in octahedral crystals.

2. Brucite of various shades.

3. Brutile, colour steel grey; lustre metallic, in acicular prisms, with longitudinal striad.

4. Blende, black and white; the white sometimes in octahedral crystals, the lustre brilliant.

5. Dysluite, in octahedral crystals, colour brown externally, internally yellowish brown; lustre metallic—(a new mineral.)

6. Ferruginous silicate of manganese, in six-sided prisms, colour pale yellow, associated with Franklinite.

7. Tourmaline, imbedded in white feldspar, in six-sided prisms, longitudinally striated; colour reddish brown.

8. Green and blue carbonate of copper. A number of large excavations were made at the Sterling mine for copper, during the revolutionary war, under an erroneous impression, that the red oxide of zinc, was the red copper ore. It was the property of Lord Sterling; hence the name of the Sterling mine. Of copper, we only find there a trace of the green and blue carbonate.

At Franklin:

1. Spinelle, black and red crystallized.

2. Ceylonite, green and bluish green, in perfect octahedrons truncated on the angles; lustre of the brilliance of polished steel.

5. Garnets, black, brown, yellow, red, and green—crystallized in dodecahedrons.

6. Silicate of Manganese, light brownish red.

7. Ferro Silicate of Manganese, of Professor Thomson, and the Fowlerite, of

Nuttall, light red or pink, foliated and splendent, has much the appearance of Feldspar, is also in rectangular prisms.

8. Lesqui-Silicate of Manganese, lamellar in scales or small plates; colour, brownish black.

9. Hornblende, crystallized.

10. Actynolite, do.

11. Tremolite, do.

12. Augite, common variety, do.

13. Jeffersonite, do. do.

14. Plumbago, foliated and crystallized in six-sided balls.

15. Brucite of various shades.

16. Scapolite, white, crystallized.

17. Wernerite, yellow, do.

18. Tourmaline, black, do.

19. Fluate of Lime, earthy and do.

20. Galena.

21. Oolite, in small grains about the size of a mustard seed, disseminated in blue secondary carbonate of lime.

22. Asbestos, connected with Hornblende rock.

23. Green Beryl.

24. Feldspar, green and white, crystallized.

25. Epidote and Pink Carbonate of Lime.

26. Arsenical Pyrites.

27. Serpentine.

28. Sahlite.

29. Cocolite, green and black.

30. Sphene, honey colour, crystallized.

31. Quartz.

32. Jasper.

33. Chalcedony.

34. Amethyst, crystallized.

35. Agate.

36. Mica, black and orange coloured, crystallized.

37. Zircon, crystallized.

38. Sulphate of Molybdena.

39. Phosphate of Iron.

40. Carbonate of Iron.

41. Steatite, foliated with yellow Garnet.

42. Phosphate of Lime, crystallized.

43. Pale Yellow-blende, of a foliated structure—lustre, vitreous.

Near Hamburgh.

1. An ore of Manganese, and iron of a light reddish brown, very compact and heavy.

2. Augite and Brucite.

In the Township of Vernon.

1. Green Spinelle and Brucite, in octahedral crystals.

In Newton Township.

1. Sulphate of Barytes in lamellar masses, and tabular crystals, in a vein traversing secondary limestone.

2. Sapphire, blue and white, in rhombs and six-sided prisms.

3. Red Oxide of Titanium.

4. Grey Spinelle in large octahedral crystals.

5. Mica, copper coloured, in hexahedral crystals.

6. Idocrase, crystallized, yellowish brown.

7. Steatite, presenting the pseudomorphous form of quartz, scapolite, and spinelle.

8. Scapolite, in four-sided prisms. For a more particular account of the Newton minerals, see Silliman's Journal, vol. XXI. page 319.

In Frankford Township.

Serpentine, of a light yellowish green, bears a fine polish, has a glistening lustre, and is quite abundant.

Swartwout's Pond, a large sheet of water, of Stillwater t-ship, Sussex co., which sends forth a tributary to Paulinskill.

Swedesboro', p-t. of Woolwich t-ship, Gloucester co., 13 miles S. W. from Woodbury, 49 miles from Trenton, and 155 from W. C., at the head of sloop navigation, on Raccoon creek, about 5 miles from its mouth; contains about 100 dwellings, an Episcopal and a Methodist church, an academy, 2 taverns, 4 stores, a merchant grist mill, and an extensive woollen factory, belonging to C. C. Stratton, Esq. The country around it is level; soil, sandy loam, fertile, and well cultivated. Battentown, a mile distant from it, contains 1 tavern, and a few dwellings.

Swede's Branch, mill stream of Chester t-ship, Burlington co., flows by a N. W. course of more than 3 miles, to the Delaware river.

Swimming River. (See *Shrewsbury river.*)

Tabernacle, village of Northampton t-ship, Burlington co., 12 miles S. W. of Mount Holly; contains a Methodist church, a tavern, and 10 or 12 houses.

Talman's Creek, small tributary of the Rancocus creek, rising in Evesham t-ship, Burlington co., near Evesham village, and flows six miles to its recipient.

Tansboro', village of Gloucester t-ship, of Gloucester co., on the road from Long-a-coming, to Great Egg Harbour river, 15 miles S. E. from Woodbury, 18 from Camden; contains a tavern, and some half dozen dwellings. Surrounded by a sandy soil, and pine forest.

Tarkiln Creek, mill stream of Maurice River t-ship, Cumberland co., rising in the t-ship, and flowing by a southerly course, of 10 miles into the Delaware bay.

Taunton Furnace, on Haines' creek, Evesham t-ship, Burlington co., 11 miles S. W. from Mount Holly, and 14 S. E. from Camden.

Tenants' Run, a tributary of South river, South Amboy t-ship, Middlesex co., flowing N. W., between 3 and 4 miles to its recipient.

Tewkesbury, t-ship, Hunterdon co., bounded N. by Washington t-ship, Morris co.; E. by Bedminster t-ship, Somerset co.; S. by Readington t-ship, and W. and S. W. by Lebanon t-ship; centrally distant N. E. from Flemington, 14 miles; greatest length, N. and S., 8; breadth, E. and W. 6½ miles; area, 23,000 acres; surface hilly; soil, on the mountain, clay and loam, and in the valley, at its foot, grey limestone, rich and well cultivated; drained by Rockaway creek, and its tributaries, flowing S. E. through the township, and by Lamington river, which runs on the eastern boundary. New Germantown, and Pottersville, are post-towns of the t-ship. Population in 1830, 1659. In 1832 the t-ship contained 8 stores, 6 saw mills, 3 grist mills, 28 tanner's vats, 2 carding machines, 2 fulling mills, 9 distilleries, 417 horses and mules, 696 neat cattle, above 3 years of age; and paid poor tax, $350; road tax, $600; state and county tax, $706 68.

Tice's Pond, at the foot of the Ramapo mountain, Pompton t-ship, Bergen co.; covers about 200 acres of ground, and is the source of a tributary of Ringwood river.

Timber Creek, Big, Gloucester co., rises by two branches, the lesser in Gloucester, and the greater in Deptford t-ship, uniting about 6 miles above the mouth. The north branch is navigable for sloops from the Delaware to Chew's landing, a distance of 8 or 9 miles, and the south, nearly to Blackwoodtown, a distance of about 10 miles. The whole length of the stream, by its meanders, may be 13 or 14 miles. It receives several small tributaries in its course, and drives some valuable mills.

Timber Creek, Little, of Woolwich t-ship, Gloucester co., rises in the t-ship, and flows N. W. 7 or 8 miles, to the Delaware river, below Chester Island. There is a mill upon it, near its head.

Tinton Falls, village, and mill site of Shrewsbury t-ship, Monmouth co., upon a branch of the Nevisink river, 9 miles E. from Freehold; contains from 15 to 20 dwellings, a grist and saw mill, 1 tavern, and 2 stores. The water of the S. E. branch of Swimming river, falls over a sand rock, filled with animal remains, and forming a cascade of about 30 feet high. From this rock flows a copious chalybeate spring, which is frequently visited by those who seek health or amusement at the boarding houses near the coast.

Titusville, post-office, Hunterdon county.

Toms' River, p-t., of Dover t-ship, Monmouth co., upon the head of Toms' River bay, and tide water, 25 miles S. E. from Freehold, 221 from W. City, and 69 from Trenton, and 6 from the confluence of the river with Barnegat bay; a flourishing village, lying on both sides of the creek, united by a wooden bridge, of near 200 feet in length; contains from 50 to 60 frame dwellings, some of which are very neat and commodious; 2 taverns, 5 or 6 stores, and a Methodist meeting. Many sloops and schooners are built here, and more than $200,000 worth of timber and cord-wood, annually exported.

Toms' River, mill stream of Monmouth co.; its main branch rises on the line dividing Freehold and Upper Freehold t-ships, and near Paint Island spring; and flows thence by a S. E. and E. course of 30 miles, into Barnegat bay. Above the village

of Toms' river, about 4 miles, it receives the south branch, which is formed by many streams from Dover and Upper Freehold t-ships; and about a mile above the village, Wrangle Brook also unites with it. It drains a wide expanse of forest land, and by the main stream and branches turns many mills and iron works.

Townsbury, post-office, Warren county.

Tranquility, small tributary of the west branch of Wading river, rises and flows about 4 miles in the neck of land, between the east and west branches of the river.

Trap, hamlet of Shrewsbury t-ship, Monmouth co., near Shark river, 11 miles S. E. from Freehold; containing 6 or 8 dwellings, surrounded by a sandy soil and pine forest.

Trenton t-ship, Hunterdon co., bounded N. by Hopewell, E. by Lawrence t-ships; S. E. by Nottingham t-ship, of Burlington co.; and S. W. and W. by the river Delaware. Greatest length N. W. and S. E. 8 miles; breadth E. and W. 6 miles; area, 10,609 acres; surface, level; soil, clay and red shale, generally well cultivated, and productive. It is drained by Jacob's creek on the north, and by the Assunpink and its tributaries, on the south. The town of Birmingham, and the city of Trenton, are within its boundary. Population in 1830, 3925. In 1832, there were in the t-ship 11 merchants, 3 fisheries, 2 saw mills, 3 grist mills, 2 ferries and bridges, 220 tan vats, 2 grain distilleries, 469 horses and mules, and 590 neat cattle, above 3 years old; and it paid poor tax, $900; road tax, $400; and county tax, $1264 98. (See *Trenton City.*)

Trenton, city, and seat of government of the state, on the left bank of the Delaware river, three-fourths of a mile above the tide, opposite the lower falls of the river, and on the north side of the Assunpink creek, Trenton t-ship, Hunterdon co., 30 miles from Philadelphia, 58 from New York; lat. 40° 13′ 41″ N.; long. 0° 21′ 15″ E. of Philadelphia, and 2° 8' 15" of Washington City. Incorporated by the act of 13th November, 1792, which established its government under a mayor, recorder, 3 aldermen, and 13 assistants, with the usual city privileges, and power to license taverns within the city; and by the act of 3d January, 1817, the mayor, recorder, and aldermen, or any three of them, of whom the mayor and recorder must be one, are empowered to hold a court of general quarter sessions. There are here, a state house, 100 by 60 feet, with bow at either end, cupola, and bell; the building is of stone, stuccoed in imitation of dark granite, and beautifully situated on the bank of the river, commanding a fine view of the stream, the airy bridge which has been thrown over it, and of the undulating shore of Pennsylvania : a house for the residence of the governor of the state; 3 fire-proof offices, a bank incorporated in 1804, with an authorized capital of $600,000, of which $214,740 only have been paid in; an academy in which the languages are taught, 3 boarding and day schools for females, and several common schools. These are, however, in the city proper; but Trenton, as known in common parlance, including the villages of Mill Hill, Bloomsbury, and Lamberton, extending 1¾ miles down the river bank, has an Episcopal, Presbyterian, Friends', Baptist, Reformed Baptist, Roman Catholic, Methodist, and African Methodist churches. Trenton proper contains 425 dwellings, 13 taverns, about 30 stores, among which are 3 bookstores, and 3 silversmith shops; 3 printing offices, each of which issues a weekly paper, viz. the Union, the True American, and the New Jersey Gazetteer; a public library, established about the year 1750, and a lyceum or literary association. Mill Hill has 78 dwellings, 4 stores, and 4 taverns. Bloomsbury, 145 dwellings, 2 stores, and 5 taverns; and Lamberton, 64 dwellings, 2 stores, and 2 taverns. The Philadelphia steam-boats ply daily, and sometimes several times a day, one from Lamberton, and others from Bloomsbury; and stages run 3 times a day by the rail-road to New York and Philadelphia. Stages also run hence by Princeton to Brunswick, and to various other parts of the country The Delaware and Raritan canal receives its feeder here, on which is an extensive basin for vessels and boats, and the main canal crosses the Assunpink east of the town, over a noble stone aqueduct. The state prison is at Lamberton, where a new prison is also being erected, adapted to the confinement of 150 convicts. The famed bridge over the Delaware, is thrown from Bloomsbury to Morrisville, a span of 1100 feet, having a double carriage-way and foot-paths resting on the chords of, and suspended from, a series of five arches, supported on stone piers. This structure has been much admired for its lightness, grace, and strength. There are on the Assunpink, within the town, two cotton mills, having 5400 spindles, and one mill for power looms, and on the Delaware, two mills for looms; the whole number of looms exceed 200.

For some years past Trenton has not been in a very thriving state, but the late improvements have given new life to business and enterprise, and much prosperity is anticipated from the completion of the canal, and particularly from the construction of the mill race, now being made by the Trenton Falls Company.

This company was incorporated by an act of the legislature, 16th Feb. 1831, with power to purchase, lease, or sell lands, mills, and water privileges useful in the creation of water power; to cut a wing dam in the Delaware river, between the mouth of the Assunpink and the head of Wells' Falls, and a race-way along the bank, not extending more than one and a half miles below the Trenton Falls; to make lateral race-ways and other works; to sell lots, sites, and privileges under the charter; and with a general power of taking lands necessary for their purposes, at the appraisement of the commissioners; and with the customary powers granted to other corporations. Their charter is perpetual, protecting the company from any tax exceeding the half of one per cent. on the actual amount of capital expended in the construction of the work, with the privilege of extending its capital to $200,000. Each share, in the election of managers, is entitled to one vote.

The capital subscribed is $90,000; the cost of constructing the work is estimated at $140,000 exclusive of the lands purchased by the company for mill sites and building lots. The canal and race-way commences at the head of Scudder's Falls, directly opposite the upper end of Slack's Island, and continues down the margin of the river, to a point opposite the centre of White's Island, where, leaving the bank, it enters upon the meadows bordering the river, through which it passes to the Assunpink, in Trenton; thence, it is designed to cross this creek by an aqueduct, and to pass through Bloomsbury, to the precincts of Lamberton, where it debouches into the river.

The fall in the river Delaware, between the head and foot of the race-way is 20 feet, of which, one foot and a half descent is given to the race-way, leaving a head and fall at the Assunpink of 14 feet, and below the foot of the Trenton Falls 18½ feet.

The entire column of the water descending the race-way is estimated at 23,868 cubic feet per minute, at the lowest known state of the water.— This at the Assunpink, will afford a power equal to 335 horses; or if all be expended below the Assunpink, equal to 575 horses: or should one-third of the water be used above, and two-thirds below the creek, the power above will be equal to 145 horses, and that below, to 384 horses. This calculation is based on a depth of six feet water only, in the race-way; the minimum supply, after all deductions for leakage and evaporation at the lowest water.

This, however, is the view of the power, in what is deemed its first stage. The work commences at the upper end of Slack's Island, which is of considerable extent, situate near the middle of the river. The main channel of the stream was formerly on the right, or Pennsylvania side of the island, but a loose stone wall having, some years since, been thrown across this channel to improve the navigation of the river, the larger portion of the water was thrown into the Jersey channel. This wall remains, but it is overflowed at the lowest water. By raising this dam and throwing the whole current of the river into this channel, or by entirely removing it, and erecting a dam from the head of the company's works to Slack's Island, and reopening the channel on the other side, the water in the raceway would be raised two feet beyond its present elevation; and in constructing their work, the company have adapted it to the reception of that body of water. A column of eight feet instead of six, would thus be gained in the race; the velocity of its current increased to 122 feet per minute, and the quantity of water to 52,704 cubic feet in the same time. The power of the water would then be equal to 960 horses at the Assunpink, or 1260 below it: or should one-third of the power be employed above, and two-thirds below the creek, it would afford the company a power above, equal to 330 horses, below, 840, in the whole 1170.

The company propose to let their lands for the erection of mills, above the Assunpink, at 30 cents, and below the creek, at from 40 to 50 cents the foot, perpetual rent, according to situation; with the right of the free use of the company's wharf, rail-road, &c.: and their lands for dwellings, in lots 20 by 75 feet, at $6 per annum. The buildings, in all cases, to be fire proof. And they propose to let the water from the main race-way for mill power, at a perpetual rent of three dollars above, and four dollars below the Assunpink creek, for every square inch area of the aperture, through which it shall be drawn off by a flume, the plan of which is in the office of the company. The aperture to be measured and made according to the standard measure, also kept by the company, and similar to that in the office of the Secretary of State, at Washington, and according to other regulations published by the company.

The advantages of this site for manufacturing purposes are perhaps unsurpassed by any in the country. Intermediately situated between the great markets of Philadelphia and New York, 30 miles from the former, and 60 from the latter—surrounded by a rich agricultural country, producing a large surplus quantity of grain of every description, and capable of quadrupling its productions—upon a river, navigable to the ocean, and for near 250 miles above the falls, flowing through a wide and fertile country, whose products may find a ready market here; having also the feeder of the Delaware and Raritan canal, connecting with the main canal in the heart of the city plot, whilst the canal itself unites with the Delaware, below the bar at Bordentown, and passing through Trenton, along the Millstone and Raritan rivers, to New Brunswick, affords a fine sloop navigation, and all the advantages of cheap and rapid water transportation from and to Philadelphia and New York:—the facility of obtaining an abundant and cheap supply of anthracite coal by the river and the Pennsylvania canal, on the opposite bank:—the rail-roads made, and in progress towards New York and Philadelphia, of which, there are two leading to the latter, one on each side of the river; that on the west running directly from the city, and that on the east from Bordentown, combine all that the manufacturer can require:—a healthy country, abundant and cheap provisions, an adequate supply of labourers, convenience in obtaining raw materials, unfailing power for its manipulation, and a chance of, and ready access to, the best markets of the country.

The following is a description of Trenton, in 1748, as given by the Swedish traveller Kalm—which the citizen will delight to compare with its present condition:

"Trenton is a long, narrow town, situate at some distance from the river Delaware, on a sandy plain. It is reckoned 30 miles from Philadelphia. It has two small churches, one for the people belonging to the Church of England, the other for the Presbyterians. The houses are partly built of stone, though most of them are made of wood or planks, commonly two stories high, together with a cellar below the building, and a kitchen under ground, close to the cellar. The houses stand at a moderate distance from one another. They are commonly built so that the street passes along one side of the houses, while gardens of different dimensions bound the other side; in each garden is a draw-well; the place is reckoned very healthy. Our landlord told us that 22 years ago, when he first settled here, (1726) there was hardly more than one house: but from that time, Trenton has increased so much, that there are at present near an hundred houses. The houses were within, divided into several rooms by their partitions of boards. The inhabitants of the place carried on a small trade with the goods which they got from Philadelphia; but their chief gain consisted in the arrival of the numerous travellers between that city and New York; for they are commonly brought by the Trenton yachts from Philadelphia to Trenton, or from thence to Philadelphia. But from Trenton, further to New Brunswick, the travellers go in wagons, which set out every day for that place. Several of the inhabitants also subsist on the carriage of all sorts of goods, which are sent in great quantities, either from Philadelphia to New York, or from thence to the former place— for between Philadelphia and Trenton, all goods go by water; but between Trenton and New Brunswick, they are all carried by land, and both these conveniences belong to people of this town. For the yachts which go between this place and the capital of Pennsylvania, they usually pay a shilling and sixpence, Pennsylvania currency, per person, and every one pays beside for his baggage. Every passenger must provide meat and drink for himself, and pay some settled fare. Between Trenton and New Brunswick, a person pays 2s. 6d., and the baggage is likewise paid for separately."

The town was founded a few years prior to 1720, by William Trent, an enterprising trader, who was distinguished for public spirit, and private character, in the provinces of Pennsylvania and New Jersey. He was at one time, Speaker of the Assembly of the former, and at another, Speaker of the Assembly of the latter, province. The site of Trenton, before it bore his name, was significantly called Littleworth. Mr. Trent died on the 29th December, 1724.

Trowbridge Mountain, a long and irregularly shaped hill, of Morris co., extending from the N. branch of the Raritan, through Mendham, Randolph, and Hanover t-ships, to the Rockaway river, ranging S. W. and N. E. It is of granitic formation; many parts of it in cultivation, but generally sterile.

Troy, hamlet of Hanover t-ship, Morris co., on the Parcipany river, about 7 miles N. E. of Morristown; contains a forge, 1 grist mill, a saw mill, and 12 or 15 dwellings. Soil, sandy loam.

Tubmill, branch of Wading river, rises in the west plains of Little Egg Harbour t-ship, Burlington co., and flows S. W. 7 miles to its recipient, about a mile below Bridgeport.

Tuckahoe Creek, rises on the line between Weymouth t-ship, Gloucester co., and Maurice river t-ship, Cumberland co., and forms, in part, the western boundary of the former co., and also, its southern boundary, separating it in the latter case, from Cape May co. Its course, for about 11 miles, is S., thence due E. for about 12 miles; emptying into Great Egg Harbour bay. It is a fine mill stream, driving several mills, at Marshallville, Etna, and other higher points, and is navigable for sloops, above the village of Tuckahoe, more than 10 miles from the ocean.

Tuckahoe, p-t. on both sides of the Tuckahoe river, over which there is a bridge, 10 miles above the sea, 46 miles S. E. from Woodbury, and by post-route 192 from Washington; contains some 20 dwellings, 3 taverns, several stores. It is a place of considerable trade in wood, lumber, and ship building. The land immediately on the river is good, but a short distance from it, is swampy and low.

Tuckerton, p-t, and port of entry, for Little Egg Harbour district, about 35 miles S. E. of Mount Holly, 65 from Trenton, and 189 N. E. from W. C.; situate on a narrow tongue of land, projecting into the marsh on Little Egg Harbour bay, Little Egg Harbour t-ship, Burlington co.; contains between 30 and 40 dwellings, 4 taverns, 5 stores, 2 Methodist churches, a Quaker meeting house. It lies upon a navigable stream, called Shord's Mill Branch, 6 miles from the bay, whence wood scows and flats ascend to the town. There is a large business done here in timber and cord-wood; and salt is, or was manufactured in the vicinity. The town is frequented during the summer season, by many persons for the benefits of sea-bathing, &c. A stage plies regularly between it and Philadelphia.

Tulipehaukin Creek, tributary of the west branch of Wading river, rises in, and has its whole course of about 8 miles, through Washington t-ship, Burlington co.

Turpentine, hamlet of Northampton t-ship, Burlington co., on the road from Mount Holly to Freehold, about a mile east from the former; contains a tavern, a store, and some 8 or 10 dwellings.

Turtle Gut Inlet, Lower t-ship, Cape May co., between Five Mile and Two Mile Beach.

Tuscomusco Creek, a small tributary of the Atsion river, Evesham t-ship, Burlington co.

Two Mile Beach, on the Atlantic ocean, Lower t-ship, Cape May co., between Turtle Gut and Cold Spring Inlet.

Union Cross Roads, hamlet of Deptford t-ship, Gloucester co., 4 miles S. E. of Woodbury; contains 3 or 4 dwellings.

Union t-ship, Essex co., bounded N. by Orange and Newark t-ships; E. by Elizabethtown t-ship; S. by Rahway, and W. by Westfield and Springfield t-ships. Centrally distant from Newark S. W. 6 miles: greatest length N. and S. 5½, breadth E. and W. 5 miles; area, 12,000 acres; surface, rolling; soil, red shale, well cultivated; watered by Elizabeth river on the east, and Rahway river on the west. Population in 1830, 1405.— In 1832 the t-ship contained 350 taxables, 56 householders, whose ratables did not exceed $30 in value; 40 single men, 2 stores, 7 saw mills, 1 woollen factory, 21 tan vats; and paid state tax, $179 65; county, 470 04; poor, $300. There is a fine body of turf here, upon the south branch of Elizabeth river.

Union or "*Connecticut Farms*," is the post-town of the preceding t-ship, situated on the road from Elizabethtown to Morristown, 4 miles N. W. of the former, 5 miles S. E. from Newark, 213 N. E. from W. C., and 47 from Trenton; contains a Presbyterian church, and within a half a mile of it, 3 taverns, a store, and about 30 dwellings.

Up-Clearing Creek, a small tributary of Cohansey creek, which flows westerly into it, from Hopewell t-sp, Cumberland co.

Upper t-ship, Cape May co., bounded N. by Tuckahoe creek, which divides it from Weymouth t-ship, Gloucester co.; E. and S. E. by the Atlantic ocean; S. W. by Dennis t-sp; and N. W. by Maurice river t-ship,

Cumberland co. Centrally distant from Cape May court-house N. E. 13 miles: greatest length N. E. and S. W. 12 miles; breadth S. E. and N. W. 11½ miles; area, 37,000 acres; surface, flat; soil, sand and clay; timber, generally oak and cedar. Population in 1830, 1067. In 1832 there were in the t-ship about 200 taxables, 173 householders, whose ratables did not exceed $30; 1 grist mill, 6 saw mills, 6 stores, 140 horses, and 560 cattle above the age of three years. There are 1 Baptist and 1 Episcopalian church, here. The t-ship paid for t-ship expenses, $77 38; county, $466 65; state tax, $150 73. It is drained by Tuckahoe river and Cedar Swamp creek. The last flows N. E. from the S. W. boundary of the t-ship, through an extensive cedar swamp into the river. On the Atlantic front is Ludlam's and Peck's Beaches, having a width of near half a mile, between which the tide flows into several marsh canals and small lagunes. The marsh may have an average width of about two miles. Tuckahoe village lies on the Tuckahoe river, partly in this, and partly in Gloucester co., having a post-office in the latter. Marshallville lies on the line between Cumberland and Cape May counties, but in the former.

Vancamp Brook, rises from two ponds at the west foot of the Blue mountain, Walpack t-ship, Sussex co., and by a S. W. course of about 8 miles empties into the Delaware river, in Pahaquarry t-ship.

Vansickles, tavern, store, and post-office, of Bethlehem t-ship, Hunterdon co., on the S. E. foot of the Musconetcong mountain, 10 miles N. W. from Flemington, 36 from Trenton, and 195 from W. C.

Varmintown, hamlet of Upper Freehold t-ship, Monmouth co., 6 miles S. E. of Allentown, and 16 S. W. of Freehold; contains a wheelwright and smith shop, and 2 or 3 cottages, in a fertile country of sandy loam.

Vauxhall, small hamlet of Springfield t-ship, Essex co., 7 miles W. from Newark, and 2½ N. from Springfield.

Vealtown, in a vale of Mine mountain, on Mine Brook, Bernard t-ship, Somerset co., 11 miles N. of Somerville; contains a mill and some half dozen dwellings.

Vernon t-ship, Sussex co., bounded N. by the state of New York; E. by Pompton t-ship, Bergen co.; S. by Hardiston t-ship; and W. by Wantage t-ship, from which it is separated by the Wallkill river. Greatest length 11, breadth 10 miles; area, 52,480 acres. The whole surface of the t-ship is covered by mountains; the Wallkill and Wawayanda mountains being on the south and east, and the Pochuck mountain on the west. It is drained north by Warwick creek and its tributaries, Black creek and Double Pond creek; south by Pacak creek, a tributary of the Pequannock, and by some small tributaries of the Wallkill river. Population in 1830, 2377; taxables in 1832, 382. There were in the t-ship in 1832, 158 householders, whose ratables did not exceed $30; 2 storekeepers, 5 pairs stones for grinding grain, 1 carding machine, 1 furnace, 3 forges, 8 mill saws, 1 fulling mill, 311 horses and mules, and 1650 neat cattle, 3 years old and upwards, and 6 distilleries. The t-ship paid for school tax, $116; state and county tax, $921 10; poor tax, $300; and road tax, $1200. Hamburg and Vernon are villages and post-towns of this t-ship. The mountains, which on the east, rise to the height of 1000 feet, are composed of primitive rock, in which hornblende is a principal constituent; the valleys are uniformly of primitive limestone. The mountains yield iron abundantly.

Vernon, p-t. of the above named t-ship, lying in the valley between the Wawayanda and Pochuck mountains, 246 miles N. E. from W. C., 88 from Trenton, and 18 from Newton. It contains a tavern, store, and from 10 to 12 dwellings.

Vienna, p-t. of Independence t-ship,

Warren co., on the Pequest creek, near the S. W. boundary of the t-sp, by the post-road 220 miles from W. C., 54 from Trenton, and 12 from Belvidere, upon the verge of the Great Meadows; contains a Presbyterian church, a store, tavern, and 6 or 8 dwellings.

Vincenttown, p-t. of Northampton t-ship, Burlington co., at the junction of Stop-the-Jade creek with the south branch of the Rancocus creek, 5 miles S. of Mount Holly, 12 miles S. E. from Burlington, 32 from Trenton, and 159 N. E. from W. C.; contains a grist mill, saw mill, 2 taverns, 4 stores, from 30 to 40 dwellings, a Quaker meeting house, and a house of public worship, free to all denominations; surrounded by a fine fertile country.

Wading River, a considerable arm of Little Egg Harbour river, which rises by two branches; the east in Dover t-ship, Monmouth co., and flows S. W. 15 miles, into Washington township; the west in Northampton t-ship, and flows S. W. about 15 miles, to unite with the east, near Bodine's tavern. The main stem flows by a south course, thence of 8 miles to the Little Egg Harbour river, below Swan's Bay.

Waertown, hamlet of Stafford t-sp, Monmouth co., upon Barnegat bay, near the mouth of Waertown creek, a small mill stream, of about 3 miles long, 35 miles S. E. from Freehold, and opposite to Barnegat Inlet; contains 10 or 12 dwellings, a tavern and store; in a sandy soil, covered with pine forest.

Wallkill Mountains. (See *Hamburg.*)

Wallkill River, rises in Byram t-ship, Sussex co., and flows by a N. E. course of 23 or 24 miles, through Hardiston t-ship, dividing Wantage from Vernon t-ship, into the state of New York, and thence by a like course of 35 or 40 miles, through Orange and Ulster counties, falls into the Hudson river, 3 miles S. E. from the village of Esopus or Kingston. This stream is remarkable for being the drain of a large and valuable tract of marsh meadow land, exceeding 50,000 acres, elevated more than 325 feet above tide water. The waters which descend from the surrounding hills, being slowly discharged from the river, cover these vast meadows every winter, and would render them extremely fertile, could they be effectually drained.

Walnut Valley, post-office, Warren co.

Walpack t-ship, of Sussex co., bounded N. E. by Sandistone t-ship; S. E. by the Blue mountain, which separates it from Stillwater t-ship; S. W. by Pahaquarry t-ship; and W. by the river Delaware. Greatest length 10 miles; breadth 4 miles; area, 15,360 acres; surface on the east, mountainous; on the west, river alluvion. Population in 1830, 660; taxables 137. There were in the t-ship in 1832, 24 householders whose ratables did not exceed $30; 1 storekeeper, 2 saw mills, 146 horses and mules, 3 years old and upwards; 354 neat cattle of like age; 14 tan vats. It paid state and county tax, $293 80; and road tax, $350. It is drained by the Flatkill, which runs centrally through the t-ship, and empties into the Delaware at the Walpack Bend; and by Vancamp Brook, which rises in Long Pond, in the Blue mountain. There is a post-office here, called after the t-ship, distant from Washington 240, from Trenton 82, and from Newton 12 miles. The Blue mountain covers nearly half the t-ship; between its base and the river is a margin, of an average width of two miles, of limestone, bordered and partly covered by alluvion, rich and highly productive of wheat, corn, &c. There is a German Reformed church in the t-ship.

Walpack Bend, a remarkable bend of the river Delaware, at the S. W. angle of Walpack t-ship, about 85 miles above the city of Trenton.

Wantage t-ship, of Sussex co., bounded N. by the state of New York; E. by Vernon t-ship; S. by Frankford and Hardiston t-ships; and W. by the Blue mountain, which separates this from Sandistone and Montague t-ships. Greatest length 11 miles; breadth 8½ miles; area, 42,880 acres; surface on the west, mountainous and hilly; on the east, rolling. Population in 1830, 4034; taxables 643. There were in the t-ship in 1832, 208 householders, 11 storekeepers or traders, 18 pairs of stones for grinding grain, 6 saw mills, 1 fulling mill, 5 carding machines, 939 horses and mules, and 3481 neat cattle, over 3 years of age; 18 tan vats, and 3 distilleries. The t-ship paid a school tax of $500; state and county tax, $1706 27; poor tax, $300; and road tax, $1500. It is drained by Deep Clove river and Papakating creek, uniting south of Deckertown, and thence flowing into the Wallkill river, which forms the whole eastern boundary of the t-ship. The Paterson and Hamburg turnpike road runs N. E., and the Newton and Bolton N. W., through the t-ship; and at their intersection, is the small village of Deckertown. There is a post-office at Deckertown, 444 miles from W. C., 86 from Trenton, and 16 from Newton; and another called Libertyville, 241 miles from W. C., 83 from Trenton, and 10 from Newton. Wantage is a rich t-ship, consisting of limestone and slate soils; the one on the east, and the other on its western side, highly cultivated. Along the Wallkill river, there is a margin of swamp, known as the Drowned Lands, caused by the collection of the waters from the high ground, in a deep and flat valley, through which the river moves sluggishly. These lands are, in places, heavily timbered.

Wardle's Beach, on the Atlantic ocean, Shrewsbury t-ship, Monmouth co., extending south from Old Shrewsbury Inlet.

Warren County, was taken from Sussex, by Act, 20th Nov., 1824, which directed, That all the lower part of the latter, southwesterly of a line, beginning on the river Delaware, at the mouth of Flat Brook, in the t-ship of Walpack, and running thence a straight course to the N. E. corner of Hardwicke church, and thence in the same course to the middle of the Musconetcong creek, thence down the middle of the said creek, to the Delaware, should be a new county. Warren is bounded N. E. by Sussex co.; S. E. by the Musconetcong creek, which divides it from Morris and Hunterdon, and W. and N. W. by the river Delaware. Its greatest length, N. E. and S. W. is 35 miles; greatest breadth, E. and W. 17 miles; area, about 350 square miles; central lat. 40° 50′ N.; long. 1° 58′ E., from W. C.

The county is divided between the primitive and transition formations. A strip of the former crosses it, in the neighbourhood of Beattystown, towards Philipsburg, and the other fills the portion N. of a line running N. W. and S. E. by Sparta, towards Belvidere, including the Blue mountain; leaving an intervening strip of primitive, of a wedge-like form, having its broader part resting on New York. From these formations we may expect a great variety of soils; and indeed all the rocks which belong to them, are singularly blended. The valley of the Musconetcong, on the N. W. side, abounds with transition limestone, bordered by a vein of dark slate; and all the valleys, whether of the primitive or transition, are fertilized by the decomposition of the limestone rock, mingling with the sand, loam and clay, washing from the mountains, making a compound, various as the rocks from which it is derived.

The metals found within the county, are magnetic iron, brown hematite, and bog ore, in several places, but principally in Scott's mountain, Jenny Jump, and on the Delaware river, near Foul Rift. A mine of magnetic iron ore is wrought in Scott's mountain, Oxford t-ship, where a furnace was established nearly a century since, and has lately been repaired and put into operation.

Zinc, or lead, appears in the hills which bound the Musconetcong valley, on the N. W.; but most probably zinc, inasmuch as these hills are in the range of the Wallkill mountain, where that metal lies in large masses. Gold and silver are said to have been discovered in the Jenny Jump mountain, but which, though possibly true, may in all likelihood, be iron or copper pyrites, which have so often been mistaken for the precious metals. Marble, steatite, or soapstone, roofing slate, and manganese, may also be obtained in the county, sufficiently near to navigation, to render them valuable in commerce. The state quarries, near the Blue mountain, are already extensively worked.

The county is marked by several prominent mountain ridges, which determine its water courses, and the surface is every where uneven. Entering it from the south, we cross the natural boundary, the Musconetcong creek, which is confined to a narrow valley, by hills, forming a continuation of the Wallkill mountain, whose north-western base is washed by the Pohatcong creek, for nearly the whole breadth of the county; and the valley of that stream is divided from that of the Pequest, by Scott's mountain, which breaks into small and diminished knolls, near the eastern extremity of the county. North of the main branch of the Pequest, but embraced by it and its chief tributary, Beaver brook, lies the Jenny Jump mountain, a narrow and isolated ridge. Beaver brook drains a valley of several miles in width, and covered with knolls of slate, and beds of limestone, and circumscribed northward by a long, unbroken, slaty ridge, which bounds the valley of the Paulinskill. Between that stream, and the Blue mountain, the mean distance may be about five miles. The Blue mountain covers the remaining portion of the county, with the exception of a small strip of alluvial, which borders the Delaware river.

As in most parts of the primitive and transition formations, the streams are rapid and precipitous, affording advantageous use of their volumes for hydraulic purposes, but are in no instance navigable. The waters of the county, without exception, seek the Delaware; and whilst that river boldly cuts its way through the mountains, these tributaries are compelled to pursue the course of the ridges whose bases they lave.

The only artificial road of the county, is that from Morristown to Philipsburg, opposite to Easton. A rail-road has been authorized by the Legislature, which is designed to unite with a similar road, opposite to Belvidere, on the Delaware, and to proceed thence to the Susquehanna river.

The business of the county is chiefly agricultural, and its staples are wheat, corn, rye, oats, and flax; and in the northern part buckwheat. Within a few years, husbandry has made great advances, and yet continues to improve. The use of lime as a manure is becoming general; and the rich valley lands yield very large crops of wheat, which find a ready market at Easton. Flax-seed is also grown in great quantities; of which 12,000 bushels are annually purchased in Belvidere, alone.

In 1830, the county contained, 18,627 inhabitants, of whom 9463 were white males, 8695 white females; 214 free coloured males, 208 free coloured females; 21 male, and 26 female slaves. Of this population, 286 were aliens, 10 were deaf and dumb, and 14 were blind. The inhabitants are chiefly of English extraction, and a considerable portion from New England parents.

By the abstract of the assessors, reported to the Legislature, in 1832, there were 102,377 acres of improved land, making nearly one-half the area of the county; 1062 householders, whose ratables did not exceed $30;

411 single men; 3489 taxables; 56 merchants, 45 grist mills, 41 saw mills, 16 carding machines, 7 furnaces for casting iron, 2 cotton and woollen factories, 2 fulling mills, 3 oil mills, and 1 plaster mill, 235 tan vats, 1 glass factory, 3 distilleries of grain, and 25 of cider; 14 carriages, with steel springs; 177 riding chairs, gigs and sulkies; 4324 horses, and 7772 neat cattle, over 3 years of age; and it paid for t-ship purposes, $5700; and for state and county purposes, $8999 20. The t-ship of Greenwich alone honourably distinguished itself, by appropriating money to *school use*, and paid for this object, $500.

The religious sects of the county are Presbyterian, Methodist, Episcopalian, Baptists, and *Chris-ti-ans*. The last has, we believe, two churches, and admits women to officiate in the ministry. These sects rank in number in the order we have placed them.

The towns and post-offices of the county are, Belvidere, the seat of justice; Finesville, Hughesville, Bloomsbury, Asbury, Imlaydale, Pleasant Valley, Mansfield, Anderson, Beattystown, Hackettstown, Alamuche, Long Bridge, Johnsonburg, Lawrenceville, Marksborough, Philipsburg, Stewartsville, New Village, Broadway, Concord, Rocksbury, Oxford, Hope, Shiloh, Columbia, Knowlton Mills, Centreville, Sodom, Gravel Hill, &c.

The courts of common pleas, orphan's courts, and quarter sessions, are holden at Belvidere, on the 2d Tuesday of February, 1st Tuesday of June, 4th Tuesday of August, and the 1st Tuesday after the 4th in November. The circuit court and sessions of oyer and terminer, and general jail delivery, are holden on the 1st Tuesday in June, and the 1st Tuesday after the 4th in November.

The county elects one member to the council, and two to the general Assembly.

STATISTICAL TABLE OF WARREN COUNTY.

Townships.	Length.	Breadth.	Area.	Surface.	Population. 1830.
Greenwich,	13	11	38,000	hilly.	4486
Hardwick,	11	8	24,320	do.	1962
Independence,	9	8½	29,440	hills and vales.	2126
Knowlton,	10	10	44,800	do.	2827
Mansfield,	15	62	33,000	mountainous.	3303
Oxford,	16	5½	42,000	do.	3665
Pahaquarry,	13	2½	12,800	do.	258
			224,360		18,627

Warren t-ship, Somerset co., bounded N. by Bernard t-ship and by Morris t-ship, Morris co., from which it is separated by the Passaic river; N. E. by New Providence; S. E. by Westfield t-ship, of Essex co.; S. by Piscataway t-ship, Middlesex co.; and S. W. by Bridgewater t-ship, Somerset co. Greatest length N. E. and S. W. 8 miles; breadth N. and S. 4 miles: centrally distant N. E. from Somerville 6 miles; area, 18,000 acres; surface, mountainous, the whole t-ship being covered with hills; bent into elliptic form, with a single narrow valley drained by Middle Brook. These hills are low, well wooded, and composed of trap rock, upon old red sandstone, whose disintegration gives a soil of stiff clay and sandy loam. They contain veins of copper ore, apparently, very rich, and said to be valuable not only for the copper they contain, but also for their gold. Several efforts have been made to work them, but none have been successfully prosecuted. Mines have been opened within 2 miles N. E. of Somerville, which were lately wrought by Mr. Cammams and Dr. Stryker, who have suspended their operations; others, within a mile of the village of Green Brook, and six of Somerville, were worked some 40 years ago. The southern base of these mineral hills is washed by Green Brook. Mount Bethel is a small hamlet at which we believe the post-office of the t-ship is kept, called "*Warren.*" Population in 1830, 1501. In 1832 the t-ship contained about 300 taxables, 56 householders, whose ratables did not exceed $30; 42 single men, 4 stores, 8 saw mills, 4 grist 'mills, 2 fulling mills, 4 tan vats, 5 distilleries, 3 carding machines, 259 horses and mules, and 873 neat cattle, over 3 years of age.

Warwick Creek, rises in Orange co., in the state of New York, from Wickham's Pond, and flows thence by the town of Warwick S. W. into Vernon t-ship, Sussex co., and into the valley between Wawayanda and Pochuck mountains; thence by a N. W. course re-enters the state of New York, and unites with the Wallkill river, in the Great Marsh. This stream gives motion to several mills.

Washington t-ship, Morris co., bounded N. by Roxbury t-ship; E. by that t-ship and Chester; S. by Tewkesbury and Lebanon t-ships, Hunterdon co.; and W. by Mansfield and Independence t-ships, Warren co., from which it is separated by Musconetcong creek. Centrally distant W. from Morristown 18 miles: greatest length E. and W. 8, breadth N. and S. 7½ miles; area, 27,500 acres; surface, mountainous, Schooley's mountain covering the western portion; on the east of which, lies the German valley, drained by the south branch of the Raritan river: the intervening country between that and the Black river, near the south-eastern boundary, is hilly. The soil of the highlands is generally clay and loam, with grey limestone in the valleys. Much of the mountain is cultivated, and with lime, brings abundant crops. The German valley is very rich, and settled by the industrious descendants of Germans. The celebrated mineral spring and houses of public entertainment, are on the mountain. (See *Schooley's Mountain.*) Springtown and Pleasant Grove are villages of the t-ship.—Population in 1830, 2188. In 1832 the t-ship contained 397 taxables, 124 householders, whose ratables did not exceed $30 in value; 8 stores, 11 saw, 6 grist mills, 3 forges, 20 tan vats, 10 distilleries, 532 horses, and 1015 neat cattle, above 3 years of age; and paid the following taxes: state, $314; county, $703 74; poor, $300; road, $500.

Washington, village of North Brunswick t-ship, Middlesex co., on the left bank of the South river, 5 miles S. E. from New Brunswick, and about 3 miles from the confluence of that river with the Raritan. There are here 2 taverns, 3 stores, and from 30 to 40 dwellings. An unsuccessful attempt has been made to cut a canal, a mile long, between the South river and the Raritan, in order to save several miles in the navigation from the town to Perth Amboy.

Washington t-ship, Burlington co., bounded N. and N. E. by Northampton t-ship; S. E. by Little Egg Harbour t-ship; S. W. and W. by Galloway and Waterford t-ships, Gloucester co.; and N. W. by Evesham t-ship. Centrally distant S. from Woodbury, 22 miles. Greatest breadth, N. and S. 19 miles; greatest length, E. and W. 20 miles; area, 112,000 acres. Surface, level; soil, generally sandy, and covered with forest. Drained S. by the Little Egg Harbour river, and its several branches; Atsion, the main branch, being on the W. boundary, and Wading river running centrally through the t-ship. Shamong, Washington, and

Greenbank, are villages of the t-ship. Population in 1830, 1315. In 1832 the t-ship contained 141 householders, whose ratables did not exceed $30; 59 single men; 287 taxables; 6 stores, 3 fisheries, 7 saw mills, 4 grist mills, 2 furnaces, 1 forge, 6 dearborns, 19 covered wagons, 4 gigs and sulkies, 333 neat cattle, 265 horses and mules; and paid state tax, $117 12; county tax, $371 10; township tax, $450.

Washington, p-t. of Washington t-ship, Morris co.; in the German valley, Schooley's mountain, on the turnpike road from Morristown to Easton, and on the south branch of the Raritan river, 18 miles W. of Morristown, 54 N. E. from Trenton, and 220 by post route from W. C.; contains 1 Presbyterian, and 1 Lutheran church, a school, 1 store, 2 taverns, and about 20 dwellings. It is surrounded by a fertile, well improved, limestone country. (See *German Valley.*)

Washington, village of Mansfield t-ship, Warren county. (See *Mansfield.*)

Waterford t-ship, Gloucester co., bounded N. E. by Chester t-ship; E. by Evesham t-ship, Burlington co.; S. E. by Galloway t-ship; W. by Gloucester and Newton t-ships; and N. W. by the river Delaware. Centrally distant W. from Woodbury 12 miles. Greatest length, N. W. and S. E., 25; breadth, 8 miles. Its form is very irregular, being deeply indented by the adjacent county of Burlington, and being near the middle of its length, scarce more than a mile in width. Its surface is level, broken only by the streams which run through it; soil, sandy, mixed in the northern part, more or less with loam, but generally light, producing tolerable grass, when manured with marl, ashes or lime, and is cultivated in fruit and vegetables for market. The southern part of the t-ship, has a sandy soil, covered with a pine forest, and is valuable chiefly on account of its timber. It is drained, N. E. by Pensauken creek; **N. W.**

by Cooper's creek, which, respectively, are boundaries; and on the S. E. by several branches of the Atsion river, of which Atquatqua creek runs along the S. E. boundary. Shell marl is found in the t-ship, in the neighbourhood of Long-a-coming, and other places. Waterfordville, and Ellisville, are villages of the t-ship, and Long-a-coming is on the western t-ship line. Population in 1830, 3088. In 1832 the t-ship contained an Episcopal church, 404 householders, whose ratables did not exceed $30, in value; 7 stores, 5 fisheries, 5 grist mills, 4 saw mills, 7 distilleries, 2 glass factories; and paid poor tax, $660 52; county tax, $1321 06; township tax, $1200.

Waterfordville, village of Waterford t-ship, Gloucester co., on the road from Camden to Moorestown, about 5 miles from either; contains a tavern, store, and 8 or 10 dwellings.

Water Street, village of Mendham t-ship, Morris co., on the line between that and Morris t-ship, and on the head waters of Whippany river, 3 miles W. of Morristown; contains a grist mill, store, and half a dozen of dwellings.

Watson's Creek, Middletown t-sp., Monmouth co., runs N. E. 2 miles, into Sandy Hook bay.

Wawayanda Mountain, Vernon t-ship, Sussex co., extends northerly, across the eastern part of the t-ship, about 9 miles. It interlocks on the S. with the Wallkill mountain.

Waycake Creek, Middletown t-sp., Monmouth co., flows N. about 5 miles, into the Raritan bay, W. of Point Comfort.

Weasel; the name of a dense settlement, of Acquackanonck t-ship, Essex co., extending for near 4 miles, along the right bank of the Passaic, between Acquackanonck village, and Paterson. There may be in the settlement, about 40 dwellings, many of which are very neat. The country is fertile, and extremely well cultivated;—land, in farms, valued at $100 the acre.

West or *Jecak Creek*, forms the S. E. boundary of Cumberland co., between that and Cape May co. It is a mill stream between 6 and 7 miles in length, upon which are Hughes' grist and saw mills.

Westfield, small village of Chester t-ship, Burlington co., on the road from Camden to Burlington, 7 miles N. of the former, and 11 S. W. from Mount Holly; contains a Friends' meeting house, and some half dozen farm houses, in a very fertile well cultivated country. Soil, sandy loam.

Westfield t-ship, Essex co., bounded N. by Springfield; E. by Union; S. E. by Rahway t-ships; S. by Middlesex co.; W. by Warren t-ship, Somerset co., and by New Providence t-ship. Centrally distant S. W. from Newark 13 miles: greatest length 7, breadth 6 miles; area, 18,000 acres; surface on the N. W. hilly, but subsiding to a plain on the south; soil, clay loam northward, and red shale southward: the latter rich and carefully cultivated. Rahway river courses the eastern, and Green Brook the western, boundary. A more abundant and delightful country is scarce any where to be found, than that along from the foot of the mountain, north of Scotch Plains through the t-ship. Westfield, Plainfield, and Scotch Plains are villages and post-towns of the precinct. Population in 1830, 2492. In 1832 the t-ship contained 475 taxables, 124 householders, whose ratables did not exceed $30; 64 single men, 5 merchants, 5 grist mills, 2 saw mills, 1 paper mill, 423 horses and mules, and 1111 neat cattle, above 3 years old; and paid state tax, $264 78; county, $692 77; poor, $420; road, $800.

Westfield, p-t. of the above t-ship, 11 miles S. W. from Newark, 218 N. E. from W. C., 52 from Trenton, and 3½ from Scotch Plains, on the road leading thence to Elizabethtown; contains a Presbyterian church, a tavern, store, and smithery, and 25 dwellings. The vicinage is level, with a stiff clay cold soil. Lands valued at an average of 25 dollars per acre.

Westecunk Creek, rises by several branches in Little Egg Harbour t-sp, Burlington co., and flows S. E. about 8 miles, through Stafford t-ship, Monmouth co., into Little Egg Harbour bay. There was formerly a forge upon the stream. There are now a grist and saw mill, and in the vicinity, some 15 or 20 dwellings. The *Palma Christi*, or castor bean, is extensively cultivated here.

West Milford, post-office of Bergen co., 248 miles from W. C., and 82 N. E. from Trenton.

Weston, p-t., on the Millstone river, and on the Delaware and Raritan canal, formerly called Rogers' Mill, about a mile and a half from its confluence with the Raritan river, and 2 miles below the village of Millstone, 3 miles in a direct line S. E. of Somerville, Somerset co., and about 30 from Trenton; contains a saw mill, grist mill, store, and some 10 or 12 dwellings.

Weymouth, blast furnace, forge, and village, in Hamilton t-ship, Gloucester co., upon the Great Egg Harbour river, about 5 miles above the head of navigation. The furnace makes about 900 tons of castings annually: the forge having four fires and two hammers, makes about 200 tons bar iron, immediately from the ore. There are also a grist and saw mill, and buildings for the workmen, of whom 100 are constantly employed about the works, and the persons depending upon them for subsistence, average 600 annually. There are 85,000 acres of land pertaining to this establishment, within which May's Landing is included. The works have a superabundant supply of water, during all seasons of the year.

Weymouth t-ship, Gloucester co., bounded N. by Hamilton; E. by Great Egg Harbour river; S. and W. by Tuckahoe river. Centrally distant from Woodbury 41 miles: greatest length N. and S. 12 miles; breadth E. and W. 10 miles; area,

50,000 acres; surface, level; soil, sandy: eastern boundary on the river, and the portion on the S. E. lying between the two rivers is salt marsh. Stephens' Creek and Tuckahoe are villages and post-towns of the t-ship. Population in 1830, 3333. In 1832 the t-ship contained 90 householders, whose ratables did not exceed $30; 4 stores, 2 grist mills, 1 carding machine, 1 blast furnace, and 2 forges called Etna, 4 saw mills, 315 neat cattle, and 90 horses and mules, above 3 years old; and paid county tax, $157 69; poor tax, $78 82; and road tax, $600.

Whale Pond Creek, Shrewsbury t-ship, Monmouth co., flows easterly about 5 miles to the ocean, about a mile below the Long Branch boarding houses. It gives motion to a mill.

Wheat Sheaf, small village on the line separating Rahway from Elizabethtown t-ship, 8 miles S. W. from Newark, and half-way between Bridgetown and Elizabethtown, 3 miles from either; contains a tavern, from whose sign it has its name; a store, and 8 or 10 dwellings.

Whippany, manufacturing village, of Hanover t-ship, Morris co., on the Whippany river, 5 miles N. E. of Morristown; contains a Methodist church, an academy, 3 stores, 1 tavern, 5 cotton manufactories, 2000 spindles, 3 paper mills, and 56 dwellings. Soil, loam, valued at 25 and 30 dollars per acre.

Whippany River, Morris co., a considerable tributary of the Rockaway, rises in Mendham t-ship, at the foot of Trowbridge mountain, and flows by a N. E. course of 17 or 18 miles, by Morristown, to its recipient about 2 miles above the junction of that stream with the Passaic. This is a fine mill stream, drives many mills in its course, and is well employed at the village of Whippany.

White Hall, hamlet on Schooley's mountain, Lebanon t-ship, Hunterdon co., 18 miles N. E. of Flemington; contains a store, tavern, smith shop, and 4 or 5 dwellings.

White Hill, landing and small village, on the Delaware river, Mansfield t-ship, Burlington co.; contains 2 taverns, 10 or 12 dwellings, and an air furnace. There is also a ferry here.

White House, p-t. of Readington t-ship, Hunterdon co., 10 miles N. E. of Flemington, 33 from Trenton, and 196 from W. C., upon Rockaway creek; contains a grist mill, some 12 or 15 dwellings, 3 stores, 3 taverns, and a Presbyterian or Dutch Reformed church. The surface of the country around it is hilly; soil, loam, clay, and red shale.

White Marsh Run, tributary of Maurice river, rises in Fairfield t-ship, Cumberland co., and flows eastwardly to its recipient, about 6 miles.

White Ponds, two small lakes, connected by a brook, lying at the west foot of Pimple Hill, in Hardiston t-ship, Sussex co., on the western line of the t-ship, distant, in a direct line N. E. from Newton, 8 miles.

Wickhechecoke Creek, rises by two branches in the hills, on the N. W. of Amwell t-ship, Hunterdon co., and flows by a southerly course of 10 miles, into the Delaware, giving motion to several mills.

Williamsville, Orange t-ship, Essex co., 5 miles N. W. of Newark, near the foot of the first mountain; contains 8 or 10 houses.

Williamsburg, or *Penn's Neck,* West Windsor t-ship, Middlesex co., on the straight turnpike, from Trenton to New Brunswick, 10 miles from the first, 15 from the second, 2 miles from Princeton, and half a mile W. from Millstone river, and Stony brook; contains a Baptist church, of wood; an Episcopalian church; 2 taverns, 1 store, and 12 dwellings. Soil, kind, sandy loam, extremely well cultivated, and productive. There are two large quarries of freestone, of excellent building stone upon the river.

Williamsburg. (See *Cedar Creek.*)

Willingboro' t-ship, Burlington co., bounded N. E. by Burlington t-ship; S. E. by Northampton; S.

W. by the Rancocus creek, which separates it from Chester t-ship; and N. W. by the river Delaware. Centrally distant N. W. from Mount Holly, 7 miles. Greatest length, 6, breadth, 4 miles; area, 7500 acres. Surface, generally level; soil, sand and sandy loam, well cultivated, and productive in grass, grain, vegetables and fruit. A small branch of the Rancocus creek, crosses the t-ship. Dunks' ferry, over the Delaware, is within it, 4 miles below Burlington. Cooperstown is the only village. Population in 1830, 782. In 1832 the t-ship contained 160 taxables; 50 householders, whose ratables did not exceed $30; 28 single men; 1 grist mill, 2 distilleries, 2 coaches, 6 dearborns, 36 covered wagons, 4 chairs and curricles, 5 gigs and sulkies, 269 neat cattle, and 176 horses and mules, above 3 years old; and paid state tax, $109 38; county tax, $381 93; township tax, $400.

Windsor, West, t-ship, Middlesex co., bounded N. E. by South Brunswick; S. E. by East Windsor; S. W. by Nottingham t-ship, of Burlington co., and by Lawrence t-ship, Hunterdon co.; and on the N. W. by Montgomery t-ship, Hunterdon co. Centrally distant S. W. from Brunswick, 17 miles. Greatest length, 7, breadth, 5 miles; area, 19,000 acres. Surface, level; soil, sandy loam and clay, generally well cultivated, and producing, abundantly, grain and grass. Drained on the E. by Millstone river; on the S. W. by the Assunpink creek; and on the N. W. by Stony Brook. The road through Princeton divides this from Somerset co. Princeton, Williamsburg, Clarksville, Dutch Neck, and Edinburg, are towns of the t-ship. Population in 1830, 2129. In 1832 the t-ship contained 448 taxables; 226 householders, whose ratables did not exceed $30; 64 single men; 6 merchants; 1 large grist mill, with 3 run of stones; 1 woollen factory, 3 distilleries, and 496 horses and mules, and 848 neat cattle, over 3 years of age; and paid state tax,

$320 49; county, $394 04; road, $200; poor, $450. Excellent free-stone, for building, is abundant in the t-ship.

Windsor, East, t-ship of Middlesex co., bounded N. by South Brunswick t-ship; N. E. by South Amboy; S. E. by Freehold t-ship, Monmouth co.; S. W. by Nottingham t-ship, Burlington co.; and N. W. by West Windsor t-ship. Centrally distant S. W. from New Brunswick, 20 miles. Greatest length, 12: greatest breadth, 6 miles; area, 24,000 acres. Surface level; soil, sandy and gravelly loam, light, and not generally productive. Drained by Millstone river, and Rocky brook, on the N. E., and by the Assunpink and Miry run, upon the S. W. Hightstown, Mill-ford, Centreville, and Cattail, are villages, the first a post-town, of the t-ship. The turnpike road from Bordentown, to New Brunswick, crosses the t-ship. Population in 1830, 1930. In 1832 the t-ship contained 487 taxables; 52 householders, whose ratables did not exceed $30; and 41 single men, 3 merchants, 3 saw mills, 4 grist mills, 1 woollen factory, 2 carding machines, and fulling mills, 32 tan vats, 13 distilleries for cider, and 484 horses and mules, and 897 neat cattle, above 3 years of age; and paid state tax, $286 77; county, $352 53; road tax, $400; poor tax, $700.

Woodbridge t-ship, Middlesex co., bounded N. by Westfield, and Rahway t-ships, Essex co.; E. by Staten Island Sound; S. E. by Perth Amboy t-ship; S. by Raritan river; and W. by Piscataway t-ship. Centrally distant from New Brunswick, N. E. 8 miles. Length, E. and W. 9, breadth, N. and S. 9 miles; area, 24,000 acres. Surface, level; soil, red shale, universally well cultivated. Drained on the N. E. by a branch of Rahway river, upon which are some mills. Rahway and Woodbridge, are post-towns, Matouchin and Bon-hamtown, villages of the t-ship. Two turnpike roads from New Brunswick, run N. E. through the t-ship, which

are crossed by another, from Perth Amboy to New Durham. Population in 1830, 3969. In 1832 the t-ship contained 700 taxables; 180 householders, whose ratables did not exceed $30 in value; 99 single men; 13 stores, 5 saw mills, 3 grist mills, 40 tan vats, 1 distillery, 585 horses and mules, 1555 neat cattle, 3 years old and upwards; and paid state tax, $594 53; county, $731 03; road, 1800; poor, $1000. This t-ship contains a portion of the thriving town of Rahway. It was incorporated by Governor Philip Carteret, prior to 1680, by one of the most liberal charters which had ever been given in America. (See *Records of East Jersey Proprietaries, at Amboy.*) In 1682, it was estimated that there were in the t-ship, one hundred and twenty families. They had then erected a court-house and prison, and had many thousand acres surveyed for plantations. Delaplaine, the surveyor-general, was one of the settlers here.

Woodbury Creek, Deptford t-ship, Gloucester co., rises by two branches; the southern called Matthew's branch, each about 3 miles above Woodbury, and unite below the town. The north branch is navigable from the town to the river Delaware, 3 miles.

Woodbury, p-t., and seat of justice of Gloucester co., on Woodbury creek, at the head of navigation, 8 miles S. of Camden, 39 from Trenton, and 145 from W. C.; contains a spacious court-house of brick, and county offices, fire proof, and of the same material, detached, and a prison, in the rear of the court-house, of stone; 1 Friends' meeting house, large, and of brick; 1 Presbyterian church, frame, with cupola and bell, the upper part of which is used as an academy; and 1 brick Methodist church; 2 common schools; 2 public libraries, one of which was founded by the ladies of the town; 2 sunday schools; a county bible society; and temperance society, which has been productive of very beneficial effects; several store-keepers refusing to sell spirituous liquors; 10 stores, 3 taverns, 4 lawyers, 3 physicians, 1 clergyman, 100 dwelling houses, and 735 inhabitants. The town, for a mile in length, and half a mile in breadth, is incorporated, for the maintenance of a fire engine and fire apparatus, for which eight public wells have been sunk; and the provisions for defence, against this devastating element, are very efficient. The creek was, 70 years since, stopped out; but the obstruction was removed in 1830, much to the convenience and health of the inhabitants. Vessels now load at the landing, in the town.

Woodruff's Gap, through Bear Fort mountain, Pompton t-ship, Bergen co. The Ringwood and Long Pond turnpike road passes through it.

Woodstown, p-t., and village, of Pilesgrove t-ship, Salem co., upon the Salem creek, 10 miles E. of the town of Salem, 161 N. E. from W. C., and 55 S. of Trenton. The town contains about 150 dwellings, 2 taverns, and 6 stores, 3 schools, 1 Friends' meeting, 1 Baptist, and 1 African Methodist church. In the neighbourhood of the town, there are some valuable marl beds—and the use of marl has much improved the agriculture of the t-ship.

Woodsville, p-t. of Hopewell t-sp., Hunterdon co., 10 miles S. from Flemington, 13 N. from Trenton, 179 from W. C., on the turnpike road from N. Brunswick, to Lambertsville; contains a store, tavern, and half a dozen dwellings, mostly new. It lies upon the slope of a gently rising ground, from which there is a delightful prospect of the surrounding country; the soil of which is of red shale, and well cultivated.

Woolwich t-ship, Gloucester co., bounded on the N. E. by Greenwich; on the S. E. by Franklin, t-ships; S. W. by Pittsgrove, Pilesgrove, and Upper Penn's Neck, t-ships, Salem co; and N. W. by the river Delaware. Centrally distant S. W. from Woodbury, 11 miles. Greatest length,

16; breadth, 7 miles; area, about 40,000 acres. Surface, level; soil, sandy, and on the S. E. covered with pine forest. Drained, westerly, by Repaupo, Little Timber, Raccoon, and Oldman's, creeks—the last of which forms the S. W. boundary. Swedesboro' and Battentown, are villages—the first a post-town of the t-ship. Population in 1830, 3033. In 1832 the t-ship contained 333 householders, whose ratables did not exceed $30; 8 stores, 9 grist mills, 4 saw mills, 3 fulling mills, 1 tannery, 8 distilleries, 1433 neat cattle, and 699 horses and mules above the age of 3 years.

Wrangleboro' or *Clark's Mill*, village, on Nacote creek, of Galloway t-ship, Gloucester co., about 37 miles S. E. from Woodbury; contains a store, one or more taverns, and one mill, and 15 or 20 dwellings.

Wrangle Brook, considerable tributary of the south branch of Toms' river, Dover t-ship, Monmouth co., uniting with the main branch, about two miles above Toms' River village.

Wrightsville, on the road from Allentown to Freehold, Upper Freehold t-ship, Monmouth co., 5 miles from the former, and 14 from the latter; contains 8 or 10 dwellings and a Quaker meeting house; soil, sandy. In the rear of the village, upon Cattail creek, are some bog meadows, which, in hot weather, are covered, in places, with an efflorescence of sulphate of iron (copperas).

Wrightstown, Hanover t-ship, Burlington co., 10 miles N. E. from Mount Holly, and 10 S. E. of Bordenton; contains 2 taverns, 2 stores, a Methodist church, and some 15 or 20 dwellings; surrounded by a very fertile country.

Yard's Branch, of Paulinskill, rises in the Blue mountains, in Pahaquarry t-ship, and flows S. W. through Knowlton t-ship to its recipient, near the village of Sodom, having a course of about 8 miles.